# FAMILY COMMUNICATION

# LEA'S COMMUNICATION SERIES

*Jennings Bryant/Dolf Zillmann, General Editors*

Selected titles in Applied Communication
(Teresa L. Thompson, Advisory Editor) include:

For a complete list of titles in LEA's Communication Series, please contact Lawrence Erlbaum Associates, Publishers, at www.erlbaum.com.

# FAMILY COMMUNICATION

Chris Segrin
*University of Arizona*

Jeanne Flora
*University of LaVerne*

**LEA** LAWRENCE ERLBAUM ASSOCIATES, PUBLISHERS
**2005** Mahwah, New Jersey                    London

| Senior Acquisitions Editor: | Linda Bathgate |
| Assistant Editor: | Karin Wittig Bates |
| Cover Design: | Kathryn Houghtaling Lacey |
| Textbook Production Manager: | Paul Smolenski |
| Full-Service Compositor: | TechBooks |
| Text and Cover Printer: | Hamilton Printing Company |

This book was typeset in 11 / 13 pt. Dante, Bold, Italic.
The heads were typeset in Franklin Gothic, Bold, and Bold Italic.

Lawrence Erlbaum Associates, Inc., Publishers
10 Industrial Avenue
Mahwah, NJ 07430
www.erlbaum.com

**Library of Congress Cataloging-in-Publication Data**

Segrin, Chris.
    Family communication / Chris Segrin, Jeanne Flora.
        p.    cm.—(LEA's communication series)
    Includes bibliographical references and indexes.
    ISBN 0-8058-4797-9 (case : alk. paper)—ISBN 0-8058-4798-7 (pbk. : alk. paper)
    1. Communication in the family.    2. Interpersonal relations.    3. Family—Research.
4. Family assessment.    5. Problem families.    I. Flora, Jeanne.    II. Title.    III. Series.

    HQ728.S373    2005
    306.87—dc22

                                                                2004013165

Books published by Lawrence Erlbaum Associates are printed on acid-free
paper, and their bindings are chosen for strength and durability.

Printed in the United States of America
10   9   8   7   6   5   4   3   2   1

# Contents

# Preface

Few if any relationships are more important, salient, long lasting, and central to people's well-being than their family relationships. These include spouses, parents, children, and siblings, to name but a few. Although these relationships are often defined by genes and institutionalized ceremonies such as marriage, they are built, maintained, and destroyed by communication.

*Family Communication* carefully examines state-of-the-art research and theories of family communication and family relationships. In addition to presenting cutting-edge research, we focus as well on classic theories and research findings that have influenced and revolutionized the way scholars conceptualize family interaction. This book was written to fulfill the need for a text that presented a thorough and up-to-date presentation of scientific research in family communication for teachers and students of family communication as well as for professionals who work with families. Toward that end, we critically selected and evaluated research and translated that knowledge into a language that is understandable to a broad range of readers. Undergraduate readers should find the information easy to understand, whereas advanced readers, such as graduate students and professionals, will also find it a useful reference to classic and contemporary research on family communication and relationships.

*Family Communication* is divided into four main sections. Part I, "Introducing Family Communication and Basic Family Processes," introduces readers to fundamental issues in the study of family communication. These include, for example, questions of how "family" is defined, dominant theories in family science, and basic family communication processes, such as conflict, intimacy, decision making, power, roles, and rules. Part II, "Communication in Family Subsystems," explores what is known about communication in different types of families or family relationships. Consequently, this section contains chapters on topics such as courtship and mate selection, marriage, parent–child, sibling, and grandparent–grandchild relationships. Parts III and IV examine more problematic issues in family communication. Our experience with teaching family communication suggests that people are often interested in the topic, not to learn why their family is so happy and content but to gain a better understanding of some problematic issues in their family. Part III therefore covers "Communication During Family Stress." In this section, we look at theoretical models of how families react to and handle stress, normative and nonnormative family stressors, divorce, remarriage, and the creation of stepfamilies. Throughout this section, we note where "stressors" can actually have positive consequences for the family, and how family communication patterns can mitigate some of the ill effects of family stressors. Finally, in Part IV, "Family Interaction, Health, and Well-Being," we consider the role of family communication in mental and physical health, in addition to the role of communication in family violence and abuse. This section concludes with a critical analysis of organized efforts at improving aspects of family communication through therapies, enhancement, and enrichment programs. Readers who wish to learn more about the research methods and measures used to study family will find an overview of family research methodologies in the Appendix.

As readers of *Family Communication* will learn, this area of inquiry is truly interdisciplinary. Researchers from the fields of Communication, Family Studies, Nursing, Psychology, Social Work, and Sociology have made remarkable contributions to our current knowledge of family communication processes. Even with our specific emphasis on communication in families, works from these different academic disciplines are evident throughout the book.

We are pleased to acknowledge the support and counsel of our editor at Lawrence Erlbaum Associates, Linda Bathgate, along with the editorial and production staff members at LEA for their diligent work on this book. We would also like to thank John Caughlin (University of Illinois) for his feedback and helpful suggestions as well as Melissa Taylor and Peggy Flyntz (University of Arizona) for their editorial assistance. Special thanks also are extended to our respective universities, University of Arizona and University of LaVerne, and to our families and friends for their support.

# I

# Introducing Family Communication and Basic Family Processes

# CHAPTER ONE

# Defining Family Communication and Family Functioning

It is often said that there are no individuals in this world, only fragments of families. This idea reflects the fact that interactions and experiences in the family shape the course of our entire lives and are forever carried with us. Shortly after most people physically depart from their family of origin, they initiate a new family of orientation. The family is therefore an unending cycle in which people are constantly involved at multiple levels.

The study of family communication has a long tradition. Some of the most influential works in the field were conducted around the time of World War II and are still influencing the way scholars think about families today. The past 15 years have witnessed more exciting new developments in the field of family communication that are fundamentally reshaping the way people think about functional and dysfunctional family interaction. New developments are providing badly needed information about current family problems. With recent attention and increased focus on problems such as divorce, child abuse, domestic violence, and mental health problems, scholars, therapists, members of the clergy, and students of communication have begun to realize that these problems are in fact *communication* problems. By better understanding the forms, functions, and processes of family communication, people hope to be able to comprehend how and why these problems exist, and perhaps begin to take steps toward preventing them in the future. In addition to concerns about family problems, people also hope to understand issues such as what makes for a happy marriage, what parenting techniques are associated with positive child outcomes, and how to maintain meaningful relationships with family members over the entire life span. These too are fundamentally communication issues.

Although personal experience is a valuable teacher, and there is often a kernel of truth in cultural folklore and media portrayals of family, we believe that answers to many pressing questions about family communication are evident, or emerging, from the scientific research conducted by family communication scholars. Indeed, as we illustrate throughout this book, the evidence from scientific studies regarding family interaction sometimes contradicts the messages people receive from the media or from their own cultural and family folklore. In this book, we carefully examine state-of-the-art research and theories, as well as classic research and theories that contribute to the understanding of complex family interactions.

In the past, literally thousands, if not millions, of families, parents, stepparents, spouses, children, grandparents, aunts, cousins, and uncles from all walks of life have been studied by family researchers. One primary theme stemming from this research is that there is no "one" version of the American family. If there were one clear, specific recipe for a happy family, there would be little need to study families. In chapter 2, we present the concept of equifinality. *Equifinality* refers to the fact that the same end state may be reached in many different ways. For example, there is not one path to a successful marriage. There may be some common themes to successful marriages, but there are many different ways couples can go about their courtship, negotiate roles, or deal with conflict and still achieve a successful marriage. The take-home message is that families are diverse. To help describe and explain this diversity, scholars have developed numerous typologies of families and family interaction. We present many of these important typologies throughout the chapters of this book. We also show how scholars have relied on these typologies to answer pressing questions about family interaction and even predict the nature of family interaction.

In this opening chapter, we address basic questions about families and family interaction. We explore, "What does the word 'family' mean?" and "What is a useful definition of family?" This analysis will show there is not one universally accepted definition of family, but each definition has distinct advantages, disadvantages, and implications. We also explore common labels for family forms. In studying definitions of family, we encounter other questions, such as "What tasks and resources are family members expected to perform and provide for one another?" "What kind of interaction defines 'family'?" and "How is family interaction different from interaction in other relationships?" In answering these questions, we also provide a general definition of communication, and discuss how communication constitutes family and is situated at the heart of family processes. Next, we present demographic data that highlight family trends related to marriage, family form and size, and divorce and remarriage. Although they do not accurately depict all families, the data point to general family trends that we explore further in later chapters of the book. Finally, people often ask, "What makes for optimal family interaction or family functioning?" Although this is a question we address throughout the book, in this chapter, we present two models of family functioning that start us on the path toward answering this question: Olson's circumplex model and the McMaster model. We close this chapter by examining how issues of cultural diversity influence what scholars and laypersons view as optimal family interaction.

## EXAMINING DEFINITIONS OF FAMILY

What is family? Must members be related by blood? Is a civil or religious ceremony necessary or sufficient to the definition of family? Are two students who are in a romantic relationship and who share an apartment a family? Are children necessary or sufficient for family? Must a family have as its core a man and a woman? Is commitment necessary for family? What makes a family group different from any other social group we belong to?

If you are having trouble answering any of these questions, you are not alone. Currently, there is not one universally accepted definition of family, and it is not likely that we will progress toward one soon (Settles, 1999). Definitions of family attempt to lay out necessary and sufficient criteria for creating a family. Criteria address family form, function, and interaction. Issues of *form* address who is "in" the family and by what objective means they are connected (e.g., marriage, blood, adoption). Issues of *function* concentrate on the tasks performed and expected family functions. Issues of *interaction* address the communication processes that connect individuals as family members and show how communication constitutes family. Wamboldt and Reiss (1989) classified definitions of family into three types. The first type, *structural* definitions, defines family by form, whereas the second and third types, *task-orientation* definitions and *transactional* definitions, define family by function and interaction, respectively. In the following sections, we look at the advantages and disadvantages of defining family by form, function, and interaction. We also examine common family forms and functions. Toward the end of this discussion, we present a definition of family that has been especially useful for us, in part because it relies on structural, task-orientation, and transactional components.

## Defining Family by Form: Structural Definitions

Structural definitions lay out specific criteria that make clear who is in the family and who is not (Fitzpatrick & Badzinski, 1994). Structural definitions do not depend on the quality of the family interaction or task performance, and they are not dependent on subjective feelings of group identity or affection. Rather they define family simply by form. Popenoe's (1993) definition of family illustrates one classic example of a structural definition. The criteria for membership are clear and, common to many structural definitions, a hierarchy of family members is assumed. According to Popenoe's definition, family is "a relatively small domestic group of kin (or people in a kin-like relationship) consisting of at least one adult and one dependent person" (p. 529). This definition implies that family shares a household and that a dependent (e.g., most commonly a child, but possibly a handicapped or elderly adult) who is related by blood (or a bloodlike relationship, as in the case of adoption) must be present. Popenoe's definition implies that a sexual bond is not necessary or sufficient to form a family. As one of the more narrow structural definitions, Popenoe's definition does not consider a married or cohabiting couple a family. However, a single parent (whether married previously or not) who lives with one or more dependents is considered a family.

The U.S. Census Bureau also defines family structurally, but takes a more broad approach and disregards the necessity of a dependent. According to the U.S. Census Bureau (2002), family is "a group of two people or more related by birth, marriage, or adoption and residing together" [in a household] (p. 4). In other words, as long as individuals are related by blood or law and live together, they are considered family. Plausibly, two brothers, two cousins, or an adult mother and daughter who live together fit this definition of family. Compared to Popenoe's definition, the U.S. Census Bureau's definition comes closer to depicting the total number of households in the United States. However, the U.S. Census Bureau is careful to note that the terms household and family are not synonymous. A household is simply one or more persons living together in a housing unit, and not all households are family households. Following the U.S. Census Bureau's definition, examples of nonfamily households could include a person living alone or a person sharing a home exclusively with people to whom he or she is not related or married, such as two or more friends, roommates, or intimate partners without a legally recognized relationship.

Even with their variety, structural definitions are similar in that they clearly specify who is in the family and who is not by using external, objective criteria. The simplicity of structural definitions makes them appealing to people who are forced to make external decisions about what family is without much information about the inner fabric of any given family. In fact, structural definitions have thrived most with demographers, policymakers, and those in the legal arena.

Just as the simplicity of structural definitions seems useful, limitations are very apparent. Can objective criteria define family, or must people turn to more subjective definitions of family based on interaction and function? Perhaps "behavior trumps biology" in defining family (Sappenfield, 2002). For example, an individual may structurally be a member of a family, but because of negative behavior or frequent absence, he or she is not considered by others to be "family." Furthermore, many common structural definitions have not been adequate enough to encompass some family forms including nonresidential stepfamilies, foster families, and gay or lesbian families. Even though families of diverse structure are not considered "family" according to some structural definitions, they may very well be perceived as "family" if they function as "vital emotional units, based primarily on love and affection, that provide psychological security and nurturance to their members" (Peterson & Steinmetz, 1999, p. 3). In a study of children's perceptions of family, Newman, Roberts, and Syrè (1993) explored whether children define family by function, form, interaction, or all three. They asked children who ranged in age groups of 4 to 6, 7 to 9, 10 to 12, 13 to 15, and university age, "If a person [from another planet] asked you, what would you say to help him or her figure out what a family is?" (Newman et al., 1993, p. 954). Responses were coded to determine how many made reference to biological ties (e.g., people bonded through blood relations), legal ties (e.g., a man and a woman are married), co-residence (e.g., people with whom you live), affective ties (e.g., people who love each other), shared activities (e.g., people with whom you eat your meals), family roles (e.g., a dad, mom, brother, or sister), or other (e.g., a whole bunch of people). The children defined family in several ways. However, affective ties were most frequently mentioned by participants (60%), whereas co-residence was second most frequently mentioned (38%). Responses varied by age, with older children more likely to mention the affective criterion. Overall, this study indicates that communication, as manifested in the affective ties, may do more to constitute family than would structural criteria.

### Examining Family Forms From a Structural Perspective

Contemporary perceptions of family are increasingly diverse in structural form. Peterson and Steinmetz (1999) suggest that the diversity of family forms is akin to the diversity a biologist finds in a strong and adaptive ecosystem. Like the biologist, we too must have a way of naming and describing the diversity of forms in our ecosystem of families. We next explore labels for specific family forms, keeping in mind that as family forms evolve, our names for these family forms have evolved and are still evolving.

A *family of origin* refers to relatives who are connected by blood or traditional sociolegal contracts such as marriage or adoption. A family of origin includes parents, grandparents, siblings, cousins, aunts, uncles, and so forth. Family of origin usually refers to the family into which one is born. In contrast, a *family of orientation* is further limited to individuals who share the same household and, again, are connected by blood, a sociolegal contract, or act as if they were connected by a sociolegal contract (e.g., such as a committed gay or lesbian couple). Family of orientation is thought of as the family one chooses (e.g., choosing a mate) or creates (e.g., creating a child), although it may or may not include children.

A *nuclear family* consists of two heterosexual parents and one or more children. Some definitions of nuclear family further limit the definition, by requiring biological children, fathers who are in the paid labor force, and mothers who are homemakers (Peterson & Steinmetz, 1999). As family forms have become more diverse, the percentage of nuclear families has been declining to the point that it is no longer the standard against which other family forms are measured. According to the U.S. Census Bureau (2001), the proportion of married couple households with their own children declined from 40% of all U.S. households in 1970 to 24% in 2000. For this reason, Peterson and Steinmetz state that "it makes no sense to continually 'normalize' a form of the family that is attainable only by a minority and may have been dominant only briefly in our history" (p. 2).

A *binuclear family* is an original family split into two by divorce. Both families include whatever children were in the original family. One family is headed by the mother who may remain single or remarry, and the other family is headed by the father who may remain single or remarry (Ahrons & Rodgers, 1987). A *single-parent family* refers to a parent, who may or may not have been married, and one or more children (DeGenova & Rice, 2002). According to the U.S. Census Bureau (2001), single-parent families increased from 11% of all households in 1970 to 16% in 2000. Keeping in mind that the terms household and family are different, another way to look at this is that the percentage of single-parent *families* grew to 31% in 2000 (U.S. Census Bureau, 2001). In a *stepfamily*, "one or both of the married adults have children from a previous union with primary residence in the household" (DeFrain & Olson, 1999, p. 318). For many, the term stepfamily is preferred over the term "blended family" because "the label [blended family] fosters unrealistic expectations that the new family will quickly and easily blend together into a harmonious family" (DeFrain & Olson, p. 318).

A *cohabitating family* "consists of two people of the opposite sex living together, sharing sexual expression, who are committed to their relationship without formal legal marriage," and who may or may not have children (DeGenova & Rice, 2002, p. 4). As we discuss further in this chapter, cohabitation has increased dramatically in the last 40 years. A *gay or lesbian family* "consists of a couple of the same sex, living together and sharing sexual expression and commitment. Some gay or lesbian families include children, usually the offspring of one of the partners" (DeGenova & Rice, p. 4). Finally, a *child-free family* refers to a married couple who voluntarily decides not to have children (DeFrain & Olson, 1999).

## Defining Family by Function: Task-Orientation Definitions

Task-orientation definitions define family primarily by function, though in some cases they comment on form as well. Most commonly, task-orientation definitions view family as at least one adult and one or more other persons who perform certain tasks of family life such as socialization, nurturance, development, and financial and emotional support.

In one classic example of a task-orientation definition, Lerner and Spanier (1978) define family as a social unit that accepts responsibility for the socialization and nurturance of children. According to this definition, there are no structural limits on the social unit that accepts responsibility for the child. The social unit may involve one mother, two grandparents, or an adult who is not even related to a child biologically or legally.

A decision by the California Supreme Court illustrates that task performance and interaction are often valued more than family structure. The court awarded legal custody of a child to a man, Thomas, who had no biological relation to the child and was never married to the child's mother, and the mother did not even want him to have anything to do with her son. According to Sappenfield (2002):

> Thomas had met the child's mother when she was already three months pregnant. They moved in together a few months before the birth in 1995, and Thomas' name was on the birth certificate. After an on-again, off-again relationship [for four years]...the biological father nowhere to be found and the mother struggling with drug abuse, Thomas took custody of the boy and sought to become his permanent and legal provider. (p. 2)

Putting unprecedented scrutiny on blood ties, the court ruled that Thomas was indeed the boy's legal father (with no adoption processes necessary) because he had lived with the child for long periods of time, consistently referred to the child as his son, and offered significant financial and emotional support to the child. Essentially, the California court ruled that an adult could grow into the role of father or mother, because psychosocial caretaking tasks and financial support meant more in the end to the child's welfare than did biological ties. We should point out that in contrast to this example, there are plenty of examples of courts upholding blood ties and essentially devaluing psychosocial caretaking. This is a fear that adoptive parents know all too well.

Clearly, the task-orientation definitions set themselves apart from structural definitions in that they are more flexible. Whoever fulfills the tasks demanded of family members is considered family, regardless of his or her structural connection to the other members. This flexibility is often viewed as an advantage of task-orientation definitions. What becomes problematic for many task-orientation definitions is deciding what tasks *must* be performed in order to term someone family. Among the various task-orientation definitions, there is not perfect consensus. Task demands vary by family stage and type. For example, some couples do not have children and the task of socializing and nurturing children is not what defines them as family. For them, Lerner and Spanier's (1978) definition of family (as a social unit that accepts responsibility for the socialization and nurturance of children) is not so useful. So is it possible to define all the specific tasks that are required to define a group of people as family? There are some tasks that appear to be common to task-orientation definitions, and we discuss these common expectations for family tasks and functions in the next section.

### Common Family Tasks and Functions

Sociologists are credited with first viewing the family as a social institution that functions to meet the needs of the individual and society. Nurturing and socializing children has traditionally been viewed as the most primary and important function of the family

(Murdock, 1949; Reiss, 1980). This traditional view of course assumes nuclear families as the primary reference point. A more modern view of family functions acknowledges the need to nurture and socialize family members in general, whether they are children, adults, or elderly members, regardless of whether they entered the family through birth, marriage, adoption, or co-residence.

Nurturing family members involves providing basic care, emotional support, and financial support. Upon birth and for many years beyond, people rely on their families for food, clothing, and shelter. Emotional support provides family members with a sense of belonging, love, affection, kinship, companionship, and acceptance. Provision of at least basic care is not only a social and moral expectation but also a legal obligation because courts can take a child away from a family or certain family members if they do not provide sufficient care. Norms regarding parental responsibility for provision of care often become complicated after divorce. Nearly 50% of nonresidential, divorced parents have no contact with their children, and less than 15% have weekly contact (Ganong & Coleman, 1999; Seltzer, 1991). Child support laws attempt to spell out some expectations for nonresidential parents. However, many divorced parents fail to pay child support or do so insufficiently. Norms are also complicated after remarriage. A handful of states have laws requiring stepparents to provide financial assistance to their stepchildren (Fine & Fine, 1992) and, in a few cases, stepparents have been legally required to pay postdivorce child support to stepchildren (Ganong & Coleman).

Families are also expected to socialize members. Young children usually learn basic manners and social skills from their parents. Prior to formal education, most young children learn from their family how to recite their ABCs, to count, or to distinguish and name colors. Recreation is even a form of socialization in which children learn important roles for functioning inside and outside the family. Parents also pass on a variety of cultural traditions and values, including cultural stories, holiday rituals, political ideologies, or religious convictions. In addition, the family encourages its members to adapt to changes in society. Children even socialize parents, in what Peterson and Hann (1999) term "reciprocal socialization." For example, children may teach parents about societal advances in computer technology. Children may even help other family members adapt to larger changes in societal values, such as society's redefined roles of women or revised views about civil rights or sexual orientation.

Not all families fulfill these functions of care and socialization. As a result, educational, governmental, and religious organizations have taken on some obligations and duties once left to the family (Ganong & Coleman, 1999; Hareven, 1991). Many children rely exclusively on their school for breakfast and lunch, before and after school care, emotional support, not to mention socialization and intellectual development. The debate between public versus private responsibility for the young and the elderly remains charged.

## Defining Family by Interaction: Transactional Definitions

Transactional definitions represent a third approach to defining family and give central importance to the communication among individuals and the subjective feelings generated by interaction. Burgess and Locke (1953) proposed one of the first transactional definitions when they defined family as "a unit of interacting personalities." Naturally, many family communication scholars favor the transactional definitions. Transactional definitions do not intend to ignore the tasks demanded of family members. Rather, they extend the task-orientation definitions, arguing that a family is more than a group of people who perform certain tasks for one another. Although the distinction is not perfect, task-orientation definitions place more emphasis on the instrumental role of family, and transactional definitions highlight the interaction in the family. According to transactional definitions, what makes a group of people a family is that they perform their tasks within a certain system of interaction. Describing the interaction and subjective feelings that define the family system, Wamboldt and Reiss (1989) define family as "a group of intimates [whose interaction generates] a sense of home and group identity; complete with strong ties of loyalty and emotion, and an experience of a history and a future" (p. 728). The meaning and boundaries of family are often symbolized through family stories, family rituals, and other symbolic communication. Overall, the focus is not on the family's task performance but on the interaction *among* communicators (Whitchurch & Dickson, 1999). Interaction among family members according to the transactional perspective is characterized by the following: intimacy, interdependence, commitment, feelings of family identity, emotional ties, self-defined symbols and boundaries for family membership, and an ongoing history and future.

An advantage of task-orientation and transactional definitions is that they are more fluid and broad than most structural definitions. They allow us to name as family groups of people who traditionally would not be considered family. Furthermore, it is true that individuals' well-being is often more related to the psychosocial tasks performed by those around them as well as subjective feelings of intimacy and family identity, rather than to biological ties. The advantage of these definitions is simultaneously a disadvantage. Task-orientation definitions and transactional definitions are too broad for some purposes. For example, even people who are not "family" may fulfill psychosocial caretaking tasks, for example, teachers, babysitters, close friends. And even people who are not "family" may generate subjective feelings of home, identity, loyalty, strong emotion, and an experience of history and future, for example, fraternities and sororities and religious groups. Compared to structural definitions, psychosocial definitions imply that family is more voluntary in nature. This voluntary nature provides freedom, but at what cost? To what extent can people choose the tasks and subjective feelings that define family? For example, is it acceptable not to take on the task of caring for an older family member just because one does not feel an emotional connection with him or her? Is it acceptable to deny someone family status because one does not have feelings of home or loyalty with them?

After this discussion of various definitions, readers may wonder how the authors define family. Even though we feel that simple definitions of family are useful in some circumstances, we relied on a multifaceted definition of family to guide our choices about the type of research to include in this book. We prefer DeGenova and Rice's (2002) definition, which refers to structural, task-orientation, and transactional components in one definition. According to DeGenova and Rice, "family is any group of persons united by the ties of marriage, blood, or adoption, or any sexually expressive relationship, in which (1) the adults cooperate financially for their mutual support, (2) the people are committed to one another in an intimate interpersonal relationship, and (3) the members see their individual identities as importantly attached to the group with an identity of its own" (p. 2). Still, we are careful to note that there is not one universally accepted definition of family, and for the time being, there may be benefits to a variety of definitions.

## Implications of Family Definitions

So why do we need to define family anyway? Herein lies the great quandary. On one hand it seems that each individual should define for himself or herself what family is. However, people are continually motivated to define family for scientific, political, legal, and social reasons. For instance, scientists must take the task of defining family seriously, because what is known about the dynamics of families and treatment of perceived problems of families is highly influenced by one's definitions and theoretical lens (Settles, 1999, p. 147). McHale and Grolnick (2002) argue that family scholars have frequently used structural definitions to define family with a nucleocentric bias, resulting in an overwhelming number of studies of intact heterosexual couples raising children in nuclear families. However, as researchers grapple with how to broaden their definitions of family, they are reminded that any good scientific definition must specify what something is and what it is not. So when researchers conduct a study on families, a good definition makes clear who is included in the study. Definitions that are too broad are useless for scientific purposes.

Defining family is also important for political and legal reasons, because "a unit defined as family may be in line to receive such special benefits as housing, health care, and sick leave" (Popenoe, 1993, p. 529). In other words, "families will be acknowledged or forgotten as they are accorded family status" (Settles, 1999, p. 147). A good number of high-profile legal cases depict the struggle that often ensues when a wealthy person dies and relatives and former partners battle over inheritance. When money is involved, specific definitions of family suddenly become important. Knowing how to define family becomes important in other legal decisions regarding protection of contractual relationships among cohabitants, biotechnological developments such as in vitro fertilization and surrogate parenthood, visitation rights of grandparents, or land-use laws that recognize family-like living arrangements such as group homes within the meaning of "single family" land use (Melton & Wilcox, 1989). More than any other time in history, family scholars are significantly influencing legal and political decisions regarding family.

Finally, for social and practical reasons, people want to be able to explain to their social world who is in their family. Many people have very complicated answers to seemingly simple questions about who their family is. Even in personal conversations, people often use phrases such as "they are like family to me" to describe close friends, and people commonly distinguish, for example, their biological father from the person they really consider to be their "dad."

## FAMILY TRENDS AND DEMOGRAPHICS

In the following section, we explore demographic data related to trends in marriage, death, divorce, remarriage, single parenting, and family size. Why are family communication scholars interested in the demographic qualities of families? As we mentioned, family communication scholars argue that communication constitutes family and is vital to defining family reality. The various family forms we review represent different social constructions of family reality. We also argue later in this book that processes such as marriage and divorce are essentially communication processes. Events such as the birth of a child or the death of a family member fundamentally reshape interaction in the family system. We need to understand the demographic trends that are influenced by and influence family communication. For help, we turn to the U.S. Census Bureau, one of the richest demographic resources for the study of families (Rosenthal, 2001).

## Marriage Trends

According to the U.S. Census Bureau (2001), "marriage is still very much a part of American life" (p. 10). By age 65, about 95% of men and women in the United States have been married. However, since 1970, people have been delaying marriage. The proportion of women 20 to 24 years old who had never married doubled between 1970 and 2000, from 36% to 73%. During that same time, the number of never-married women between the ages of 30 and 34 tripled, from 6% to 22%. Delays in marriage have sharply increased for men as well. The number of unmarried men between the ages of 20 and 24 rose from 55% in 1970 to 84% in 2000. For men of ages 30 to 34, the never-married group jumped from 9% to 30%. Clearly, the median age at first marriage is rising for both men and women, and these changes are depicted in Figure 1.1. Over the last century, the age at first marriage was lowest for both men and women in 1956—at ages 22.5 and 20.1, respectively. Note that in 1890, the age, 26.1, at first marriage for men is not so different from the age, 26.8, at first marriage for men in the year 2000. For sure, many economic, social, and political events, some of which we discuss in chapters 5 and 6, have had strong influences on marriage trends.

In 2000, 3.7% of all households were termed "unmarried-partner households" (U.S. Census Bureau, 2001). This category could include cohabiting couples, whether homosexual or heterosexual. However the U.S. Census Bureau speculates that this number underrepresents the true number of heterosexual cohabiting couples or gay and lesbian couples, because such persons are sometimes reluctant to classify themselves and may describe themselves as friends or roommates. Even still, between 1980 and 1993, the known number of cohabiting couples doubled to nearly 4 million (Cohan & Kleinbaum, 2002; U.S. Census Bureau). Rates in recent years appear relatively stable. Data on cohabitation and marriage have an interesting relationship. Increasing cohabitation rates appear to be offsetting declining rates in marriage. Although people are delaying marriage, they are not, to the same degree, delaying the age at which they first enter a cohabiting union. In addition, nearly half of all first marriages begin with cohabitation (Bumpass, Sweet, & Cherlin, 1991).

## Death, Divorce, Remarriage, and Single-Parenting Trends

The U.S. Census Bureau (2001) reports that life expectancy increased from 46 years for men and 48 for women in 1900 to 74 years for men and 79 for women in 1997. Although life expectancy has increased for both males and females, higher male mortality rates mean

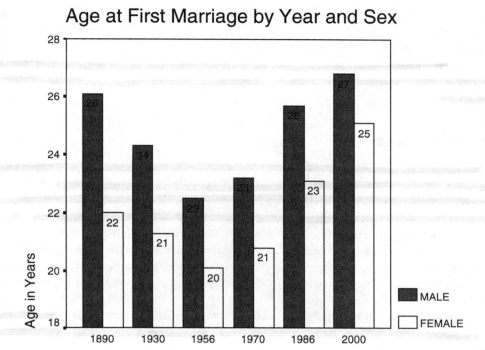

FIG. 1.1.   Age at First Marriage by Year and Sex.

*Note:* Data from *Estimated Median Age at First Marriage, by Sex: 1890 to the Present: January 1999* [Table MS-2] by U.S. Census Bureau. (1999, January). World Wide Web: http://www.census.gov/population/socdemo/ms-la/tabms-2.txt and *Median Age at First Marriage of the Population 15 Years and Over by Sex: Selected Years, 1970 to 2000* [Figure 3] by U.S. Census Bureau, America's Families and Living Arrangements. (2001, June). World Wide Web: http://www.census.gov/prod/2001pubs/p20-537.pdf.

women have a greater likelihood of living alone than do men. Among the population 75 years and over, 67% of men were living with their spouses in 2000 compared with only 29% of women the same age. Because women, on average, marry older men (by 2–3 years) and live longer (by about 5 years), women can expect to live the last 7 to 8 years of their lives as widows.

Divorce causes even more marital dissolutions than does death. About half of all marriages initiated in recent years will end in divorce. In chapter 11, we further discuss trends in divorce and the dramatic increase in divorce rates over the last 30 to 40 years. Most divorced people and many widowed individuals remarry. As a result, almost half of all marriages are remarriages for one or both partners, and many of these remarriages involve children from one or both partners (Bumpass, Sweet, & Castro Martin, 1990; Ganong & Coleman, 1999). Remarriage often happens quickly, with the median number of years between divorce and remarriage at 3 years for women and 4 years for men (U.S. Census Bureau, 2001).

Divorce and remarriage restructure families. According to the National Survey of Families and Households, about one third of children live with a stepparent (Bumpass, Raley, & Sweet, 1995). The number of single mothers and single fathers is also rising dramatically. In 2000, of those households that are considered family households, 26% were single-mother families (more than triple the number in 1970), whereas 5% were single-father families (more than five times the number in 1970; U.S. Census Bureau, 2001). The increase in single-parent families is related both to (a) the increase in divorce rates and (b) the increase in never-married mothers and fathers who may be delaying marriage.

## Family Size Trends

After World War II, birthrates climbed to a high level and remained high for the next 20 years (from 1945 to 1965), producing a group of people termed *baby boomers*. Presently, the increase in childless women, delays in marriage, and the economic implications of raising children are some of the factors that contribute to smaller family sizes. From 1970 to 2000, the percentage of family groups that have four or more children decreased from 17% to 6% (U.S. Census Bureau, 2001). Figure 1.2 depicts declines in household size between 1970 and 2000 (although keep in mind that the terms household and family are not synonymous). Note that between 1970 and 2000, the average number of people per household declined from 3.14 to 2.62.

Though people are having fewer children now compared to in the past, more adult children are living at home, and adult children are more likely to return to their parents'

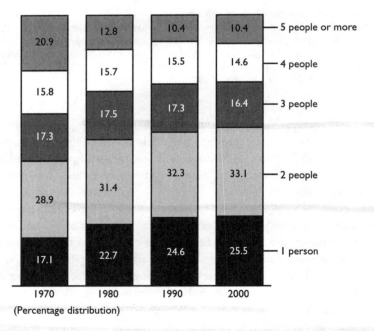

FIG. 1.2.   Household Size Between 1970 and 2000.

*Source:* U.S. Census Bureau, Current Population Survey, March Supplements: 1970 to 2000.

*Note:* Figure from *Households by Size: Selected Years, 1970 to 2000*: [Figure 2] by U.S. Census Bureau. (2001). *America's families and living arrangements: Population characteristics*, World Wide Web: http://www.census.gov/prod/2001pubs/p20-537.pdf.

home after departures for education or work (Mitchell & Gee, 1996). In 2000, forty-three percent of women and 56% of men ages 18 to 24 lived at home with one or both of their parents.

## DEFINING COMMUNICATION AND ITS CHARACTERISTICS

Like definitions of family, there are numerous definitions of communication that reflect diverse perspectives in the communication discipline. Indeed, most readers have likely been exposed to at least a basic definition of communication. We prefer a definition of communication that highlights many of the basic issues addressed by communication theorists: *Communication is a transactional process in which individuals create, share, and regulate meaning.*

Communication scholars have long been interested in the means by which humans communicate. Watzlawick, Beavin, and Jackson (1967) proposed that humans use both digital and analogic codes to communicate. In *digital codes*, meaning is conveyed symbolically. *Symbols* are arbitrary and conventional units of meaning. In other words, there is no necessary relationship between the symbol and the thing or idea that the symbol represents. Words and numbers are two common examples of symbols. As long as members of a language community agree that the word "hungry" represents that physical state, then it becomes a symbol. People simply choose the sounds produced by those letters to stand for that physical state. Members of a language community use the same symbols and recognize them as conventional units of meaning. One assumption inherent in family communication research is that each family is a unique miniculture (Whitchurch & Dickson, 1999). Minicultures develop their own symbols. The meaning assigned to those symbols is only understood by those who are a part of the miniculture. For example, family minicultures have nicknames, family jokes, or references that only members of the family understand.

*Analogic codes* communicate meaning by being similar to what they convey. The code is the thing, not a distant representation of the thing. Thus, there is a direct relationship between the code and the meaning expressed. For example, a no smoking sign that uses an analogic code would show a picture of a cigarette with a diagonal line through the cigarette to indicate that cigarettes are not allowed. In contrast, a no smoking sign in a digital code would simply read "no smoking," relying on symbolic words. Many nonverbal behaviors are analogic codes. For example, facial movements are the expressions of real emotions, not just a distant representation of an emotion. A great deal of family communication occurs through nonverbal analogic codes. Parents communicate with their newborn infants almost entirely through analogic codes (e.g., the cry or yawn of a baby), and even as their children age, some parents become quite skilled at decoding their child's expressions (e.g., knowing the child is distressed by the expression on his or her face).

But is all behavior communication? Watzlawick et al. (1967) originally proposed, "one cannot not communicate." That is, every behavior is communicative. Indeed in families, members may know each other so well that they can determine the intent behind most behaviors, or so they think they can. Bavelas (1990) later conceded that all behavior is not communicative, though it may have informative value (p. 599). Thus, one individual's interpretation is not the same as communication. Communication is a mutual process that extends beyond one person's interpretations. Communication relies on intersubjectivity. *Intersubjectivity* refers to shared meaning, or a state where a person understands the other and is understood by the other. In families, a great deal of history and common experience allows individuals to reach a level of intersubjectivity that they would not otherwise achieve in more casual relationships. Long-time married couples often report that they achieve this intersubjectivity—they understand what their partners are thinking and feeling—even when few, if any, words are exchanged. However, even couples that know each other well often resort to lengthy exchanges in order to understand each other. And sometimes they never understand each other and simply have to do the best job they can at attempting to understand and coordinate their behavior (Pearce, 1976).

The success of communication is dependent on *feedback*, or the interpretations and evaluations one receives about the message. Feedback indicates that it is possible and in fact common for people to disagree about the meaning of any given symbol. As illustrated in subsequent chapters on marital communication or parent–child communication, family members often become confused about what other members "meant" by their verbal or nonverbal behavior. For example, parents may define a "fun" activity very differently from the way their children do, and they eventually are prompted by the child to clarify and regulate a new, shared meaning. Watzlawick et al. (1967) term this process "reframing," whereby family members step outside the situation or the norms of the family system and look at things in a new light.

Watzlawick et al. (1967) proposed another axiom that is central to the study of family communication: "Every communication has a content and relationship aspect such that the latter classifies the former and is therefore a metacommunication" (p. 54). *Content messages* refer to what is said, and *relationship messages* refer to how it is said and the impact it has on the relationship. Relationship messages are often communicated through nonverbal behavior. To Watzlawick et al., relationship messages are always most important. Much of the study of family communication is the study of relationship messages. Marital partners in conflict may find they underestimated or overestimated the amount of impact that their communication had on their partner. Parents may offer the same content message to two children, but the relationship message is sent or interpreted differently by each child. *Metacommunication*, then, refers to communication about communication, where the communicators say "This is how I see myself . . . this is how I see you . . . this is how I see you seeing me" (Watzlawick et al., p. 54). Metacommunication is an important skill for families, particularly when things go wrong in family communication. In distressed family relationships, metacommunication is typically absent or constant (i.e., the members are constantly battling over interpretations of content or the nature of the relationship).

Our definition of communication also implies that people create, share, and regulate meaning in a transactional process. As a process, communication is an ongoing, complex, changing activity (Dance, 1967). Every family's communication is continuous, with a unique history, present, and future. Past experiences in the family clearly influence present interactions. Communication defines the family's present reality and constructs family relationships. Families are constantly renegotiating their reality into the future. Rather than attempting to understand the family from one specific instance of communication or from one family member, the family should be understood as a whole. Because most families are not just dyadic relationships, the transactional process is complex. In this relatively new area of family communication, many scholars who originated from the area of interpersonal communication naturally focused most of their attention on various family dyads (e.g., parent–child communication, marital communication; Whitchurch & Constantine, 1993). For sure, family communication research has and still does benefit from this tradition. Thanks to the nudging of scholars from the area of group communication, family communication scholars today are increasingly focusing on whole family interactions (Socha, 1999). Communication, even if just between a dyad, always occurs in a whole family system. Although some believe that family communication is simply the study of communication in the context of families, most family scholars assert "the family is the central organizing construct of study, not a context for communication" (Whitchurch & Dickson, 1999, p. 690).

## MODELS OF FAMILY FUNCTIONING

### Olson's Circumplex Model

Perhaps the premier model of family functioning was developed by family systems theorist David Olson (1993; Olson, Sprenkle, & Russell, 1979). Olson suggested that there are two primary dimensions of family behavior that are vital to their functioning. These are termed *adaptability* and *cohesion*. A third dimension of family behavior, communication, is presumed to allow families to change their degree of adaptability and cohesion in response to the demands they face.

The adaptability dimension of family behavior refers to "the ability of a marital/family system to change its power structure, role relationships, and relationship rules in response to situational and developmental stress" (Olson et al., 1979, p. 12). More recently, Olson has referred to this dimension of family behavior as "flexibility" (Olson, 1993). Families that are highly adaptive change easily in response to environmental demands. Families with low adaptability have a fixed or invariant style of functioning and interacting. In times of crisis or bounty, their behavior remains fairly constant. Family adaptability is manifested in how assertive family members are with each other, the amount of control in the family, family discipline practices, negotiation, how rigidly family roles are adhered to, and the nature and enforcement of rules in the family. In the circumplex model, there are four different levels of family functioning that represent different points on the highly adaptable to nonadaptable continuum. Running from low to high adaptability, these include the rigid, structured, flexible, and chaotic families. A profile of such families, as a function of the different family adaptability behaviors, is presented in Table 1.1. According to Olson, the midlevel or balanced families (i.e., flexible or structured) are the most functional, whereas extreme families (i.e., chaotic or rigid) are assumed to be the least functional. This is because rigid families are unable to change their power structure and interaction patterns to appropriately meet the demands and challenges they face. At the same time, chaotic families represent something of a free-for-all with no clear idea on any given day of who is in charge or who is occupying what roles.

**TABLE 1.1**
Levels of Family Adaptability in Olson's Circumplex Model
of Family Functioning

| Concepts | Chaotic (Extreme Adaptability) | Flexible (High Adaptability) | Structured (Mod.–Low Adaptability) | Rigid (No Adaptability) |
|---|---|---|---|---|
| Assertiveness/ Passiveness | Opposite styles (rules unclear) | Generally assertive | Generally assertive | Opposite styles (vacillates) |
| Control | Limited leadership | Egalitarian (fluid leadership) | Democratic with clear leader | Authoritarian leadership |
| Discipline | Lenient | Democratic with unpredictable consequences | Democratic with predictable consequences | Autocratic and overly strict |
| Negotiation | Endless negotiation and poor problem solving | Good negotiation and Problem solving | Good problem solving and rules for negotiation | Limited negotiation and poor problem solving |
| Roles | Dramatic role shifts | More fluid family roles | More defined family roles | Rigid roles (stereotyped) |
| Rules | Dramatic rule shifts and many implicit rules; rules arbitrarily enforced | Rule changes and more implicit than explicit rules | Few rule changes, mostly explicit rules; rules enforced | Rigid, extreme rules; rules strictly enforced |

Reprinted from Olson, D. H. (1993). Circumplex model of marital and family systems: Assessing family functioning. In F. Walsh (Ed.), *Normal family processes* (2nd ed., pp. 104–137). New York: Guilford with permission.

The second major dimension of family behavior in Olson's circumplex model is family *cohesion*. This dimension represents "the emotional bonding members have with one another and the degree of individual autonomy a person experiences in the family system" (Olson et al., 1979, p. 5). Like family adaptability, the family's cohesion is evident in a number of family behaviors that include their emotional bonding to each other, the regulation and maintenance of boundaries, the nature of family coalitions, how the family shares time and space, family versus individual friends, and family decision-making patterns. Very cohesive families spend maximum time together, make decisions as a family, and are strongly bonded to each other emotionally. Noncohesive families tend to have members who "do their own thing," have their own friends, spend little time together, and maintain more personal than shared family space. As with the adaptability dimension, Olson and his colleagues suggest that there are four different family types on the cohesion dimension that represent different points on the continuum. From low to high cohesion, these family types are: disengaged, separated, connected, and enmeshed. A profile of such families, as a function of the different family cohesion behaviors, is presented in Table 1.2. Once again, Olson argues that it is the midlevel or balanced

**TABLE 1.2**
Levels of Family Cohesion in Olson's Circumplex Model of Family
Functioning

| Concepts | Disengaged (No Cohesion) | Separated (Low–Moderate Cohesion) | Connected (Moderate–High Cohesion) | Enmeshed (Extreme Cohesion) |
|---|---|---|---|---|
| Emotional Bonding | Independent (low) | Low–moderate | High–moderate | Dependent (high) |
| Internal/External Boundaries | Open external boundaries | Open internal boundaries | Closed external boundaries | Blurred internal boundaries |
| Coalition | Weak coalition (family scapegoat) | Clear marital coalition (husband–wife stronger) | Strong marital coalition (united front) | Strong parent–child coalition |
| Time | Maximum time away from family | Time alone (space) & time together important | Time together more important than space | Maximum time together |
| Space | Maximum separate physical space | Maintain private space and family space | Maximum family space and minimum private space | Minimum private space |
| Friends | Few family friends; many individual friends | Some family and individual friends | More time with family friends— some individual friends | Family friends more important; few individual friends |
| Decision Making | Individual decisions | Most decisions are individual based; able to make joint family decisions | Individual decisions are shared; made with family interests in in mind | All decisions made by family |

Reprinted from Olson, D. H., Sprenkle, D. H., & Russell, C. S. (1979). Circumplex model of marital and family systems: I. Cohesion and adaptability dimensions, family types, and clinical applications. *Family Process, 18*, 3–28 with permission.

families (i.e., separated or connected) who are the most functional, with the extreme-level families (i.e., disengaged and enmeshed) being the least functional. The reasoning is that disengaged families exhibit insufficient bonding to each other and excessive autonomy from the family. The enmeshed families on the other hand exhibit extreme emotional bonding to each other, overidentification with the family, blurred boundaries, and insufficient autonomy to function effectively outside of the family context.

The communication that takes place among family members is considered to be a third important aspect of family behavior. In the circumplex model, family communication is seen as a *facilitating dimension*. By this, Olson and his colleagues (1979) mean that communication allows the family members to move on the adaptability and cohesion dimensions. As families grow, develop, and change it is often necessary for them to adjust their adaptability and cohesion in order to maintain optimal functioning. Positive communication behaviors such as self-disclosure, clarity, attentive listening, demonstration of empathy, and staying on topic are assumed to facilitate such adjustments in adaptability and cohesion (Olson, 1993). On the other hand, negative family communication behaviors such as criticism, denial of feelings, excessive conflict, and failure to listen are assumed to impede the family's movement on the adaptability and cohesion dimensions. Consequently, when it would be optimal for families to alter their adaptability or cohesion, they remain stuck at one point on the continuum, unable to change their behavior. This contributes to dysfunctional responses to environmental stressors.

By combining the adaptability (or flexibility) and cohesion dimensions, it is possible to plot families on a two-dimensional space. This plot, depicted in Figure 1.3, constitutes the circumplex model of family functioning. Families who could be plotted on the periphery of the circumplex model are considered to be *extreme* families. That is to say that they

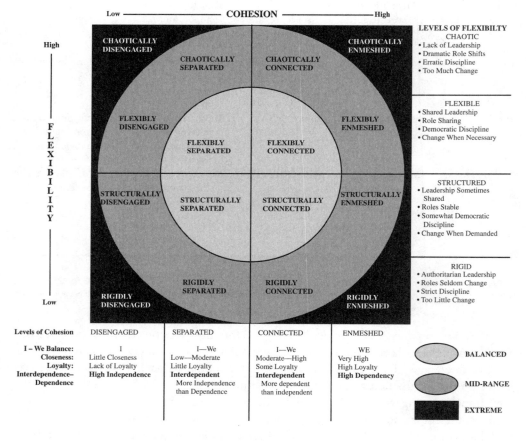

**FIG. 1.3.** The Circumplex Model of Family Functioning.
Reprinted from Olson, D. H., Sprenkle, D. H., & Russell, C. S. (1979). Circumplex model of marital and family systems: I. Cohesion and adaptability dimensions, family types, and clinical applications. *Family Process, 18*, 3–28 with permission.

have either very high or very low adaptability or cohesion. These are assumed to be the least functional families. Families whose behavior places them somewhat closer to the middle of the circumplex model are characterized as *midrange* families. These families are moderately functional because they are balanced on at least one of the two dimensions of family behavior. Finally, the families whose behavior locates them at the center of the circumplex model are considered to be the most functional. Their location at the center indicates that they are balanced on both dimensions of family behavior.

It is important to bear in mind that families can change their position on the circumplex as they evolve over time (Olson, 1993). In fact, the most functional families will alter their adaptability and cohesion to levels that are most appropriate to their stage of the family life cycle. For example, newlywed couples may be extremely high on the cohesion dimension but somewhat low on the adaptability dimension. However, as time passes and they have children, cohesion levels may naturally decline and adaptability levels may increase substantially. The presence of multiple children in the home ordinarily calls for substantial adaptability in order to keep the family functioning at an appropriate level. Keep in mind that it is the family's positive communication skills that are hypothesized to allow for movement on the adaptability and cohesion dimensions. This is an important ability for maintaining family functioning during times of stress (see chap. 9 for more details on the circumplex model and family stress).

In some of the original analyses of the circumplex model, Olson and his colleagues found that balanced or midrange families had the highest level of family functioning (e.g., Olson et al., 1979; Russell, 1979). Further evidence for this curvilinear (i.e., inverted U) relationship between adaptability or cohesion and family functioning has been documented in research conducted since then (e.g., Kawash & Kozeluk, 1990; Olson, 2000; Rodick, Henggeler, & Hanson, 1986; Thomas & Olson, 1993; Yahav, 2002). However, there is also some evidence to suggest that there are linear relationships among adaptability, cohesion, and positive family outcomes (Farrell & Barnes, 1993; James & Hunsley, 1995; Perosa & Perosa, 2001; Shields & Clark, 1995). Especially for family cohesion, some research shows that more is better. At the present time, scientists do not completely agree on the exact nature of the relationships among adaptability, cohesion, and family functioning. It may be that the measures of family cohesion, for example, do not effectively discriminate between connected and enmeshed families. Another possibility is that enmeshed families may be rare in our society, so they may not show up in research studies very often. This could make it look like more cohesion is better for family functioning. We suspect that, at least in theory, families with extraordinarily high levels of cohesion probably do not function as well as those that are moderate in cohesion. The confused roles and boundaries that are associated with very high cohesion, the failure to develop a unique identity apart from the family, and the lack of friends aside from "family friends" would ordinarily not be conducive for optimal family outcomes.

## The McMaster Model of Family Functioning

Unlike Olson's (1993) circumplex model that plots family functioning in a two-dimensional space, the McMaster model of family functioning (Epstein, Bishop, & Levin, 1978) is based on six conceptual dimensions of family functionality. Even though there are many more dimensions in the McMaster model, many of them are closely related to adaptability and cohesion (Noller & Fitzpatrick, 1993), so it is more similar to Olson's circumplex model than what may appear at first glance. The McMaster model was developed with attention to clinical application. One of the underlying philosophies of the McMaster model is that family functioning is better described by transactional and systematic properties of the family than by intrapsychic characteristics of individual family members. Consequently, family assessment from the perspective of the McMaster model focuses on structural and organizational properties of the family, along with appraisals of the transactions among family members (Epstein, Baldwin, & Bishop, 1983).

The first dimension of the McMaster model of family functioning is *problem solving*, which is the family's ability to resolve issues that threaten their functional capacity. It is assumed that the most functional families work through common stages of problem solving such as identifying the problem, deciding on alternative solutions, and monitoring actions. Like Olson's (1993) model, the McMaster model has a *communication* dimension. This is the exchange of information among family members in a way that is both clear and direct. This dimension of family behavior is measured in the McMaster model with items such as "People come right out and say things instead of hinting at them," "We are frank with each other," and "When someone is upset the others know why" (Epstein et al., 1983). We should note that in the McMaster model, the general term "communication" is used to describe healthy, functional behaviors. For sure, most communication scholars are careful not to use the term *communication* as loosely, given communication can also refer to dysfunctional behaviors (e.g., see chap. 15). The *roles* dimension of the McMaster model describes the established patterns of behavior in the family for handling various functions and tasks. In the McMaster model, the most functional families are those in which members each have a role and are accountable for performing the duties associated with that role. The fourth dimension is termed *affective responsiveness* and reflects the extent to which family members are able to experience and express a range of emotions. In the most functional families, the expression of emotion is accepted regardless of its nature. In more dysfunctional families, emotions are either suppressed, or only a limited range of emotional expression (e.g., only happiness) is tolerated. A related dimension called *affective involvement* represents the family's interest in and connection to each other. This dimension is very similar to the cohesion dimension in Olson's model. Affective involvement implies that family members place value on one another's activities. Like the cohesion dimension of Olson's circumplex model, in the McMaster model it is assumed that the relationship between affective involvement and family functioning is curvilinear. There is such a thing as too much affective involvement. Similarly, too little affective involvement would mean that family members generally do not care about each other, so this too would be seen as dysfunctional. The sixth and final dimension of the McMaster model of family functioning is *behavior control*. This variable reflects the way that the family expresses and maintains standards for the behavior of its members. In the model, there are four different behavior control profiles: flexible, rigid, laissez-faire, and chaotic. The rigid and chaotic styles are seen as extremes in low or high flexibility, respectively. These are not considered to be functional profiles for a family's behavior control. However, the laissez-faire and flexible styles are less extreme. In the McMaster model, flexible behavior control is viewed as most functional. In this model, behavior control is seen as an issue in situations involving danger, expressing psychological needs and drives, and social behavior. Like the affective involvement dimension, there is such a thing as too much and too little behavior control. The best functioning families have moderate amounts of behavior control in most circumstances.

## THE INFLUENCE OF CULTURE

In the opening of this chapter, we remind readers that people have implicit, personal theories of family life that are shaped by experiences in their own family minicultures, their interactions with other families around them, their cultural background, and the media. These personal theories about family life affect views of family competence. In the following sections, we examine how issues of cultural diversity influence what scholars and laypersons view as optimal family interaction.

"In sharp contrast with earlier times, latterday family diversity is more likely to be celebrated than castigated" (Aponte, 1999, p. 111). Even still, family scholars in the social scientific tradition are only beginning to explore the relationship between culture and family communication (Diggs & Socha, 2004; Goodwin, 1999). Current knowledge about marital and family communication is informed mostly by intact European-American middle-class couples raising children in nuclear families (Flannagan et al., 2002; McHale & Grolnick, 2002). Admittedly, a great deal of the research we review in this book has a Eurocentric framing. One alternative to a Eurocentric perspective is an Afrocentric approach. With an Afrocentric framing, the researcher views family life from "the lived experiences of Africans and African Americans" (Socha & Diggs, 1999, p. 12; see also Asante, 1988). An Afrocentric approach to family life is characterized, in part, by (a) definitions of family that emphasize extended family versus just the nuclear family; (b) family values of collectivism, spirituality, and openness; and (c) an awareness of the family's story or struggle regarding race and racism. There is a pressing need for more cultural sensitivity and awareness in family communication research, as represented by the Afrocentric perspective. As Gudykunst and Lee (2001) argue, people cannot "assume that family communication is the same within or across ethnic groups. Research based on European American families may or may not generalize to non-European-American families" (pp. 82–83). In addition to specific Eurocentric or Afrocentric approaches, there are obviously other cultural frames of reference related to the study of family communication.

Using a cultural variability approach to the study of family communication, researchers examine a family's or individual family member's orientation toward major cultural values (Hofstede, 1980; Socha & Diggs, 1999; Ting-Toomey, 1999). A family's cultural heritage does not always inform one about family communication patterns, because "not all members of ethnic groups identify with their ethnic groups or maintain their cultural practices" (Gudykunst & Lee, 2001, p. 83). For this reason, *self-construals*, the way people view themselves in relation to others, are better predictors of communication styles than larger cultural dimensions such as individualism–collectivism (Gudykunst et al., 1996). Some people from collectivist cultural backgrounds, for example, who would typically be expected to stress family harmony and collectivist norms, instead act according to individualistic values. Markus and Kitayama (1991) introduced the concepts of interdependent and independent self-contruals. People with an *independent self-construal* tend to view themselves as unique individuals, separate from others, who do not have to consult others before deciding how to act. People with an *interdependent self-construal* view themselves as interconnected to their ingroups. Gudykunst (1994) explains that people all use both independent and interdependent self-construals, but one style tends to dictate their behavior in most contexts. Still, as Gudykunst (1994) describes, some people from the United States who have a predominately independent self-construal may have an interdependent self-construal with regard to their family. For this reason, Gudykunst and Lee recommend assessing a person's family-specific self-construal in order to better understand family communication. In this way, it is possible to assess an *individual's* orientation (not a general culture's orientation) toward Hofstede's cultural values (e.g., individualism–collectivism, masculinity–femininity, power–distance) in reference to the individual's family.

*Individualism–collectivism* refers to a person's focus on the self versus the group. This dimension is likely to affect individual perceptions about appropriate family cohesion. It may also influence perceptions about the extent to which parents should nurture their young and teach them to contribute to the common family good or instead teach them to be independent and stand out from the crowd.

Lynch (1998) states:

> What one person views as nurturance, another may view as spoiling. For example, [many parents throughout the world nurture children] by having them sleep in their parents' bed; following them around in order to feed them; keeping them in close physical proximity through holding, touching, and carrying long after they can walk alone. Many families in the United States would describe themselves as nurturing, but they expect more independence. Infants may sleep alone in rooms of their own soon after birth; feedings are scheduled, and young children are expected to stay in a particular chair or area for meals; and children spend far more time in infant swings or playpens than on the laps of their caregivers. (p. 59)

Depending on one's orientation toward individualism–collectivism, the preference for openness or the objection to enmeshed bonding implied by Olson's model is culturally influenced (Parks, 1982). Individualism–collectivism even relates to family structure issues. Some families, such as African American families and Latino families, are typically large with extended family networks that are active in daily life, in the form of childcare, shared housing, or socializing. Other families are small with just one or two adults responsible for the household, family activities, and support.

*Masculinity–femininity* refers to whether sex roles are defined and differentiated (i.e., masculine) versus whether roles are flexible and interchangeable (i.e., feminine). Naturally, this dimension relates to perceptions about roles and rights in marriage, as well as to socialization of children. *Power–distance* refers to the extent to which a person respects authority and hierarchy (i.e., high power–distance) versus viewing all persons as equal in status (low power–distance). This dimension would seem to influence family rules and negotiation, as well as respect for family members and family tradition.

Besides looking at cultural values and interaction norms, another way of examining family diversity is by exploring how family structure (e.g., family size) varies according to cultural considerations (see Aponte, 1999, p. 117). As for family size, Mexican American families have the largest average family size (4.1 persons), compared to Chinese American (3.6), African American and Puerto Rican (both 3.5), Japanese American (3.1), and non-Hispanic-White (3.0) families. Extended family households are proportionally the highest among recent immigrants from Latin American as well as Asian countries (Aponte). African American families have the highest divorce ratio, and less than 80% of African American women between the ages of 35 and 44 had ever married in 1990 (Aponte, 1999). In comparison, non-Hispanic-White families have the lowest divorce ratio, and 92.1% of non-Hispanic-White women in the same age range have married. Naturally, then, there is also a higher proportion of births to unmarried African American women than to non-Hispanic-White women.

Aponte (1999) cautions that data presenting family structural differences by culture should be interpreted carefully because: "The range of variation *within* groups on any specific item (e.g., family size) is usually far greater than the gap *separating* groups on the item (difference in average size). Additionally, it is well known that many differences between groups actually reflect socio-economic standing, or more simply 'class,' rather than 'culture' or 'ethnicity'" (p. 111). As people marry across cultures and adapt family functioning across cultures, classification systems become more complicated. Finally, Diggs and Socha (2004) encourage researchers to view "culture" with a broader lens, so as to systematically study the impact of other variables besides race on family communication. Other variables include socioeconomic class, mental and physical health, religion, and rural versus urban environments.

Throughout this book, we point the readers to boxed inserts that highlight the media's influence in and portrayal of family life, with regard to various topics in the book. In Box 1.1, we summarize descriptive work by James Robinson and Thomas Skill (2001) regarding the portrayal of cultural and structural diversity in families on television from the 1950s to the 1990s.

## CONCLUSION

Defining family is a complicated issue. There is not one universally accepted definition of family, and any given individual defines family differently depending on his or her purpose. We learned in this chapter that family is commonly defined by structure, tasks performed, or interaction, and that family communication scholars place special emphasis on interaction as a defining feature. We also examined labels for common family structures as well as common expectations for tasks performed and interactions exchanged among family members. These labels will provide a language for describing families throughout the book. In addition, the family tasks and interactions hint at many of the family processes we will examine in subsequent chapters. To some, defining family seems mundane. However, important scientific, legal, and social implications rest on family definitions.

In upcoming chapters, we explore many of the family trends depicted by the demographic data on families presented in this chapter. We also continue to explore the defining features of family communication, including the complex nature of content and

---

**Box 1.1**
**Television Portrayals of Cultural and Structural Diversity in Families**

*Reflections on TV portrayals of family from Robinson and Skill (2001)*

- "Since first appearing in 1968, the number of African American families has increased to 14% in the 1990s. During that same time, families of other races have been nearly nonexistent" (p. 158).
- "The divorce rate of TV families has jumped from 2.9% during the 1970s to 15% in the 1990s" (p. 158).
- "Whereas the percentage of nuclear families was higher during the 1950s, the percentage of nuclear families has been fairly stable at about 25% for the past 35 years" (p. 158).
- "Single parents have been and remain significant factors in leading families on television, accounting for 24% in the 1950s, 32% in the 1960s, 24% in the 1970s, 34% in the 1980s, and 31% in the 1990s" (p. 159).

What can we discern from these descriptive data regarding portrayals of television families? Robinson and Skill (2001) argue that the slowly growing diversity in television families reflects the public's increasing acknowledgment and validation of such families. The benefit for viewers, according to Robinson and Skill, is that they will come to understand the family systems concept of equifinality. Recall that the principle of equifinality suggests that multiple paths, or in this case, multiple family configurations and cultures, can be functional and satisfying. Yet, television still appears to be out of touch with the way families look and act in the real world. Regarding portrayals of racial and ethnic diversity, television families still do not proportionally reflect the diversity of race and ethnicity reflective of families in America today. Regarding diversity in family roles and lifestyles, Robinson and Skill write, "Although some voices in the popular media consider many televised family portrayals to be uninvited role models for atypical or dysfunctional family configurations or lifestyles, numerous studies confirm that television is at best a 'close follower' of real-world trends and lifestyles" (p. 140).

Do you think television family portrayals have become any closer to real-world families from the 1990s to now? To what extent are non-White families or gay or lesbian families being portrayed in TV now? Finally, is it important for TV families to reflect real families?

---

Reprinted from Robinson, J. D., & Skill, T. (2001). Five decades of families on television: From the 1950s through the 1990s. In J. Bryant & J. A. Bryant (Eds.), *Television and the American family*, 2nd ed., (pp. 139–162). Mahwah, NJ: Lawrence Erlbaum Associates with permission.

relationship messages and the role of communication in constituting family meaning. In addition, the models of family functioning (Olson's circumplex model and the McMaster model) that we present in this chapter point to many of the issues concerning family interaction that we explore in depth. Finally, we introduce in this chapter how culture and societal influences such as the media impact the way people define family and determine what they feel is functional family interaction.

CHAPTER TWO

# Theoretical Perspectives on Family Communication

In this chapter we review a number of influential theories of family communication and relationships. Although not all of the theories discussed in this chapter were explicitly developed as theories of family interaction per se, each has been widely and fruitfully applied in the scientific study of families.

What is a theory, and why do social scientists develop theories? Simply put, a theory is an explanation of a fact pattern. Social scientists generally do not develop theories to explain individual cases or incidents. Rather, theories are developed to explain how and why certain things happen, particularly when those things happen repeatedly. For example, scientists and therapists realized that a lot of couples who get divorced exhibit certain patterns of destructive conflict. For that reason, they attempted to develop a theory that explains how and why conflict can harm a marriage (see chaps. 4 and 11 for further analysis of this issue). If only a handful of divorced couples had problems with conflict, scientists probably would not have been motivated to develop an explanation for why conflict harms marriage. Scientific theories serve a number of useful functions. Perhaps the most basic function of a theory is to *explain* how and why a phenomenon occurs or operates. A related function of theories is to *predict* when a phenomenon might or might not happen. For example, in recent years there has been great interest in developing theories of divorce that allow for prediction of who will divorce and who will stay married. In addition, theories sometimes allow scientists and therapists to *control* a phenomenon. If a valid theory of divorce explains the phenomenon as caused by dysfunctional communication patterns, instituting training seminars or therapy techniques that address those communication problems might be a useful way to lower the divorce rate.

In this chapter, we present an analysis of family systems theory, symbolic interaction theory, social learning theory, attachment theory, and the dialectic perspective. Notice how each theory offers different explanations of how and why family interactions function as they do. It is important to keep in mind that no theory offers the one and only explanation for a fact pattern. There are often multiple explanations for why family interactions function as they do. The utility of a theory is therefore determined, at least in part, by how well it holds up under empirical scrutiny. In other words, are the available data consistent with the propositions of the theory? All of the theories discussed in this chapter have been associated with numerous studies that support the essential components and elements of the theory.

## FAMILY SYSTEMS THEORY

### Historical Background

As social scientific theories go, family systems theory has unique beginnings. In fact, family systems theory emerged from a line of work that was more closely related to engineering and biology than to families or human relationships. Family systems theory was derived from general systems theory (GST), which is a theoretical perspective developed for explaining how elements of a system work together to produce outputs from the various inputs they are given. A "*system*" is nothing more than a "set of elements standing in interrelation among themselves and with the environment" (Bertalanffy, 1975, p. 159). Two key figures in the development of GST were biologist Ludwig von Bertalanffy and mathematician and engineer Norbert Wiener (e.g., Bertalanffy, 1968; Wiener, 1948). Wiener is most noted for his work on *cybernetics*, which is the science of self-correcting systems. An early application of GST came from work on antiaircraft gunnery during World War II. An essential realization of this work was the necessity to constantly compare the aim of the weapon, and the resultant course of its munitions delivery, to the position of the target. When the ammunition was being delivered too far ahead of the plane or too far behind, the operator of the weapon had to take this into consideration and adjust the aim of the antiaircraft gun. In the abstract, this concept is known as *cybernetic feedback* and would be an essential component of GST.

Whitchurch and Constantine (1993) identified three basic assumptions of GST. First, systems theories can unify science. The principles of GST are thought by many to cut across traditional academic boundaries. That is to say, they apply to systems in the natural as well as in the social sciences. For this reason, concepts and processes that describe the functioning of an automobile engine (mechanical engineering) could be equally applicable to a description of the functioning of a family (family science), or the functioning of a particular ecosystem (biology). A second assumption of GST is that a system must be understood as a whole. This concept, known as *holism*, is fundamental to all systems approaches. A system cannot be understood by merely studying each of its components in isolation from each other. There is little to be learned about the functions and outputs of an automobile engine by carefully examining the alternator and oil filter. That would not be much more useful than trying to learn about a family by carefully studying their cat and their daughter. The concept of holism implies that "the whole is greater than the sum of its parts." To understand the system, one must look at it holistically, considering all elements and how they relate to each other. A third assumption of GST is that human systems are self-reflexive. *Self-reflexivity* means that we can develop our own goals and monitor our own behavior. This is inherent in the fact that human systems are cybernetic systems that can process feedback, which is what allows for adjustments in behaviors in order to reach a goal.

### The Family as a System

At first glance, the connection between "family" and such concepts as engines, antiaircraft artillery, and ecosystems may not be obvious. However, the family is a system that operates in accord with many of the same principles as these other systems. At the same time, the family is a special type of system with some characteristics that set it apart from some other types of systems. The family is often characterized as an open and ongoing system (Broderick, 1993). Systems that are *open* take input from the environment and produce output back to the environment. The input that families take from the environment includes things as simple as food bought at the grocery store to more complex matters such as information on the best colleges to send their children to. Output also includes a vast range of things from garbage to professional work to children who become members of society. Although no family is truly a closed system, families vary in the extent to which they are open. Families that are extremely open are said to have permeable *boundaries*. Boundaries are simply dividing lines that determine who is in and who is out of the system (Yerby, Buerkel-Rothfuss, & Bochner, 1995). The permeable boundaries of the very open family suggest that people can come and go with ease, into and out of the family system. Such a family, for example, may allow a distant cousin to move in for an extended period of time. At the same time, a teenage child might move out of the home to study in Europe as an exchange student. Families that are less open are more inclined to keep to themselves and send clear messages about the limited extent to which they will tolerate "outsiders" entering into the system.

Any system that is *ongoing* has a past, present, and future. If one considers the extended family, most families could be viewed as perpetual. Obviously, we all have ancestors, and barring some catastrophe, our families will all continue long after we are gone. In the grand scheme of things, when people think about their families (e.g., parents, siblings, grandparents, aunts, and uncles) they are really considering a mere snapshot in time. The greater ongoing system has a very long history and is sure to have a very long future.

The fact that families are open and ongoing systems means that they have a number of qualities that distinguish them from other types of systems (Broderick, 1993). For instance, all open and ongoing systems are *dynamic*. The relationships among their elements and the environment are not static; rather, they change over time. The way that a mother relates to her child at age 1 is very different from the way she relates to her child at age 15. The qualities of open and ongoing systems are *emergent*. The elements of the family interact to produce something that is more than just a collection of individuals. Systems theorists often make an analogy to baking a cake. Combining eggs, flour, sugar, and milk and baking it results in something very different from a mere collection of the individual ingredients. Families have a similar quality of emergent properties. Families also exhibit regular patterns from which we can deduce *rules*. For example, observing a family over a long period of time might reveal that whenever a member has a birthday, he or she is excused from any household chores. To the extent that this pattern is evident, one could say that this is a "rule" in the family. It is also the case that these patterns of interaction, or rules, are *hierarchically structured*. This means that rules exist at different levels of abstraction, and some take precedence over others (see chap. 4). Open and ongoing systems also *regulate relationships among their components*. In order to maintain the integrity of the system, it is essential to have some rules or patterns that hold the elements together and allow for the smooth functioning of the overall system. Parents who scold their children for fighting with each other are, in the abstract, attempting to regulate their relationships. Constant and intense fighting among family members could otherwise threaten the family's well-being and ability to realize their goals. Finally, open and ongoing systems *regulate relationships between the system and the environment.* All families exist in a greater society ecosystem or suprasystem. Because they are open, interaction with elements outside of the immediate family system is essential. For this reason, families develop rules and patterns of conduct for these interactions, with the goal of protecting the integrity of the family system. A family rule that children cannot go out on dates until they are 15 is an example of a rule designed to regulate relationships between the family and the external environment.

The family's distinction as an open and ongoing system helps to delineate it from a variety of other systems. However, the family is not the only open and ongoing system. Many animal societies and environmental ecosystems could also be characterized as open and ongoing systems. To more fully appreciate the concept of family systems it is necessary to look closer at some of the family processes that are inherent in family systems theory.

## Major Processes in Family Systems Theory

System processes are the characteristics that describe how the family system functions as a whole unit (Bochner & Eisenberg, 1987). One way to understand family systems theory is to examine the family processes that are assumed to play an important role in the family's day to day functioning.

### Mutual Influence

According to family systems theory, all family components are interdependent. That is to say, what happens to one member affects all other members of the family. The actions of every family member will influence the actions of other family members. Family systems theorists feel that families are constantly in the processes of influencing each other, and that this process never ends. So, for example, a child graduating from college is not just an individual achievement; it is a family event. For parents, it may represent the culmination of years of child rearing, a reduced financial burden, and the possibility of a more distant relationship with the child as he or she moves away to start a new job. To a sibling, this event may represent more freedom to use the family car, no longer having to share a bedroom, and the absence of a reliable tennis partner. Either way, the graduation of one member of the family impacts all other members of the family. Keep in mind, however, that there is no linear cause (child graduates) and effect (more distant relationship with the child) relationship in this hypothetical family. The act of going to college, graduating, and moving away to take a job is also influenced by the family. For example, a child without a close relationship to his or her parents might be more likely to move out of state after graduation. The concept of mutual influence suggests that all family members influence each other.

### Stability

All families seek some level of regularity in their lives. Regularity brings predictability, and at least some degree of predictability allows for smooth functioning of the family.

The tendency to seek stability is called *morphostasis*. Patterns, routines, and rules all allow families to function with some level of stability. A total lack of stability, or chaos, could easily destroy a family system. In a state a chaos, family roles are unclear, the behavior of family members is unpredictable, and important tasks may go undone because everyone thought that someone else would do them. Alternatively, family members may waste energy duplicating one another's efforts. It is easy to see how such a scenario would make the family such an inhospitable place as to motivate most of its members to leave the system. Although some degree of flexibility and change is healthy for the family (see section on family functioning in chap. 1) all families need and seek some stability.

### Change

Just as families need some stability, healthy families must experience some change. In fact, families are also driven to seek change. This tendency is known as *morphogenesis*. Morphogenesis is the tendency to reorganize and evolve over time. As family members marry, have children, age, and die, the family evolves. This is a natural and unavoidable evolution. Families also exist is a larger society, and as society itself changes, so do most families. Fifty years ago family members may have looked down on a mother who took a full-time job while her children were still young. Given the changing economic and social conditions of society, families today may be more inclined to not only accept but also honor someone who takes on so many tasks.

### Feedback and Calibration

Families are information processors. They perform the cybernetic function of examining their own behavior and trying to correct it so as to achieve goals. In a feedback loop, the family examines its output, and if that output is not meeting the goal or reaching some standard, they send a message (which becomes new input) to correct the behavior that led to the deviant outcome. An obvious example of this would be rearing children. Families will often correct or punish deviant behavior of their children in hopes that the children will ultimately grow up in accord with some standard defined by the family. The goal of feedback and control is to reach some level of *homeostasis*, or equilibrium. A married couple with full-time jobs that often keep them apart from each other may plan a vacation together to allow them to re-establish some balance between separateness and connection in their relationship. *Negative feedback*, also know as error-actuated feedback, occurs when the family initiates corrective action upon awareness of a deviation from some standard. This is the way that most thermostats operate. Once the temperature deviates from a set point, the thermostat sends a signal to the furnace or air conditioner to produce more heating or cooling. Parents who punish their children for bad behavior operate on negative feedback. *Positive feedback*, or deviation-amplifying feedback, works to enhance changes from a set point. For example, if a young adult child who lives with his parents and works a part-time job suddenly starts looking into colleges to attend, the parents might respond by verbally encouraging him, offering financial assistance with tuition, and relieving him of household chores so that he can pursue his studies. In this way, the parents use feedback to actually encourage change in their son's behavior, once they realize that he is contemplating a change from the norm of his part-time job.

### Equifinality

The concept of equifinality refers to the fact that the same end state may be reached in many different ways. Different families can achieve the same goals by traveling down very different paths. Consider, for example, the goal of providing for the family. Some may do this through the father's employment. In other families, both the mother and the father work. In still other families, teenage children may work and contribute some of their wages to the family. In all cases, the family system generates income to provide for their needs, but in very different ways. The family systems concept of equifinality is useful and important because it is a reminder that there is no single version of family well-being and functionality. Instead, there are many different ways that families can pursue the same goal. A related systems concept, *multifinality*, indicates that the same set of inputs may lead to different outputs. Two middle-class, suburban families with similar incomes and resources may end up raising very different children. This is because different families will process the same inputs differently.

These, and additional concepts and processes in family systems theory, are assembled in Table 2.1.

## Evaluation of Family Systems Theory

Family systems theory is the dominant paradigm in family science. It has been noted that "Many, if not most, family communication specialists have a systems theory world-view" (Whitchurch & Dickson, 1999). Nevertheless, family systems theory has been criticized on several grounds (see Klein & White, 1996, and Whitchurch & Constantine, 1993, for reviews). One position is that family systems theory is not really a true theory, but rather a philosophical perspective. There is some ambiguity and generality in family systems theory that makes it hard to generate concrete, testable hypotheses. Also, some people feel that family systems theory goes too far in emphasizing the role of *all* family members in influencing the phenomena that the family experiences. If a father loses his job, more often than not he is more responsible for that outcome than the family's 1-year old child is. On a related point, family systems theory has also been criticized by feminist scholars who argue that systems conceptualizations do not recognize the fact that women and children often have less power and resources than do men. For that reason, it may be unwise to view the contribution of women and children to family matters as equal to that of men. This criticism has become particularly heated when topics such as family violence and sexual abuse are discussed. Although systems theorists would not "blame" the victim, they would try to understand family problems as a function of the relationships among family members, instead of the behavior of an individual perpetrator. Whitchurch and Constantine argue that this later critique is based on a misunderstanding of GST, and that recent developments in family systems theory actually recognize different levels of power in the family through the concept of hierarchy.

**TABLE 2.1**
Key Concepts in Family Systems Theory

| *Family Systems Concept* | *Definition* |
| --- | --- |
| • Boundaries | The border between the system and its external environment |
| • Enmeshment | A lack of differentiation between family members so as to minimize the development of individual identities |
| • Equifinality | The idea that the same end state can be reached by many different paths |
| • Feedback | The family's response to a behavior or process that is observed |
| • Goals | The family's desired outcomes or end states |
| • Holism | The family can only be understood by examining it in its entirety; the whole is more than the sum of its parts; also known as nonsummativity |
| • Homeostasis | Maintaining a state of equilibrium through feedback and calibration |
| • Interdependence | The idea that all components of the system are interrelated; what happens to one happens to all; the actions of one element affect the actions of the others |
| • Morphogenesis | The family's tendency to evolve and change with time |
| • Morphostasis | The tendency to seek stability or equilibrium |
| • Multifinality | The idea that the same set of inputs can lead to different outputs in different families |
| • Mutual Influence | Family members influence each other |
| • Negative Feedback | Error-actuated feedback that is engaged when actions deviate from a family standard; this feedback attempts to suppress the deviation |
| • Positive Feedback | Deviation-amplifying feedback that is designed to stimulate and enhance deviation for a norm |
| • Requisite Variety | Having the necessary range of resources and responses to adequately address the demands encountered in the environment |
| • Rules | Prescribed patterns of behavior in the family; they contribute to the family's stability |
| • Subsystem | A smaller system within the family system such as husband–wife or parent–child |
| • Suprasystem | The larger system in which the family is embedded such as the extended family or society more generally |

## SYMBOLIC INTERACTION THEORY

### Historical Background

Even before the development of symbolic interaction theory, 20th-century pragmatists, such as John Dewey and William James, began to argue that reality is not objectively "set in stone"; rather, it is constantly changing. This way of thinking about reality was somewhat novel for the early 20th century. Furthermore, this new notion of reality advocated that participants constantly co-create a subjective social reality as they interact. Inspired by the ideas of these earlier thinkers, George Herbert Mead is credited with articulating the foundations of the theory later named symbolic interaction (SI) theory. Along with Mead, Manford Kuhn is recognized for contributing to and affirming the unique ideas of SI. Mead was a very popular and respected teacher at the University of Chicago, and, after his death, his students compiled lecture notes from his classes to produce a book they titled *Mind, Self, and Society* (1934). One of Mead's students, Herbert Blumer (1969), termed Mead's theoretical tenets "symbolic interaction theory."

Mead and others were interested in the way humans create, react to, and redefine the shared, symbolic meanings in their social environment. Mead began with the premise that words and nonverbal behaviors are the primary symbols to which humans assign meaning. He stressed the idea that meaning only occurs when people share common symbols and interpretations in a state of intersubjectivity. He also elaborated on the idea that symbolic meanings are heavily influenced by perceptions, including people's own perceptions and other people's perceptions of them and the social structure around them. For example, imagine a college student who comes home over a break from school with baskets full of dirty laundry. Her mother washes and folds the clothes for her. What does this behavior symbolize? Because SI sees meaning as occurring between people, we cannot know the meaning until we study the mother and daughter's interaction and perceptions. Perhaps (a) the daughter perceives herself as mature and self-sufficient; (b) based on prior interaction, the mother views and accepts the daughter as self-sufficient; and (c) the two come to a common interpretation that the mother is not obligated to do the laundry, but chooses to do so as a symbol of care for her busy daughter. In another mother–daughter relationship, this very same behavior could symbolize an obligatory caretaking duty full of resent, guilt, and the perception of a lazy daughter.

Mead (1934) and Blumer (1969) felt that the study of human beings required methods different from those of the study of physical objects or laws of nature. This is because human behavior can only be understood by knowing what it means to the person who is actually performing the behavior. Because SI emphasizes individuals' perceptions and the intersubjectivity shared by participants, it is difficult to observe and understand communication from the outside. Not until researchers know the perspective of the individual, can they understand him or her. Mead and Blumer advocated the use of case studies and examination of stories and personal histories in order to understand people's behaviors from the perspective of the people themselves.

Today, SI can be thought of as a diverse collection of theories rather than as a particular theory (Klein & White, 1996). Over time, many branches of the theory developed (e.g., social construction theory, role theory, and self-theory), emphasizing slightly different aspects of symbolic, human interaction. For instance, social construction theory spun off SI to explain co-constructed meaning rather than shared meaning. That is, social construction theory builds on the ideas of SI to further emphasize that "meaning does not reside inside one person's head, waiting to be shared with another. Rather, meaning exists in the practice of communication between people" (Turner & West, 2002, p. 61; see also Chen & Pearce, 1995). To illustrate the social construction of meaning, consider what happens when people become grandparents for the first time. They are often assigned a new title (i.e., grandma, nana, grammy, etc.), which is already loaded with basic cultural meaning. However, the title takes on further meaning as the grandparent–grandchild relationship develops. Through family interaction, the family co-constructs what they mean by the term *grandma*. In some families, grandma is a distant relative who sends gifts on holidays. For others, Grandma is a primary caretaker, acting more like some "moms." In sum, society's expectations for grandparents influence the meaning assigned to the role, but an additional layer of meaning is generated through the family's own interaction.

## Central Themes, Assumptions, and Concepts in SI

There are at least three central themes of SI and several underlying assumptions associated with these themes (Klein & White, 1996; LaRossa & Reitzes, 1993; West & Turner, 2000). Each theme relates to one of the three concepts that title Mead's (1934) book, *Mind, Self, and Society*. The first theme involves the importance of meanings for human behavior and relates to Mead's concept of *mind*. Three assumptions reveal this theme (Blumer, 1969; West & Turner, 2000, p. 76):

1. Humans act toward others on the basis of the meaning those others have for them.
2. Meaning is created in interaction between people.
3. Meaning is modified through an interpretive process.

This collection of assumptions acknowledges that human minds have the capacity to use symbols to represent thought. In particular, people rely on common, significant symbols that have shared, social meaning. As a symbol system, language works because people act in accordance with shared meanings. Even though people have many shared symbols, symbolic meaning is always being modified in interaction. Through perspective taking and other interpretive processes, people come to understand others' views. For instance, in symbolic role-taking, people try to take another person's perspective, or step inside his or her mind, in order to see how another person sorts out meaning. Very young children have a difficult time perspective taking. In a game of hide and seek, young children may think that if their own eyes are closed, then no one else can see them. They soon learn that what they see is not what other people see.

The second theme addresses how humans develop self-concepts and relates to Mead's (1934) concept of *self*. Two assumptions reveal this theme (LaRossa & Reitzes, 1993; West & Turner, 2000, p. 78):

1. Individuals develop self-concepts through interaction with others.
2. Self-concepts provide an important motive for behavior.

Mead (1934) describes the *self* as an *I* and a *Me*. During interaction, the *I* simply acts, impulsively and spontaneously. The *Me* is more reflective, concerned with how people come across to their social world. The *Me* employs social comparisons and considers the way other people view the self. More specifically, the *Me* attends to reflected self-appraisals. *Reflected self-appraisals* refer to the appraisals or evaluations other people make of the self. The extent to which another person's view affects one's self-concept depends on how much one values the other person's opinion. Young children often take the comments of their primary caretakers very seriously, because they have few other referents in their lives. Some college students, on the other hand, only take their parents' opinions with a "grain of salt" because they are receiving a great deal of reflected self-appraisal from other important sources including friends, romantic partners, professors, and so forth.

As SI indicates, the way people view their *self* motivates their future behavior. For example, people who have been told they are bad at math and who view themselves as bad at math have little reason to be motivated to major in math. Their self-concept may even set forth a self-fulfilling prophecy, whereby they see little reason to try hard at math because they already perceive they are bad. Putting forth little effort at math helps them meet their already low expectations.

Finally, the third theme describes the relationship between individuals and society and relates to Mead's (1934) concept of *society* (West & Turner, 2000, p. 79):

1. People and groups are influenced by cultural and social processes.
2. Social structure is worked out through social interaction.

Mead (1934) states that *society* is comprised of particular others and generalized others. *Particular others* refer to close significant others, such as family and friends, and *generalized others* refer to the larger community or society. According to SI, people act in the context of societal norms and values, whether they be the norms and values of their particular others or generalized others. For example, family members know what is normal behavior for their family culture (i.e., their particularized others), and they act with those norms in mind. Some families have a ritual of eating dinner together around a table every night. Other families do not expect members to eat at the same time or in the same place. Just as the interaction in one's family creates a set of norms and values, society (i.e., generalized others) influences what is viewed as normal family interaction. The media, for instance, is one societal force that shapes standards for family interaction.

## Evaluation and Application to Family Communication

Sociologist and symbolic interaction theorist Ernest W. Burgess was "the first to define family in terms of its interaction: 'a unity of interacting personalities,' by which he meant a family as a living, changing, growing thing, 'a unity of interacting persons,' rather than 'a mere collection of individuals'" (as cited in Whitchurch & Dickson, 1999, p. 691). Burgess' pioneering approach viewed interaction as the defining feature of families. His work became a theoretical cornerstone of family research. SI inspired a new way of studying families, by examining family interaction and the creation and maintenance of family symbols and themes.

In particular, SI has guided research on topics such as the socialization of family members, symbolic interpretations of family events, and family identities and narratives. As Steinmetz (1999) states: "We are not born with a sense of who we are, but must develop a sense of 'self' through symbolization with other people" (p. 375). Symbolic interaction draws attention to the critical role that parents, siblings, and other outside forces play as socializing agents for children (Bohannon & White, 1999; Cheng & Kuo, 2000). Children observe appropriate behavior for certain roles, and they receive reflected self-appraisal from the significant others in their family. Second, SI explains how families symbolize both routine and extraordinary events, though a great deal of attention has been given to extraordinary events, such as marriage, death, or major family illnesses (Book, 1996; Rehm & Franck, 2000; see also chap. 3). Informed by the society around them, families develop rituals for family events, such as weddings or funerals, or rituals for routine events, such as bedtime rituals to put a child to sleep. Finally, families generate stories to symbolize one family member's identity or the whole family identity (Hequembourg & Farrell, 1999; Stone, 1988).

There are a number of obvious strengths and weaknesses of SI. As a strength, SI highlights that meaning is dynamic and subjective, and understandings are worked out as family members interact with one another and with society. The problem is that researchers sometimes have a difficult time studying family meanings and symbols because they are often so subjective. Apart from actually living with a family, the only way researchers can learn about these subjective understandings is by asking family members to report their perceptions and tell their own story. Some family members may not even be aware of their own subjective meanings, and, if they are, they may be unwilling to report or may adjust their story for someone outside the family. Nonetheless, SI and its theoretical offshoots continue to inspire a great deal of research in family studies.

## SOCIAL LEARNING THEORY

### Background

Social learning theory was developed by Stanford University psychologist Albert Bandura (Bandura, 1977). Bandura developed social learning theory, not as a theory of family communication per se, rather as a more general theory of behavioral acquisition. More recently, Bandura has expanded social learning theory into the more general social cognitive theory (e.g., Bandura, 1986, 1994). However, for purposes of the present discussion we will contain our presentation largely to explanation of the basic principles of social learning theory.

In the premier study of what was later to become social learning theory, Bandura, Ross, and Ross (1963) documented that children will imitate a model who is reinforced for performing certain behaviors. To explore this issue, they randomly assigned nursery school students to watch a filmed portrayal of a child model. Under one condition, the model behaved aggressively and was rewarded for doing so. Under the second condition the model behaved aggressively and was punished for doing so. In the control group the model did not behave aggressively at all. Shortly thereafter, the children were allowed to play, and researchers measured their aggressive behavior during the play session. They found that children who observed the aggressive model get rewarded exhibited significantly more aggressive behavior themselves than either those under the aggression-punished condition or those in the control group. Also, those who saw the model get punished for aggressive behavior behaved much less aggressively than those under the other conditions. Bandura and his colleagues theorized that the children learned the consequences of behaving aggressively by observing what happened when the model behaved aggressively. When the model was rewarded, the nursery school children imitated or enacted the same behavior that produced the reward for the model. When the model was punished, the children seemed to avoid performing the behavior that resulted in punishment for the model. This idea of observational learning through modeling would become a central element of Bandura's social learning theory.

One can think of the process of social learning as a search for "if-then" relationships (Smith, 1982). Consistent with the more general principles of behavioral theory, according to social learning theory, people seek rewards and try to avoid punishments. Bandura notes that, fortunately, people are able to learn what brings rewards and what brings punishments at least some of the time through observing what happens to other people. Imagine what life would be like if the only way we could learn about the consequences of driving without a seatbelt, playing with a loaded gun, picking up rattlesnakes, and drinking household chemicals was through direct experience. Most people would not live to see their 20th birthday. Fortunately, we are able to learn about the consequences of these behaviors by observing other people's misfortunes. Similarly, we are able to learn about behaviors that bring more positive consequences by also observing others. Once the "if-then" rule (e.g., "If I touch a hot stove, then I will burn my hand" or "If I scream and cry, then my mother will give me candy") is learned, most people act accordingly to secure the reward or avoid the punishment.

## Learning About the Consequences of Behavior

In social learning theory, people are assumed to gain most of their knowledge about the consequences of performing various behaviors through two possible sources. The first, and most obvious, is through *direct experience*. In this rudimentary mode of learning, people acquire knowledge of behavioral consequences by actually experiencing them. For example, if a child eats a chili pepper and it burns his or her mouth, that experience teaches the child to avoid eating chili peppers in the future. If the child eats a chocolate candy bar, and it tastes good, the child would learn the reinforcing value of eating chocolate and would presumably perform the behavior frequently in the future. The idea of learning through direct experience and the rewards and punishments that are associated with our behaviors is a basic element of behavior theory, and is a mode by which even the simplest of animals can and will learn. However, because of their ability to form mental representations and their ability to abstract rules from observations of actions and their consequences, humans (and some other animals) are also able to learn through observation and the *vicarious experience* that it presents. Learning by vicarious experience happens when we take note of the effects of *other people's* behaviors. For example, if John observed his parents reward his sister with $20 for bringing home a report card with straight As, he is likely to abstract the following if-then rule: "If you get straight As in school, then mom and dad will give you money." So long as receiving money is seen by John as a positive outcome, he is likely to try to enact that behavior (i.e., working hard in school to get good grades) himself. Note that John did not learn the if-then rule by directly experiencing the effects of getting good grades. Rather, he learned the rule vicariously, through observing what happened when his sister got good grades.

## The Process of Social Learning

Let us dissect the process of observational learning, or learning by modeling, a bit further. Learning through vicarious experience is dependent on several interrelated processes. To start, there must be some *attention* paid to the model. Each day people are exposed to dozens, hundreds, and in some cases, thousands of other people. Each of these people is a potential model from whom others can learn about the consequences of enacting various behaviors. However, social learning can only happen if we pay attention to both the model's behavior and its associated consequences. Without attention to the model, there can be no observational learning. Second, there must be *retention* of the if-then rule that is learned by observing the model. That is to say, we have to form a mental representation of what was learned, and store that in memory, perhaps as a more abstract rule. Bandura (1986) notes that retention can be enhanced by rehearsal. The more people rehearse the socially learned rule (e.g., if I apologize for doing something wrong, people will forgive me) the more likely they are to have access to it at critical times, and therefore to perform the appropriate behavior for either securing rewards or avoiding punishing responses from the social environment. Next, there are a number of *behavioral production processes* that are vital to performing the observed behavior. People must have the ability to produce or enact the behavior that they observed. This often requires organization of constituent subskills into a new response pattern. Sometimes people are able to enhance their ability to perform observed behaviors by receiving informative feedback from others on troublesome aspects of their behavior. For example, a father might teach his daughter how to kick a soccer ball by modeling the behavior. If the daughter does not perform the behavior with the same competence as the father's, he might give her feedback on what she has done incorrectly in order to help her perform the behavior in the best way possible. Finally, there has to be *motivation* to perform the modeled behavior. In the previous example, the father might model the proper way to kick a soccer ball 100 times in the presence of his daughter. However, even if she pays attention to him, remembers how to do it, and has the competence to perform the modeled behavior, she will not do so unless she has sufficient motivation.

Where does the motivation to perform behavior come from? Social learning theory recognizes that incentives can be inherent in the behavior, vicariously produced, or self-produced (Bandura, 1986). Some behaviors are inherently satisfying to most people. For example, people generally like to eat ice cream. The motivation to eat ice cream comes from consequences that are inherent in the behavior itself, not from some abstract or complex rule that is learned (e.g., "eating ice cream will keep the dairy farmers in business and will therefore be good for the state economy"). Bandura refers to the effects of such behaviors as eating ice cream or drinking water when thirsty as "direct incentive." Sometimes the incentive for performing a behavior is *self-produced*. With self-produced incentives, people essentially reward themselves for a job well done. There is nothing inherently satisfying about bowling a strike. However, bowling enthusiasts will mentally congratulate themselves upon bowling a strike because they have come to value this sort of performance. To people who do not care about or understand bowling, knocking down 10 pins with a heavy ball may seem like a meaningless behavior. Most important to social learning theory, people are sometimes motivated to perform behaviors because of *vicarious incentives*. People often acquire and perform behaviors because they see other people do so and get rewarded. The fashion and clothing industry—an industry that relies heavily on modeling—is constantly trying to impart vicarious knowledge of the consequences of performing various behaviors (e.g., wear this brand of shoes and you will be a good athlete; wear this style of pants and you will look great and gain the admiration of your peers, etc.).

## Application to Family Communication

Even though social learning processes operate throughout the life span, and through observation of virtually any person, their applicability to child learning in the family context is undeniable. Smith (1982) noted that "we acquire most of our basic values and personal habits by initially observing our parents' behavior and later the behavior of admired friends and reference groups" (p. 201). Children often grow up to hold political and religious values similar to those of their parents, pursue many of the same hobbies and occupations that their parents do, and sometimes even drive the same brand of car that their parents drive. Social learning theory provides a compelling account for how and why this happens. The theory is a reminder that anything that parents do in the presence of their children can and often will communicate abstract if-then rules to the children. If the surrounding circumstances are right, these rules may then become prompts for behavior, or inhibitors of behavior, depending on the content of the mental representation.

Smith (1982) described a number of conditions that affect the success of modeling, several of which have obvious applicability in the family setting. One such factor is the *similarity* between the model and the observer. The more similar the model is to the observer, the more likely the observer is to enact the modeled behavior. Similarity between the model and the self contributes to self-efficacy in the observer. When people experience self-efficacy, they feel that they are able to adequately perform the behavior. Supposedly the thinking with models similar to the self is that "if they can do it, then I can do it." It is obvious that there is considerable perceived similarity within family groups. For this reason, family members can be ideal models of behavior. Smith also notes that modeling is more successful when models have high *status*. Certainly parents and older siblings have very high status in the eyes of young children. Because most children start out in life looking up to their parents, they naturally use their parents as a benchmark for appropriate behavior. Also, modeling is most successful when there are *multiple models*. In the family context, it is often the case that more than one person performs a particular behavior. So, for example, if two or three members of the family are avid golfers, children raised in that family will have multiple models to observe, and are consequently very likely to adopt the same behaviors (i.e., take up golfing) themselves.

Family science researchers have continued to apply social learning theory to the explanation of many functional and dysfunctional aspects of family interaction. For example, there are many who feel that people learn how to be spouses and how to be parents by observing their own parents in these roles. In the area of family dysfunction, there is compelling evidence for social learning processes in family or partner violence, substance abuse, and even divorce (e.g., Andrews, Hops, & Duncan, 1997; Mihalic & Elliot, 1997; Swinford, DeMaris, Cernkovich, & Giordano, 2000; see chaps. 11, 13, and 15 for more in-depth analysis of these family issues). When parents engage in physical violence or substance use in the presence of their children, they inadvertently communicate that this is an acceptable form of behavior. This is because young children lack the reasoning skills to independently determine what is right and what is wrong. Therefore, they use their parents as a benchmark for appropriate conduct. The idea is that, if the parents do it, it must be the correct thing to do. So if the mother and father resort to physical violence when engaged in conflict or consume large amounts of alcohol when stressed, children who observe that behavior are likely to enact it themselves later in life. Similarly, when children observe their parents' divorce, they are likely to learn the if-then rule that goes "if you have problems in your marriage, then you get divorced." This is one of several hypotheses for the intergenerational transmission of divorce discussed in chapter 11. It is apparent that social learning processes are so powerful that the if-then rules learned in family contexts and the behaviors that they prompt will often hold up in the face of intense challenges. For example, most people know that divorce and domestic violence are not positive experiences. Yet, the template for behavior that is learned in the family of origin through social learning can be nearly impossible for some people to modify or escape. Despite "knowing" that family violence is wrong, when confronted with intense conflict, that becomes the default response. As disturbing as these family patterns are, they are a testimony to the power of social learning.

## ATTACHMENT THEORY

### Background

Attachment theory was originally developed by John Bowlby and was based on his observational studies of children who experienced separation from their parents during World War II (Bowlby, 1969, 1973, 1980). Bowlby was also influenced by ethological theories that explore similarities and differences in behavior across species. Ultimately he argued that attachment processes outlined in the theory are evident in nonhuman as well as human primates and serve an adaptive function for the survival of the species. Although Bowlby developed his theory as something of an alternative to the orthodox psychodynamic view of child development that was articulated by Sigmund Freud, Bowlby's thinking still preserves many of the trappings of psychodynamic ideology.

Bowlby (1973) observed that human infants are innately driven to seek out and remain in close proximity to their primary caregivers. Indeed, this pattern of behavior is typical of most primates. Bowlby characterized attachment behavior as "any form of behavior that results in a person attaining or retaining proximity to some other differentiated and preferred individual" (p. 292). This type of behavior is viewed as "hardwired" into the brain. That is to say, people do not need to learn proximity seeking to the caregiver. Rather, this tendency is already present at birth. Bowlby felt that this pattern of behavior was the result of natural selection. Because it is adaptive to the survival of the species, those who did not seek the proximity of a caregiver as an infant were less likely to survive and pass on their genes.

### Functions of Attachment

As noted earlier, attachment processes between the infant and primary caregiver are assumed to be functional. Bowlby argued that attachment is adaptive to the survival of the species. His writings highlight four distinct functions that are served by attachment, all of which appear to be beneficial to the infant's survival and development. Perhaps the most basic function of attachment is *proximity seeking*. Infants have an innate tendency to seek out their primary caregiver. Given that this person is the source of protection and nourishment, it is obvious how this tendency serves the infant's best interests. *Separation protest* is a second function of attachment. This simply implies that the infant will resist separation from his or her primary caregiver. Behaviorally, it is evident in crying and screaming when the infant is separated from the caregiver. The *safe haven* function refers to the tendency to seek out the caregiver in times of stress or danger. Eventually children will explore their environment apart from their parents. However, attachment will readily send the child back to the presence of the parent for protection during times of stress. Finally, the *secure base* function indicates that an attachment that is felt as secure will motivate or allow the child to explore his or her environment, beyond immediate contact with the caregiver. The idea is that the secure attachment with the caregiver provides a sort of psychological foundation on which the child can mount an exploration into the unknown elements of his or her environment. If the child knows in the back of his or her mind that the caregiver is available for protection, exploration of the environment is not felt to be as risky. All of these functions of attachment should keep the infant out of harm's way and in the presence of the individual who can shelter, protect, and nourish. There can be little doubt about the adaptive nature of such processes. Infants (or animals) who enact attachment behaviors are most likely to survive the perils of early development and grow into functional adults.

## Working Models and Attachment Styles

In attachment theory, interactions between the infant and his or her primary caregiver (usually the mother) become the basis for internal *working models*. These are mental representations that summarize and organize interactions between the self and the caregiver. Early attachment experiences contribute to both internal working models of the self and internal working models of others. In the self model, the child views him- or herself as either worthy or unworthy of love and support. Experiences with a parent who is warm and responsive would obviously lead to an internal working model of the self as worthy of love. However, if early childhood experiences with the caregiver are marked by coldness and unavailability, the child will come to view the self as unworthy of love and support. As Reis and Patrick (1996) wisely observed, "just how this internalization occurs remains one of the most important and unresolved issues in attachment research" (p. 526). Internal working models of others are a mental representation of the benevolence of other people. Other models are something of a prototype of other human beings and how they can be expected to treat the child. These representations are summarized along themes of availability, responsiveness, and trustworthiness. Essentially, the child will generalize from experiences with the primary caregiver and assume that this is how most people will treat him or her. According to attachment theory, once these internal working models are established, which may happen as early as age 1 or 2, they are relatively stable throughout the remainder of the life span.

Obviously, different children have different internal working models of the self and others. These various internal working models become the foundation for attachment styles. Bowlby (1973) felt that the nature of the caregiver's response to the child was the dominant factor that determined the infant's attachment style. Originally, attachment

MODEL OF SELF

| | Positive | Negative |
|---|---|---|
| | **SECURE** | **PREOCCUPIED** |
| Positive | Comfortable with intimacy and autonomy | Preoccupied with relationships |
| | **DISMISSING** | **FEARFUL** |
| Negative | Dismissing of intimacy Counter-dependent | Fearful of intimacy Socially avoidant |

MODEL OF OTHERS (left margin label)

**FIG. 2.1.**   The Bartholomew and Horowitz (1991) Model of Attachment Styles

*Note.* From "Attachment Styles Among Young Adults: A Test of a Four Category Model;" by K. Bartholomew & L. M. Horowitz, 1991, *Journal of Personality and Social Psychology, 61,* pp. 226–244. Copyright 1991 by the American Psychological Association. Adapted with permission.

theorists suggested that there were three distinct attachment styles. People with a *secure* attachment style had caregivers who were responsive to their needs, available, and affectionate. Those with an *anxious–avoidant* attachment style had early interactions with caregivers who were cold, not nurturing, and unavailable. If the primary caregiver was inconsistent or unpredictable in his or her responsiveness to the child, the child was thought to develop an *anxious–ambivalent* attachment style. Research on attachment theory has shown that infants with different attachment styles will behave differently around their mothers (Ainsworth, Blehar, Waters, & Wall, 1978). For example, infants with a secure attachment will gladly explore their environment when in the presence of their mothers. Upon separation they become distressed but then readily settle back down when reunited with their mothers. Infants with an anxious–avoidant attachment style tend to avoid close contact with their mothers and keep to themselves. Finally, the anxious–ambivalent infants will exhibit extreme distress upon separation from their mothers. However, when reunited, these children show signs of anger and ambivalence.

More recently, a four-category scheme of attachment styles has been proposed, based on positive and negative models of the self and others (Bartholomew & Horowitz, 1991). In this model, early experiences with caregivers are thought to produce internal working models of the self that are generally positive (worthy of love and acceptable to others) or negative (unworthy of love, unacceptable to others). At the same time, children are assumed to develop internal working models of others that are either positive (others are trustworthy and available) or negative (others are unreliable and rejecting). When the internal working models of the self and others are crossed, there are four possible attachment styles: *secure, preoccupied, dismissing,* and *fearful.* These are depicted in Figure 2.1.

As evident in Figure 2.1, the four-category scheme preserves the secure attachment style of the original three-category scheme. However, it divides the avoidant styles into two substyles: the dismissing and the fearful. In each case, the internal working model of others is negative, but in the dismissing style the internal working model of the self is positive, whereas it is negative in the fearful style. It should be noted that this scheme was developed and validated largely on young adults. One might wonder how, for example, a person develops a positive internal working model of the self but a negative model of others. Infants appear much more readily willing to internalize the negative behavior of others as a negative reflection on the self. However, people who start out in life with a positive view of the self, but then have a string of bad experiences with others, could plausibly maintain their positive view of the self while holding a more negative view of other people. Note that this explanation hinges on the person's ability to *not* always internalize the negative actions of others as a poor reflection on the self. This undoubtedly entails a more adult way of thinking about the social world and its relation to the self.

## Evaluation and Application to Family Communication

Embedded within attachment theory are some very powerful ideas and statements about family communication early in life. According to Bowlby (1969, 1973, 1980) the nature of the parent–infant interaction sets a template for social relationships that the child will carry with him or her for life. Notably, much of this early parent–child communication is nonverbal. As children grow older, their attachment figures shift from parents to romantic partners and spouses (Hazan & Shaver, 1987; Reis & Patrick, 1996). This implies that communication patterns in the family of origin may be revisited in some way in the family of orientation. For example, people with secure attachment styles have a tendency to end up in traditional or independent marriages, whereas those with dismissing or preoccupied styles are more likely to be in separate style marriages (Fitzpatrick, Fey, Segrin, & Schiff, 1993) (see chap. 6 for a discussion of the different martial types). Those with a secure attachment style are also more likely to report high marital satisfaction compared to those with other styles of attachment (Feeney, 2002; Feeney, Noller, & Callan, 1994; Meyers & Landsberger, 2002). A positive view of the self (i.e., secure or dismissive attachment style) is positively associated with family outcomes such as perceived rewards from marriage and parenting (Vasquez, Durik, & Hyde, 2002). Finally, secure attachment has been linked with less destructive marital conflict patterns and more positive attitudes toward parenting (Cohn, Silver, Cowan, Cowan, & Pearson, 1992; Feeney, Noller, & Roberts, 2000). Findings such as these are useful for employing attachment theory as an explanation for the effects of family of origin experiences on later family of orientation experiences. They also draw attention to the critical role of parent–child communication in the early years of life. Even preverbal children appear very attuned and attentive to their parents' style of relating to them. This early parental communication evidently leads to self-concept development and views of the trustworthiness of others that impacts later communication patterns and relationships.

Attachment theory has been very useful for explaining why people with a history of childhood abuse often find themselves in abusive relationships as adults. This noxious form of parent–child communication has been linked with a host of negative social and psychological outcomes later in life (see chaps. 13 and 15 for a more in-depth analysis). An abused child would be expected to develop a negative internal working model of the self and therefore not feel worthy of love from others. Perhaps the child even feels that abusive conduct from others is somehow deserved or warranted. This sets up a mental representation of close relationships as normatively including abusive behavior. When such a child grows older and begins seeking romantic partners, attachment theorists speculate that this mental model of close relationships causes the person to, perhaps unknowingly, seek out others who will be abusive. In so doing, they recreate their childhood experiences and settle into a social life that is at once painful but familiar.

It would not be an exaggeration to state that attachment theory has been subject to hundreds of studies in the past 25 years. Researchers have used attachment styles to explain so many different phenomena that it begins to strain the imagination of the reader and credibility of the theory. The eagerness with which researchers have studied attachment styles in the past 15 years appears to be fueled by a variable–analytic mentality in which the search is on for any phenomenon, concept, or experience that varies as a function of attachment styles. Regardless of the utility of this approach, it obviously indicates the current mass appeal of attachment theory in the social and behavioral sciences.

One assumption of attachment theory that has been hotly debated is the stability of attachment styles. Bowlby (1969, 1973, 1980) argued that the attachment styles formed in childhood are enduring throughout the life span. However, some scientists disagree with this assumption. For example, Coyne (1999) has been critical of theories that characterize early childhood experiences as frozen in time, like the Wooly Mammoth, unable to be changed. Rather, Coyne argues that we have experiences throughout the life span that are influential in developing and changing our interpersonal perspectives. Further, he argues that early childhood experiences have only modest associations with later adult experiences such as depression. In the research literature there is at least suggestive support for the stability of internal working models and attachment styles over time (e.g., Bram, Gallant, & Segrin, 1999; Feeney et al., 2000). However, when attachment style is measured categorically (e.g., secure and dismissive), about 25% of respondents appear to change their attachment style over periods of 1 to 4 years (Feeney & Noller, 1996). Further, people may experience a different attachment style depending on the relationship. When considering their 10 "most important" relationships, 88% of respondents reported that these relationships corresponded with at least two attachment styles, and 47% reported correspondence with three attachment styles (Baldwin, Keelan, Fehr, Enns, & Koh-Rangarajoo, 1996). If attachment styles change over time and by relationship, the fundamental importance of parent–child interaction that is postulated by attachment theory could be seriously questioned.

## THE DIALECTICAL PERSPECTIVE

Every year, millions of Americans travel home to their family of origin during the holiday season. In most cases people seem eager to reunite with family members and spend time with them. Often, after a week or so, people return back to their homes, jobs, and school, and seem as eager to get back to their life away from the family of origin as they were to see the family members in the first place. Why does it happen that at one moment people want to be united with their family members, and at the next they want to leave family members behind and get back to school or work? The dialectical perspective (Baxter & Montgomery, 1996, 1997) explains that these seeming contradictions are an inherent part of our relationships with other people. Even though the dialectical approach describes forces that operate in virtually all relationships, family theorists have found its principles and ideas to be very useful for explaining the form and function of family relationships.

## Contradiction in Family Relationships

In the dialectical perspective, contradictions are seen as an inherent aspect of any relationship. Contradictions cause change in our relationships and they keep relationships growing instead of static. They are relational forces that are unified opposites. By "unified" Baxter and Montgomery (1997) suggest that the opposing relational forces are interdependent. In other words, the meaning or experience of one force is dependent on the other. For example, if one lived in a tropical climate where the outdoor temperature was consistently between 70 and 90°F is there any such thing as it being "hot" or "cold" outside? For people who live in the Midwestern United States where the weather can range from 0 to 100°F "hot" and "cold" have obvious and clear meanings. The point is that the experience of "hot" takes on meaning relative to its alternative: "cold." If there were no such thing as "cold," "hot" would not be very meaningful.

What are some contradictions, or unified opposites, that play a part in family life? One example cited by Baxter and Montgomery (1996) is *autonomy versus connectedness*. Reconsider the previous example about the family reunion over the holidays. In all close relationships, there is an obvious desire for a sense of "connectedness" among the members of the relationship. This might be established and maintained though sharing time and space, engaging in conversation, and engaging in joint activities. Without any of these, it would be hard to say that there is much of a relationship at all. However, there are very few people who want to spend 24 hours a day together. Even the closest married couples and the most attached parent–child dyads seem to desire some time on their own. Consequently, family members must strike a balance in their relationships, over time, between connectedness and separateness. These opposing forces that impinge on the relationship are known as *dialectic tensions*. Other dialectic tensions that must be managed in family relationships include *novelty versus predictability*, *disclosure versus privacy*, *stability versus change*, and *conventionality versus uniqueness* (Baxter & Montgomery; Bochner & Eisenberg, 1987). According to the dialectical approach, these oppositional forces are balanced by different families in different ways. Rarely are they handled with an "either-or" approach.

Before leaving the topic of contradictions, it is important to note that the opposing forces described in the dialectical approach are not located in the struggle between one person and another. Rather, Baxter and Montgomery (1996, 1997) note that these oppositional forces are part of the *relationship*. In other words, they are relational, not individual, forces. In a mother–daughter relationship, the disclosure–privacy dialectic is not an issue of the mother expecting and offering full disclosure while the daughter expects and maintains full privacy. That would be an antagonism between two individuals. Rather, this is a relational force that each must manage. There are surely some things that the mother wants to disclose to the daughter and some things that she would like to keep private. Similarly, the daughter would also want to disclose some things to her mother and keep some matters to herself. This dialectical tension calls on the mother and daughter to balance their desires for disclosure and privacy in a way that is comfortable for their relationship. Most people who have been in such a family relationship can attest to the difficulty of negotiating this dialectic tension.

## Praxis and Praxis Patterns

According to the dialectical perspective, "people are at once both actors and objects of their own action" (Baxter & Montgomery, 1997, p. 329). This concept is called *praxis*. People consciously and often freely make choices about how they choose to treat their family members. This is abundantly evident in messages that are sent from one family member to another. At the same time, sent messages and communication patterns have a way of influencing the relationship in such as a way as to impact the original message sender. Consider, for example, a parent with an anger-management problem. If the parent expresses anger with his child through enacting physical violence, he could be seen as a sender of dysfunctional verbal and nonverbal communication, but at the same time, he will be *acted on* by his own communication. Assume, for example, that the Child Protective Services were made aware of the abuse, took the child from the family home, and had the father arrested. Suddenly, his act of communication has massive consequences that come back and act on him and his relationship with the child.

Different relationships use different mechanisms for managing the dialectical tensions that they experience. These mechanisms or tactics are called *praxis patterns*. Baxter and Montgomery (1996, 1997) divide these tactics into those that are dysfunctional and those that are functional. One of the common but dysfunctional praxis patterns is *denial*. Here, members of the relationship simply deny the presence of the contradiction by only honoring one of the poles while excluding the other. In a family that felt the opposing forces of conventionality and uniqueness, family members would be using denial if they simply ignored the pull for uniqueness and honored only the drive for conventionality. Another dysfunctional praxis pattern is *disorientation*. This happens when there is no real "management" of the oppositional forces in the relationship. Rather, members of the relationship resign themselves to the fact that these contradictory motives are inevitable and negative. Consequently, they are likely to find themselves in double-bind situations where any behavior or communication will feel like it clashes with one of the opposing relational forces.

Baxter and Montgomery (1996, 1997) have also identified a series of more functional praxis patterns. These are more effective means for managing the dialectical tensions in such a way as to minimize negative relational outcomes. One functional praxis pattern called *spiraling alternation* involves alternating between the opposite poles of a dialectic at different points in time. For example, every Sunday family members may get together for dinner, honoring connectedness, but it may be understood that every Saturday night everyone is free to do their own thing or go out with their friends, honoring the desire for autonomy. In *segmentation*, members of the relationship honor opposing poles of the dialectic, not over time, but over topic or activity domain. For example, a family might be very open when it comes to discussing spiritual beliefs and finances, but very private when it comes to discussing sexuality. By having open communication on some topics and treating others with a "hands-off" attitude the family alternates between the two poles of the disclosure–privacy dialectic. *Balance* is a praxis pattern in which members of the relationship try to respond to both ends of the opposition by seeking a compromise. One problem with balance is that neither polarity is fully satisfied at any point in time. *Integration* is something of an ideal in conflict resolution and management of dialectical tensions. When members of a relationship integrate, they find a way of simultaneously satisfying both polarities of a dialectical tension. Baxter and Montgomery (1996) suggest that in some cases family dinnertime can be seen as an integration praxis pattern in which the family bond is established and maintained, and yet individual actions and accomplishments are recognized and embraced though the input of individual members into the interaction. With *recalibration* members of the relationship create "a transformation in the expressed form of the contradiction such that the opposing forces are no longer regarded as oppositional to one another" (Baxter & Montgomery, p. 65). With this praxis pattern, members of the relationship find a way to reframe the contradiction "such that the polarities are encompassed in one another" (p. 65). The phrase "if you love something, set it free" may be a reflection of this mentality. By freeing one's partner to behave as he or she will, members of a relationship can experience security through that freedom. Finally, the praxis pattern of *reaffirmation* "celebrates the richness afforded by each polarity and tolerates the tension posed by their unity" (Baxter & Montgomery, p. 66). In some ways, the "for better or worse" part of a marriage vow may represent reaffirmation for some married couples. If the couple accepts both the good times and the bad, and realizes that they will have a better and stronger relationship as a result of working through each, they may be enacting a reaffirmation praxis pattern.

## Evaluation and Application to Family Communication

The dialectical approach has proven to be very useful to family theorists and researchers who are interested in explaining various family processes and tasks. For example, the work of Bochner and Eisenberg (1987), which predated the formal development of the dialectical approach, argued that there are two dialectical tensions that are central to family functioning. They characterize the first as *integration versus differentiation*. All families are made up of individuals with their own unique identities. At the same time, families as a collective unit have an identity. One task that faces all families is honoring the desire for a collective identity as a family unit versus allowing individuals within the family to develop their own unique identities as individuals, or their own unique relationships with other family member (e.g., mother–daughter and between two siblings). Another dialectic that has a substantial impact on family functioning according to Bochner and Eisenberg is *stability versus change*. Most families have predictable patterns of interaction. These might be reflected in activities such as the family dinner, picking up children from school, or watching television together in the evening. Some degree of predictability is desirable for most families. On the other hand, too much stability in the family can lead to stagnation. As families evolve through time, they experience changes that are internal to the system (e.g., birth of a child) and changes that are external to the system (e.g., societal changes). There is some need to adapt to these changes, but without entirely abandoning the family's traditions and destroying any sense of predictability in family interaction. According to Bochner and Eisenberg, managing these two important dialects is a significant task that families must address in order to maintain their integrity.

The work of Bochner and Eisenberg (1987) shows how the assumptions and ideas of the dialectical approach can be fruitfully employed for describing certain family processes. At the same time, the dialectical approach does not have all of the elements of a formal theory such as social learning theory. For this reason it more difficult to use the dialectical approach for prediction or intervention to change or improve family functioning. Its major utility is in *explaining* the nature of family relationships. Also, some of the concepts in the dialectical perspective can be difficult to grasp, much less identify, in a practical setting. For example, the praxis patterns of integration, recalibration, and reaffirmation are somewhat vaguely conceptualized and therefore difficult to observe or identify in an actual family setting. Further, these praxis patterns may not be as common as other praxis patterns such as denial, segmentation, or balance.

## CONCLUSION

In this chapter we explore several theories that are and have been very influential in the field of family science. These general theories have inspired hundreds of research studies and numerous more specific theories that draw on many of the postulates of the theories presented here. We start by examining *family systems theory*. According to this perspective, family processes can only be understood by examining the family in its totality. All family processes and events are thought to be connected to the larger family system and social suprasystem in which the family itself resides. Families are assumed to have emergent qualities that make them more than just the sum of their individual parts. *Symbolic interaction theory* highlights the vital role of the family in creating self-concepts and understandings of the world. Symbolic interaction theorists feel that meaning is at least to some extent negotiated through our interactions with other people. Because the family is the primary source of social interactions and relationships, it has a monumental role in shaping people's self-concepts and what it means to be a father, sister, grandmother, and so forth. Although meanings are negotiated through social interactions over the entire life span, the process starts in the family. *Social learning theory* explains how people acquire behaviors through observing other people perform behaviors, along with the consequences that they experience subsequent to the behavior. Learning by modeling is a fundamental process in social leaning theory. When people observe a model perform a behavior and get rewarded for doing so, they are likely to start performing the behavior themselves. Like symbolic interaction theory, social learning theory has obvious applications to family interaction because the family provides a multitude of compelling models for children to observe. *Attachment theory* focuses on early infant–caregiver interactions as the basis for forming enduring internal working models of interpersonal relationships. An internal working model is a mental representation of the self as worthy or unworthy of love and attention and others as reliable and trustworthy or rejecting and uncaring. Attachment theorists feel that the nature of early interactions with a caregiver will inform young children's internal working models which then influence the nature of their interpersonal relationships well into adulthood. Finally, we examine the *dialectical perspective*. This approach to understanding family processes is built around dialectical tensions or functional contradictions that are an inherent part of any family relationship. In the dialectical perspective, family members are seen as having to balance or manage tensions such as connectedness–separateness, stability–change, and novelty–predictability. The dialectical perspective also explains how families manage dialectical tensions through a variety of techniques known as praxis patterns.

Of all the theories that we discuss in this chapter, only *family systems theory* was explicitly developed as an explanation of family dynamics (although it was derived from the more general version of systems theory). All of the other theories were developed as explanations of more general interpersonal processes. However, the family either plays a prominent role in the reasoning of the theory (as in attachment theory) or the theory has obvious and immediate applicability to the family. In either case, scholars have seized on these theories as some of their primary tools for explaining and understanding family interactions and relationships. Throughout the remainder of this book, we present numerous specific applications of these influential theories. Their continued application to the understanding of issues such as child abuse, alcoholism in the family, marital satisfaction, divorce, and parent–child interaction is a testimony to the utility of these family interaction theories.

# CHAPTER THREE

# Family Interaction Patterns: Norms and Networks, Routines and Rituals, Stories and Secrets

Many people claim to be in the constant pursuit of more "family time" (Daly, 2001). Each year people make a (New Year) resolution to spend more family time together: to eat dinner together more often, to spend more time talking to their children, to take a family vacation. Some dual-earner couples go to great lengths to rearrange job schedules in order to spend more time with their children. People even turn down jobs to spend more time with their families. As Rivenburg (2002) argues, the "family thing" is so revered in our society that people have invoked the "more time with family" excuse as a face-saving way to quit a job before getting fired. Even if it is only an excuse, the fact that people view more family time as a viable excuse reveals that our society at least claims to respect family time. But are people spending more time interacting with our families now than at other times in the past? What is family time anyway? And what matters more? The quantity of time we spend interacting with family members or the quality and symbolic meaning of the interaction?

In this chapter, we begin to answer questions about the amount of time families spend together by exploring norms and networks for family interaction. Then we spend a majority of the chapter studying the meanings that are formed and renegotiated through symbolic family interaction. Our analysis of family routines reveals the patterns that emerge in family interaction. Often these patterns become ritualized, meaning they take on symbolic meaning. For example, the routine of a mother brushing her young daughter's hair before bed every night may be more than an instrumental task. The task takes on the status of ritual when it is repeatedly enacted as a means of symbolizing something—possibly care and attentiveness in the relationship. In rituals, the actual interaction is less important than what the interaction symbolizes. Everyday rituals (e.g., a child's bedtime ritual and dinnertime rituals) can help make sense of daily family life and symbolize family roles, rules, and bonds of connection. During times of stress and transition, rituals, even ones so simple as the dinnertime ritual, can take on heightened meaning and impact. Formal rituals (e.g., weddings, religious holidays, and graduations) serve to transmit family values and publicly mark transitions in a way that produces memories. Some rituals even symbolize negative family themes (e.g., when an annual family Christmas celebration predictably reveals power struggles and strained relationships).

The symbolic content of family interaction is also revealed and reconstructed in the stories family members tell and the secrets they keep. Even when we are "just talking" about the events and routines in our lives, we are telling stories and censoring information. Family stories often have symbolic meaning. They can function to socialize members, affirm belonging and connect generations, and present implicit or explicit judgments about behavior. Naturally, in this chapter, we explore the functions of family stories and how they vary by type and narrative form. Some family stories purposely leave out information. This leads us to a discussion of family secrets. We explore the complex decisions family members make about what to tell and criteria for when and who to tell. Together, rituals, stories, and secrets are the types of family interaction that create a symbolic identity for the family. As we discussed in chapter 2, families exhibit the systems theory concept of nonsummativity. That is, the family is more than the sum of its parts. All these symbolic forms of interaction combine to create the family's spirit, identity, and its relationship to the outside world (Steinglass, Bennett, Wolin, & Reiss, 1987).

## INTERACTION NORMS AND NETWORKS

According to Daly (2001), the concept of "family time" is a relatively new notion. The notion stems from Victorian times and peaked in the family-centered decade of the 1950s. In Box 3.1, we study the notion of family time from a historical perspective and explore television's romanticized portrayal of family time.

To say that family time is different from work time does not really describe what family time is. When people talk about spending family time together, they have an idiosyncratic definition of what family time is. Daly (2001) warns that this usually involves some romanticized ideal of family togetherness, positive interactions, and child centeredness. Family time is romanticized as time together that involves everyone having fun or strengthening bonds of intimacy. The phrase "spending family time together" rarely refers to negative interactions (e.g., eating dinner together in an atmosphere of tension and underlying conflict, as does the family in the popular film *American Beauty*). And the phrase rarely indicates time spent together doing mundane or less enjoyable tasks such as cleaning the house. Clearly, there is a difference between what society romanticizes as family time and the total amount of time that family members spend together. Society's way of distinguishing family time was to develop the phrase "quality time," which is different from ordinary or negatively toned family interactions (Shaw, 1992).

Barnett (1998) warns that operational definitions of family time in research are far from the romanticized definitions of family time that individuals have in mind. In fact, scholars rarely use the term family time. They instead study more specific variables, usually related to the quantity of time adults or parents spend at work or how much time children spend watching TV. As Sandberg and Hofferth (2001) note, we know far more about the quantity of time families spend in specific activities than we do about the quality of time family members spend together because such data are more difficult to collect on a large scale. This has led to recent attempts in the last few decades to examine

### Box 3.1
### Family Time: Historical Perspective and Television's Portrayals

*Historical Perspective*

Prior to industrialized technology, most time was spent with family. Parents and children lived and worked in their family units, unless they were sent to live as a servant or apprentice in another family's home (Coontz, 2000). Even though few mothers worked outside the home, much of their time was intensely devoted to running the family farm or business. The advent of "wage labor under the factory system not only separated the public sphere of paid labor from the private domain of personal meanings, but also bracketed family time as different from work time" (Daly, 2001, p. 284). Daly suggests that the privileged class in late-19th-century Victorian Protestant culture popularized leisure and family time by making the family dinner and children's bedtime communication rituals. The living room parlor became a place for family conversation, and Sundays became a day for family time and rest from work that took one away from the family.

More recently, the 1950s have been dubbed as one of the most family- and child-centered decades in America—and also one of the most atypical decades. In the 1950s, 60% of children grew up in a home where the father went out to work and the mother stayed at home focusing on time with family—"a higher percentage than before or since" (Coontz, 2000, p. 287). Family historians like Coontz suggest that other decades, including recent ones, have been child and family focused; but what makes the 1950s unique is that women's and men's roles were more specialized compared to certain times before and most times since the 1950s when men and women were more equally devoted to family time, labor, and childcare.

*Television's Portrayals*

Some Americans appear nostalgic for a 1950s family that was actually quite rare in history. This type of family was popularized and further romanticized by television. Considering the fact that television ownership and viewing exploded in the 1950s, it is easy to understand why the 1950s family was the first family to be popularized on a large scale by television. "In 1948, fewer than 1 in 200 homes had a television set; by 1956, over half had a set and, by 1962, nine out of ten homes were equipped with television" (Douglas, 2003, p. 7). Even now, when Americans judge the state of the modern family, many draw comparisons to the heralded 1950s television family—a family portrayed to be even more family centered than the actual 1950s family. Consequently, some conclude that the modern family is in decline because it does not match up to 1950s television portrayal of families who lived in a "perfect" suburbia, enjoyed affluence, prioritized home and children, lived in mutual love and parental authority, and had clearly delineated gender-specific roles (see Douglas). Is the American family really in decline? Further, to what extent is the modern television family a reliable indicator of decline or improvement in the family? Some argue that modern television families are actually more functional and more realistic. For sure there is more variety in the way television families and their time together are portrayed.

the quality of time family members spend together. Such attempts have obviously given family communication scholars a full research agenda.

## Interaction Norms

In this section, we explore some of the research on the *quantity* of time families spend together, given that we spend much of the rest of this text examining issues related to the *quality* of family interactions. Observation is the most accurate way to determine how much time family members spend together. But observational methods are usually too intrusive, costly, and time intensive. The most valid and reliable alternative involves time diaries (Sandberg & Hofferth, 2001). Respondents are asked, for example, to report on their activities in 24-hour periods. They record information about their activities, time spent in each activity, and the people involved in the activity. Sandberg and Hofferth explored data from two time diary studies, both conducted at the University of Michigan with similar methodologies, but one included data from 1981; and the other, from 1997. Specifically, they compared the total time children spent with their parents, not distinguishing whether the parents were (a) engaged with the child in an activity or (b) simply present but not engaged. Overall, they found that American children spent *more* time with their mothers in 1997 versus in 1981, and no less time with their fathers. When considering two-parent families, "children's time with mothers, fathers, and both parents has increased dramatically . . . but these increases are not paralleled for children in single-parent families" (Sandberg & Hofferth, p. 434). The increase in single parenthood presents an obvious decrease in time parents have to spend with children (Sandberg & Hofferth). However, it should be noted that in single-parent households, parents spent no less time with children in 1997 versus in 1981. There simply are more single-parent households, as documented in chapter 1.

Several societal forces compete to challenge how or to what extent children spend more time with parents now. It seems at first counterintuitive that parents are spending more time with children. How could they spend more time when there appears to be so much data supporting the thesis that Americans are overworked and that the amount of hours adults spend in the labor force has dramatically increased over the last 4 decades (Hochschild, 1997)?

Contrary to popular belief, there are some well-supported arguments for why parents may actually be spending similar amounts of time or even more time with children. Jacobs and Gerson (2001) clarify that overall changes in working time are actually modest. They say the changes appear dramatic for several reasons. First, the increased participation of women in the workforce makes it appear that work time is increasing for all individuals, when the notable changes are occurring mostly for women. Increases in women's working hours do not necessarily translate to fewer parent–child interactions to the extent that fathers can adjust their work schedules to compensate for mother's increased time at work and to the extent that fathers desire to be more involved in their children's lives now more than in decades such as the 1950s. This appears to be the case in two-parent families in which mothers are working.

The argument that some fathers are spending more time with their children still does not fully explain how mothers can be spending more time with children when mothers are also working more. Jacobs and Gerson (2001) argue that only some mothers may be spending more time in the labor force. In other words, only some segments of the population have increased work hours, whereas other segments of the population have similar work hours or just modest changes. One segment of the population that appears to be working more is that of highly educated workers who hold prestigious jobs and occupations. Jacobs and Gerson highlight the pressure for these workers to log incredibly long workweeks. Further, there are even solid arguments that time spent doing housework is declining. More of the time once devoted to housework may be directed toward interacting with family members.

Probably the strongest explanation for why parents, and especially mothers, are spending more time with their children pertains to child-rearing trends. Although individualism is still prized highly in the United States, trends of child-centered parenting encourage parents to spend more and more time with children (Alwin, 1996). That is, even if some mothers are working more, they simultaneously make it a priority to devote more of the time they do have to their children. Overall, even though some structural reasons, such as single-parent families and maternal labor participation, relate negatively to parent–child time, these structural changes are outweighed by behavioral changes (Sandberg & Hofferth, 2001). These behavioral changes include the increased time that fathers, and parents in general, are devoting to children and the decreased time devoted to housework and other priorities.

What is the big deal with spending family time together? Time spent in family activities is assumed to promote positive relationships and individual development. There is a fair amount of research to suggest this is the case. For example, Hofferth and Sandberg (2001) found that children who spent more hours eating meals with their family had lower levels of behavior problems than did those who spent fewer hours eating together. This is possibly because children and parents can discuss events of the day or offer emotional support to each other during the dinner activity. Time spent in shared leisure activities is also positively associated with family satisfaction (Orthner & Mancini, 1990), likely for many of the same reasons. In the parent–child relationship, most communication occurs during another activity. In 1997, children spent only 45 minutes per week in which sitting and talking was the main activity (Hofferth & Sandberg).

Time spent in joint activities also appears to be positively related to the relational satisfaction of married couples, particularly when there are opportunities for interaction (Baxter & Dindia, 1990; Orthner & Mancini, 1990; Presser, 2000). Married couples have been estimated to spend anywhere from 1 hour and 15 minutes to 2 hours and 45 minutes conversing on a daily basis (Kirchler, 1989). Further, happy couples spend more time than unhappy couples discussing events of the day and personal topics. Presser found that in some cases, nonstandard work schedules are correlated with marital instability because the work schedule discourages interaction time and quality. "Specifically, it was the night and rotating shifts that significantly increased the odds of marital instability, and this was only for couples with children" (p. 107). Presser explains that for these couples, it may be extremely difficult to get sleep during the day when children are present. Lack of sleep leads to physiological stress and in turn exacerbates marital tensions and the quality of communication between partners and children. Presser further acknowledges that social interaction is the glue that holds relationships together. But ultimately, the *quality* of social interaction is more important than the *quantity* of interaction or the activity in which the interaction occurs.

*Quantity versus quality of time together.* Family scholars have recently argued that quantity and quality of time are very distinct concepts. The quality of time family members spend together says far more about their relationships than does the quantity of time spent together, especially for married couples. Guldner and Swensen (1995) suggest the evidence that increased time together causes increased relationship satisfaction is empirically very suspect. Research on commuter marriages (Govaerts & Dixon, 1988), long-distance romantic relationships (Guldner & Swensen), and couples separated by military careers (Pavalko & Elder, 1990) indicates no necessary relationship between satisfaction and geographic separation. Dainton and Aylor (2001) found that when people in long-distance romantic relationships had at least some limited opportunities for face-to-face interaction, they experienced no less uncertainty and trust and no more jealousy than did persons in geographically close relationships. When Reissman, Aron, and Bergen (1993) experimentally increased the amount of time married couples spent together and compared them to a control group, they found no greater increase in satisfaction for those couples who were instructed to spend more time together.

The problem is that some prior research has assumed that time spent together in what appear from the outside to be "positive" activities (e.g., joint leisure activities or holiday rituals) always elicits positive affective exchanges. When this assumption is tested, we see that it is not the activity but the interaction and subjective feelings generated during the activity that affect couple or family satisfaction. However, for years scholars have overgeneralized that spouses' joint pursuit of leisure activities enhances their satisfaction with marriage (Crawford, Houts, Huston, & George, 2002, p. 448). Crawford et al. followed couples over a decade studying not only how much time they spent in joint and separate leisure activities but also how much they liked the activities in which they participated. They found that the joint pursuit of activities that both spouses liked was positively related to husbands' satisfaction, but not to that of the wives. Further, their "principal longitudinal finding was that husbands' pursuit of activities that they liked but their wives disliked, both with and without their wives, was the most important factor in reducing their own satisfaction, as well as that of their wives" (Crawford et al., p. 448). As we have found in our own research, what is really at stake in joint activity time is the quality of interaction. The exhibition of socially skilled interactions and perceptions of partner positivity during leisure time make such time together more satisfying (Flora & Segrin, 1998). Although positive interactions could happen in a variety of activities, Flora and Segrin manipulated couples' activity types in the lab to see whether certain activities more than others promoted positive interaction. Couples in the study were randomly assigned to participate in one of three activities (a) relax on the couch together, (b) play a vertical checkers game in which there were negative consequences for losing, or (c) watch a popular TV show together. These activities were found to vary particularly in the amount of social interaction and competitiveness they elicited. Overall, the relax activity was most satisfying to couples, likely because it produced more opportunities for high-quality interaction. But surely couples find rewarding interaction in a variety of activities, and some couples are so dissatisfied that not even the best of activities can elicit positive communication. Thus, more time together and more communication do not necessarily translate to better relationships.

## Communication Climates and Networks

### Family Communication Climates

Over time, families establish a communication climate. McLeod and Chaffee (1972) suggested two fundamental communication orientations that contribute to this environment. Ritchie and Fitzpatrick (1990; Fitzpatrick & Ritchie, 1994; Ritchie, 1991) later labeled these two orientations the conformity orientation and the conversation orientation. *Conformity orientation* refers to the degree to which families create a climate that stresses homogeneity of attitudes, values, and beliefs (high conformity) versus heterogeneous attitudes and beliefs, greater individuality, and uniqueness and independence of family members (low conformity; Koerner & Fitzpatrick, 1997). High-conformity interactions also stress harmony, conflict avoidance, interdependence of networks, and obedience to parents (Koerner & Fitzpatrick, 2004). *Conversation orientation* refers to the degree to which family members create a climate where all are encouraged to participate freely and frequently in interaction without limitations regarding time spent and topics discussed (high conversation) versus less frequent interaction with only a few topics that are freely discussed (low conversation; Koerner & Fitzpatrick, 1997). High-conversation families share a lot of activities, thoughts, and feelings (Koerner & Fitzpatrick, 2004).

Based on their conversation and conformity orientation, families can be classified into four types (McLeod & Chaffee, 1972; see also Fitzpatrick & Ritchie, 1994). As depicted by Figure 3.1, families high in conversation and low in conformity are termed *pluralistic.* In pluralistic families, communication is open, frequent, and unconstrained, and members are encouraged to think independently. *Consensual* families are characterized by a tension between pressure to agree and an interest in open communication and the exploration of new ideas. Members of *laissez-faire* families have few interactions about limited topics. Emotional involvement among members is typically low and members look outside the family for emotional connection. Finally, *protective* families emphasize conformity and obedience.

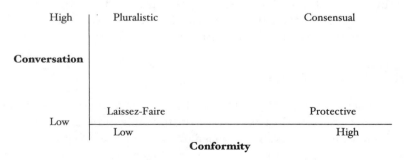

FIG. 3.1.   Family Types Based on Conversation and Conformity Orientations

Family communication orientations of conformity and conversation relate to family norms for exchanging and concealing information (Ritchie, 1997). The conformity orientation is associated with traditional values, respect for authority, and rules curbing expression. The conversation orientation is related to accepting and openly confronting conflict, and it is also associated with open sharing, independence, and autonomy in the parents' marriage (Fitzpatrick & Ritchie, 1994; Ritchie). Children from high-conformity-orientation families are more susceptible to peer pressure and less willing to test out new ideas at home than are children from high-conversation-oriented families (Dixson, 1995; Ritchie & Fitzpatrick, 1990). A family's conformity orientation is also reflected in the specific speech acts used by parents and children alike. For example, Koerner and Cvancara (2002) found families high in conformity contained members who used more advice, interpretation, and questions, compared to families low in conformity, whose members used more acknowledgment, reflection, and confirmation in their conversations. Overall, the speech acts of people from high-conformity families appeared to be relatively more self-oriented; namely, they viewed conversations from their own frame of reference. In comparison, the other-oriented nature of people from low-conformity families meant that they were relatively more likely to view conversations from the other person's perspective (Koerner & Cvancara). In chapter 4, we explore how such family communication climates relate to the experience of family conflict.

There are a variety of reasons why families adopt communication orientations related to conformity and conversation. The work of Kohn (1997) and Ritchie (1997) proposes that family communication climates are related in part to educational attainment and the workplace environment of parents. Kohn initially argued that a process of learning generalization encourages parents to adopt a family interaction pattern that is similar to that of their workplace environment. For example, parents who work in jobs that require conformity and deference to authority will encourage those same values in their children. In the same way, parents who work in jobs that require self-expression, self-direction, and autonomy will encourage those values in their children. Even if parents do not explicitly teach a communication orientation, the family communication climate is a context for implicit modeling and reinforcement (Elwood & Schrader, 1998). According to the learning generalization process, applying work communication patterns to home may be in the best interest of the child. Children will become familiar with the communication patterns that will be useful for them in later social and work environments, assuming they have the same work and educational goals as do their parents. Indeed, Ritchie found that a communication environment in the parents' workplace that favors openness, autonomy, and initiative is related to conversation orientation in the family.

### *Family Interaction Networks*

Family interactions can also be conceptualized as a network. Family communication networks attempt to model who talks to whom in the family and with what frequency. The concept of family networks has been applied to two-generation families (i.e., networks involving parents and children) as well as to multigeneration families (i.e., extended family networks). Family communication textbook writers Galvin, Bylund, and Brommel (2004) describe network structures that are useful for describing two-generation family networks. Although these network structures have not been the subject of much empirical research, they are descriptively heuristic. In a *centralized interaction network*, one member of the family acts as the hub of communication. This member talks to every other member and then passes information along to the rest of the family. The central member keeps the family in touch, because the rest of the members do not talk to each other with as much frequency, if at all. Two types of centralized structures are the *wheel network* and the *Y-network*. In the wheel network, the central member at the hub connects all the rest of the members at the spokes of the wheel. Everyone communicates through the one key figure. In the Y-network, the central member acts as gatekeeper. The gatekeeper talks to every other member, but only allows some messages to get through to members. The Y-structure depicts one or two members who are kept out of the loop of information, upon the discretion of the gatekeeper.

*Decentralized networks* do not have one single member who is the hub of information. In one type of decentralized network, the *all-channel network*, everyone talks to everyone else with similar frequency. It is common for members to share information with several members, sometimes repeating the same story over again. It is not uncommon for families with an all-channel network to discuss things all together. In the decentralized *chain network*, family members relay messages through a chain of family members. Although there is not one central member, alliances exist such that some members will only talk to certain other members. Members on opposite ends of the communication chain may rarely or never talk to each other. Any information they have about the opposite member is filtered through the chain of members in between.

Rather than simply label types of family communication networks, the family communication research literature has been more apt to study whether age, time, or topic affects who talks to whom in family networks. For example, Guerrero and Afifi (1995a) confirmed common lay beliefs that teenagers exhibit more topic avoidance with their parents than do preteenagers. Topic avoidance remains relatively common through the time the child launches from home or moves away to college. This change in network patterns is typical and age appropriate (Caughlin & Golish, 2002). Individualistic cultural norms set the expectation for teenagers to mature so as to one day become independent of their parents. Topic avoidance represents the teen's desire to figure things out alone, take ownership over information, and set new boundaries in the relationship. Admittedly, many parents and children struggle as they attempt to negotiate new network boundaries and channels (Petronio, 1994). As one might expect, parents' dissatisfaction with the parent–child relationship is related to perceptions of their child's avoidance (Caughlin & Golish). Later in this chapter's discussion of family secrets, we explore the process of topic avoidance and privacy dilemmas in greater depth.

Keeping in mind that network structures change with age, Guerrero and Afifi (1995a) maintain that once young adult children have established autonomy from their parents, they often feel a renewed desire to become closer to their parents and less need to practice topic avoidance. Studying network contact later on in the life span, Patterson (1995) found that older adults (average age 74) had significantly more contact with their family networks than did younger adults (average age 22). Interestingly, the younger adult group did not report any less affinity for their families. Patterson noted that although family network contact appears to fluctuate over the life span, affinity for one's family appears relatively stable. Throughout the book, we explore how the addition of family members (e.g., birth of a child, marriage, or in-home care of an elderly member) or the loss of family members (e.g., through death, divorce, or an adult child who moves out of the house) changes communication frequency in the family network. In chapter 8, we specifically explore the role of extended family networks.

### Standards for Family Communication Climates and Networks

As a counterpart to our discussion of *actual* family norms and networks, communication scholar John Caughlin reminds us that people hold standards for how they wish their family communication would be. In his three-part study on family communication standards, Caughlin (2003) begins by using open-ended questions to assess the content of people's family communication standards. As one might expect, people held a variety of standards, and some articulated multiple standards, whereas others reported just one or a few. Caughlin notes that there are inherent idiosyncrasies in family communication standards. An individual's cultural values, for instance, inform standards of family communication such as openness or avoidance. Caughlin developed a 10-factor measure of the most commonly mentioned standards for "good family communication." These standards include openness, expression of affection, emotional and instrumental support, politeness, use of appropriate humor and sarcasm, routine interaction, clear and effective discipline, avoidance of personal or hurtful topics, maintenance of structural stability (e.g., "have one person in the family who everyone else always listens to and obeys"), and mind-reading (e.g., "know what's going on in other family members' lives without asking"). The measure assesses (a) the extent to which an individual endorses any of the 10 most common standards, (b) how the communication in that individual's family is different from the standard, and (c) whether the individual feels the difference is positive or negative.

Indeed, Caughlin (2003) found that unmet family communication ideals accounted for poorer family satisfaction. Even after accounting for whether the ideals were met or not, simply holding certain relationship-focused ideals, such as openness, expression of affection, emotional and instrumental support, regular routine interaction, was positively associated with satisfaction. It could be that holding positive relationship standards indicates a motivation to work toward those standards or a heightened satisfaction that a standard held has been fulfilled. Beginning to study standards and patterns for family network interaction leads us to a more in-depth discussion of family routines and rituals.

## FAMILY ROUTINES AND RITUALS

A *family ritual* is defined as symbolic communication: "that owing to the satisfaction that family members experience through its repetition, is acted out in a systemic fashion over time" (Wolin & Bennet, 1984, p. 401). In other words, rituals have special meaning that establish and preserve the family's identity (Jorgenson & Bochner, 2004; Wolin & Bennet). The interaction and behavior related to the ritual symbolize something greater for the family. "In the context of the family system, it is typically the family unit that in some way is honored in a ritual's enactment" (Baxter & Clark, 1996, p. 254). Family reunions, for example, typically symbolize the perseverance of family unity over generations. As we note in our discussion of symbolic interaction theory in chapter 2, families develop symbolic rituals for both routine and extraordinary events. However, rituals are different from routines. Routines are repetitive behaviors that are crucial to the structure of family life, but they lack the symbolism and the "compelling anticipatory nature" that rituals possess (Viere, 2001). Routines are converted to rituals when they move from instrumental to symbolic acts (Fiese et al., 2002). Admittedly, the boundary separating ritual from nonritual is not clear-cut (Wolin & Bennett). The two are commonly distinguished by the notion that "routines are activities that family members have to do rather than want to do. . . . Rituals that lose meaning or become mundane may take on routine status for families" (Viere, p. 286).

Rituals are thought to be symbolically important to the family's relational and psychological well-being. For example, Fiese and Tomcho (2001) found that the more meaning married couples found in their religious holiday rituals, the more relationship satisfaction they experienced. For these satisfied couples, interaction surrounding religious holidays was not merely a routine void of meaning but rather a ritual that reaffirmed their own affection and intimacy. In her work on communication rituals in intercultural weddings, Wendy Leeds-Hurwitz (2002) argues that the wedding ritual typically (a) confirms the existence of a united support community from both partners, (b) symbolizes the blending of each partner's cultural background and the transmission of cultural values, and (c) highlights membership in a new family and the unique identity of the couple. Although rituals are frequently viewed as positive forms of family interaction, we discuss later in this section that rituals can also be characterized by family dysfunction and stress. Holiday rituals or wedding rituals are intended to be some of the most positive rituals that families ever experience. Instead, they frequently spark some of the most heightened stress families ever experience (Leeds-Hurwitz).

Wolin and Bennett (1984) describe three main types of family rituals: patterned family interactions, family celebrations, and family traditions. *Patterned family interactions* are the least formal but most frequently enacted. They include family regularities such as dinnertime, bedtime, leisure activities, or the treatment of guests in the home, so long as these events have a larger symbolic value. For example, the ritual may symbolize how the family feels about each other and about other people, or what appropriate roles and rules are. Imagine a family that ritualizes dinnertime so that certain members prepare the meal; seating around the table is consistent, and children must remain at the table until everyone is finished eating and only then may they ask to be excused. Such a dinnertime ritual may symbolize the family's roles and rules and honors the family's unified time together.

Family traditions and family celebrations are more formal than are patterned family interactions. *Family traditions* include birthdays, anniversaries, family reunions, or family vacations. The nature of the celebrations and the meaning attached to them are unique to each family. Obviously, families vacation in different ways. To some, a camping vacation is the perfect escape from daily life. To others, this type of vacation is more exhausting and stressful than daily life. *Family celebrations* are more culture specific and often follow some relative standardization with other families. Family celebrations include rites of passage (e.g., baptisms, graduations, weddings, and funerals), religious celebrations (e.g., Christmas, Easter, and Passover), and secular holidays (e.g., Thanksgiving and Fourth of July). These more formal and infrequent rituals have a variety of functions. Family celebrations are a means of transmitting values. Indeed, Fiese and Tomcho (2001) found that meaningful aspects of religious holiday rituals are transmitted across generations and have the potential to enhance satisfactory family relationships. Rituals such as graduations and weddings, which are related to life-cycle transitions, introduce new statuses and change perceptions of people (Troll, 1988). For instance, graduation rituals may help a child to be perceived as an adult. Overall, rituals mark time by socially producing memories about events, transitions, and patterns in life.

A growing body of research has documented the protective and therapeutic roles of rituals in the face of family stress related to issues of alcoholism, illness, life-cycle transitions, or divorce and remarriage. Cheal (1988) theorized that rituals could be mechanisms of tension management. The behavioral routine stabilizes family life in the midst of a crisis that has the capacity to drastically alter family patterns. In addition, the ritual reminds the family of important symbolic meanings or brings new meaning at a time when the family is vulnerable to the loss or misconstrual of meaning.

In the 1970s and 1980s, Wolin and Bennett (1984) began to explore the relationship between alcoholism and family rituals. They were concerned with three "critical crossroads" in the relationship between family rituals and alcoholism. The first involved the family of origin's response to parental alcoholism, particularly the extent to which the alcoholism disrupted family rituals. Here, they were interested in whether rituals would protect a child from the effects of an alcoholic parent or at the other extreme enable the alcoholism to continue. The second and third crossroads involved the spouse selected by the child and the couple's establishment of rituals in their new family. The second and third crossroads related to the extent to which parental alcoholism would be transmitted to the child. In a series of studies, Wolin and Bennett explored the child's ritual heritage (i.e., the rituals related to one's family of origin background) and ritual establishment (i.e., the "crucial" choices children from an alcoholic home make when they select a mate and establish their own rituals).

Bennett, Wolin, Reiss, and Teitelbaum (1987) articulate the link between family rituals and alcoholism in the following way:

> As with most chronic illnesses, alcoholism can become a powerful organizer of family life, altering the details of daily routines as well as special occasions. Not all families suffer the consequences of alcoholism in the same way, however. While some are clearly able to protect their daily routines and most valued activities, others are unsuccessful in keeping the ravages due to the alcoholic drinking under control. (p. 112)

Bennett et al.'s (1987) research spawned interest in the effects of "ritual disruption." This important concept refers to whether a family's rituals are subsumed by the alcoholism or kept distinctive from the problem-drinking behavior. In *subsumptive families*, the alcohol use disrupts and controls the practice of family rituals. In fact, the alcohol abuse is a negative ritual in itself. In *distinctive families*, the family rituals remain distinct from the alcohol abuse. In families where rituals, namely, the dinnertime rituals, are kept intact and distinctive from the alcoholic problems, children are less likely to develop alcoholic problems of their own (Bennett et al.). Thus, under potentially stressful child-rearing circumstances, rituals (i.e., positive rituals) offer a protective factor. Bennett et al.'s research exposed other shielding factors related to spouse selection and selective engagement in nonalcoholic family rituals. Regarding transmission of alcoholism, children who came from alcoholic families received additional protection by choosing spouses and in-laws who promoted rituals that were not dominated by an alcoholic identity.

In much the same way that positive family rituals protect alcoholic families, routines and rituals are often effective means for managing illness in the family. Markson and Fiese (2000) found evidence that meaningful family rituals appeared to protect children from anxiety-related health problems. Similarly, Fiese (2000a) found that families were most successful at managing a child's asthma when they had established daily routines regarding asthma care. These routines involved giving the child daily doses of medicine at prescribed times (e.g., mealtime), refilling prescriptions, establishing behaviors for dealing with asthma attacks, keeping track of inhalers, and vacuuming the house. Managing these routines allowed other social and familial routines and rituals (e.g., school attendance, dinnertime, and vacations) to be less disrupted.

Even as families deal with ordinary daily stressors and transitions, routines and rituals help organize family life. This may explain why some parents and young children alike suffer when their "normal schedule" is disrupted. Jencius and Rotter (1998) found, for example, that for children bedtime rituals contributed to less sleep disturbance (e.g., protest against bedtime, trouble going to sleep, or waking up in the middle of the night), so long as the rituals involved the child, emphasized continuity statements, and were conducted with some flexible choice rather than with extreme rigidity. Examples of *child involvement* in bedtime rituals included a child turning on his or her own bathwater, helping to make lunch for the next day, or helping pick out clothes for the next day. *Continuity statements* included references to tomorrow that gave faith to the child that there will be a tomorrow with events to expect. Examples of *giving the child choice* within reason involved telling the child that dad can read two long books or three short books or letting the child choose what the bedtime snack or bathtime activities will be. To some families, bedtime patterns are simply routines with little symbolic meaning. To other families, bedtime patterns truly take on ritual status. That is, the bath, teeth brushing, a bedtime story, prayer, and lying down with the child in bed are imbibed with symbolic relational messages. Jencius and Rotter argue that for some parents who both work during the day, the bedtime ritual takes on greater symbolic meaning, because they have limited opportunities to symbolize their care and affection.

Continuing throughout the life span, Fiese found that when families develop predictable family routines and rituals during middle childhood years, children perform better in school (2000b) and adolescents have a higher self-esteem and sense of belonging (Fiese, 1992). Rituals have the capacity to bring stability and meaning, especially at times when children are vulnerable to other chaotic experiences outside the family. Rituals even help buffer potential stress and chaos during transitions inside the family. This appears to be the case for stepfamilies, who benefit from balancing new family rituals to embrace their new family while still honoring the old family traditions (Braithwaite, Baxter, & Harper, 1998). Similarly, couples that transition to parenthood benefit from maintaining some of their old relationship maintenance rituals (e.g., still taking time for a night out without the baby) while they simultaneously develop new rituals with their child (Bruess & Pearson, 1995; Fiese, Hooker, Kotary, & Schwagler, 1993). Further, new rituals developed in association with the birth of a child can provide grandparents with an opportunity to be involved with grandchildren (e.g., to help celebrate a grandchild's birthday; Fiese et al., 2002).

Clearly, there is a great deal of research that highlights the positive functions of family rituals. But what happens when once-positive rituals lose their symbolic meaning, when rituals originate as a symbol of dysfunction, or when rituals become rigid and do not fit the needs of the family? The point is that rituals are not uniformly positive. Negative family rituals can seriously harm the family's well-being. Unfortunately, many maladaptive rituals are also transmitted across generations. Based on earlier work by Wolin and Benett (1984), Viere (2001) summarized six typologies of family ritual use. The typology depicts how families vary in their commitment to ritualizing and their ability to adapt rituals to time and new circumstances. This typology also helps understand how and why rituals may have a positive or negative effect on the family.

1. *Underritualized.* Families who do not celebrate or mark family changes and who do not join in larger societal rituals.
2. *Rigidly ritualized.* Families who cannot adapt their rituals over time. Ritual behaviors are closed, prescribed, and must occur in the same way every time.
3. *Skewed ritualization.* One particular ethnic or religious tradition or one particular side of the family is ritualized at the expense of the other. Or one particular behavior is ritualized excessively, often with a negative intent or impact.
4. *Hollow ritualization.* The family celebrates events out of obligation, and there is little meaning or process in the event. This often occurs when rituals are not adapted over time and create stress for family members.
5. *Interrupted ritualization.* Sudden changes (e.g., death, illness, and war) keep the family from celebrating the rituals they would otherwise celebrate.
6. *Adaptable ritualization.* The family keeps the rituals meaningful by flexibly changing the events, roles, and rules related to the ritual when necessary.

Baxter and Clark (1996) studied a family's commitment to rituals and hypothesized that their ability to adapt rituals would both be related to the degree of support and control in family communication patterns. Their results indicated that families who were more committed to their rituals expressed more supportive communication (as measured by having a conversation orientation). We should note that they only studied rituals that were intended to be positive. Clearly, some families are committed to rituals that are negative and not able to adapt their commitment to the old ritual so as to be compatible with the family's current needs. Adolescent children commonly get embarrassed when their parents fail to adapt childhood rituals. Essentially, the adolescent outgrows the ritual faster than the parents do. For example, "practices evident in celebrating a young child's birthday (e.g., funny hats, games, and candy) may not be responsive to the kind of birthday party the child wants during his or her adolescence" (Baxter & Clark, p. 256). Not suprisingly, Fiese (1992) found that mother–adolescent disagreement about commitment to family rituals (e.g., mom thinks the dinnertime ritual is more important and meaningful than does her teenager) was negatively related to adolescent feelings of belonging.

Van der Hart (1983) pointed out that families that have little involvement and commitment to their rituals are in danger of hollow rituals. These families often show a high degree of role prescription. For example, the family must go to grandma's house for lunch every Sunday. And grandma always serves roast beef. Little meaning is attached to the gathering and there is no room for change. Rigid role prescriptions can also skew the practice of rituals. For example, imagine a mother who takes on all the duties associated with cooking the Thanksgiving meal and thinks of the holiday as work, while the rest of the family gets to enjoy themselves (Shaw, 1992). Or as Galvin and Brommel (1999) describe, a spouse may engage in a skewed work ritual, where he or she works an obnoxious amount of hours in order to gain distance from the family or avoid problems. Family scholars still have much more to learn about negative family rituals. Roberts (1988) proposed that rigidly ritualized symptoms such as binge eating, alcoholic drinking, spousal abuse, and drug abuse often appear in families lacking more meaningful positive rituals. We attempt to shed more light on negative rituals such as those in Part IV of this book.

Finally, inclusion in family rituals defines who is an insider and who is an outsider. Family rituals construct boundaries that may partially or totally exclude family members whose position in the family is ambiguous, controversial, or whose identity and beliefs are not compatible with the rest of the members (Oswald, 2002). In some families, the family status and inclusion of gay and lesbian persons is disputed. Oswald found that the quality of family relationships, namely, parent–child and sibling relationships, and the visibility of the same-sex relationship predicted whether gay and lesbian persons and their partners were invited to family rituals. In earlier research, Oswald (2000) contends that certain types of family rituals, namely, heterosexual weddings, are commonly problematic for gay, lesbian, bisexual, and transgender family members. The problem may stem from a frustration that some relationships in one's family are positively ritualized while others are not.

## FAMILY STORIES AND SECRETS

### Family Stories

Families naturally tell stories during the course of interaction. It is common to hear family members say to one another, "Do you remember when . . . " or "One time we all . . . " (Fiese et al., 1999; Fiese, Hooker, Kotary, Schwagler, & Rimmer, 1995). In recent decades, family scholars have recognized that these stories, whether they occur naturally or are prompted by a researcher's questions, provide a window to the symbolic content of family life. Family stories are defined as "verbal accounts of personal experiences that are important to the family, and typically involve the creation and maintenance of relationships, depict rules of interaction, and reflect beliefs about family and other social institutions" (Fiese et al., 2001, p. 260). This definition gives us a starting point, but we would be remiss not to acknowledge that family stories can also be about negative family interactions and can involve the destruction of relationships (Vangeliti, Crumley, & Baker, 1999). Whether positive or negative, stories serve several important functions in the family, all related to the process of symbolic meaning-making. Some of the primary functions of family stories are to remember events, interpret and judge events, socialize members, affirm belonging, and connect generations (Jorgenson & Bochner, 2004). Family stories are often prompted by certain situations (e.g., dinnertime, funerals, holidays, and bedtime) and center around common topics (e.g., how a couple got together, how a family originated whether by birth or adoption, how the family handles adversity, what it means to be a member the family, or how parents struggled with issues of growing up or making decisions).

### Functions of Family Stories

We begin by exploring the functions of storytelling in the family. One primary function of stories is to help families remember events by marking information and experiences in time. This is what Vangelisti et al. (1999) term the "referential function" of stories. As Fiese et al. (1999) say, family stories form a "family scrapbook" over the generations (p. 3). Even though a primary function of stories is to remember events, Karney and Coombs (2000) note that people are not reliable historians. The scrapbook gets adapted over time by inconsistent memories, exaggerations, and denials. One may wonder if the bad memories of family members pose a problem for researchers. To the contrary, if family members had accurate, unbiased memories, researchers would probably be far less interested in their stories. The fact that family members are telling stories that they *choose* to tell versus ones that are historically accurate gives the researcher an insider's perspective as to what events and experiences are most symbolic and in what way. For example, a collection of studies in which married couples retrospectively tell the events of their relationship development indicate that how a couple remembers the events of their past is related to their current satisfaction and future marital outcomes (Buehlman, Gottman, & Katz, 1992; Flora & Segrin, 2003). In basic terms, dissatisfied couples seem to forget the once pleasant events in their relationship development. Satisfied couples cling to the pleasant memories of the past and possibly even exaggerate their positive nature. Imagine, for example, that each time a husband tells the story about their first date, the story gets revised and perhaps exaggerated such that now the food at the restaurant was not just good, but exquisite, and now his date was not just dressed nicely, but was stunning. Other research shows that married couples do well to forget some of their partners' faults and instead dwell on their partners' strengths in the process of storytelling (Karney & Coombs). In this way, the ongoing revision of relationship stories becomes transformative and re-defines reality in a positive or negative light (Berger & Kellner, 1964; Wamboldt, 1999).

Intertwined with the referential function, some stories have an *evaluative function*, whereby interpretive assessments regarding events and experiences are revealed in the stories (Vangelisti et al., 1999). By examining stories, we can access people's perceptions and attitudes and see how they alter the construction of meaning in their relationships

(Bochner, Ellis, & Tillmann-Healy, 1997; Buehlman et al., 1992; Vangelisti et al.). Vangelisti et al. summarize the symbolic impact of family stories:

> When people tell stories about their family, they provide listeners with clues as to how they feel about family members and what they think makes for "healthy" and "unhealthy" family interaction. The issues they choose to discuss or avoid, the attributions they make about family members' behavior, and the way they position themselves vis-à-vis the story line can reveal interesting information about how they view family relationships. (p. 336)

Karney and Fry (2002) examined the stories that married couples told about their relationship development, and how these stories were related to their retrospective satisfaction and their predictions of future marital satisfaction. What is unique about their study is that they specifically examined how couples think their relationship has changed over time. They found that what couples appear to care about the most is how their relationship has been changing over time rather than how they judged their relationship at any previous point in time. In particular, "spouses who perceived the greatest improvements in their satisfaction were significantly more optimistic about the future of the marriage, whereas remembered levels of satisfaction were not significantly associated with spouses' future predictions" (p. 234). According to this study, the evaluative function of narratives is important in a temporal sense. We do not evaluate events in a vacuum. Rather, some of our most impactful evaluations are based on comparisons we make to previous events in the relationship scrapbook.

Evaluations of family events are also related to people's expectations for ideal family interaction. Vangelisti et al. (1999) illustrated this in a two-part study. Participants were asked to write a story telling about an event that they felt best described their family. After explaining why they thought the story happened the way it did, participants were asked to "re-write the story so it described what they believed was an 'ideal' family," unless they already considered their family to be ideal" (p. 340). In the first part of the study, Vangelisti et al. found that stories reflecting themes of care, togetherness, adaptability, reconstruction (e.g., the family being reunited or reconciled), and humor were positively associated with family satisfaction. Stories with themes of disregard, hostility, chaos, divergent values, and negative personality attributes were negatively related to family satisfaction. Thus, the stories revealed what it was that made people satisfied or dissatisfied with their family relationships. When evaluating positive events, discrepant themes between one's own family stories and the ideal family stories were related to family satisfaction. For example, the more people felt that the positive themes for their own family stories exceeded their ideal family regarding these themes, the more satisfied they were with their own families. In turn, people had less family satisfaction when their own family stories had more negative themes than their ideal family stories. The evaluative function of stories is strongly linked to people's expectations for what makes a good family. More recently, Vangelisti and Alexander (2002) suggest that when spouses' ideal standards for a spouse are unmet, one of their last remaining coping mechanisms is to construct a story that rationalizes the disappointing situation through excuses, justifications, and other similar means.

Another major function of stories is to *socialize members of the family*. One of the most obvious examples is a parent telling a story or recounting a childhood experience as a way to share values, manners, and lessons. Stories have morals to them, and family members often use such stories strategically (Yerby, Buerkel-Rothfuss, & Bochner, 1995). For example, Fiese et al. (1995) found that once children were of preschool age, parents began to tell stories that included themes of achievement and personal success. Theoretically, this storytelling is a way to socialize children into roles the parent hopes the children will enact later in life. Once the children are at an age where they can engage in symbolic role-taking, these stories can have an impact, because the children can imagine how they could conduct their life and make choices in order to replicate the themes of the story. On the other hand, very small children can hardly imagine roles outside of themselves. Prior to preschool age, Fiese et al. found that parents told stories with more themes of affiliation, belonging, or closeness versus themes of achievement and personal success. In the study, the parents of very young children were utilizing the *belonging function* of storytelling. Perhaps because their children were so young and developmentally dependent, parents were particularly motivated to affirm the child's connection to the parent and build the child's collective identity through such stories. Fiese et al. even noted, "we were struck by the relatively high incidence of storytelling in families with infants," which they note is likely useful for linguistic development and stimulation, even if the infant could not understand the story (p. 768). Another appealing explanation is that parents benefit from telling belonging stories to infants because the parents are also beginning to solidify their own new bond with the child. Indeed, the meaning of what family is and who belongs in a family is constituted through stories (Harold, 2000).

Fiese et al. (1995) also note that themes of family stories are clearly culture bound. For example, families who adhere to values of extreme individualism may see less need to constantly tell stories that highlight themes of connection, belonging, and interdependence, especially as children get older. Other families may constantly emphasize such themes throughout the family, regardless of family stage.

### *Analyzing Family Narratives*

Cowan (1999) makes a fine distinction between narratives and stories. Narratives refer to the form; and stories, to the thematic content. Prior to the 1990s, scholars examined stories for their thematic content, and certainly much can be ascertained from such an examination as we have just presented. However, in the 1990s, a group of researchers formed the Family Narrative Consortium (FNC) in order to systematically develop a research methodology to study narrative form. Specifically, they were interested in how family narrative form relates to family interaction patterns, marital satisfaction, and child adjustment (see Fiese et al., 1999, 2001). Jorgenson and Bochner (2004) point out that there has been some resistance to analyzing the narrative form of stories, because occasionally the emotion and meaning of the story are lost in the effort to predict outcomes and analyze a story with predetermined categories. Further, stories should not be detached from the experiences in which they were formed; stories are a part of family relationships (Bochner & Ellis, 1995).

Nonetheless, the FNC identified three components they felt were central to the study of family narratives as a form of interaction: narrative coherence, narrative interaction, and relationship beliefs. The FNC developed several scales to measure each of the three components of narratives. Members of the FNC also collaborated on a series of studies, which we describe here, intended to validate the scales.

*Narrative coherence* refers to how an individual constructs and organizes a narrative. Coherence is often called the "syntax" of a narrative (Fiese et al., 2001). It also involves the consistency of the narrative and the match between the story's affect and content. Dickstein, St. Andre, Sameroff, Seifer, and Schiller (1999) hypothesized that a family's ability to produce a coherent narrative regarding family life would be related to the presence of maternal mental illness. Indeed, they found that "mothers with major depression and currently experiencing psychiatric symptoms created less coherent accounts than nonill mothers" (Fiese et al., p. 268). Mothers with psychiatric symptoms also told stories with more negative narrative interaction—a component we discuss in a moment. In another test of the validity of the narrative coherence scales, Grotevant, Fravel, Gorall, and Piper (1999) found that parents who went through open-adoption processes had more coherent narratives related to the child's heritage than those who made confidential or mediated adoptions. Confidential adoptions had more incomplete details that affected the narrative's coherence. Assuming that coherent birth stories are related to psychological well-being, the authors suggested that this finding might have important implications for adoption programs or therapies that help prospective parents develop a "story" of the child's heritage.

*adoption*

The second component, *narrative interaction,* refers to the way two or more members construct and tell the story together. It involves studying the "act" of storytelling. The FNC developed scales to measure couple narrative style (i.e., how the couple tells a story together). On the narrative style scale, negative referents include discrepancies, differences of opinion, parallel stories, and occasions of anger, whereas positive referents include additions to the partner's story and synthetic interaction. A related scale measures coordination of the couple or family members (e.g., positive coordination in the form of "we" statements, asking for others' opinions and clarification, polite turn taking versus negative referents such as statements of disconforming exclusion). Finally, a confirmation and disconfirmation scale distinguishes generally validating behaviors and statements from nonvalidating ones. Using a semistructured interview, Wamboldt (1999) asked couples to tell stories primarily about their current relationship and some about their family of origin. They found that a couple's relational satisfaction was related to positive narrative interaction. In other words, it appears to be important that the couple jointly constructs their relationship reality in a positive, affirming way as reflected by the scales. The benefits of interactive, affirming relationship storytelling to the well-being of married and dating couples has been demonstrated in measures of storytelling related to the Oral History Interview (Buehlman et al., 1992; Flora & Segrin, 2003). We discuss this in chapter 6, our chapter regarding marriage.

Positive narrative interaction also appears to have beneficial effects on the family in general. Fiese and Marjinsky (1999) interviewed families about their mealtime practices and had the couple tell a story to their child about a mealtime when the parent was a child. They found that "couples who worked together to tell their story also worked together with their children in positive exchanges at the dinner table" (Fiese & Marjinsky,

p. 65). They explained their findings by noting that "good couple behavior is related to good family behavior" (Fiese & Marjinsky, p. 65).

The third component the FNC identified in narratives is *relationship beliefs*. One scale measuring this component, the Relationship Expectations Scale, examines how members of the family view relationships (e.g., manageable, reliable, safe versus dangerous, unfulfilling, and restrictive). Another scale related to the relationship beliefs component measures the extent to which the family is willing to share personal and sensitive information with an interviewer. Studying the impact of relationship beliefs, Fiese and Marjinsky (1999) found that secure relationship beliefs expressed about the current family were related to positivity at the dinner table.

## Family Secrets

Stories can reveal information and hide information. Baxter and Wilmot (1985) suggest that the best way to really understand a social organization, such as the family, is to analyze the strategies used by the unit to control the flow of information. One of these such strategies is the family secret. Vangelisti (1994a) found that almost all families have secrets. As we mentioned earlier, people are unreliable historians, sometimes unintentionally, because they simply cannot remember the facts, and other times intentionally, because they want to keep something a secret. Naima Brown-Smith (1998) opens her review of family secrets with the following example:

> Madeleine Albright left the Republic of Czech with her parents when she was just 2 years old. After arriving in the United States, she was raised as a Catholic. Over the years, Albright's parents talked often and openly with her about their history. Conversation topics included what it was like to live in Prague, the historical figures they knew there, as well as their role in Czech politics. However, Albright's parents kept hidden the family's true heritage . . . [Later, the former U.S. Secretary of State received] letters that revealed that she was really of Jewish descent. Indeed three of her grandparents were Jews killed by Nazis in the Holocaust. Not only did this revelation affect the Albright family's identity but also Madeleine Albright's political image, as many people now question the integrity of her story, claiming that she was aware of her heritage but deliberately hid it. (p. 20)

Decisions to keep certain information a secret or not are complex, and families often have implicit or explicit rules about what information should remain a secret. Secrets vary by topic and function. Some families and family members are more prone to tell secrets than are others. In this section, we explore these decisions in the context of family interaction. But first, we define family secrets and consider theoretical grounding for the study of family secrets. The study of family secrets is a relatively new topic for family scholars, a topic that proves to be very interesting juxtaposed against the already impressive amount of scholarship devoted to family stories and interpersonal disclosures.

### Defining Family Secrets and Theoretical Grounding

Caughlin and Petronio (2004) view secrets as a special instance of privacy in which information is intentionally revealed. Communication scholar Sandra Petronio (1991, 2000, 2002) introduced Communication Privacy Management Theory (CPM) and specifically applied the theory to family groups (Caughlin & Petronio; Petronio, Jones, & Morr, 2003). CPM details how people manage privacy. Petronio (2002) argues that people feel they have ownership over their private information and a right to control the flow of such information to others. CPM uses the metaphor of boundaries to refer to the mental limits people set regarding information they own and information others own. People have both personal and collective boundaries (Karpel, 1980; Petronio et al.; Vangelisti, Caughlin, & Timmerman, 2001). Personal boundaries are set by individuals to control information they feel they own. Personal boundaries lead to *individual secrets*. *Whole or shared family secrets* are those that the entire family keeps from outsiders. Such secrets represent the use of collectively negotiated boundaries (Vangelisti & Caughlin, 1997). Sometimes coalitions of family members may keep an *internal* secret from the rest of the family (Brown-Smith, 1998).

How do family members decide what to keep a secret, what to tell, and who to tell? CPM proposes that most families have rules regarding the regulation of private information (Petronio, 2002; Petronio et al., 2003). Sometimes rules are preexisting, and members become socialized to them implicitly or explicitly. For example, some families, as a rule, do not talk about money in public. This rule may be communicated explicitly by saying, "We don't talk about money in public," or implicitly by predictably changing the topic if it comes up. On other occasions, families, or coalitions in families, mutually negotiate rules, although this effort is often the subject of great conflict. Still in other situations, individuals find themselves in a "predicament where no clear privacy rules used in the family can easily apply" (Petronio et al., p. 33). CPM suggests five criteria that shape the formation of family rules (Petronio; Petronio et al.). Rules are affected by (a) cultural expectations, (b) gender expectations, (c) individual motivations, (d) judgments about the benefit to risk ratio, and (e) the context.

Decisions about how to manage private or secretive information result in what CPM terms "family privacy dilemmas." Petronio et al. (2003) describe *internal* family privacy dilemmas that refer to boundaries among family members:

> We know that families encounter dilemmas that stem from being confidants within the family, from accidentally discovering problematical information, and from snooping on other family members. . . . In general, the conundrum surrounds the contradictory expectation that, on one hand, family members may wish to maintain some level of separateness and autonomy if the consequence of a decision to manage the dilemma has the potential to hurt themselves or other family members. This paradox underscores the joint position of being both a *group* member and, simultaneously, *an individual member of a group.*

Vangelisti et al. (2001) examined privacy dilemmas regarding boundaries between the family and the people *external* to the family. Specifically, they studied individuals' criteria for revealing whole family secrets to an outsider. Their study produced 10 common criteria people use when deciding whether to disclose a whole family secret. When asked, "How likely are you to tell the secret . . . " the 10 most common criteria are as follows.

1. Intimate exchange (e.g., if we were having a heart to heart discussion)
2. Exposure (e.g., if I were confronted or it would be found out anyway)

3. Urgency (e.g., if I could not hold it in any longer or he/she were the only person I could tell)
4. Acceptance (e.g., if the person would still accept me)
5. Conversational appropriateness (e.g., if we were discussing a topic related to it)
6. Relational security (e.g., if I trusted that the person would not tell anyone else)
7. Important reason (e.g., if I thought it was essential that the person know)
8. Permission (e.g., if my family members thought it was okay to tell)
9. Family membership (e.g., if he or she was going to marry into my family)
10. Never (e.g., I would never tell)

The *relational security* and *important reason* criteria yielded interesting results. Relational security appeared to stand as a "minimum criterion" for revealing family secrets. That is, if the right amount of relational security were not present in the first place, then the individual would not even consider telling, and subsequently the other criteria would hardly matter. However, for the important reason criterion, people reported that if there were a pressing reason to tell, they would consider doing so even if they were otherwise unlikely to tell. So this criterion superceded others. People who strongly identified with their secret, felt their family secret was intimate, or perceived the secret to be negatively toned were more likely to require that more of the criteria be fulfilled before they would tell another. Further, even though a person may feel psychologically close to another person, they still reported strongly considering most of the criteria before they would divulge a secret, though they were less likely to say they would never tell. The point is that even if we feel psychologically close to someone, we still may maintain secrets and go through complex decision processes before we tell.

### Functions and Types of Family Secrets

Vangelisti et al. (2001) point out that secret keeping is often portrayed as negative. In some cases, it may indeed be negative. There is some evidence that the suppression of negative emotion (i.e., keeping something in) takes a toll on one's mental and physical health (Caughlin & Petronio, 2004; Petrie, Booth, & Pennebaker, 1998). The more romantic partners perceive that their partners avoid conversation topics with them, the less satisfied they are with the relationship (Caughlin & Golish, 2002). In the same study, Caughlin and Golish found that parents' dissatisfaction with their relationship with their child increased the more they perceived their child was avoiding conversation topics. Afifi and Guerrero (2000) even point out that, in some cases, people understand that pervasive secret keeping is antithetical to relationship development, and they in fact strategically use topic avoidance to destroy or deescalate a relationship.

The desire to protect ourselves from the negative fallout of a revealed secret is one of the primary reasons for keeping a secret (Afifi & Guerrero, 2000). Derlega, Winstead, and Folk-Barron (2000) echo this concern in the context of persons living with HIV or AIDS. On one hand, disclosing the diagnosis is necessary for garnering social support from one's intimate partner or family. However, one must weigh the benefits against the potential negative fallout. Due to a similar fear of negative reaction, adolescents and young adults frequently avoid discussing relationship experiences, dangerous behaviors, and especially sexual experiences with their parents (Guerrero & Afifi, 1995a). Adolescents and young adults are more likely to discuss such topics with siblings than parents, and they usually choose a same-sex person when disclosing sexual matters (Guerrero & Afifi, 1995b). Contrary to popular belief, adolescent daughters exhibit similar levels of topic avoidance with parents as compared to sons, except that daughters are a little more likely to talk about their friendships with their parents (Guerrero & Afifi, 1995a). Before we paint the picture that children avoid discussing all such topics with their parents, Guerrero and Afifi (1995a) remind us that children do communicate with their parents about many potentially sensitive topics. Researchers are continuing to explore how parents and children negotiate discussion of sensitive topics.

Topic avoidance is not always motivated simply by fear. Sometimes individuals feel that talking about a certain topic is futile or even uninteresting (Afifi & Guerrero, 2000). Individuals may also feel that the relationship can be maintained or protected by avoiding topics. Roloff and Ifert (2000) describe how intimate partners withhold complaints, suppress arguments, and declare some topics off limits all in an effort to manage conflict and protect the relationship. For it to benefit intimate relationships, topic avoidance must be conducted selectively not universally, be freely chosen not coerced, and require good communication skills and an attitude of tolerance (Roloff & Ifert).

The view of secrets as entirely negative is narrow and inaccurate (Bochner, 1982; Caughlin & Petronio, 2004). As we have seen, secret keeping for relationship protection may be a positive function. For a variety of other related reasons, secret keeping can have positive effects on relationships (e.g., keeping a secret to overlook a family member's faults, to prevent greater family distress, or to maintain a positive surprise) (Vangelisti, 1994a). Secrets can even create a bond between the members who are "in the know" (Vangelisti). It is often flattering and affirming to be the recipient of confidential information (Petronio et al., 2003).

Secrets vary by topic and type. In 1994, Vangelisti developed three categories of secrets: taboo secrets, rule violations, and conventional secrets. *Taboo secrets* concern topics that are condemned or stigmatized by the family and society. Topics pertaining to abuse, sexuality, unwanted or premarital pregnancies, mental health, substance abuse, or marital problems are often considered taboo secrets. Secrets involving *rule violations* center around family rules that have been broken (e.g., breaking curfew). *Conventional secrets* pertain to activities or topics that are not necessarily wrong, but family members feel are inappropriate to discuss, particularly with nonintimates (e.g., personality conflicts, religion or ideology, and how much money one makes). This category could also include secrets that are perceived to be positive (e.g., birthday surprises). Interestingly, the topic of the family secret is not a good predictor of whether people will disclose the secret or not (Vangelisti & Caughlin, 1997). People have idiosyncratic perceptions about whether their secret is a serious one with regards to their own family. Instead of the secret topic, people's perceptions of the intimacy of the secret topic appear to be better clues as to whether a person will disclose the secret (Vangelisti & Caughlin). In summary, managing private or secretive information is a complex process that varies greatly by individual and family. Decisions to tell depend on rules, implicit boundaries, anticipated consequences, and who one is disclosing to. The nature of a family is greatly informed by what the members tell and what they keep.

## CONCLUSION

Family members obviously spend a great deal of time together compared to some other types of relationships. Despite common cries that the family spends less time together now than in the past, solid evidence indicates this in not necessarily the case. In general, American children spend more time with their mothers now than they did 2 decades ago, and they spend similar amounts of time with their fathers. In two-parent families in which the mother works, fathers' time with children has dramatically increased. Still the quantity of time spent together, whether in a parent–child relationship or in a marital relationship, does not always translate to high-quality interactions and positive exchanges. The quality of time together makes a much larger impact.

After spending so much time interacting, family members develop a regular communication climate. As Ritchie and Fitzpatrick (1990) explain, communication environments in part stem from the family's expectations regarding conformity and conversation orientations. Families also develop interaction networks regarding who talks to whom, with what frequency, and about what topics. As Caughlin (2003) argues, family members are constantly comparing their actual interaction norms and networks to the standards they hold regarding how they wish their family would interact.

Sometimes the communication of family members takes on heightened symbolic meaning in the form of family rituals, stories, and secrets. With regard to rituals, the actual interaction or activity becomes less important than what it symbolizes. As Leeds-Hurwitz (2002) states: "Communication is the primary vehicle by which we create community, perform ritual, convey identity, and discern meaning, for it is through concrete interaction that we create these more abstract concepts" (p. 29). Some family rituals act as a positive stabilizing force in the face of family stress. Others are the source of family stress. As for family stories, they are often told with an implicit or explicit function in mind—to help the family remember important events, to socialize members, to pass judgment on behavior, or to emphasize family ties. Family stories and interaction undoubtedly contain omissions. Certain events and experiences are kept as secrets, sometimes by the whole family and sometimes just by certain members. Petronio's (1991, 2000, 2002) CPM theory explains how people set mental boundaries regarding whether information should be revealed to any, some, or all in the family. These boundaries are guided by implicit and explicit rules that individuals and families have regarding the flow of information. Together, the family's symbolic interactions, in the form of rituals, stories, and secrets, reveal the family's unique identity and its relationship to the outside world.

# CHAPTER FOUR

# Family Interaction Processes: Power, Decision Making, Conflict, and Intimacy

In this chapter, we continue to explore not just *how* families interact, but *what* their interaction is about. Namely, we study four family processes that in obvious or underlying ways dominate much of family interaction: (a) establishing or wielding power, (b) making everyday or special decisions, (c) dealing with conflicts, and (d) building or maintaining intimacy. Think of any recent family interaction, and it is likely the interaction dealt with one or more of these processes. Because power, decision making, conflict, and intimacy are such fundamental communication processes, a primary goal of this chapter is to introduce and conceptualize each process. With this foundation, we continue in subsequent chapters to examine research regarding the way these family processes assert themselves in specific family contexts (e.g., in parent–child, marital, sibling, or whole family interactions).

An important point we make in this chapter is that power, decision making, conflict, and intimacy are ongoing communication *processes*, even though lay persons often speak of them as discrete events (e.g., "We made a decision" or "We had a conflict"). With a process perspective, we are concerned with the origin, intensity, and direction of family communication (Sprey, 1999). For example, what causes a family conflict to develop as it does? Is there a chain of events that predicts conflict intensity and kind? What direction will the conflict take in the future? As Sprey says, to study a family process is to study what "has happened, is happening, and may happen" in the family (p. 668). We should also note that although we isolate each process for the sake of discussion in this chapter, processes of power, decision making, conflict, and intimacy are interrelated in real-life family interactions. For example, family decisions are clearly related to who holds the power as well as to issues of family conflict and intimacy.

## POWER

The models of family functioning we examine in chapter 1 implicitly recognize that power processes are central to family interaction. The adaptability dimension in Olson's circumplex model addresses power processes manifested in assertiveness, control, discipline, roles, and the enforcement of rules. Issues of power are also inherent in the McMaster model's dimensions of behavior control and problem solving. These models refer to how power is manifested, but they do not define power or explicitly describe how power processes develop in families. Admittedly, family scholars have struggled to define and measure power. Broderick (1993) explains: "Literally hundreds of studies have been done on family power, who wields it and at whose expense. The matter has turned out to be complicated and elusive. As a result the scholarly literature on family power is voluminous, complex, and often contradictory" (p. 164).

## Conceptual Views of Power

### Power as Ability

Power is commonly viewed as an ability or potential to achieve desired goals and outcomes (Levine & Boster, 2001; McDonald, 1980). Applied to families, power is "the ability to change the behavior of other family members" (Cromwell & Olson, 1975, p. 5). Safilios-Rothschild (1976) conceptualized two different abilities related to changing behavior: the ability to *orchestrate* and the ability to *implement*. Individuals with orchestration abilities "make only the important and infrequent decisions that do not infringe upon their time, but that determine the family life style and the major characteristics and features of their family" (Safilios-Rothschild, p. 359). People with orchestration abilities can delegate smaller decisions to other family members as well as the implementation of larger decisions. Implementation abilities refer to the power one has to implement decisions, but this power is dependent on the orchestrator. More recently power has been viewed as the ability to change not only behavior but also emotion. Laboratory studies of marital interaction prompted definitions of power as the ability of one partner's affect to influence the other partner's subsequent affect (Gottman, Driver, Yoshimoto, & Rushe, 2002).

Note that conceptualizations of power as potential or ability are different from those that view power as outcome. Levine and Boster (2001, p. 29) point out that viewing power as outcome is tautological. By viewing power as outcome, power can only be determined in retrospect. That is, someone is considered powerful because they influenced someone; they influenced them because they are powerful. Levine and Boster suggest that the term "compliance-gaining" more accurately represents the implementation of power, whereas the term "power" simply denotes potential or ability.

### Power as an Interactional Process

Power is not an individual trait, but rather a multidimensional, dynamic process that occurs within interaction. Simply stated, in order to be powerful, one must have another who is willing to submit or willing to accept influence (Gottman, Coan, Carrère, & Swanson, 1998). According to power-dependency theory "person A's power over B is determined by B's dependence upon A. Likewise, B's power over A is a function of A's dependence upon B" (Levine & Boster, 2001, p. 30). In other words, parents have power over their young children because their children depend on them for basic necessities. When those same parents grow older, and in turn become dependent on their own children, the children often transition to a position of power over their parents.

The term *process* also highlights the ongoing, dynamic nature of power. Sprey (1972) introduces the concept of powering, which refers to "the ongoing confrontation" of power inputs among family members (p. 236). Past power inputs affect current and future power inputs, and often serve as justifications (e.g., "I should get to decide this time because you decided the last time" or "This is the way it has always been and always will be"). Furthermore, as a dynamic multidimensional process, power inputs take various forms, affect other family processes, and occur within a changing family system. Thus, to understand power, we must understand something about the family system and the messages used to implement the power.

### Power as Affected by Perception and Culture

Power is largely a matter of perception and context. Being powerful requires that other people perceive themselves to be dependent or under one's control. When an adolescent takes the view that "my parents can't control me and I don't need anything from them anyway," the parents lose power from the adolescent's perspective. The view that power is influenced by perception is grounded in symbolic interaction theory (see chap. 2), which argues that meaning is created in interaction between people and modified through communicative and interpretive processes. Families negotiate their own unique symbolic meanings. In some families there is little room for negotiation and adolescents cannot even envision an alternative power structure. In other cases, parents and adolescents are constantly reestablishing power processes in their relationship.

In addition, one's cultural values influence perceptions of power as well as norms for power processes. Two of Hofstede's (1980) cultural dimensions are inextricably related to family power processes: power–distance (e.g., the degree to which people in a culture view individuals as equal) and masculinity–femininity (e.g., the degree to which people in a culture view sex roles as gender specific; Gudykunst & Lee, 2001, p. 79). Child-rearing practices in high power–distance cultures emphasize that children should obey their parents (Hofstede, 1994). In low power–distance and high-femininity cultures, mothers and fathers dominate children less and emphasize gender role equality in the family (Goodwin, 1999). Further, in masculine cultures (e.g., Japan), where sex roles are gender specific, women are more likely to seek marital partners with masculine traits such as wealth and status versus personality and affection (Goodwin). Pyke (1999) even demonstrates how individualist and collectivist cultural orientations influence power processes between adult children and aging parents. According to Pyke, aging parents in collectivist families often receive high levels of care, but pay for this care with a decrease in power whereby they accept the influence of their adult children. Collectivist elders are more likely to "back down" from conflict, mind their own interests rather than offer advice and criticism to their children, and in fact repress their own interests in favor of their children's. In comparison, aging parents in individualist families retain more power, but pay for it with less family assistance. Because individualist elders do not look to their children for as much care, they apparently perceive more freedom to express their own opinions, advice, and criticism to their children. Pyke's research is also a good example of how power processes are interactional and related to other family processes, in this case, processes of intimacy and care.

## Sources of Power

Now that we have examined common conceptualizations of power, we turn our attention to sources of power in the family. That is, how do individuals become powerful? Sprey (1999) equates studying family communication processes to the study of other natural processes. When studying the course of a tornado or the flow of a river, "it makes sense to study its beginning to speculate about its duration and future path" (Sprey, p. 668).

### Bases of Power

French and Raven (1959) describe the following sources or bases of power: reward, coercive, legitimate, expert, and referent power. These bases of power were not specifically developed to apply to the family context, but because they assume power is interactional, they inform research on family interaction. The assumption that power is interactional suggests that one person does not inherently hold power, but individuals grant power to others. *Reward power* relies on a person's (source's) ability to reward another (target) and the target's perception of that ability and reward. In other words, the rewards only become a source of power if the target wants the rewards the source has to offer. Imagine, for example, a parent who says to a college-age son, "I'll pay for your college education only if you major in engineering." If the son does not care much about a free college education in light of the expectations, then the money is not a source of power or influence. Bettinghaus and Cody (1994) argue that the influence sparked by reward power will bring about changes in public behavior, but not necessarily changes in private beliefs. For example, the son in the previous example may go on to major in engineering in order to get a free education, but privately believe that engineering is not the best major for him. Grolnick and Gurland (2002) add that parents can use rewards, token economies, or contingency programs to get their child's compliance, but they cannot expect these tactics to boost the child's self-regulation: "If parents want their daughter to clean her room right now, they should promise her a candy bar, but if they want their daughter to recognize the value of keeping her room clean and to do so willingly without being reminded, the candy bar will not work" (p. 24).

*Coercive power* stems from expectations on the part of the target that the source will administer punishments if he or she (target) does not conform to the influence attempt. This of course requires that the source has the ability and awareness to administer punishment to bring about change. Imagine a child who knows that throwing a temper tantrum in the grocery story will cause mom to give in and buy the candy that he or she wants. The strength of coercive power lies in the magnitude of the negativity associated with the threatened punishment. To many parents, a public temper tantrum is embarrassing, and that embarrassment is a form of social punishment. It is no wonder that some parents comply with their children, buy the candy, and effectively rid themselves of the public embarrassment. Other parents are not embarrassed or punished by public temper tantrums, and such behavior is not a strong source of coercive power. Again, compliance due to coercive power is more likely to change public behavior than private beliefs (Bettinghaus & Cody, 1994). For example, the parent may buy the candy, but privately believe it is not the best thing to do for the child.

*Legitimate power* addresses power based on the positions one holds or the roles one plays. When a mother argues that the reason her child should comply with her is because, "I'm your mother, and I said so," she is assuming that her position grants her the "right" to make a request. The target feels obligated to comply to the extent that he or she has some internalized respect for the legitimacy of the source's position (e.g., the child believes it is important to respect parents). Because of this internalized respect for the source's position, Bettinghaus and Cody (1994) argue that legitimate power leads to changes in both public behavior and private beliefs. Further, families often reference cultural norms that indicate who holds legitimate power. For instance, some families grant fathers more power than mothers because a masculine cultural orientation dictates that fathers are the head of the house (Goodwin, 1999). These families adhere to what Bernstein (1971) first called positional power structures (i.e., power based on beliefs in tradition or status) versus person-oriented power structures (i.e., power granted to a person based on individual needs and personalities, without regard to traditional positions in the family).

*Referent power* refers to power based on liking and identification. According to referent power, individuals comply with the requests of family members whom they like or identify the most with. This may explain why "daddy's little girl" is so powerful. She gets what she wants because she is favored more than are other family members. Referent power also stems from identification and shared interests. Some children grant power to a same-sex parent or to a parent with similar interests because the child identifies with the parent. Buerkel-Rothfuss, Fink, and Buerkel (1995) found, for example, that satisfaction in the father–son relationship was related to the intergenerational transmission of communication styles from father to son. Parents often capitalize on referent power when teaching manners to small children (e.g., "Be a big boy like your dad and use your fork and spoon"). Referent power leads to changes in private beliefs and public behavior (Bettinghaus & Cody, 1994).

Finally, *expert power* explains the power a target grants to a source because the target believes the source has superior training or ability. One spouse may have more power over financial decisions in the family because he or she simply has more expertise in managing money. The key is that the source has some information or background that the target respects but does not have. This type of influence leads to changes in public behavior and private beliefs (Bettinghaus & Cody, 1994).

### Social Exchange Theory

Some of the major theoretical perspectives we introduce in chapter 2 relate to power processes in the family. In this chapter we introduce another theory that relates, in part, to power in the family. *Social exchange theory* (Thibaut & Kelly, 1959) is based on the premise that people view their relationships in economic terms, considering the costs and rewards in their relationships. As rational beings, people seek out more rewards than costs, and this balance affects relationship satisfaction. Furthermore, people evaluate their relationships based on a comparison level (i.e., the standard they feel they should be receiving in terms of costs and rewards) as well as on a comparison level for alternatives (i.e., the rewards they think are available in other relationships). The theory assumes that people can make *rational choices* about how to maintain their relationships based on costs and rewards. However, in most cases, it is not just one relational partner making choices about the relationship. Both individuals simultaneously make choices. This results in what Huston and Burgess (1979) call a "bartering of rewards and costs" and an evaluation of the relationship rather than simply of another individual apart from the relationship (p. 4). Hence, it is important to remember the "social" part of social exchange theory. In some cases, though, it is not possible for family members (e.g., young children or an abused spouse) to make choices about remaining in a relationship based on costs and rewards. Further, many family relationships are relationships of obligation, in which individuals have little option of dissolving the relationships, even if costly.

Costs and rewards come in many forms. Foa and Foa (1976) suggest six resources that have exchange value in relationships. Abstract resources include information, love, and status. Concrete or material resources include money, goods, and services. Not every resource is weighted equally. Consider marriages with clearly separated roles: One spouse makes the money and the other takes care of the home. In some such marriages, making money and taking care of the home are weighted as equal resources and power is egalitarian. In other marriages, the breadwinner claims more power because making money is weighted as a more important resource.

One criticism of social exchange theory is that it is difficult to test the theory because we cannot attach a concrete value to each resource. Rather, resource value is a matter of perceptions (Sabatelli & Shehan, 1993). Tichenor (1999) found that when the breadwinner is male (e.g., a traditional marriage), couples typically weight making money as a more important resource than taking care of the home. In status-reversal couples, where the primary breadwinner is female, "economic resources have a relatively minimal impact on women's power in terms of control over money, decision making, and the division of domestic labor" (p. 638). Studies of status-reversal couples indicate that exchange theories have failed to explain power dynamics in marriage. Status-reversal wives, in general, still bear the larger burden of domestic labor. Yet in the Tichenor study, wives as a group did not see the labor burden as unfair because they judged their success as a wife by how much they contributed to home life rather than by how much money they made. "Stay-at-home fathers and husbands who contribute a smaller proportion of the family income are accorded [the power of] provider status that is unthinkable for women in similar circumstances" (Tichenor, p. 649). Adding another nuance to the argument, Steil (1997) found that power is accorded differently depending on whether women have children. Women with children appear to have more household responsibility and less influence than their husbands do, regardless of whether they earn as much or more than their husbands. For women without children, influence increased and household expectations decreased to the extent that they were able to earn more money.

Tichenor (1999) argues that much of power in marriages and families is *hidden power*—covert power that cannot be observed or calculated according to social exchange theory. Hidden power may be related to gender ideology or to other implicit ideologies, and it reveals itself in communication (e.g., family stories, secrets, and rules) and family structure (e.g., roles). "Clearly, there is a material component to equality in marriage, but it is not income nor status that translates into power. It is the [symbolic] meaning attached to these contributions that seems to be primary" (Tichenor, p. 649).

## Family Roles Related to Power

Family power structures are revealed in the roles family members play and the rules they enforce. In *patriarchal* families, power centers around one powerful male, generally a father or grandfather. This person takes on the primary leadership role, making decisions and rules, while the rest of the members follow. Tsushima and Viktor (2001) argue that less powerful family members are typically more adaptable role takers and followers simply because they have learned to be adaptable as a coping mechanism: "The powerless need to adjust to the powerful more than the reverse" (p. 268). *Matriarchal* families are similar to patriarchal ones, except that a mother or grandmother takes on the primary leadership role. In single-parent families, where there is no other adult in the home to share and negotiate power, matriarchal or patriarchal power structures are common (Tsushima & Viktor). In the United States, African American couples tend to be more egalitarian than White couples, and in Latino couples, more than in White or African American couples, the wife is more likely to be a "housewife" (Goodwin, 1999).

In families with *democratic authority*, the leadership role is not yoked to one specific member, and there may in fact be more than one leader (e.g., mother and father). All family members have some role in decision making, and even nonleaders are consulted for input. Families that are high in conversation orientation pride themselves on a democratic authority, whereby all members are encouraged to voice opinions in an unrestrained way (Koerner & Fitzpatrick, 2004; see chap. 3). Regarding democratic authority between marital partners, Craddock (1988) found that Australian couples who had congruent egalitarian expectations for marital roles were more satisfied in the areas of personality issues, communication, conflict resolution, leisure activities, and family and friends than were couples in which the male had traditional role expectations and the female had egalitarian expectations. Even though research on U.S. couples has shown that there are multiple ways to structure roles and make marriage successful (Fitzpatrick, 1988a; Gottman, 1994), mismatched role expectations and power imbalances appear to be increasingly problematic for couples as gender expectations are transformed (Gottman & Notarius, 2002). In fact, Cook et al. (1995) found that asymmetries in power or influence were predictive of divorce. Still, in some research, mostly dated research or masculine culture-specific research, husbands report less satisfaction when their wives have more say in decision making (Steil, 1997).

Some families have a *child-centered* power structure. Here the children's wishes and intentions dictate the family's course of action. The parents literally build their lives around the children. These families exhibit role reversals (e.g., children leading parents) and often some boundary confusion (i.e., confusion over what behavior is appropriate for a parent or child). Although single-parent families are not necessarily child centered, children in such families theoretically have more influence than children from two-parent families (Ahuja & Stinson, 1993). Finally, in *dispersed* families there is no central leader or it is not clear who is in charge. Members do their own thing without regard for other family members.

Although it is appealing to quickly attach a label, such as patriarchal or child centered, to describe a family's power and role structure, Broderick (1993) advises caution. He argues that patterns of family power are often not stable across time and context.

For example, family roles can differ from pubic to private spheres. Females may be submissive in public and dominant in private, or vice versa (Goodwin, 1999; Sillars, 1995). Broderick further proposes that understanding power in families must begin with an analysis of rules that undergird power processes (p. 166). Power is manifested in the creation and enforcement of family rules.

## Family Rules Related to Power

Family rules can be organized according to four levels: (a) the family paradigm, (b) midrange policies, (c) metarules, and (d) concrete rules (Broderick, 1993). The *family paradigm* refers to a "set of shared assumptions, expectations, and commitments that constitute each family's operational philosophy of governance" (Broderick, p. 166). The family paradigm represents overarching ideals that fundamentally set the tone for more specific rules in the family. Broderick offers three examples of paradigms. In a *competitive paradigm*, each member looks out for himself or herself, prioritizing individual concerns over the group. One can imagine how this paradigm is manifested in concrete rules and tenets of the family—tenets such as "You've got to look out for yourself" or rules such as "You snooze, you lose" (i.e., whoever lays claim to a resource first owns it). In a *policy-governed paradigm*, individuals submit to family-governed policies. Broderick presents concrete rules compatible with the policy-governed paradigm: "In this family there are bedtime rules for children according to their age. You are six; your bedtime is 8:30" or "There is no need to yell at each other. Let's all take turns speaking" (p. 167). A *principled-interaction paradigm* requires that members are mature enough to internalize principles such as mutual respect, empathy, and equity, without being reminded of these principles in specific rules. Family paradigms represent the family's typical style of functioning. However, when families face unusual circumstances, they may be required to default to rules consistent with another paradigm or to change the paradigm entirely in dramatic or severely stressful situations.

*Midrange policies*, the second level of rules, are "less generic than the overarching family paradigms . . . but still broad enough to subsume a wide range of [concrete rules]" (Broderick, p. 169). Midrange policies direct members to how they should generally act in certain contexts (e.g., "Each child should participate in his or her fair share of the family chores"). Note, though, that this rule is not so concrete as to spell out what specific chore should be conducted and how. Because midrange rules are directed toward certain sectors of family life (e.g., chores, manners, and time with friends), Broderick calls them "sector specific." *Metarules*, the third level of rules, are sometimes thought of as rules about rules. Metarules are rules that describe the circumstances in which the most specific level of rules, *concrete rules*, apply. Thus, if a concrete rule states that "Mario must take the trash out each week," the metarule comments on how this rule is played out. The metarule may state that if Mario is sick, then he does not have to fulfill his duties. At the level of metarules, family members negotiate their rules. Metarules might be negotiated through bargaining for resources in the competitive family, through policy debate in the policy-governed family, and through appeals to clarify issues or work toward the common good in the principled family (Broderick).

Concrete rules can be articulated in a regulative or constitutive nature. Either way, they are specific. Regulative rules provide a guide to behavior. Regulative rules tell family members what behavior is appropriate, obligatory, and prohibited and are often verbalized as "You must" or "You have to" (e.g., "You must say please and thank you"). Gralinski and Kopp (1993) found that when dealing with infants and young toddlers, mothers enforce only a few regulative rules, mostly ones related to safety issues (e.g., "Don't touch the stove" or "Hold hands to cross the street"), basic preservation of family possessions (e.g., "Don't play with the remote control," or "Don't write on walls"), and basic social rules (e.g., "Don't bite"). However, at about 18 months of age, mothers dramatically increase their reliance on a wide variety of regulative rules, in particular, introducing rules about relating with other people and social or family etiquette. In addition to regulative rules, constitutive rules interpret the meaning of behaviors (e.g., "Talking back to your parents is a sign of disrespect").

Overall, family rules are relationship agreements specific to the family system. As we indicate in chapter 3, some rules are explicit, meaning they are evident in conversation and sometimes verbally agreed to. Other rules are implicit; they are unspoken, inferred from the way people interact, and may remain unspoken until they are violated. Implicit rules are often linked to hidden or covert power. For example, most families have topics that are secret or taboo, and implicit rules are particularly notable for preventing issues from being raised.

## DECISION MAKING

Like power, decision making is an ongoing family process, influenced by the past and sure to influence future decisions. Decision making is related to other family processes, most notably to power processes because powerful members have more influence in decisions. Some family members think carefully together about how decisions will affect the family as a whole (e.g., Olson et al.'s (1979) connected and enmeshed families), whereas others care less about how their individual decisions impact the family (e.g., Olson's separated or disengaged families). Here, we explore the nature of family decision making as well as models and styles of family decision making.

### The Nature of Decisions

Families make some decisions that are rather simple or even trivial (e.g., what television show to watch) and others that are more complex and serious (e.g., whether to move an aging parent to a care home). Decisions are commonly distinguished as instrumental or affective. *Instrumental decisions* involve solving functional issues and are often, though not always, more basic. Examples include deciding what to buy at the store, what house to buy, what to eat. *Affective decisions* are based on emotions. They involve resolving conflicts and choices related to values, roles, and feelings. When partners agree that they have drifted so far apart that it is no use investing in the relationship any more, they are making an affective decision regarding the way they feel about the relationship.

Realistically, many of the decisions made in life have both instrumental and affective components. For example, deciding how to care for an aging parent involves affective issues of emotion and values as well as instrumental issues regarding how the care will take place.

Family scholars are beginning to devote more attention to how families make decisions during times of crisis and change or as a result of crisis and change (Settles, 1999). Examples include decisions related to getting married, divorced, or remarried, dealing with troubled adolescents, or dealing with aging parents and age-related decisions such as retirement or choosing a college. In one such example, Allen, Baucom, Burnett, Epstein, and Rankin-Esquer (2001) studied how or whether decision making changes in remarried couples. They found that remarried spouses held standards for greater shared decision making power than they did in their previous marriage(s). Interestingly, however, the remarried individuals in Allen et al.'s study did not endorse greater standards for shared decision making than did a comparison group of first-married individuals. Because the study relied on retrospective accounts rather than on longitudinal data, it is difficult to tell if the remarried individuals actually had more decision-making power than they did in their own first marriages or whether their accounts were affected by factors such as inaccurate memories (Allen et al.).

Many of the decisions families make are everyday decisions related to dealing with children, economic matters (e.g., purchases), or work. Marketing consumer researchers capitalize on such decisions. They want to know who makes the decisions in the family regarding their product and then how to influence the primary decision maker. Marketing researchers Lee and Beatty (2002) show that mothers who contribute more income to the family have significantly more influence in everyday purchasing decisions. Other marketing studies focus on the influence parents have on children's consumption patterns in clothing and fast foods and on choices adolescents make about higher education, drug use, career choices, and peer groups (Settles, 1999). Over a decade ago, Lackman and Lanasa (1993) reported that children between the ages of 4 and 11 personally spend 5 billion dollars a year, and influence the spending of another 130 billion dollars. According to Labrecque and Line (2001), children often underestimate the degree of influence they actually have in instrumental family decisions, such as what restaurant to choose. Not surprisingly, in families where adolescents have more power to make decisions about what to eat, food choices are less healthy (De Bourdeaudhuij & Van Oost, 1998). Even in larger instrumental decisions, such as buying a car, Hsiung and Bagozzi (2003) found that adolescent children were consistently persuasive, though they did not wield nearly the amount of influence as did parents. Kirchler, Rodler, Hölzl, and Meier (2001) even add that when parents disagree, it is not uncommon for children to influence or even settle purchasing disputes.

## Models and Styles of Decision Making

Because the family system is an ever-changing unit, every decision a family makes is unique, even if the type of decision is repetitive. Although we cannot predict the exact nature of any given decision, models and styles of decision making point to common methods of decision making and common processes that operate to influence decisions.

We first examine Turners' styles of decision making and then explore Settles' model of family decision making.

### Turner's Decision-Making Styles

Long ago, Turner (1970) identified three common family decision-making styles: consensus, accommodation, and de facto. On one hand, Turner's decision-making styles now seem to be a rather simplistic view of a very complex family process. Yet, unlike some other general group decision-making models, Turner specifically had the family in mind. More recently, group communication scholars have brought a modern sophistication to the study of group decision making (see Hirokawa & Salazar, 1999), and given that the family is a group (Socha, 1999), there is a need to integrate group and family decision-making research.

The first of Turner's decision-making styles, *consensus,* requires that all family members agree before a decision is made. This is the least common decision-making style. It is easy to understand why consensus rarely happens when one considers how hard it is to get *all* the members of a family to agree on one decision. Yet some families take consensus decision making very seriously and find great satisfaction in it. Epstein et al. (1983), who conceptualized the McMaster model of family functioning that we discuss in chapter 1, name seven steps that encourage consensus decisions in the family. They include (a) identifying the problem, (b) communicating the problem, (c) developing alternatives, (d) making a decision on one alternative, (e) putting the decision into effect, (f) monitoring the action, and (g) evaluating and modifying the decision. Clearly, enacting these steps demands that the family has adequate time and social skills.

*Accommodation* decision making involves acquiescing or adapting to the decision of another family member. One or two family members decide and the rest of the family members go along with the decision. Accommodation decisions are influenced by power processes, as more powerful members usually decide based on their overt or covert power. Less powerful members then accommodate. Sometimes family members choose to accommodate, when the outcome of the decision is not that important to them. Other times family members feel forced to accommodate. Imagine parents who decide to relocate to a new region of the country and the children have no choice but to go. Decisions by majority vote are also an example of accommodation decision making, whereby the minority must accommodate to the majority of family members. One of the strengths of accommodation is that decisions are made quickly, compared to time-consuming processes of consensus decision making. With its strengths, accommodation is potentially problematic when the same family member makes the decisions all the time and the needs of other members are not considered. This is often the case in rigid families, described by Olson's circumplex model in chapter 1. When there is no room for negotiation, tensions do not get aired and members are more likely to react to perceptions of overly strict and autocratic family functioning.

Finally, in de facto decision making, the situation decides for the family. An example of de facto decision making is when the family does nothing or cannot agree, and eventually, after the passing of time, the decision either resolves itself or is determined by situational factors. Imagine a family who cannot decide whether their young children

FIG. 4.1.   Settles' (1999) Model of Family Decision Making.

*Note.* From *Handbook of Marriage and Family* (p. 161), by B. H. Settles, 1999, New York: Kluwer Academic/Plenum Publishers. Copyright 1999 by Plenum. Reprinted with permission.

should attend private or public school. After endless discussions that get them nowhere and procrastination in the application process, the family eventually realizes that the deadline has passed for applications to the private school. The decision is made by the situation, and the children attend public school. Like the accommodation decision-making style, de facto decisions occur frequently in families.

### Settles' Model of Decision Making

Settles' (1999) model of decision making (see Figure 4.1) explores the degree of choice families have when making decisions. The model considers processes that operate to expand or limit a family's degree of choice or, using the model's term, their *area of choice*. Although Turner's decision-making styles take a microlevel approach, studying the actual decision-making process itself, Settles' model takes a macrolevel perspective, describing the social, familial, environmental, and individual forces that affect family decisions. The type of choice and degree of choice a family has regarding any given decision are affected by the following factors: awareness, roles, social structure, resources, skills, personality, norms, and other constraints. In the model, these factors form a boundary around the area of choice. This boundary can be expanded or contracted to depict the degree of choice. Settles also explains that the boundary may not necessarily be symmetrical, because the boundary can be expanded by some factors and constricted by others.

The first factor, *awareness*, refers to the degree to which the family is aware of the decision and options related to the decision. It also encompasses the family's perception of the decision. At one extreme, families may not be aware of a decision, or if they are, they may not perceive many options. For example, microcultures such as the Amish purposely limit outside influences that could introduce them to options in the larger world. This lack of awareness constricts the area of choice. Is this always negative for families? Settles (1999) proposes there is sometimes freedom in limitations. For example, living in a very remote, rural, or mountainous area is perceived as freeing to some, though it limits the area of choice. On the other extreme, some families are highly conscious of their decision and the options available to them. This high level of awareness can both relieve and overwhelm families.

The second factor in the model involves *roles*. Individuals who participate in a variety of roles are likely to have had diverse life experiences, introducing them to different types of people, skills, groups, and interests. Experience with multiple roles expands the area of choice. In comparison, people who play few roles and play them rigidly only have limited ways of acting on and viewing decisions.

With regard to *social structure*, most families hope for mobility in order to expand their area of choice. Settles (1999) explains that the social structure of contemporary society offers many individuals and families flexible opportunities for geographic mobility, educational and vocational mobility, and even class mobility. Theoretically, the opportunity for social mobility gives families more options when making decisions.

*Resources* and *skills* are two other factors that affect the area of choice. Important resources include time, energy, money, material goods, expert advice, and social or physical support. Skills, including communication skills, trade skills, or academic skills are important in part because they open many resources to families. Besides affecting the size of the area of choice, communication skills are a means for discussing options and ultimately making decisions that stem from the area of choice.

*Personality*, including "a person's predispositions, inclinations, and sense of the self[,] is useful for identifying choices that a person will be comfortable in examining" (Settles, 1999, p. 162). As Settles further describes, a personal phobia (e.g., a social phobia) limits options regarding specific decisions, such as participation in the community. *Norms*, or expectations of appropriate behavior, impact the area of choice as well. Legal and social norms influence the choices parents have for nurturing and disciplining children or the choices couples have for dissolving a marriage. Conforming to norms restricts choice, and this can be useful for social order. On the other hand, deviating from norms allows more choice, which has costs and benefits. Finally, Settles explains that "at any one time there may be events that precipitate decision-making or planning or that limit individuals and their families from assuming control over their life course" (e.g., wars, famines, economic shifts, and plants closing; p. 162). In the model, Settles terms these events "other constraints."

Settles' (1999) model is useful because it acknowledges that decision-making processes in an open system, such as the family, are influenced by elements both internal and external to the system. Even seemingly simple decisions are embedded within unique, complex systems. *Requisite variety*, a concept from family systems theory, explains that systems are asked to respond to everything they encounter using a variety of skills and factors. According to Settles' model, families respond to decisions using a variety of factors. Ultimately the degree of choice they have regarding decisions is related to the variety (or lack of variety) of skills, resources, awareness, and constraints, around them.

# CONFLICT

Of the four family communication processes we discuss in this chapter, conflict has arguably received the most attention (Sillars, Canary, & Tafoya, 2004). This attention has not come without regard to the way other family processes, such as power, decision making, and intimacy, affect the course of conflict. In fact, these other relational processes are often the very topic of conflict (e.g., conflict over who gets to make decisions). In this section, we simply introduce conflict as a family process. In doing so, we define conflict; discuss types, topics, and frequency of family conflict; and present two selected family conflict models.

## The Nature of Family Conflict

According to Hocker and Wilmot (1998) conflict is a struggle between or among two or more interdependent parties who perceive "incompatible goals, scarce resources and interference from the other" (p. 12). For sure, family members live interdependently within the family system. Noller and Fitzpatrick (1993) are not exaggerating when they say that within a family system anything can become an issue (p. 102). Family members share so many resources and so much time that conflict is normative and inevitable (Sillars et al., 2004). Researchers who have examined family conflict have primarily focused on "the 'relational dimension' of communication, that is, *how* families communicate about conflict and what this suggests about their relationship, not what they disagree about, what they do about it, or even how well conflicts are resolved" (Sillars et al.). Because we spend considerable time in subsequent chapters studying the relational implications for how family members communicate about conflict (e.g., in marriages or sibling relationships), we now devote some attention to the content of family conflict.

### Conflict Topics

Topics of family conflict involve *content* issues (e.g., household chores, and money) and *relationship* issues (e.g., love, power, and parental attention). However, this distinction is hardly ever clear-cut. Conflicts about seemingly simple content topics, such as which sibling gets to bat first in a game of softball, may be embedded in larger relationship conflicts such as sibling power struggles and conflict over parental attention. Regarding the topic of conflicts in marriage, Storaasli and Markman (1990) found that topics involving friends, religion, and jealousy tended to decrease over time, whereas topics regarding sex, communication, and recreation tended to increase over time (see also Rogge & Bradbury, 2002). Carpenter and Halberstadt (2000) explored mothers' reports of topics that stimulate anger and subsequently conflict in families with children. Mothers felt that parents' anger in the family was typically due to expectancy violations (e.g., children back-talking or a spouse not devoting sufficient attention to the family). Mothers felt that their children's anger was most often due to goal blockages (e.g., not letting the child have snacks between meals).

Family conflict stems from both external and internal environments. In an open family system, members receive inputs from the external environment that interfere with all of the interdependent members of the family system. For example, if dad loses his job (an external input), it can trigger a series of conflicts internal to the family, related to heightened family stress, rearranged goals, or scare resources. Some conflict stems from the internal family environment and may only be overtly expressed among some family members. Yet again, all the members of the family likely feel the effects. Married couples with children soon learn, "It's not just you and me, babe" (Cummings, Goeke-Morey, & Papp, 2001). Marital conflict influences children; children influence marital conflict (Erel & Burman, 1995; see chap. 7). Just as marital conflict spills over to other family relationships, sibling conflict also appears to affect the larger family system (see chap. 8). Perlman and Ross (1997) found that conflict among siblings is one of the most frequently reported family management problems. Sibling conflict is often distressing to parents; however, their efforts to resolve conflicts may give rise to more negativity in the sibling relationship (McHale, Updegraff, Tucker, & Crouter, 2000). Thus, the family system is presented with dilemmas regarding how to respond to conflict that is overtly expressed by only some of the members.

### Conflict Types

Gottman (1999) describes solvable and perpetual types of conflict. *Solvable* conflicts can be resolved, whereas perpetual conflicts are a part of family life forever. An example of a solvable conflict is a family who cannot decide where to go on vacation. With the right conflict resolution tactics, the family may eventually come to a mutually agreeable decision about where to vacation. *Perpetual* conflicts are deeply rooted in disagreements over larger issues (e.g., values, roles, and personality traits) and, as the term *perpetual* suggests, they resurface again and again in families and never get resolved. An example of a perpetual conflict is a couple experiencing value differences in how to raise their children. According to Gottman, over half of the problems in marriages are perpetual problems. Because most of these perpetual problems will not be resolved, Gottman advises that couples find ways to cope with these problems (e.g., by keeping open dialog and humor about the issues). Gottman and Silver (1999) say that some problems are "inevitably part of a relationship, much the same way chronic physical ailments are inevitable as you get older. They are like a trick knee, a bad back . . . we may not love these problems, but we are able to cope with them, to avoid situations that worsen them, and to develop strategies and routines that help us deal with them" (p. 131).

Although successful couples appear to have a knack for dealing with and repairing problems that come up in their marriage over time, less successful couples lack the skill to successfully deal with conflict and are too oppressed by the relationship context to deal with conflict appropriately. Sillars et al. (2004) argue that although skills are crucial to conflict management, contextual factors should not be discounted. What is a concrete and easy way to resolve conflict in the context of a nondistressed relationship may be a more profound and difficult issue to resolve in the context of a distressed relationship. Further, the context of any one family or relationship may change over time. Noller and Feeney (2002) found that "less happy spouses make a concerted effort over the first year or so to create a more constructive climate of marital interaction. By the time two years of marriage have passed, however, they seem to revert to the more destructive patterns they used earlier" (p. 137). Finally, a contextual factor such as cultural preferences and norms for dealing with conflict, influences what family members perceive as "ideal skills" for dealing with conflict (Ting-Toomey & Oetzel, 2001).

Not all types of conflict are negative for the family system. Moderate amounts of conflict related to topics of autonomy and assertion of individuality are common in the parent-child relationship and are a normal part of child development (see chap. 7). Psychological separation theory (Hoffman, 1984) argues that individuation and independence are important to adolescents' adjustment, though this occurs within the parameters of one's cultural orientation. During this time, adolescents develop some degree of emotional autonomy or emotional uncoupling from parents. They learn to make independent decisions and disagree more with parental opinion (Steinmetz, 1999). When these conflicts occur within the context of parental support and acceptance, they encourage development of the youth's necessary skills at becoming independent. They also help prepare parents for the detachment associated with launching the child from the home as a young adult.

In courtship and marriage, many types of conflict are healthy for partners as a means of revealing their individual preferences and dreams that, if denied, could lead to more destructive conflict later. Noller and Feeney (2002) found that premarital reports of frequency of conflict were correlated with more satisfaction for husbands later on in the marriage. In other words, these husbands appeared to benefit from discussions of conflict issues early on in the relationship. It is interesting to study topics and types of family conflict, but we see later in our chapters on intimate partnerships (chap. 6) and divorce (chap. 11) that the intensity of conflict and the way people deal with it are really what determine whether conflict has a positive or negative impact on relationship quality.

### Conflict Frequency

With regard to conflict *frequency*, we stress again that the occurrence of conflict is inevitable in families—even in the best of families. However, Vuchinich (1987) suggests "nondistressed families (those not experiencing problems so serious that they seek professional help) seem to be able to strike a delicate balance between enough conflict to realize the positive benefits, but not too much conflict, which would disrupt family relationships" (p. 591). Just what does this "delicate balance" look like, and who is most likely to start and stop family conflicts? In a fascinating study, Vuchinich recorded 64 family dinners in nondistressed families. The duration of the dinners averaged 15 minutes with an average of 3.3 verbal conflict episodes per dinner. A verbal conflict episode was defined as a square-off where one person initiates an opposition and the other returns an opposition.

Results indicated that one third of the potential conflicts were "nipped in the bud." The conflict was avoided or corrected before it ever happened. Some oppositions were framed as a correction or command, the correction or command was accepted, and no further conflict ensued (e.g., a child was told to quit eating with her fingers, and the child agreed). Of the potential verbal conflict episodes, there was a one-third avoid to two-thirds fight ratio, which suggests these nondistressed families did indeed balance conflict avoidance and conflict engagement. No single family role (e.g., mothers, fathers, and children) appeared to dominate the initiation of verbal conflicts. Parents initiated nearly half of the conflicts, and children initiated just over half. However, fathers only had half as many conflicts initiated against them compared to mothers, daughters, and sons.

According to Vuchinich (1987) family conflicts are usually stopped in one of four ways:

1. *Submission.* One person in the conflict "gives in" to another by agreeing or going along with the other.
2. *Compromise.* The disputing members each "give a little" and find a "middle ground" that they both can accept.
3. *Standoff.* The members drop the conflict without resolution by agreeing to disagree and move on.
4. *Withdrawal.* One party leaves the interaction by refusing to talk or leaving the room. Family conflict is disrupted by negative affect and, unlike the other three methods, the family is not able to smoothly transition to other activities.

Of these four methods, 61% of the conflicts eventually ended in a standoff.

Does conflict frequency vary by family stage, the type of family relationship, or the quality of the relationship? Regarding conflict frequency between spouses, even though some conflicts are inevitable or useful for married couples, research has consistently revealed that distressed spouses report more conflict than do nondistressed spouses (Noller & Feeney, 2002). In addition, premarital conflict patterns and frequency are good predictors of later conflict and dissatisfaction (Kelly, Huston, & Cate, 1985). In marriage, there is evidence that women are more likely to bring up conflict topics (Cowan & Cowan, 1995) contributing to a pattern that has been named the (wife) demand–(husband) withdrawal pattern of interaction. In this pattern, women raise more issues and press for change, whereas men resist and withdraw from dealing with conflict. Conflict frequency has also been associated with marital stages. This is reflected in Karney and Bradbury's (1995) vulnerability–stress–adaptation model. Most notably, the stress associated with the birth of the first baby makes couples who already have communication and relationship vulnerabilities susceptible to more conflict, especially destructive conflict, and less able to successfully adapt to being parents. Likewise, Crohan (1996) found that couples experience heightened conflict as they make the adjustment to marriage.

When Sillars et al. (2004) summarized research on conflict frequency across family relationships, they found that marital partners reported only a few overt conflicts a *month*, parents and children reported a handful of conflicts a *week*, and young siblings in close contact have been observed to have numerous conflicts within just 1 *hour*. On one hand, we could conclude that conflict is most dramatic in the sibling relationship. However, Sillars et al. are quick to point out that the number of conflicts may not be as significant as the intensity and type of conflict. In addition, it is difficult to compare spouses' and children's reports of conflict, which may be biased, to researchers' observations of conflict.

## Models Related to Family Conflict

There are many models of conflict in general. Here we focus on two communication models related to family conflict. The first relates to how conflict varies according to the family's communication climate, and the second depicts Rusbult and Zembrodt's exit–voice–loyalty–neglect model.

### Family Communication Climate and Conflict Patterns

In chapter 3, we discuss how family communication climates are distinguished by their conversation orientation and conformity orientation. Recall that families high in conversation and low in conformity are termed *pluralistic*. Communication is open, frequent, and unconstrained, and members are encouraged to think independently. Regarding conflict, Koerner and Fitzpatrick (1997) found pluralistic families to be characterized by extremely low conflict avoidance and low expression of negative feelings. Because of the freedom that pluralistic families have to express any topic, even negative topics, it seems at first glance counterintuitive that these families had a low expression of negative feelings. However, Koerner and Fitzpatrick speculate that because these family members have the freedom to discuss any topic, they, more than other families, preemptively deal with issues before they build up and thus experience more positive relationships.

*Consensual* families are characterized by a tension between pressure to agree and an interest in open communication and the exploration of new ideas. The conflict episodes of consensual families contain a lot of venting of negative feelings. However, this venting does not necessarily endanger the closeness of members because they also seek social support from one another and try to deal with conflict positively.

Members of *laissez-faire* families have few interactions about limited topics. Emotional involvement among members is typically low and members look outside the family for emotional connection. Conflict episodes are rare because they are usually avoided. Should conflict occur, it is usually uneventful because members do not care about seeking approval or support. Thus, there is little reason to express hostility.

Finally, *protective* families emphasize conformity and obedience. They largely avoid conflict, but occasionally vent negative feelings in bursts of hostile and unproductive conflict tactics. As a result, members have many unresolved conflicts with one another and are distressed by this underlying conflict, unlike members of laissez-faire families who do not appear to care much about whether they disagree.

Orrego and Rodriguez (2001) found that compared to young adults from pluralistic families, young adults from protective families experience a more conflictual separation–individuation process when they leave home to attend college. They resent their parents' demands for strict obedience and conformity, feel more guilt over unresolved issues, and consequently experience more problems adjusting to college. Conflict style in family of origin even appears to influence the way young adults deal with conflict in their own romantic relationships. In particular, people who grew up in families with high-conformity orientation (whether protective or consensual) exhibit more negative conflict behaviors in their romantic relationships, in the form of verbal aggression and forceful and coercive attempts to resist others (Koerner & Fitzpatrick, 2002a).

### Exit–Voice–Loyalty–Neglect Model

The exit–voice–loyalty–neglect (EVLN) model (Rusbult & Zembrodt, 1983) categorizes how people respond to conflict square-offs or destructive acts against them. The model has two primary dimensions: constructive versus destructive responses and active versus passive responses. Crossing the two dimensions yields four labels that globally characterize how families deal with conflict (Simpson, Ickes, & Orina, 2001, p. 41). *Exit* refers to destructive and active responses, such as walking out during an argument. Exit responses are thought to be most damaging to relationships. *Voice* involves constructive and active responses, such as openly discussing problems. Voice behaviors typically strengthen and improve relationships. *Loyalty* refers to constructive and passive responses, like waiting and hoping for problems to go away. Loyalty behaviors may be productive for relationships if the problems cannot be immediately resolved or might eventually diminish on their own. Finally, *neglect* involves destructive and passive responses, like refusing to discuss problems. Neglect typically leads to relationship stagnation and disrepair.

The EVLN model appears to capture common and natural responses to conflict. One weakness is that it does not adequately acknowledge that whether a given response is constructive or destructive depends on the situation or cultural context at hand (Simpson, et al., 2001). For example, voice behaviors should be put off when family members are "too tired, too upset, or don't have all the information they need to discuss the issue" (Noller & Fitzpatrick, 1993, p. 108). Furthermore, voice behaviors, in some situational or cultural contexts, may threaten another's face and turn a small conflict into a greater threat to the relationship (Gudykunst, 1994).

## INTIMACY

Like power, decision making, and conflict, intimacy is a family process that takes place over time, and ebbs and flows with the changing family system. The models of family functioning we examined in chapter 1 acknowledge that healthy families share intimacy, manifested in emotional bonding (Olson's circumplex model) and affective involvement and responsiveness (McMasters' model). In this section, we conceptualize intimacy as a process, examine how communication is a means for intimate self-expression and response, and begin to explore the challenge of maintaining intimacy in family life.

### Conceptualizing Intimacy

According to Greeff and Malherbe (2001), most definitions of intimacy "emphasize one or more of the following characteristics: behavioral interdependency, fulfillment of needs, and emotional attachment" (p. 248). It is important to distinguish the contributions that each characteristic makes to the process of intimacy. Reis and Patrick (1996) refer to this as studying the subprocesses that contribute to intimacy.

#### Behavioral Interdependence Versus Emotional Closeness and Needs

*Behavioral interdependence* is sometimes termed *closeness*. It emphasizes the impact that one person's behavior has on another and the degree of shared activity. Berscheid, Snyder, and Omoto (1989) view closeness as high behavioral interdependence manifested in four properties of interconnected activities: "(1) the individuals have *frequent* impact on each other; (2) the degree of impact per each occurrence is *strong*; (3) the impact involves *diverse* kinds of activities for each person; and (4) all of these properties characterize the interconnected activity series for a relatively long *duration* of time" (Kelly et al., 1983, p. 13). Because families live together as a domestic unit, they have frequent opportunities for a variety of interconnected activities. The activities and shared time among family members have a strong impact on them from the moment they are born.

However, Reis and Patrick (1996) caution against using the concepts intimacy and behavioral closeness interchangeably. Many relationships are behaviorally close relationships, but not necessarily intimate (e.g., long time co-workers or activity-centered friendships; Reis & Patrick, p. 536). On the other hand, some couples or families do not need a high degree of behavioral interdependency in order to feel emotional intimacy. For example, some couples are able to maintain emotional intimacy in spite of being physically separated due to incarceration (Segrin & Flora, 2001), military careers (Pavalko & Elder, 1990), or other reasons. In these cases, intimacy is primarily maintained through communication. Even when communication between partners is severely restricted, some partners rely on cognitive processes (e.g., stories that keep memories alive) to remind them of the intimate responses and connections they once had or will have again with their spouse (Segrin & Flora). In a moment, we continue to explain why many feel intimacy is better defined by emotional closeness than by behavioral closeness.

Intimacy, according to Reis and Patrick (1996), "refers to an interactive process in which, as a result of a partner's response, individuals come to feel understood, validated, and cared for" (p. 536). In this definition, intimacy is yoked most closely to emotional closeness and the positive fulfillment of emotional needs, rather than to behavioral interdependence. As Berscheid et al. (1989) propose, behavioral interdependence often evokes strong emotions, but not necessarily positive emotional experiences in relationships.

According to Reis and Patrick's (1996) definition of intimacy, desires to emotionally connect with another prompt individuals to risk expressing themselves. This *self-expression* occurs in verbal (e.g., self-disclosure) and nonverbal (e.g., emotional expressions) forms. Individuals also desire others to *respond to their self-expressions* with understanding, validation, and care. Next, individuals make *interpretive judgments* about whether their partner's response to their self-expression fulfills their needs. Because of the nature of interpretive judgments, any given response may fulfill the needs of one partner and not of another. Figure 4.2 illustrates this intimacy process described by Reis and Patrick's definition (i.e., self-expression, partner response, and evaluation of the response).

### Theoretical Roots of Intimacy Needs

Before we go on to explore the process of self-expression and response depicted by the model, we first examine some theoretical roots of intimacy needs. The intimacy process fulfills needs inborn in all humans. As we discuss in chapter 2, attachment theory suggests that we long to be intimately attached to another from the moment we are born, and this longing does not end when we become adults. However, the ideal degree of intimacy that we seek varies by person, depending on factors such as attachment style, family history, culture, and personality (Reis & Patrick, 1996). Exploring the role of family history in intimacy needs, Lauer and Lauer (1991) found that adults (with an average age of 35) from intact–happy families were less likely to be in a romantic, intimate relationship than those from an intact–unhappy, death-disrupted, or divorce-disrupted family. Lauer and Lauer

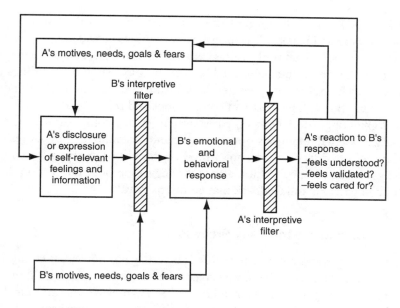

FIG. 4.2.   Reis and Patrick's (1996) Model of Intimacy.
*Note.* From *Social Psychology: Handbook of Basic Principles* (pp. 523–563), by H. T. Reiss and B. C. Patrick, 1996, New York: Guilford. Copyright 1996 by Guilford Publications. Guilford Press. Reprinted with permission.

suggested "those from disrupted and intact–unhappy families have an intimacy deficit that makes it more imperative for them to be in an intimate relationship, particularly the intense kind of relationship involved in marriage, cohabitating, or dating steadily" (p. 289).

Needs for intimacy are intricately tied to expectations for intimacy. According to Cooper (1999), prior to the last 2 centuries, families were primarily considered productive and reproductive units, with fewer expectations for emotional intimacy. However, as people increasingly select mates for romantic, rather than for dynastic reasons, intimacy expectations increase. Today, marital and family relationships in the United States have high expectations for intimacy. Spouses are expected to be strong, emotional allies. Intimacy expectations have not only changed over time but also vary by cultural background. In Japan, for example, people generally expect to have a more intimate relationship with a close friend than with a spouse (Gudykunst & Nishida, 1986).

Regardless of one's expectations, the result of unfulfilled intimacy expectations is loneliness. In intimate relationships such as marital or family relationships, loneliness is particularly distressing because it is inconsistent with expectations that such relationships should be highly intimate (Flora & Segrin, 2000). Just as not enough intimacy can lead to loneliness, excessive attention or too much intimacy can contribute to loneliness. Andersson, Mullins, and Johnson (1990) concluded that overinvolved parents who stress excessive intimacy in the parent–child relationship can be just as noxious as underinvolved, neglectful parents when it comes to producing lonely children. Parental overinvolvement can produce narcissistic children who develop unrealistically high expectations for intimacy that can never be fulfilled in their own adult, intimate relationships (see Segrin, 1998).

Finally, Reis and Patrick (1996) argue that symbolic interaction theory relates to perceptions of intimacy in relationships: "Relationships with others provide a mechanism for the development of the self. That is, the self is constructed through reflected self-appraisals, in which feedback from others helps establish and modify self-understanding" (p. 538). Thus, humans seek a relationship context in which to express themselves and socially define themselves through processes of comparisons and reflections. In the family context, there is great opportunity for comparisons (e.g., sibling comparisons) and reflective feedback (e.g., parental appraisals or confirming and disconfirming messages), though such comparisons and feedback do not always contribute to the intimate connections many family members hope for. Intimacy, according to symbolic interaction theory, is a function of comparisons and feedback that emotionally validate the self.

## Self-Expression and the Intimacy Process

Intimacy is "reflected and constructed" through verbal and nonverbal communication (Turner & West, 2002, p. 200). Here we explore the construction of self-expressive messages and later the responses to such messages. Self-expressive messages include self-disclosure, emotional bids (both verbal and nonverbal) for recognition, support, affection, connection, and a collection of other nonverbal behaviors. Of these expressions, scholars have devoted an enormous amount of research to self-disclosure (e.g., Altman & Taylor, 1973; Greeff & Malherbe, 2001; Reis & Patrick, 1996). Self-disclosure involves verbally sharing personal or private information with another in an intentional way. Through self-disclosure, family members come to know each other—to know their likes, dislikes, hopes, and fears.

In addition to self-disclosure, another way family members try to express themselves is through the *bids* they make to one another (Gottman & DeClaire, 2001). Bids stem from a natural desire to feel intimately connected. "A bid can be a question, a gesture, a look, a touch—any single expression that says, 'I want to be connected to you'" (Gottman & DeClaire, p. 4). Occasionally family members directly express their need for connection (e.g., A husband says to a wife, "Let's spend more time together"). Often, bids are subtler than direct self-disclosures. Gottman and DeClaire give specific examples of subtle bids:

*Vocalizing:* such as laughing, chuckling, grunting, sighing, or groaning in a way that invites interaction or interest.

*Affectionate touching:* such as a back-slap, a handshake, a pat, a squeeze, a kiss, a hug, or a back or shoulder rub.

*Affiliating gestures:* such as opening a door, offering a place to sit, handing over a utensil, or pointing to a shared activity or interest. (p. 31)

Clearly, much of the emotional bidding process involves nonverbal behaviors. Indeed, Patterson (1983) concluded that one of the primary functions of nonverbal behavior is to express intimacy. Some or all of the following behaviors cluster together to express intimacy through nonverbal involvement: more forward lean, closer proximity, more eye contact, more direct and open body orientation, more touching, more positive facial and vocal expressions, more frequent and intense interruptions, a faster speaking rate.

The specific use of nonverbal behaviors to indicate intimacy to other family members varies by relationship type and age. In the marital relationship, spouses use a whole collection of nonverbal behaviors to communicate intimacy in a sexual way. In the healthy parent–child relationship, nonverbal behaviors communicate intimacy, but differently. Harrison-Speake and Willis (1995) examined adults' perceptions of appropriate and inappropriate touching behaviors between parents and children (ages 2–14). In the cases of lap-sitting, kissing, and bathing, participants indicated more approval for mothers than for fathers touching children. As children aged, participants approved of less touching. However, mothers were granted significantly more latitude for intimate touch of older children than were fathers. In the father–son relationship, family-of-origin patterns appear to influence nonverbal expressions of intimacy and affection in the family of orientation, as exemplified by Floyd and Morman (2000). Grown men with highly unaffectionate fathers tend to compensate for their lack of affection received by giving more affection to their own sons. Men with highly affectionate fathers are likely to be most verbally and nonverbally affectionate with their own sons. Fathers who are least affectionate with their own sons are those who received only moderate amounts of affection from their own fathers (compared to men who received very high or very low levels of affection).

## Partner Responsiveness and the Intimacy Process

The intimacy process begins when one person expresses self-relevant thoughts, feelings, and bids to another person (Reis & Patrick, 1996). The intimacy process develops when partners respond to self-expressions by communicating understanding, validation, and care. As we focus on the role of the partner responses in the intimacy process, we should be clear to highlight the acute difference between intimacy and self-disclosure (Greeff & Malherbe, 2001; Reis & Patrick). Self-disclosure is a common covariant of intimacy, but not all self-disclosures contribute to greater intimacy. The risk of self-disclosure involves whether the other person will accept the information and feelings shared. Self-disclosures that promote negative feelings can draw family members apart. For example, recall our discussion of family secrets in chapter 3, where we explained the dilemma family members face in discerning whether the revelation of a secret will help or harm the relationship with the receiver. For example, persons who are lesbian or gay face the risk of a negative response when and if they decide to come out to their families of origin. Contrary to "generic therapeutic values" that encourage honesty and revelation of family secrets, self-revelation is not always in the person's best interest and does not always lead to greater intimacy (Green, 2000):

> Those who decide on their own to come out already have better family relationships prior to the disclosure and realistically anticipate improved family relationships after the disclosure. By contrast, those who have decided on their own to remain closeted may have poorer family relationships to begin with, and they may correctly be anticipating permanent deterioration or termination of family relationships following the disclosure of sexual orientation. (p. 264)

Thus, self-disclosure and intimacy are not synonymous, and the intimacy process depends on responses of understanding, care, and validation.

Intimacy, in the emotional bidding process (Gottman & DeClaire, 2001), depends on whether the partner responds by accepting the bids. Bids are accepted by figuratively turning toward the person and offering confirming messages. Confirming messages involve acknowledgment of the bid and often a response in kind, in the form of support, expression of positive feelings, agreement, reciprocal nonverbal behaviors, and so forth. Bids can be denied by figuratively turning against the person with disconfirming, defensive, contradictory, or critical responses. Bids can be ignored, as when someone is too preoccupied to notice the bid or too busy to respond. At first glance, the process of making bids and responding to them is a seemingly minute and mundane part of family interaction. However, Gottman and DeClaire argue that the emotional bidding and responding process is at the heart of intimacy.

In 1997, Harvey and Omarzu proposed the minding theory of relationships. This theory acknowledges that intimacy depends on mutual self-expression and mindful responses. However, it uniquely expands on the role that cognitions and perceptions play in the response process. In other words, self-expressions must be cognitively accepted and partner responses must be perceived as confirming. The minding theory of relationships names five cognitive components hypothesized to enhance intimacy and satisfaction: (a) building a foundation of relationship knowledge, (b) accepting the relational knowledge, (c) assuming an optimistic attributional style, (d) feeling that the first three components are reciprocated by the partner, and (e) continuing these minding patterns over time.

To begin, building a foundation of relationship knowledge is based on mutual self-disclosure. Self-disclosure provides one with a mental "map" of the other person (Gottman, 1999). This map contains knowledge of the other's history, likes, dislikes, current stressors, current joys, and so forth. One must pay attention, or be mindful, to the self-disclosure of others. Mindless dismissals of self-disclosure keep one from developing a detailed mental map of the other, and eventually parents say to children or spouses say to one another, "I feel like I don't really know you." Second, as Omarzu, Whalen, and Harvey (2001) say, "knowledge alone is not enough" (p. 346). The theory hypothesizes that romantic partners and family members share greater intimacy when they feel that the information they share is accepted and respected, even when opinions, values, and habits differ.

The third element of minding theory involves attributions. That is, minding stipulates that partners or family members give each other the benefit of the doubt when they account for the other's behavior. The listener remains more receptive to the speaker by assuming that negative events were caused by something outside the relationship, and positive events were caused by the partner's inherent virtues (Omarzu et al., 2001). The fourth component of the theory explains that the minding behaviors and optimistic thinking patterns must be reciprocal. When minding works to stimulate intimacy, both persons are seeking knowledge about the other, accepting the knowledge even with its differences, and making positive attributions about the other. Finally, these minding patterns must be continued over time. Partners and family members constantly change and there is never a time to stop minding. Minding theory implies that married couples should continually mind their relationships with some of the same vigor they used in their dating period. Parents should update the mental map of their children, staying abreast of their changing interests and feelings and reasonably respecting the development of their individual tastes and opinions. Intimacy is constructed in a mutual process of self-expressions, partner responses to those expressions, and positive perceptions of this process.

## CONCLUSION

Family processes involving power, decision making, conflict, and intimacy are like fingerprints. No one decision or conflict is the same. Yet, scholars have created useful models and theories to help explain the nature of these family processes. Power refers to the ability to change the behavior or affect of another. It is an interactional process, meaning that in order to be powerful, one must have another who is willing to submit. Family power is theoretically rooted in social bases of power, resource exchange theories, and gender and relational hierarchies. Family power can also be observed in family roles and rules.

Processes of family decision making are intimately tied to who holds the power in the family. Interestingly, children often underestimate the amount of influence they actually have, especially in instrumental decisions. Family decisions are both instrumental (functional) and affective (emotion driven), and decisions are affected by family structure, developmental changes, and external inputs to the family system. Turner (1970) models the microprocesses of decision making in families by pointing to three common styles of decision making: consensus, accommodation, and de facto. Settles (1999) proposes viewing family decision making on a macrolevel, exploring social, familial, environmental, and individual forces that affect family decisions.

Family members live so interdependently that conflict is bound to occur. Conflict stems from content or relationship issues, and from the internal family environment or the external environment. Family conflicts vary by topic, type, and frequency. Not all conflicts are destructive for family relationships; however, conflict mutually influences all family members, even if only some are overtly involved. Koerner and Fitzpatrick (1997) argue that a family's conversation and conformity orientation relates directly to the way they deal with conflict. Further, the exit–voice–loyalty–neglect model categorizes the multiples ways family members respond to conflict square-offs.

Finally, all people have needs for intimacy, though only some fulfill these needs in the family context. Intimacy revolves around partner A's self-expressions; partner B's response to A; and partner A's perception about whether he or she felt understood, validated, and cared for by the response. Self-disclosures and nonverbal bids for attention often stimulate intimacy, but they do not always elicit a favorable response. Harvey and Omarzu (1997) propose that intimacy requires a heightened level of "minding," where people make conscious attempts to stay connected to their partners and family members. Maintaining intimacy presents a constant challenge for family members. Now that we have at least conceptualized these basic family processes, we examine them in subsequent chapters with regard to specific family events and relationships.

# II

# Communication in Family Subsystems

# CHAPTER FIVE

# Courtship and Mate Selection

Research and theory on premarital relationships and mate selection have a "long and venerable history in family studies," and for good reason (Surra, 1990, p. 844). Premarital relationships are not only influenced by family background factors (Seiffge-Krenke, Shulman, & Klessinger, 2001) but also play a major role in the way one experiences family life in the future. Cate and Lloyd (1992) name courtship as the "first (and perhaps most crucial) stage in the family life cycle" (p. 2). An assumption inherent in most premarital relationship research is that relationships do not begin on their wedding day. Some, if not much of the architecture for later relational quality is already present premaritally (Flora & Segrin, 2003; Karney & Bradbury, 1995). What are some of these risk factors for poor marital quality that are evident premaritally? In this chapter, we highlight risk factors such as age, length of courtship, interaction patterns, and many other factors that couples transport from their courtship into their marriages (Hill & Peplau, 1998).

Next, what are the factors that draw two people into marriage? For sure, not all premarital relationships advance to marriage. Some people date knowing they only have a short-term interest in the partner. Some people date having long-term interest, but the relationship does not work out for a variety of reasons we will explore. Both men and women are more selective about their partners in situations that they intend to be longterm (Stewart, Stinnett, & Rosenfeld, 2000). Greater selectivity is warranted when the partners are looking to spend their lives together or raise children together. We begin the chapter by examining individual, dyadic, and external factors that influence the choice of a mate. Over time, these factors have been incorporated into models of mate selection. We review several of these models, including evolutionary psychology, social exchange, stage, and interpersonal process models.

Finally, in what ways are dating couples different from married couples? And do couples ever consider themselves to be a "family" before marriage? Perhaps because serious dating relationships are a testing ground for marriage, we recently found in our own research that serious, long-term dating couples and young married couples were not significantly different in their relationship satisfaction or their relational bond (i.e., their expressions of unity, fondness and affection, negativity, and disappointment; Flora & Segrin, 2003). Further, some premarital partners behave in ways that were once reserved for traditional marital or family relationships (Cate & Lloyd, 1992). There has been a staggering increase in the number of couples who cohabit (i.e., live together) prior to marriage or as an alternative to marriage (Bumpass & Sweet, 1989; Cate, Levin, & Richmond, 2002; Cohan

**Box 5.1**
**TV Game Shows' Portrayals of Dating and Courtship**

Since their inception, television, films, magazines, novels, pop music, and many other media genres have portrayed courtship and mate selection processes. Sometimes these portrayals are very realistic. However, in many instances, they are trivialized, sexualized, oversimplified, and stereotyped in order to offer audiences tantalizing, humorous, satirical, or short-term glimpses of dating life. In the last half-century, TV game shows and reality shows have developed an appetite for dating, courtship, and interpersonal attraction. Hetsroni (2000) observes that there have been two types of courtship games on television. The first type involves shows such as the 1960s to 1970s *Newlywed Game*, where husbands and wives were separately asked the same questions about each other and their relationship. Couples who had the most answers in common won a prize, under the assumption that they had a courtship process that helped them get to know each other better than did the other couples. The second type, of more recent interest, involves a male or female who selects a mate among numerous candidates and rounds of elimination. This second type of show was popularized by *The Love Connection* in the 1980s and generated more interest in the 1990s and early 2000s, with MTV's *Singled Out* and other major network productions such as *Who Wants to Marry a Millionaire*, *Blind Date*, *The Bachelor*, *The Bachelorette*, and numerous other shows with related premises such as *Change of Heart* or *Temptation Island*.

It is obvious why the networks like such shows: They are typically inexpensive and good at least for short-term ratings. Why do audiences like them so much? Such shows are a mix of sport, fairytale, and comedy. Avins (2002), for example, argues that people are "voyeurs" who "find sport in the brutality of modern courtship" (p. F1). Similarly, Farhi (2002) interviewed numerous people who admitted that the shows were "cheap and tacky," but that they were seduced by the fairytale image of people trying to find the "perfect" match (p. C1). Further, people get a chance to laugh at themselves and see some of the crazy things they may actually do in the dating process. Is there any harm in these TV dating game shows? Hetsroni (2000) feels that dating game participants place far more emphasis on physical characteristics and sex-related qualities of potential mates rather than on lifestyle, psychological, and communication qualities. Perhaps participants can afford to look primarily at superficial qualities knowing that they may not necessarily be with these partners for the long term. Besides, Roug and Lowry (2002) argue that most audiences understand that TV dating game shows are just comedies and that most people watch with the notion that they would never act like most of the contestants.

Ward (2002) presents an alternative perspective. At least with regard to TV (e.g., soap operas), films, and music videos, Ward feels that media portrayals of courtship for the most part negatively influence young people's notions of what constitutes proper and common dating behavior. Ward's correlational and experimental data show that young adults who consume a lot of television are more likely to endorse attitudes indicating that sexual relationships are recreationally oriented, that pregnancy and sexually transmitted diseases are not major risks in casual sex, that most of their peers are "doing it," and that sexual stereotypes (e.g., men are sex driven and women are sex objects) hold true. As Ward says, we need more research to address whether endorsement of such attitudes actually leads to risky behaviors. What do you think?

& Kleinbaum, 2002). It is also more common and more acceptable than ever for couples to have children outside marriage (Cate et al.). Thus, many people at least subjectively consider themselves to be a "family" before marriage. Even the many couples that do not cohabit enter their marital unions with a well-developed relationship culture and pattern of interactions. Indeed, many feel that a couple's interaction does more to constitute a mate relationship than does the presence of a marriage license.

Overall, the intent of this chapter is to present social scientific research findings on courtship and premarital communication. While reading through this chapter, it may be interesting to compare media portrayals of courtship to the real-life processes presented in this chapter (see Box 5.1).

## FACTORS THAT INFLUENCE PREMARITAL RELATIONSHIPS AND MATE SELECTION

Premarital relationships are affected by individual, dyadic, and external factors. Cate et al. (2002) define individual factors as personality characteristics, individual dispositions, personal preferences, or individual needs. Dyadic factors, or relationship-level factors, consider the match between two partners (i.e., partner complementarity) and dyadic interaction. External factors involve forces outside the relationship, including outside individuals and circumstances that impact the relationship. We begin by examining how individual factors are related to partner choice and the extent to which these individual factors affect the course and stability of premarital relationships.

### Individual Factors

#### Relationship Readiness

There are several factors that affect an individual's readiness for the kind of serious relationship that could lead to marriage. One such factor is age. As we mentioned in chapter 1, the average age of first marriage has increased dramatically for both men and women over the last half-century (from 20.1 years for women and 22.5 years for men in 1956 to 25.1 years for women and 26.8 years for men in 2000). Increases in marriage age reflect a variety of social forces, including increased education for men and especially for women, greater societal acceptance of being single, and economic pressures that make it difficult to financially support a marriage, such as costs of a home or children. For example, Hill and Peplau (1998) report that as early as the 1970s, women who sought advanced degrees were less likely to marry their college partner, waiting instead to marry once they completed their advanced degree. For these and other reasons, many people do not feel they are ready to advance a relationship to the level of marriage until they are older.

Delay of marriage may have some positive benefits. For the most part, length of courtship is positively related to marital adjustment and satisfaction (Cate & Lloyd, 1992; Hill & Peplau, 1998; Lewis & Spanier, 1979). Teenage marriages are especially prone to divorce (Cate & Lloyd). It may be that having a longer courtship and marrying at a later age, when one has more education and economic grounding, translate to greater individual maturity and stability in the interaction of premarital partners (Cate & Lloyd).

### Individual Needs, Beliefs, and Family Background

During the 1990s, researchers explored how individual attachment needs and self-beliefs, such as self-esteem, affect premarital relationship stability (Cate et al., 2002). Such research posed the following questions. Do individuals with a secure attachment style have more stable premarital relationships? Are individuals with higher self-esteem more likely to stay in a premarital relationship? These questions were prompted by earlier research (Burgess & Wallin, 1953), which suggested that individuals who were self-confident before marriage had more successful marriages (Hill & Peplau, 1998). In some of this research (e.g., Feeney & Noller, 1992; Kirkpatrick & Davis, 1994), there is little or mixed evidence that individual factors of self-esteem or attachment have a direct effect. However, Cate et al. suggest that the direct and possibly indirect relationship between attachment and premarital relationship quality deserves more attention. In a 6-year longitudinal study, Seiffge-Krenke et al. (2001) found that adolescents who experienced a "reliable alliance" with their parents went on to experience more connectedness (i.e., happiness, friendship, trust, and acceptance) as well as more attraction in their adult romantic relationships. The authors concluded that the adolescents might have transferred their attachment security with their parents to their romantic relationships. Duemmler and Kobak (2001) noted that especially for males, attachment security with mothers and fathers is associated with greater increases in commitment during the early phases of a romantic relationship. Likewise Feeney (1999) found that males with a dismissing attachment style, or more attachment insecurity, experienced recurrent conflicts as they attempted to manage tensions for togetherness and autonomy in their romantic relationships.

Related to but different from self-beliefs are relationship beliefs. There is compelling evidence to suggest that certain beliefs individuals hold about relationships relate to relationship success. These beliefs include realistic expectations about the work involved in relationships (Demo & Ganong, 1994; Hill & Peplau, 1998), optimistic views or positive illusions that emphasize the strengths of one's partner and relationship (Murray & Holmes, 1999; Murray, Holmes, & Griffin, 1996), and motivation to be in a romantic relationship (Kurdek, 1991). Overall, self- and relationship beliefs are thought to have some impact on relationship stability; however, it is difficult to separate the role of individual beliefs from dyadic factors, because individuals are not in a vacuum in relationships.

### Mate Preferences and Values

Buss, Shackelford, Kirkpatrick, and Larsen (2001) propose that individuals have mate preferences and values, and these values have evolved with tides of cultural change. Buss et al. compared 18 different mate preferences of heterosexual men and women across several different time periods (1939, 1967, 1977, 1984–1985, and 1996) and across geographically diverse regions of the United States (e.g., Texas, California, Massachusetts, and Michigan). Although there were a few regional differences (e.g., individuals from

Texas placed greater value on chastity of mates and similar religious background), the overwhelming majority of differences occurred not across regions, but across the 57-year time period. The most dramatic evolution of mate selection values pertains to preferences for chastity, physical attractiveness, financial resources, cooking and housekeeping, and mutual attraction and love.

### Chastity

From the early 1900s through the mid-1980s, people gradually viewed chastity as a less important mate characteristic. There was, however, a small increase in the importance that both sexes placed on chastity between the mid-1980s and mid-1990s. Buss et al. (2001) suggest that during the late 1980s and early 1990s, people became more aware of AIDS and other sexually transmitted diseases, which may have prompted them to reconsider the value of chastity. Even still, people today name several other mate characteristics that are more important to them than chastity. Why has chastity traditionally been an important mate selection characteristic, and to what extent have changing values in chastity been reflected in research on premarital couples?

Since ancestral times, men, especially, have been concerned about the chastity of their female mates. Ancestral men wanted to be sure they were investing in offspring to whom they were genetically related. Women's sexual infidelity posed a risk (Shackelford & Buss, 1997). In the 1930s, researchers suggested that another reason for valuing chastity was because premarital sexual restraint was associated with marital success (Hill & Peplau, 1998). Curious about whether this association held during the "sexually liberated 70s," Hill and Peplau report results from the Boston couples study. In this study, the researchers sampled 231 college dating couples in 1972 and followed the couples for 15 years. Although results from this study are not totally generalizable, because the participants were all White, well-educated Bostonians, the fact that the researchers collected comprehensive data on a range of premarital predictors and followed the participants over 15 years makes this a rare and noteworthy study. Among the many variables examined, Hill and Peplau reported that earlier age at first intercourse for men and women in the study did not appear to affect short-term dating outcomes, but did negatively affect later marital stability. Further, women with more sexual partners were more likely to break up with their dating partner (Hill & Peplau, p. 258). The magnitude of these correlations, however, was rather small. More recent research (e.g., Teachman, 2003) found that when women engage in premarital sex only with the man they eventually marry, they are no more likely to divorce than women who refrain from sex until marriage. On the other hand, women who have premarital sex with more than one partner have a slight increased risk of marital disruption

### Physical Attractiveness

Over the last half-century, both men and women have gradually viewed physical attractiveness as an increasingly important quality for a mate. In fact, men and women report that physical attractiveness is important, regardless of whether their partner is a short-term or long-term interest. Still, men value physical attractiveness more than women do, as have men in the past (Shackelford & Buss, 1997). For men, physical attractiveness rose from the 14th most important characteristic in 1939 to 8th in 1996. For women, it increased from 17th in 1939 to 13th in 1996. Buss et al. (2001) note that the cosmetics, diet, and cosmetic surgery industries have capitalized on and perpetuated this trend.

What makes for physical attractiveness? Some individuals believe that beauty is in the eye of the beholder (i.e., beauty is bound to individual-specific or cultural-specific preferences). Although this is sometimes the case, there is actually a great deal of consensus across individuals and across cultures concerning what makes for an attractive mate. Much of the consensus relates to the role of body and facial symmetry (e.g., a straight smile or leg length proportional to body length). Humans across all cultures have been found to rate symmetrical bodies and faces as more attractive than asymmetrical ones, although these findings have met some recent challenges. For example, Kowner (2001) contends, "people in reality do not judge facial beauty based only on static features [and whether or not they are symmetrical]. In fact, since prehistoric times, humans have increasingly stressed the role of communication through facial expressions which are often asymmetric" (p. 461).

Riggio, Widaman, Tucker, and Salinas (1991) argue that physical attractiveness is just one component to attractiveness. They view attractiveness as a multifaceted concept based on facial beauty, body attractiveness, attractiveness of dress, and dynamic expressive style. Although facial beauty, body, and dress are usually fixed or static variables that can be measured using a still photograph, one's style of expression is a dynamic variable that involves verbal and nonverbal communication skills and role-playing skills. Riggio et al. found that, among college students, facial beauty and expressive style were the most important components in an individual's overall judgments of another person's attractiveness. Thus, communication, manifested in expressive style, may supercede some physical considerations. Knapp and Vangelisti (2000) remark that "most people have had an experience when someone they thought was only moderately attractive actually became much more attractive to them" (p. 167). *Initial* perceptions of attraction are often based only on physical characteristics, sometimes simply static physical characteristics (e.g., we view a picture of someone). Once one begins to interact with another person, that person's communication and expressive style, including dynamic asymmetrical expressions, figure into one's perceptions of attractiveness.

### Financial Resources, Cooking and Housekeeping, and Mutual Attraction and Love

Good financial prospects have become increasingly important to women *and* men. This change is most dramatic for men, who in earlier decades had few expectations and preferences for an economically resourceful mate. It appears, however, that mate preferences regarding a partner's earning power interact with age and gender. Sprecher, Sullivan, and Hatfield (1994) found that younger persons (i.e., ages 19–22) were more willing to marry someone who earned less than they did. However, the older women became, the less willing they were to marry a man who earned less than they did. As for cooking and housekeeping, men place much less value on these qualities than they once did. Women's preferences for a mate with cooking and housekeeping skills have remained notably low over time, even though many women appear to need more help with cooking and housekeeping now that they are entering the workforce in greater numbers.

Finally, mutual attraction and love were not considered primary (i.e., top two) mate selection values until 1967. Currently mutual attraction and love are the top mate selection values for men and women. This value preference reflects the increasing importance people of the past half-century have placed on the companionate, interactional nature of marriage. Overall, individuals' mate selection values have changed over the past half-century, and the mate preferences of men and women have gradually, though not completely, converged.

Research on mate selection values is useful, yet it is difficult to use group-level data pertaining to mate preferences to predict the mate choice of a specific person (Houts, Robins, & Huston, 1996). In other words, we cannot understand the mate selection process simply by studying an individual's preferences. We do not always act on our preferences. Plus, relationships depend on the interplay of preferences and values for both individuals. Courtship and mate selection are influenced by many dyadic factors (e.g., the extent to which two people are compatible in preferences and in the nature of their interaction) and external factors (e.g., circumstances and social network factors). Clearly, relationships are not the result of *one* individual's preferences. Each partner has to prefer the other, and the circumstances must be right. Houts et al. explain: "In reality, individuals who are seeking a compatible mate must make many compromises if they are to marry at all" (p. 18).

## Dyadic Factors

Compared to individual and external factors, dyadic factors command the most attention from premarital relationship researchers, particularly from those in the field of communication. Most of the attention centers on issues of partner compatibility and the way interaction constitutes romantic relationships. Here the concern is not on the individual, but on the match between two individuals.

### Introducing the Role of Similarity and Attraction in Partner Compatibility

"It is an axiom of research on interpersonal attraction that similarity leads to liking, and empirical studies demonstrate that intimate relationships tend to be homogamous" (Hill & Peplau, 1998, p. 266). Having stated this "axiom," we now examine the extent to which intimate partners really are homogamous and explore support for and contentions to the belief that similarity breeds liking.

Individuals who are alike on a characteristic are *homogamous* for it. When individuals pair with mates according to homogamy, they are *assortively matched* (Murstein, 1986). For example, partners who have the same education are assortively matched for education. Assortive matching is concerned with whether individuals are more alike than what would be expected by chance. Most early research on assortive matching examined sociocultural variables such as age, ethnicity, education, socioeconomic class, and physical attractiveness. As we detail in the following section, there is clear evidence for assortive matching with regard to these sociocultural variables. Although many have found weak evidence for assortive matching based on general personality variables, there is fascinating evidence for assortive matching with regard to some personal characteristics that relate to mental health.

### Assortive Matching for Sociocultural and Personal Variables

Historically, couples have assortively matched for *age*, especially in first marriages. Still men and women are not perfectly matched on age, with men traditionally being older by a year or two. In the past, this was explained by the fact that fewer women went to college and that men were expected to contribute more economic support to the marriage (Murstein, 1986). Today, more women than men attend college, and women are making more financial contributions to the relationship than ever before. Some speculate that this age gap for first marriages may close in the next century.

Individuals report more acceptance of interracial marriage than ever before, and rates of intermarriage are increasing. In 1960, fewer than 4 in 1,000 U.S. marriages were interracial relationships (Crowder & Tolnay, 2000). More recently, 3 in 100 marriages in the U.S. were classified as interracial (U.S. Census Bureau, 1998). In reality, assortive matching for *race* is still relatively strong. Gaines and Brennan (2001) further summarize rates of racial outmarriage: 7% for African Americans, 28% for Mexican Americans, 30% for Asian Americans, and over 50% for Native Americans. Attitudes toward interracial marriage changed greatly after civil rights reforms of the 1960s; however, Black–White marriages still only represent 1 in 4 of the interracial marriages in the United States (Gaines & Brennan; U.S. Census Bureau, 1998). In addition, Black men are more likely to marry White women, compared to marriages between White men and Black women (Crowder & Tolnay). Overall, Asian American-Anglo and Latino-Anglo couples have led the way in interracial marriage (Gaines & Brennan). Interestingly, when Shibazaki and Brennan (1998) compared interethnic and intraethnic couples, they found no differences between the couples in relationship satisfaction or reasons for entering the relationship. Individuals in interethnic relationships did report less societal approval of their relationship and less self-esteem, among some other minor differences.

There has traditionally been strong evidence of assortive matching by *education* and *socioeconomic class* (Murstein, 1986). Houts et al. (1996) offer a common explanation for why such assortive matching occurs. People may not consciously look for mates of similar education and socioeconomic class, but society is organized so that people of similar class are more likely to come into contact with each other. For example, people who attend college effectively place themselves in a pool of other college students, most of whom have similar goals for attaining a college degree and at least share the socioeconomic means to enter college. Tuition and entrance requirements at some elite universities demand particular homogamy of socioeconomic class.

Regarding assortive matching for *physical attractiveness*, Walster (1966) first found support for a phenomenon called the matching hypothesis. The matching hypothesis proposes that people of similar levels of attractiveness will pair with one another. The matching hypothesis exemplifies the occasional divergence between mate preferences and actual mate characteristics. That is, although many people say they would prefer to have a highly attractive mate, and some average-looking people dream of being matched with a supermodel, people commonly end up with someone of a similar level of attractiveness. According to the matching hypothesis, an average-looking woman would set herself up for constant rejection, if she repeatedly asked out only highly attractive men. Highly attractive men, who are likely being courted by other highly attractive women, would choose the attractive prospects over the nonattractive prospects who have less "mate value" (Shackelford & Buss, 1977). Likewise, some average-looking people prefer to be with other average-looking people because they feel they will not have to engage in excessive "mate guarding" to keep their highly attractive mate away from other desiring people (Shackelford & Buss). The matching hypothesis is based on the notion that physical attractiveness gives mates a certain degree of mate value. However, physical attractiveness is not the only thing that gives people mate value. Sometimes people exchange their financial value for another's physical attractiveness value (e.g., a physically unattractive but rich man matched with a highly physically attractive woman). Knapp and Vangelisti (2000) explain that a high self-esteem gives a person (a) the perception that he or she has high mate value; (b) the motivation to seek out a mate who has high value, perhaps even higher actual value; and (c) the "tough skin" to deal with rejection from a potential partner. In sum, who we date is often a reflection of our own level of attractiveness or other valuable qualities that can substitute for our attractiveness.

In addition to these sociocultural variables, it appears that people seek out others who are similar to the self on other seemingly less desirable qualities. For example, people select interpersonal partners with psychiatric conditions similar to their own (du Fort, Kovess, & Bolvin, 1994; Merikangas, Weissman, Prusoff, & John, 1988; Merikangas & Spiker, 1982), including *depression* (Merikangas, 1984; Rosenblatt & Greenberg, 1991). Sophisticated studies of depression in married couples and their first-degree relatives that establish a family history of depression (e.g., Merikangas & Spiker; Merikangas et al.) provide compelling evidence for the assortive matching hypothesis. Ordinarily, some may be inclined to view similar symptoms of depression in husbands and their wives as evidence of emotional transmission from one spouse to the other through repeated interactions. However, evidence of a family history of depression in each spouse points to the conclusion that the spouses were most likely "matched" on symptoms of depression from the start of their relationship. Because similarity is such a powerful force in interpersonal attraction (Byrne, 1971; Newcomb, 1961), it is reasonable to assume that the assortive matching effect permeates the formation of most close relationships—even on such undesirable qualities as psychological distress (Merikangas; Segrin, in press).

### Assortive Matching for Interaction Variables

At this point, we have examined assortive matching for sociocultural and personality characteristics, such as age, ethnicity, education, socioeconomic class, physical attractiveness, and depression. Houts et al. (1996) suggest: "The mate selection literature, which now reads much like a Lands' End catalogue of criteria that people are said to use to select mates . . . needs to focus more attention on what factors actually affect dating, [and] the interpersonal quality of premarital relationships" (p. 18). Toward this end, Houts et al.

examine partner similarity in *leisure interests* and *role preferences*. They argue that in order to select a mate, people date, and the dating period is primarily defined by the interaction that occurs during joint leisure pursuits. In leisure pursuits, partners evaluate their similarity in leisure interests and their role preferences. Because marriage has increasingly become a companionate relationship, leisure and role compatibility are assumed to affect the quality of interaction in relationships, whereas "social similarities (e.g., ethnicity, religion) are likely to be only modestly associated with how well couples get along on a day-to-day basis" (Houts et al., p. 9). Similarity in leisure and role preferences may be rooted in sociological similarities, but not necessarily. Houts et al. studied 168 couples and examined similarity in leisure pursuits related to interests in sports, exercise, culture, outings, relaxation, television, and partying. They also examined similarity in role preferences related to housekeeping, repairs and outdoor maintenance, food preparation, financial tasks, and shopping. Couples who had similar role preferences were those who agreed on who should complete certain tasks: the husband, wife, or both. Results indicated that the couples in the study were assortively matched with regard to leisure preferences and role preferences. In addition, the husbands who indicated the greatest feelings of love and the most relationship maintenance behaviors were those who had more similar leisure interests with their wives. Couples who were less similar in their role preferences reported more conflict and negativity in their marriage. Finally, homogamy of social characteristics, such as age, education, and religion, did not predict similar leisure preferences among the spouses. Thus, social homogamy did not lead to psychosocial homogamy (i.e., leisure and role preferences).

In 1994, Burleson, Kunkel, and Birch studied the extent to which romantic partners had similar values about communication and if similar values enhanced attraction and satisfaction in the relationship. Similar to the Houts et al. (1996) study, Burleson et al.'s study followed the premise that satisfying romantic relationships are based on whether the partners have enjoyable interactions and a good time together. They essentially explored whether similar communication values led to the kind of enjoyable interactions that would benefit a relationship. In general, Burleson et al. found that romantic partners did not exhibit similar communication values. However, the more similar partners were in the way they valued affectively oriented communication skills, the more partner attraction and relationship satisfaction those partners experienced. Burleson et al. concluded that people do not appear to choose partners based on similar communication values, but the more similar partners' communication values are, the more attraction and satisfaction they experience. Overall, it appears that assortive matching is common for many sociocultural and interactional variables, but certainly not all. Further, it is difficult to tell whether "birds of a feather flock together" by choice or convenience. In other words, does assortive matching stem from conscious choices for homogamy or unconscious homogamy due to convenience and social environment?

### Does Similarity Really Breed Attraction?

We now move on to the reason scholars have shown so much interest in homogamy. Similarity has long been assumed to produce attraction and relationship satisfaction. As Burleson et al. (1994) hypothesized, similarity of communication values may make interactions more enjoyable. Yet some people seek out dissimilar others for the very same reason—to make interaction more enjoyable. Some people desire a partner who has different strengths that are complementary as well as different weakness so as not to compound problems. Aron and Aron's model of self-expansion (1986, 1997) proposes that people desire to expand themselves through the course of a relationship. Self-expansion is enhanced by participation in novel activities that reduce boredom. A partner who is dissimilar may promote activities that are novel and arousing to the other throughout the course of the relationship. What makes the study of similarity and attraction so difficult is that there are so many types of similarities and differences to consider. There is also a difference between perceived similarity and actual similarity. In addition, partners can grow to become more similar or different over the course of a relationship.

By far, the most attention and controversy surrounds the relationship between *attitude* similarity and attraction. Byrne's (1969) "reinforcement affect model" of attraction suggests that people are attracted to others who view the world in the same way as they do because it validates their views. Ah Yun (2002) summarized some of the major challenges to the "axiom" that attitude similarity breeds attraction. One challenge offered by Sunnafrank and his colleagues (Sunnafrank, 1985, 1986, 1992; Sunnafrank & Miller, 1981) is that communication moderates the effect that attitude similarity has on attraction. This argument maintains that attitude dissimilarity can be an aversive force in new relationships and can even keep two people from achieving an opportunity to interact (Ah Yun, p. 148). However, if given the opportunity to interact, the communication is often pleasant, and, over time, communication can help overcome some of the differences. After a brief initial interaction, similar people do not like each other any more than do dissimilar people (Sunnafrank & Miller).

A second challenge to the attitude similarity and attraction axiom is the *repulsion hypothesis* (Rosenbaum, 1986). "According to the repulsion hypothesis, attitude similarity does not heighten interpersonal attraction, because similarity is expected. However the discovery of attitude *dissimilarity* is unexpected and aversive, resulting in interpersonal repulsiveness that decreases interpersonal attractiveness" (Ah Yun, 2002, p. 148). Thus, attitude similarity does not increase attraction, but attitude dissimilarity decreases attraction.

Ah Yun (2002) completed a meta-analysis, comparing results from 80 studies on the relationship between attitude similarity and attraction. He concluded that attitude similarity is associated with attraction to some extent. Interaction, at least in the early stages of a relationship, moderates, or in effect lessens, the effect that attitude similarity has on attraction.

### Verbal and Nonverbal Communication in Premarital Relationships

During the dating period premarital partners develop their style of interaction. It is the communication of premarital partners that forms and constitutes their relationship (Rogers, 2001). Much of the communication in initial interaction is highly scripted (Kellermann, 1995). For example, partners often expect initial interactions to be a pleasant exchange of introductions and small talk. As the relationship progresses, people forgo some of the scripts involved in the "meeting and dating game"; however, they may adhere to other scripts throughout the course of the relationship (Harvey & Weber, 2002, p. 50). Knapp (1978; 1984; Knapp & Vangelisti, 2000) highlighted the scripts that characterize

**TABLE 5.1**

Relationship Stages, Representative Scripts, and Relationship
Stage Descriptions

| Stage | Representative Scripts | Relationship Stage Descriptions |
|---|---|---|
| Initiating | "Hi how ya doin'?"<br>"Fine. You?" | We've recently met (or I'd like to meet this person). As I scan him or her I am deciding whether he or she is "attractive" or "unattractive" and deciding whether to initiate communication. I am thinking: "I see you, I am friendly, and I want to open channels for communication to take place." |
| Experimenting | "Oh, so you like to ski . . . so do I."<br>"You do? Great. Where do you go?" | We are beginning the process of experimenting—trying to discover the unknown. We exchange demographic information and our conversation often seems controlled by a norm that says "if you tell me your hometown, I'll tell you mine." Small talk is the key means of communicating here. This relationship is generally pleasant, relaxed, uncritical, casual, and full of questions. |
| Intensifying | "I . . . I think I love you."<br>"I love you too." | We have a good amount of personal disclosure, and we have begun to get a glimpse of some previously withheld secrets. We disclose about a lot of things, and often about how our relationship is developing. We have begun to speak more informally. We say "we," and express our commitment directly (such as saying "I really like you" or "We work well together"). As we begin to get close, we do so with caution, waiting for confirmation before proceeding. |
| Integrating | "I feel so much a part of you."<br>"Yeah, we are like one person. What happens to you happens to me." | Our two individual personalities are almost fused or blended. Our verbal and nonverbal communication shows that we are alike. We dress alike, have the same interests, and others begin to treat us as a "couple." When they invite us places, they invite us both. We're as close as family members often are. |
| Bonding | "I want to be with you always."<br>"Let's get married." | In a public ritual, we have announced to the world that a commitment has been formally contracted. It is during this stage that we become engaged, get married, go into business together, or move in together. Communication is at its highest level and often we don't even have to talk because we know each other so well. Our families and friends are blended. |

*Note.* From Mark L. Knapp and Anita L. Vangelisti *Interpersonal Communication and Human Relationships* (4th ed.) ⓒ 2000, Published by Allyn and Bacon, Boston, MA. ⓒ 2000 by Pearson Education. Reprinted by permission of the publisher. Also from "Development of Relationship Stage Measures," by S. A. Welch and R. B. Rubin, 2002, *Communication Quarterly, 50,* pp. 24–40. Copyright 2002 by Eastern Communication Association. Adapted with permission.

stages of meeting and coming together in a dating relationship (Table 5.1). More recently, Welch and Rubin (2002) developed descriptions of the relationship stages (also in Table 5.1) associated with these scripts.

### Initiating and Experimenting

During the *initiating* and *experimenting* stages, nonverbal cues are powerful, perhaps even more powerful that verbal cues. In her research on open communication and self-disclosure in new relationships, Montgomery (1986) revealed that people pay more attention to the style of disclosure, which is heavily influenced by nonverbal behaviors, than to the actual content of the disclosure. Immediately, one can think of the multitude of nonverbal behaviors important to flirting. In 1985, Moore cataloged a variety of nonverbal courtship or flirting behaviors, including glancing, leaning forward, smiling, nodding, touch, hair flip and head toss, object caress (e.g., touching the edge of a glass), laugh, and lip lick. Moore (1998) has also documented how refusal or disinterest in a partner is indicated nonverbally, for example, by looking away, turning away, frowning, and yawning. More recently, Moore (2002) found that men and women decode nonverbal courtship behaviors differently. For example, men rate refusal behaviors as less negative than do women. Men also rate flirting behaviors as more positive than do women, or as communicating stronger positive intent toward the relationship. Moore provides a fascinating, though controversial, evolutionary psychology framework to explain the difference in male's and female's perceptions of flirting. She suggests that because women bear children, they have a lot more investment in romantic relationships. Thus, they benefit from making careful and sometimes timely decisions about a mate in order to find someone who will help support their investment. With theoretically less investment, men want to more quickly take advantage of sexual opportunities. Thus, Moore explains: "Using subtle behaviors to signal interest may allow women to stall decision making leading to greater intimacy until they have had time to asses adequately partners' qualifications. For a man being prepared to see interest on the part of a potential partner but also pressing for attention even when lacking is adaptive" (p. 104).

Because partners have not been together long enough to develop shared interpretations and joint interpersonal meanings, they act based on implicit assumptions and personal meanings (Cushman & Whiting, 1972). Mongeau's research on the early stages of romantic relationships also demonstrates that males and females differ in their sexual attitudes and sexual expectations in early dating stages (Mongeau & Carey, 1996). Specifically, males, to a much greater extent than females, approach a first date with heightened sexual expectations when the female initiates the date (Mongeau & Carey). In other words, the fact the female verbally initiated the date seems to translate to an expectation that she may be likely to initiate or be open to other sexual interests on the first date—an expectation that is often violated.

### Intensifying and Integrating

One primary way premarital relationships are different from marital relationships is that premarital partners do not have the same kind of formal barriers to keep them from leaving a relationship (i.e., premarital partners are not legally bound to one another by a marriage license). The voluntary nature of premarital relationships prompts partners to think about how committed they are to their relationship. Premarital partners use verbal lines (e.g., I love you) and nonverbal behavior (e.g., holding hands and kissing) in the *intensifying* stage of their relationship to communicate feelings of commitment. In the *integrating* stage, partners use communication to indicate how much the other is a part of his or her life. They may directly say how bonded they feel with their partner (e.g., "You are such a big part of my life"), or they may indirectly indicate how integrated their lives are (e.g., by introducing their partner to family and important people in their life).

Participants in Aron, Dutton, Aron, and Iverson's (1989) study reported that the two most common predecessors to falling in love included (a) discovering another person likes you and (b) discovering desirable characteristics in another. Interaction is a means by which partners confirm desirable characteristics. Through interaction, partners confirm reciprocal liking, when they find out that the other wants a relationship. As relationships progress, participants are faced with decisions about the best way to communicate liking to the other person, considering the range of possible intimacy expressions including sexual intimacy. People must also consider whether their desires for how to express intimacy and how to intensify the relationship are compatible with their partners'. For example, do partners agree that it is appropriate to display affection in public? Do partners agree about the extent to which they want to engage in sexual activity (e.g., kissing or sexual intercourse)? O'Sullivan and Gaines found that a majority (81%) of college students report at least some ambivalence regarding decisions related to participating in sexual activity. When partners accepted sexual invitations, they reported doing so because of relationship or intimacy concerns, and relatively few reported that they felt obligated or believed that intimacy would "fix" things. However, O'Sullivan and Gaines also emphasized the need for clearer communication about sexual intentions and desires between dating partners.

As partners choose to intensify their relationship, they become increasingly interdependent. Greater interdependence translates to more opportunities for conflict. Siegert and Stamp (1994) provide an interesting analysis of conflict in dating relationships by studying how romantic partners handle the "first big fight" in their relationship.

> The experience of conflict is pivotal to both the development and the dissolution of close relationships. As such, a salient conflict such as an FBF [first big fight] may influence the relationship in several ways. Its outcome may reaffirm and strengthen a couple's commitment to their relationship through an increased understanding and acceptance of their differences on various issues. On the other hand, its negotiation may push people apart by bringing to the surface basic incompatibilities in attitudes, beliefs, and/or expectations. It may also be an important first step in establishing standards of appropriateness for future conflicts. (Siegert & Stamp, pp. 346–347)

Based on their study of how premarital couples handle their first big fight, Siegert and Stamp made three conclusions. First, fights, especially the "big" fights they studied, can both reduce uncertainty and increase uncertainty. After some fights, couples understand each other better as well as understand reasons behind their partner's actions. Yet other fights increase uncertainty by leaving partners with questions about the relationship and decisions about how to handle information that is revealed. Second, fights often test relationship commitment. Partners must decide how hard they want to work to overcome fights and how much conflictive issues will get in the way of commitment. Third, partners' communication distinguished those premarital relationships that survived the first big fight from those that did not. Survivors engaged in joint problem solving, and both partners had the ability and willingness to make some sacrifices and adjustments in behavior. The motivation to resolve conflicts in dating relationships, through the use of positive resources such as open discussion and concern for the partner, appears to be directly related to strong intimacy and commitment.

### Bonding Communication and Transferring Interaction Patterns to Marriage

More interdependent lives mean more opportunities for conflict, but also the potential for greater perspective taking, because partners can potentially understand each other better. Stets (1993) explored conflict and perspective taking as dating relationships progress from casual, somewhat serious, serious, to engaged relationship stages. Ultimately, at the engaged stage, couples exhibit *bonding* communication, as they declare to each other and the social world that they want to marry. Results from Stets' study indicated that perspective taking usually increases as relationships develop. Further, this increase in perspective taking is crucial in moderating the tendency for conflict to also increase with relationship seriousness. Further, control attempts decreased from the "somewhat serious" stage to the "serious stage," as couples "settled in" to their relationship and understood their partner more.

Scholars are learning that interaction patterns during courtship have a significant impact on later marital outcomes. Many laypersons believe that the interaction in a relationship changes once the relationship is officially bonded (i.e., once they get married); however, this appears not to be the case. Around 2 decades ago, Kelly et al. (1985) found that conflict during courtship was a very good indicator of conflict and dissatisfaction in the marriage. There is also a *sleeper effect* such that the effect of conflict during courtship sometimes does not show up until later (Notarius, 1996). Even serious conflict during courtship does not appear to affect a couple's satisfaction with their relationship at that time, but it does predict dissatisfaction with the partner and the marriage up to 5 years later (Markman, Renick, Floyd, Stanely, & Clements, 1993). For these reasons, the study of premarital communication is an important complement to studies on marital relations (Flora & Segrin, 2003; Karney & Bradbury, 1995).

## External Factors

In addition to individual and dyadic factors, external factors influence mate choice. As we described earlier, external factors involve forces outside the relationship, including outside individuals and circumstances that impact the relationship. Namely, two of the most influential external factors involve proximity and the social network.

### Proximity and Partner Availability

Some external factors that affect premarital relationships involve demographic trends in society. One such factor is simply the availability of partners. In 1968, Eckland proposed that our chances are about 50–50 "that the 'one and only' lives within walking distance" (p. 16). In other words, proximity may have more to do with mate selection than the romantic notion that there is one destined match among the millions of available partners. Glick (1988) popularized the term "marital squeeze" to refer to the lack of available marriage partners. Glick originally used the term to refer to an oversupply of women in decades prior to the 1980s (Surra, 1990). The marital squeeze meant that women had to compete for a fewer number of available male partners, and some women were forced to remain single. However, after the 1980s, men began to experience more of a marital squeeze (Surra). An exception, however, is for African American women who still are faced with an undersupply of African American men, that is, if being assortively matched for race is considered important (Crowder & Tolnay, 2000; Surra, Gray, Cottle, & Boettcher, 2004).

In the 1970s, a group of researchers (Pennebaker et al., 1979) tested whether there was any empirical evidence to support the notion that people are willing to compromise their standards for a partner when there are few available choices. They literally put the title of Mickey Gilley's country western song *Don't the Girls Get Prettier at Closing Time* to the test. They found that both men and women rated patrons of several bars as more attractive when the bar neared closing time as compared to earlier in the evening. Although they did not control for the effects of alcohol, it may be that people are more willing to compromise their choices when they feel a "squeeze" of partners. They may simply be reacting to the anxiety of being alone.

### Social Network Influences

In some societies, social networks are highly involved in the selection of a mate, as in the case of arranged marriages. In the United States, the vast majority of marriages involve spouses who self-select one another. Even in these marriages, people are often curious about the extent to which their social network can damage or enhance their dating relationship. What difference does is make if your parents or friends do not like the person you are dating? Most evidence indicates that interference or disapproval negatively affects the relationship and support enhances the relationship (Klein & Milardo, 2000; Schmeeckle & Sprecher, 2004; Surra, 1990). There is not much support for the *Romeo and Juliet effect* (i.e., the idea that couples become stronger in spite of interference; Sprecher & Felmlee, 1992). It appears, however, that specific actions that are supportive or interfering are not as influential as are the perceived subjective reactions of other people (e.g., What will other people think of me if I date this person?). In other words, people are more concerned about what others will think (i.e., their general disapproval or encouragement) versus what they do (Parks & Eggert, 1991; Sprecher & Felmlee).

Daters also carefully observe how their partners interact with their network (e.g., "Do they get along with my family?"). Social network members sometimes even indirectly socialize dating partners (e.g., your new boyfriend observes the way other couples in your family network behave, and he infers your family's expectations for your relationship).

If third parties decide to interfere with a romantic relationship, they most commonly do so in the middle stages of the relationship. The premise is that interference in the beginning stages may not be necessary. Why bother because the relationship may never progress to a serious level anyway? Interference at the latest stages, for example, after engagement, is also less common. At this stage, interference could alienate the couple from the network and damage chances for any type of relationship in the future (Surra, 1990). In general, (a) network support enhances relationship progress and interference hampers it, and (b) interference tends to occur in the middle stages of a relationship.

## MODELS OF MATE SELECTION

To this point, we have examined variables that influence premarital relationships separately. Scholars have organized and integrated many of these variables into models of mate selection. Some of the most primary models of mate selection include evolutionary psychology models, social exchange models, stage models, and interpersonal process models.

### Evolutionary Psychology Models

Evolutionary psychology examines behavior and psychological mechanisms that evolved when our ancestors attempted to adapt to problems in order to survive as a species. According to this perspective, mate selection has adapted to enhance reproductive success and the propagation of genes (Buss & Kenrick, 1998; Buss & Schmitt, 1993; Shackelford & Buss, 1997; Sprecher et al., 1994; Wu, 2001). When individuals choose mates today, they are not consciously thinking about maximizing reproduction (Kenrick, Groth, Trost, & Sadalla, 1993). Instead, they are conditioned subconsciously to prefer traits and characteristics that maximize reproduction.

Although males and females appear to seek out some similar qualities in the opposite sex, evolutionary psychology models have traditionally focused on differential preferences between the sexes (Kenrick et al.). According to evolutionary psychology theories, when selecting mates, men seek traits in women that are indicative of physical fitness and the ability to successfully bear children.

> Our ancestral humans did have access to three classes of cues that provide probabilistic evidence of a woman's age and health status: (a) features of physical appearance (e.g., full lips, clear skin, smooth skin, clear eyes, lustrous hair, symmetry, good muscle tone, [appropriate hip to waist ratio], and absence of lesions), (b) observable behavior (e.g., sprightly, youthful gait and high activity level), and (c) social reputation (e.g., knowledge gleaned from others about a person's age and prior health history). (Buss & Schmitt, 1993, p. 208)

The theory predicts that women would seek qualities in a male that are indicative of resource provision (e.g., a good job, a good income, and strength). Because women bear a greater burden than men with childbirth and rearing, it is more important for them to find a mate with the potential to provide resources over the long term. Because men are not as burdened by childbirth and rearing, they are primarily looking for women with good reproductive potential. Thus, men and women have different costs and contributions associated with reproduction.

Men and women are accorded mate value based on their contributions to the reproductive goal, though men and women are valuable for different reasons. Mate value is often positively correlated in relationships, such that men with greater resources, or greater mate value, are more likely to marry women who are more physically attractive (Shackelford & Buss, 1997). Evolutionary psychology further suggests that relative to women, men are more selective about marriage partners than casual sex partners (e.g., a one night stand) (Kenrick et al., 1993). In other words, men, especially, are more selective about partners with whom they intend to produce children. Women appear to have similar levels of selectivity whether for a 1-night stand or for a marriage partner, perhaps because they would bear a direct burden if they became pregnant in either situation. The higher level of investment, particularly parental investment, in marriage prompts partners to engage in mate guarding. Women must guard their mates from "mate poachers" who could lure their partner and his resources away (Schmitt & Buss, 2001). Men must also guard their mates to ensure that their investments are worthwhile. Men want to be sure that they are investing resources in children who are truly their own, not those of a mate poacher. Even today, for example, there is some evidence to suggest that stepparents are more likely to abuse a stepchild, in whom they have no genetic investment, versus a biological child (Daly & Wilson, 1988).

Evolutionary psychology theory has been extended and critiqued. Kenrick, Li, and Butner (2003) extended the theory, arguing that mate choice is influenced by the interplay between evolutionary psychology forces and pressures of one's social environment. "Culture is not a phenomenon outside the stream of human evolution but an emergent dynamic that interacts with the decision rules of the individuals who make up societies" (Kenrick et al., p. 22). In other words, cultural forces, such as availability of resources (e.g., availability of partners) or changing cultural preferences also influence mate selection. Further, critiques of evolutionary psychology theories suggest that although self-reported mate preferences correspond with the theory, it is unclear whether people actually select mates based on their evolutionary preferences (Surra, 1998). Again, environmental or cultural factors may keep one from acting on preferences. A great question in evolutionary psychology is at what point culture influences decisions. Furthermore, feminist perspectives often take issue with the theory, arguing that it overemphasizes reproduction as an influence to mate choice.

## Social Exchange Models

Social exchange theory (presented in chap. 4) suggests that the development of close relationships is based on the satisfactory exchange of rewards between partners (Thibaut & Kelly, 1959). Partners are satisfied and motivated to remain in a relationship when the rewards exceed the costs, the rewards meet or exceed the comparison level, and the comparison level for alternatives is low. Rusbult (1980; interdependence theory) enhanced the basic ideas of social exchange theory by emphasizing that high rewards, low costs, along with high *investment* in the relationship lead to feelings of commitment to a relationship (Drigotas & Rusbult, 1992).

Social exchange theory is an appealing idea, although it has been difficult to test the theory. This is in part due to the fact that costs and rewards are hard to define, because people may have different views of costs and rewards. In addition, social exchange theory assumes that people make rationally calculated decisions and are cognitively aware of costs and rewards—an assumption that has been questioned by researchers (Berger & Roloff, 1980). Some more recent research has suggested that issues of equity and social exchange are most critical very early on in relationships or once partners become dissatisfied with their relationship. Early in relationships, gross differences in social exchange cause people to look over some potential partners. Once relationships are underway, smaller issues of social exchange are ignored, and exchange value is not a primary contributor to relationship satisfaction. This appears to be the case in relationships that are *communal*, meaning investment is not predicated on exchange value and immediate rewards, as in *exchange* relationships (Mills & Clark, 1994). However, many people start to count the costs once they become dissatisfied, as a means of justifying and further fueling their dissatisfaction with the relationship (Sprecher, 2001).

## Stage Models

Prior to stage models of courtship, researchers purported that one feature or one single dimension, for example, attitude similarity, physical attractiveness, or need fulfillment, motivated mate selection decisions. Duck (1998) calls these early models "switch-on" models. If the one feature is satisfied in a potential partner, then the relationship is a "go." Many of these early models were not very successful at predicting eventual mate selection or relationship success. Initial attraction, for example, is a very poor predictor of the eventual "success" of a marriage. However, these early models provided the framework for later, more complex models.

### Winch's Complementary Needs Model

One early and historically important model is the *complementary needs model* developed by sociologist Robert Winch (1958). Winch argued that homogamy of social characteristics is a strong influence on marital choice, but only for preliminary screening to determine a field of eligible spouses. Past the preliminary screening, partners seek out one primary characteristic in a partner: complementary needs. Two needs are complementary if the process of satisfying partner A's needs also satisfies the needs of partner B. For example, partner A enjoys being submissive, and partner B enjoys being dominant. Or, partner A likes to work on the car, and partner B needs someone to keep her car in good running condition. Despite its initial appeal, most researchers other than Winch have failed to find empirical support for the theory (Cate & Lloyd, 1992). In his explanation for the lack of support for Winch's theory, Murstein (1986) argues that people are not always aware of their needs. Even if they are, they do not always select mates based on those needs. Finally, research indicates that people's ideal partners are often more like their ideal selves, rather than someone who is different (Murstein).

### Murstein's Stimulus–Value–Role Model

Researchers soon surmised that people progress toward long-term commitments by filtering *various* pieces of information concerning compatibility, not just one. Further, people filter information at various stages in the relationship. This thinking led to filter theories and stage models of mate selection. Earlier in the chapter, we discussed one example of a stage model, Knapp and Vangelisti's (2000) progression of relationship stages on the path toward marriage.

Another popular stage model is Murstein's stimulus–value–role (SVR) model (Figure 5.1).

SVR is an exchange theory suggesting that in a free-choice situation, attraction and interaction depend on the exchange of assets and liabilities that each partner brings to the relationship. Assets are commodities (i.e., behaviors and qualities) the individual possesses that are capable of rewarding another. Liabilities are behaviors or qualities associated with an individual that are costly to others. The variables that can influence the course of development of the relationship can be classified under three categories: stimulus, value comparison, and role.

On first contact, people are in the *stimulus stage*. Here, people form first impressions based on physical appearance, status, poise, or other readily available information

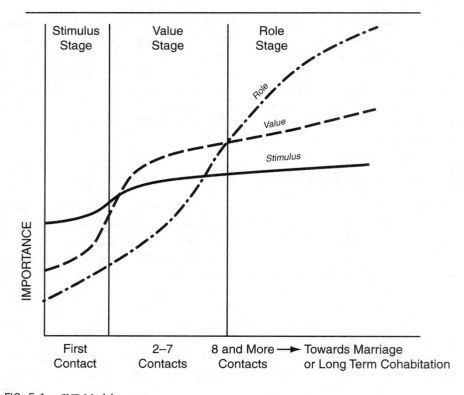

FIG. 5.1. SVR Model

*Note.* From B. I. Murstein, *Paths to Marriage*, p. 135, copyright © 1986 by Sage. Reprinted with permission of Sage Publications, Inc.

involving career, reputation, and professional aspirations. This stage is crucial because if one person does not possess sufficient stimuli or assets to attract the other, no further contact will be sought. In the *value comparison* stage, approximately contacts 2 to 7 in Murstein's initial research, the partners focus on attitudes, beliefs, needs, and desires. Stimulus issues are still a concern; however, value comparisons take center stage. Partners gather information through verbal interaction, saving the most intimate, controversial values until the later contacts. If couples have survived the stimulus and value stages, they have established a reasonably good relationship.

The primary focus now, in contacts 8 and beyond, turns to whether they can function in compatible roles. A primary feature of the *role stage* is evaluating whether the course of one partner's roles fits with respect to the other partner's roles. For example, if partner A sees herself going on to medical school and practicing medicine in an underdeveloped nation, will partner B be able to achieve his role desires in that location? Murstein suggests that successfully completing each stage prepares a couple for marriage, although some couples continue to work on the factors related to these stages throughout a marriage, and many couples do marry without experiencing each stage.

Murstein has found support for his theory (1986), although the theory has not been well supported by others. The theory has also been critiqued on the grounds that some of the stage boundaries seem arbitrary or have little theoretical justification (Cate, 1992). For example, some couples may consider roles before values or along with values. Further the timing of each stage may vary by couple. Still, SVR is one of the most well-developed stage models. Many of the criticisms against it are critiques that pertain to stage models in general. Duck (1998), for example, wrote, "I now realize that filtering theories [or stage theories] overemphasize thought and cognition, and they really only propose a more sophisticated sequence of motors to be switched on" (p. 74). In other words, the stage models may just be a more expanded version of the early one-dimensional "switch-on" models, and there still remain questions regarding why the stages are ordered as they are. In response, Murstein (1987) has suggested that couples realistically gather information regarding each stage throughout the relationship. However, a growing dissatisfaction with the stage models motivated the development of interpersonal process models.

## Interpersonal Process Models

Static factors such as social similarity and attitudinal similarity may influence the early development of relationships. However, interpersonal process models of courtship recognize that the actual interaction within relationships is the primary force in the long-term development of relationships. Interpersonal process models also acknowledge that courtship is affected by multiple variables and that there are multiple paths to marriage. Relationships do not necessarily change in linear stages.

One group of researchers (Huston, Surra, Fitzgerald, & Cate, 1981; Surra, 1987; Surra et al., 2004) popularized a method for retrospectively studying changes in commitment leading up to marriage and reasons for such changes. Specifically, the researchers used a graphing method in which they asked participants to report how likely (e.g., 70% chance) it was that they would marry their partner at certain points in time or after certain relationship events (e.g., first kiss, first holiday together, and first big fight). They

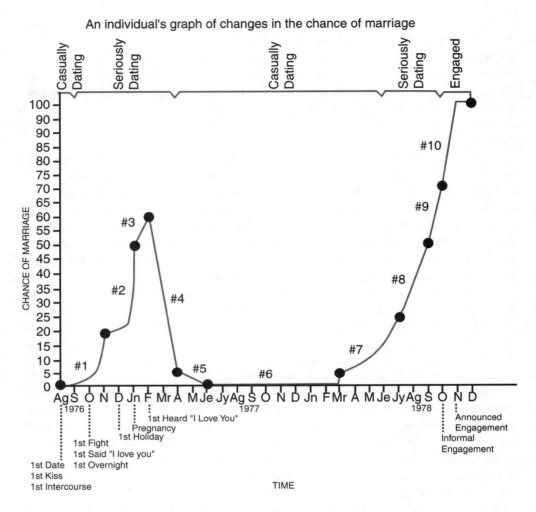

FIG. 5.2.    Surra's (1987) Method of Graphing Turning Points in Commitment

*Note.* From C. A. Surra, *Journal of Social and Personal Relationships*, 4, pp. 17–33, copyright © 1987 by Sage. Reprinted with permission of Sage Publications.

also asked participants to report what processes (e.g., conflict, preconceived beliefs, events with special meaning, and self-disclosure) affected upturns or downturns in their certainty toward marriage. This research was inspired by the work of Bolton (1961), who advocated studying subjective inferences about relationship development as a counterpart to objective inferences made by researchers. Figure 5.2 depicts an example of the method used to graph turning points.

Using these methods, Surra and her colleagues identified four courtship patterns: (a) *accelerated types*, in which partners moved gradually and rapidly in their certainty toward marriage; (b) *accelerated–arrested types*, in which partners moved rapidly toward marriage early on, but lost some momentum later; (c) *intermediate types*, in which partners progressed steadily toward marriage, but at a more moderate pace; and (d) *prolonged types*, in which partners had unusually long and sometimes rocky courtships.

These retrospective research techniques have spawned numerous other researchers to "take an insider's perspective, and examine individuals' own explanations for their decisions about marriage" (Surra & Hughes, 1997, p. 5). Attention is focused specifically on the turning points that affect commitment in relationships (e.g., Baxter & Bullis, 1986; Baxter & Erbert, 1999; Baxter & Pittman, 2001; Siegart & Stamp, 1994; Surra & Hughes). In other words, turning points are critical events that are perceived by the partners to have affected the trajectory of the relationship. Some turning points affect the relationship positively (e.g., saying "I love you") and others affect it negatively (e.g., finding out your partner went on a date with someone else). Finding out negative information often increases uncertainty in the relationship (Planalp & Honeycutt, 1985). Surra and Hughes found that more than half of couples experience unpredictable and nonlinear relational trajectories, as indicated by their significant turning points. Surra and her colleagues (Surra, Arizzi, & Asmussen, 1988; Surra & Hughes) also found that the turning points or reasons for changes in relationship commitment represent some predominant themes, namely, relationship-driven reasons and event-driven reasons.

*Relationship-driven commitments* reflect turning points based on "behavioral interdependence (e.g., time spent together and activities done together) and positive and negative attributions about the relationship (e.g., how comfortable the are with one another"; Surra & Hughes, 1997, p. 8). Commitment changes inspired by relationship-driven reasons are usually gradual changes that occur over time as partners thoughtfully consider their compatibility. Compared to event-driven commitments, relationship-driven commitments typically have fewer significant downturns, and less conflict and negativity, more satisfaction, and partners feel surer about their desires to be seriously involved. Surra and Hughes further argue that relationship-driven commitments follow the courtship patterns suggested by existing mate-selection models that emphasize compatibility testing over time. *Event-driven commitments* are marked by more frequent and dramatic downturns, followed by upturns, followed by downturns, and so on. That is, they have a more "rocky" path (Surra & Hughes). Changes in event-driven commitments are inspired by external events, possibly involving the social network (e.g., disapproval or approval of the parents), unexpected circumstances (e.g., pregnancy or a job change), or timing (e.g., it was time for me to get married). Event-driven commitments experience more conflict, less satisfaction, and more ambivalence about the relationship.

Studies based on the subjective insider's perspective have relied heavily on the theoretical perspective of relational dialectics (Baxter, 1990; Baxter & Erbert, 1999) and chaos theory (Weigel & Murray, 2000). Both theoretical perspectives acknowledge that relationships do not develop in a linear fashion. The relational dialectics perspective argues that in a relationship it is natural to experience opposing forces and events. For example, Surra and Hughes (1997) remark that some people may find the "passionate, changeable" nature of relationships appealing. Further, chaos theory explains how "seemingly insignificant events, such as a careless comment during an argument or the chance meeting with an old boyfriend, may become devastating for a couple. The careless comment or chance meeting may cause a ripple of other events that can drastically alter the course of the relationship" in a way that traditional mate-selection theories would not predict (Weigel & Murray, p. 430).

# COHABITATION

Prior to the 1960s, a majority of people in the United States considered cohabiting (i.e., living together in a nonmarital union) to be deviant behavior (Seltzer, 2000). More recently, over half of first marriages begin in cohabitation, and rates are even higher (e.g., over two thirds) for remarriages (Stewart, Manning, & Smock, 2003). Cohabitation is so common that many researchers view it as a stage of courtship (McGinnis, 2003; Seltzer, 2000). Indeed, many couples themselves say cohabitation is a necessary stage in their courtship (Bumpass, Sweet, & Cherlin, 1991; McGinnis, 2003). Cohabitation is often viewed as a way to "test" the relationship prior to marriage. However, Seltzer (2000) indicates that an increasing number of cohabitants see cohabitation as an end, not a "prelude" to marriage. Homosexual couples have historically seen cohabitation as an end, although same-sex marriages or commitment ceremonies are on the rise. For heterosexual couples, the trend to cohabit as an alternative to marriage is relatively recent. In the 1990s, only 35% of cohabitors who formed unions at age 25 or older married their partners within 3 years of starting to live together, compared with 60% in the 1970s (Seltzer). Given these statistics, it is not surprising that cohabitation is also a setting in which many couples bear their first child, if they have not done so prior to cohabitation. For some in the White community and many in the African American community, cohabitation follows the birth of children (Pinsof, 2002). However, in the African American community especially, many couples do not choose to cohabit after or before the birth of the child (Pinsof). Child rearing is becoming increasingly independent of cohabitation or marriage.

In some cases, cohabitation has been hypothesized to contribute to a decline in the number of divorces. As Bumpass and Lu (2000) argue, some "high-risk" relationships that would have been sure to end in divorce instead dissolve during cohabitation. However, researchers have consistently found that marriages preceded by cohabitation are more likely to end in separation or divorce (Bumpass & Lu; Sweet & Bumpass, 1992). Is this really true? And if so, why or in what instances? To answer these questions, we explore the validity of the arguments that "people who cohabit are different" *and* that "cohabitation changes people" (Seltzer, 2000).

## People Who Cohabit Are Different

There are three primary hypotheses to explain the idea that people who cohabit are different from those who do not cohabit. The first hypothesis argues that the positive relationship between cohabitation and marital instability is an artifact of *union duration* (Cohan & Kleinbaum, 2002). This argument is based on the evidence that marital satisfaction typically declines over time in a relationship. If it is the case that cohabiting causes couples to delay marriage, compared to noncohabitants, then cohabitants are further along the trajectory toward relational decline. The union duration hypothesis has received only mixed support (Cohan & Kleinbaum).

Another explanation for the higher rates of marital instability among cohabitators is *selection effects* (Bumpass & Sweet, 1989; Cohan & Kleinbaum, 2002). Selection effects refer to the idea that many people who cohabit also possess characteristics that are risk factors for divorce: lower income, less education, parental divorce, being non-White, younger age, lower religiosity, premarital pregnancy and childbirth, and greater acceptance of divorce (Cohan & Kleinbaum). According to the selection effects explanation, marital instability is not a result of cohabitation per se, but is related instead to the kind of people who tend to cohabit. There is some support for this argument. However, as cohabitation has become more normative, some of the characteristics that once separated cohabitors from noncohabitors are gradually dissipating. In particular, cohabitors who intend to marry do not differ greatly from noncohabiting couples with regard to many of these characteristics (Skinner, Bahr, Crane, & Call, 2002). Still, some propose that even when these selection characteristics are controlled, people who cohabit may be at greater risk for divorce than those who do not (Cohan & Kleinbaum).

A third hypothesis, the *social context* explanation, contends that cohabitors receive less social support for their relationship than do conventional couples. Dykstra (1993) found that cohabitors received less support from their families. Friends and family may either pressure the cohabitating couple to marry or, to the contrary, deny the relationship the respect offered to a married couple. Marriage ceremonies formally invite friends and family into a supportive context for the relationship, and decisions to cohabit are often individual decisions that do not explicitly invite family support. However, Skinner et al. (2002) reveal that short-term cohabitating couples (i.e., couples living together until they get married) are not as stigmatized by their social networks as are long-term cohabitors. Many short-term cohabitators express intentions to marry and have social networks that accept cohabitation as a stage of relationship development. Such couples that cohabit for a short term have marital quality similar to married couples that do not cohabit (Skinner et al.). Evidence seems to indicate that *some* cohabitors, particularly long-term cohabitors, lack external support for their relationship, which contributes to relational instability.

## Cohabitation Changes People

Brines and Joyner (1999) argue that cohabitation inhibits joint investment in the relationship. They found, for example, that in comparison to married couples, cohabitators were more likely to emphasize autonomy, equality, and fairness with regard to a number of relationship issues involving time, household chores, and money. It appears that many cohabitators keep careful watch over their investment in the relationship and the balance of exchange between partners. Without a formal relationship contract (i.e., a marriage contract), partners can theoretically leave at any time. The uncertainty of the relationship's future, says Brines and Joyner, motivates people to monitor how much they should invest in an uncertain relationship. That is, they take on a quid pro quo attitude (i.e., You scratch my back and I'll scratch yours). Although people in marriages are not immune to it, this attitude may be especially prevalent in cohabitating relationships. As Gottman (1999) contends, "unhappy couples are the ones who keep count of positives given and received, whereas happy couples are positive unconditionally" (p. 12). In sum, cohabitation may breed less joint commitment and investment in the relationship and more acceptance of divorce.

Do spouses who cohabited prior to marriage have poorer communication in their marriages compared to those who did not cohabit? Cohan and Kleinbaum (2002) directly addressed this question in one of the first studies on cohabitation to examine marital behavior and communication through observation. They found that premarital cohabitation is associated with more "destructive and divisive" communication (e.g., verbal aggression, coercion, negative escalation) during problem solving. Spouses who cohabited before marriage were less successful at providing support to their partners and soliciting support from them (Cohan & Kleinbaum). Both couples with single and multiple cohabitation experiences exhibited poorer communication in their marriages than those with no cohabitation experience. However, people with multiple cohabitation experiences were worse off than those with just a single cohabitation experience with their spouse. Similarly, Skinner et al. (2002) found that not all cohabitating unions are the same. Spouses who cohabit for a short term, with a clear intention to marry, are more like married couples who did not cohabit than long-term cohabitors. Long-term cohabitors usually have a heightened level of uncertainty about the future of their relationship.

## CONCLUSION

The vast majority of people marry, or at least cohabit with an intimate partner, sometime in their life. Pairing with a mate depends on individual, dyadic, and external factors. Individual factors such as relationship readiness, mate preferences, and individual beliefs are influential. For example, individuals who marry young or who have negative self and relationship beliefs have less successful relationships. Over the last half-century, individuals' mate preferences have evolved such that individuals now place less priority on chastity and cooking and housekeeping and more emphasis on physical attractiveness, financial resources, and mutual love and attraction.

Courtship, however, is not a one-way street. Our mates must choose us as well. Together, potential partners consider dyadic factors such as assortive matching, leisure and role compatibility, and dyadic interaction. In particular, the interaction between partners constitutes a relationship reality and relationship norms that will continue with the couple over time. One of the most important conclusions from this chapter is that premarital communication prior to marriage directly sets the stage for marital interaction.

Although partners create a relationship culture, their relationship is not in a vacuum. The external environment impacts mate parings. People must deal with external circumstances that affect a partner's availability as well as pressure against or support for the relationship from the couple's social network. Couples are better off when they have a supportive social network.

With the multitude of factors that affect mate parings, researchers have struggled to construct models of mate selection. Several prominent models of mate selection became popular during the last century, for example, evolutionary psychology, social exchange, stage, and interpersonal process models. These models have met varying degrees of support and are still being developed. Models that reflect the communication and psychological complexities of courtship are most useful.

Another major change over the last few decades is the increase of cohabitation prior to marriage. Cohabitation is so common that some now consider it to be a stage of relationship development. Not all cohabiting relationships are the same, and people who are long-term or multiple cohabitors seem to be at the most risk for relationship problems. As a follow-up to our study of courtship and mate selection, we explore in chapter 6 the communication behaviors that help to maintain marriages and intimate partnerships over time.

CHAPTER SIX

# Marriage and Intimate Partnerships

Approximately 90% of Americans expect to marry at some point in their lives, and most expect their marriages to be successful (DeFrain & Olson, 1999). But what does it mean for a marriage to be successful? Are successful marriages simply ones that remain intact for multiple years? Common sense suggests that marital success is about more than just remaining married. One is not hard pressed to find couples that are married, but not happily married or committed to their marriage. In this chapter, we begin by examining what makes for a successful marriage. Next, we explore how successful marriages are maintained over time. Work by some of the best researchers in marital communication focuses attention on the behaviors and perceptions characteristic of spouses in successful marriages. In other words, how do successfully married spouses behave and communicate in their marriages, or how do they think about their marriages so as to set themselves apart from less successful spouses? Finally, how specific is the "formula" for a successful marriage or intimate partnership? Is there more than one way to make a marriage work? Our examination of various "couple types" proves that there is more than one way for intimate partnerships to work. Although there are some general principles common to successful marriages, not all successful couples approach relational processes in the same manner. We also explore similarities and differences in heterosexual and homosexual intimate relationships. We close the chapter by examining whether the same things that make for success early in a marriage work in long-term marriages.

## WHAT IS MARITAL SUCCESS?

Throughout history, marital success has been judged according to both institutional and companionate criteria. Institutional criteria measure the extent to which marriage meets the instrumental needs and desires of an individual and society. For example, does the marriage preserve socioeconomic structure, produce children, or uphold religious tradition? Companionate criteria measure the extent to which marriage fulfills psychological needs and desires, including emotional security, happiness, intimacy, or, as Cooper (1999) describes, the "sentiments" of marriage (p. 22). Some scholars argue that a little over a century ago an extreme historical shift took place, in which the sentiments of romantic love usurped institutional considerations, particularly in the Western world (e.g., Shorter, 1975). Other moderate perspectives argue that at most any point in history, marital success has required attention to both institutional and companionate goals (Cooper; Orbuch, Veroff, Hassan, & Horrocks, 2002). Today, societal judgments of marital success in the United States heavily emphasize companionship, intimacy, and sentiment, although institutional criteria are often still considered. The extent to which spouses favor companionate criteria over institutional criteria appears to be influenced, in part, by cultural context. For example, mutual love and attraction appear to be valued in most all cultures; however, spouses with individualist self-construals place an even greater emphasis on their socioemotional connection and the expression of romantic love than do spouses with collectivist self-construals (Ting-Toomey, 1991).

## Researchers' Judgments of Marital Success

Researchers commonly judge marital success with one or more of the following measures: stability and duration, satisfaction and adjustment, and commitment. *Stability* refers to whether a marriage remains intact or dissolves (Wright, Nelson, & Georgen, 1994), and duration refers to the number of years the marriage remains intact. Currently, marriages in the United States have around a 50% likelihood of remaining intact until the death of one of the spouses. In chapter 11, we discuss the dramatic increase in the divorce rate over the past half-century and reasons for the rising divorce rate. Being in a stable marriage does not guarantee that spouses will be satisfied with or committed to their marriage. For a variety of reasons, spouses may remain in a marriage though they lack satisfaction or certain types of commitment. For example, some spouses say they remain married "for the children." It is also plausible that a marriage may become unstable (i.e., it may dissolve), even when one or both of the partners remains committed or even satisfied.

*Satisfaction* and *adjustment* are also used to assess marital success. Satisfaction refers to the extent to which a partner subjectively feels enjoyment, contentment, and love in the relationship (Hendrick, 1988). Compared to satisfaction, adjustment is defined more broadly. Adjustment refers to whether spouses have mastered the tasks necessary for marriage (Wright et al., 1994), so that they are not only satisfied but also skilled in dealing with marital issues such as agreement, conflict, expression of affection, or companionate activities (Spanier, 1976). Considerable evidence suggests that martial satisfaction and adjustment fluctuate over the course of the marriage, with the largest declines in satisfaction occurring in the early years of marriage. Reasons for the rise and fall of marital satisfaction and adjustment over the life span are further discussed in chapters 10 and 11.

Although researchers have traditionally examined marital satisfaction and adjustment with much more vigor than commitment, the trend toward examining *commitment* as a measure of marital success is rapidly increasing. In the 1990s, Johnson proposed three separate dimensions to commitment that could be measured separately: personal commitment, moral commitment, and structural commitment (Johnson, 1991; Johnson, Caughlin, & Huston, 1999). *Personal commitment* refers to a person's desire for staying in a relationship and is affected by one's attraction to the partner, the relationship, and the couple identity. *Moral commitment* involves the moral obligation one feels to remain in a relationship. One may feel morally obligated to a set of values, to another person, or to the particular value of consistency. *Structural commitment* consists of the constraints or barriers to leaving a relationship. Constraints could include a lack of alternative partners, pressure from one's social network to remain in the relationship, an unwillingness to enter the procedural tasks of ending a relationship, or an unwillingness to part from the time and resources put into the relationship.

Overall, researchers generally assume that marital success is marked by stability, along with high marital satisfaction and adjustment and commitment. Although stability, satisfaction and adjustment, and the various types of commitment have been found to be separate constructs that measure different aspects of a relationship, there are still moderate to high correlations among these measures (Flanagan et al., 2002; Flora, 1998). In other words, it is likely that high satisfaction, high commitment, and high stability are yoked together for most couples, even though researchers can find several exceptions to this case.

## Spouses' Judgments of Marital Success

Along with researchers, spouses obviously have personal standards for gauging the success of their marriage that may or may not correspond with researchers' conceptualizations of marital success. To further complicate judgments of marital success, spouses' sentiments about their marriage vacillate over the course of time. For example, when reflecting on their marriage, some spouses can specifically point to "good" years and "bad" years in their marriage. Dialectical tensions push and pull at spouses' feelings about the marriage. Sahlstein and Baxter (2001) describe dialectical tensions regarding commitment. They point out that changing feelings and contradictions concerning commitment can be manifested in two different ways. *Antagonistic contradictions* represent two partners who feel differently about a relationship force or sentiment. For example, spouses may each feel different levels of commitment toward the relationship at one given point in time. Antagonistic contradictions represent "a person against a person" (Sahlstein & Baxter, 2001, p. 117). Nonantagonistic contradictions represent two parties who together recognize the existence of relational contradictions, and they work through those contradictions mutually. For example, the spouses simultaneously experience a desire to renew their commitment or to stress commitment to other things. Nonantagonistic contradictions represent "a force against a force" (Sahlstein & Baxter, 2001, p. 117). The major difference is that in antagonistic contradictions, the spouses are "not on the same page." They each feel differently about the relationship. In nonantagonistic contradictions. the spouses' feelings change over time, but they change together. Spouses' ability to deal with dialectical tensions concerning commitment in a compatible, nonantagonistic way is related to their marital satisfaction.

## Predicting and Understanding Marital Success

The next question is what predicts marital success? Within empirical research, there is a long tradition of using *sociodemographic* and *intrapersonal* factors to predict marital success. Sociodemographic factors such as age at marriage, religiosity, socioeconomic status, and intrapersonal factors such as neuroticism or trait anxiety have been linked with varying degrees to marital success (Caughlin, Huston, & Houts, 2000; Karney & Bradbury, 1997). For example, divorce is negatively correlated with marrying at a later age and frequent attendance at religious services, and marital satisfaction is negatively correlated with neuroticism and trait anxiety. Even today, sociodemographic and intrapersonal factors can be fruitful predictors of divorce or marital satisfaction.

Huston, Caughlin, Houts, Smith, and George (2001) argue that spouses bring both positive and negative intrapersonal attributes into marriage. These attributes, for instance, family history or personality, endure stably over time. People start out their marriages with these attributes and continue their marriages with them. In fact, Huston et al.'s *enduring dynamics* model argues that most partners enter into their marriage with their "eyes open" to their partner's and relationship's faults. The effects of these attributes are also relatively constant over time, meaning they impact the couple early in the marriage as well as later in the marriage (Karney & Bradbury, 1997). For example, "a personality trait like neuroticism may be associated with lower marital satisfaction at all times. . . . In contrast, interpersonal processes, reflected in variables such as marital interaction, are likely to develop over time as marital satisfaction develops" (Karney & Bradbury, p. 1088). Are these intrapersonal processes capable of affecting interpersonal processes? Huston et al. found evidence for an emotional contagion process, whereby wives who are married to husbands with high trait anxiety essentially "catch" their husband's bad moods. And do these bad moods affect the spouses' interaction? Such questions beg for interpersonal interaction to be studied along with intrapersonal factors. Alone, sociodemographic or intrapersonal factors do not fully reveal the actual causes of marital breakup or changes in satisfaction.

Beginning in the 1950s and exploding in the 1970s, social scientists introduced *interpersonal process* models of marriage. In combination with intrapersonal models, interpersonal models helped to more fully explore the causes of marital breakup and distress (Gottman & Notarius, 2002). These models were focused on understanding the nature of communication between spouses, the impact of communication on the marriage, and the influences on communication patterns within the marriage. Sometimes, interpersonal processes researchers study marital interaction by directly observing spouses' interactions within the marriage. These types of investigations commonly involve observing spouses' interact either in a research laboratory or in a naturalistic setting. Admittedly, interactions in the laboratory may not reflect naturalistic interaction, but naturalistic interaction is difficult to observe. Overall, observational methods afford considerable precision for researchers to assess specific phenomenon.

Besides direct observation, researchers can also ask couples to report about their own marital interaction through methods such as surveys, diaries, or interviews. Although often not as precise or controlled as direct observation, these methods allow researchers to study a greater scope of marital behaviors and, in the case of diaries, may better capture everyday interactions (Huston et al., 2001; Noller & Feeney, 2004). Further, if both spouses keep separate diaries of their interaction, researchers can link one partner's reports with the other partner's evaluations and check for biased reporting (Caughlin & Huston, 2002).

### The Core Triad of Balance and the Emotional Bank Account

In 1999, Gottman articulated his "core triad of balance" theory, which argues that marital interaction should be understood from three domains of human experience: behavior, perception, and physiology (p. 33). Behavior refers to the verbal and nonverbal behaviors that spouses exchange. Perception refers to the way people cognitively process behaviors and events. Two people may perceive the same behavior differently. The domain of physiology refers to the way one's body feels and functions (e.g., heart rate and breathing) as a result of behaviors and perceptions in the relationship. According to Gottman, these three domains are overlapping, interactive, and influenced by interpersonal processes. Furthermore, marital success rests on regulating each domain at a "stable, steady state" (Gottman, p. 33). One could think back to the systems theory notion of homeostasis (see chap. 2). When the negative threshold of any domain in the triad is exceeded, the marital system becomes unstable (Carrère, Buehlman, Gottman, Coan, & Ruckstuhl, 2000).

Several researchers, including Gottman (1999) and Markman have used the analogy of an emotional bank account in marriage. For example, in Markman's relational bank account model of marital satisfaction and erosion (RBA; Clements, Cordova, Markman, & Laurenceau, 1997; Markman, 1984), positive relational behaviors (e.g., affection, intimacy, compliments, and agreements) are equivalent to "deposits" in the account. Negative relational behaviors (e.g., conflicts, disagreements, criticisms, and complaints) function as "withdrawals." Marital satisfaction is related to the "balance" of the RBA. In order to keep a positive balance, spouses must make more deposits to the relationship than withdrawals. Gottman has even gone so far as to say that most stable, happy couples maintain around a 5:1 ratio of positive to negative behaviors, and that the ratio appears to be even larger for these couples when they discuss nonconflict topics such as the events of the day. Some marital researchers take issue with this ratio, claiming that it is too simplistic or even dangerous to reduce positive and negative behaviors to a ratio. Not all scholars arrive at the same ratio, and positives and negatives may not cancel each other out so neatly. Further, some argue that it can be difficult to identify what a positive or negative behavior is. As Gottman and Levenson (2000) found, anger is not always a destructive emotion in marriage. Some expressions of anger may lead to positive outcomes later on in the marriage. Still, Gottman's general message is important. The relationships of stable, happy couples are defined by positivity more than negativity, from both the spouses' perspective and the researchers' perspective.

Further explaining the progression toward marriage, Markman (1984) observed:

> The bank account model predicts that all premarital couples begin their marriage with a history of positive interactions (or they probably would not be planning marriage). However, these positive interactions are not necessarily the product of good communication. For example, premarital couples may be "in love with love" and the idea of getting married, and these romantic feelings screen out negative events and highlight positive events. (p. 264)

What Markman suggests is that premarital couples view their relationship through rose-colored glasses. The warning signs for eventual marital distress are there, but they just do not look at them. Noller and Feeney (2002) found that women commonly proceed with marriage even when they are aware of and dissatisfied with maladaptive conflict processes in the relationship. Individual investment in the relationship and the wedding as well as societal pressure cause some engaged people to replace their doubts with unrealistic optimism. In summary, relationships are not only about behaviors but also about how people perceive and cognitively edit those behaviors.

In the next sections, we explore a primary question of this chapter: How do couples maintain a relationship? We examine this question by looking at the behaviors and perceptions that help maintain marriages. Of Gottman's (1999) three domains of marriage, (behavior, perception, and physiology), behavior and perception have received the most attention from communication researchers. Upcoming chapters explore the third domain, physiology (see chap. 14), as well as traits and processes linked to marital distress and divorce that emerge or endure in marriages (chaps. 10 and 11).

## BEHAVIORS AND RELATIONSHIP MAINTENANCE

To study the behaviors used to maintain intimate relationships, researchers have conducted countless studies using both observation of spouses' behavior and self-report methods. Results of these studies have prompted some researchers to summarize and categorize relationship maintenance behaviors. For example, Stafford, Dainton, and Haas (2000) draw from a well-developed program of research (see Canary & Stafford, 2001) to present the behaviors that married couples report using to maintain their marriage. These maintenance behaviors are described in Table 6.1.

Similarly, Gottman's long-standing program of research identifies seven principles that are characteristic of successful marriages. Table 6.2 describes the seven principles and provides examples.

The intent of relationship maintenance is for couples to enact the maintenance behaviors preemptively, rather than waiting until the health of the marriage has deteriorated. Contrary to popular belief, a majority of relationship maintenance behaviors are the seemingly small, routine behaviors that keep a healthy marriage going. Stafford et al. (2000) distinguish routine behaviors, which include the ordinary and even mundane behaviors that partners pursue on a daily basis, from strategic behaviors, which refer to behaviors that are "consciously and intentionally enacted to meet a particular goal—in this case, relational maintenance" (p. 307). It should be noted that neither Stafford et al. nor Gottman's (1999) lists of maintenance behaviors is meant to be exhaustive. The mass of literature on marriage provides other suggestions for behaviors that maintain a marriage. Nonetheless, these lists offer a starting point for studying maintenance behaviors in marriage. There is considerable overlap between the two lists. Most notably, both lists point to the importance of negotiating, through interaction, relational processes and influences such as (a) intimacy and affection and (b) conflict and roles.

### Communication Behaviors That Express Intimacy and Affection

Noller and Fitzpatrick (1993) summarize many of the ways partners express love to one another, including self-disclosure, nonmaterial evidence of love (e.g., expressing positive affect, support, and spending time together in joint activities and rituals), physical expressions of affection (e.g., hugging and kissing), tolerance of unpleasant aspects of the partner, and material evidence for love (e.g., giving gifts). Here, we explore some of these nonmaterial, communicative expressions of intimacy and affection.

TABLE 6.1
## Stafford, Dainton, and Hass (2000): Relationship Maintenance Scale

Assurances

1. I say "I love you."
2. I show my love for my partner.
3. I imply that our relationship has a future.
4. I tell my partner how much she or he means to me.
5. I talk about our plans for the future.
6. I stress my commitment to him or her.
7. I show him or her how much he or she means to me.
8. I talk about future events (e.g., having children or anniversaries or retirement).

Openness

9. I encourage my partner to share his or her feelings with me.
10. I simply tell my partner how I feel about the relationship.
11. I talk about my fears.
12. I disclose what I need or want from the relationship.
13. I like to have periodic talks about our relationship.
14. I am open about my feelings.
15. I talk about where we stand.

Conflict Management

16. I apologize when I am wrong.
17. I cooperate in how I handle disagreements.
18. I listen to my partner and try not to judge.
19. I am understanding.
20. I am patient and forgiving with my partner.

Shared Tasks

21. I help equally with the tasks that need to be done.
22. I offer to do things that aren't "my" responsibility.
23. I do my fair share of the work we have to do.
24. I perform my household responsibilities.
25. I do not shirk my duties.

Positivity

26. I act cheerful and positive around him or her.
27. I try to be upbeat when we are together.

Advice

28. I tell my partner what I think she or he should do about her or his problems.
29. I give him or her my opinion on things going on in his or her life.

Social Networks

30. I like to spend time with our same friends.
31. I focus on common friends and affiliations.

**TABLE 6.2**
Gottman's (1999) Seven Principles for Making Marriage Work

1. Enhance your love maps

   Description: Being intimately familiar with each other's world, remembering major events in each other's history and keeping updated on the facts and feelings of your spouse's world.

   Examples: My spouse is familiar with my current stresses.
   I feel that my spouse knows me pretty well.
   I can tell you in detail my first impressions of my partner.

2. Nurture fondness and admiration

   Description: Maintaining a sense that the other person is worthy of being respected and liked and expressing respect and liking.

   Examples: I can easily list three things I most admire about my partner.
   I often find some way to tell my partner "I love you."
   My partner appreciates the things I do in this marriage.

3. Turn toward each other

   Description: Responding to a partner's bids for attention, affection, humor, or support in both small and large ways.

   Examples: My partner is usually interested in hearing my views on things.
   We enjoy doing even the smallest things together, like folding laundry or watching TV.
   At the end of a day my partner is glad to see me.

4. Let your partner influence you

   Description: Letting your spouse influence your decision making by taking his or her feelings and opinions into account.

   Examples: I don't reject my spouse's opinions out of hand.
   I try to communicate respect even during our disagreements.
   I usually want my partner to feel that what he or she says really counts with me.

5. Solve your solvable problems

   Description: Identifying and solving those problems that are minor irritants or situational disagreements rather than letting them carry over to other areas of your lives.

   Techniques: Start up conflicts softly rather than harshly.
   Learn how to repair previous behavior.
   Monitor and regulate your negative affect (emotion).
   Learn how to compromise.
   Become more tolerant of each other's imperfections.

6. Overcome gridlock

   Description: Identifying and dealing with perpetual problems that will always be present in the marriage.

   Techniques: Explore the hidden issues that are causing the gridlock.
   Rather than solve the problem, learn to enter dialogue about these issue and share dreams behind the conflict.

(Continued)

**TABLE 6.2**

(Continued)

---

7. Create shared meaning

   Description:  Creating and sharing a relational culture with symbols and rituals that represent what it
   means to be a part of the relationship.

   Examples:    We share many of the same goals in our life together.
                We both value special celebrations (like birthdays, anniversaries, and family reunions).
                We have ways of becoming renewed and refreshed when we are burned out or fatigued.

---

*Note.* From *The Seven Principles for Making Marriage Work* by John M. Gottman, Ph.D., and Nan Silver, Copyright © 1999
by John M. Gottman, Ph.D., and Nan Silver. Used by permission of Crawn Publishers, a division of Random House, Inc.

### *Self-Disclosure and Secrecy*

As for self-disclosure, research indicates that not only is it crucial in the development of
dating relationships, but also self-disclosure continues to be important in marriage (Derlega, Metts, Petronio, & Margulis, 1993; see also chap. 4). As spouses grow and change over
the course of the marriage, self-disclosure is a means for them to stay connected. For example, compared to less satisfied couples, satisfied couples spend more time "debriefing"
each other about the events of the day (Vangelisti & Banski, 1993). As one might expect,
self-disclosure has frequently been related to greater emotional involvement (Rubin,
Hill, Peplau, & Dunkel-Schetter, 1980) and to greater relationship satisfaction (Derlega
et al.). Furthermore, Derlega et al. clarify that the quality of self-disclosure contributes
to marital satisfaction more so than the quantity of sharing. Some spouses spend a lot
of time together, but they do not really know each other. In other words, the spouses
are living emotionally parallel lives. Several of the maintenance behaviors described by
Stafford, Dainton, and Haas (2000; e.g., assurances and openness) and Gottman (1999;
e.g., enhancing love maps and nurturing fondness and admiration) rely on self-disclosure
as a means of increasing understanding and maintaining emotional intimacy. Indeed,
Montogomery (1981) defined quality communication in marriage as a "process by which
marriage partners achieve and maintain understanding of each other" (p. 21).

Is self-disclosure always related to marital satisfaction? Finkenauer and Hazam (2000)
found that in some limited situations, a lack of self-disclosure, or secrecy, may be positively related to marital satisfaction (see also chap. 3). For some couples, there may be
difficult topics or conflictive issues that are best left avoided. These difficult topics could
include criticisms (e.g., "you're really too fat") or issues that repeatedly lead to gridlocked
conflict. In these special cases, secrecy or restraint may stem from a partner's tolerance of
unpleasant aspects of the other. In other words, the secrecy may be a form of respect and
acceptance. Finkenauer and Hazam further suggest "people who are satisfied with their
marriage may be competent communicators who possess the skill to diagnose when to
use disclosure versus secrecy in a way that ensures relational satisfaction" (p. 259). Such
social skills involve decisions about whether the benefits of secrecy outweigh the costs

for the relationship. For sure, decisions to keep some things secret in a marriage may have immediate benefits, but long-term costs. Finkenauer and Hazam are careful to warn that individuals who use an extreme amount of secrecy or seem to have a disposition characterized by secrecy tend to be less satisfied with their marriages. Furthermore, the suspicion that one's partner keeps information from him or her is negatively associated with marital satisfaction. Negotiating self-disclosure is an important part of marriage, and, with only a few exceptions, high amounts of self-disclosure enhance emotional intimacy.

### Verbally Encoding Positive Affect and Support Messages

In addition to self-disclosure, there are several other nonmaterial ways of maintaining intimacy and expressing affection, many of which include the verbal and nonverbal encoding of positive affect and support as well as the decoding of affect and other emotional bids. Beginning with verbal behavior, Gottman's (1999) suggestion to "nurture fondness and affection" and Stafford et al.'s (2000) identification of "positivity" and "assurances" emphasize the importance of encoding verbal expressions of positive affect. Compared to other maintenance behaviors, positivity and assurances appear to be more influential in enhancing perceptions of marital satisfaction later on in the relationship (Weigel & Ballard-Reisch, 2001). That is, these behaviors have a strong carry over effect. Verbal expressions of positive affect and affirmation have been found to be especially important for husbands, who typically have a smaller social network from which to receive positive self-affirmations (Orbuch et al., 2002). Other ways spouses report communicating intimacy are calling their partner by public or private nicknames (e.g., Honey or Baby), teasing them in an affectionate or sexual way, or using other expressions idiosyncratic to the relationship (Noller & Fitzpatrick, 1993). Yet another way to build positive affect in a relationship is to offer verbal support for one's partner. Cutrona and Suhr (1994) found that one of the most common ways spouses support each other is by offering advice, welcomed advice, that is. The married couples in Stafford et al.'s study also reported that they offered advice to partners as a means of helping their partners and maintaining the marriage.

### Nonverbally Encoding and Decoding Intimacy and Affection

Compared to rewarding verbal behavior, encoding rewarding nonverbal behavior appears to be as important or even more so for marital satisfaction (Noller, 1992). A number of individual behaviors, such as gaze or touch, indicate conversational involvement and intimacy. Conversational involvement is just one way of "turning toward your partner" (i.e., responding to a partner's request to be attentive and engaged; Gottman & Silver, 1999; see chap. 4). For example, researchers have known for a long time that couples that score higher in romantic love engage in more eye contact (Rubin, 1970). More recent research has found that whether complaining to or complimenting one another, the eye contact of husbands is positively correlated with marital well-being, even more so than the eye contact of wives (Flora & Segrin, 2000a). Gottman (1994) found that husbands are particularly prone to withdraw from negative conflict interactions. If it is that case that husbands' eye contact communicates "I'm taking the time to be attentive to you," then it may be cherished by wives because it nonverbally indicates the very opposite of withdrawal—involvement.

Intimacy is also a function of nonverbal behaviors such as increased touch, increased facial expression, convergence of paralanguage, and tie signs (Patterson, 1988). Tie signs (Morris, 1977) are public displays of intimacy and commitment such as holding hands, putting arms around the other's waist, or wearing wedding rings. The use of these nonverbal behaviors to express intimacy varies in quantity and kind throughout the course of a marriage. For example, Guerrero and Andersen's (1991) study on public touch in romantic relationships found that touch had a curvilinear relationship with relational stage. Couples in early or late and stable stages of their relationship touched less in the waist and hand areas than did those in the intermediate stage of their relationship. By implication, married couples, presumed to have more stable and secure relationships, may not publicly touch as much as some dating couples who use public touch as a means of stating their newly increasing intimacy to their partner and social world. Married couples may also experience fluctuation in their amount of private touch over the course of the marriage. For example, in a study of women in the early years of marriage, Greenblat (1983) found that the frequency of intercourse declined from an average of nearly 15 times per month during the first years of marriage to about 6 times per month during the sixth year. There was, however, a wide frequency, ranging from 4 to 45 times per month for couples married less than 1 year. Though frequency of intercourse may vary over the course of the marriage, affection and physical closeness continue to be strong needs throughout the life span.

Just as the frequency and meaning of touch vary greatly among married couples, facial expressions are complex reflections of emotion in marriage. Relying on earlier work on facial expression by Ekman and Friesen (1978; see also Ekman, 2003), Gottman, Levenson, and Woodin (2001) examined what facial expressions reveal about marital quality. Previously, Ekman drew attention to two different types of smiles. The *Duchenne smile* (named after the researcher who first identified it) refers to a smile of genuine, felt happiness. The Duchenne smile activates the muscles not only around the mouth and cheeks to form a smile, but also most importantly the skin around the outer corner of the eye wrinkles. In an unfelt smile, or a "fake" smile, the mouth and cheek muscles move to a lesser degree and the eye muscles do not wrinkle. During videotaped interviews with married couples, Gottman et al. found a higher frequency of the genuine Duchenne smiles in spouses who had positive perceptions of their marriage. Spouses with poor perceptions of their marriage exhibited more unfelt smiles, as well as more facial expressions of contempt, anger, and fear.

Successfully encoding nonverbal messages is an important indicator and motivator of marital satisfaction, but accurately decoding nonverbal messages is arguably more important. Koerner and Fitzpatrick (2002b) found that for both husbands and wives, accurately decoding relational positive affect, and distinguishing it from nonrelational negative affect, is associated with greater marital satisfaction. *Relational affect* refers to affect about the relationship (i.e., caused by the relationship), whereas *nonrelational affect* refers to affect caused by something outside the relationship. Spouses benefit from being able to decode positive, relational affect and identify what their partner finds positive in the relationship. Koerner and Fitzpatrick explain that recognizing what is good allows a spouse to replicate that good behavior. For example, when a wife recognizes that her husband experiences positive affect when they make dinner together and share conversation over a meal, she can take measures to repeat that joint activity. Even more so than wives, husbands' satisfaction is positively affected by their ability to decode nonrelational negative affect in their wives' messages. That is, when a husband recognizes that his wife's negative affect is caused by something outside the relationship rather than him, he is better poised to be supportive rather than defensive.

### Joint Activities and Rituals

Finally, intimate partnerships are often maintained when the couple spends time together in joint activities and rituals. Stafford et al. (2000) report that spending time with shared social networks (e.g., shared friends) enhances the marital relationship. Other researchers have found that time spent together in joint activities, particularly leisure activities, is positively related to relational satisfaction (Canary, Stafford, Hause, & Wallace, 1993). Flanagan et al. (2002) suggest that one of the reasons joint activity can serve a protective function for relationships is because of the interdependence it encourages, and "more interdependence is theorized to lead to more closeness and commitment between partners" (p. 113). For example, Baldwin, Ellis, and Baldwin (1999) found that spouses who were both runners and ran together experienced above-average marital satisfaction. However, as we discussed in chapter 3, not all joint activities are relationship enhancing. For instance, one can imagine a couple that hates to play tennis together because they perpetually argue or become overly competitive. A growing amount of research suggests that the effect of joint activity on relationship satisfaction may be moderated by social skills and positivity (Flora & Segrin, 1998), expectations regarding the activity (Flanagan et al.), whether the activity is exciting and self-expanding versus boring or simply pleasant (Reissman, Aron, & Bergman, 1993), and whether the activity is interactive versus parallel or passive (Holman & Jacquart, 1988).

Shared rituals are a form of joint activity that possess the potential to be relationship enhancing, depending on many of the moderating variables just listed. Gottman (1999) suggests that rituals are a way a couple may create shared meaning, if the ritual represents something valued and positive in the relationship. Couples may have rituals for celebrating their anniversary (e.g., a weekend trip away to celebrate their love) or rituals for nursing a sick spouse back to health (e.g., making a favorite meal as a sign of support and care).

In summary there are many behavioral expressions of intimacy and affection that spouses use either routinely or strategically to maintain their marriage. Clearly, the needs for and means of sharing intimacy and affection vary by couple and over the course of a marriage. Negotiating the encoding and decoding of intimacy is a central part of marriage.

## Communication Behaviors Used to Negotiate Conflict and Roles

Maintaining any long-term intimate relationship requires partners to negotiate conflict and roles. The preponderance of data on conflict resolution indicates that it is one important determinant of marital success (Bradbury & Karney, 1993; Gottman, 1993a).

Researchers have identified specific conflict patterns predictive of divorce, and these patterns are examined in detail in chapter 11. The present chapter examines how couples approach conflict in order to maintain their marriage. Research indicates that successful marriages find ways to decrease risk factors and increase protective factors when dealing with conflict (Flanagan et al., 2002).

It is important to note that when dealing with conflict, partners in successful marriages *decrease* their risk factors, but they do not completely rid their marriage of risk factors. Even the best of marriages have times when partners reciprocate destructive negative affect, criticize (personally attack) one another, express contempt, become defensive, or stonewall (i.e., emotionally withdraw) during conversation. One of the ways successful couples distinguish themselves from unsuccessful couples is by maintaining a stable steady state, so that conflict behavior does not exceed a negative threshold (Gottman, 1999).

### Using Repair Attempts and Solving Solvable Problems

What then are the protective factors that successful marriages depend on when dealing with conflict? One of the most important factors is a couple's ability to effectively repair a situation when expressions of negative affect begin to get out of control and exceed the negative threshold (Gottman, 1999). Gottman explains that a repair attempt "can be almost anything, but it is generally the spouses acting as their own therapist. They comment on the communication itself, or they support and soothe one another, or they express appreciations to soften their complaints" (Gottman, p. 48). Other ways of soothing negative affect during conflict may include apologizing or expressing interest, humor, or affection (Gottman et al., 1998). Ultimately, repair attempts are difficult to define, because they tend to be very idiosyncratic to the couple. For example, breaking up a tense, conflictual moment with humor may work with one couple and infuriate another.

Many of the conflicts couples deal with are deeply rooted in value or personality differences. Such conflicts surface again and again, and often seem unsolvable to couples themselves. In a moment, we discuss how couples can deal with these perpetual problems. However, other problems in marriage are situational and theoretically solvable. Although not all couples have the ability to solve even those problems that are "solvable," successful couples rely on several tactics to approach such problems. Before we review those tactics, we first provide an example from Gottman and Silver (1999) of what a solvable problem is and an answer (pp. 136 and 139):

> The problem: Helena gets together with her friends every Monday night. Jonathan wants her to take a ballroom dancing class together with him, but the only night the class is held is Monday. Helena doesn't want to give up her girls' night out.
>
> The answer: They could switch off weekly between dancing class and Helena's girls' night out. Or maybe her friends would be willing to switch the night. Or Jonathan could find another dancing class on another night or on the weekend. Or one of them could simply agree not to push it.

The married couples in Stafford et al.'s (2000) study reported that they maintained their relationships by approaching conflict in the following ways: apologizing when they were wrong; cooperating to handle disagreements; listening without judgment to one another; being understanding, patient, and forgiving. Observational research confirms that in many cases couples do enact these behaviors when actually dealing with conflict. For example, Gottman (1999) has found that successful couples are more likely to (a) use repair attempts, which could include offering apologies; (b) accept influence and suggestions from the spouse (especially from the wife), which requires some degree of listening to one's partner; (c) compromise more, which involves cooperation, and (d) express less destructive negative affect (especially when starting up conflicts in the case of wives), which likely requires patience and forgiveness.

### Controversy Surrounding the Active Listening Model

Interestingly, strategies recommended by some therapists and textbooks for dealing with conflict now appear to have mixed findings or even no positive association with marital success. One such strategy is the active listening model. Since its inception in the 1970s, the active listening model has been highly influential in marital therapy. The active listening model involves using "I" statements versus "you" statements to express feelings during conflict. It also requires listeners to paraphrase and summarize the speaker's feelings and message content and then to validate the speaker's feelings. Active listening would sound like the following exchange:

**Speaker:** "I feel mad when you spend all your time playing golf every Sunday."
**Listener:** "It sounds like this makes you very mad. You'd like it if I spent more time at home on Saturdays. I can understand why this would make you upset."

Gottman et al. (1998) found that couples hardly used active listening during actual conflict, and when it was used, it predicted nothing. In other words, active listening did not hurt couples, but neither did it help couples like some scholars and therapists predict. For a listener, it is difficult and perhaps unrealistic to be empathic when one feels attacked by the other. Gottman (1999) argues that a therapist may be able to actively listen, but for a spouse, active listening asks one to do "emotional gymnastics" at the very moment one feels emotionally attacked. Indeed, even though spouses say that listening without judgment is one way they maintain their relationships, Sillars, Roberts, Dun, and Leonard (2001) found that spouses rarely take their partner's perspective during conflict. Even happy couples appear to respond in kind to negativity (e.g., they get angry and say what they feel in response) and forgo empathic responses to negativity. However, happy couples do not allow the negativity to escalate in a global way. That is, they do not harbor the conflict and let it seep into other areas of the marriage. Instead, they soon deescalate the negativity, perhaps with an idiosyncratic repair attempt, rather than with the formulaic active listening model. Other researchers, such as Stanley, Bradbury, and Markman (2000) counter that Gottman (1999) has overstated the case, and the active listening model still has merit, even if it is tough for couples to perform. However, evidence in support of the active listening model is mixed, and some feel it suggests a style of listening that is too scripted.

### Dealing With Perpetual Problems

Dealing with tough conflicts, according to Gottman (1999), relies on a deep fix that is rooted in the strength of the marital friendship. Developing a strong marital friendship requires having strong mutual respect and understanding for one another. The strength of the marital friendship is particularly important as couples try to deal with perpetual problems. Perpetual problems are "issues with no resolution that the couple has been dealing with for many years" (Gottman, p. 96). One might also call these problems "enduring" problems (Huston et al., 2001). Regardless, of the name, the point is that a great number of problems in marriage are perpetual ones, not solvable ones (Gottman; Roloff & Johnson, 2002). Examples of perpetual problems include dealing with personality, attitudinal, religious, or communication differences that seem to underlie conflicts in an intense way. These problems resurface again and again, and couples often become gridlocked. In other words, as soon as the topic arises, the couple comes to an emotional standstill and cannot even talk about the problem. Gottman and Silver (1999) provide an example of a perpetual problem and answer (pp. 136 and 138):

> The problem: Elise wants to spend less time with Joel and more time with her friends. Joel says this makes him feel abandoned. Elise says that she needs time away from him. He seems very needy to her, and she's feeling suffocated by him.
>
> The answer: This problem suggests a core difference between Elise and Joel in their personalities and what they need from each other to feel close and connected. This difference is unlikely to change—they'll just need to adjust to it.

Gottman explains that even successful couples do not overcome most perpetual problems, but their strong respect for one another encourages them to find ways to dialog about the problems, understand why the differences exist, and discover ways to live with the differences so that both persons' desires can be honored to some extent. Caughlin et al. (2000) are careful to clarify that successful couples do not necessarily *accommodate* to perpetual problems. That is, they do not just forget about the problem and try to be happy. Rather, they find ways to *endure* the problem when it surfaces (e.g., through dialogue and respect), in a way that keeps the problem from escalating.

An ugly alternative to the "respect" approach to perpetual problems is the "control" approach. In their research on relational control in marriage, Millar and Rogers (1988; see also Rogers, 2001) define *one-up messages* (i.e., attempts to direct or assert rights), *one-down messages* (i.e., requests or acceptances of another's control movements), and *one-across messages* (i.e., neutral messages). The higher the proportion of one-up messages, the more domineering a person is. However, being domineering does not lead to being dominant. Being dominant requires another to accept one's control movements (i.e., match your one-ups with one-downs). Two spouses who issue a high proportion of one-up messages are both domineering, but neither is dominant. According to Rogers, this battle of domineeringness leads to "an ongoing unsettledness over relational issues" (p. 27). There is an inverse relationship between domineeringness and marital and communication satisfaction, especially when wives are domineering. Couples who deal with perpetual problems by constantly trying to control and change the other in a domineering way only exacerbate the perpetual problem.

### Negotiating Roles

One topic that often sparks conflicts betweens spouses is how to arrange roles in a marriage. A considerable amount of research has examined issues of task sharing in couples. The married couples in Stafford et al's (2000) study reported that they attempted to share household tasks as a means of maintaining their relationship. An increasing amount of research has found that helping out with household tasks has many relational benefits because it can communicate affection or commitment to the spouse (see Canary & Stafford, 2001). Dual-career husbands, especially, are helping out with household tasks now more than in previous decades (DeFrain & Olson, 1999; Gilbert, 1993). Juxtaposed with South and Spitze's (1994) finding that women complete 70% of the housework even if they work outside the home, Canary and Stafford review a collection of research that indicates a growing equity in the division of household labor. However, household chores still have a tendency to be more gender segregated than are child-rearing tasks or financial management tasks (DeFrain & Olson). Even so, Canary and Stafford highlight Gilbert's assertion that "Men's greater involvement in relationships, caring, and parenting likely is the hallmark of the 1990s" (p. 43). In marriages where husbands and wives are working toward a more equitable relationship, husbands appear to be more willing to share power and accept the influence of their wives, who are encouraging (hopefully by requests that are introduced without harsh negative affect) shared involvement in household tasks.

DeFrain and Olson (1999) estimate that nearly two thirds of women in the United States work outside the home, some as single mothers and others in dual-career couples. The nature of the dual-earner couple is further explained by Rosenfeld, Bowen, and Richman (1995), who found three types of dual-earner couples, all differing in their adjustment to demands at work and demands at home. The *collapsing* couple type involved a wife who was poorly adjusted to her demands at home and at work, and a husband who was poorly adjusted to his demands at work and only moderately adjusted to his demands at home. In the *work-directed* couple type, the husband and wife were both well-adjusted to their roles at work, with the wife moderately adjusted to her demands at home and the husband poorly adjusted. In the *traditional* couple type, the wife was highly adjusted at home, but poorly adjusted at work. In other words, she may have put her family first and career second. Rosenfeld et al. found that the work-directed marriage was most positive for wives. These wives had fulfilling careers and were able to at least moderately keep up at home. However, some husbands in the work-directed marriage may feel they must "sacrifice" a traditional wife. The traditional marriage appeared to be most positive for husbands' home and work adaptation. Because their wives had only a secondary commitment to their jobs, husbands in the traditional marriage could fully respond to their career demands as their wives picked up the load at home. However, Rosenfeld et al. point out "there is no inherent reason this trade-off needs to be the wife's 'sacrifice'" (p. 281).

Flanagan et al. (2002) argue that relationship behaviors reflecting teamwork and sacrifice can be protective factors in marriage. With regard to roles, however, one couple may define the concepts of teamwork and sacrifice different from another. To one couple, teamwork may mean splitting household chores equally. To another, teamwork could mean one spouse taking care of the home and the other working outside the home. Though they play different roles, both spouses perceive their roles as benefiting the joint team effort. Perceptions are also pivotal to the concept of sacrifice. Sacrifice can enhance marital quality as long as personal sacrifices are perceived as contributing to the greater good of the relationship rather than being harmful to the self (Whitton & Stanley, 1999). Thus, behaviors and perceptions are intricately tied, and we soon explore the important role of perceptions in marriage.

## PERCEPTION AND RELATIONSHIP MAINTENANCE

At the same time spouses exchange behaviors with one another, they cognitively process those behaviors and their sentiment for the relationship. The very same behavior may be perceived differently depending on the spouse and the marriage. Upon receiving flowers from her husband, one wife may perceive the gift as an indication of her husband's thoughtfulness and care. For a wife in a different marriage, an offering of flowers may be perceived as her husband's inadequate attempt to put a quick fix on a recurring problem. An impressive amount of research has explored how marital success is related to certain types of perceptions spouses make about the marriage and the behaviors within it.

### Attributions

*Attributions* are specific perceptions people make about the reasons or causes of another person's behavior. Marital researchers have given special attention to causal and responsibility attributions. Causal attributions answer what produced a behavior, and causes can be viewed as *internally motivated* or *externally motivated*, *stable* (i.e., an enduring personality trait) or *unstable* (i.e., a one-time situational cause), or *global* (i.e., touching the relationship in a far-reaching global way) or *specific* (i.e., affecting just one specific area of the relationship; Abramson, Seligman, & Teasdale, 1978; Fincham & Bradbury, 1991). Spouses in satisfying marriages are more likely to offer internal, stable, and global attributions for positive spousal behaviors, and external, unstable, and specific attributions for negative spousal behaviors. For example, a satisfied wife may attribute her husband's motivation to give her flowers (a positive behavior) to internal (e.g., "he's such a thoughtful guy"), stable (e.g., "he always does nice things like this for me"), or global causes (e.g., "this gift is a symbol of how much he cares about our relationship"). Responsibility attributions address whether a person behaved according to appropriate expectations. Although responsibility and causal attributions have both received attention, responsibility attributions appear to be especially pivotal to perceptions of marital conflict (Davey, Fincham, Beach, & Brody, 2001). Davey et al. illustrate how a responsibility attribution can compound a negative causal attribution to explain an event (p. 721). When a spouse comes home late from work, the other spouse may make a causal attribution (e.g., "she didn't keep track of time again"), followed by a responsibility attribution (e.g., "she only thinks about herself and her own needs"), which puts an additional sting on the conflict.

## The Effect of Sentiment Override and Cognitive Editing on Attributions

In 1980, Weiss introduced the concept of sentiment override, described as a phenomenon in which "spouses' responses to a partner behavior are determined largely by their general sentiment toward the partner rather than by anything about the behavior itself" (Fincham, Bradbury, & Scott, 1990, p. 139). The notion of sentiment override is similar to the concept of positive illusions, which we discussed in chapter 5. Like dating partners, married individuals may have positive (or negative) illusions about the relationship that cloud their objective interpretation of behaviors in the marriage (Rusbult, Van Lange, Wildschut, Yovetich, & Verette, 2000). Naturally, sentiment override is inextricably linked to spouses' attributions. In an example of the sentiment override effect, Flora and Segrin (2000a) found compelling evidence to suggest that positive relational sentiments could override the experience of some negative affect, during interactions where spouses were complaining to one another. When they had an overall positive sentiment toward the relationship, spouses did not interpret complaints from their partner so negatively. Essentially, spouses were viewing each other "through rose-colored glasses."

Although we mentioned earlier in this chapter that accurate decoding of nonverbal behavior is related to marital satisfaction, Noller and Feeney (2002) present some special exceptions. In their 2-year longitudinal study, Noller and Feeney found that wives who were satisfied with their marriage early in the study tended to be less accurate at decoding their husband's negatives messages throughout the course of the study. The wives did not interpret their husband's negative messages to be as negative as an unbiased observer might have. It appears inaccurate decoding marked by optimistic attributions and perceptions buffers negativity in marriage. The benefit of positive sentiment override is that it may decrease a spouse's desire to reciprocate and escalate negativity in a marriage, because there presumably is little or no negativity to reciprocate in the spouse's biased mind (Hawkins, Carrère, & Gottman, 2002; Notarius, Benson, Sloane, Vanzetti, & Hornyak, 1989).

Spouses have also been found to engage in *cognitive editing*, a process slightly different from the sentiment override effect. In the case of editing, spouses are not necessarily biased in their immediate perceptions of a behavior, but when they subsequently respond to the behavior, they "edit out" the negative behavior in a way that is consistent with their overall feelings toward the relationship (Gottman & Notarius, 2002; Notarius et al., 1989). Later on, the spouse remembers only the edited version of the interaction. They remember what they want to remember. Examples of cognitive editing include denial, embellishment, or selective abstraction. In cognitive editing, a remark may be accurately perceived, but ignored. In sentiment override, however, the negative remark would be inaccurately perceived in the first place to match the spouse's existing positive or negative feelings toward the relationship.

## Oral Histories of Marriage

When researchers listen to couples talk about events and feelings surrounding their marriage, it is difficult to separate what really happened and what did not happen from the cognitive bias inherent in attributions, sentiment override effects, and editing processes.

Depending on a researcher's goal, it may not always be necessary to untangle the objective from the subjective when studying a marriage. In some cases, knowing how the couple *views* their marriage is most important.

There is a story behind every marriage. This story might include details of how the couple first met, what they did on their first date, when they decided to get married, and memories of the good times and bad times in their marriage. When people tell the story of their marriage, they often unwittingly reveal insights into their fondness for their partner, their philosophy of a good marriage, and the extent to which they have developed a shared identity as a "couple." Even more impactful, the way married couples view their past predicts their future marital stability and satisfaction (Buehlman et al., 1992; Flora & Segrin, 2003; Segrin & Flora, 2001). Using a technique called the Oral History Interview (Krokoff, 1984), couples are asked a series of general open-ended questions about their marriages. Tapes of these interviews are then analyzed for various themes that are evident in their way the couples individually and jointly talk about their marriage. Couples who are most satisfied and stable in their marriage are those who express a strong marital bond when telling the story of their past. The strength of the marital bond is evident in themes that express high *fondness and affection* (i.e., pride, compliments, and affection), high *we-ness* (i.e., indications of spousal unity), high *expansiveness* (i.e., elaboration about the partner and marriage), low *negativity* (i.e., criticisms or lack of compliments), low *disappointment* (i.e., disillusionment in the marriage), low *chaos* (i.e., unexpected, out of control problems), and high *glorifying the struggle* (i.e., recognizing hard times but feeling good about working through them).

## COUPLE TYPES

Successful marriages are capable of regulating "rich climates of positivity in the marriage," but often "very different, rich climates" (Gottman, 1999, p. 88). The systems theory concept of equifinality suggests that there is more than one way to achieve a similar end state. Separate programs of research by Gottman (1994) and Fitzpatrick (1988a) have identified various types of couples, who differ in many regards, but are all reasonably capable of making marriage work. In addition to studying Gottman and Fitzpatrick's couple types, we also explore two other types of couples in this section: homosexual couples and long-term married couples.

### Gottman's Couple Types

Gottman (1994) identified three types of couples: Volatile, Validating, and Conflict-Avoiding couples. Each couple type maintains a relationship climate in which positivity outweighs negativity, but they achieve this climate in different ways. The couple types differ in the way they exert influence, resolve conflict, and communicate about emotions (see Table 6.3). Still, each couple type can have a stable marriage. Each type also appears to support successful parenting.

Gottman uses the term "mismatches" to describe marriages in which spouses are different types (e.g., a Volatile spouse with a Conflict-Avoiding spouse). The term *mismatch*

**TABLE 6.3**
Gottman's Volatile, Validating, and Conflict-Avoiding Couples

---

**Volatile Couples:**

These spouses are the most emotionally expressive of the three types. They fiercely value openness and honesty. Their strong expressions of both negative and positive emotion prompt them to disagree passionately, but soon reaffirm their relationship and the other's personality with positive expressions of affection, humor, or teasing. In order to achieve a climate richer in positivity rather than in negativity, the many disagreements they lift up are met with large amounts of positive affect. This ratio keeps spouses from feeling hurt by negative emotional expressions, and they in fact foster a great deal of romance in the relationship. Disagreements are often interpreted as signs of involvement and caring. Both partners are likely to bring up issues and influence the other early on in discussions, and neither withdraws. Spouses appreciate the individual expression in their union and see it as the glue that holds them together.

**Validating Couples:**

These spouses are more moderate in their emotional expressions. Though they can become very emotionally expressive, they do so only concerning very important issues, and they usually consider the timing of their emotional expressions. Spouses are careful to initiate their complaints in a softened way. If necessary, they become increasingly expressive as the conversation continues. However, they pride themselves on ending a conversation or influence attempt by solving a problem in a way that benefits the couple as a team. Validating couples view themselves as a team, and they place a premium on companionship and togetherness.

**Conflict-Avoiding Couples:**

These spouses attempt to minimize or even completely avoid conflicts. Rather than spending time disagreeing, they focus on the areas of their relationship that reflect shared beliefs and solidarity. They may compromise or agree to disagree because their primary goal of accepting the other supercedes conflicts. As Gottman (1994) describes, any forms of emotional expressions by the conflict-avoiding couple are usually "low key" and "tempered." Conflict-avoiding couples are sometimes falsely accused of lacking the insight or ability to deal with conflict. To the contrary, conflict-avoiding couples may be so empathic about their partner and relationship that they take great care to build solidarity and accept their partners as they are.

---

*Note.* From *What Predicts Divorce: The Relationship Between Marital Processes and Marital Outcomes*, by J. M. Gottman, 1994, Hillsdale, NJ: Lawrence Erlbaum Associates. Adapted with permission.

hints at Gottman's feeling that these spouses are not well-suited for one another. The adjustments they will be required to make in order to make the marriage work will be very difficult. Gottman claims that mismatched partners enter marriage with a heightened frequency and intensity of perpetual problems. They struggle to overcome disagreements about when and how to exert influence, resolve conflict, and communicate about emotions. Gottman (1999) describes a likely scenario in a match of a Conflict–Avoider and a Volatile: "the avoider quickly feels that he or she has married an out-of control crazy person. The volatile believes that he or she has married a cold fish and feels unloved, rejected and unappreciated" (p. 96).

## Fitzpatrick's Marital Typology and Couple Types

Prior to Gottman's work on marital types, Fitzpatrick and her colleagues (Fitzpatrick, 1984, 1988a) introduced a well-developed and validated marital typology. The typology

**TABLE 6.4**
Fitzpatrick's Traditional, Independent, and Separate Couples

---

**Traditionals**:

These couples value stability and hold to conventional relational ideologies and customs (e.g., the woman takes the man's last name, infidelity is inexcusable, gender roles are traditional, relational stability is preferred over relational change). They are highly interdependent, as evident by their frequent sharing, companionship, and regulated time together (e.g., scheduled meal times). They are likely to be expressive and engage in conflict when the issue is serious, though in a cooperative rather than assertive way.

**Independents:**

These couples hold very nonconventional values about relationships (e.g., believing the relationship should not constrain individual freedom and should exhibit novelty). They are highly interdependent in their emotional connection, though they may maintain separate physical spaces and lack the timed routines that characterize Traditionals. Independents are very expressive, report some assertiveness, and embrace conflict.

**Separates:**

These couples espouse ambivalent relational ideologies, often supporting traditional marriage and family values, but simultaneously supporting the individual freedom and ideology of change and uncertainty that Independents uphold. Sometimes the public and private behaviors of separates are contradictory (e.g., they may publicly support conventional relationship values, but privately behave in an unconventional way). Separates are not very expressive with one another. They maintain emotional and physical space from their spouses as they find emotional support outside the marriage. The little interdependence separates have may be expressed through regulated time together. They avoid open marital conflicts.

---

*Note.* Adapted from Fitzpatrick (1984, 1988).

developed from an understanding of basic dimensions in marriage, some of which Gottman later used to define his stable couple types. The three bipolar dimensions include *conventional versus nonconventional* relationship ideology (i.e., ideology of traditionalism vs. ideology of uncertainty and change), *interdependence versus autonomy* (i.e., sharing, autonomy, undifferentiated space, and temporal regularity), and *conflict avoidance versus conflict engagement* (i.e., conflict avoidance and assertiveness). Fitzpatrick developed the Relational Dimensions Instrument (RDI), whereby spouses can individually report their tendencies across these dimensions. Depending on results of the RDI, individuals may be defined by one of three types: Traditional, Independent, or Separate (see Table 6.4).

Fitzpatrick reports that of the more than 1,000 couples who have taken the RDI over the years, about 60% of couples have spouses who are matched in their marital orientation (e.g., both are Traditionals). Fitzpatrick terms these couples "Pure" types. Of the 60% Pure types, each of the three Pure types is represented similarly, at around 20%. The remaining 40% are termed "Mixed" types (e.g., the wife is Traditional and the husband is Separate). Of the variety of Mixed types that exist, none seem to appear more frequently than do the others.

Years of research have validated that the couple types differ in their use of power, conflict strategies, self-disclosure, communication of emotions, expectations, and marital satisfaction (see Douglas, 1999). Although Fitzpatrick (1988a) stresses that each couple type can represent a satisfying, functional marriage, she and others have found levels of satisfaction to be slightly higher among Traditionals and lowest among Separates (Douglas; Fitzpatrick & Best, 1979). In 1994, Gottman compared his couple types to Fitzpatrick's Pure types, pointing out several similarities between Traditionals and Validating couples, Independent and Volatile couples, and Separate and Conflict-Avoiding couples.

## Gay and Lesbian Couples

Fitzpatrick and Gottman's research on couple types is highly influential, in part, because of the awareness it raises about the variety of ways in which intimate partnerships can work. Along with studying diversity in relationship processes, family scholars have recently reflected an interest in the diversity of *people* in intimate partnerships. There is a preponderance of data on White, heterosexual couples (Flanagan et al., 2002), and this research is sometimes not generalizable to other populations. Research on same-sex partnerships indicates some similarities to heterosexual couples, but many important differences.

### Similarities Between Heterosexual and Homosexual Couples

Compared to heterosexual couples, homosexual couples appear to be more similar than different in their overall affective appraisals of relationship quality. For example, Kurdek (1998a) compared relationship satisfaction in married, gay cohabiting, and lesbian cohabiting couples who were all at comparable stages in their relationship. Levels of relationship satisfaction in heterosexual partners did not differ from either gay or lesbian partners. All three couple types showed decreases in satisfaction over the 5-year study; however, the rate of change in satisfaction did not differ among the couple types. Other compelling evidence indicates that commitment levels are similar among married, gay-cohabitating, and lesbian-cohabitating couples (Kurdek, 1995), and that commitment over time is driven by similar processes of affection and companionship (Kurdek, 2000). More recently, Kurdek (2003) found that even though the dissolution rates of gay and lesbian partners are similar, in some cases lesbian partners report slightly more liking, trust, and equality and less decline in their relational quality over time, compared to gay partners. Still, Kurdek found that overall, gay and lesbian partners are similar on most other relationship variables, and the few differences are not large in magnitude.

To what extent are relationship processes and structures similar between heterosexual and homosexual couples? In an effort to better understand homosexual relationships, Fitzpatrick and her colleagues administered the RDI to 165 homosexual participants (including both gay and lesbian couples), in order to categorize participants as Traditional, Independent, or Separate (Fitzpatrick, Jandt, Myrick, & Edgar, 1994; Noller & Fitzpatrick, 1993). Results from the homosexual sample indicated 51% Traditionals, 29% Separates, and 20% Independents. There were some significant differences between the male and the female samples. When compared to a major random sample of heterosexual partners, the data from lesbian participants indicated more Traditionals. The gay male sample had about the same proportion of Traditionals, but more Separates than the heterosexual sample. Noller and Fitzpatrick caution that the sample of homosexual partners may not be representative of the general population of homosexual partners because the couples in the study were contacted through the Couples National Network. Because of their participation in the network, these couples may have had an above average interest in developing close network ties and prorelationship ideals.

Homosexual couples must negotiate many of the same relational processes as heterosexual couples, including conflict, intimacy, power, or roles. In another example of similar relationship processes in heterosexual and homosexual couples, Kurdek (1994) reported that intimacy and power were the two top areas of conflict for gay, lesbian, and heterosexual couples. Same-sex partners reported similar frequencies of conflict as heterosexual partners in four of the six conflict areas studied (Kurdek). Also, gay and lesbian couples did not appear to differ in their frequency of conflicts.

### Differences Between Heterosexual and Homosexual Couples

One of the most major differences between heterosexual and homosexual couples is the lack of institutional and social support for homosexual relationships. The implications of this difference are far-reaching. In a majority of states, same-sex marriages are not legally recognized. Couples in such unions are denied privileges available to married couples, such as inheritance, medical decisions, insurance, taxes, or property transfers. Because most same-sex relationships are not recognized civil unions, there are fewer support systems and barriers to relationship dissolution. Indeed, same-sex couples have significantly higher dissolution rates (Blumstein & Schwartz, 1983; Kurdek, 1998a). However, systems that provide support can also impart stress. Same-sex couples may be relieved of some of the stressors that partners in dissolving heterosexual relationships face (e.g., divorce costs and relationships with in-laws). With a lack of institutional barriers to dissolution, Kurdek comments that it is remarkable that as many homosexual couples remain together as long as they do. He emphasizes that same-sex couples must find creative ways to make their relationship succeed in the face of a hostile social environment. Some of these creative coping mechanisms may involve cognitive processing (e.g., the capacity to glorify the struggle or adjust expectations) and careful construction of supportive social networks. When Haas and Stafford (1998) examined relationship maintenance behaviors in gay and lesbian partners, they found that shared networks were particularly important maintenance behaviors—perhaps more important than for heterosexual couples. Merging the partners' social networks and becoming involved with one another's family and friends symbolized coming out and public commitment to the relationship. In a supportive context, making an invisible relationship visible can garner support. Other rituals that heterosexual couples have for garnering support (e.g., engagements and marriage ceremonies) are not as common for homosexual couples.

Homosexual couples lack the number of role models that heterosexual partners have. Furthermore, they cannot assign role relationships according to sex, as some heterosexual couples do. Cohabitating lesbian couples have been found to have more equity in their relationships than do married, heterosexual couples (Kurdek, 1998a). Lesbian partners also report more intimacy in their relationships than do married, heterosexual couples (Kurdek). To explain the greater intimacy in lesbian relationships, Kurdek says that if females are socialized to define themselves in terms of their relationships more than males are, then lesbian relationships may benefit from a "double-dose of relationship enhancing influences" (p. 554). Kurdek also tested the hypothesis that same-sex couples would exhibit more constructive problem solving than would married, heterosexual couples, because same-sex couples approach problems from the same gender perspective. Contrary to his hypothesis, same-sex couples did not differ from married couples in problem-solving abilities. For many researchers, studying homosexual couples provides a way to see whether differences between partners in heterosexual relationships can be attributed to gender differences or roles differences (Nussbaum, 2000). In Box 6.1, we examine how gender differences in *heterosexual* couples get exaggerated in popular culture. With regard to the same-sex couples in Kurdek's study, constructive problem solving appeared to be more related to factors such as conflict resolution styles or investment in the conflict, rather than to gender differences. In a more specific, observational study of communication and conflict behavior in same-sex couples, Gottman's early data reveal that compared to heterosexual couples, same-sex couples start off their conversations with more positivity, the positivity has more impact, and the negativity has less impact (Nussbaum). On the downside, same-sex couples in the study were not as successful at repairing a negative situation once it began to escalate.

---

**Box 6.1**
**Mars and Venus: An Exaggeration of Gender Differences?**

Marriage scholars worry that some of the ideas perpetuated by the media and self-help books about how to make marriage work actually have a detrimental rather than beneficial effect on people's lives. Zimmerman, Haddock, and McGeorge (2001) persuasively argue that one such highly controversial book is John Gray's (1992) *Men are from Mars, Women are from Venus.*

The 1992 Mars and Venus book was on *The New York Times* bestseller list for 339 weeks, and it outsold all other hard-cover books published in the United States in the 1990s. This first book inspired (and continues to inspire) a series of other John Gray books, audiotapes, videotapes, and a board game, not to mention widespread media interest on shows such as *Oprah*. Zimmerman et al. (2001) respond, "Unfortunately, for a book with such immense influence, much of the material is potentially detrimental to its readers and to their intimate relationships" (p. 55). Why then do people like the book? The book is flashy. The information is relayed with humor. And, the gender stereotypes portrayed by the book play up exaggerations of gender differences that readers are already familiar with from media or other cultural myths.

What do Zimmerman et al. (2001) point to as the myths in the Mars and Venus philosophy? Their five major criticisms center around what they view as Gray's (1992) extreme exaggeration of gender differences related to the way men and women communicate and act in intimate relationships.

1. **Stereotypic descriptions of women and men:** Women are portrayed as emotionally unstable, illogical, inefficient, overwhelmed with negative emotions and problems, and desperate for conversation and emotional connection. Men are portrayed as emotionally inept, insensitive, lazy, helpless, and as having fragile egos that are insulted by advice from women. Men are also described as logical and independent, having good problem-solving skills and the ability to control most emotions, except anger. Men are portrayed to be better suited for the public sphere; and women, for the

private sphere. Zimmerman et al. (2001) argue that the idea that men and women are instinctually different in these ways is not supported by research. Many perceived gender differences are usually situational, not instinctual, and can be explained by socialization, power differentials, and social inequities rather than by instinct.

2. **Traditional division of labor:** The Mars and Venus philosophy assumes that women are mostly responsible for housework and childcare, even if they are employed. Men are allowed time to resort to their "caves" after a hard day's work, and women are not to interrupt them. Men should also be praised for the occasional things they do around the house, whereas women are just expected to pick up the slack at home without acknowledgment of help

3. **Responsibility for change and relationship quality rests on female partners:** The Mars and Venus philosophy assumes that women are mostly responsible for achieving and maintaining relational success. Toward this end, women are the ones who need to accommodate their communication style and expectations to match men's "natural" style. Women should never try to change or improve men. In times when men need to listen to women, Gray (1992) suggests that it is possible for men to fake listening.

4. **Priority of male partner's needs:** The Mars and Venus philosophy suggests that a man's need to withdraw to his "cave" overrides a woman's need to talk or obtain help with house and child-care tasks. Further, women should not give advice to men, because it may hurt their feelings.

5. **Threats of male anger and dire consequences:** The Mars and Venus philosophy suggests that if men have to listen to women too much, men will become frustrated. In particular, offering advice may make men angry. Finally, women need to accommodate to men's needs for either intimacy or space to withdraw to their "cave." Without either, men may become angry or forget that they love their wives.

---

Even though Gray (1992) popularized the idea that husbands and wives are very different, scientific research on communication and relationships shows that men and women probably have more similarities than differences. Rather than metaphorically describing men and women as inhabitants of different planets, Dindia (see Wood & Dindia, 1998) provides a more accurate metaphor by stating "men are from North Dakota and women are from South Dakota."

## Long-Term Married Couples

Family scholars have recently expressed growing interest in the maintenance of long-term marriages. Maintaining intimacy and negotiating conflicts are ongoing challenges for couples. Carstensen, Gottman, and Levenson (1995) found that compared to middle-aged couples (mean age 44 for husbands and 43 for wives), older couples (mean age 64 for husbands and 62 for wives) displayed (a) less negative affect (e.g., anger, disgust, belligerence, and whining) and (b) more affection. Regarding negative affect, it is difficult to tell whether older couples have less severe marital problems or are simply less emotionally engaged in their problems. In an examination of responsive listening behaviors in middle-aged versus long-term marriages, happy older couples and happy middle-aged couples both displayed more positive and fewer negative emotional expressions while listening than did their unhappy counterparts (Pasupathi, Carstensen, Levenson, & Gottman,

1999). However, happy older couples avoided eye contact and did not back-channel as much when dealing with conflict as did happy middle-aged couples. Still, these less responsive listening behaviors did not take a toll on the intimacy and marital satisfaction of older couples. As the researchers suggest, "as conflicts become more and more familiar, the listening spouse in a conflict conversation must provide less evidence for having heard and understood the speaking spouse's statements. . . . It may be that when happy older couples avoid eye contact and do not backchannel, they actually avoid escalating a conflict" (Pasupathi et al., p. 187). Indeed, Caughlin (2002) found that in some marriages that last beyond 10 years, satisfaction is actually enhanced over time when husbands' withdraw from their wives' demands. This finding contradicts the typical conclusions regarding the pattern termed *demand–withdrawal*. In fact, in chapter 11, we discuss how this pattern, which involves one partner, usually the wife, making constant demands and the other partner consistently withdrawing, is associated with divorce. Caughlin explains, however, that in long-term marriages, the demand–withdrawal pattern may be dissatisfying at the current moment, but it may help avoid the escalation of problems that could take a toll on future satisfaction.

What about Carstensen et al.'s (1995) discovery of more affection in longer term marriages? In their qualitative study of 20 older married couples, Dickson and Walker (2001) concur that many husbands become more emotionally expressive over time. Compared to their wives, later-life husbands were more emotionally expressive, more open and willing to talk about their relationship, and more validating when their wives talked about the relationship. Overall, most people in long-term marriages report being happy with their marriages—usually happier with them in later life than in midlife (Goodman, 1999). However, this may be due in part to the fact that many of the unhappy marriages were dissolved earlier. Finally, it appears that many, though not all, of the same behaviors that promoted intimacy earlier in a marriage still promote intimacy later in marriage (Cooney & Dunne, 2001).

## CONCLUSION

"Traditionally, the marital relationship has been the centerpiece around which the family is created and grows" (Flanagan et al., 2002, p. 99). As this chapter illustrates, the complexities of marital relationships are reflected in the many types of ways spouses make their marital union work. Gottman identified three types of stable couples: Validating, Volatile, and Conflict-Avoiding. In many ways, these stable couple types are analogous to Fitzpatrick's couple types: Traditional, Independent, and Separate. We also discussed other types of couples, namely, gay and lesbian couples, that are both similar to and different from the traditional heterosexual, married couple. Overall, the point made by this discussion is that there is more than one way to conduct a successful marriage or intimate partnership.

Commensurate with societies' interest in the companionate nature of marriage, researchers over the last 30 to 40 years have sought to understand the interpersonal processes that characterize successful, intimate partnerships. Researchers emphasize that the behaviors and cognitions of partners are pivotal and intricately tied with one another.

The ability to regulate these two domains so they do not exceed negative thresholds is undoubtedly one of the toughest challenges couples face. Spouses must regulate an array of behaviors, including behaviors that communicate intimacy and affection as well as behaviors used to negotiate conflict and roles. Those couples that succeed appear to foster intimacy by (a) skillfully encoding and decoding verbal and nonverbal messages, (b) taking the time to really get to know their partners and nurture fondness and admiration, and (c) spending at least some time in meaningful joint activities and rituals. Although there are a variety of ways to negotiate roles and conflict, successful couples maintain an underlying (a) respect for one another that allows them to maintain dialog about tough problems, (b) willingness to accept influence and repair mistakes, and (c) attitude of teamwork and positive sacrifice toward task sharing.

The fact that spouses' behaviors are so intricately tied to cognitions means that spouses are constantly mentally processing the behaviors they exchange. Successful couples appear to have a positive bias in the way they perceive their spouses' behavior. This bias, which includes positive attributions, positive sentiment override, and cognitive editing, can be heard even as couples casually talk about their relationship.

All couples face the challenge of maintaining their relationship over the long term. Some long-term couples adapt their methods for relationships maintenance over time. Most rely on a collection of maintenance behaviors that have worked for years. Although the face of any marriage is constantly evolving, researchers feel that generally high levels of satisfaction, commitment, and stability characterize successful marriages.

# CHAPTER SEVEN

# Parent–Child Communication

The parent–child relationship is the most primary *intergenerational* relationship in the family, and to some, the very relationship that defines a family. Recall the definitions of family we explored in chapter 1, some of which named an adult and a dependent as the necessary ingredients for family (e.g., Popenoe's definition). Unlike mate relationships, which are usually relationships of choice, children do not choose their parents. Regardless of whether parents consciously choose to have children, the parent–child relationship is one of obligation to some extent. Societal structure and the child's needs obligate parents to care for their child. Children are born dependent on their parents and require the aid of their parents longer than do most other animal species.

As we begin to review research on parent–child communication, one immediate question is who are the parents and children that are the subject of such research. Until the 1970s, most empirical research on parent–child communication was actually research on *mother–child* communication (Grolnick & Gurland, 2002). Parenting was a task reserved primarily for mothers, because divided sex roles, especially those typical of the mid-1900s, encouraged fathers to place their primary focus on resource allocation in the workforce (Mintz, 1998). Mothers were thought to have a direct and exclusive influence on their children, for better or for worse. Mothers were lauded for providing children with secure bonds and proper socialization, and they were also blamed for problems the child developed. This view led to a trend termed "mother-blaming"—a term insinuating that people have overestimated the effect of mothers' behavior on children, when not all child problems stem exclusively from the influence of mothers (Grolnick & Gurland). Influences from peers, fathers, the family system, external events, genetics, and numerous other sources contribute to multiple and complex interactions between the child and his or her environment. Although research on mothering still dominates parenting research, family scholars have recently witnessed an intense focus on the role of fathers and the larger family system in parent–child interaction. Some suggest that fathers teach, model, or mentor children in ways that complement the skill repertoire of mothers (Furstenberg, 1998, p. 296). Others suggest that mothers and fathers may not be so different in their child-care competencies or even in their interactions with children (Gauvain, Fagot, Leve, & Kavanagh, 2002). The diversity of parent–child relationships is enormous, due to differences in age and sex (e.g., mother–infant, father–adolescent daughter), as well as other complex variables such as family structure, culture, and class. In this chapter, we focus primarily on parents and preadult children, reserving our discussion of adult children and parents to chapters Eight and Ten.

## OVERVIEW OF PARENT–CHILD INTERACTION PERSPECTIVES

Parent–child processes have been the subject of literally thousands of studies. Although we cannot comprehensively review all these studies in one chapter, we attempt to illuminate some of the major themes related to communication processes in the parent–child relationship. Research on parent–child interaction can be roughly organized according to three perspectives: *unidirectional, bidirectional*, and *systems* approaches (Peterson & Hann, 1999; Stafford & Bayer, 1993). A "central tenet" of the unidirectional view is that characteristics and communication of the parent directly affect the child (Stafford & Bayer, p. 52). Parents must provide warmth and support to their children as well as discipline and control. How should parents balance these two seemingly different tasks? We explore this question and examine various parenting styles that address how parents balance these tasks. We also study the impact of various parenting practices on child outcomes such as self-concept, communication competencies, and self-control (Stafford & Bayer). Overall, the unidirectional approach views children as clay to be molded by the parent.

The bidirectional view is concerned with the reciprocal relationship between parents and children. For example, how do parents and children mutually influence and communicate with one another? The bidirectional view is less interested in whether socialization originates with the parent or child (Peterson & Hann, 1999). Further, this perspective does not suggest that parents and children necessarily affect each other in similar ways or that the nature of the reciprocal influence is similar over time. The bidirectional approach is useful for studying reciprocal forms of interaction (e.g., infants and caretakers reciprocally responding to one another) and attachment bonds that develop between parents and children.

Finally, the systems approach to parent–child interactions depicts parent–child interactions in the context of larger family and social systems. If the parent–child relationship is not an isolated relationship, then what forces outside the relationship affect it? We study social roles for being a mother, father, single parent, son, or daughter. In addition, interactions in the larger family system (e.g., marital interaction) also affect the parent–child dyad. Further, parents and children interact with people and forces outside the family (e.g., career demands) who affect and are affected by parent–child interactions.

## THE UNIDIRECTIONAL APPROACH

The unidirectional approach has focused on two major parenting dimensions that we prefer to term *warmth* and *control*. Grolnick and Gurland (2002) aptly point out that the parenting literature is full of confusing terminology. Researchers often use different terms to refer to the same concept. For example, one researcher may use the term "warmth"; and the other, "support" to refer to the same idea. However, factor analysis of parenting questionnaires over the past 30 to 40 years has revealed that regardless of terminology, warmth and control are two dimensions of primary importance in parenting (Grolnick & Gurland, p. 10). The balance of warmth and control is arguably the most important and challenging aspect to parenting (Baumrind, 1971; Grolnick & Gurland; Maccoby & Martin, 1983; Schaefer, 1959), and this challenge appears to peak during toddlerhood and adolescence (Laursen & Collins, 2004; Noller, 1995). In this section, we study how parents communicate warmth and control, how the delivery of warmth and control affects child outcomes, and finally how parental behavior has been classified into parenting styles.

## Parental Warmth Messages and Their Effect on Child Outcomes

Warmth messages are verbal and nonverbal behaviors that make the child feel cared for, supported, loved, and accepted. Peterson and Hann (1999) argue: "Perhaps the closest thing to a general law of parenting is that supportive, warm, sensitive, and responsive childrearing is associated with the development of social competence in the young" (p. 336). How do parents communicate messages of warmth to their children? And what are optimal quantities and qualities of warmth messages for healthy child outcomes?

### Nonverbal Warmth Messages to Young Children

During infancy, nonverbal messages involving touch, physical proximity, gaze, facial expression, and paralanguage are a primary means for parents to communicate warmth and involvement. Although infants are obviously limited in their capacity to express themselves, they are born with sensory abilities that prepare them to "assimilate into the communicative system" (Van Egeren & Barratt, 2004). Infants may not consciously understand the intentions behind some parental nonverbal and verbal messages, but at the very least, a functional, communicative connection develops between the parent and the child. Hertenstein's (2002) research on parent–infant touch reveals that processes of conditioning and social learning characterize parent–infant interactions. In other words, infants learn that certain types of touch are related to emotional states and reactions.

Like many of the nonverbal channels available to parents of infants, touch can communicate both positively and negatively valenced emotions. We discuss some of these negative messages in a moment. However, as a form of warmth and involvement, touch is noted for both soothing infants and arousing their attention. Knowing that infants typically get upset when their caregivers stare at them with a prolonged expressionless face, Stack and Muir (1990) instructed one group of mothers to touch their 5-month infants while staring at them with an expressionless face and the other group not to touch their infants while staring with an expressionless face. The infants who were touched smiled more and grimaced less. The authors concluded that touch has the power to soothe infants, perhaps even when other nonverbal channels are unavailable.

Although touch is a potent means of interacting with a child, researhers have devoted far more attention to the nonverbal channels of paralanguage, facial expression, and gaze (Hertenstein, 2002). Beginning with paralanguage, *motherese*, more recently termed *infant-directed speech* or *baby talk*, refers to the way caregivers modify their speech for infants and young children who are learning language (Barratt, 1995; Van Egeren & Barratt, 2004). Infant-directed speech is marked by high pitches, frequent and diverse changes in intonation, shorter utterances, longer pauses, vocal intensity, and simplified speech (Haslett & Samter, 1997). For example, when parents say to an infant, "What's wrong?" or "You're so special," they do not usually use a monotone voice. Many drastically alter their vocal pitch and intensity when talking.

Infants are drawn to human voices in general compared to other sounds (Jusczyk, 1997), and they are particularly attracted to infant-directed speech (Van Egeren & Barratt, 2004). Even at just a few months, infants recognize the paralinguistic variations in pitch and phonetic structure (Jusczyk; Papousek, Bornstein, Nuzzo, Papousek, & Symmes, 1990). Because children recognize that it is aimed at them, infant-directed speech is a way for parents to signal they are involved with and care about the child. One could also think of infant-directed speech as a parent's bid for attention from the child.

Parents package other nonverbal behaviors, such as gaze and facial expression, together with vocalizations to indicate involvement and warmth. Across all cultures, infants produce more frequent and more positive vocalizations when engaged in mutual gaze with a caregiver (Keller, Schoelmerich, & Eibl Eibesfeldt, 1988; Van Egeren & Barratt, 2004). As for facial expression, infants begin to recognize facial expressions of emotion around 3 months of age (Haslett & Samter, 1997). Infants between 4 and 6 months can reliably distinguish among facial expressions of anger, fear, and surprise. Although parents rely heavily on nonverbal expressions to indicate warmth to young children, not all parents appear to successfully communicate warmth messages to their children nonverbally. Adolescent mothers, for example, have been found to vocalize less and smile less to their infants (Barratt & Roach, 1995). Likewise, depressed mothers are less nonverbally sensitive in their interactions with infants (Embry & Dawson, 2002).

### Parental Warmth Messages as a Foundation for Social Competency

These early nonverbal and verbal messages of warmth and involvement pave the way for children's developing social competency. One important aspect of social competence is learning to balance sociability and autonomy (Peterson & Hann, 1999). Recall the assertion from attachment theory that secure and safe infants are more likely to explore their environment away from the parent, knowing that they can always return to their secure base if necessary. Warmth messages such as soothing physical touch or other responsive nonverbal behaviors on the part of the parent can indicate to the infant that he or she is safe and secure and consequently free to explore in an autonomous way (Hertenstein, 2002). Although it may seem counterintuitive at first glance, consistent levels of positive involvement with very young children may actually encourage them to be more independent and willing to explore situations in which they will learn important lessons and social skills.

Communication skills are another important component to social competence. Early on, infant-directed speech plays a role in enhancing young children's communication skills. Given that infants and young children are noted for short attention spans, the paralinguistic variety of infant-directed speech helps the child stay involved and attentive to learning (Stafford & Bayer, 1993). In addition, the simple sentence structure models for the child how to make his or her own first simple sentences. For example, the mother will say to the child, "Doggie barks," and the child learns to repeat the sentence.

Infant-directed speech may also help the child learn turn taking (i.e., when to talk and respond). For example, the mother will ask a question and suggest to the child how and when to respond to the question (e.g., "How old is Katie? Say 'two'"). This is an early form of scaffolding. *Scaffolding* refers to intentionally structuring an event to enhance a child's learning (Haslett & Samter, 1997). Parents constantly use scaffolding to teach behavioral skills as well communication skills. For example, some parents let their children help cook by giving them structured tasks they can handle in order to learn skills (e.g., measuring water in a measuring cup). Some parents also use scaffolding to teach other age-appropriate social skills, such as helping the child to order food on his or her own at a restaurant in order to learn to communicate in a new context. The goal of scaffolding is to help the child for a period of time so that he or she eventually can complete tasks autonomously.

Unfortunately, some parents confuse age appropriate scaffolding and involvement with parental intrusiveness (Barber & Harmon, 2002). Gottman, Katz, and Hooven (1997) describe one form of parental intrusiveness, which involves taking over for the child as soon as the child has trouble with a task. For example, as soon as the child has trouble reading, the parent takes over and reads the rest of the book. Parental intrusiveness in the parent–adolescent or parent–young adult relationship is particularly noxious. Imagine parental intrusiveness in the form of the parent who immediately calls the coach when the teenager does not get a starting position on the baseball team, or the parent who calls the boyfriend as soon as the teenager begins having trouble with the boyfriend. Sometimes parental intrusiveness stems from the parent's intent to be supportive, involved, and helpful to the child. However, parental intrusiveness is just the opposite—unhelpful to children. Children do not develop age-appropriate social skills to deal with social situations and problems of their own because they are used to their parents taking care of everything for them.

### The Interaction Between Verbal and Nonverbal Warmth Messages

When most people think of warmth messages, explicit verbal statements come to mind (e.g., telling a child he or she is loved; Cutrona, 1996). Indeed, children benefit from hearing parents' explicit verbal expressions of warmth and involvement. Consistent and genuine messages of warmth and involvement contribute to a positive self-esteem in children (Stafford & Bayer, 1993) and adolescents (Noller, 1995). Bowlby (1973) reminds us that from ages 1 to 6, separation from a parent is a very real fear for a child. Consistent, explicit verbal expressions of warmth and assurance may allay some of these fears. For example, parents of children who are reluctant to go into the preschool classroom for the first time, might assure the child that they will be right outside the classroom to pick up the child after preschool. Children do not fully develop a sense of time until around age 8 (Piaget, 1977). Children benefit from being frequently reminded of their parents' love, warmth, and involvement, both verbally and nonverbally. Recall Jencius and Rotter's (1998) argument in chapter 3 that young children appeared to be soothed when their bedtime ritual included continutity statements from the parent (e.g., "I'll see you in the morning" or "When you wake up, we have a lot of things to do tomorrow. We're going to...").

Obviously, verbal and nonverbal warmth messages often co-occur. However, even when the verbal channel is available to them, parents may still communicate a majority of their most meaningful warmth messages through nonverbal means alone. For example, a parent and child may simply engage in an activity together (e.g., playing a game, reading a book, or watching a movie). In some cases, behavioral involvement is a more important form of support than are explicit verbal messages. For example, attending an adolescent child's band recital (i.e., behavioral proximity) may be as important, if not more so, than simply verbally congratulating the child on performing in the recital (i.e., verbal support), but not attending.

That fact that verbal and nonverbal messages co-occur is an indicator to children that some messages of verbal support are inconsistent with nonverbal behavior (Baumrind, 1995). *Inconsistent warmth messages* involve the parent telling the child he or she is loved, but not acting as if the child is loved. Somewhat related, Seligman (1995) warns against what we might call *hollow warmth messages*. Such messages involve unconditional positive praise that is not contingent on anything the child does. Clearly children benefit from feeling unconditional love and security from their parents. The problem, according to Seligman, is that in this "era of feel-good parenting," some parents excessively shower their children with undeserving, unrealistic, "Pollyanish" praise (e.g., telling the child "You are the best kid" or "You are so good") even when the child performs inappropriately or poorly. This leads to two negative outcomes for children. First, the child is prone to become passive, knowing that praise will come no matter how he or she acts. Second, "the child may have trouble appreciating that he has actually succeeded later on when he really does succeed and Mom praises him sincerely. . . . He will have trouble learning that his actions work when they actually do" (Seligman, p. 287). Further, by overemphasizing how a child feels to the exclusion of what the child does, children are prone to become less persistent, more bored, more depressed, and less motivated to master skills. Overall, it is not surprising that self-esteem is more closely related to (a) genuine, specific support rather than to ingenuine, nonspecific support; (b) actual support received rather than perceived support; and (c) actual success and mastery rather than simple feel-good statements (Cutrona, 1996; Seligman).

Finally, some parents simply do not communicate messages of warmth at all, or if they do, it occurs in such a disguised way that the message is ineffective. For example, parents may think that by teasing the child they are expressing warmth, when the child interprets the teasing as criticism or mockery. Likewise, whenever some parents offer a support message, they tag on a statement of criticism. As in marital relationships where one negative statement can wash out five or more positive statements, Gottman argues that the same may be true for parent–child relationships (Gottman & DeClaire, 2001).

Overall, the relationship between parents' and children's expressiveness begins in infancy and continues as children age and throughout adulthood (Halberstadt, 1991). For sure, the nature of parents' warmth and expressiveness does and should change as the child matures. Children benefit from warmth, support, and involvement that are administered in consistent, genuine, and age-appropriate ways. For years, researchers have suggested that too little warmth and involvement are problematic for children. Perhaps less obvious, too much involvement or poorly administered support is also problematic. It can be interpreted as overprotective or ingenuine.

# Parental Control Messages and Their Effects on Child Outcomes

Parental demands and control are more likely to be accepted by the child when accompanied by high levels of support and responsiveness (Baumrind, 1995). Yet Baumrind further adds warmth "does not imply unconditional acceptance; a warm and loving parent may also be a firm disciplinarian" (p. 58). We turn our attention now to a second major parenting dimension: control. The control dimension is also labeled in multiple ways in the research literature. The terms *control, controlling, restrictive,* and *autocratic* generally refer to the degree of control parents have over their children. Within the control dimension, the terminology is especially confusing because a "controlling" parent usually has a negative connotation, whereas parents who are "in control" are viewed favorably (Grolnick & Gurland, 2002).

We should also note that parental control has been differentiated according to behavioral control and psychological control (Barber, 1996; Barber & Harmon, 2002; Gray & Steinberg, 1999; Miller-Day & Lee, 2001). *Behavioral control* refers to the regulation of the child's behavior through behavioral monitoring and limit setting. *Psychological control* refers to the emotional and cognitive autonomy that parents allow children. Psychological control may include expressions of disappointment, parental intrusiveness, love withdrawal, guilt induction, or other techniques that appeal to pride, guilt, and shame (Miller-Day & Lee). People should be just as concerned about extreme psychological forms of parental control as they are about extreme behavioral forms of control. However, the two forms of control are often intertwined. As with the warmth dimension, parents have numerous ways they can communicate behavioral and psychological control messages, including both verbal and nonverbal means. Next, we examine the variety of parental control messages and the effect of control messages on child outcomes.

## Psychological Control

*Disappointment* is a potent means of psychological control because it capitalizes on children who seek to please their parents. Naturally, children attempt to meet parental expectations to receive positive reinforcement and to avoid guilt. As Miller-Day and Lee (2001) explain, parents have a variety of options for communicating disappointment as a means of psychological control (p. 8). Parents may express *situational disappointment* (e.g., "My mom was disappointed that I didn't try out for the volleyball team) or *enduring disappointment* (e.g., "I'm a failure to my mom"). Further, parents can express disappointment through *direct verbal strategies* ("she or he tells me directly" or "she or he criticizes me") *indirect verbal strategies* ("she or he makes little comments"), *nonverbal strategies* ("she or he sends the message with body language"), or *avoidance* ("she or he doesn't communicate disappointment. I usually hear it from someone else"). Miller-Day and Lee found that most young adults perceived that their parents expressed disappointment directly more than indirectly. However, compared to fathers, mothers were perceived to make more indirect verbal criticisms that were perceived to be critical "digs" at the child. Mothers also appeared to rely on nonverbal expressions more than verbal expressions. Daughters perceived their mothers to be more critical when disappointed, and sons perceived their fathers to be more critical when disappointed. Those young adults who felt their parents were less critical in their expressions of disappointment perceived that they had more personal control.

Most all parents express disappointment to their children at one point or another. Some expressions of disappointment may be useful or motivating for children and others destructive, depending on how they are administered. When parental disappointment is laced with direct or indirect criticism or mockery, it is especially destructive for children (Gottman et al., 1997; Miller-Day & Lee, 2001). In addition, children internalize global disappointment as contempt and a "trait of failure" (Gottman et al.) . As Seligman (1995) suggests: "Any time you find your child to be at fault, it is important to focus on specific and temporary personal causes, if truth allows, and avoid blaming the child's character or ability" (p. 63). Specific, constructive complaints that prompt an optimistic character in a child sound like the following, "Tammy, you are really misbehaving today. I don't like it at all" (Seligman, p. 64). On the other hand, an example of a global, destructive criticism that leads to a pessimistic character is: "Tammy, what's wrong with you? You are always such monster" (Seligman, p. 64).

*Parental intrusiveness*, which we discussed earlier in the chapter, is also a form of psychological control. It is marked by anxious parental overinvolvement and overprotectiveness. Intrusive parents control most aspects and decisions in the child's life. Parents truly become controlling. Through intrusiveness, the parent manipulates the child's emotional experiences and impairs the individuation process (Barber & Harmon, 2002; Peterson & Hann, 1999). So controlled by the parent, the child is not allowed to develop his or her own interests and opinions apart from the parent. In interviews with active and remitted bulimic women regarding factors that maintained their disorder, women indicated that their parents were intrusive, though not globally intrusive (Rorty, Yager, Rossotto, & Buckwalter, 2000; see also chap. 13). They described their parents as intrusive in areas where they desired more personal privacy (e.g., personal appearance, weight, shape, personal space, and private thoughts and feelings). Alternatively, they felt their parents were underinvolved in areas where they wished for greater care and attention (e.g., emotional support). Some parents are so intrusive in the child's life that boundaries between the parent and child become blurred or violated. The parent might draw the child into inappropriate roles. In extreme cases, some parents draw the child into a "peer-like" relationship by entering into a competitive or sexual relationship with the child (Stroufe, 2002).

The balance of involvement is tricky for parents. Children desire their parents to be involved in their lives, and even high school students benefit from parents' high involvement (Grolnick & Gurland, 2002). However, this high involvement is best in the form of support rather than in controlling behavior. Pomerantz and Ruble (1998) found that involvement administered in a "controlling" way makes children feel (a) an external not internal force caused them to do well (e.g., received a reward for doing well in school), (b) performance and results were more important than actually learning (e.g., parent picks the child's topic for the report), and (c) they were incompetent (e.g., parent helped the child before the child asked for it; Grolnick & Gurland, p. 19). On the other hand, involvement in an "autonomy-granting" manner (a) made the children feel they were the cause of good behavior, (b) indicated that learning was most important (e.g., the child was encouraged to pick his or her own topic), and (c) communicated confidence with the child (e.g., standing by the child while encouraging him or her to figure out the problem by himself or herself) (Grolnick & Gurland, p. 19). In summary, parents' attempts to dominate and control their adolescents have deleterious effects on the adolescents' mental health and do not allow them to learn to monitor and regulate their own behavior. In the best case scenario, adolescents who have been subject to controlling parenting develop a strong sense of self-control and discipline, but they are so used to doing what their parents tell them to do, that they do not develop skills to cope apart from their parents (Roberts & Steinberg, 1999). Adolescents appear to be better off when their parents are supportive and involved, provide structure and standards, yet still grant them autonomy. These adolescents tend to have better mental health, more self-confidence, and more self-competence because they have internalized appropriate standards and coping behaviors themselves (Roberts & Steinberg).

*Love withdrawal* is another process of psychological control in which parents threaten to withdraw love and attention as a form of punishment. The parent may turn his or her back, leave the house, or refuse to speak to the child. The withdrawal of love is intended to punish the child by capitalizing on feelings of dependency and fear and inducing guilt. The child is caught in a relationship that binds him or her to the parents in dependency, and then manipulates the fact that the child is dependent in a way that the parent can get what he or she wants. Usually what the parent wants is to discourage the child's autonomy or discourage deviation from parental expectations (Maccoby & Martin, 1983).

The fact that children want their parents to be supportive and involved in their lives may be the very reason that love withdrawal is such a powerful technique for gaining compliance. However, the psychological manipulation involved in most extreme forms of love withdrawal (e.g., threatening to leave the child, locking the child in a room, or telling the child you will not love him or her until he or she cleans up the room) promotes low self-esteem, feelings of blame and guilt, and possibly other long-term consequences that have not been fully researched (Grolnick & Gurland, 2002; Stafford & Bayer, 1993). Administered poorly, the child-rearing technique termed "time out" can be a form of love withdrawal (Stafford & Bayer). In a time out, the parent removes the child from the problematic situation and isolates him or her for a short period of time in another room, perhaps by making the child sit in a chair or face the corner. Time outs can be effective if they are coupled with specific reasoning to help the child internalize the expected behavior and if the child is reassured of the parent's love before or after just a short time out. Part of the idea behind a time out is to give the child time to calm their emotional flooding. Flooding refers to overwhelming feelings of anger, fear, or sadness, so powerful that the flooded person cannot reasonably deal with much else at the moment (Ekman, 1984; Gottman, 1994). As Gottman et al. (1997) remark, no one, not a parent or child, can reason when emotionally flooded. Because reasoning is also an important component to time outs, we should point out that the time out technique assumes that the child is old enough to reason. In this way, the child can recognize the problematic behavior and reason why is it wrong after he or she calms down. Obviously, a time out administered to a 1-year-old for a long period of time is inappropriate and will likely not accomplish this level of reasoning. In an adapted form of the time out, some parents, for example, require a time out for the toy the children are fighting over, rather than a time out for the children. This technique is intended to communicate that the parent does not globally want to withdraw love from the child but does not like the way he or she is playing with the toy. Thus, it is not the child who is bad, but the action that is bad (Seligman, 1995, p. 289).

Somewhat similar to love withdrawal, *guilt induction* is another psychological means of control. Guilt induction prompts the child to internalize family and parental problems, even when the problems may realistically be rooted in the parent or some external force. Nonetheless, the child feels he or she caused the problem and deserves blame. Abusive parents are noted for skewing attributions of blame so that blame is placed on the child (Wilson & Whipple, 2001). For the child, undeserved and extreme internalization of guilt often leads to depression, suicide, or other related symptoms (Barber, 1992; Peterson & Hann, 1999).

### Behavioral Control

As we mentioned, the line between psychological and behavioral control is blurred. Coercive communication behaviors, whether verbal or nonverbal, are really extreme forms of psychological *and* behavioral control. With coercive verbal communication, the parent attempts to control the child's behavior without offering reasons and rational explanations. Baumrind (1995) explains coercive communication:

> Parents are being coercive when they typically issue superfluous commands accompanied by threats and promises, but not by reasons. When parents are being coercive they focus the child's attention on their powerful status rather than on the harmful consequences of the act that they wish to correct. Coerciveness may undermine internalization by irking the child and provoking opposition so that the child disobeys when the coercive parent is absent. (pp. 61–62)

The following statement is an example of verbal coercion: "If you don't say your sorry, I'll send you to your room." Coercion can also occur in the nonverbal form of physical punishment or overly punitive behaviors (e.g., spanking, slapping, and hitting). Typically, coercive nonverbal behavior from parents declines between toddlerhood and adulthood (Laursen & Collins, 2004).

Most parents admit there are times when they are simply concerned about compliance. They need to stop a child's destructive behavior immediately or they need to remove a child from a dangerous situation. The parent is not concerned about teaching a lesson at that moment. In other cases, the child may not be old enough to internalize regulations or too emotionally flooded to reason. To control these situations, many parents issue directives, declarative statements (e.g., they yell "Stop" before the child crosses the street or touches the hot stove), or physical restraint (e.g., they pull the child back from crossing the street). Once parents are successful at securing immediate compliance, they may be able to reason with the child about the situation, if the child is old enough. Clearly, there is a time and place for such directives and physical control. Younger children appear to respond to directive messages, so long as they are delivered in the context of positive affect, but older children do not respond well to directives, even if they are issued with positive affect (Krcmar, 1996). Stafford and Bayer (1993) conclude that parents who primarily communicate with a *controlling communication style* (i.e., they mostly issue directives, declaratives, negative acknowledgments; and infrequently ask questions) impede the communication competence of their children when compared to parents who only occasionally use controlling communication and primarily use a *conversing communication style* (i.e., using frequent questions and positive acknowledgments). Further, abusive parents tend to use controlling messages and behaviors uniformly, rather than assessing what the situation calls for (Wilson & Whipple, 2001). Abusive parents then continue their controlling style even after the child has complied (i.e., continuing to scold the child after compliance; Wilson & Whipple).

But the question remains even for parents who typically use a conversing style: To what extent should they use tactics of coercion or punitive behaviors at all? Many scholars, concerned about child abuse, categorically reject the use of physical punishment. Baumrind (1995) asserts that harsh physical punishment has "no corrective purpose" and is "pathogenic," particularly when it is delivered in an arbitrary, inconsistent, unstructured manner in a "disorderly home" (p. 67). Indeed, inconsistent discipline is characteristic of parents who are physically or psychologically abusive. Although scholars can agree that extreme forms of physical punishment are entirely inappropriate and destructive for children, what about spanking? Gottman et al. (1997) argue that spanking often occurs at times when parents could have and perhaps should have used other alternatives to control behavior. One of the major concerns with spanking is that it may spur children to become aggressive themselves when they are faced with conflict, and it may damage a child's self-esteem. It appears high levels of spanking and low levels of reasoning do prompt children to use more aggression toward their parents and peers (Gottman et al.; Larzelere, Klein, Schumm, & Alibrando, 1989). However, both Baumrind and Gottman et al. contend that children who have received infrequent spankings in the context of a generally positive parent–child relationship appear not to suffer harmful effects. Baumrind writes: "Corporal punishment administered in private for willful defiance rather than for childish irresponsibility, not in anger, and not to children younger than eighteen months or to teenagers, may well be effective and harmless in that is does not generate hostility, persistent dysphoria, or maladjustment" (p. 68). Needless to say, the appropriateness of physical punishment is a controversial topic among scholars and parents alike. Opposite of the punishments parents administer in coercion, parents can also offer rewards to secure compliant behavior. Some parents offer tangible rewards (e.g., "I'll give you $5 if you clean your room"). Opposite of disappointment, some parents offer intangible rewards of praise and acknowledgment to secure compliance, for example, "Wow, you got your pajamas on all by yourself; What a big girl" (Baumrind, p. 70). As we discussed in chapter 4, controlling children through reward systems, or likewise controlling them through coercive punishment, secures compliance for the moment but does not lead to internalization of values. This occurs because the child has little or no reason to alter his or her behavior other than to avoid the punishment or receive the reward (Wilson & Whipple, 2001). Further such strategies are limited in helping to develop social competence, and in some cases, they damage social competence. However, sometimes parents are only concerned about securing momentary compliance, and in this case, rewards and punishments are effective. Overall Grolnick and Gurland (2002) argue, what is "good" parenting depends on what we desire for our children:

> If the goal of socialization is simply to produce obedient, compliant children, the goal can easily be attained through the constant and controlling imposition and enforcement of rules. If, however, the goal of socialization is not just for children to comply, but to engage in behaviors volitionally and to accept and endorse the behaviors or develop a value for them, parents must facilitate children's internalization of the regulation of their own behavior. (p. 20)

### Firm Control

Methods of *firm control* stress self-discipline through firmness, reasonable demands for children, provision of guidance and limit setting, without being autocratic and overly punitive (Peterson & Hann, 1999, p. 333). Firm control involves monitoring and imposing restrictions, but not in an intrusive or overly directive way. Proponents of firm control do not advocate extreme forms of monitoring to the point of parental intrusion. They also do not advocate deficient monitoring or permissive parenting where the parents fail to set standards for the child and let him or her behave in any manner. Techniques of firm control encourage a form of parental induction that is different from guilt induction. The intent behind parental induction is to encourage children to think about "(1) why rules are necessary, (2) why their misbehavior is unacceptable, (3) how their behavior impacts others, and (4) how they might make their behavior more acceptable and make amends for any harm they have done" (Peterson & Hann, p. 334).

The hope is that children will come to internalize parental standards and expectations, so that eventually, the child will be able to monitor his or her own behavior. In other words, the child will be able to determine when his or her behavior is inappropriate and what he or she should do about it. Unlike guilt induction, where the child is unpredictably and arbitrarily controlled to internalize blame, the type of parental induction encouraged by firm control frees the child from control. Learning to internalize reasonable standards and behavior ultimately enhances the child's autonomy, because he or she can learn how to act within reason, and even how to respectfully disagree from parents' viewpoints.

Firm control is also thought to be a more proactive parenting style, curbing some misbehavior before it happens, as opposed to a reactive style where the parent responds to the problematic behavior. Parents can avoid some misbehavior before it happens by monitoring and staying involved in the child's life and by equipping the child with skills to cope with problems on his or her own. For very young children, one proactive strategy is engaging the child's attention in a positive activity instead of waiting for misbehavior to occur and then using discipline (Holden, 1983). For example, parents traveling with their small child on an airplane might bring activity books for the child or engage them in conversation, rather than allow them to become bored and prone to misbehavior. The link between the proactive style and positive outcomes for adolescents are found in the reasoning that proactive parents use with children. Conversations that reveal the parents' reasoning, standards, and behavioral interpretations allow the child to have a good sense for what is right and wrong behavior.

Clearly parents have to set reasonable limits on behavior, as methods of firm control advocate. However, Ginott (1965/1994) suggests that although parents can set limits on behavior, they should not set limits on feelings. Children deserve a choice in some matters that affect them. These matters may include domains such as food, clothes, homework, music lessons, and allowance (Gottman et al., 1997). In this choice making, children learn to develop their own interests and opinions. They develop themselves as individuals. They learn how to make decisions and the consequences of decisions—something that will be a lifelong process. Overall, Gottman et al. suggest, "[children] need to learn our values (like caring about how other people feel), and they learn these values largely from the way we treat them and how parents treat one another, not through lecture" (p. 23).

## Parenting Typologies and Styles

Researchers have labeled parenting styles to categorize the way parents balance warmth, control, and other important dimensions. Baumrind (1967, 1968, 1971) developed one of the most well-known taxonomies of parenting styles. Her taxonomy, based initially on extensive observations of parents and 3- and 4-year-old children, addresses how parents balance control and warmth when communicating with their children. Baumrind uncovered three distinct parenting styles, Authoritative, Permissive, and Authoritarian, detailed in Table 7.1.

In 1971, Baumrind suggested a fourth *neglecting style*, though it never received as much attention as the other three styles. This neglecting style referred to a disproportionately small group of parents who appeared detached, neglecting, and indifferent, when compared to involved and nurturant parents.

Baumrind regarded the authoritative (democratic) parenting style as the most effective means for molding competent and content children. Indeed, she found that children with authoritative parents are more self-reliant and have more self-control and better moods. Children of permissive parents have low self-control and self-reliance and have been characterized as immature. Baumrind described children of authoritarian parents as passively hostile, vulnerable to stress, lower in positive moods, and disaffiliative. Such adolescents are less likely to have developed their own sense of identity, have lower self-esteem, and are so used to using their parents' standards or external moral standards to make decisions, that they do not have good judgment of their own. Not surprisingly, in a study of the frequency and content of college students' e-mail to parents (Trice, 2002), students from authoritative (democratic) families e-mailed their parents the most, but sought less specific academic and social advice from parents, compared to students from authoritarian families who sought the most advice. Students from permissive families e-mailed the least and also sought the least academic and social advice. All of these groups of students, however, sought about the same degree of financial assistance from their parents.

A more recent question regarding Baumrind's parenting styles is whether the authoritative (democratic) parenting style is most effective for all family contexts. Some have suggested that the authoritative style is most applicable and effective for advantaged children (i.e., White, middle-class children living with both biological parents) (Steinberg, Mounts, Lamborn, & Dornbusch, 1991). Socha, Sanchez-Hucles, Bromley, and Kelly (1995) explain that compared to White parents, Black parents stress more obedience and

**TABLE 7.1**
Parenting Styles

| Parental Style | Characteristics |
| --- | --- |
| **Authoritative Style** (Sometimes termed *democratic style*) | Parents balance high nurturance with firm control and age-appropriate demands. They clearly communicate to the child what they require. These parents are especially good at using reason and facts to argue for compliance and to maintain firm control. At the same time, they are also willing to accept a child's opinion or refusal to comply, if the child presents a well-reasoned argument. Thus, there is give and take, or useful negotiation between parents and children. The parent has standards for the child, but is not coercive or restrictive in gaining compliance. Parents are involved and affectionate with their children, to an extent that is satisfying and useful for the child. Parents also use more positive reinforcement than punishment. |
| **Permissive Style** | Parents offer moderate amounts of nurturance and are particularly noted for exercising little control. Parents enforce few rules, make few demands, and allow the child to regulate his or her own activities. These parents view themselves as resources to the child rather than enforcers of standards. These parents often give in to their child's complaining or pleading. When they do attempt to seek compliance from the child, it is often through coercive tactics of guilt or diversion of the child's attention rather than through well-reasoned conversations. |
| **Authoritarian Style** | Compared to the other two styles, these parents are the most highly demanding, yet their high demands are not followed by reasoning. The parents are typically unresponsive to the child's needs, discourage verbal responses or reasoning from the child, and are unlikely to change their demands should their children appeal for such change. These parents favor punitive measures to control a child's will. They believe in and promote respect for authority and respect for order and tradition, and argue that the child should accept their word as it is. Their strict demands are sometimes grounded in strict theological standards. Again, compared to the other two styles, these parents express the lowest levels of affection, empathy, and support for their children. Hence, they have little positive emotional rapport with their children. Punishment is favored over positive reinforcement. |

*Note.* Adapted from Baumrind (1995) and Stafford & Bayer (1993).

control, but in a way that is ecologically valuable. This means that parents are teaching their children skills that will help them adapt to their environment, which in the case of the African American child often means an environment of racism. Socha et al. argue that respect for authority, rules, safe behavior, and achievement, stressed through obedience and high control, is adaptive especially for low-income and working-class African American children. An alternative explanation is that parenting techniques involving obedience and high control stem from pressure and stress experienced by parents in such environments (Florsheim et al., 2003; Socha et al.).

More recently, Amato and Fowler (2002) found that the core principles of authoritative (democratic) parenting are linked with positive child outcomes across diverse family contexts, including race, ethnicity, family structure, education, income, and gender. Even when they compared groups as different as White, married, nonpoor mothers and Black, single, poor mothers, Amato and Fowler found that authoritative parenting was generally associated with the best child outcomes.

## THE BIDIRECTIONAL APPROACH

The unidirectional approach has been heavily critiqued for overemphasizing the role of parents on child outcomes and excluding the effects of other external and systemic influences. Maccoby (2002) argues that these criticisms are partly justified, but not entirely. Most researchers in the unidirectional tradition do not claim that parents exclusively influence children. Rather the unidirectional approach helps us isolate specific variables for study and is useful so long as results are interpreted along with those from the bidirectional and systemic approaches. Bidirectional approaches to parent–child communication have blossomed over the past 15 to 20 years (Maccoby, 2002). The bidirectional view is concerned with the reciprocal relationship between parents and children and how parents and children mutually influence and communicate with one another (Parke, 2002). This mutual influence begins once the child is born, if not before, and parents and children constantly influence each over the course of their lives. In this section, we examine just some of the bidirectional processes in the parent–child relationship, such as responsiveness, synchrony, and attachment.

*Reciprocal responsiveness* refers to whether caregivers respond appropriately and contingently to their children and whether children respond to their parents in such a manner (Baumrind, 1995). *Synchrony* in interaction refers to a person's ability to maintain a shared focus in the relationship (Peterson & Hann, 1999). Synchrony and responsiveness require that the participants are attentive and aware of each other's needs or responses (Haslett & Samter, 1997).

Mothers (or caregivers) are initially more responsive to infants' cues than infants are to maternal cues (Van Egeren, Barratt, & Roach, 2001). Researchers suggest that early mother–infant interactions are dominated by the infant (Gottman & Ringland, 1981; Van Egeren & Barratt, 2004). The infant makes a signal that elicits a response from the mother. The infant has a great capacity to control the parent, so long as the parent is attentive and motivated to respond. However, infants become contingently responsive to their mothers by at least 4 months (Van Egeren & Barratt). Beginning at 4 to 9 weeks, face-to-face responsiveness and communication increase dramatically, as infants learn to smile. Most parents then react to the infants newly learned facial expressions with increases in their own vocalizations, facial expressions, and gestures.

Depressed mothers, unfortunately, display less synchrony (Embry & Dawson, 2002). In other words, depressed mothers find it difficult to focus on their infants and provide contingent responses. They are less likely to mimic their infants' positive emotional expressions and states (e.g., return a smile when the infant smiles). When non-depressed adults become unresponsive for some reason (e.g., they close their eyes), infants react by becoming more animated and attempting to establish contact (Van Egeren & Barratt, 2004). The infant becomes distressed if bids to communicate subside or continually fail, which is often the case with depressed parents. When infants seek out closeness or a response, but are chronically rejected, they then learn to purposely avoid their caregiver in times of stress (Stroufe, 2002).

Reciprocity and synchrony help parents and children develop emotional bonds to one another beyond infancy. Communication researcher April Trees (2000) conducted a fascinating study regarding the impact of responsiveness and synchrony in the parent–young adult relationship. She examined the extent to which young adults felt their mothers' actual nonverbal behaviors were supportive and whether movement synchrony (e.g., beginning and ending movements at the same time) affected perceptions of support. Trees videotaped the interaction of mothers and their adolescent children while they discussed a "relational problem," which for most young adults involved a problem with a friend, romantic partner, co-worker, or roommate. After the interaction, Trees asked the young adults to complete a survey indicating how supportive they felt their mother was. In addition, using a video-recall procedure, the young adults were asked to watch selected segments of the video and report how appropriate they felt their mother's nonverbal behavior was at that moment. Trees' goal was to establish initial links between (a) nonverbal sensitivity and appropriateness and support and (b) synchrony and support. In general, the young adults reported feeling that their mothers' responses were more supportive when the mothers displayed vocal warmth and interest and kinesic and proxemic attentiveness. In addition, more movement synchrony between mothers and young adults was associated with young adults' perceptions that their mothers were more supportive.

Synchrony affects perceptions of support; but how much synchrony should parents display when children are experiencing negative affect? First, it is important to recall that synchrony, as we defined earlier, is not necessarily behaving in the same way as the child, but rather maintaining a shared focus on the relationship. One mistake some parents make is to respond to their child's flood of negative affect with their own flood of emotions. Clearly it is easier to say than to do, but parents often need to take their own time outs before responding. Carson and Parke (1996) found that fathers who are more likely to respond to their children's negative affect with negative emotional displays of their own have preschool children who are less socially skilled (i.e., less willing to share, more verbally aggressive, more avoidant of others, and more likely to become physically aggressive) than their preschool classmates. Carson and Parke concluded that these children were not learning adequate emotional regulation skills from their fathers.

Further, Haim Ginott (1965/1994) suggests that the best way parents can support a child who is experiencing negative affect is to listen to them. Appropriately responding to children's emotions is important, but "statements of understanding *precede* statements of advice" (Gottman et al., 1997, p. 20). Many parents rush in to give advice before they really understand the child's emotions. Influenced heavily by the work of Ginott, Gottman et al. point out that some parents respond to children's emotions by dismissing them or disapproving of them. Following is an example of a response that dismisses a child's sadness. The child is upset because a page is torn in one of his favorite books. The parent says, "C'mon, it's just a book" or "Cheer up." What is just an insignificant children's book to the parent is a big deal to the child. In addition, learning to deal with this moment

**TABLE 7.2**
Emotion Coaching

---

*Steps to Emotion Coaching*

---

1. **Notice low-intensity emotions.** The parent must be aware of the child's emotions (e.g., sadness or anger) before they escalate to more high-intensity emotional expressions.

   **Emotion-coaching response:** The parent is aware enough to detect that the 6-year-old who is trying to color a picture is becoming annoyed by the younger sibling who is trying to take away some of the crayons.

   **Emotion-dismissing response:** The parent does not notice or care to acknowledge the low-intensity emotions.

2. **See the negative emotion as an opportunity for teaching or intimacy.**

   **Emotion-coaching response:** The parent is aware that now is a useful time to help understand and teach the child, before the child becomes too flooded with negative emotions. The parent also sees this moment as a chance to emotionally connect with the child.

   **Emotion-dismissing response:** The parent sees the child's emotion as an unreasonable demand and the child should get out of the negative state as quickly as possible.

3. **The parent empathizes with the child and validates his or her emotions.**

   **Emotion-coaching response:** The parent might soothe the child, calm the child, and use affection. Obviously, this validation is communicated very differently depending on the age of the child (e.g., imagine a teenager vs. small child). Note that if the parent is the target of the negative emotion, the parent may be too emotionally flooded and defensive to soothe the child.

   **Emotion-dismissing response:** The parent invalidates the emotion and tries to get the child to move on by saying, "Grow up" or "Go to your room" or "Don't be a baby."

4. **The parent helps the child verbally label the emotion the child is having.**

   **Emotion-coaching response:** Does that bother you (make you angry) that you don't have some of the crayons to use for your picture?

   **Emotion-dismissing response:** No response.

5. **The parent helps the child problem solve.**

   **Emotion-coaching response:** Although the parents accepts the child's emotions, he or she may help the child set limits ("It's OK to be angry, but not OK to hit your brother"). Thus, the parent helps the child determine appropriate behavior and brainstorm for strategies and goals for dealing with the problem. They may also help the child determine consequences for inappropriate behavior.

   **Emotion-dismissing response:** No response.

---

*Note.* From *Meta-Emotion: How Families Communicate Emotionally,* by J. M. Gottman, L. F. Katz, and C. Hooven, 1997, Mahwah, NJ: Lawrence Erlbaum Associates. Adapted with permission.

of sadness is important in preparing the child to deal with other emotions of sadness later in life. Gottman et al. suggest that a better way for a parent to contingently respond to children's emotions is through emotion coaching. The steps of emotions coaching are listed in Table 7.2 along with examples of emotion-coaching versus emotion-dismissing responses.

The parent–child relationship can be described as a constant back and forth. Parents change children; children change parents; they change each other. These bidirectional influences affect *parent–child attachment* over the life span. When infants are born, they attach to their parents. However, parents' baby talk and messages of love do as much to enhance their own attachment to the child as the child's attachment to them. During adolescence, the attachment relationship between parents and children typically undergoes large changes. Parent–child conflict during adolescence not only is normative but also prompts the dyad to revise attachment expectations and renegotiate roles (Hock, Eberly, Bartle-Haring, Ellwanger, & Widaman, 2001; Laursen & Collins, 2004). Laursen and Collins even go so far as to suggest that conflict during adolescence actually strengthens the parent-child attachment for the short and especially long-term, by stimulating communication about the relationship. Having a secure attachment before and during adolescence allows parents and adolescents to better resolve conflicts related to adolescent autonomy. When parents remain a secure base for the child, even through the changes of adolescence, they encourage the child to safely explore and develop age-appropriate autonomous behavior. Sufficient levels of support along with gradual opportunities for autonomy encourage processes of individuation and encourage adolescents to experiment with social skills specific to relationships outside the family (Noller, 1995; Perosa & Perosa, 1993).

Much has been written about adolescents' experience separating from their parents, but little attention has been given to how parents respond to separation from their adolescents (Hock et al., 2001). Hock et al. indicate that it is normal for parents to express feelings of missing a child who has grown more independent or left home. Parents, and especially mothers, indicate feeling more warmth and affection toward their adolescents than adolescents report feeling toward their mothers. Some argue that mothers' optimistic feelings of attachment may be an attempt to counter their adolescents' impending detachment (Laursen & Collins, 2004; Noller & Callan, 1990). Parents who express overly high anxiety about adolescent distancing may be "unaware of or deny that distancing is normal and appropriate for their children; alternatively, these parents may 'personalize' their adolescents' movement to extrafamilial relationships: that is, they may view such movement as rejection. The tension associated with 'losing the child to others' could reflect jealousy and possessiveness" (Hock et al., p. 294). For sure, the parent–child relationship evolves during adolescence, and some of this disengagement is normative. Adolescence is just one turning point in the parent-child relationship. Golish (2000) reminds readers that there are many complex bi-directional turning points that continue to evolve throughout adulthood.

## SYSTEMS APPROACH

Compared to the bidirectional and especially to the unidirectional approach, the systems approach to parent–child communication has generated much less research. However, Peterson and Hann (1999) feel that a systems approach is the most "conceptually accurate" way to view parent–child interaction. Systemic models take into account familial and social forces in the parent–child relationship. The strength of systemic models is simultaneously a challenge, because systems approaches consider such a complex array of variables. In this section, we briefly examine how communication patterns in the parent–child relationship interact with social forces external to the family. For example, we look at social roles and expectations for mothering, fathering, co-parenting, and single parenting. System approaches are also noted for analyzing the whole family context and the impact that other relationships in the family have on parents and children (Belsky, 1981; Parke, 2002). Complete systems studies rarely occur, because researchers are almost always exploring just a part of the system (e.g., one dyad or triad).

## Parent–Child Interaction and Social Roles

### The Role of Father

The act of being a father or mother is guided by socially prescribed roles that evolve over time. The larger social system influences how parents act. Morman and Floyd (2002) argue that over the last 4 centuries, and even within the last century, role expectations for fathers have cycled back and forth between being "a detached, authoritarian father and one of being a companionate nurturant father" (p. 398). The current generation of fathers report that their relationships with their sons have higher levels of closeness, relationship satisfaction, and affectionate verbal and nonverbal communication than did their relationships with their own fathers (Morman & Floyd). Yet, fewer men are experiencing fatherhood now than in the 1960s (Eggebeen & Knoester, 2001). This is partly because more men are opting not to have children, and partly because some men are biological fathers, but not involved in "fathering" (i.e., involved in their children's lives; Eggebeen & Knoester). Compared to recent decades, fathers have clearly increased the amount of time they spend with their children (Silverstein, 2002). However, fathers on the whole still spend significantly less time with their children than mothers (Stafford & Dainton, 1995). Silverstein adds that fathers in dual-shift, working-class families spend the most time with their children. Out of necessity, they must assume child-care responsibilities when mother is at work. Fathers in upper-middle-class families that pay for someone other than the mother to care of the child spend the least amount of time with their children. Doherty and Beaton (2004) explain that wives expectations for how involved their husbands should be as fathers appear to influence their husbands' involvement more so than husbands' own expectations influence their involvement.

When compared to other men, men who are fathers have similar psychological and physical well-being. However, fathers are more involved in civic and social organizations (e.g., church, school organizations, and service clubs) and more involved in intergenerational family connections. In addition, fathers with children at home actually average more work hours per week and are less likely to be unemployed than men without children or fathers with grown children (Eggebeen & Knoester, 2001). There are still strong expectations for fathers to live up to the "provider" role. Indeed, fathers appear to be strongly influenced by outside expectations for role performance.

### The Role of Mother

Attention to the role of mothers in families, compared to fathers, has and still does overwhelm the research literature. While fathers have been negatively stereotyped as detached and authoritarian, mothers have been negatively stereotyped as overly sensitive and involved and blamed for problems children develop. As with fathers, many of the negative stereotypes of mothers have been exaggerated. However, adolescents indicate that they are closer to their mothers and share feelings more openly with them (Noller & Callan, 1991). Mothers also become more distressed after conflict with their adolescents, perhaps in part because some mothers see their role as family peacemaker and conciliator (Laursen & Collins, 2004). As we mentioned earlier, the larger social system influences how parents act out their roles. In Box 7.1, we explore how the media influences young females' images of motherhood. Then in the following sections, we examine social forces such as maternal employment and single parenting that affect how the role of mother is played out.

---

**Box 7.1**
**Images of Motherhood in the Media**

Dutch researchers Ex, Janssens, and Korzilius (2002) studied whether or in what ways young females' television viewing is related to their images of motherhood. The sample in their study included 166 female adolescents (age 15–17) and young women (age 20–22) who were not yet mothers and who had various educational backgrounds. Ex et al. were interested in the females' viewing habits with regard to eight family-centered television series, all of which portrayed a mother. Six of these eight television series were American (*The Cosby Show, Roseanne, Married with Children, Growing Pains, The Bold and the Beautiful,* and *Beverly Hills 90210*), and two others were a Dutch soap and a Dutch sitcom. Ex et al. measured the female's viewing behavior (i.e., how much television they watched in general, which of these specific programs they watched) and their motivation for viewing (i.e., relaxation and entertainment, information, comparison, social use, escape, and affinity). They also measured whether the females in the study had a "traditional orientation" toward motherhood or a "self-assertive and relational orientation" toward motherhood. Those females who scored high on the traditional orientation felt that ideal mothers should devote themselves entirely to the family and be overly concerned about the needs of their children and the family. Those who had a self-assertive and relational orientation viewed ideal mothers as having concern for their own views, independence, and self-reliance as well as being open and considerate of others outside the family.

Results indicated that the total amount of general television viewing (regardless of whether the viewing involved one of the eight television shows or some other program) was unrelated to females' views of motherhood. However, watching certain family-centered shows, as opposed to other programming, was related to images of motherhood. Specifically, the more females watched *The Bold and the Beautiful, Beverly Hills 90210*, and the two other Dutch programs the more they had traditional self- and ideal images of motherhood. In other words, some sitcoms and soaps, particularly those that portray traditionally oriented television mothers, are related to young females' views of their future and ideal traditional motherhood. Finally, females who were motivated to watch television for relaxation, entertainment, and affinity with television, versus those who watched for more goal-directed reasons like information and comparison, had more traditional views of motherhood. Ex et al. (2002) say that it is hard to tell if certain motivations for viewing actually induce a traditional view of motherhood. Or, perhaps the kind of individuals who watch for relaxation, entertainment, and affinity, usually younger persons with less education, have more traditional views of motherhood already.

How do you think your own television viewing habits have or have not influenced your views about ideal parenting?

Much about mothering has changed since the 1950s and 1960s. Day-to-day interaction with children is affected by social circumstances, such as maternal employment. As we learned in chapters 3 and 6, numerous studies indicate that mothers are working more. More children than ever are parented by dual-career parents. Yet we also learned in chapter 3 that mothers are spending more time with their children now than they did 2 decades ago. Grolnick and Gurland (2002) argue that whereas "work status may or may not affect parenting, work stress clearly does" (p. 26). Work stress spills over to parent–child interactions, resulting in parents who are more emotionally and behaviorally withdrawn from their children and less caring and loving in their behavior.

Another important social and contextual factor impinging on a growing number of mothers is the challenge of heading a single-parent family. A growing number of fathers are involved in single parenting, but mothers by far are more likely to assume this role. One of the greatest challenges faced by single parents is a lack of economic resources (DeFrain & Olson, 1999; Grolnick & Gurland, 2002). Many single mothers never had a spouse to help support them and the child, and those who are divorced suffer greatly when the former spouse does not pay child support. In other single-parent families, the former partners or spouses are involved in co-parenting and cooperate financially, though they are no longer romantically involved. Still, many single-parents are tightly bound to their jobs in order to support the family. Consequently, children in single-mother families do not spend as much time with their mothers, compared to children in intact families. The single parent's lack of time also contributes to less parental authority and supervision in single-parent families (Knok, 1988). Many single parents are too pressured to fully engage in parenting. Other problems single parents often report are stress, loneliness, and a lack of social support. When single parents experience stress and exhaustion, and they have no partner or social network to offer social support, their stress often "spills over" into their parenting, in the form of permissive or punitive parenting tactics or lack of follow-through on punishment (Grolnick & Gurland; Simons & Johnson, 1996).

Many adolescent single mothers receive support from their parents and families of origin. In fact, Florsheim et al.'s (2003) study of adolescent African American and adolescent Latino parents found that the quality of the mother's relationship with her parents predicted her adjustment to parenthood. Florsheim et al. also found that adolescent African American parents were less likely to stay romantically involved after the birth of a child than were adolescent Latino parents. However, African American fathers were no more likely than Latino fathers to disengage from parenting. Overall, many single parents face difficult parenting challenges that stem from economic disadvantage, lack of support, and heightened stress, although intact families are not immune to such challenges. In chapter 12 we explore the addition of a stepparent to the single parent family.

Another diverse type of parent–child relationship includes lesbian or gay parents and their children. One distinction in such relationships is whether (a) the child entered the family in the context of a heterosexual relationship that eventually dissolved when one partner came out as lesbian or gay, or (b) whether the child was born or adopted by parents who already had a lesbian or gay identity (Patterson, 2000). Patterson describes that children of the first type are more likely to experience stress and reorganization somewhat akin to divorce, unlike children of the second type who have not experienced these transitions. Family scholars who have studied mothering and fathering in same-sex households or custody and visitation rights of homosexual parents (Parke, 2002; West & Turner, 1995) conclude that the sexual identity and gender of the parent is less important than the nature of interaction with the child. Allen and Burrell's (2002) meta-analysis of the impact of sexual orientation of the parent on the child found that "the parent's heterosexuality or homosexuality is not related to any adverse outcome in the child's development" (pp. 136–137). Further, there do not appear to be any negative consequences to granting a homosexual parent custody or visitation rights any more so than granting those same rights to a heterosexual parent.

## Parent–Child Interaction Within the Family System

What is appealing about a systems perspective is that it encourages us to consider the impact of coparenting (i.e., mothers and fathers parenting together) and the effect of the family system on the child (Doherty & Beaton, 2004). Research on co-parenting examines the triadic connection among mother, father, and child, rather than just the parent–child relationship. Such research indicates that when alone with the child, many parents act different from when they are in a triadic relationship (Doherty & Beaton; McHale, Lauretti, Kuersten-Hogan, & Rasmussen, 2000; Stafford & Bayer, 1993). McHale (1997) introduced the concept of *covert* co-parenting processes. Such processes involve interaction between the parent and child when the other parent is absent that either strengthens or undermines the child's sense of family integrity (McHale, Lauretti, Talbot, & Pouquette, 2002, p. 147). For example, when one parent is absent, some parents make disparaging remarks to the child about the absent parent, whereas others make positive, complimentary remarks. When parenting alone, some parents uphold discipline strategies that are consistent with those used in the presence of the other parent, whereas others introduce inconsistent discipline strategies. McHale et al. (2002) argue that in distressed marriages, parenting is more inconsistent, such that parents exhibit more differences when alone with the child versus when with the other parent and child together. In some cases, dysfunctional *cross-generational coalitions or triangulation* develops. In such cases, the spouses are split over some conflict, and one parent "gangs up" with the child against the other parent. Obviously, the child is prone to feel caught in loyalty conflicts between the parents (Buchanan & Waizenhofer, 2001).

In what way is the quality of the marital relationship linked to the quality of the parent–child relationship? Erel and Burman's (1995) meta-analysis examined two hypotheses regarding this link: the compensatory hypothesis and the spillover hypothesis. The *compensatory hypothesis* argues that a poor marital relationship prompts a stronger parent–child relationship, or vice versa. In other words, a parent who is dissatisfied in the marriage may seek intimacy and satisfaction in the parent–child relationship and may devote more involvement and investment in the parent–child relationship. The compensatory hypothesis suggests that the involvement and intimacy of a healthy parent–child relationship intrudes on or detracts from the marital relationship. Erel and Burman found a clear lack of support for the compensatory hypothesis.

The *spillover hypothesis* argues that positive marital relations lead to positive parent–child relations, and alternatively, marital disharmony "spills over" to create parent–child disharmony. Erel and Burman (1995) found strong empirical support for this hypothesis. It appears parents who have a more satisfying and supportive relationship with one another are more available to respond sensitively to the child's needs. Parents who are experiencing distress and conflict in their own relationship are likely to be irritable and emotionally drained and therefore less attentive, sensitive, and involved with their children (Buehler & Gerard, 2002). Parents may even take out their own frustrations about the marital relationship on the children in the form of harsh discipline or scapegoating (Buehler & Gerard; Erel & Burman). In *scapegoating*, the parent focuses on the child's faults and problems as a distraction or outlet for his/her own problems.

Further contributing to the spillover hypothesis effect, social learning theory predicts that children's behavior would be influenced by vicariously modeling their parents' behavior. When they observe destructive conflict interactions between their parents, children experience strained parent–child relationships, not to mention poorer problem-solving skills, poor adjustment, and lower peer competence in their interactions apart from their parents (Buehler & Gerard, 2002; Goodman, Barfoot, Frye, & Belli, 1999). According to Cummings et al. (2001), this negative spillover is especially evident after children observe their parents involved in physical aggression, nonverbal conflict or the silent treatment, intense conflicts, conflict about child-related themes, and withdrawal. By contrast, not all marital conflicts result in negative spillover effects. In fact, observing parents deal with interparental conflict constructively may model useful social skills for children. Such constructive conflicts are emotionally regulated, mutually respectful, and ones that are either resolved or progress toward resolution. We should also note that spillover effects can occur in the opposite direction, such that strained parent–child relations place stress on the marital relationship. Living with a disturbed child or one who requires special care may place stress on parents that spills over to the marital relationship. We discuss this scenario more in our review of nonnormative family stress in chapter 10.

## CONCLUSION

In this chapter, we examine communication between parents and children from three approaches. The unidirectional approach isolates the one-way effects of parents on children. By far, this approach has the longest tradition in the parent–child literature and has accumulated the most data. Namely, we explore how parents administer warmth and control messages to children, and the effect of such messages on child outcomes. It appears parents must strike a balance such that their warmth messages are sensitive and consistent, yet not overly intrusive. Likewise, control messages are most effective when they provide well-reasoned structure that prompts the child to internalize right and wrong behavior as opposed to controlling, coercive directives that do not enhance the child's self-competence and may even prompt the child to rebel. The importance of balancing warmth and control in the parent–child relationship is consistent with Olson's (1993) recommendation for balancing cohesion and adaptability in the whole family system. Within the unidirectional approach, we also pointed to various parenting styles, the most famous of which include Baumrind's (1971) authoritative, permissive, and authoritarian styles. Of Baumrind's (1971) parenting styles, the authoritative style is most highly recommended.

The bidirectional and systems approaches respond to the need to study complexities in parent–child relationships. Namely, the bidirectional approach examines how parents and children mutually influence one another through processes of responsiveness, synchrony, and attachment. This mutual influence begins upon birth. Infants cry, parents respond, and the attachment bonds between parents and children develop and change with the years. Parents and children alike often struggle with maintaining appropriate levels of attachment. Some parents, for instance, struggle to "let their children go" as they become adolescents and young adults. Parents and children appear to benefit from synchrony, which refers to not necessarily acting in the same way, but at least to maintaining a shared interest in the relationship and interaction. When a child becomes upset, for example, the synchronous parent does not necessarily respond in kind, but is aware of the child's emotions and if appropriate sympathizes or helps problem solve.

Finally, the systems approach challenges us to look outside the dyadic parent–child relationship. Whole family interactions or co-parenting interactions often differ from dyadic parent–child interactions. In addition, the quality of other family relationships (e.g., the marital relationship) and larger societal expectations (e.g., parental role expectations) impinge on parents and children. More often than not, stress from other relationships or outside forces spills over to the parent–child relationship.

# CHAPTER EIGHT

# Sibling and Extended Family Relationships

In the study of family interaction, marital relationships and parent–child relationships command a majority of attention. In this chapter, we explore communication in other types of family relationships, sibling and extended family relationships, that play fascinating and complex roles in family life. The sibling relationship is particularly unique because it is the one family relationship that frequently lasts a lifetime. This chapter helps us understand why no two sibling relationships are alike and how sibling interaction can vary so much across the life span. To begin, sibling relationships are affected by factors such as age, sex, birth spacing, birth order, number of siblings, the family context within which they originate and exist, and differential treatment by parents. Some spend little time with their siblings, perhaps due to differences in age, geographic distance once they become adults, or living arrangements that separate step- or half-siblings after a divorce and remarriage. For others, sibling relationships are intense and complex relationships that persist over the life span. Many people wonder whether siblings have a positive or negative impact on people's lives. As we will see, siblings can have both positive and negative effects on communication competencies and well-being (Stafford, 2004). Sibling relationships are marked by frequent and intense conflict (Katz, Kramer, & Gottman, 1992) and also by remarkable caregiving and support (Stafford). Cicirelli (1996) may have said it best: At any stage, the sibling relationship may be marked by "closeness, rivalry, or indifference" (p. 67).

Do sibling relationships matter much in adulthood? Throughout adulthood sibling contact waxes and wanes, though most siblings make intentional efforts to maintain their relationship beyond their obligatory family ties. In a moment, we will learn that these maintenance efforts are beneficial, given that the sibling relationship is commonly a source of support and shared history late in life.

In the second half of the chapter, we examine extended family relationships. As with sibling relationships, extended family relationships do not fit one mold. In some families, extended family relationships are alive and strong, whereas other families focus their primary attention on the nuclear family rather than on the extended family. As we will see, many argue that definitions of and interactions in extended family relationships are influenced by sociocultural and contextual factors. We explore some of those factors. For example, we describe socioemotional selectivity theory and the intergenerational stake hypothesis, which explain how and why reliance on family as a social network varies with age. Is it really true that grandparents feel more investment in the grandparent–grandchild relationship than do grandchildren?

We spend considerable time studying the grandparent–grandchild relationship, because it is one of the most popularly researched extended family relationships. There are numerous ways grandparents play out their role and communicate with grandchildren. We examine factors that promote positive grandparent–grandchild relationships. Finally, we briefly explore how adult children relate to and care for their parents and in-laws, with an emphasis on the factors that cause strain or joy in such relationships.

## SIBLING RELATIONSHIPS

### Defining the Sibling Relationship and Exploring How Sibling Relationships Vary

Sibling relationships are unique in that they span more time than any other family relationship, often lasting from childhood to old age. During childhood, those who have siblings spend more time in the presence of their siblings than any other family relationship. McHale and Crouter (1996) found that 11-year-olds spent about 33% of their out-of-school time (close to 3 hours a day) in the presence of their siblings. Behind the sibling relationship, relationships with mothers took up about 23% of children's time. Compared to sibling relationships in childhood, adult–sibling relationships vary significantly in the amount of time siblings spend together. As we discuss in a moment, some siblings maintain a high degree of closeness and contact throughout the life span. Other siblings maintain a more formal relationship with minimal, if any, contact. Cicirelli (1996) argues that even when siblings are separated by distance, as is often the case in adulthood, or even when siblings spend minimal time together, the relationship still exists. Cicirelli proposes that the sibling relationship exists not only in overt interactions but also in covert cognitive and affective ways. This means that even when siblings go for periods of time without interacting, the relationship still exists in their minds and feelings.

Like many of the other family relationships we study in this book, sibling relationships vary by form, function, and the subjective feelings generated by them. Cicirelli (1996) defines several different sibling types. *Full siblings* have common biological parents, which means they share much of their genetic make up, with 33% to 66% of their genes in common (Cicirelli). Full siblings often share many aspects of their environment as well. As we will see later in this chapter, just because siblings share the same environment, they do not experience that environment in the same way. Yet, because of this shared history, people often turn to their sibling relationships for validation about childhood experiences (Teti, 2002).

Most sibling research pertains to full sibling relationships, although many other sibling types are common in family life. *Half-siblings* share just one biological parent, whereas *step-siblings* share no biological parents but are linked by the marriage of their parents. Some half- and step-siblings live together; others do not. White and Reidmann (1992a) found that children in remarriages give priority to their full siblings, over half- and step-siblings.

Even though people have significantly lower contact with their half- and step-siblings in adulthood, they still maintain relatively frequent contact throughout adulthood. Having no full siblings encourages more contact with step- and half-siblings. White and Reidmann also note that only 5% of step-siblings are so estranged that they do not even know where their step-sibling lives. *Adoptive siblings* are the result of the legal adoption of a child into the family. Finally, *fictive siblings* represent people who have been labeled sibling, perhaps due to custom or affection, although there is no biological or legal connection. For example, sometimes outsiders are taken into a family and treated as a brother or sister.

Birth spacing, birth order, sex of siblings, and number of siblings further contribute to the complexity of sibling relationships and make it difficult to generalize research results. Most children experience the birth of a sibling within the first 4 years of their life (Baydar, Hyle, & Brooks-Dunn, 1997). Dunn (1983) describes how birth spacing can invoke two different types of sibling relationships. *Reciprocal sibling relationships* are characterized by siblings who interact in a peerlike way by creating similar experiences for one another. Reciprocal relationships are usually seen in siblings who are close in age, developmental status, or interests. For example, children in a reciprocal sibling relationship often play together at the same level. The reciprocal sibling relationship offers children an opportunity to refine developmental competencies and peer-related social skills (McCoy, Brody, & Stoneman, 2002). In a moment, we explore the argument that siblings who are close in age in a reciprocal relationship are more prone to sibling rivalry (Minnett, Vandell, & Santrock, 1983). Obviously, siblings close in age are competing for similar resources, toys, and parental attention. *Complementary sibling relationships* occur in siblings who are at different developmental stages and competencies, often because of a larger age difference. During interaction, the older sibling fulfills the caregiving, teaching, or leading role. The younger sibling is guided by the older siblings and imitates the older siblings' behavior. As Teti (2002) indicates, complementary sibling relationships sometimes take on elements of the parent–child relationship (i.e., the older or more powerful sibling acts as a parent to the other sibling).

During adolescence and adulthood, the way siblings exchange advice and support is one indicator of whether they have a reciprocal or complementary relationship. Siblings in a reciprocal relationship are more likely to exchange advice in an egalitarian way. In a complementary sibling relationship, the older sibling gives advice and the younger sibling seeks advice, nurturance, or life direction (Buhrmester, 1992; Tucker, Barber, & Eccles, 1997). In adulthood, age is not a good indicator of whether siblings have a reciprocal or complementary relationship. Siblings commonly have a more egalitarian, or reciprocal, relationship in adulthood, regardless of age differences (Tucker et al.). The increasing competence of younger siblings appears to diminish the power differentials (Buhrmester & Furman, 1990).

There is some evidence to indicate that siblings perceive their relationship differently based on birth order or sex. Buhrmester (1992) found that during adolescence older siblings are likely to view their younger sibling as an annoyance, even though younger siblings may simultaneously view their older sibling with admiration and perceive more intimacy in the relationship. These discrepant perceptions are especially prevalent when the older sibling reaches adolescence, but are usually not perceptions that persist throughout adulthood. Besides age, sex of siblings is related to differences in perceptions of the sibling relationship and sibling interaction. Compared to males, females report greater intimacy, admiration, and affection for their sibling relationships (Buhrmester; Clark-Lempers, Lempers, & Ho, 1991). Female–female sibling dyads use relationship maintenance behaviors more often, and they offer and accept more advice and intimate disclosures than male–male or cross-sex dyads (Myers & Members of COM 200, 2001; Tucker et al., 1997).

Overall, Teti (2002) argues that "sibling constellation variables," such as birth spacing, birth order, sex of sibling, and number of siblings, are interesting, but of little value when trying to predict sibling interaction and relationship quality. First, these constellation variables fluctuate so much according to each sibling dyad. Second, the complexity of sibling relationships is attributed to far more than these surface constellation variables. Sibling interaction is greatly influenced by individual factors such as personality or unique family system forces such as parenting styles or family divorce and remarriage.

## Preadult Sibling Relationships

### The Transition to Siblinghood

Family systems theorists propose that the introduction of a sibling to the family system causes major stress, or change, for all members of the family system, including the older sibling. Psychodynamic interpretations from the early to mid part of the 1900s characterized the stress introduced by a sibling as a negative force for the older sibling (Teti, 2002). The birth of a younger sibling was thought to induce rivalry and jealousy on the part of the older sibling, as well as resentment regarding the attention parents devote to the newborn. Is there any evidence to support these claims?

There may in fact be some detrimental effects related to the introduction of a sibling. However, the detrimental effects are not directly related to the introduction of the sibling per say, but rather to other changes in the family system that accompany the sibling in some families. Baydar, Greek, and Brooks-Gunn (1997) found that sometimes the introduction of an additional child leaves less time for positive parent–child interaction with the older child and prompts parents to increase their controlling and punitive communication behaviors. This is detrimental to the older child's vocabulary development. In addition, the introduction of a sibling, particularly when closely spaced in age, takes a toll on the economic well-being of the family. The additional child places more stress on the system overall and means parents may not be able to afford activities and opportunities for the older child. Blake (1989) found that people from families with four children receive on average a year less schooling than those from families with two children, because resources are spread thinner. In addition, the birth of a younger sibling is related to an increase in behavioral problems in preschool and elementary school-aged children (Baydar, Hyle, & Brooks-Gunn, 1997). However, these behavioral problems are temporary and usually diminish in about a year. Baydar, Hyle et al. (1997) also note that increases in behavior problems are based on reports by mothers, who may simply be perceiving more behavior problems as a result of their own stress associated with a new baby.

To the contrary, there may also be some positive effects from the introduction of a sibling, which in turn cancel out some of the negative aspects. When a sibling is born, families are less likely to rely on daycare, now that they have the expense of two children versus one. In certain cases, older siblings benefit from less daycare and a parent who is solely focused on the children (Baydar, Greek, & Brooks-Gunn, 1997). Further, some older siblings react in a positive and nurturing way to the birth of a sibling. At first, the older sibling may help with newborn care by dressing, diapering, feeding, and holding and touching the baby (Nadelman & Bagun, 1982). Later the older sibling may teach, lead, or take responsibility for the growing sibling. These nurturing skills are important lessons that usually pay off for older children later in life, when they are called on to use nurturing, teaching, or leading skills in a job or use caregiving skills in their own family of orientation (Teti, 2002). Cicirelli (1994) cautions, however, that the benefits older children experience from enacting a caregiver role are curvilinear. Moderate caregiving by older siblings enhances their academic achievement, but heavy caregiving responsibilities hinder older siblings' academic achievement because they do not have time to attend to their own responsibilities. Overall, Teti suggests that a high-quality, secure relationship between parents of the older child before the birth of the sibling promotes children's adjustment to the birth of a sibling. When this is the case, the transition to siblinghood may not be so disturbing.

### Sibling Caregiving, Support, and Socialization

Until researchers began to systematically study sibling relationships in the 1970s, siblings were primarily characterized in terms of rivalry and competition (Teti, 2002). However, siblings appear to provide many prosocial behaviors for one another beginning with caregiving and support. Indeed in some contexts, such as non-Western cultures or lower income families in the United States, older siblings are called on to a great extent to care for younger siblings (Brody, Stoneman, Smith, & Gibson, 1999; Teti, 2002). At a very early age, siblings demonstrate support and caregiving skills. Dunn and Kendrick (1982) found that siblings as young as 2 and 3 years old appeared to be in touch with their younger brother's or sister's feelings. These toddlers could comment to their parents about their infant sibling's emotional state or what they thought the infant liked or disliked. In turn, younger siblings very soon become attached to their older siblings, sometimes turning to them for comfort or security, especially in the absence of a parental caregiver. During middle childhood and adolescence, siblings often grow closer and show support to one another in the face of life events with a negative impact (Dunn, 1996). However, Dunn is quick to note that siblings do not grow closer in response to all negative life events. In Dunn's research, most of the negative life events around which siblings reported drawing closer were not severe life events. In the case of marital separation and divorce, there is mixed evidence regarding whether siblings respond with increased conflict or increased support to one another.

There is no doubt that siblings actively socialize one another. The sibling relationship is often called a "training ground" for social skills and peer competencies (Parke & Buriel, 1998; Stafford, 2004). In this training ground, siblings experiment with positive, prosocial behaviors (e.g., skills for comforting, empathy, conflict management, or academic achievement) and negative, antisocial behaviors (e.g., aggression, teasing, or risky and delinquent behaviors). Tucker, Updegraff, McHale, and Crouter (1999) explored how older siblings socialize prosocial behaviors such as empathy and perspective-taking skills in the younger sibling. Earlier research by Perner, Ruffman, and Leekam (1994) indicates that children with siblings have better perspective taking skills than only children. Minus some exceptions, Tucker et al. found that simply having a sibling is not what encourages the development of perspective taking skills, but rather having a good relationship with a sibling. In general, when siblings reported a positive relationship and when the older sibling exhibited positive behaviors (e.g., doing nice things for the sibling and trying to make the sibling feel better), younger siblings exhibited more empathy. Younger boys' empathy was promoted by having a positive relationship with an older brother versus an older sister. The younger brothers appeared to focus on same sex models more, although the positive behaviors of older sisters did make some impact. Though younger sisters' empathy was enhanced by positive behaviors in older siblings, younger sisters, but not brothers, also appeared to develop empathy skills in response to older sisters who were negative (e.g., hurt the sibling, were mean to the sibling). Tucker et al. speculated that either (a) it was adaptive for the younger sisters to be empathically aware of their hostile older sisters' feelings in order to defend themselves or (b) girls in general are socialized to feel more responsible for the negative feelings of others.

Certainly sibling relationships are not the only place children can learn perspective-taking skills. This may be one reason why Kitzmann, Cohen, and Lockwood (2002) found that the quality of only children's friendships was no lower than children who had siblings. Though the only children in Kitzmann et al.'s study had similar quality friendships as children with siblings, we should note that elementary-school-age (6–12 years) only children were more likely to be victimized and aggressive in their peer group. Kitamann et al. suggest that having a sibling may help children learn important conflict management skills earlier in life.

We cannot assume that siblings always promote social competencies; siblings sometimes inhibit social competencies (Stafford, 2004). Just as siblings can learn useful conflict management skills from one another, they also learn and model aggressive behaviors (Bank, Patterson, & Reid, 1996; Patterson, Dishion, & Bank, 1984). In addition, many siblings socialize risky behaviors in one another. For example, alcohol use by a nearby sibling is a risk factor for adolescent drinking and abuse (Conger & Rueter, 1996; see also chap. 14). One plausible reason is that alcohol use by an older sibling models, facilitates, and legitimizes drinking and association with friends who drink. Overall, Teti (2002) argues that the socialization role of siblings is complex and poorly understood, and it is difficult to make general conclusions. We can safely say that siblings prompt both positive and negative socialization effects.

### Sibling Competition and Conflict

Sibling relationships are commonly noted for their competition and conflict. To some extent this charaterization is true. Some amount of conflict and discord is normative in sibling relationships. In fact, nonaggressive sibling conflict may actually promote social development and teach children to tolerate negative affect and manage conflict (Katz et al., 1992; Kramer & Baron, 1995). However, conflict among siblings can become destructive and extreme. Prolonged hostile conflict among siblings is detrimental for children's well-being. Stocker, Burwell, and Briggs (2002) found that such conflict predicted children's increased anxiety, depressed mood, and delinquent behavior. Others indicate that extreme conflict among siblings predicts disturbed behavior into adulthood (Patterson, 1982). Naturally, the more verbally aggressive messages (i.e., messages that attack a person's self-concept to deliver psychological pain) individuals receive from their siblings, the less satisfied they are with their sibling relationship (Teven, Martin, & Newpauer, 1998). Stocker et al.'s sophisticated research methods even allow us to conclude that the influence of sibling conflict on child well-being is independent of the influence of hostile conflict behaviors from parents.

Siblings are prone to rivalry and competition, particularly when they feel resources or parental attention are in short demand. Interestingly, it appears that siblings often act, whether consciously or unconsciously, in ways that will reduce competition and social comparisons. *Sibling deidentification* is a process in which individuals specifically aim to develop an identity unique from their siblings (Schacter, 1982; Teti, 2002). Sibling deidentification is most evident in late childhood. During this time, children become aware of their own identity and how they can uniquely shape themselves through the choices they make. For example, a child may differentiate himself or herself from a sibling who excelled in a particular sport or hobby, by choosing an alternative hobby. Theoretically, sibling deidentification is more important for siblings who are close in age and competing for the same resources and parental or social attention. Teti further argues that we can only understand sibling rivalry and competition in the context of the larger family system. If sibling deidentifiaction is a way for children to respond to expectations or scarce resources in the family system, then we must understand that what it takes for a sibling to "deidentify" from another is related to the unique expectations of that family system. In some families, this requires carving out a niche very different from that of a sibling.

Are there productive ways to curb destructive sibling conflict and competition? In a unique study, Kramer and Radey (1997) tested whether 4- to 5-year-old siblings who were exposed to social skills training to get along with their younger siblings actually made prosocial improvements in their interaction. The researchers took baseline measurements of the siblings' interaction in their home before the training. The multiweek training involved instruction, modeling, role-playing, and positive feedback in the research laboratory as well as in the home. For example, facilitators discussed ways to initiate play with a younger sibling and appropriate versus inappropriate behaviors. The training also involved modeling with dolls that they pretended to be siblings, as well as free-play time in which siblings were prompted or praised for their behavior. The researchers set up a control group who read books and watched videos about how to get along with siblings, but received no direct instruction. Compared to the control group, those who received the direct social skills training demonstrated more of the social skills they learned during actual interaction later on. Parents of those in the training group reported decreased levels of sibling rivalry, competition, antagonism, power differentials and more sibling warmth. Kramer and Radey concluded that it is possible to teach children effective ways to relate to a sibling early on so as to set the sibling relationship on a positive trajectory.

### Parental Involvement in Sibling Relationships

In Kramer and Radey's (1997) study, the social skills training was facilitated by trained graduate students who were obviously not related to the children. This begs questions regarding the extent to which parents are effective at intervening in sibling conflict and further the degree to which parents should be involved in sibling conflict. Kramer and Baron (1995) describe the real concerns that parents have about how to help their children develop positive sibling relationships. Not only are they concerned about expressions of conflict and antagonism among siblings, but also parents are disturbed, potentially more disturbed, when they observe less warmth in the sibling relationship than they expect. Kramer and Baron go on to explain that sometimes parents' high expectations for siblings to get along with each other are unrealistic in light of children's developmental level. For example, some children are too young to understand the concept of sharing with a sibling.

When siblings are in conflict, parents face the dilemma of whether to step in and solve the problem, let the siblings work the problem out on their own, or indirectly coach them. Clearly the severity of the conflict and the developmental stage of the child makes a difference. McHale, Updegraff, et al. (2000) found that parents who try to step in and solve conflicts between their adolescent siblings usually promote even more negative sibling relationship qualities. Furman and Giberson (1995) concur that parents who try to micromanage their children's conflicts deny them the opportunity to refine their own conflict management skills. In contrast, positive sibling relationship qualities among adolescents are promoted when parents spend time together in everyday, shared activities with the sibling dyad (McHale, Updegraff, et al.). For adolescent children, casually promoting cohesion among the sibling dyad and family unit works better than a direct intervention once problems develop. This more autonomous parenting style fits especially well with adolescents who are typically autonomy seeking.

Part of what makes it tough for parents who intervene is the danger that siblings will perceive differential treatment on the part of the parent. Differential treatment by parents is actually very common and children are highly aware of it. Kowal, Kramer, Krull, and Crick (2002) found that siblings perceive differential treatment in over a third of their parents' behaviors. Furthermore, siblings agree on the occurrence and direction of differential treatment about a third of the time. A great deal of research suggests that differential treatment of siblings has negative effects, promoting sibling antagonism, resentment, and distress (Teti, 2002). Yet Kowal et al. found that children rate 75% of cases of preferential treatment as fair and tolerable. As Kowal et al. say, "issues of equity rather than equality appear to be most salient to children, at least during early adolesence" (p. 304). If they perceive the differential treatment to be "logical" and if they have a positive relationship, siblings handle differential treatment better. For example, older siblings may understand that a younger sibling needs to be treated differently given age and developmental demands. What this means is that siblings' subjective evaluations appear to matter more than do objective evaluations. Subjective evaluations also reveal that some children dislike the fact that they are preferentially treated because it makes them feel awkward that they are getting something that they do not deserve.

## Adult Sibling Relationships

### Early and Middle Adulthood

Research generally indicates that siblings remain important forces in each other's lives throughout adulthood. Two thirds of people report that a sibling is among their closest friends (White & Riedmann, 1992b). The sibling relationship does, however, wax and wane throughout adulthood. White's (2001) analysis of sibling relationships over the life course indicates that sibling contact decreases in early adulthood and then resurges in later adulthood. For example, at around 16 years of age, siblings gradually give and receive less help from each other than they do in earlier years. Declines in sibling contact and the sibling bond are consistent with the individuation process that most young adults experience as they physically and psychologically detach themselves from their families of origin (White, 2001). White found that levels of contact remain "remarkably stable" from age 45 to 85. On average, siblings talk with or visit one another once or twice a month throughout adulthood. White remarks that siblings are clearly among the "second tier" in adults' social networks, with the adults' new family of orientation in the "first tier." In many cases, siblings experience a "substantial resurgence" in helping exchanges after age 70.

There are several factors that contribute to variance in sibling contact. To begin, contact frequency varies widely according to proximity, with nearby siblings sharing significantly more contact, especially as they age. Siblings with more education and higher incomes have more contact (Treas & Lawton, 1999). Presumably, financial resources facilitate sibling contact, especially when distance is involved. Sibling contact also changes in response to life circumstances, although the effects are small and not so consistent. Marital dissolution is a life circumstance that is related to increases in sibling contact and exchange, whereas new marriages and geographic distance (e.g., due to employment) are related to less sibling contact. Marriage alters siblings' previous interaction patterns, particularly if the new spouse is disliked by the other sibling (Cicirelli, 1996). Some believe that having children reduces sibling contact, because the sibling with children is so involved with his or her first-tier family. However, there is evidence that having children boosts sibling contact because siblings are concerned about maintaining ties in the form of active relationships with aunts, uncles, and cousins (White, 2001). Overall, it is difficult to make large generalizations about the impact of life-course events on sibling contact and bonding.

Myers and Members of COM 200 (2001) found that adults in their mid- to late 20s actively use relationship maintenance behaviors in their sibling relationships. In other words, most adults have a commitment to their sibling relationships that extends beyond obligatory family ties. Further, relationship maintenance behaviors such as positivity, openness, assurances, sharing networks, and sharing tasks are all related to sibling liking. Adult siblings use shared task maintenance behaviors most frequently, and openness least frequently. Shared tasks include helping each other, sharing household chores, sharing care of elderly parents, babysitting, and participating in and putting on family events and holidays. Myers and his students note that these behaviors are not always fun, but they are an instrumental part of the sibling relationship and represent an attitude of sacrifice and shared burdens. To explain why openness is the least used maintenance behavior, Myers and his students point to the idea that sibling relationships are less voluntary and not built on self-disclosure like a romantic relationship or friendship. Siblings tend to be more open with their friends when it comes to most topics except those that revolve around their parents (Pulakos, 1988).

Just as positive sibling behavior persists into adulthood, negative aspects of the sibling relationship, such as rivalry, do not always end when siblings enter adulthood. In adulthood, sibling rivalry is commonly transformed into comparisons (Adams, 1999). In individualist, success-oriented societies, siblings compare "how they are doing" in relation to their siblings, matching up career achievements, financial resources, houses, kids, kids' achievements, and even parental attention. Siblings make these comparisons openly and subtly (Adams). Along with rivalry, outright sibling conflict often continues into adulthood. Sometimes the topics of conflict shift along with family life-cycle stages. For example, adult siblings may disagree over how to cooperate regarding care for an aging parent. In many cases, sibling conflicts are rooted in the same perpetual issues that sparked conflict in childhood (e.g., power struggles or differential treatment).

Gold (1989) explains that the way siblings negotiate contact, closeness, involvement, acceptance, emotional and instrumental support, envy, and resentment results in five different types of sibling relationships, described in Table 8.1.

Gold (1989) found that 78% of adult sibling relationships were intimate, congenial, or loyal types, and the remaining other types were apathetic or hostile. Bedford (1995)

**TABLE 8.1**
Sibling Types in Adulthood

| | |
|---|---|
| Intimate siblings: | The siblings are highly devoted and psychologically close to one another. They exhibit high affection, acceptance, self-disclosure, and empathy, as well as a lack of envy and resentment. The sibling relationship takes priority over most other relationships. |
| Congenial siblings: | Siblings are affectionate and close; however, they clearly place more value on marital and parent–child relationships. |
| Loyal siblings: | The siblings adhere to cultural norms for their relationship. They support each other during times of crisis and see each other at family events. They have regular, but not frequent contact. |
| Apathetic siblings: | The siblings are mutually disinterested in one another and see little of each other because their lives have gone in different directions. They are not, however, hostile or rivalrous. |
| Hostile siblings: | Siblings exhibit strong negative feelings toward one another, in the form of envy, resentment, negative affect, and they are preoccupied with the negative state of the relationship. |

*Note.* Adapted from Gold (1989).

notes that a majority of adults believe their sibling(s) would come to their aid in crisis, regardless of the quality of their relationship. One could imagine intimate, congenial, loyal, or perhaps even apathetic or hostile siblings coming to one another's aid if the situation truly called for extreme measures.

### Later Adulthood

Positive aspects of *young adult* sibling relationships include (a) companionship, (b) aid and services, (c) emotional support, and (d) cooperation in care for the elderly. Positive aspects in *older adult* sibling relationships also involve (a) companionship and (b) aid and services. But slightly different from young adult sibling relationships, older adult sibling relationships may include (c) emotional support, often in the form of reminiscence and shared memories; and (d) resolution of rivalry and comparisons earlier in life (Adams, 1999, p. 87; Goetting, 1986).

Providing socioemotional support through shared reminiscing may be an even more important role for elderly siblings than providing aid (Mares, 1995). Ultimately, some elderly persons can pay for others to provide care and aid (e.g., in a nursing home), but they only have limited people in their social network who can share memories dating back to childhood. White (2001) stresses how unique it is that later-life siblings share such a lifelong string of memories: "Siblings may be the only members of older individuals' social networks who can not only remember World War II, but who can also remember them in 1940" (p. 566).

Sister–sister sibling pairs tend to be the most intimate and keep in the most contact later in life, just as in earlier life (Riggio, 2000). Cicirelli (1989) found that older men and women who feel closer to a sister are less depressed than those who do not. Sisters are also likely to help their bereaved sister during the transition to widowhood (Lopata, 1973). Brother–sister dyads are next closest, and brother–brother sibling pairs least intimate in later life, though some argue that brothers possess strongly intimate feelings about their siblings, but they just do not reveal their feelings as outwardly (Bedford & Avioli, 2001).

Some of the increased intimacy that siblings feel later in life may be attributed to the fact that they have let go of some resentment, rivalry, or conflict that characterized their relationship earlier. Sibling rivalry fueled by parents' preferential treatment appears to negatively impact childhood sibling pairs more than later-life sibling pairs (Riggio, 2000). With parents no longer living, later-life siblings are not so immediately reminded of the differential treatment. Later-life siblings may be able to put earlier conflicts in perspective or may have simply learned to avoid topics that generate conflict in their relationship.

## EXTENDED FAMILY RELATIONSHIPS

## The Extended Family as a Social Network

The phrase *extended family* refers to "social relationships among those related by blood, law, or self-ascribed association that extends beyond the marriage or committed part- ner couple, and the immediate family of parenting adult(s) and dependent children"

(Schmeeckle & Sprecher, 2004, p. 350). Extended family is sometimes referred to as "secondary kin," and differentiated from immediate family or first-tier kin (Adams, 1999). Modern-day immediate families are increasingly complex as a result of factors such as cohabitation, divorce, and stepfamilies. Extended family networks then become exponentially diverse and complex (Schmeeckle & Sprecher).

There are a variety of factors that affect contact and bonding with extended family members, including technology, culture, and life-course stage. Technological advances such as telephones, airplane travel, and computer-assisted communication (e.g., e-mail) allow geographically dispersed family members to maintain active ties more so than in the past (Schmeeckle & Sprecher, 2004). However, access to these technological tools for staying in touch with family depends on economic resources. Having more education and greater economic resources can lure people away from their extended family to pursue career opportunities. But again, these privileges can increase contact with extended family, to the extent that one has the economic means for travel, e-mail, and phones (Johnson, 2000). Although many believe that people who experience low socioeconomic conditions increase contact with extended family networks to alleviate the conditions of poverty, Roschelle (1997) found the opposite case to be true: As socioeconomic conditions increase, so does participation in social support networks such as extended family.

Under the umbrella of culture, researchers have examined how cultural factors such as socioeconomic class, ethnicity, gender, and age affect contact with extended family. Socioeconomic class and ethnicity have been pinpointed as factors that relate to living with extended family members. Interestingly, the percentage of extended family households decreased to a low of 10% in 1980, but then gradually increased to 12% in 1990 (Glick, Bean, & Van Hook, 1997). Glick et al. tested whether changes in waves of immigration had anything to do with the increase in extended family living. Mexican, Guatemalan, and Salvadoran immigrant families did account for some of the increase, primarily because of the number of young single adults who emigrated from these countries to live with relatives. However, immigration explained only a little of the overall increase in extended family households in the total population. There are other social and economic trends that contribute to extended family living (e.g., single teen mothers living with their parents or adult children and grandchildren living with parents because cost of living pressures preclude a separate residence).

Overall, there is mixed evidence regarding the extent to which extended family relationships vary according to ethnicity. A large body of literature suggests that many minority families in the United States maintain strong network ties. For example, Kamo (1998) argues that Confucian regard for *filial responsibility* (i.e., responsibility for parents exercised by children) prescribes many Asian American families to interact with older extended family by way of respect and obligation. This is manifested in high personal contact, financial and physical support for the elderly, and coresidence involving multigenerational arrangements. Even Asian American families that are not driven by Confucianism, for example, Filipino American families, adhere strongly to values of respect and obligation. Research indicates a great deal of variance in Latino families, because Mexican American families are often different from Cuban or Puerto Rican families (Williams & Torrez, 1998). Still, there is some evidence to indicate that compared to Black and White families, Mexican American families are larger, have more frequent intergenerational contact, and have greater expectations for intergenerational assistance. As we discuss later in the chapter, African Americans are more likely to live in extended family households than are European Americans (Hunter & Taylor, 1998). If they live in close proximity, African American family members are likely to remain in close contact. African American grandmothers, especially, play a central role as authority figures and sources of support and consistency.

Contrary to the arguments that minority families in the United States maintain stronger network ties with extended family, results of Roschelle's (1997) research indicate the following: "African Americans, Chicanos, and Puerto Ricans are not more familistic than non-Hispanic White families. In fact, Anglo men and women give to and receive from network members more child care help and household assistance than do African Americans, Chicanos, or Puerto Ricans" (p. 181). Roschelle further argues that family scholars have exaggerated the idea that present-day minority families participate more actively with extended family out of values for familism. The issue is clearly a complicated one that interacts with multiple factors such as socioeconomic class, contextual factors (e.g., rural vs. urban families), and changing values. Based on their research, Riedmann and White (1996) concur that there is no consistent evidence that one ethnic group has stronger adult sibling ties or that any group is characterized by weaker ties (p. 125). Some researchers suggest that differences in kinship ties among ethnic groups in the United States are most evident in the oldest generation. Johnson (1995, 2000) found significant differences in the kinship ties of Whites and Blacks, but the differences were among participants in the study who were over 85 years old. Johnson concludes that differences in kinship networks between Whites and Blacks appear among "White oldest old" and "Black oldest old." In Johnson's sample, Black respondents were more involved in family life, received more instrumental and expressive support from family, stayed in more frequent contact with them, and relied on siblings and siblings' children far more than White respondents. It could be that the role of extended family in minority families is gradually transforming.

One active part of many African American and Latino kin networks that is not seen commonly in European American kin networks is *fictive kin* (Schmeeckle & Sprecher, 2004). Fictive kin are treated as relatives though they are not related by blood or law. For example, a close adult female may be assigned the title "aunt" and treated as such, though there is no blood relation. Compared to European Americans, African Americans are more likely to enact the principle of substitution (Luckey, 1994). In substitution, older childless persons treat their nieces and nephews as their own children. Godparents, another type of fictive kin especially common in Latino families, represent adults who are given the honor and challenge of providing an additional support network for children.

Research has produced a consistent message regarding gender and extended family ties. Women are more involved in maintaining family ties than men, and older women do more of the work to maintain family ties than younger women (Adams, 1999, p. 87). Schmeeckle and Sprecher (2004) emphasize that men are involved in maintaining family ties, just not to the same degree as women in most families. Compared to men, women are more commonly designated and socialized to be "kinkeepers," who are in charge of maintaining family ties. Women indeed report more obligation to care for and assistant kin (Stein, 1992). But even though women feel more obligation, Stein found that men are more likely to experience psychological distress (e.g., depression, neuroticism) in conjunction with their feelings of obligation. Why is it that feelings of obligation are not associated with psychological distress in women to the degree they are in men? This is especially puzzling given women experience *more* feelings of obligation than men. Stein argues that when people have the opportunity to repay obligations, they feel less distress because they can actively take personal control over ridding themselves of obligatory feelings. Norms and expectations for women to assist kin, host family gatherings, and initiate contact may be an outlet for repaying obligations and reducing psychological distress, and this outlet is not as readily available to men.

### Socioemotional Selectivity Theory

To explain the relationship between age and reliance on the family network, we introduce *socioemotional selectivity theory* (Carstensen, 1993, 1995). The theory proposes that as people get older, they begin to feel that their time is limited. As a result, their preferences for social contact and social partners change. Namely, they favor emotionally meaningful relationships that have immediate benefits, such as family relationships or familiar relationships, over peripheral relationships that tend to offer information and satisfy ambitions that will benefit one in the long term. Carstensen explains three goals that motivate social contact and describes how attention to these goals changes as a result of life stage (see Figure 8.1).

The first goal, *emotion regulation*, refers to the desire for emotional comfort and gratification. This goal is especially strong in infancy, and then again later in life when people invest their limited time in their most emotionally meaningful relationships. The goal of *information seeking* prompts people to seek out contact with people who are the best sources, even if those people are novel and unfamiliar. When information seeking, people

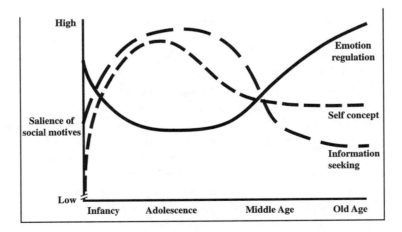

**FIG. 8.1.**    Socioemotional selectivity theory: Three salient social motives across the life span.
*Note:* From "Evidence for a Life-Span Theory of Socioemotional Selectivity," by L. J. Carstensen, 1995, *Current Direction in Psychological Science, 4*, pp. 151–156. Copyright 1995 by Blackwell Publishers. Reprinted with permission.

are trying to understand the world, what other people are like, and what culture is like. Carstensen explains that information seeking peaks from adolescence to young adulthood. By later life, people have already experienced life and may be less interested in information seeking because they have "been there and done that." Developing and maintaining *self-concept* is a third social goal that encourages people to consider their place in the social world, consider how they compare with other people, and monitor their view of themselves and other people's view of themselves. The self-concept goal peaks in adolescence.

As socioemotional selectivity theory predicts, social network sizes vary by age (Lang & Carstensen, 2002; Lang, Staudinger, & Carstensen, 1998). Older adults have smaller social networks than do young and middle aged adults. Younger and middle aged adults who prioritize social acceptance have larger social networks, a greater proportion of friends, and receive advice more often. Older adults who prioritize emotional regulation goals have smaller social networks and receive less advice. Indeed, this pattern appears to be adaptive for older adults. Social contacts that do not promote emotional gratification may even strain older persons. Many older adults find emotional gratification in their family relationships, particularly their nuclear family relationships. Those who do not have nuclear family available, perhaps those who never married, remained childless, or prematurely lost a spouse and children, appear to compensate by investing in a small network of other emotionally meaningful relationships (e.g., close friendships). Such persons still appear to have the same number of emotionally close relationships in later life than those with nuclear family available. The age-related social network patterns predicted by socioemotional selectivity theory appear to be similar in European Americans and African Americans (Fung, Carstensen, & Lang, 2001). Socioemotional selectivity theory may have some interesting implications for other types of extended family relationships, such as the grandparent and grandchild relationship.

## Grandparent–Grandchild Relationships

Harwood (2000a) argues that compared to marital communication or parent–child communication, grandparent–grandchild (GP–GC) communication has been relatively ignored in the family communication research literature. With the introduction of Szinovacz's (1998) edited *Handbook on Grandparenthood*, Bengtson and Robertson's (1985) *Grandparenthood*, and numerous journal articles in the last two decades exploring the complexities of GP–GC relationships and communication within them, attention is rapidly growing. In this section, we begin by exploring variations in the role of grandparenting. Attention to the role of grandparents gained momentum when researchers began to (a) classify types of grandparents, (b) explore variation in functional and cultural grandparenting roles, and (c) study how divorce impacts the way the grandparent role is experienced (Allen, Blieszner, & Roberto, 2000). A second emphasis in the research literature involves studying GP–GC communication as well as relationship development and decline between grandparents and grandchildren. Much of this research explores (a) communication topics and patterns, (b) predictors of solidarity in the GP–GC relationship, and (c) predictions of the intergenerational stake hypothesis and socioemotional selectivity theory.

## Variations in the Grandparenting Role

### Prevalence and Timing

Over the course of the last hundred years, increasing life expectancies mean people are more likely to have grandparents living when they are born. Uhlenberg and Kirby's (1998) work on demographic trends in grandparenthood projected that in 2000, two thirds of all children began their lives with a complete set of grandparents. In 1900, less than one fourth of newborns began their lives with all grandparents alive. Decreasing family sizes also mean that compared to the past, children today have fewer siblings or cousins, but more living grandparents.

Before concluding that grandparenthood is on the rise, it is important to consider other demographic trends that offset the likelihood that people will know their grandparents or be a grandparent. Even though people are living longer, an increasing number of people never have a grandchild. Uhlenberg and Kirby calculated that rates of grandchildlessness will reach 25% for those entering old age after 2020. Of women aged 60 to 64 in 1900, 16.4% were grandchildless. In addition, women are delaying childbirth, which counters grandparents' chances of getting to know their grandchildren before grandparents die. Matthews and Hamilton (2002) report that the mean age of U.S. mothers who gave birth was 24.6 in 1970 and 27.2 in 2000. The mean age of mothers for a first birth was 21.4 in 1970 and 24.9 in 2000. Most striking, from 1990 to 2001, the number of women who gave birth increased by 14% for women 30 to 34, by 28% for women 35 to 39, and by 47% for women 40 to 44. Equally notable, the number of teenage pregnancies has decreased to historically low levels (Ventura, Hamilton, & Sutton, 2003).

People have expectations regarding the "model age" for becoming a grandparent. Hirshorn (1998) introduced the idea of *"on-time"* versus *"off-time"* grandparenthood. In off-time grandparenthood, people experience the role of grandparenthood earlier or later than they expected. Experiencing the role off-time can leave grandparents feeling deviant, isolated or lacking in social support (Hirshorn). In a moment, we discuss grandparents who become primary caretakers of their grandchildren, sometimes because of an off-time birth such as a teenage pregnancy. In the other direction, some people experience anxiety due to the fact that they are not grandparents by the time they expected to be.

### Grandparent Types

In 1964, Neugarten and Weinstein developed one of the first typologies of grandparenting styles. Their typology included five styles. (1) The *formal style* describes grandparents who maintain a clear line between parents and grandparents. They might occasionally babysit, provide special gifts, or minor services, but they are sure not to offer advice on childrearing to parents. (2) The *fun-seeker style* involves grandparents who have the view that the GP–GC relationship should be one of pleasure and leisure. They look to have fun with their grandchildren rather than establish lines of authority. Sometimes the fun involves indulging in special activities and treats. (3) In the *surrogate parent style*, the grandparent, usually the grandmother, takes on a parenting role and may even substitute for the children's mother. The surrogate parent role is called on when the mother cannot take care of the children because of employment or other reasons. (4) Grandfathers commonly enact the *reservoir of family wisdom* style. Here, the grandparent represents an

**TABLE 8.2**
Typology of Grandparenting Styles

1. *Influential*:    These grandparents are physically present and highly involved in the grandchildren's lives on a weekly and sometimes daily basis. They feel they have an intimate relationship with their grandchildren and act as a confidant for their grandchild. They sometimes advise their grandchildren and talk about their grandchild's future. They offer instrumental help in the form of financial assistance, helping the grandchild find a job, etc. Authority and discipline are also part of the grandparents' role.
2. *Supportive*:    Unlike influential grandparents, supportive grandparents do not enter into a role of authority and discipline with their grandchildren. They see their grandchildren very often, though perhaps not as frequently as the influential grandparents. They encourage their grandchild's talents and attend their grandchild's activities. They are similar to influential grandparents in many other ways, maintaining intimacy and offering instrumental support. But again, they do not enter the parent-like authority role.
3. *Passive*:    These grandparents are mildly to moderately involved in their grandchildren's lives. They do not provide instrumental support or engage in authority and discipline. They do not engage in a lot of activities with their grandchild or attend many activities. Still they report being a friend to their grandchild, a confidant on a few limited topics such as parents and the future, and feel that their grandchildren learn some skills from them. Passive grandparents are more likely to live far away from their grandchildren or have a large number of grandchildren to juggle.
4. *Authority oriented*:    Like the passive grandparents, authority-oriented grandparents are less involved in social activities with their grandchild. Instead, they see themselves as authority figures and enforce discipline for their grandchildren. They readily provide wisdom and advice. They do provide some instrumental assistance to their grandchildren as well. Younger grandparents are more likely to be authority oriented.
5. *Detached*:    These grandparents are the least involved in their grandchildren's lives. They have little interaction, share few activities, do not describe themselves as close to their grandchildren, and do not know their grandchildren well. Occasionally, they provide financial assistance.

*Note*. Adapted from Cherlin & Furstenberg (1985, 1986) and Mueller, Wilhelm, & Elder (2002).

authoritative figure with traditional power. This powerful figure hands down resources, lessons, and skills. (5) Finally, the *distant figure* style depicts grandparents who have little or no contact with their grandchildren. When they do have contact it usually involves a fleeting appearance at a family ritual or holiday.

Cherlin and Furstenberg (1985, 1986) developed another popular classification of grandparenting styles. This classification was later replicated and extended by Mueller, Wilhelm, and Elder (2002). The classification also involves five grandparenting styles described in Table 8.2.

Mueller et al. (2002) further note that *influential* and *supportive* grandparents are usually embedded within a highly cohesive family system. Compared to other types of grandparents, these grandparents also tend to be more educated, have fewer grandchildren, live closer to their grandchildren, and are sometimes involved in farming. *Passive* and *detatched* grandparents tend to live farther away, be on the paternal side, have a large number of grandchildren, lack encouragement from the parent generation, and not be involved in farming. *Authority-oriented* grandparents tend to be younger, employed full time, encouraged by the parents to play an authority role, and more likely to be on the maternal side.

### Grandparents Who Function as Primary Caretakers

For many, grandparenthood is a time of great joy, filled with relaxed, leisure-based interactions with grandchildren. A significant number of grandparents, however, play the role of primary caregiver to their grandchildren. Goodman and Silverstein (2001) report that in 1997, six percent of children under age 18 were living in grand-parent headed households. In addition, grandparent-headed households are the norm for 13% of African American children, 5.7% of Hispanic children, and 3.9% of non-Hispanic White children. Grandparents who have sole responsibility for their grandchildren often take on this role in response to disruptive family events that preclude parents from taking primary responsibility for their children. Such events may include the parents' incarceration, addiction, death, mental illness, teen pregnancy, or child abuse. Minkler and Roe (1993), for example, highlighted the strains experienced by urban African American grandmothers raising children whose parents were consumed by the crack cocaine epidemic. We should also point out Jimenez's (2002) argument that African American grandmothers do not always assume primary caretaking responsibilities in response to family stress or deficit. Instead, African American families may indeed have a cultural heritage of kinship solidarity that prompts grandmothers to assume involved caretaking responsibilities regardless of the family situation.

Grandparents who are primary caretakers interact with their children differently than do other grandparents. On one hand, they experience the joys of raising a child more directly, as they watch children grow, learn, and participate in activities. However, grandparents also report a long list of stressors associated with the primary caretaker role (Waldrop & Weber, 2001). These stressors include the following: tension and trauma lingering from problems that precluded the parent from providing care, balancing work and care for the grandchild, financial burden, ambiguity over the grandparent's legal authority over the child, poor health, and a lack of social support or coping outlets. Children who live with a grandparent and no parent present are twice as likely to be in families below the poverty level than children living with both a parent and grandparent (Fields, 2003). In light of these stressors, it is not surprising that undertaking the primary caretaking responsibilities for grandchildren is associated with a higher risk for depression (Soloman & Marx, 2000). Waldrop and Weber describe the most common coping mechanisms used by grandparents who are primary caretakers. In order of those most highly utilized, the coping mechanisms include: taking action to stabilize the child's situation, talking about feelings, relying on religious faith, working hard rather than dwelling on problems, focusing on the grandchild's needs, reaching out to others (e.g., volunteers and friends), and indulging in bad habits that make them feel better for the moment (e.g., overeating, increased smoking, drinking too much coffee, or staying up late).

### Cultural Variations in the Grandparenting Role

Several family scholars argue that cultural considerations influence how the grandparent role is enacted. One such cultural consideration involves rural versus urban families. King and Elder (1995) found that grandparents in rural farm families live closer to and have more contact with their grandchildren than do grandparents from nonfarm families. The increased contact among farm families is especially notable when considering paternal grandparents.

A few researchers point to the issue of language compatibility between the generations, particularly among immigrants to the United States. Schmidt and Padilla (1983) studied the importance of speaking Spanish within Hispanic American families and language compatibility between grandparents and grandchildren. Language compatibility obviously affects the degree to which GP and GC can communicate. Further, grandchildren who can speak English but choose to speak Spanish with their grandparents may do so as a symbol of respect for cultural heritage and values. Similar issues of language compatibility play a role in many Asian American GP–GC relationships (Kamo, 1998).

Hunter and Taylor (1998) describe the grandmother role in African American families as one of high status with regard to authority. Compared to grandparents in European American families, grandparents in African American families not only accept more responsibilities for caregiving, but they also view themselves as playing a more central role in the family (Hunter & Taylor). According to Cherlin and Furstenburg (1985), African American grandparents rarely enact a passive grandparenting style. Rather, they usually take on influential or authority-oriented styles, stressing parent-like authority and high involvement and or support.

### Divorce and Grandparenting

With regard to divorce and grandparents, researchers have focused on two different scenarios. One involves the role that grandparents play when children are experiencing the divorce of their parents. The second involves the impact of grandparental divorce on GP–GC relationships. When parents divorce, grandchildren's contact with grandparents may be mediated by the parents more so than before. This can make the GP–GC relationship vulnerable (Lussier, Deater-Deckard, Dunn, & Davies, 2002). In fact, young children have little control over seeing their grandparents. As one might expect, contact is lowest between the grandchild and the non-resident-parent grandparents versus the resident-parent grandparents. Lussier et al. also found that in general, closeness to grandparents is related to lower levels of emotional and behavioral problems among children who have experienced parental divorce. There are some important caveats, however. If after the divorce, children are living with their mother alone, their mother and a stepfather, or in an arrangement of shared custody between mother and father, then closeness to maternal grandparents is related to better child adjustment. If children are living with their father and a stepmother, then closeness to maternal grandparents is associated with lower adjustment. Among children living with single mothers, closeness with paternal grandparents is also linked with poorer adjustment.

As the baby boom generation ages, many more grandchildren will be involved with grandparents who have divorced previously or even grandparents who divorce after grandchildren are born. Grandparental divorce appears to have negative consequences for the GP–GC relationship (King, 2003). Even though many grandparents who have experienced a divorce are still involved with their grandchildren, King found that views about the importance of the grandparent role are not as strong in grandparents who have ever divorced. Divorced grandparents also have less contact, participate in fewer shared activities with the grandchild, and report weaker bonds with their grandchildren. These negative effects are greater for paternal grandparents and for grandfathers than for grandmothers. King argues that weaker bonds with grandchildren may also stem from strained adult child–parent relationships or the fact that ever-divorced grandparents tend to live farther away from their grandchildren. On the positive side, King found that if the grandparent–parent relationship is strong, the GP–GC relationship may be buffered from these negative consequences. In addition, ever-divorced grandparents are more likely to discuss a grandchild's problems than never-divorced grandparents. King speculates that grandparents who have experienced difficult times or weaker GP–GC bonds may be detatched from grandchildren so as to discuss problems more objectively. With regard to stepgrandparenting, Cherlin and Furstenburg (1986) found that the age of the stepgrandchild affects the step-GP–GC bond. The older the stepchild is when the parents remarry, the less priority the stepparents place on the stepgrandparent role.

## Communication and Relationship Solidarity in the GP–GC Relationship

### Communication Patterns and Topics

Researchers have summarized a number of factors that are influential in GP–GC communication patterns (Elder & Conger, 2000; Mueller et al., 2002). The first is *geographic proximity*. The closer grandparents live to their grandchildren, the more opportunity they have to be involved in their grandchildren's lives. Opportunity, however, does not always translate to frequent contact or a quality relationship. Some grandparents and grandchildren maintain a high-quality relationship in spite of distance, with the telephone and travel commonly playing a role. A second factor is the *quality of the parents' relationship with the grandparent*. Mueller et al. note that parents serve as gatekeepers or mediators in the GP–GC relationship. Parents can hinder or facillitate interaction between the two. In addition, Hagestad (1985) suggests that in some cases grandparents and grandchildren do not have direct exchange and interaction until the grandchild reaches adulthood. Prior to that the middle generation, the parents, mediate most of the interaction.

The third factor involves the *matrifocal tilt*. Family ties on the maternal side of families tend to be stronger, particularly family ties between grandparents and grandchildren. Fourth, *age of the grandparent and grandchild* can influence contact and involvement. Younger grandparents, who often are healthier, tend to be more active with their grandchildren. Older grandchildren, in adolescence and young adulthood, commonly detach from family relationships as they develop interests outside the family and no longer need intense care. Fifth, Elder and Conger (2000) describe that the *number of grandchildren*, if large, can limit time available to spend with grandchildren and, if small, can maximize time available. Sixth, after *parental divorce*, maternal grandparents especially tend to be more involved in their grandchildren's lives. Finally, numerous other factors such as *religion, family rituals, rural residence*, and *having known one's own grandparents or learned about them through intergenerational history* are all positively related to grandparents' involvement in grandchildren's lives (King & Elder, 1997; Mueller et al., 2002).

Regarding topics of conversation in positive GP–GC relationships, Lin, Harwood, and Bonnesen (2002) found that family and education are the two most commonly discussed topics. Given Harwood and Lin's (2000) finding that grandparents express a great deal of pride in their grandchildren's accomplishments, educational accomplishments and school activities are a likely topic of conversation. Leisure activities and friendships are other frequently mentioned topics. Grandparents and grandchildren tend to avoid topics relating to health and topics related to the age of the grandparents. Discussing the age of the grandchildren does not appear to be as taboo, however. Lin et al. are clear to note that the topic of GP–GC conversations is always moderated by how they talk about a topic, not just what the topic is, as well as who initiates topics.

### Predictors of Solidarity and the Intergenerational Stake Hypothesis

Harwood (2000b) reveals several predictors of relational solidarity and communication satisfaction in the GP–GC relationship. These predictors include: *perceptions of kindness, grandparents' perceptions of grandchildren's involvement in and support of the relationship,* and *grandparents' storytelling behavior.* In other research Harwood (2000a; see also Lin & Harwood, 2003) found that for grandparents and grandchildren alike, *perceptions of the other's communication accommodation* are strong predictors of feelings of solidarity in the relationship. *Communication accommodation* refers to attuning one's communication style or conversation topics to be similar to (convergence) or different from (divergence) a conversation partner's (Lin & Harwood, p. 539). Communication adjustments are based on one's perceptions or stereotypes of the other person. Of course it is possible for people to overaccommodate or underaccommodate. Harwood (2000a) specifically found that in the GP–GC relationship, communication accommodation is most beneficial when partners appropriately converge to show displays of affection and respect, share personal thoughts and feelings, indicate attentiveness and support, and perceive the other as complimenting them. Neither overaccommodation nor underaccommodation was related to relational solidarity. Not suprisingly, Harwood and Lin (2000) also found that grandparents are especially touched when grandchildren take the initiative to call or visit on their own. These same grandparents mentioned a great deal of pride in their role and pride in the goals that their grandchildren are achieving. Even though grandparents reported disliking the distance that separates them from their grandchildren, in positive GP–GC relationships, grandparents do not blame grandchildren for the distance, but rather blame the distance on external circumstances.

Finally, we should introduce the *intergenerational stake hypothesis.* This hypothesis predicts that compared to grandchildren, grandparents will be more committed to, more interested in investing in, and perceive more closeness in the GP–GC relationship. Indeed, there is empirical support for this hypothesis. Harwood (2001) confirmed that grandparents view more closeness in the GP–GC relationship than do grandchildren. In addition, grandchildren perceive the GP–GC relationship to be more active than do grandparents. Harwood suggests that grandparents and grandchildren may have different expectations for the relationship. If they are expecting more interaction than grandchildren, grandparents may feel the relationship is not as active (in comparison to their expectations), when grandchildren feel it is. The intergenerational stake hypothesis is somewhat compatible with socioemotional selectivity theory's prediction that older persons desire to invest in close, meaningful relationships, such as family relationships, whereas younger persons invest more in peripheral relationships. Crosnoe and Elder (2002) reveal one example of the intergenerational stake hypothesis at work in college-aged grandchildren's relationship with grandparents. Grandparents often perceive that they have a generational stake in mentoring their grandchildren and being involved in their transition to college. But grandchildren often do not see the grandparents' involvement as necessary or useful, that is, unless the grandparent also has a similar educational background.

## Adult Children in Relationship With Parents and In-Laws

Once children become adults and create their own family of orientation, the adult child–parent relationship is considered by many an "extended family relationship" (see Schmeeckle & Sprecher's (2004) definition of extended family earlier in the chapter). To some extent, learned patterns of interaction between parents and children remain the same as children transition to adulthood (Aquilino, 1997). There appears to be continuity in the areas of emotional closeness and control and conflict. Yet the transition of children to adult roles undoubtedly brings about some change in interaction. Aquilino argues that adult child–parent relationships improve when children enter roles that the parents have previously occupied (e.g., the child goes to college, gets married, or begins a similar career). There is an exception, however, when it comes to parenthood. Late-life parents report less emotional closeness, more conflict, and more power issues with their adult children who are parents versus those who are not parents (Aquilino). It is difficult to determine why this is the case. Perhaps in some circumstances, having children leaves less time, creates more stress, and brings up new issues to negotiate, such as expectations for babysitting and discipline.

Lawton, Silverstein, and Bengtson (1994) suggest that greater frequency of contact generally breeds more affection in the adult child–parent relationship. However, what motivates adult children to remain in contact with their mothers may not necessarily be the same as that with fathers. Feelings of affection are noted for motivating adult children to make contact with mothers, whereas instrumental (i.e., task-related) or obligatory reasons are more likely to motivate adult children to make contact with fathers.

When adult children take on primary or even secondary caretaking responsibilities for their aging parents, contact dramatically increases, especially if the caretaking involves co-residence. Caring for an elderly parent is stressful for many adult children, particularly as the intensity of the care increases. Bethea (2002) found that living with an elderly parent is associated with modest decreases in communication satisfaction in the adult child's marriage, compared to those couples that do not live with a parent. Even though the couples in Bethea's study had been married over 30 years, having an elderly parent present still altered their communication satisfaction. One might think that these long-term married couples would have patterns of communication so established that they would not be affected by the presence of an elderly parent. This appears not to be the case. We should also note that the couples in Bethea's study that took a parent into their home had higher communication satisfaction to begin with than the couples that did not take in an elderly parent, so we should put their decreases in satisfaction in perspective. Williams and Nussbaum (2001) further argue that contrary to popular opinion, caregiving does not appear to be an "overwhelmingly negative burden" in the lives of most adult children (p. 158). Clearly, individual cases vary a lot. We discuss the issue of adult children giving care to their parents even more in chapter 14.

Finally, what impact do in-laws have on the lives of adult children? Popular jokes about in-law relationships stereotype them as negative. In particular, relationships between mothers-in-law and daughters-in-law are commonly characterized as negative, competitive, and filled with resentment over having to share the son or husband (Lopata, 1999). It appears that the quality of in-law relationships is positively related to marital stability, satisfaction, and commitment (Bryant, Conger, & Meehan, 2001). What this suggests is that in-law relationships have the capacity to be positive, supportive relationships, although they can also be negative. This was the case even for the couples in Bryant et al.'s study that had been married several decades. Many people believe that in-laws and social networks are influential in dating relationships or new marriages (see chap. 5), but Bryant et al. suggest that in-laws continue to play a role throughout the life span. Lopata suggests that once grandchildren are born, grandparents may be motivated to have a better relationship with their son-in-law or daughter-in-law because they want to be involved with their grandchildren. However, the birth of children is sometimes related to greater ambiguity in the in-law relationship (Fischer, 1986; Lopata), perhaps due to issues regarding how much to involve in-laws versus one's own parents with child-rearing issues. On the whole, in-laws are another part of the extended family network, but a part that researchers have yet to fully explore.

## CONCLUSION

Traditionally, family scholars have treated sibling relationships and extended family relationships as peripheral family relationships in comparison to the parent–child or marital relationship. However, as we see in this chapter, the sibling relationship can be a very intense relationship, especially during childhood. Family systems theorists propose that the transition to siblinghood can be a major change in one's life, though most children are too young to clearly remember what it was like when their sibling closest in age was born. During childhood, people typically spend as much time with their siblings than with any other family member. Sibling interaction is notably complex in childhood. Siblings can be caregivers and confidants as well as competitors and antagonizers. Siblings socialize one another in positive and negative ways. The sibling relationship is also affected by parental involvement. Siblings are very aware of differential treatment by parents, although children do not always perceive differential treatment negatively. In early and middle adulthood, time spent with siblings decreases, yet many people count a sibling as one of their closest friends. In late adulthood, many people rely on siblings for the kind support, companionship, and reminiscing that can only be offered by someone who has shared the history of a lifetime. Overall, two primary factors have catapulted sibling relationships to the forefront of many researchers' minds: (a) the intensity and complexity of sibling relationships in childhood, and (b) the fact that siblings relationships can be uniquely lifelong family relationships with potential benefits in middle and late adulthood.

It is not just family scholars who have treated extended family relationships as peripheral relationships. Many families themselves place little emphasis on such relationships. Others, however, place great stake in the extended family. People's perceptions of and interactions in extended families are influenced by sociocultural and contextual factors. Many scholars believe that extended family ties are stronger, or at least more important, among older persons, women, rural families, and ethnic minority families. Although this is true to a large extent, a few notable researchers in the last decade have cautioned that family scholars have sometimes exaggerated the idea that present-day minority families participate more actively with extended family out of values of familism.

Indeed, socioemotional selectivity theory predicts that later in life, people are more invested in emotionally meaningful relationships such as family relationships. In the grandparent–grandchild relationship, grandparents often feel more investment in the relationship than do grandchildren. There are numerous ways grandparents play out their role and communicate with grandchildren. Some grandparents literally are the primary caretakers of their grandchildren. In another extreme, some grandparents enact a detached style with little or no contact with their grandchildren. Although the research on grandparents is more descriptive than prescriptive, many speculate that the most satisfying grandparent–grandchild relationship involves grandparents who fall somewhere between primary caretakers and detatched grandparents.

The adult child–parent relationship is another extended family relationship that researchers are just beginning to understand. It is a relationship that can be filled with support and affection, sometimes beyond what was experienced when the child was younger. Many adult children are at least moderately involved in caregiving to the parents who once cared for them. Finally, contrary to many people's notion that their in-laws will not affect their marriage, married adults relate to and appear to be affected by their relationships with their in-laws, even after years of marriage. In the end, if we truly want to understand the family system as a whole, siblings and extended family relationships deserve careful study. They are part of what makes family life a complex web of relationships.

# III

# Communication During Family Stress

# CHAPTER NINE

# Models of Family Stress and Coping

Stress is an inevitable part of family life. Although there are few certainties in the modern family, it is safe to assume that all families will experience stress and that coping with stressors will be an ongoing activity in all families. Why is stress such a ubiquitous part of family life? In some cases, families generate stressors of their own through problematic interactions among themselves (Pearlin & Skaff, 1998). Most parents who have raised an adolescent child and most people who can remember their family interactions during adolescence have experienced such stressors. In other cases family members encounter problems in their roles outside of the family boundary (e.g., student, employee, and friend) that can adversely impact relationships and activities within the family (Pearlin & Skaff). This happens, for example, when a parent gets laid off at work. For reasons such as these, it has been argued that "All stressors either begin or end up in the family" (Olson, 1997, p. 261).

In this chapter we attempt to answer a number of fundamental questions about the role and impact of stress on family relationships. For example, what are the different types of stressors that families must deal with? Do all stressful events have a negative impact on the family? Through examining various models of family stress we attempt to explain the process by which families respond to stress. Questions about the role of communication in addressing and managing stressors are taken up as well. There are also a number of important questions about the family's response to stress. How do families cope with stressors? Exactly how does social support from the family help to deal with stressful experiences and situations? The answers to these questions reveal complex and intriguing associations between the family and the stressors they face.

When studying the effects of stress on the family, it is important to distinguish stress from stressors. Olson, Lavee, and McCubbin (1988) define *family stressors* as "discrete life events or transitions that have an impact upon the family unit and produce, or have the potential to produce, change in the family social system" (p. 19). On the other hand, *family stress* is the response of the family to the stressor; it involves the tensions that family members experience as a result of the stressor (McCubbin et al., 1980). When do stressors produce stress? According to family systems theorists (see chap. 2) families develop a requisite variety of rules of transformation (Burr & Klein, 1994). This means that families usually have enough rules for how to handle different situations that they are able to transform inputs (e.g., stressors) into outputs in such a way that their basic needs, functions, and goals can be sustained. The family experiences stress when they do not have the requisite variety of rules to meet the challenges of certain stressors. In other words, they do not have the means to handle the change that is necessitated by the stressor while still fulfilling their basic goals and functions.

People often think of family stressors and stress in negative terms. However, it is important to keep in mind that stress can stimulate growth and important transitions for families. Successfully managing stress can fundamentally alter family relationships and interactions, sometimes in a very positive way. At the same time, stress can sometimes permanently damage, and even destroy, family relationships. Often the key to explaining the consequences of stressors on the family can be found in a careful examination of their communication behaviors. Stress can alter family communication patterns; but family communication patterns can equally alter the family's experience and reaction to a stressor.

## TYPES OF FAMILY STRESSORS

There are an almost infinite number of events or situations that families might find stressful. One useful way to think about family stressors is to consider those that are normative or predictable versus those that are nonnormative or unpredictable (Cowan, 1991). _Normative family stressors_ involve those changes or progressions in family life that occur for most families, usually coming with the passage of time. These involve, for example, marriage, birth of the first child, and death of an elderly family member. Normative stressors are viewed as ubiquitous in that they occur in most families, and expectable because they can easily be anticipated (McCubbin et al., 1980). _Nonnormative family stressors_, on the other hand, are difficult to foresee because they happen somewhat at random, and do not occur in every family. These include, for example, the serious illness of a child, involuntary separations from the family, and divorce. Because of the random nature of nonnormative stressors, they are often experienced as more traumatic for family members. At the same time, the ability to see normative stressors impending on the horizon does not necessarily lessen their impact on the family environment.

It is important to understand that the distinction between normative and nonnormative family stressors is imperfect. As we argue in chapter 10, the "normative" family stressors that accompany progression through the family life cycle may not really be normative in modern society. Untimely death, divorce, and childlessness mean that many families never experience some of the stressors that are commonly considered to be normative. Similarly, those stressors that are characterized as "nonnormative" may not be as unpredictable as once thought. At least some "unpredictable" family stressors such as marital distress and divorce are clearly foreshadowed in couple's communication behaviors.

Both normative and nonnormative family stressors contribute to what family systems theorists refer to as _morphogenesis_ (Olson et al., 1979). That is the tendency of a family to develop and change over time. The inevitability of normative family stressors implies that there will always be morphogenetic forces impinging on all families. During periods of relative calm, families also experience _morphostasis_, which is the tendency to remain at a steady state, or follow the status quo. The experience of both normative and nonnormative stressors typically disrupts morphostatic tendencies and at least temporarily engages morphorgenetic tendencies of the family.

Another useful way of understanding and classifying family stressors was developed by Adams (1975). Adams argued that there are two distinct dimensions to family stressors. The first has to do with how *temporary versus permanent* the family stressor is. Some stressors such as raising an adolescent child are inherently temporary. By necessity, such stressors will eventually pass. Other stressors, such as the death of a family member, are permanent. These are stressors that the family will bear over the long run. Keep in mind that temporary and permanent really represent end points on a continuum. There are of course many stressors, such as long-term illness, that fall somewhere in between these two extremes. The second conceptual dimension proposed by Adams concerns the *voluntary versus involuntary* nature of family stressors. As strange as it may sound at first, family members sometimes voluntarily enter into situations that can be very stressful. For example, a married couple may undergo a period of separation or seek a divorce on their own volition. Other stressors such as infertility or raising a troubled child are more involuntary in nature. Like the temporary–permanent dimension, voluntary and involuntary are best viewed as end points on a continuum. Some stressors like early retirement or optional layoff from work might be viewed as a situation that is a response to both voluntary and involuntary forces. It may be tempting to conclude that voluntary stressors are easier to cope with than those that are involuntary because people often have some control over them. However, voluntary stressors carry with them more personal responsibility and blame that can create considerable mental anguish for family members.

A more recent theory of family stress conceptualizes stress as occurring at one of three different levels of abstraction (Burr & Klein, 1994). Burr and Klein based their conceptualization of different levels of stress on group theory and the theory of logical types (Watzlawick, Weakland, & Fisch, 1974). Group theory explains how change can occur within a system that as a whole stays constant. The theory of logical types explains how members experience a metamorphosis whereby they move from one logical level to a higher one. Combining elements of these theories, Burr and Klein (1994) proposed a developmental theory of family stress based on different logical levels of stress and with the assumption that families will first try to adjust very specific concrete processes in order to deal with stress before resorting to more fundamental and abstract changes to the family system.

*Level I stress* causes the family to cope by changing its role expectations or rules. If changes in these role expectations or rules are effective at handling the stressor, the family is assumed to enter into a period of recovery as they gain mastery over the stressor. Burr and Klein (1994) suggest that for many families, the birth of a child represents a Level I stressor. In most families, husbands and wives have to assume a new role (i.e., father and mother) and certain rules may need to be enacted to address the stressor (e.g., someone needs to feed the child when she or he wakes up in the morning). For most families, such changes are sufficient for effectively coping with the stressor. When Level I processes are unsuccessful, the family is in a more difficult situation, characterized as Level II stress.

When families encounter *Level II stress* rearranging rules and making simple changes in roles are not sufficient to allow the family to effectively deal with the stressor. Rather, the family must make more fundamental changes, usually in their approach to relating to each other. For example, when a family attempts to handle the stress of raising an adolescent child, they may develop new rules such as a curfew and make role adjustments such as having the child assume responsibility for some household chores. If this approach is not effective, the family may need to rethink its approach to discipline, responsibility, and the way that they relate to the child. Instead of just assuming that the parents' rules and intentions will automatically be followed, they may need to reconsider how they relate to the child, perhaps by now creating adverse consequences when rules and obligations are not followed. This may change the fundamental nature of the parent–child relationship from caretaker and provider to authority figure and enforcer. When such Level II processes are ineffective, the family is in an even more difficult situation, characterized as Level III stress.

The experience of _Level III stress_ causes the family to question its most basic assumptions, and the very fabric of the family is in trouble (Burr & Klein, 1994). The family's most basic orientation and philosophy of life must be examined, and often changed or discarded. Returning to our example of raising the adolescent child, assume that the child is involved in criminal activity, charged with assault, and sentenced to a juvenile detention facility. In this case, the parents may feel overwhelmed and defeated, despite their best efforts at raising the child. They may have to psychologically relinquish at least part of their relationship with and emotional connection to their child in order to cope with the severe stressor that they are experiencing. In this case, the very nature of what it means to be a family and a parent is called into question, reexamined, and altered in response to the stressor. The idea that parents are ultimately responsible for the actions of their children may have to be abandoned. Burr and Klein note that in Level III stress, families often have to deal with fundamental questions of whether people are good or bad, their spiritual beliefs, and how much emotional distance from family members is necessary and desirable.

## MODELS OF FAMILY STRESS

### The ABC-X Model

Perhaps the premier model of family stress was developed and described by Hill (1949) as part of his now-classic research on the stress of separation and reunion following World War II. During World War II many men were enlisted into the military and shipped overseas as part of their military service, often leaving their wives and children behind to face an uncertain future. During the war, many women entered the work force for the first time and earned their own salaries. When the war ended and soldiers came home many families had yet another set of adjustments to make. Adopting a systems perspective, Hill realized that the stress experienced by the family was not just the result of a particular event such as the husband's departure from the home due to active military duty. Rather, there were a number of systemic variables that seemed to influence which families experienced high degrees of stress and which managed without as much difficulty.

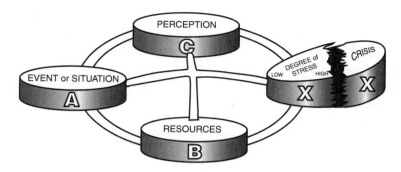

FIG. 9.1.    Hill's (1949) ABC-X Model of Family Stress.

The ABC-X model gets its name from four interrelated factors that are theorized to describe the experience of family stress. The A factor represents the *event or situation* that the family encounters. This interacts with the B factor which is the family's *resources*. The event or situation also interacts with the C factor, the family's *perception* of the event. Collectively the A, B, and C factors produce the *stress or crisis* reaction which is the X factor. Hill's ABC-X model is depicted in Figure 9.1.

### Stressful Events or Situations (A)

In the family context, stressful events have been described as "an occurrence that provokes a variable amount of change in the family system" (McKenry & Price, 2000, p. 6). Notice how McKenry and Price's definition of the stressful event is focused on *change*. The underlying assumption is that anything that alters the status quo has the potential to produce stress. Most families develop routines that allow for smooth functioning without having to constantly renegotiate roles, argue over rules, and so forth. When stressful events occur, these routines are upset. Roles that used to be functional for the family are now lost or seriously altered. Rules that used to ensure family harmony and well-being may now have to be adjusted or broken once the event or situation is encountered. McKenry and Price also note that not all "stressful" events or situations are negative. Even positive events can produce stress in the family. The inheritance of a large sum of money from a distant relative or a job promotion can each be associated with stress. Remarkably, the stress associated with these seemingly positive events or situations can sometimes be as disruptive to family functioning as the stress from what are ordinarily viewed as negative events such as the death of a family member or the loss of a family member's job. Later in this chapter we discuss one common classification scheme for stressful family events based on their predictability or unpredictability.

### Family Resources (B)

Resources are traits, abilities, and qualities of individual family members, the family system, and the greater community in which the family is embedded that can be used to address the demands imposed by the event or situation (McCubbin & Patterson, 1985).

Family systems theorists generally feel that resources reside in individuals, the collective family unit, and the societal ecosystem in which the family is a part. Family resources can mitigate the ill effects of many situations. For example, if a family member is laid off at work, but other family members have good jobs and incomes, these resources can lessen the potentially negative impact of the situation on the family. Therefore, family scientists say that resources may act as a *buffer* against the potentially negative consequences of stressful events. On the other hand, some families may lack resources to protect against the negative effects of certain events. Consider for example a rural farm family that is isolated and has few close friends or relatives. Even a fairly modest event such as the brief hospitalization of one of the parents has the potential to create substantial turmoil for the family and the care of their farm. In this way, family scientists suggest that the lack of resources can create a *vulnerability* to stress when certain events or situations are encountered.

### Family Perception (C)

The family's perception is their appraisal, assessment, or definition of the event or situation. How people appraise life events and situations is strongly tied to how stressed they are in response to those situations (Lazarus & Launier, 1978). There is remarkable variation in how different families appraise the same event. For instance, in some families the departure of a young adult child might be a time of intense sadness. Parents may fear the loss of the child's companionship, worry about how the child will make it on his or her own, and lament missed opportunities for interaction with the child that may never be recaptured. However, other families may view this as a celebration, fueled by pride in the child's successful transition to adulthood and independence, or by a "good riddance" attitude. The great American songwriter John Mellencamp once wrote, "There is nothing more sad or glorious than generations changing hands." This statement is an elegant account of both the dualism inherent in many family events as well as of the dramatic range of feelings that family members might have concerning a given event. Families that cope best with stressful events are those who are able to recast or reframe the event in a positive light. This allows family members to (a) clarify issues, hardships, and tasks and render them more manageable; (b) decrease the intensity of emotional burden created by the event; and (c) encourage members to carry on with the family's fundamental tasks (McCubbin & Patterson, 1985; McKenry & Price, 2000). There are many different ways of looking at the same event. Like resources, positive appraisals can buffer against the ill effects associated with potentially stressful events.

### Stress and Crisis (X)

The X factor in Hill's ABC-X model is the stress and crisis actually experienced by the family. This is thought to be a product of the event, the family's resources, and the family's perceptions of the event. The family's stress experience is their reaction or response to the event or situation (filtered through their resources and perceptions). Stress and crisis are two different types of reaction to challenging events and situations.

*Crisis* is an overwhelming disturbance in the family's equilibrium that involves severe pressure on and incapacitation of the family system (Boss, 1988; McKenry & Price, 2000). When a family is in a state of crisis they are in genuine disorder and are unable to function normally or effectively. Customary roles and routines are often abandoned and boundaries are dramatically changed when a family is in crisis. Alternatively, *stress* denotes a change in the family's steady state. So long as these changes do not overtax the family's resources and coping skills, there may be no negative outcomes for the family. As McKenry and Price note, crisis is a dichotomous variable. The family is either in a state of crisis or not. Stress is a continuous variable. A family can experience varying degrees of stress. Because stress merely represents a change or disturbance in the family's normal state and routines, it is easy to see why stress is not inherently bad. Many families may benefit from some stress. The experience of stress can sometimes cause families to abandon harmful practices as when family members try to prepare healthy meals after one family member had a heart attack.

## The Double ABC-X Model

Hill's (1949) *ABC-X* model of family stress has been very influential over the past 50 years (Huang, 1991). However, the model was refined by McCubbin and Patterson (1982) in recognition of the fact that family stress unfolds over time, and that families develop new perceptions and new resources after they initially experience the event or situation. Accordingly, McCubbin and Patterson developed the double *ABC-X* model of family stress. This expanded version of the original ABC-X model is depicted in Figure 9.2.

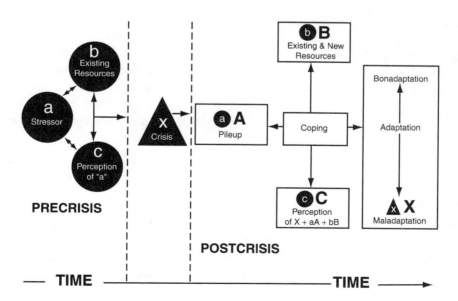

FIG. 9.2.   McCubbin and Patterson's (1982) Double ABC-X Model of Family Stress.

*Note.* From H. I. McCubbin and J. M. Patterson, *Family Stress, Coping, and Social Support,* 1982. Courtesy of Charles C Thomas, Publisher, Ltd., Springfield, Illinois.

As evident in Figure 9.2, the double ABC-X model is divided into precrisis and postcrisis stages. The variables in the precrisis stage are identical to Hill's (1949) original ABC-X model (i.e., stressor, resources, perception, and crisis). The postcrisis factors were included to better explain how and why families adapt to the stressful situation once it is encountered.

### Stressor Pileup (aA)

McCubbin and Patterson (1982) note that stressors rarely occur in isolation from other problems. Often stressful events are associated with other issues, events, and situations that are themselves stressful to the family. These authors suggest that there are several types of stressors that contribute to stress pileup in the family. First, the *initial stressor event* has its own set of hardships that can move the family into a state of crisis. Second, *family life changes* are often ongoing at the time that the initial event is experienced and happen regardless of the initial stressor. Finally, *consequences of family coping* efforts often bring on an additional set of stressors. For example, if a child is diagnosed with a serious illness, that illness could function as an initial stressor on the family. At the same time that the family is dealing with this stressor, they may also be in the process of launching their oldest child and caring for an aging grandparent. These family life changes only further compound the family's stress over the sick child. If an overwhelmed parent turns to heavy drinking in order to cope with the demands of these stressors to soothe his or her nerves, this coping mechanism may bring on further stressors such as a drunk driving conviction, missed work, and failure to meet other obligations due to intoxication. Collectively, all of these different stressors that come in the wake of the child's illness constitute stressor pileup and potentially make a bad situation even worse. In a study of families with autistic or communication-impaired children, stress pileup proved to be the most consistent and strongest predictor of family adjustment (Bristol, 1987). Menees and Segrin (2000) found that children who were exposed to the stress of an alcoholic parent were anywhere from two to four times more likely than children without an alcoholic parent to have been exposed to additional family stressors such as parental separation, divorce, or unemployment. These findings illustrate McCubbin and Patterson's point that family stressors rarely occur in isolation and that the pileup of stressors has a major impact on family outcomes.

### Existing and New Resources (bB)

In the double ABC-X model there are two types of family resources. The first are the family's existing resources at the time of the initial stressor. These are available at the time of initial impact and allow the family to minimize the immediate consequences of the stressor and, in the best case scenario, prevent the family from entering into a state of crisis. The second set of resources is characterized as *coping resources* (McCubbin & Patterson, 1982). These are personal, family, or social resources that are developed or strengthened in response to the initial stressor. Coping resources might include social support that is mobilized after the initial stressor, or new skills that the family develops in order to handle the initial stressor. Recall from the discussion of stress pileup that sometimes these post-crisis-coping efforts may bring on new stressors as well. Ideally, the family's postcrisis resources will be factors that help to minimize the negative effects of the stressful event or situation, while allowing the family to effectively adapt to this new challenge in their lives.

### Perception (cC)

The double C factor in the double ABC-X model (McCubbin & Patterson, 1982) is the family's perception of (a) the initial stressor event and (b) the stress or crisis produced by that event, as well as any stress pileup that followed. Like the original C factor, this factor entails the family's perception and definition of the situation that they find themselves in. McCubbin and Patterson state that the family's postcrisis perceptions involve religious beliefs, redefining the original situation, and endowing the situation with meaning. Over time, people tend to look at many stressful situations differently from when they first encountered them. When families reframe an event in a more positive light, the amount of stress that they experience may be minimized. For instance, if a troubled adolescent is picked up by the police and jailed for theft, the family may initially be shocked and upset. The parents may feel like failures and fear for their child's future. However, as time progresses, the family may reframe the initial stressor in more positive terms. For instance, they may feel that contact with the criminal justice system might be a "wake-up call" for the troubled adolescent. Perhaps he or she might be required to enroll in a drug treatment program because the theft was committed so that the adolescent could get money to buy drugs. They may feel that this will scare the child and put him or her back on track, away from a life of crime. In this way, the family is seeing new meaning and even some potential benefits to what was originally a stressful and shocking event. The double C factor in this model is an explicit recognition of the fact that perceptions are not static. They evolve and change over time.

### Family Crisis and Adaptation (xX)

The double X factor in the model is the family's ultimate adaptation to the crisis. McCubbin and Patterson (1982) define adaptation as "the process of stimulus regulation, environmental control, and balancing to achieve a level of functioning, which preserves family unity and enhances the family system and member growth and development" (p. 45). Stimulus regulation and environmental control involve literally taking control of the situation that produced the initial stress and the surrounding environment (e.g., immediate family, extended family, and local community) in which the family exists. In stimulus regulation, the family selectively lets in or shuts out demands that are imposed by the stressful event. In some cases they may have to resort to denial in order to accomplish stimulus regulation. In environmental control the family tries to influence the type and quality of demands that are placed on them. Balancing entails making accommodations or compromises in order to adjust to the stressor and perhaps assimilating the stressful event or situation into their daily lives and routines. Some stressors such as the death or chronic illness of an immediate family member are permanent and often unchanging in their nature. These require family members to make equally permanent changes in the structure of their roles and routines, thereby assimilating the stressor into the fundamental fabric of the family's life. Unlike the X factor in the precrisis state (crisis), the X factor in the postcrisis state (adaptation) is really a continuum. The family's degree of adaptation can range from maladaption (from the French word "mal," meaning bad or poorly) on the low end to bonadaptation (from the French word "bon," meaning good) on the high end. A family in a state of maladaption is in crisis. However, a family in a state of bonadaptation is probably functioning *better* after the stressor than before. Bonadaptation implies that the demands on the family unit are matched by the resources that they have available (McCubbin & Patterson). For some families that mobilize their resources and reframe stressful events in a positive light, the experience can lead to a form of hypercoping in which the family functioning is literally improved following the stressor.

### Additional Concepts in the Double ABC-X Model

Proponents of the double ABC-X model of family stress often use concepts in addition to events, resources, perceptions, and stress in order to understand how families function under stress. McCubbin and Patterson (1982) suggest that vulnerability and regenerative power are useful for understanding how families defend themselves against a crisis and how they recover from a crisis. *Vulnerability* is the family's ability to prevent stressors from creating a crisis situation. As we mentioned earlier in this section, the family's resources (B) play a major role in determining their vulnerability. For the most part, the more resources the family has available, the lower their vulnerability is. *Regenerative power* is the family's ability to bounce back and recover from a crisis. Like certain lizards that can rapidly regrow a severed tail, some families have a remarkable ability to recover from states of crisis. This concept is similar to what some refer to as resiliency (Olson et al., 1988). According to the double ABC-X model, those families with good resources, optimistic perceptions, and functional coping responses should have high regenerative power. Finally, research on the double ABC-X model has highlighted the role of *boundary ambiguity* (McCubbin & Patterson). Boundary ambiguity occurs when family members are unsure about who is in or out of the system and who occupies what roles. When a father goes off to war, for example, the remaining family members may be uncertain about who will take over the family functions that were previously taken care of by the now absent father. Perhaps a close relative will spend more time with the family and help out. This may raise questions about how to treat that person. Is he or she now a member of the immediate family? These sorts of questions and dilemmas can be stressful for the family and contribute to stressor pileup.

### The Role of Family Communication in the ABC-X and Double ABC-X Models

Although not explicitly labeled as a component of either model, family communication plays an important role in both the ABC-X and the double ABC-X models. In most cases, family communication could be viewed as a resource (B) that could help to buffer against the ill effects of stress or as a vulnerability factor in the case of families with poor communication. Family communication plays a vital role in processes such as social support, coping, information exchange, and problem solving. A study of stress among intergenerational farm families revealed that participants, especially members of the older generation, saw family communication (e.g., showing positive feelings) as a resource for coping with their stress (Weigel & Weigel, 1993). For families that have clear, direct, open, and responsive styles of communication, that pattern of behavior literally becomes a resource on which they can draw during times of stress. Alternatively, families with ambiguous, indirect, and minimal communication patterns would be more vulnerable to the experience of stressful events and situations. This is because they would have a hard time mobilizing the family resources that would allow them to effectively cope with and respond to the demands imposed by the stressful event. In extreme cases, these problematic family communication patterns can become stressors in their own right. In chapter 13, we discuss how dysfunctional family communication patterns such as expressed emotion and communication deviance can function as a stressor that exacerbates the course of certain mental health problems experienced by family members.

The beneficial effect of family communication as a resource in times of stress is illustrated in a study on the transition to parenthood among adolescent African American and Latino couples (Florsheim et al., 2003). These researchers followed 14- to 19-year-old mothers and their partners as they became first-time parents. Most were still living in their family of origin. They found that young parents who had good relationships with their own parents, as indexed by supportive interactions and minimal conflict for example, maintained good relationships with their partner and exhibited lower risk for parental dysfunction (i.e., parental stress and child abuse potential). Despite the fact that these young couples were experiencing a major life stressor, good communication and relationships with their parents and each other proved to be associated with better outcomes for the family.

Another important role of family communication in the ABC-X models is in the process of perception (C). The family's perception or definition of a stressor is theorized to play a vital role in their ultimate reaction and adaptation to the event or situation. Family perceptions develop largely as a result of the family's communication about the stressful event. Recall from chapter 2 that according to the theory of symbolic interaction, shared realities are created through interaction with other people. What does a parent's layoff from work mean to a young child? What does a mother's diagnosis of breast cancer mean to her adolescent children? Answers to questions such as these emerge as a product of the family's communication about the stressor. Particularly for younger family members who may not understand the stressful event, there is at best a vague notion of what the stressor implies for the family. In healthy families, parents and children talk about the meaning and impact of the stressor. Often parents may try to shield their younger children from the stress that could be associated with the event or situation. In so doing, they minimize the potentially aversive impact of the event on the young children by trying to offer a benign definition or perception of the situation. Of course, this tactic can be taken too far such that family members remain in the dark about the true meaning of the stressor to their own detriment. In either case, however, the ultimate family perception of the event is created, shaped, revised, and sustained through family communication.

## Olson's Systems Model of Family Stress

Recall from chapter 1 that one of the major models of family functioning was developed by Olson and his colleagues and is centered around the twin concepts of adaptability (or flexibility) and cohesion (Olson, 1993; Olson et al., 1979). As we discuss in chapter 1, the most functional families according to this approach are those that are balanced in their adaptability and cohesion. However, there is some evidence indicating a linear relationship among adaptability, cohesion, and positive family outcomes (Farrell & Barnes, 1993). This perspective has been fruitfully extended to the domain of family stress and has produced a number of predications about families that are best able to handle stressors. One of the more fundamental hypotheses from this perspective is that families will adjust their levels of adaptability and cohesion in response to situational stressors and changes that result from progression through the family life cycle (Olson, 1983; Olson & McCubbin, 1982). Even though moderate amounts of adaptability and cohesion are optimal for family functioning, there are times when it is best for the family to at least temporarily alter their adaptability and cohesion in response to stressful events. Naturally, healthy families will make adjustments in response to environmental stressors. On the other hand, dysfunctional families often remain rooted at extremes on the adaptability and cohesion dimensions, unable to make adjustments in response to stressors. For example, a healthy family with moderate degrees of adaptability and cohesion might find it most helpful to increase their cohesion (in the direction of enmeshment) and increase their adaptability (in the direction of chaos) after a member of the immediate family is seriously injured in a car accident. The increased cohesion facilitates the exchange of social and emotional support. The heightened adaptability allows family members to assume each other's roles and cover for each other so that they can simultaneously attend to the injured family member while still taking care of routine family business. Of course, in a functional family, these extreme levels of adaptability and cohesion that allow the family to effectively cope with the stressor would be expected to subside as the impact of the stressor event declines. Ultimately, such families would be expected to return to "normal" levels of adaptability and cohesion as they adjust to the stressor. Olson and McCubbin are quick to point out that the most functional changes in response to stress are those that are moderate, such as a shift from flexible to structured, as opposed to a dramatic shift from chaotic to rigid.

A related prediction rooted in this perspective is that troubled families will either not change their adaptability and cohesion when stressed or make dramatic changes from one extreme to the other (Olson et al., 1979). As we mentioned earlier, some dysfunctional families are unable to adjust their levels of adaptability and cohesion in response to stressors. However, there are some dysfunctional families that dramatically swing from, say, disengaged all the way to enmeshed upon experiencing a stressful event or situation. These families come across as unstable and may be somewhat chaotic. These wild swings in adaptability and cohesion can themselves become a source of stress, potentially contributing to stress pileup. According to Olson and his associates, the most functional families will make temporary adjustments in their adaptability and cohesion in order to meet the demands of a stressor, but these adjustments are moderate, not dramatic.

What allows families to make the necessary changes in their adaptability and cohesion in order to effectively cope with stressful events? As we discuss in chapter 1, Olson (1993) suggests that family communication skills facilitate movement and adjustment along the adaptability and cohesion continua. Families with positive communication skills such as clear messages, effective problem solving, supportive statements, and demonstration of empathy are hypothesized to be able to alter their adaptability and cohesion in response to stressors. Alternatively, families that do not listen well to each other, who use indirect messages, and who are excessively critical of each other are expected to be locked into one particular level of adaptability and cohesion, usually at one of the extremes, unable to change when they encounter a stressful event or situation.

Earlier we mentioned that families need to adjust their adaptability and cohesion in response to both situational stressors and ordinary progressions through the family life cycle. In other words, a married couple with two adolescent children may need to function at a level of adaptability different from that of a retired couple with no children. Research has consistently shown that well-functioning families at different stages in the family lifestyle tend to exhibit predictably different levels of adaptability and cohesion (Olson et al., 1988; Olson & Lavee, 1989). For example, the majority of young couples without children are moderately high in both their cohesion and adaptability. Once children become part of the family, the situation changes considerably. Families with young children tend to be more structured in their adaptability, while showing slight decreases in cohesion. When teenagers become part of the picture, this pattern is even more accentuated. A much greater percentage (60%) of families with teens are separated in their cohesion compared to young couples without children (29%; Olson & Lavee, 1989). Older couples whose children have left home tend to exhibit adaptability levels that are comparable to those of young couples without children, and cohesion levels that are comparable to those of families with teens, but lower than those of young couples without children. As families progress through the life cycle and respond to the different stresses and strains that are imposed by these developmental challenges, they make moderate adjustments in their adaptability and cohesion. In functional families these changes are a natural part of the family life cycle. However, dysfunctional families show a greater tendency to remain stuck at one level of adaptability and one level of cohesion, unable to adjust in order to adequately meet the demands of the changing family life cycle.

Olson's (1997) systems model of family stress also predicts that families will first draw on internal resources before using external resources to manage family stress. Internal resources can be found within the family system. These include such things as social support, good communication, tangible assistance with tasks, financial resources that the family has, and the use of special skills that family members can use to manage the stressor. External resources are located outside the family system and include such things as community-based assistance programs, professional counseling or therapy, and law enforcement intervention. Using this knowledge, one could accurately assume that families who tap into external resources (e.g., calling the police to help settle domestic disputes or visiting the community food bank to get food) are under a great degree of stress. Contact with these external agencies suggests that they were unable to bring resolution to their problems or meet the demand of the stressor with the resources that they had within the family system. It implies that the family has effectively exhausted its internal resources for addressing the stressor.

## The Vulnerability–Stress–Adaptation Model of Marriage

Thus far we have examined several models of family stress that take a systemwide perspective to understanding the family's experience of and response to stress. A more recent addition to the roster of family stress models was proposed by Karney and Bradbury (1995) in their vulnerability-stress-adaptation model of marriage. This model differs from other family stress models in some important ways. First, this is a model that is specific to the marital subsystem. Second, unlike those models that begin with the stressful event or experience, Karney and Bradbury's model explicitly assumes that marital partners have preexisting vulnerabilities that color husbands' and wives' reactions to stress. Finally, the model assumes that the presence of stress affects the stability and satisfaction of the marriage. In other words, the quality of this family subsystem is partially a function of the stress that the couple experiences. The vulnerability–stress-adaptation model is depicted in Figure 9.3.

In the vulnerability-stress-adaptation model, *stressful events* are assumed to have an impact on *adaptive processes* in the marriage (depicted as path A in Figure 9.3). Adaptive processes are those behaviors that spouses exchange, such as positive communication and problem solving, that allow them to adjust to their roles within the marriage and to cope with challenges that they encounter. The experience of stress tends to have a negative influence on these processes (Karney & Bradbury, 1995), which can then threaten the quality of the marriage. The model also assumes that spouses bring with them certain backgrounds or *enduring vulnerabilities* that influence both adaptive processes (path B) and the experience of stressful events (path C). Enduring vulnerabilities are backgrounds and traits that husbands and wives bring into their marriage. Consider,

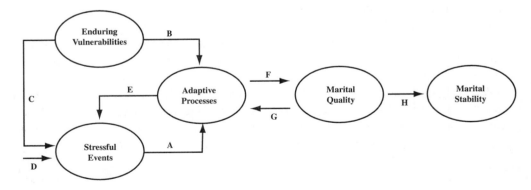

FIG. 9.3.    Karney and Bradbury's Vulnerability–Stress–Adaptation Model of Marriage.

*Note.* From "The Longitudinal Course of Marital Quality and Stability: A Review of Theory, Method, and Research," by B. R. Karney and T. N. Bradbury, 1995, *Psychological Bulletin, 118,* p. 23. Copyright 1995 by the American Psychological Association. Reprinted with permission.

for example, poor communication skills as an enduring vulnerability. First, people with poor communication skills will presumably have a harder time adjusting to their role as husband or wife. Negotiating expectations, clarifying preferences, and blending into extended family systems are all interpersonal tasks that present challenges to people with poor communication skills. At the same time, the model predicts that people with poor skills will actually experience more stressful events. This phenomenon is characterized as the stress generation effect (Segrin, 2001a). Someone with poor communication skills may experience excessive arguments with his or her partner and have a hard time creating positive interactions and experiences within the marriage. The net result of this enduring vulnerability is that the couple may actually experience more stressful events.

Similar to the double ABC-X model (McCubbin & Patterson, 1982), Karney and Bradbury's (1995) model assumes that adaptive processes will influence the likelihood of encountering stressful events (path E). Couples with good adaptive processes can cope well with stressful events and keep them from piling up. On the other hand, couples with poor adaptive processes will respond to stress in such a way as to actually increase the probability of experiencing more stressful events. Karney and Bradbury note that this sets up a vicious cycle in which stressful events tax the couple's capacity for adaptation, which in turn contributes to worsening of the events, which only serves to further hinder the couple's capacity for adaptation. These adaptive processes play a vital role in the vulnerability–stress–adaptation model because they are seen as proximal and reciprocal causes of *marital quality* (paths F and G). Marital quality is the couple's overall evaluation of and satisfaction with their marriage. Marriages that have good adaptive processes (i.e., the partners exchange positive behaviors, have rewarding interactions, and adjust well to tasks in the marriage) are assumed to have higher quality than those with poor adaptive processes. At the same time, the quality of the marriage is assumed to influence adaptive processes. Naturally, partners who are happy with their marriage are more likely to exchange positive behaviors, treat each other graciously, and work hard at solving marital problems compared to partners who are unhappy with their marriage. In this way, marital quality can actually enhance couples' adaptive processes.

Ultimately, the vulnerability–stress–adaptation model assumes that marital quality is a proximal predictor of *marital stability* (path H). Marital stability simply refers to the duration of the marriage, and in particular, whether the couple stays together. Research findings generally show that marital satisfaction has stronger effects on marital stability than on most other variables that have been examined as potential predictors of marital stability (Karney & Bradbury, 1995). However, Karney and Bradbury are quick to point out that this effect is still only moderate in magnitude. They suggest that this may be due to the fact that most unstable (i.e., broken-up) marriages are marked by dissatisfaction, but not all stable (i.e., in tact) marriages are marked by satisfaction.

## FAMILY COPING WITH STRESS

The concept of coping or adaptation figures prominently in most theoretical models of family stress. Family coping involves the active strategies and behaviors that families enact in order to manage and adapt to stressful situations (McCubbin & Dahl, 1985).

In the ABC-X model, coping is considered to be a family resource, and in the double ABC-X model coping is assumed to influence stress pileup, resources, perceptions, and adaptation to the stressor (McCubbin & Patterson, 1982). Family coping has a powerful impact on the relationship between stressful events and the family's stress reaction to those events. There are a number of hypotheses that explain this relationship (McCubbin et al., 1980). First, effective family coping behaviors are thought to decrease vulnerabilities to stressors. Second, family coping strategies can strengthen or maintain family resources such as cohesiveness, organization, and adaptability. Third, effective coping in the family can reduce or eliminate stressor events and their negative consequences. Finally, family coping behaviors may actively alter the environment by changing social circumstances surrounding the stressor and its experience.

## Taxonomies of Family Coping Strategies

There is a wide range of coping strategies that families will enact when they encounter stressors. These run from tactics that are generally helpful for reducing the ill effects of the stressor to strategies that can actually worsen the impact of the stressor. For example, psychologists Robert and Anita Plutchik developed a taxonomy of eight basic strategies that families use to cope with stress (Plutchik & Plutchik, 1990). *Mapping* is coping with a problem by trying to obtain more information about it. *Avoidance* involves coping with a problem by removing the family members from situations that produce the stressor. Families that use *help seeking* cope with stress by asking for help from other family members, neighbors, coworkers, or experts. *Minimization* is an attempt to cope by psychologically reducing the importance, significance, or seriousness of the stressor. Some families cope through *reversal* in which they act the exact opposite of how they feel. For example, the angrier they get with someone, the more polite and generous family members may behave toward that person. When families cope with *blame* they try to make themselves feel good by assigning responsibility for the problem to other people or external factors. *Substitution* is a coping strategy in which families employ indirect methods to solve a problem. Substitution is most often used when there are no direct methods for dealing with a problem. For example, family members who feel stressed out by their jobs and school will often take a pleasant vacation. Quitting work or school is not an option, but the vacation allows the family time to relax and at least temporarily escape the stressor. Finally, *improving shortcomings* is a technique that families use when they carefully consider how they contributed to the stressor and then try to improve aspects of their lives in order to deal with the stressor and prevent its reoccurrence. Note that not all of these coping strategies involve actual behaviors. Sometimes family members will cope with a stressor not by acting or communicating but by denying the problem or changing the way that they think about it.

For Plutchik and Plutchik (1990), communication is a fundamental element of families' efforts at coping with stressful events. They observe that "for every problem, however small or large, there are many possible solutions. . . . it has been our experience that most people tend to use one style of communication most of the time. When this particular style does not work, they become angry and frustrated rather than simply switching to an alternative approach" (p. 36). Plutchik and Plutchik are suggesting here that effective coping almost always entails some flexibility in the substance and style of family members' interactions following the stressor. Families that are locked into one style of communicating are, in the long run, going to have more trouble coping with stressors than are families that can adjust their style of interaction to meet the demands of the situation.

A complementary taxonomy of family coping methods was developed by Burr and Klein (1994) in which they identified seven highly abstract strategies that have emerged from research on family coping. Each of these strategies is in turn associated with a number of less abstract, or more specific, strategies. Burr and Klein's (1994) taxonomy is summarized in Table 9.1. One noteworthy aspect of this taxonomy is Burr and Klein's explicit recognition of family communication as an actual coping strategy (see also Olson, 1997). They find that certain positive communication behaviors such as being open and honest, carefully listening to each other, and paying careful attention to each other's nonverbal behaviors can function as effective coping mechanisms for family members in times of stress. Presumably many of these communication tactics work by putting family members "on the same page" as they are confronted with a stressor. When family

**TABLE 9.1**
Burr and Klein's Conceptual Framework of Family Coping Strategies

| Highly Abstract Strategies | Moderately Abstract Strategies |
| --- | --- |
| • Cognitive | – be accepting of the situation and others<br>– gain useful knowledge<br>– change how the situation is viewed or defined (reframe) |
| • Emotional | – express feelings and affection<br>– avoid or resolve negative feelings and disabling expressions of emotion<br>– be sensitive to others' emotional needs |
| • Relationships | – increase cohesion (togetherness)<br>– develop increased trust<br>– increase cooperation<br>– increase tolerance of each other |
| • Communication | – be open and honest<br>– listen to each other<br>– be sensitive to nonverbal communication |
| • Community | – seek help and support from others<br>– fulfill expectations in organizations |
| • Spiritual | – be more involved in religious activities<br>– increase faith or seek help from God |
| • Individual Development | – develop autonomy, independence, and self-sufficiency<br>– keep active in hobbies |

*Note.* From W. R. Burr, and S. R. Klein. *Reexamining Family Stress: New Theory and Research,* p. 133, copyright © 1994 by Sage Publications. Reprinted with permission of Sage Publication, Inc.

members misunderstand each other, the effects of a stressor can be intensified. These communication strategies substantially decrease the likelihood of such an occurrence. It is also worth noting that what Burr and Klein refer to as "communication" is actually a collection of strategies, some associated with message production (e.g., exchanging information and being honest) and some with message reception (e.g., listening and being sensitive).

When most people think about coping with a problem, they tend to think about the things that we do to lessen the impact of a stressor and to effectively resolve the difficulties that it presents. However, researchers agree that family coping strategies can have both positive and negative effects (McCubbin et al., 1980; Plutchik & Plutchik, 1990). Recall from our discussion of the double ABC-X model that certain coping strategies can lead to stress pileup. This happens when family coping literally becomes a source of stress. How does this happen? McCubbin et al. suggest that there are at least three ways that family coping strategies can actually be a source of stress. First, some coping strategies may indirectly damage the family system. If a family tries to shield its children from the crime-ridden neighborhood in which they live by sending them to an exclusive private school on the other side of town, the exorbitant tuition that they pay may actually create financial hardships that effectively become a family stressor in their own right. Second, some family coping strategies cause direct harm to the family system. When family members turn to drugs or alcohol as a means of coping with hardship they may experience secondary stressors that are directly linked to these behaviors such as drunk driving convictions and missed work. Third, some family coping mechanisms create further stress by interfering with the adaptive behaviors that could enhance the family's well-being. For example, some family members may use denial as a coping mechanism. Unfortunately, this will do nothing to motivate family members to pursue effective solutions to the problem that plagues them. In the meantime, the problem may actually worsen. It is clear that effective coping strategies certainly have the potential to greatly minimize the negative effects of stressors. At the same time, there are some families that employ coping strategies that are literally antagonistic to effective solutions to their problems. In such cases the coping strategies literally produce more stressors, contributing to stress pileup.

As families cope with the stressors that they encounter, they directly and indirectly teach coping mechanisms to their children (Chambers, 1999; Kliewer, Fearnow, & Miller, 1996). Kliewer et al. suggest that one way this happens is through *coaching*. In coaching, parents directly instruct their children on how to handle the various problems they en-counter. Coaching might entail explaining the meaning of the stressor to the child and recommending concrete methods for addressing the stressor. This advice is often consis-tent with the parents' own preferred coping styles. Another mechanism by which families transmit coping strategies to their children is through *modeling*. Recall from chapter 2 that social learning theory explains how children will pick up behaviors by observing their parents enact those behaviors, especially when there are positive outcomes connected to the coping behaviors. Kliewer and her associates found that mothers who used less active coping strategies had daughters who also used less active coping strategies. Mothers who modeled avoidant coping methods also had sons who reported more avoidant coping strategies. These results suggest that children will often pick up their parents' preferred mechanisms for coping by simply observing them in stressful situations. So, if a parent comes home from a difficult day at work and proceeds to drink large amounts of alcohol and then starts to exhibit a more pleasant mood, children who repeatedly observe this coping strategy would be very likely to eventually enact the same behaviors when they are stressed.

## Family Coping and Stress Appraisal

Psychologists refer to the assessment of stressors and the degree to which they are threatening as *primary appraisal* and to assessment of coping resources for dealing with those stressors as *secondary appraisal* (Lazarus, 1966). Presumably family coping strategies are effective either when they alter primary appraisals by removing the stressor or making it seem less threatening or when they alter secondary appraisals by enhancing perceptions of family members' ability to handle the stressor (Wills, Blechman, & McNamara, 1996). Consistent with this notion, a study of dual-worker couples revealed that the best predictor of marital adjustment was not the hardships that they experienced but rather their communication (a coping resource) and their relational efficacy (i.e., the couple's appraisal of their ability to deal with problems; Meeks, Arnkoff, Glass, & Notarius, 1986). Menees (1997) also found that children of an alcoholic parent had highest self-esteem when they coped with stressors via family problem solving and ventilation. Young people who engage in family problem solving work together with their parents to address their stressors. Although it may seem ironic that this would be an effective strategy in children of alcoholics, the fact that the stressor emerged from the family of origin makes that same family an especially powerful force for shaping the child's primary and secondary appraisals. Ventilation is a coping strategy that involves talking with other people to get things out in the open rather than keep them to oneself. This sort of coping may engage other people and solicit input from them that could be vital in altering primary and secondary appraisals for the better. Sometimes just talking to other people about a problem can make the problem seem not so bad.

## Communal Coping

Many of the family coping strategies covered earlier in this section could be enacted by family members individually. However, there are many cases where families (e.g., parents and their children and wives and their husbands) cope with problems together as a unit. This phenomenon is known as *communal coping*. Communal coping refers to appraising and acting on a problem in the context of a relationship by pooling resources and efforts to address the problem (Lyons, Mickelson, Sullivan, & Coyne, 1998). According to Lyons and associates, the key to communal coping is that family members perceive the stressor as "our" problem versus "my" or "your" problem. Furthermore, they decide as a unit that the problem is "our" responsibility. Seeing the stressor as "our" problem reflects an appraisal that is communal rather than individual in nature. Seeing the required action as "our" responsibility implies that coping strategies and solutions will be enacted by the family as a whole rather than by just one person in the family. Lyons et al. explain that the process of communal coping can be broken down into three main components. The first component is a *communal coping orientation*. This is the belief that the family must join together in order to effectively address the problem. Second, communal coping involves *communication about the stressor*. Because communal coping is inherently social, family members must discuss the details of how the problem happened, what they think can be done to address it, and how it will affect the family, for example. Finally, there must be some *cooperative action* in communal coping. This simply means that family members collaborate to develop strategies and enact remedies to deal with the stressor.

Research findings consistently show that communal coping is very effective and is generally associated with positive outcomes for families dealing with stressors. For example, pregnant women experience fewer symptoms of depression to the extent that their partners (e.g., spouses and family members) use active prosocial coping strategies such as joining together to deal with the problems that they experience (Monnier & Hobfoll, 1997). Men's success in adjusting to and recovering from a heart attack is dependent on the efforts of their wives who create changes in the couple's diet and daily routine, as well as the couple's ability to work together to make lifestyle changes (Coyne, Ellard, & Smith, 1990).

Sometimes one subunit in the family can work together to shield other family members from the ill effects of stress. During the 1980s there was a severe economic downturn in rural economy that had devastating effects on families and their farms. Family scientists Rand and Katherine Conger studied how rural families coped with the stressor imposed by these austere circumstances (Conger & Conger, 2002). They found that children and adolescents in the family do not experience stress directly as a result of the economic conditions but rather through the responses of their parents to the financial hardships facing the family. Consequently, if husbands and wives exhibited strong social support toward each other, they were generally unlikely to show outward signs of emotional distress and their children therefore did not experience significant trauma as a result of the family's financial hardships. Conger and Conger theorized that if parents can contain their emotional distress and interpersonal conflicts, while maintaining their parenting skills (e.g., being nurturant and involved with the children), their children can weather the storm without any real adjustment problems or emotional distress of their own. One way that rural families pulled together during the terrible farm economy was to maintain close ties between the parents while simultaneously demonstrating affection, warmth, and minimal hostility toward the children. In these cases the parents worked together to provide a positive atmosphere for their children so that the children could prosper developmentally despite the adverse circumstances that faced the family.

## FAMILY SOCIAL SUPPORT

Social support is one of the most important and fundamental forms of family communication. It could be argued that a primary function of the family is to provide social support to its members. People often view the family as the last bastion of social support when support from anyone else cannot be found during times of stress. The beneficial effects of social support have been conclusively established over decades of scientific research. The availability of social support significantly enhances people's general well-being and happiness in addition to their ability to withstand a variety of major stressors such as serious illness (Coyne & Smith, 1994). On the other hand, people who lack available social support appear to be at risk for developing a range of physical and mental health problems.

Social support is enacted through interpersonal communication and sometimes through instrumental behaviors. Its beneficial effects appear to result from several social–psychological processes. According to the *buffering model* (Cohen & Wills, 1985) social support mitigates the ill effects of stress by reducing the appraised threat and reducing the stress response that typically follows physical or psychological threat. Supportive communication allows people to work through their emotional reactions to stressful events and to develop relief-generating reappraisals that alleviate or minimize stress (Albrecht, Burleson, & Goldsmith, 1994; Burleson & Goldsmith, 1998). The *main effect model* holds that involvement in caring relationships provides a generalized source of positive affect, self-worth, and belonging that keeps psychological despair at a minimum (Cohen, Gottlieb, & Underwood, 2000). The family is an especially likely source of such caring relationships.

In the family context most acts of social support could be classified into one of three general categories (Wills et al., 1996). *Emotional support* is the availability of a family member with whom one can discuss problems, concerns, and feelings. Ordinarily, a provider of emotional support is a good listener who is not critical, blaming, or judgmental. Sometimes a family member who provides emotional support need not do anything more than listen and be available. *Instrumental support* is offered when a family member provides assistance with various tasks. In the family, this might mean help with household chores, a ride to school, or assistance with auto repairs. When family members provide *informational support* they give guidance, feedback, and resource information that is helpful in addressing a problem. Parents are often providers of informational support to their children. So, for example, when a child attends his or her first formal high school dance, parents may offer suggestions on things like an appropriate suit or dress to wear, places to go out to dinner, and where to go to buy flowers. This kind of information can greatly reduce the stress of such an experience by helping to reduce uncertainty.

Social support from the family has a number of beneficial effects for maintaining well-being in the face of a variety of stressors and life circumstances. For instance, social support from the family is negatively related to substance abuse in adolescents (Wills, 1990; Wills et al., 1996). Among adults, family social support is positively associated with life satisfaction, health, and positive mood (Walen & Lachman, 2000). Family social support is also positively associated with intentions to behave in less risky ways among HIV-positive gay men (Kimberly & Serovich, 1999). For young adults with an alcoholic parent, family social support was significantly associated with increased self-esteem (Menees, 1997). Just as the presence of family social support can enhance well-being and buffer against the negative effects of stress, the lack of supportive relationships in the family can be detrimental to well-being. Children who do not receive very much social support from their families are more harmful to others, uncooperative, withdrawn, and exhibit higher levels of hopelessness (Kashani, Canfield, Borduin, Soltys, & Reid, 1994).

There can be no question that social support from the family can have a number of beneficial effects for family members. But what are the mechanisms that produce these positive effects? Family researchers believe that there are numerous pathways between family social support and positive outcomes (Wills, 1990). One basic function of social support is to *reduce negative affect*. When people are aware of the availability of social support from their family, they may worry less about problems and perceive them as more manageable. When people do become sad or anxious, readily available social support from family members can help to minimize these feelings. Also, family social support may *promote health-protective behaviors*. Wills suggests that family networks aid people in both recognizing symptoms and seeking medical attention when illness is suspected. One common explanation for why married men are generally healthier than unmarried men is because their wives point out their symptoms of illness and urge them to seek medical attention. Conversely, people with little social support available are more likely to be involved in health-damaging behaviors such as smoking, alcohol, or drug use. Additionally, family social support can *promote positive affect*. As we mentioned earlier, the main effect model for social support holds that family social support causes us to feel valued and cared for. This promotes a positive emotional state, feelings of belonging to a group or community, and feeling appreciated by others. Family social support may be associated with leisure experiences, enjoyment of shared activities, and help with instrumental tasks, all of which promote a positive mood in the recipients of the social support.

## CONCLUSION

We begin this chapter by examining different ways of classifying family stressors. Clearly "family stress" is not a generic phenomenon. Issues such as whether the stressor is normative versus unpredictable, temporary versus permanent, or voluntary versus involuntary can have a substantial effect on the extent to which the family experiences stress as result of exposure to various stressors. Family scientists have developed a number of theoretical models to explain how families experience and respond to stress. These include the ABC-X and double ABC-X models, along with the systems and vulnerability–stress–adaptation models. Although each of these models differs in the components and mechanisms that are specified to explain family stress, each is useful for understanding how family communication influences and is influenced by stress. For example, in the ABC-X model, family communication could certainly be thought of as a resource. In Olson's (1997) systems model, communication is the mechanism that allows family to alter their adaptability and cohesion to appropriately respond to the stressor. Finally, in Karney and Bradbury's (1995) vulnerability–stress–adaptation model, marital communication could be an enduring vulnerability as well as an adaptive process. In all models, there is a possibility that family communication itself could be the stressor or at least generate stressors. Coping involves the strategies that families use to deal with stressors. Like stressors themselves, coping strategies are diverse ranging from functional to dysfunctional and individual to communal. Many involve specific types of communication and messages exchanged between family members in order to address the stressor. Finally, we discuss social support as a fundamental and important type of family communication that is vital for responding to stressful events.

There are few family processes as consequential as the family's means and mechanisms for dealing with stress. All families will experience stress. Some families respond to stress in a ways that make them a stronger and more competent social structure. However, stress literally defeats and destroys other families. What differentiates those families that grow from those that fall apart in the face of stress is the nature of the family's communication, coping tactics, and their predisposition to attack problems instead of each other.

Later, in chapters 13 and 14 we revisit the vital role of supportive communication in the family as it relates to physical and mental health problems. More immediately, the next three chapters of this book examine various family stressors such as divorce and forming stepfamilies in more detail. Many of the concepts and mechanisms outlined in the models of family stress that were presented in this chapter will be useful for understanding how families experience and respond to these various stressors.

# CHAPTER TEN

# Normative and Nonnormative Family Stressors

All families experience stress from time to time. Stressors may cause the family to increase their interactions with each other in order to cope with the event and to reorganize their relationships. In some cases, stressors pull family members away from each other physically and psychologically, thus decreasing their interactions. In either case, family stressors are a powerful force in shaping family communication and relationships. As discussed in chapter 9, family stressors can be roughly organized into those that are normative, or predictable, versus those that are nonnormative, or unpredictable. Earlier we noted that this distinction is somewhat imperfect as certain "nonnormative" family stressors such as divorce are fairly common and predictable, whereas other "normative" family stressors such as raising and launching children do not happen in every family. Nevertheless, this distinction is prominent in the family science literature and provides a useful framework for organizing and understanding the unique aspects of different family stressors.

In this chapter we review several normative and nonnormative family stressors. In so doing, we will attempt to answer questions such as "What are the major stressors that families experience?", "What are some of the factors that lead up to or follow these stressors?", and "What is the role of communication in the experience of different family stressors?" This analysis will show that family stressors each have their own unique qualities and challenges. At the same time, some phenomena are common to most family stressors. For example, most family stressors cause a shift in roles and interactions within the family. Additionally, the family's functioning before the stressor is usually the best predictor of their functioning during and after the stressor. Stressors amplify problems that are already present in troubled families. Families that function well during times of relative harmony usually weather stressors better than families that have a great deal of conflict and contention. We start this chapter with an analysis of normative family stressors that are associated with the family life cycle. This is followed by an examination of several nonnormative, but still fairly common, family stressors.

## NORMATIVE FAMILY STRESSORS

Normative, or predictable, family stressors can be thought of as stages in the life cycle of the family. All families progress through various stages of development, and the transitions through these various stages are often times of great stress for family members (Carter &

TABLE 10.1
Carter & McGoldrick's Stages of the Family Life Cycle With Associated
Social/Relational Tasks

| Family Life Cycle Stage | Primary Social/Relational Tasks |
| --- | --- |
| • Leaving Home: Single Young Adults | – redefine relationships with parents to be less dependent<br>– develop intimate peer relationships<br>– establish self-identity |
| • The Joining of Families Through Marriage: The New Couple | – negotiate and accommodate expectations for marriage<br>– recalibrate idealized feelings toward partner while maintaining relational satisfaction<br>– negotiate and reconstruct social networks |
| • Families With Young Children | – adjust marriage to make space for child(ren)<br>– childrearing and socialization<br>– adjust relationships with grandparents |
| • Families With Adolescents | – adjust relationship with child to allow for more autonomy<br>– manage increasing parent-child conflicts<br>– refocus on middle-stage of the marriage<br>– focus on care of elderly parents (grandparents) |
| • Launching Children and Moving On | – adjust back to a marital dyad<br>– develop adult relationships with grown children<br>– expand the family supersystem to include in-laws<br>– cope with death and disability of elderly family members |
| • Families in Later Life | – maintain couple interests in the face of physical decline<br>– cope with death and disability of elderly family members<br>– support younger and older generation<br>– cope with the loss of spouse, siblings, and peers<br>– negotiate relationships for assistance with self-care<br>– review life goals and prepare for death |

*Note.* From Carter, B. & McGoldrick, M. The Expanded Family Life Cycle, 3/e/© 1999. Published by Allyn and Bacon, Boston, MA. Copyright © by Pearson Education. Reprinted by permission of the publisher.

McGoldrick, 1999; McGoldrick, Heiman, & Carter, 1993). This is known as the "critical-transition hypothesis" (Aldous, 1990). When families undergo critical transitions, they are hypothesized to experience stress and changes in family interaction patterns. Carter and McGoldrick developed an influential taxonomy of family life-cycle stages. Their model begins with single, young adults leaving home, and progresses to the transition to marriage, families with young children, families with adolescent children, launching children and moving on, and finally aging families in later life. In Table 10.1, we summarize the key social and relational tasks associated with each stage of the family life cycle. It is important to note that even though these stages of the family life cycle are referred to as "normative," it may not actually be "normal" for a family to progress through each and every stage, or to progress through them in the order that they are presented in the table. As noted earlier, unpredictable family stressors like divorce and sudden death, as well as variations in family forms such as childless and remarried couples, can seriously interrupt or alter the family's progression through these different stages.

## Social or Relational Tasks

In this section we consider five normative family stressors that represent transitions in stages through the family life cycle. Such stressors are often viewed as "developmental stressors" because they are part of the typical development of most families. These stressors include the transition to marriage, the effects of parenthood on marriage, launching children, and the aging family. Each of these has a dramatic impact on the nature and structure of family relationships. Because there is a separate chapter in this book devoted to parent–child relationships (chap. 7), in this section we focus on those stressors that have an impact on marriages and the greater family system. In chapter 7 we focus more exclusively on some of the issues and problems associated with parenting such as relations between parents and their adolescent children.

## The Transition to Marriage

Marriage is a somewhat paradoxical transition in the family life cycle. On one hand, it represents a departure from the family of origin. On the other hand, it represents a merger of two family systems into a larger, more complex supersystem. Not only does marriage create a spousal relationship, but it also creates an extensive set of relationships with in-laws, and in some cases creates an "empty-nest" situation in the family of origin. The changing landscape of the family of origin relationships and the development of a new family of orientation requires substantial adjustment for all family members involved. Despite the fact that marriage is a time of celebration and joy in most families, it also presents a series of tasks that can be experienced as stressful.

One of the fundamental challenges faced by couples making the transition to marriage is discussion and reconciliation of differing expectations and intentions for their marriage. People approach marriage with expectations that have been shaped by their families of origin, their friendship networks, and the media (Axinn & Thornton, 1992; Segrin & Nabi, 2002; Starrels & Holm, 2000; Surra, 1988). One of the first challenges faced by engaged couples is the negotiation and accommodation of each other's intentions for the marriage. This is essentially the creation of a shared couple identity. Communication tasks range from the mundane (e.g., What color towels should we buy?) to the profound (e.g., Should we have children?). Most people enter into marriage with at least a rough idea of where they stand on the more profound issues. Negotiating these expectations between partners is vital to the success of the marriage. Refusal to discuss expectations offers no escape from their consequences. Eventually partners will have to make choices about things such as jobs, children, relations with extended family members, houses to buy, and leisure pursuits that will inevitably bring potentially competing expectations into sharp focus.

Another major task for the couple making the transition to marriage involves the negotiation and reconstruction of changing social networks (Lederer & Lewis, 1991). As couples progress toward marriage, interactions with friendship networks, especially more superficial contacts, diminish. Marrying couples also inherit each other's social networks and must be able to find their place within those networks. One of the most obvious examples of this involves relationships with extended family members. There are several potential problems here that can create stress for the newlywed couple (McGoldrick, 1988). One problematic pattern occurs when a spouse (or both spouses) is strongly enmeshed in his or her family of origin and continues that pattern after marriage. This can create feelings of guilt, intrusiveness, and unclear boundaries that interfere with the couple's ability to establish their own unique identity. A second problematic pattern occurs when a spouse marries to gain "independence" and completely cuts off communication with his or her family of origin. The irony is that failing to resolve contentious issues through open communication ensures that the spouse will remain emotionally bound to his or her family of origin through powerful feelings of anger and resentment instead of being truly independent (McGoldrick et al., 1993). Finally, some couples maintain a pattern of interactions with extended family that involves some closeness, some conflict, and avoidance of certain issues. This very common pattern may be functional at times, but also causes underlying tensions to surface at times of transition in the family (e.g., weddings, funerals, major illness, and children leaving home). Couples can become ensnared in these matters, and the extended family's issues can spill over into and affect their marriage.

Despite the fact that newlywed couples are remarkably satisfied with their marriages, some evidence for the stressfulness of this transition is evident in studies that measure spouses' love for each other during this time of transition. To illustrate, Tucker and Aron (1993) measured partners' passionate love (intense longing for union with the partner) about 2 months prior to and 8 months after marriage. Surprisingly, they found small *decreases* in passionate love over this transition. Related findings indicate that during the first 2 years of the marriage, couples' love for each other decreases and their conflicts increase (Huston & Houts, 1998). It should be noted that this decrease in spouses' love for each over the transition to marriage was not dramatic, yet it does appear to be a reliable phenomenon that is perhaps reflective of the stress associated with adjusting to this new role. Also, there is considerable variability in how much love declines over the newlywed years, and it is the slope of that decline (i.e., how far and how fast it drops) that is predictive of subsequent marital dissolution (Huston, Caughlin et al., 2001). These findings indicate that another important task associated with the transition to marriage is a sort of emotional recalibration of the intense, and perhaps idealized, feelings toward the partner that existed during courtship.

## Effects of Parenthood on Marriage

The transition to parenthood is one of the most dramatic changes to occur in the course of a marriage. Although this transition is not experienced in all marriages, about 90% of all married couples have children and must therefore make the necessary adjustments to accommodate a significant shift in the social structure of their lives. Prior to the birth of children, a married couple is a family composed of one dyad. However, the birth of a single child dramatically increases the complexity of family relationships. Now there are three different dyads and a family triad. Of course, the birth of additional children increases family relational complexities exponentially. Despite the fact that there are strong parentalist pressures in our society and a great deal of positive cultural folklore associated with having children, it is apparent that children introduce stressors into the lives of parents that have a considerable impact on the landscape of their marriage. Psychologists John Gottman and Clifford Notarius (2002) recently concluded that "After 15 longitudinal studies, it is now generally accepted that the transition to parenthood is a stressful period for marriage" (p. 172). In the following sections, we explain some of the reasons for this stress.

### Changes in Marital Satisfaction

The most commonly studied effect of the transition to parenthood is a change in marital satisfaction. Numerous early studies showed that marital satisfaction declines as the first child is born. Researchers generally arrived at this conclusion through one of two methods. First, studies that compared married couples with children to childless married couples generally indicated that those with children had lower marital satisfaction. Second, studies that followed couples during the early years of their marriage, through pregnancy and birth of the first child, also revealed that marital satisfaction decreased in conjunction with parenthood. Unfortunately, the conclusions that can be drawn from such studies are limited for several reasons. Studies that compare couples with and without children often confound marital duration with the presence of children (Belsky, 1990; Huston & Vangelisti, 1995). Because most married couples have children relatively early in the course of their marriage, childless couples are likely to be those who have only been married for a short period of time. When compared to a sample of married couples with children, who have usually been married for a longer period of time, differences in marital satisfaction may be due to the different durations of their marriages. Most couples experience decreases in their marital satisfaction over the first 10 years of their marriage, irrespective of the presence of children (Kurdek, 1993; Lindahl, Clements, & Markman, 1998). A similar problem applies to studies that follow young couples through the birth of their first child. If marital satisfaction reliably decreases for most married couples over the first 10 years of their marriage, decreasing satisfaction after a child is born cannot necessarily be attributed to the presence of the child. It could just be the result of time. What is needed is a control group of childless couples for comparison who are followed over a similar period of time.

Currently, there is some disagreement in the scientific community about whether the birth of the first child is meaningfully associated with decreases in marital satisfaction (Clements & Markman, 1996). Several researchers have presented data from sophisticated studies to suggest that marital satisfaction stays relatively stable over the transition to parenthood (Huston & Vangelisti, 1995; Kurdek, 1993; Lindahl et al., 1998). Nevertheless, other equally sophisticated studies still indicate that the transition to parenthood is marked by declining marital satisfaction for the mother and father (Feeney, Noller, & Ward, 1997; Hackel & Ruble, 1992; Shapiro, Gottman, & Carrère, 2000). For example, Feeney et al. compared couples who never had children, those who had children who were no longer living at home, and those who still had children living at home. Even after statistically controlling for the length of their marriage, those who had children living at home had the lowest marital happiness of the three groups. Hackel and Ruble (1992) very cleverly followed couples from pregnancy to postpartum and compared them to a group who were childless but still intending to have children at a future date. This essentially equates the two groups on their ultimate desires for children. After the first child was born, couples reported lower marital satisfaction, and this was not simply due to the passage of time. Hackel and Ruble (1992) also asked couples to list the three most positive aspects of their current experience. Prior to pregnancy 85% listed their marriage as one of the most positive elements in their lives. During pregnancy, this figure dropped to 50%; and postpartum, only 33% of the men and 16% of the women listed their marriage as one of the three most positive aspects of their lives. Shapiro et al. followed newlywed couples for the first 6 years of their marriage. During that time, a little over one third of the couples became parents. The marital satisfaction scores of the wives who became mothers declined on average 10.63 points per year during the study. On the other hand, marital satisfaction of the wives who remained childless declined an average of 1.12 points per year (Shapiro et al.). Clearly the marital satisfaction of parents and nonparents declined over the first 6 years of their marriage, but this decline was much more dramatic for those who became parents.

The Shapiro et al. (2000) study described here produced another important finding: 33% of the wives who became mothers experienced an *increase* in marital satisfaction with the transition to parenthood. Combined with evidence from some studies showing that marital satisfaction remains stable over the transition to parenthood, it is now clear that not all couples experience decreases in marital satisfaction as a result of parenthood. Consequently, scientific attention is now beginning to shift toward explaining why (or why not) marital happiness declines as some husbands and wives become fathers and mothers.

### Traditionalization of Gender Roles

One of the most striking marital changes that accompanies parenthood is a shift to a more traditional division of labor where the wife takes care of the interior household chores and child rearing and the husband takes care of exterior household chores and finances (Belsky, 1990; Huston & Vangelisti, 1995; MacDermid, Huston, & McHale, 1990). The traditionalization of gender roles may suit some couples rather well, especially those with traditional ideologies (MacDermid et al.). On the other hand, wives who are low in stereotypically feminine traits are at high risk for decreasing marital satisfaction when roles become traditionalized with the transition to parenthood (Belsky, Lang, & Huston, 1986). Unfortunately, as many wives approach motherhood they expect that the division of household labor will become more egalitarian after the child is born. Often, the exact opposite happens, with husbands actually doing a smaller percentage of household work after the child is born (e.g., MacDermid et al.; Nomaguchi & Milkie, 2003). The violation of these expectations has been identified as a key ingredient in the declines of wives' postpartum marital satisfaction (Cowan, Cowan, Heming, & Miller, 1991; Hackel

& Ruble, 1992; Ruble, Fleming, Hackel, & Stangor, 1988). As husbands cut back on their contributions to household tasks, many wives perceive unfairness in the relationship, which in turn leads to increased marital conflict and distress (Grote & Clark, 2001; Ruble et al.).

### Planning and Timing

The stress of transition to parenthood is closely tied to the timing and planning of pregnancy. Most marriages fare best when the husband and wife have a period of time to adjust to their new roles without the added burden of parenthood. Early-first-birth couples, defined as those who have a child when the wife is age 24 or younger, experience more dramatic declines in marital satisfaction with the transition to parenthood compared to those couples who delay childbirth for a greater period of time (Helms-Erikson, 2001; see also Kurdek, 1998b). In general, the longer a couple is married before having a child, the happier they are with their marriage (Helms-Erikson). In addition to timing, planning plays a vital role in the maintenance of marital satisfaction over the transition to parenthood. The most stressful life events are often the ones that happen unexpectedly. About 50% of all pregnancies in the general population are unplanned (Henshaw, 1998). Couples who experienced unplanned pregnancies exhibit greater decreases in marital satisfaction than those whose pregnancies were planned (Cox, Paley, Burchinal, & Payne, 1999; Snowden, Schott, Awalt, & Gillis-Knox, 1988). Couples who delay childbirth and who plan the birth of their first child clearly have more time to contemplate and adjust to their new roles as parents. This undoubtedly contributes to their ability to maintain a happy marriage as they transition to parenthood.

### The Changing Nature of Marital Interactions

Children and spouses compete for finite resources—each other's time and energy. The birth of the first child is often accompanied by significant changes in the nature of spouses' interactions. Expressions of positive affection decline, conflicts increase, spouses spend less time together as a dyad, communicating less with each other and focusing a greater proportion of their interactions on the child (Belsky, 1990; Huston & Vangelisti, 1995; Kurdek, 1993). The amount of time that coupes have available for leisure time significantly decreases with parenthood, and what leisure activities the couple is able to engage in are generally centered around the child (MacDermid et al., 1990). Even though the nature of marital interactions changes substantially with the birth of the first child, the maintenance of certain interaction patterns may have a prophylactic effect to ward off the declines in satisfaction that characterize the marriages of many first-time parents. For instance, husbands and wives who exhibit good problem-solving communication prenatally experience greater marital satisfaction before the child is born and experience a smaller decline in satisfaction after the child is born, relative to those couples with poor problem-solving communication skills (Cox et al., 1999). Also, wives' marital satisfaction can be sustained and perhaps even increased over the transition to parenthood when husbands express high awareness of their wives while talking about their relationship and when they express fondness and affection toward their wives (Shapiro et al., 2000).

On the other hand, wives' satisfaction decreases when husbands express disappointment in the marriage and negativity (Shapiro et al., 2000).

## Launching Children

Popular literature and cultural folklore each suggest that launching children is stressful for family members. Perhaps this is why the term *empty-nest syndrome* is often used to refer to this stage of the family life cycle. Some people have observed that parents, especially mothers, experience depression and emptiness after their children leave home. Some also believe that this is a time of heightened conflict between spouses who may have kept their differences concealed while the children were living at home. Despite the fact that there are a number of significant challenges and tasks associated with this transition, scientific research indicates that there are many positive aspects of this stage in the family life cycle.

### Children Leaving Home

The most common reasons why children move out of their parents' home are school, marriage and cohabitation, a desire for independence, military duty, and employment (Ward & Spitze, 1996). There is some evidence that family of origin structure is systematically related to the motivation to leave home (Mitchell, 1994). In a large study of children aged 15 to 24, Mitchell found that those living in stepfamilies were five to six times more likely to leave home, compared to those living with both parents or a single parent (see also Cooney & Mortimer, 1999). At the same time, those living in a stepfamily or in lone-parent households were particularly prone to leaving home in order to get away from conflict and establish independence. Regardless of the particular motivation for leaving home, this transition demands significant changes in the adult child's repertoire of behaviors. Tasks that were previously taken care of by parents, some of which may have been outside the child's awareness, must now be assumed by the child himself or herself. Although many children are eager to leave their parents' home, there is undoubtedly a degree of stress associated with all of the new responsibilities that must be assumed. One of the fundamental family interaction tasks facing the child is the recalibration of his or her relationship with the parents. Most children welcome the autonomy from their parents, but at the same time desire to maintain a reasonable degree of contact and closeness with them. Too much reliance on parents after moving out may threaten their sense of independence and accomplishment, whereas too little may leave them feeling abruptly disconnected. Thus, this is a time when children have to recalibrate relationships with their parents to achieve a new level of balance between autonomy and connectedness.

### Parents of Children Leaving Home

Does the departure of children represent a crisis for parents? Is there really such a thing as the empty-nest syndrome as portrayed in the popular press? For the most part, launching children is associated with positive outcomes for parents. Over the transition to the empty-nest stage, mothers report increases in positive mood and general well-being, and decreases in negative mood and daily hassles (Dennerstein, Dudley, & Guthrie, 2002). For most parents, the departure of adult children may mean a new sense of freedom, diminished responsibility, increased privacy (Barber, 1989), and pride in seeing adult children establish their own identity and role, especially in cases where children leave for school, military, or employment. Whatever remorse is associated with the departure is evidently outweighed by these sources of happiness.

Like their emerging adult children, parents face their own set of social tasks during this phase of the family life cycle. Just as children must recalibrate relationships with parents at this stage, so too must parents realign relationships with their adult children. Again the task is to find a balance between autonomy and connection that is comfortable not only for the parent but also for the *relationship*. Many parent–child relationships struggle with this balancing act for years after the child has physically left the home. In addition to recalibrating parent–adult child relationships at this stage, parents also face the tasks of situating themselves in an expanding family structure and resolving relationships with their aging parents (McCullough & Rutenberg, 1988). As parents launch their children, marriages, in-laws, and grandchildren are often just around the corner. This means that parents will find themselves in an expanding set of family relationships that may at times compete for attention from their adult children. Once children are launched, it would be understandable for parents to focus their attention on relationships with their aging parents. McCullough and Rutenberg (1988) argue that a healthy relationship between the older two generations is vital for the successful launching of young adult children. Middle-aged parents who are either emotionally cut off from their own parents or overinvolved with them are anticipated to have problematic responses to the departure of their young adult children.

### Parent–Child Relationships

According to role identity theory, people develop a sense of meaning and purpose in life from the roles that they identify with and enact (Thoits, 1983). For parents who are heavily invested in their role and who derive considerable satisfaction from being a parent, it is reasonable to think that the departure of children might be associated with declines in general well-being and mood. However, most currently available evidence suggests that this is a happy time for parents. Perhaps one reason for this, consistent with role identity theory, is that parents essentially continue being parents long after their children have left the home. Most studies show that despite their physical absence, parents and children still stay in close touch with each other (White & Edwards, 1990). Frequent visits, letters, and phone calls are common among adult children and their parents, allowing them to maintain what are generally characterized as close relationships after launching (Lye, 1996). Lye found that adult children and parents commonly exchanged emotional support and advice, with the one exception being divorced fathers and their adult children. In essence, the arrangement struck between many young adult children and their parents represents a win-win situation: The children acquire their long-sought independence and the parents appear able to still derive satisfaction and enjoyment from their role as parents, with fewer constraints and responsibilities associated with the newly adjusted role. In many cases this actually improves the parent–child relationship. Barber (1989) explains that as children move out on their own, they often develop a newfound appreciation for their parents and are less critical of them. As young adults tackle the challenges faced by establishing independence, many gain a perspective that may cast their parents in a new light that is much easier to appreciate.

Young adults' decision to move out of the home has often been explained by social exchange theory (see chap. 2). Children are assumed to weigh the costs and benefits of staying versus leaving the home. According to social exchange theory, they would be expected to choose the living arrangement that yields the most valued benefits. However, as sociologist Lynn White notes, this perspective could be equally applied to parents' roles in launching their children (White, 1994a). There is no reason to assume that this transition is initiated purely by children. White observes that well-to-do parents might exchange their own resources to subsidize their children's departure in order to gain privacy and freedom of their own. This might be achieved, for example, by paying a child's rent for an apartment or housing bill for a college residence hall.

### *"Empty-Nest" Marriages*

After children leave home, the marital relationship between the parents regains prominence (McCullough & Rutenberg, 1988). Because many parents are in their mid-40s when they launch their children, it is reasonable to assume that they will live together as a couple without children in the home for 30 years. Parents who were previously consumed with child-rearing responsibilities now have the opportunity to refocus their attention to their spouse and their marriage.

For the most part, middle-aged parents' marital satisfaction appears to increase somewhat when their grown children leave the home (Barber, 1989; White & Edwards, 1990). In some cases, there may be little change in feelings between the spouses immediately after their children leave home (e.g., Dennerstein et al., 2002), but for the majority of marriages, the newfound freedom and lessened financial responsibilities associated with this stage of the family life cycle appear to spill over into greater marital happiness. With that said, we should note that there is a particular subset in the population of married couples who appear to be headed for trouble when their children leave home. The usual scenario for these couples involves troubles in their relationship that predate the launching of their children (Pryor, 1999). These might include low cohesion, conflict, and boundary confusion. However, they hang on to their marriages, perhaps out of a felt obligation to the children. Then, when the children leave home and the couple realizes that there is nothing left to their marriage, they split up. The hallmark of such marriages is early child rearing (Heidemann, Suhomlinova, & O'Rand, 1998).

Heidemann and her associates carefully studied a nationally representative sample of over 5,000 women and found that those who entered the empty-nest phase early in their marital career were far more likely to divorce after their children left home, in contrast to those who entered the empty-nest phase later in their marital career. To illustrate, a couple who has been married for 20 years at the onset of the empty nest has a nearly 300% increase in the risk of divorce compared to the risk for marriages in general. On the other hand, those who have been married for 35 years when they reach the empty nest stage experience a 40% *decrease* in the risk of divorce when their last child leaves home (Heidemann et al., 1998). One obvious difference between couples that experience the empty-nest stage at 20 as opposed to at 35 years into their marriage is that the former group clearly did not delay childbearing. In other words, those couples never had the opportunity to establish a solid foundation as a married couple before the strains of parenting fell upon them. However, couples who spent some time together as husband and wife before they became mom and dad seem to experience more positive marital outcomes as their children leave home. Of course, another plausible explanation is that those who entered the empty nest state later in their marriage are also older, and thus have fewer attractive alternatives available to them. In either event, we should note that the phenomenon of divorce during the empty-nest stage accounts for only about 10% of all divorces. Most couples who are going to divorce do so well before their last child leaves home, and most marriages that survive the child-rearing years are happy and bound for perhaps even more happiness as the children leave home.

## The Aging Family

As family members grow older, they face several challenges that are particular to this stage of the family life cycle. Among these are retirement, changing health, caregiving by the middle-aged generation, and relationship loss (Mancini & Blieszner, 1994; Walsh, 1988). This stage of the family life cycle is associated with dramatic changes in both family structure and family roles. Family members who were once care providers often become recipients of care. The declining health of some family members means their roles in the family must be redefined. The death of family members often requires others to "step up to the plate" and assume new roles, regardless of their enthusiasm for doing so. In this section we briefly discuss the impact of retirement, changing health and caregiving, and relationship loss on the aging family. For further analysis of this stage of the family life cycle, readers are referred to the section on grandparent relationships in chapter 8 and to chapter 14 where we analyze family interaction and physical health.

### Retirement

One of the hallmark signs of the aging family is retirement. This is a pivotal transition in life about which people can feel extremely ambivalent. On one hand, retirement represents freedom from the demands, responsibilities, and routines of employment. Many families look forward to the retirement years as times when they can go on long vacations together, spend time with each other, and visit friends and extended family members. At the same time, retirement can represent a profound loss of a valued role, particularly for people whose role identity is closely tied to the work that they do (Walsh, 1988). Retirement also affects the way that a family structures its time. The retiree will now be spending at least twice as much time in the home as before. The spouse of the retiree may have to alter his or her normal routine to accommodate this change (Mancini & Blieszner, 1994). This could be a source of happiness or stress. Most evidence suggests that aging married couples maintain previously established patterns in their relationship, especially in the gender stereotyped division of labor (Mares, 1995).

### Changing Health and Caregiving

One of the inevitable aspects of aging is a change in physical abilities and health. Many elderly people are able to effectively accommodate these changes without requiring much assistance. However, these changes often mean that the elderly family member may need to rely on others for certain things (e.g., going to the grocery store, preparing meals, and housekeeping). Walsh (1988) notes that only about 5% of the elderly need such intense care as to require institutionalization, but that eventually as many as 85% will require some family caregiving for their daily functioning. Some researchers have cleverly demonstrated that modern communication technologies such as videophones and e-mail dramatically help maintain family relationships (especially with grandchildren and great-grandchildren) and quality of life for institutionalized elderly people (Lansdale, 2002; Mickus & Luz, 2002). When the assistance of family members is needed, there is a fairly reliable pattern, with spouses being most likely to provide care, followed by adult children, and then siblings (Davey, 2000). Whereas some have argued that grandchildren may be involved in caregiving to aging family members (Williams & Nussbaum, 2001), others have concluded that this is rarely the case (Johnson, 1988). Like so many other normative family stressors, the family's adjustment to caring for its elderly members is associated with the quality of the past relationship between the caregiver and care recipient (Davey). When such family members have a history of positive interactions, the caregiving experience appears less stressful for all parties involved. But if there was a pattern of strained relationships prior to the elderly person's need for care, there is more stress and perceived burden by family members.

### Relationship Loss

Invariably, aging family members will face relationship loss. The most stressful form of relationship loss involves the death of a spouse. Because women have a longer life expectancy then men, about 75% of the time this means that a woman loses her husband and must adjust to widowhood. One of the best predictors of adjustment to loss of a spouse is the ability to plan for widowhood in advance (Mancini & Blieszner, 1994). People who have the opportunity to discuss widowhood with their spouses, family members, and other widows, before the spouse actually dies, seem to resolve their grief more successfully after the death (Hansson & Remondet, 1987). These findings illustrate just how important family communication is right up until the end of life. After the death of a spouse, the surviving family members can be an especially vital source of social support. Because most women over the age of 50 do not remarry after the death of a spouse (Mares, 1995), remaining family relationships may take on a new importance, especially if there is a need for care on the part of the widowed spouse.

Murray (2000) described three primary factors that influence how well the family adjusts to the death of one of its members. The first factor is *timing and concurrent stressors in the family life cycle*. If the death is perceived as "on time" as opposed to "premature," family members are better able to adjust and work through their grief. However, if there are other stressors or transitions that are active at the same time (e.g., birth of a child or a young adult child moving out of the home), the family will have a more difficult time coping with the loss. Second, the *function and position of the person prior to his or her death* will have a big impact on the family's adjustment to the loss (Brown, 1988). For example, in a rigidly structured family that is built around a patriarch, the death of that individual can send shock waves through the family that will leave them permanently disorganized. Finally, *conflicted relationships with the deceased* can lead to complicated bereavement. Unresolved conflicts, bitter feelings, and estrangement can add to the lament over losing a family member, particularly as the surviving relative realizes that the opportunity for communication and resolution of these problems is no longer available.

## NONNORMATIVE FAMILY STRESSORS

In this section we analyze the impact and function of several nonnormative family stressors. These stressors are sometimes called "unpredictable family stressors" because they are not part of the "normal" family life cycle. However, as we cautioned earlier, this is an imprecise classification as many of these stressors are in fact somewhat predictable and happen to so many families as to question their distinction as "nonnormative." In the pages that follow we discuss marital distress and separations from the family as examples of nonnormative family stressors. Each of these has a massive impact on the form and function of family relationships. Each dramatically alters family interaction patterns, and in some cases, the stressor is actually caused by altered family interaction patterns. For discussions of additional nonnormative family stressors see chapter 11 (Divorce) and chapter 14 (Major Illness).

### Marital Distress

It is safe to say that virtually all marriages go through periods of distress. It is equally safe to say that communication is at the heart of most cases of marital distress. Fitzpatrick (1988b) observed that there are three sets of factors that predict marital distress: premarital factors (e.g., personality and values), social and economic factors, and interpersonal relationship factors. Among these, interpersonal relationship factors are the largest set. Marital communication patterns have proven to be key predictors of subsequent declines in marital satisfaction (Rogge & Bradbury, 1999a). Problems with communication seem to predispose couples to marital distress, and marital distress seems to damage the quality of husbands' and wives' communication with each other (Wright et al., 1994).

Prior to marriage, most of the problems and stressors that couples face are matters exterior to their relationship. These might involve negotiating relationships with each other's friends and parents, jealousy about relationships with other people, and initiating a career, for example. Upon getting married, couples face a new set of developmental challenges, reflecting matters that are largely interior to their relationship such as maintaining intimacy, communication problems, and shared time together (Storaasli & Markman, 1990). Many people are unprepared for the demands imposed by these challenges and consequently experience marital distress.

## Marital Satisfaction Reliably Changes Over Time

One of the more reliable findings in family science is that married couples' satisfaction with their relationship reliably decreases over the first 3 to 6 years of marriage (Johnson, Amoloza, & Booth, 1992; Karney, Bradbury, & Johnson, 1999; Kurdek, 1998b; Lindahl et al., 1998; Vangelisti & Huston, 1994). Two hypotheses for this are that the presence of children causes marital satisfaction to decline and that the "honeymoon" effect eventually wares off causing couples to see each other and their problems more realistically. The good news is that this level of satisfaction rebounds 15 to 20 years into the marriage after the children start leaving home. This has led to the commonly held belief that over time marital satisfaction levels form a U curve, with highest levels early, and then late, in the relationship. Vaillant and Vaillant (1993) challenged this assumption with findings from their 40-year study of Harvard graduates. They found that satisfaction levels were relatively stable over the different periods of measurement. However, this sample was exceptionally well educated, virtually all White, and financially well off.

The U-curve pattern of marital satisfaction has also been seriously challenged by findings from a 17-year study that documented slight decreases in marital satisfaction over time, with no eventual increase in more advanced marriages (Van Laningham, Johnson, & Amato, 2001). Van Laningham and her associates convincingly demonstrated that the upturn in marital satisfaction in later years that has been observed in many past studies is the result of a cohort effect (i.e., couples who have been married 20–30 years are couples who grew up in a different era with different values from those of couples who have only been together for 3 or 4 years). By implication, one would not expect to see an upswing in satisfaction 20 to 30 years from now among couples who are currently newlywed. The research findings from Vaillant and Vaillant (1993) are a reminder that not all people will experience higher degrees of distress during the middle years of their marriage. About 30% of the husbands and 15% of the wives in one study showed *increases* in satisfaction during the early years of their marriages (Karney et al., 1999). And unfortunately, the Van Laningham, Johnson, and Amato (2001) study indicates that not all couples should expect an increase in marital satisfaction in the later years of their marriage.

## Marital Distress Is Strongly Associated With Negativity in Husband–Wife Interactions

When distressed married couples discuss important matters in their relationship, their communication is marked by disagreement, criticism, and guilt induction (Haefner, Notarius, & Pellegrini, 1991; Hooley & Hahlweg, 1989). These conversations are often the source of considerable negative affect, or emotion, for the distressed couples, and this is evident in their behaviors (Gottman & Notarius, 2002; Krokoff, Gottman, & Roy, 1988). It is not particularly surprising that distressed couples exhibit negativity during their interactions and that these interactions are the source of a lot of negative emotions. Undoubtedly, the negative communication behaviors and negative emotions displayed in these interactions are causally related.

One pattern that distinguishes the interactions of distressed and nondistressed couples is not simply the amount of negativity and negative affect but rather the *reciprocity* of negative affect (Gottman & Levenson, 1986; Hooley & Hahlweg, 1989; Krokoff et al., 1988). When couples exhibit negative affect in their interactions, specific emotions such as anger, disgust, contempt, sadness, and fear are evident in their verbal and nonverbal behaviors. In distressed couples, the expression of these negative emotions seems to trigger similar expressions from the spouse. This is evident, for example, in a pattern called "cross-complaining" (Gottman, Markman, & Notarius, 1977). In cross-complaining, complaints are met with complaints. For example, if the husband said "you need to stop buying so many things with the credit card," a cross-complaining response for his wife might be, "well why don't you try to save some money instead of blowing it all on computer equipment?" In the first utterance, the husband complains to his wife, expressing his anger over her use of their credit card. In her response, she counters with an angry complaint of her own about his frivolous spending habits. In the conversations of distressed couples these cross-complaining loops are common. Needless to say, this is not a very fruitful approach to conflict resolution.

Is the expression of negative affect, and the tendency to reciprocate such expressions from a spouse, an antecedent or a consequent of marital distress? A number of researchers have attempted to address this issue by conducting longitudinal studies of positivity and negativity in marital interactions. Research findings suggest that negative affect in marital relationships is predictive of subsequent declines in satisfaction. For example, Kurdek (1998b) found that wives' tendency to feel negative emotions when confronted with various problems predicted their, *and their husbands'*, declines in marital satisfaction over the following 6 years. A similar finding, but for the opposite sex, was found by Huston and Vangelisti (1991). In their study, newlywed husbands' and wives' negativity (e.g., acting bored or uninterested, showing anger or impatience, and criticizing or complaining) predicted decreases in wives' satisfaction over the ensuing 2 years. Husbands' pessimism (e.g., expressing ambivalence about the future and a lack of commitment to working on the relationship) during a laboratory interview has proven to be predictive of declines in marital satisfaction 2 years later (Gee, Scott, Castellani, & Cordova, 2002). When couples were observed during a conflict resolution discussion, negativity (e.g., blame, accusation, criticism) by either spouse was predictive of decreases in wives' satisfaction measured 1 year later (Gill, Christensen, & Fincham, 1999). On a more upbeat note, husbands' and wives' positivity (e.g., expressing understanding and acceptance) during that same conversation predicted *increases* in wives' satisfaction 1 year later (see also Gee et al.).

Flora and Segrin (2000a) asked married couples to complete the following sentence "I wish you were more . . . " and discuss their answers for 7 minutes. The more speaking turns each spouse took in this conversation, the more their satisfaction dropped in the following 6 months. Also, couples were asked to engage in a complimenting interaction where they completed the sentence "Of all the wonderful qualities you possess, the one that I appreciate the most is . . . ," and discussed this for 7 minutes. The more negative affect husbands reported in these supposedly "positive" interactions, the more their satisfaction declined over the subsequent 6 months. Watching these couples in the complimenting interaction, we were struck by how hard it was for some to complete the sentence. Being married to a spouse who finds it difficult to offer a compliment is disappointing and one potential source of negative affect.

Just as the presence of negativity in marital interactions warns of future declines in satisfaction, so too does negative affect reciprocity foreshadow troubles. Couples' marital satisfaction has been shown to decrease over a 3-year period when wives reciprocated their husbands' negative affect while discussing the "events of the day" (Levenson & Gottman, 1985). It is interesting that if a husband did *not* reciprocate his wife's negative affect during the conversation, her satisfaction declined. Gottman and Levenson explain that this may be due to men wanting to vent and then be left alone, whereas women may want to have their negative feelings explicitly responded to by their partner.

Before we create the impression that negativity in marital interaction is all bad, it is important to note that the expression of negativity can be functional in at least some cases. In one notable investigation, the tendency for wives' to respond to their husbands with disgust or anger was negatively associated with their current satisfaction (as expected) but *positively* associated with their satisfaction 3 years later (Gottman & Krokoff, 1989). In other words, the more negativity wives communicated toward their husbands during a conflict resolution, the happier they were later on in the marriage, despite their unhappiness at the time that they expressed this negativity. Some have characterized this as a "confrontation effect," noting that in the long run it may be better to confront the spouse with one's own anger and frustration. As we noted earlier in this book, not all couples take the same approach to handling their conflicts. For couples that characteristically avoid conflict, the wife's expression of disgust or contempt during a marital interaction predicted her current dissatisfaction with the marriage, but her future improvements in satisfaction (Krokoff, 1991). However, for couples that were conflict engagers, the expression of disgust and contempt had the effect of decreasing satisfaction over time. Thus, it appears that conflict-avoiding wives can benefit from at least occasionally expressing anger to their husbands. Alternatively, conflict-engaging couples have to strike a precarious balance between openly expressing their grievances and maintaining happiness. For such couples, the expression of anger in marital interactions seems to be harmful to wives' long-term satisfaction.

### The Demand–Withdrawal Pattern Is Harmful to Marital Satisfaction

Demand–withdrawal is a pattern of marital interaction that has been repeatedly linked with distress and even divorce. In the demand–withdrawal pattern, one spouse (usually the wife) presents a complaint, demand, or criticism. The other spouse (usually the husband) responds by withdrawal and defensiveness (Christensen, 1988). Couples seeking a divorce or who are in marital therapy report more demand–withdrawal patterns in their interactions than do happily married couples (Christensen & Shenk, 1991). This dysfunctional interaction pattern appears to reflect an unresolved discrepancy within the couple over desires for closeness versus distance. As might be expected, the tendency for either husbands or wives to be in the demand role is associated with their desire for change in their partner (Caughlin & Vangelisti, 1999). However, Caughlin and Vangelisti found that husbands' desire for change was also associated with a *wife-demand and husband-withdrawal* pattern during a conversation that the couple had in their home. Wives' desire for change was only associated with the predictable wife-demand and husband-withdrawal pattern during the conversation. Caughlin and Vangelisti noted that in some cases, the desire for change might be over a couple-level issue that will occasionally put both spouses in the demanding role, with the attendant partner withdrawing.

Husbands and wives appear to have differing reactions to the demand–withdrawal pattern. In one study of newlyweds, partner *hostility* proved to be the strongest predictor of decreases in marital satisfaction at the third anniversary for wives, but partner *withdrawal* was the strongest predictor of declines in satisfaction for husbands (Roberts, 2000). Stereotypically, people think of the nagging wife and the withdrawn husband. However, it is when these roles are reversed that marital satisfaction is harmed the most. Wives' marital satisfaction is damaged far more by their husbands' hostility than by their husbands' withdrawal. And although husbands' marital satisfaction also appears to be eroded by wives' hostility, their wives' withdrawal harms marital satisfaction even further (Roberts). At the same time, it should be noted that the demand and withdrawal pattern might be a marker of marital dissatisfaction regardless of who is in the demand mode and who is in the withdrawal mode (Caughlin, 2002). Furthermore, in some established marriages, the demand and withdrawal pattern can lead to *increases* in wives' satisfaction in the near future (Caughlin; see chap. 6).

As destructive as the demand and withdrawal pattern of marital interaction may be, there are communication behaviors that can counter its ill effects. Caughlin and Huston (2002) found that a demand and withdrawal pattern of interaction was negatively associated with both husbands' and wives' satisfaction, regardless of who was in the demand role and who was in the withdrawal role. However, when partners otherwise expressed a lot of affection toward each other (e.g., expressing approval, compliments, and "I love you"; and showing physical affection outside of intercourse) the correlation between the demand and withdrawal pattern and the marital satisfaction was near zero. When the demand and withdrawal pattern occurs in the context of a relationship that is otherwise characterized by messages that express positive regard and liking toward the partner, marital distress is minimized.

### Perceptual Inaccuracy Leads to Marital Discord

Another hallmark sign of marital distress is a perceptual inaccuracy in which spouses negatively misevaluate their partners' messages such that they perceive messages as more negative than they are intended to be (Noller, 1984). Ordinarily, this is studied in the lab by having couples interact while sitting at a "talk-table." The talk table is a device that allows couples to flip a toggle switch to determine who has the floor. It also has a series of buttons that each spouse can push to rate the positivitiy or negativity of the message that is currently being sent. Spouses who converse at a talk table are instructed to rate the intent of their messages, and their partners are instructed to rate the impact of the messages. A preponderance of messages that are rated negatively by the speaker (intent) or listener (impact) is predictive of subsequent declines in marital satisfaction (Markman, 1981, 1984). Further, couples whose marital satisfaction erodes over the years are those who cannot agree on the intent and impact ratings (Markman, 1984). Markman views this as a sort of communication skills deficit, where the husband and wife are unable to send messages to each other in such a way that intent equals impact. What is particularly interesting is that nondistressed wives may actually be happy because they *over*estimate their husbands' positive intents (Notarius et al., 1989).

Recent refinements on the intent equals impact model of perceptual accuracy call into question whether this is truly a communication skills deficit. For many distressed couples messages are often sent with a genuinely negative intent, especially among wives (Denton, Burleson, & Sprenkle, 1994). Thus, the problem may lie not so much in the mismatch of spouses' intents and perceived impacts but with their motivation to send negatively valenced messages to their partner. Also, what might be more important for the marriage than absolute perceptual accuracy (i.e., message intent equals message impact) is a *matching* of spouses' skill levels in producing and interpreting such messages (Burleson & Denton, 1992). Burleson and Denton found that married couples were happy so long as their communication skill levels were matched. In other words, a husband who had a hard time sending messages that were interpreted in accord with his intentions could be satisfied so long as his wife was equally poor in her communication. According to this matching hypothesis, the couples that are headed for martial distress are those in which the husband and wife are mismatched in their communication abilities.

### Marital Distress Is More Obvious in Nonverbal Than Verbal Communication

Sometimes what separates interpersonal success from interpersonal failure is not *what* is said but *how* it is said. Distressed couples tend to misunderstand each other's nonverbal communication behaviors, and usually they are unaware of these misunderstandings (Noller, 1984). This may be due in part to the fact that distressed couples are more prone to send discrepant messages where the vocal or visual aspects of the message are positive but the words are negative (Noller). Obviously, these messages are difficult to interpret because they send contradictory signals.

It is often the case that a couple's nonverbal behaviors are more strongly associated with their distress than their verbal behaviors are (Hooley & Hahlweg, 1989). In an interesting test of this hypothesis, Vincent, Friedman, Nugent, and Messerly (1979) asked distressed and nondistressed married couples to have a neutral conversation and then to have a conversation in which they pretended to be "the most happy, blissful, and contented couple that they could imagine" (fake good) or "the most unhappy, conflicted, and distressed couple they could imagine" (fake bad). An analysis of their interactions showed that couples' verbal behaviors in the neutral and fake conditions were significantly different for both couples. In each case, they altered the nature of their discourse to be consistent with the instructions. However, their nonverbal behaviors were indistinguishable in the neutral versus the fake conditions. The implications of these results are clear: Distressed couples can easily conceal their dissatisfaction with each other by altering their verbal behavior, but even when pretending to be happy, their nonverbal behavior gives them away. Gottman et al. (1977) also analyzed videotaped interactions of distressed and nondistressed couples and observed that "Nonverbal behavior thus discriminated distressed and nondistressed couples better than verbal behavior" (p. 469). Of course, this is not to say that marital distress is not evident in verbal behavior. Rather, when couples are being observed, it is their nonverbal behavior that most likely reveals their distress.

### Communication Behaviors That Predict Future Marital Distress Are Evident Premaritally

Researchers who study couples before marriage and then again after marriage generally find that although marital satisfaction may change over time, couples' communication patterns are relatively stable (Kelly et al., 1985; Noller & Feeney, 1998; Noller, Feeney, Bonnell, & Callan, 1994; Prado & Markman, 1999). Many of the problematic communication behaviors reviewed earlier in this chapter such as negativity, criticism, conflict, and poor perceptual and sending skills can be identified before a couple even marries (Huston & Houts, 1998). These findings lead to an astonishing conclusion. *The communication behaviors that will ultimately lead to the demise of marriage are already in place before the husband and wife marry.* The fact of the matter is that "irreconcilable differences" that are commonly cited as a cause for divorce may well have been in place before the wedding day. According to Gottman and Markman's bank account model (reviewed in chap. 6), most couples start out with a positive balance that causes them to be content with their relationship. Even though negative behaviors, or "withdrawals," may be evident at the time of marriage, it takes some time for couples to accumulate enough of these to actually distress their marriage. Huston and his associates (e.g., Huston, Niehuis, & Smith, 2001) use the term "enduring-dynamics" to characterize the hypothesis that patterns established early in the relationship persevere and lead to later declines in marital happiness. Although there is sound evidence for the enduring dynamics model, it should also be pointed out that negative changes in feelings and behaviors can also be identified in couples headed for divorce (Huston, Caughlin et al., 2001). Consequently, many marriages end up on the rocks because of both enduring patterns of interaction that predate the marriage and changes in the marriage that lead to disillusion.

## Separation From the Family

The concept of "togetherness" figures prominently in most people's ideas of marriage and family. People marry, in part, with the hope of spending time with their spouse. When people have children, it is at least assumed that they have an interest in raising the child and spending leisure time with him or her. Unfortunately, these ideals and expectations are interfered with for families that experience separations. In this section we review the causes and consequences of family separations. The focus here is not on the sort of separations that distressed couples agree to, perhaps as a prelude to divorce, but rather on separations that are to some extent involuntary and caused by matters external to the family relationship. These stressors seriously alter the family system by necessitating dramatic shifts in roles and creating unfulfilled desires for intimacy and companionship. In addition, the stressors often create new financial and child-rearing burdens. Family separations fundamentally alter communication among family members, often eliminating face-to-face interaction all together and forcing members to communicate over the telephone, through e-mail, and through written letters.

The two primary reasons why married couples are sometimes physically separated from each other (known as "martial noncohabitation") are military duty and incarceration in jail or prison (Rindfuss & Stephen, 1990). Recently, it has become more common to see spouses living apart for job reasons. Such couples are said to have a "commuter marriage." These types of marital separations are especially common among young married couples in the 18 to 24 age range. Over 10% of young Black married couples and 5% to 6% of young White couples experience marital noncohabitation. Evidence of the stressfulness of these separations is clear from statistics showing that marital noncohabitation significantly increases the likelihood of divorce (Rindfuss & Stephen). Rindfuss and Stephen explain this effect by noting that the longer couples are apart, the more they may have changed in each other's absence. When they resume living together, the adjustments that are needed to reaccommodate the spouses into each other's lives may be more than what their marriage can bear.

### Separations Caused by Military Duty

It is interesting to note that one of the dominant theories of family stress, Hill's ABC-X model (see chap. 9), was developed from studying families that had to deal with the stress of having their husband or father go to the military during World War II and return home again. Military duty brings stressors that are common to most family separations such as child-rearing burdens and unfulfilled desires for contact and companionship. Additionally, during wartime, there is the enormous burden of uncertainty about the family member's eventual return. Will he or she be killed in action or injured? Will combat permanently change his or her personality? Concern over these matters adds a serious psychological burden to many families of military personnel.

Active military duty appears to be associated with decreases in marital satisfaction (Schumm, Bell, & Gade, 2000). In this investigation, married soldiers who were deployed to the Middle East in the mid-1990s showed a noticeable drop in their marital satisfaction while on active duty, apart from their spouses. Upon their return, most experienced an increase in martial satisfaction that was generally equivalent to predeployment levels. However, Schumm and his colleagues found that this stressor proved to be too much for some marriages. Particularly for couples who had marital problems prior to the deployment, this separation was associated with increased rates of marital dissolution over the ensuing 2 years. In a related investigation, wives of soldiers deployed in Operation Desert Storm reported significantly increased emotional distress while their husbands were away (Medway, Davis, Cafferty, Chappell, & O'Hearn, 1995). The Medway et al. study is noteworthy for documenting what appears to be a spillover effect for mother's stress. The more personal distress the mother reported, the more her children exhibited behavior problems while their father was away. Regardless of whether the children were reacting to their stressed-out mother, or whether the mother was stressed because of her children's behavior problems, it is apparent that this family stressor had a systemwide impact. Consistent with the concept of interdependence in family systems theory, the problems and stresses experienced by one family member clearly had an impact on other members of the family.

### Separations Caused by Incarceration

Imprisonment can have a devastating effect on the family system. Like other forms of family separation, it creates burdens for child rearing and unmet needs for companionship. Because imprisonment is far more likely to happen to fathers than to mothers, it often creates a massive financial burden on the family, due to the loss of the father's income. In addition, this is a family stressor associated with a powerful stigma. Many family members are not comfortable disclosing to others that their spouse's or parent's absence is due to imprisonment. Communication with the incarcerated family members becomes extremely restricted to letters, occasional visits that are generally supervised, and perhaps, on rare occasion, a phone call.

Long-term prison sentences can destroy many marriages. Spouses not only have to wait years, decades, or in some cases indefinitely for reunion with their partner, but also have to cope with feelings of anger, shame, and resentment for being deserted without contributing to the reason for the abandonment (Kaslow, 1987). Because imprisonment often involves long-term family absences, family roles once served by the now-imprisoned member must be divided up among the remaining family members. This can be a source of additional stress and resentment.

The marital separation imposed by incarceration contributes to increased loneliness for inmates (Segrin & Flora, 2001). However, the quality of inmates' marriages can be a source of hope that helps to maintain psychological adjustment while in prison. Segrin and Flora found that inmates who had a positive relational history with their spouse were able to maintain a higher degree of marital quality (i.e., satisfaction and commitment) while in prison. This in turn appeared to minimize their experience of loneliness. So, although incarceration has an obvious negative effect on family relationships, strong family relationships can be extremely beneficial to the individual doing time in prison.

Nowhere is the family systemwide impact of imprisonment more apparent than in the effects on children of incarcerated mothers. When mothers are imprisoned, family members have to deal with stigmatization, loneliness, arranging visitation schedules for the mother and her children, and, most notably, arranging for long-term care for the children (Hale, 1988). This chore is sometimes taken up by grandparents. The dilemma of child care and its attendant financial burdens illustrates the obvious stress pileup that is associated with the imprisonment of family members. The primary stressor (imprisonment) brings with it a host of other stressors that the family must address, especially when young children are involved. The management of these stressors has important societal implications, as prisoners who are able to maintain some degree of visitation with family members and who are ultimately released into an intact family environment are far less likely to re-offend and return to prison (Hale).

### Separations Caused by Employment

It is sometimes difficult for spouses to find suitable jobs in the same city. For this reason, some couples choose to pursue occupations in different geographical locations, resulting in what is commonly referred to as a "commuter marriage." Commuter marriages present a unique set of stressors to the family system. Unlike many other forms of family separations, such as imprisonment, commuter marriages are not often associated with the loss of one spouse's income—In fact, the arrangement is designed to preserve and perhaps even enhance the income of both spouses. However, such families must still deal with unmet needs for companionship, perpetually shifting family roles, and when children are involved, increased child-care burdens that are not unlike those of divorced families. Like imprisonment, research shows that there is often a stigma associated with commuter marriages (Groves & Horm-Wingerd, 1991; Magnuson & Norem, 1999). Society sometimes looks down on people who "put their career before their marriage" and may also frown on parents who take a job that keeps them from their children. Often the assumption is that there must be something wrong with the marriage.

People in commuter marriages will often cite some actual benefits to the arrangements. Most commonly, these include greater career opportunities, independence, and a greater appreciation for family relationships (Groves & Horm-Wingerd, 1991; Jackson, Brown, & Patterson-Stewart, 2000). Although this may sound counterintuitive, people in commuter marriages often say that, because of their limited time together, they have a greater appreciation for family and tend to make the most of their interactions, being more honest and frank with each other. However, there are a number of drawbacks to commuter marriages. For example, spouses spend a great deal of money on travel and maintenance of a second residence. As noted previously, people in commuter marriages sometimes receive negative remarks from other people, in addition to having to deal with their own isolation and lack of emotional support. When children are involved parental absence can create an extra burden on the spouse who attempts to maintain his or her career *and* care for the children single-handedly. Unfortunately, the burdens imposed by these stressors can take a toll on marriage. Spouses whose careers keep them apart, even if they still live together, are at increased risk for divorce (Presser, 2000). Presser found that young married men who had children and worked nights had a six times higher divorce rate over a 5-year period than those who worked days. Her analysis showed that "the amount of time spouses spend alone together is not the sole or even primary explanatory factor for marital instability; rather the changing nature of family life generated by different work schedules might be the critical issue" (Presser, pp. 104–105). Like research findings on military duty, the couples that best handle the stress of commuter marriages are those who had a solid and stable relationship before initiating the arrangement, and who maintain good communication patterns throughout (Magnuson & Norem, 1999).

## CONCLUSION

In this chapter we explore the function of several normative and several nonnormative stressors on the family. It is important to bear in mind that the family life cycle from which normative stressors emanate is just a heuristic tool for describing and organizing certain family stressors. Not all families experience all of these stressors and not all experience them in the same order. Also, many of the so-called "nonnormative" stressors, such as occasional declines in marital satisfaction, are in fact rather common. Perhaps the two most frequently recurring themes in the research on particular family stressors are heterogeneity in family responses to stress and the powerful relationship between prestress family adjustment and poststress adjustment. Heterogeneity in response means that not all families handle stressors the same way. As we learn in chapter 2, in the presentation of family systems theory, the concepts of equifinality and multifinality suggest that families can take different routes to the same end point, and that families can take the same input but all end up at different end points. These concepts are clearly illustrated in the research findings on family stressors (e.g., Fitzpatrick, Vangelisti, & Firman, 1994). In addition, the best predictor of the family's adjustment to a stressor is their adjustment before the stressor occurred. Distressed families will often be seriously impaired by stressors. Well-functioning families, on the other hand, appear able to handle stressors and readjust without as much difficulty, regardless of the nature of the stressor. In all cases, stressors present numerous communication tasks to families and invariably cause dramatic changes in family interaction patterns that sometimes return to normal and sometimes remain permanently changed.

# CHAPTER ELEVEN

# Divorce

Most people enter into marriage with high hopes and the best of intentions. However, the chances of staying together "until death do us part" are no different than calling heads or tails when flipping a coin. Divorce is commonly regarded as one of the most serious stressors a person can experience, ranking right up there with death of a spouse or child. Perhaps because people start off with such high hopes, the dissolution of a marriage can be devastating. The wreckage left behind in the wake of divorce does not just involve husbands and wives, but often children, in-laws (who are often grandparents), mutual friends, family homes, and acrimoniously divided property.

Divorce has received more research attention for its effects on the family system than perhaps any other family stressor. Over the past 50 years, divorce has become increasingly prevalent in American society. Scientists believe that divorce is best understood as a process, not as a discrete event. For some people this process takes years to unfold. For others, the process may consume decades. Because most divorces involve children and extended family, its implications as a stressor are far reaching and often long lasting. Although divorce is ordinarily conceptualized as an "unpredictable" family stressor, as opposed to a normative or developmental family stressor, it turns out that divorce can actually be predicted fairly well from an analysis of married couples' communication behaviors. In addition to being predictable *from* family communication patterns, divorce also has an effect *on* family communication patterns and relationships. Therefore, it may be most appropriate to think of divorce as a family stressor that is midway between the predictable-unpredictable continuum.

In this chapter we address several fundamental questions about divorce such as "How common is divorce?", "Who gets divorced?", and "What are the societal and individual factors that predict divorce?" We then turn our attention to marital interaction and divorce. In particular, what are the communication patterns that suggest a couple is on their way to divorce? Finally, we examine the question of whether and how divorce has an effect on children.

## DEMOGRAPHY OF DIVORCE

The term *demography* refers to the statistical study of human population characteristics, particularly as they are influenced by such phenomena as fertility (births), marriages, and mortality (deaths). Before analyzing the relationships between family communication and divorce, it is instructive to briefly review some basic facts about divorce.

Information compiled by the National Center for Heath Statistics indicates that 50% of all first marriages will experience a disruption (i.e., divorce or separation) within the first 20 years of the relationship (Bramlett & Mosher, 2001). Of those who separate, 75% divorce within 2 years and 90% divorce within 5 years. Consequently, it is estimated that about half of all marriages initiated in recent years will ultimately end in divorce (Cherlin, 1992; Goldstein, 1999; Kreider & Fields, 2002). When one considers that these estimates do not involve desertions (one spouse permanently leaving the other without a legal divorce), it is obvious that marrying couples today have perhaps less than 50/50 odds at long-term success. Despite all of the attention paid to divorce as a family stressor, societal problem, and legal matter, it is not a new phenomenon. In the 1930s, two in every six marriages ended in divorce (National Center for Health Statistics, 1973), and with the exception of a sharp spike in the divorce rate right after World War II, there was a gradual increase in the divorce rate up to the 1960s. During the 1960s and 1970s the divorce rate accelerated dramatically. In the United States, 1974 marked the first year that more marriages ended in divorce as opposed to in death. That pattern has not changed since. Today, death causes about 78% as many marital dissolutions as divorce does (Glick, 1988). The divorce rate finally leveled off in the 1980s, and there is some evidence to suggest that the divorce rate has dropped just slightly in the past few years. A detailed trend study showed that divorce proneness (e.g., thinking about divorce and discussing divorce with the spouse) did not change over the period of 1980 to 2000 despite the fact that marital interaction (e.g., eating dinner, visiting friends, and recreation) reliably decreased in the United States during this same time period (Amato, Johnson, Booth, & Rogers, 2003). The stability of divorce proneness in recent years appears to be the result of positive forces such as greater family income, decision-making equality, and support for the norm of a lifelong marriage offsetting the negative effects of spouses leading increasingly separate lives.

Why has there been such a dramatic increase in the divorce rate over the past 30 to 40 years? What are the causes of divorce today? The answers to these questions are not simple. Like most phenomena involving people, there appear to be multiple factors that influence divorce. We first consider societal and individual factors associated with divorce and then examine communication and social interaction behaviors associated with divorce. According to family systems theory, the family exists in a larger ecosystem (i.e., society) and takes input from that system. To fully understand divorce as a family stressor, it is vital to consider the role of the larger societal system on the family. Also, as a system, the family is made up of individual parts, each of which has qualities of their own that will influence the family system that they belong to.

## SOCIETAL FACTORS

In the past 50 years, there have been a number of dramatic changes in American society that that have clearly impacted the divorce rate. The women's movement of the 1960s and 1970s saw dramatically increasing numbers of women obtaining college degrees and entering the workforce. Consequently, the economic constraints that faced women who wanted to get out of bad marriages were no longer as powerful as they had been in the past. There is a positive association among married women's employment, income, and probability of divorce (Teachman, Polonko, & Scanzoni, 1999). Currently, about two thirds of all divorces are initiated by women (Brinig & Allen, 2000), suggesting that societal norms that improved women's welfare and agency also removed some of their barriers to leaving an undesirable marriage.

As the women's movement of the 1960s was taking off, members of the "baby-boom" generation (people born shortly after World War II) were becoming adults. At this time there was a growing emphasis on individualism and self-fulfillment that is still an influential force in society. Americans place great value on their personal and civil rights. Today, most people expect marriage to be a means of achieving considerable personal and emotional fulfillment. Historically, many marriages were initiated as a means of securing economic well-being and independence from parents. Although these factors are still evident to some extent in society, people have come to expect, if not demand, much more from their marriages. When these expectations for fulfillment are not met, many people choose to end their marriage, presumably with the goal of finding a better partner.

Cultural attitudes toward divorce have also changed dramatically over the past 50 years. There was a time when divorced people were looked down on. However, as increasing numbers of people divorced, society started to view divorce as a more normative phenomenon. This "normalization" in turn, may have removed yet another perceived barrier to divorce for some segments of society. Changing societal views toward divorce are clearly reflected in reformed divorce laws. Divorce used to involve a civil court proceeding that resembled the trail of a lawsuit. During the 1970s, most states enacted no-fault divorce laws that dramatically streamlined the process of getting a divorce. During that decade the number of divorces in the United States almost tripled (Faust & McKibben, 1999). In addition to normalizing divorce and prompting less stringent divorce laws, changing societal attitudes toward divorce were also reflected in changing views of family functions. In a 1985 survey, only 18% of respondents felt that an unhappily married couple should stay together when there are children in the family (Thorton, 1989). Collectively, these phenomena indicate that society has become more accepting of divorce as a legitimate course of action for individuals who are dissatisfied with their marriage.

## INDIVIDUAL RISK FACTORS

Nobody enters into a marriage with a blank slate. People bring their attitudes, past experiences, occupations, and education with them into marriage. Many of these factors appear to have an appreciable impact on the likelihood that a couple will get divorced or remain married. Below we highlight 10 individual-level risk factors that have been documented to increase the likelihood of divorce (see Faust & McKibben, 1999, and Karney & Bradbury, 1995, for more in-depth reviews).

First, there is a negative association between *age* at marriage and probability of divorce. The younger people are when they marry, the more likely they will get divorced. This relationship holds up to about age 35, after which divorce rates for first marriages begin to increase. Second, *premarital pregnancy* seriously increases the risk for divorce. Faust and McKibben (1999) argue that premarital pregnancy causes hasty marriage that stops the mate-selection process, in addition to limiting educational and career opportunities. These stresses, combined with family disapproval, place an overwhelming burden on many marriages. Third, divorce rates vary by *race and ethnicity*. Blacks have a substantially higher divorce rate than do Whites or Hispanics, and the divorce rate for Asians and Pacific Islanders is lower than that for Whites and Hispanics. Fourth, married couples *with children* are slightly less likely to divorce than are couples without children. Although this effect is weak, it reflects the fact that many couples have a preference for raising their children in a dual-parent household, even when the quality of their marriage is suspect. Fifth, *premarital cohabitation* increases the likelihood of later divorce. There is an interesting set of circumstances surrounding premarital cohabitation that helps to explain its apparent ill effects on later marriage. Individuals who cohabit before marriage have fewer traditional views of marriage, are more approving of divorce, are more likely to be involved in drugs and alcohol abuse, experience more difficulties with the law, and have lower education levels than those who do not (e.g., Booth & Johnson, 1988; Bumpass et al., 1991). It therefore stands to reason that it may not be cohabitation per se that mars a future marriage, but the type of person who cohabits, along with his or her attendant stressors, that detracts from the longevity of subsequent marriage.

A sixth personal risk factor is *parental divorce*. As we show later in this chapter, people whose parents divorced are themselves more likely to divorce than people whose parents never divorced. Seventh, *socioeconomic status* is inversely related to the probability of divorce. People who are better off financially typically have higher education levels and perhaps better interpersonal skills learned in educational and business settings that contribute positively to the success of their marriages. Eighth, many people enter into marriages with *unrealistic and idealized notions* of what marriage entails. Demo, Fine, and Ganong (2000) argue that when these romanticized ideals for marriage are combined with the high premium placed on personal fulfillment, marital stability is undermined. This is because the realities of marriage rarely meet idealized expectations. Ninth, *remarriage* is a powerful risk factor for divorce. Second marriages have a divorce rate that is at least 10% higher than first marriages (Bramlett & Mosher, 2001). Like cohabitation, this effect may be due to the personal qualities of those who remarry (the same qualities that previously led to divorce), as opposed to remarriage per se. Finally, *religion* can influence the likelihood of divorce. Religiosity is negatively correlated with divorce, especially when both spouses share the same religious beliefs. Because most religions discourage divorce, the effect of religiosity on marital stability may stem in part from greater perceived barriers to divorce in addition to a value of traditional family roles.

## MARITAL INTERACTION PATTERNS THAT PREDICT DIVORCE

Notwithstanding the effects of societal and personal factors on divorce, much of what apparently causes marriage to come undone can be found in the substance and form of marital interactions. Before we examine some of these communication variables that are predictive of marital decline, it is important to dispel two common misconceptions about marital relations and divorce. First, marital satisfaction is not a strong predictor of later divorce (Karney & Bradbury, 1995). This is because there is a large number of people who are relatively dissatisfied with their marriage but stay married anyway (Huston, Caughlin et al., 2001). Consequently, knowing a couple's present satisfaction with their marriage may not be very useful for predicting their likelihood of divorce 10 years later. Although most marriages headed for divorce are marked by dissatisfaction, not all dissatisfied marriages end in divorce. For economic, family, moral, or personal reasons, many people who are in distressed marriages remain in the relationship instead of seeking a divorce.

A second misconception about marital communication and divorce is that conflicts and disagreements harm marriages and move them toward divorce. As we show in more detail in the following sections, it is not the sheer frequency of conflicts and disagreements that strongly predicts subsequent divorce, but rather the *form* of these conflicts and disagreements that predispose couples to divorce. In one study of over 1,000 married people, respondents were asked about their experiences with various marital problems such as a spouse not being home often enough, drinking or using drugs, being too critical, or spending money foolishly (Amato & Rogers, 1997). Even though the total number of problems was a significant predictor of divorce over the ensuing 12 years, experiences of specific relationship problems such as a spouse being too domineering, critical, or not talking to the other were actually stronger predictors of divorce. These variables suggest that the nature of a couple's interactions better predicts martial outcomes than just the total number of their marital problems.

Perhaps one of the greatest accomplishments in family science over the past 25 years has been the documentation of marital interaction patterns that predict divorce. As this analysis shows, the markers for divorce are often evident long before the legal divorce is executed. For example, a recent longitudinal investigation followed 199 White and 174 Black newlywed couples over a period of 14 years (Orbuch et al., 2002). By the 14th year of this study, just over 40% of the couples had divorced. Those husbands or wives who reported higher levels of destructive conflict interactions (those that involved yelling, insulting, and having to have the last word) were more likely to be divorced by the end of the study than were couples who did not engage in these destructive behaviors. However, the simple frequency of marital conflicts was not significantly predictive of divorce. Also, the odds of divorce were negatively associated with husbands feeling affirmed emotionally by their wives (i.e., she makes him feel good about his ideas, she is caring toward him, she makes him feel good about the kind of person he is).

The deleterious effects of dysfunctional conflict have also been documented by Rogge and Bradbury (1999b). They found that the use of violent conflict tactics early in a marriage was predictive of divorce over the following 4 years. The Amato and Rogers (1997) study mentioned previously used reports of married couples' problems in 1980 to predict who would be divorced by 1992. Many of the problems that were significant predictors of divorce were essentially communication problems. These included being too domineering, being critical of the spouse, not talking enough with each other, and not being home often enough. A similar collection of negative conflict behaviors such as negative escalations (e.g., name calling and bringing up past transgressions), criticism, withdrawal from arguments, and making overly negative interpretations of the partner's behavior have been strongly associated with married people contemplating divorce (Stanley, Markman, & Whitton, 2002). These results highlight the corrosive effect of dysfunctional conflict behaviors—either aggressive engagement or withdrawal—as well as the protective effect (at least for husbands) of emotional affirmation from the spouse on marital stability.

Since the late 1970s, psychologist John Gottman and his associates have been studying married couples in their laboratory and tracking their marital satisfaction and stability over subsequent years (e.g., Gottman, 1979, 1994; Gottman & Levenson, 1992, 2000). In a typical study, couples come to the lab, complete a series of questionnaires about themselves and their marriages, participate in an interview about their marriage, and engage in a 10- to 15-minute conflict resolution interaction while being videotaped. Gottman and his associates then recontact the couples over subsequent years to track the well-being of their marriage. A number of key findings have emerged from this program of research that inform our understanding of the marital processes that lead up to divorce.

## The Behavioral Cascade Toward Divorce

Gottman and his colleagues discovered processes referred to as "cascades" that lead up to divorce (Carrère & Gottman, 1999; Gottman, 1993b, 1994; Gottman & Levenson, 1992). The steps in the cascade form what is known as a Guttman scale. In a Guttman scale, presence at each stage implies that prior stages have already been passed. For example, educational degrees form a Guttman scale. All people with bachelor's degrees already hold a high school diploma. Similarly, all people with master's degrees have already passed through the high school and bachelor's stages of educational attainment.

Gottman's research on married couples shows that there is a hallmark cascade of corrosive communication behaviors that mark the trajectory toward divorce. Analyses of couples' laboratory interactions while trying to resolve a conflict in their relationship revealed a series of behaviors that are ominous signs of impending deterioration for the relationship. This behavioral cascade is depicted in Figure 11.1 and starts with a behavior Gottman calls "complain/criticize." All married people express their dissatisfaction to their spouses from time to time. However, couples on their way to divorce have a tendency to weave criticism in with their expression of dissatisfaction. For example, the following statement could be viewed as a complaint: "I have a lot of things to do before the party tonight. It would be nice if you could help out a little." People in marriages that are cascading toward divorce have a tendency to add a degree of insult or blame to their complaints. An example of such a complaint and criticism might be "I have so much to do to get ready for the party tonight. It would be nice if you could give me a hand for once instead of sitting in front of the television." In the second example, the same complaint is presented, but this time it is coupled with a criticism of the partner and a clear implication that this person is generally not very helpful. What elevates complaint to the level of criticism is the addition of blame, often executed with terms such as "you always" and "you never" (Gottman, 1999).

The next step in the behavioral cascade is *defensiveness*. When people get defensive in marital interactions they try to protect themselves from criticism and avoid blame. In so doing they deny any responsibility for wrongdoing. Usually, people get defensive when

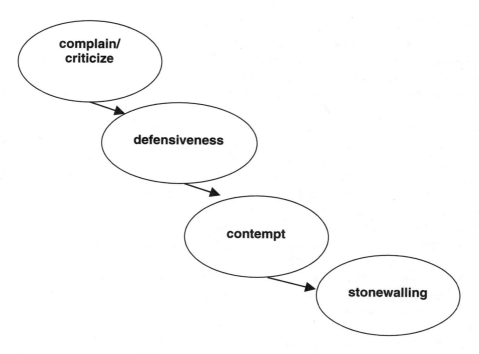

FIG. 11.1.   Gottman's Behavioral Cascade Model of Marital Dissolution (a.k.a. "The Four Horsemen of the Apocalypse").

*Note.* From *What Predicts Divorce: The Relationship Between Marital Processes and Marital Outcomes*, by J. M. Gottman, 1994, Hillsdale, NJ: Lawrence Erlbaum Associates. Copyright 1994 by Lawrence Erlbaum Associates. Adapted with permission.

they perceive that they are under attack and being victimized in some way. Gottman finds that defensiveness is sometimes coupled with whining. These "that's not fair" and "I didn't do anything wrong" messages are often delivered in a high-pitched tone, with a stretched-out syllable at the end. According to Gottman (1994) whining has an "innocent victim" posture behind it. It should be obvious that defensiveness basically shuts down the process of conflict resolution. If a spouse will not accept responsibility for any wrongdoing and puts up his or her guard, perhaps with a bit of whining added in for good measure, it easy to see how conflict discussions will get no where.

The third link in the chain of corrosive communication behaviors is *contempt*. There is perhaps no single communication behavior that is as destructive to marriage, and healthy relationships more generally, as is contempt. When people express contempt, they mock or insult their partner. Their communication sends the message "you are stupid" or "you are incompetent." In the lab this is manifest as hostile humor, mockery, or sarcasm (Gottman, 1994). Contempt is also communicated through a particular facial expression that involves pulling back one corner of the mouth and perhaps rolling the eyes. In its extreme form, contempt is literally a sign of bitter put down and hatred toward the partner. Once again, it is fairly obvious that by this stage of the cascade toward divorce, spouses feel and behave so viciously toward each other that they are creating irreparable damage to their marriage.

The final stage in the behavioral cascade is *stonewalling*. When people engage in stonewalling, they show no signs of receiving messages from their partner. Their facial expressions are often blank and they may not even make eye contact with their spouse. Obviously, people who stonewall make no contribution to an ongoing conversation aside from sending the nonverbal message that "I'm not listening to you" or "you're not even here." Some people are surprised to learn that the final stage of the cascade toward divorce is a behavior like stonewalling that has more to do with silence than with yelling and screaming. However, this is more understandable upon considering the fact that stonewalling is a manifestation of emotional divestment from the marriage. People stonewall when they no longer care enough about the relationship to put forth the effort to engage in conflict. As negative as some conflicts may sound, at least they indicate that the couple sees enough value in the future of their relationship to fight for what they believe in. But when people stonewall, they have more or less given up on the relationship. This type of communication behavior represents a psychological departure from the marriage and is a sign of impending doom.

The net result of these four communication behaviors is so destructive to marriage that Gottman characterizes them as "The Four Horsemen of the Apocalypse." He stresses that "if these negative patterns of interaction are not reversed in time, there is a point of no return, after which not much can be done to save the marriage" (Gottman, 2000, p. 217). In other words, couples that characteristically progress through this downward spiral in their conflicts can literally seal their fate through destructive communication behaviors.

## The Distance and Isolation Cascade Toward Divorce

There is an additional cascade model that illustrates husbands' and wives' reactions to their conflicts that is also descriptive of the road leading to divorce. Gottman refers to this as the distance and isolation cascade. This cascade model is illustrated in Figure 11.2.

The distance and isolation cascade starts with a phenomenon that has proven to be very important in the marital interaction literature: *flooding*. Flooding occurs when a spouse feels caught off guard and overwhelmed by his or her partner's negative emotion. This feeling of being overwhelmed is so powerful that spouses will do anything to escape from the situation. When flooded, people feel like their partner's negative emotions seem to come from out of nowhere—that they were unprovoked and unexpected. The feeling of aversion that is associated with flooding leads to a *perception that the marital problems are severe*. People who are flooded cannot comprehend their spouse's negativity. This perception contributes to an appraisal of their problems as serious and perhaps impossible to resolve as a couple, because the motivation is to get away from the spouse's negativity rather than to engage them in an effort to bring resolution to the marital problems. The next stage in the distance and isolation cascade is a *desire to work problems out individually rather than together*. At this stage spouses do not see their partner as a conduit to resolution of their difficulties. Rather, they feel that they need to "save themselves" and "go it alone." This in turn prompts *the creation of separate lives*. At this stage spouses begin to spend less time together and establish their own identities and

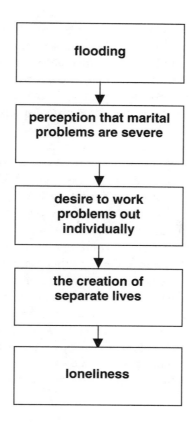

FIG. 11.2.   Gottman's Distance and Isolation Cascade.

*Note.* From *What Predicts Divorce: The Relationship Between Marital Processes and Marital Outcomes*, by J. M. Gottman, 1994, Hillsdale, NJ: Lawrence Erlbaum Associates. Copyright 1994 by Lawrence Erlbaum Associates. Adapted with permission.

routines without each other. The final stage in this cascade is loneliness. Although it may sound paradoxical to feel lonely while simultaneously being married, marriages that have degenerated to this austere condition no longer supply the type of emotional fulfillment and social companionship that most people associate with marriage. For such people loneliness is the psychological end of the line in their marriage.

## Positivity and Negativity in Marital Interactions

In addition to the cascade models of marital interactions and divorce, Gottman's work has illuminated the role of positivity and negativity in marital interactions. Traditionally, many people have felt that negative interaction behaviors such as conflicts have negative effects on marital longevity, whereas positive interaction behaviors like compliments, praise, and expressing affection help to hold marriages together. However, it is not the sheer frequency of negative or positive interaction behaviors that predicts marital outcomes; rather, their ratio. In stable marriages, also referred to as *regulated* marriages, spouses exhibit a ratio of positive to negative interaction behaviors that is overwhelmingly skewed toward the positive (Gottman, 1993b, 1994). In marriages that are headed for divorce, referred to as *nonregulated* marriages, couples exhibit fewer positive behaviors (e.g., humor and agreement) and more negative behaviors (e.g., put down, criticism, and defensiveness) in their interactions. These findings show that some marriages can remain happy and in tact despite a high frequency of negative communication behaviors between the husband and the wife, as long as they are disproportionately balanced with more positive communication behaviors.

Positivity and negativity in marital interactions appear to affect marital outcomes at different points in time. Gottman and Levenson (2000) discovered this by following a group of married couples over a 14-year period. By the end of the study, they compared those couples who had divorced sometime during the first 7 years of their marriage (early divorce) to those who divorced some time after 14 years of marriage (later divorce). The presence of negative communication behaviors, such as the Four Horsemen of the Apocalypse (i.e., criticism, defensiveness, contempt, and stonewalling) is most evident in couples headed for an early divorce. On the other hand, the *lack* of positive marital communication behaviors (e.g., showing interest, humor, and affection-caring) predicts later divorcing couples. It seems that negative martial communication behaviors such as defensiveness and contempt make marriages almost intolerable. They will destroy a marriage very quickly. However, the absence of positive behaviors appears to more gradually erode marital quality. It is easier to tolerate a lack of positivity in marriage than the presence of angry, hostile behaviors from a partner. But eventually those marriages that lack positive interactions between spouses are seen for what little they are worth and terminated.

## ACCOUNTS OF MARITAL HISTORIES THAT PREDICT DIVORCE

It is possible to accurately predict which couples will eventually divorce by analyzing the way that they tell the story of their marriage (Buehlman et al., 1992; Carrère et al., 2000). Using a technique called the Oral History Interview (described in chap. 6), researchers find that couples whose relationship stories are marked by very little *fondness* toward the partner, *we-ness*, *glorifying the struggle*, high levels of *marital disappointment*, and *chaos* are extremely likely to divorce over the ensuing 3 to 5 years (Buehlman et al.; 1992; Carrère et al.). These studies show that as husbands and wives talk about their marriage, there are markers in their discourse that indicate that their marriage is headed for trouble. For example, couples at risk for divorce will talk about their marriage with many references to "I," "me," and "mine," whereas those who are less likely to divorce use terms like "we," "us," and "ours." Similarly, happy couples will acknowledge that they have had some tough times in their relationship. However, they look back at these times of struggle as endeavors that ultimately made them stronger and better as a couple. Couples headed for divorce will also willingly admit to problems in their relationship. However, these couples come across as damaged by their struggles. Instead of emerging from the hard times stronger and better, they feel defeated by their struggles. What is astonishing is the fact that these markers (e.g., chaos, we-ness, and glorifying the struggle) are evident even when the marriages are in tact and relatively satisfying to each partner. Divorce is a family stressor that can be predicted not only by how couples communicate *with* each other but also by the way that they talk *about* each other and their marriage.

## PROCESSES THAT PREDICT DIVORCE VERSUS DISSATISFACTION

Earlier in this chapter we explain that not all dissatisfied marriages end in divorce. Some very dissatisfied couples will remain together indefinitely. It is perhaps therefore understandable that the psychological and social processes that predict marital dissatisfaction are not necessarily one and the same as those that predict divorce. Family scientist Ted Huston and his associates have been analyzing and reporting data collected from their Process of Adaptation in Intimate Relationships (PAIR) Project that speak to this issue (e.g., Caughlin et al., 2000; Huston, Caughlin, et al., 2001; Huston, Niehuis, et al., 2001). In this project, Huston and his colleagues (Huston, Caughlin, et al., 2001) followed 168 newly wed couples over the course of 13 years.

Findings from this investigation indicate that marital happiness can be explained by an *enduring dynamics* model. This simply means that what predicts marital satisfaction for those couples who stay married are relatively enduring qualities and traits that people bring to their marriage. For example, people's trait anxiety is associated with the deterioration of marital happiness, but not necessarily with divorce (Caughlin et al., 2000). It is of some interest to note that the association between anxiety and marital distress can be explained, at least to some extent, by communication behaviors. This is because trait anxious people exhibit negativity in their interactions and also elicit negativity from their spouses.

In contrast to the enduring dynamics model, a *disillusionment* model appears to provide better prediction and explanation of those couples that eventually divorce. The disillusionment model explains divorce as stemming from a loss of love and affection and feelings of ambivalence about the marriage. Initially, many couples start out with idealized views of marriage and each other. Disillusionment happens when these idealized views become hard to maintain and are challenged by realities that simply do not sustain the attractive notions that many people hold for their marriage. Note how disillusionment is different from *emergent distress*. In emergent distress, negativity and problems develop and escalate. Findings from the PAIR project indicate, however, that divorce is better explained by disillusionment, which is a deterioration of positive feelings and behaviors, than by emergent distress, which is an escalation of negative feelings and behaviors (Huston, Caughlin, et al., 2001).

## POSTDIVORCE FAMILY RELATIONS

Divorce has a massive impact on family systems at least as powerful as the death of an immediate family member. People sometimes incorrectly assume that after a divorce there is no longer any relationship between the divorcing parties. However, family systems inevitably move on after divorce, albeit in a different form. When children are involved, spouses still have to negotiate and maintain some sort of relationship in order to effectively manage their roles as fathers and mothers. Nevertheless, divorce dramatically changes the nature of family relationships and interaction patterns.

What happens to marital relationships after divorce? Graham (1997) studied recently divorced parents and found that there are several different postdivorce relational trajectories into which divorced couples fall. The most common was called the *gradual relational progress* trajectory (Graham). These couples slowly and steadily developed a functional postdivorce relationship, where their commitment to the relationship actually increased steadily over time. The second most common relational pattern involved the *disrupted progress* couples. Husbands and wives on this trajectory started out with high hopes for an amiable postdivorce relationship but experienced significant emotionally charged events that hurt their relationship, after which they gradually began to recover and increase their commitment to the relationship. Less common patterns involved *sustained adjustment* where couples maintained their relationship at a fairly high and steady level of commitment, the *disjointed erratic cycle* where couples experienced dramatic and repeated increases and decreases in the quality of their relationship; and the *eventual deterioration* pattern where couples started out with high hopes for a functional postdivorce relationship, but ultimately could not work things out and drifted apart. It is important to bear in mind that the couples in Graham's study were all parents; thus, they had a compelling reason for trying to redefine and salvage some sort of relationship after the divorce. Research on divorced couples and families shows that many actually experience some success at maintaining functional postdivorce relationships (Ellwood & Stolberg, 1991; Graham), and that for couples with children, divorce certainly does not mark the end of their relationship with each other.

Despite the fact that many divorced couples are able to maintain a functional or cooperative relationship for the sake of child rearing, it is equally common for spouses to blame their partner instead of themselves for relational problems (Honeycutt, 1993). When looking back at positive communication behaviors in the marriage (e.g., compliments, expressing support) divorced spouses take personal credit. However, when they recall negative communication behaviors in their relationship (e.g., being domineering, criticizing) divorced couples see their partner as responsible for such conduct. Happily married couples tend to do the exact opposite—They take blame for negative communication behaviors, and report that it is their partners who are making the positive contributions to their interactions (Honeycutt). Taken together, these findings suggest that although many married couples are able to manage a functional postdivorce relationship, they still harbor some bitter sentiments and blame toward their partner and tend not to see themselves as the cause of the marital breakdown.

Divorce produces significant changes in people's social relationships, not only with each other but also with their social networks. After divorce, many people are forced to move to a new residence, and half of the time people lose friends because of divorce (Wang & Amato, 2000). Just as social networks merge as people form long-term committed relationships, social networks fall apart as people break up their relationships. Not surprisingly, the development of new intimate relationships is positively associated with adjustment to divorce (Wang & Amato). Involvement in these relationships may decrease attachment to the former spouse and have positive effects on overall happiness.

## THE EFFECTS OF DIVORCE ON CHILDREN

There are few issues in family science that are as contentious as the effects of divorce on children. Writers in both the scientific and the lay press have vigorously debated whether divorce has ill effects on children. Some argue that parental divorce causes serious and long-lasting troubles for children, whereas others state that most children are resilient and recover rapidly from any negative effects associated with their parents' divorce. A large body of scientific evidence supports a perspective that is somewhere in between these two extremes.

### Research Findings

In 1991, sociologists Paul Amato and Bruce Keith conducted a meta-analysis of the research literature on parental divorce and the well-being of children (Amato & Keith, 1991a). A meta-analysis is a statistical analysis of existing studies that combines the effects found in these studies to produce an "overall" estimate of, in this case, the extent to which divorce influences childhood well-being. Amato and Keith (1991a) analyzed 92 studies that involved over 13,000 children, comparing those whose parents were divorced to those who lived with parents that were still married. In about 70% of the studies they found that children from divorced families scored lower on measures of well-being than did children from intact families. The measures of well-being included school achievement, conduct, psychological adjustment, self-concept, social adjustment, and parent–child relations.

At first glance, these results appear rather ominous. Children from divorced families seem to have pervasive problems. However, there are several caveats that are absolutely vital to understanding these effects. First and foremost, Amato and Keith (1991a) found that the effects for parental divorce on children's well-being, although statistically significant, were weak in magnitude. Across all the studies reviewed, the median effect size for parental divorce on childhood well-being was $d = .14$. This means that children from divorced parents scored on average .14 $SD$ below that of the children from intact marriages on the various measures of well-being. A concrete example might help to illustrate the meaning of this difference. Suppose that the average high school grade point average is 2.75, with a $SD$ of 0.75 (this would imply that 68% of all high school students have a GPA between 2.00 and 3.50). A difference of .14 $SD$ units would indicate that children from intact families would have an average GPA of 2.80, whereas children from divorced families would have an average GPA of 2.70.

Amato and Keith (1991a) also found that the effects of parental divorce on children's psychological adjustment, social adjustment, and on their relationships with their parents were most pronounced for primary-school through high-school-age children. For preschool- or college-age children, the negative effects of parental divorce are noticeably weaker or nonexistent. The effects of parental divorce on children seem to be decreasing in those studies conducted more recently. Studies conducted in the 1950s and 1960s tended to reveal much stronger effects for parental divorce than do studies conducted more recently, although recent evidence suggests that this trend may be leveling off (Reifman, Villa, Amans, Rethinam, & Telesca, 2001). In a follow-up meta-analysis of 67 studies conducted in the 1990s, Amato (2001) found that the negative effects of divorce on children were at their lowest in the 1980s, but then started to gradually get stronger in the 1990s. It appears that as divorce became more commonplace in society, its negative effects on children decreased in magnitude. However, recently this trend might be starting to reverse (Amato).

Divorce appears to have a number of negative consequences for children, across a wide range of domains. However, these effects tend to be weak in magnitude, most pronounced for middle-age children, and weaker today than they were 40 to 50 years ago. With that stated, *why* does parental divorce affect children? Several hypotheses have been offered to explain these effects (Amato, 1993; Amato & Keith, 1991a).

## Parental Absence Perspective

Parenting is a demanding task, and people generally feel that two parents living and working together can do the job better than just one. By being able to assist each other with parenting responsibilities and provide multiple role models, two-parent households are assumed to be optimal for children's social and psychological adjustment. Amato and Keith (1991a) found a clever way to test this hypothesis by comparing children from intact families to children from families that experienced the death of a parent. Their results provided some support for the parental absence perspective in that children who experienced the death of a parent had lower scores on academic achievement, conduct, psychological adjustment, and self-esteem than did children from intact families. Because their results showed that children from divorced families had even lower well-being than did children from families that experienced the death of a parent, one cannot view divorce and parental death as equally deleterious to children's well-being. As an aside, children living with stepparents had significantly more adjustment problems than did children living with both biological parents, again questioning the parental absence perspective and showing that the addition of a stepparent does not "solve" the parental absence problem (Amato & Keith, 1991a).

## Economic Disadvantage Perspective

Divorce commonly results in poorer economic conditions for children, at least temporarily. On average, a custodial mother's standard of living decreases 30% after a divorce, and in 1993 about half of all single-mother families were living below the poverty level (Hoffman & Duncan, 1988; Saluter, 1994). Studies that have examined the relationship between family socioeconomic status and children's well-being indicate that reduced family income is partly, but not entirely, responsible for some of the problems experienced by children of divorce. The lower standard of living that often follows divorce may have its strongest effect on children's academic achievement, because of reduced access to resources such as good schools, books, and computers.

## Family Conflict Perspective

As indicated earlier in this chapter, divorce is often preceded by periods of dysfunctional conflict. The family conflict perspective holds that the ill effects of divorce on children are largely the result of children's years of exposure to bitter conflict in their families. This hypothesis has been evaluated by comparing children from intact high-conflict families to children from intact low-conflict families (Amato, 1993; Amato & Keith, 1991a). The results clearly demonstrate greater problems with conduct, psychological adjustment, and self-concept among children from high-conflict, intact families, particularly when the children are involved in the conflicts (Burns & Dunlop, 2002). In fact, *children from high-conflict intact families have more adjustment problems than do children from divorced families* (Amato & Keith). Furthermore, children exposed to high levels of family conflict actually experience *beneficial* effects when their parents divorce (Booth & Amato, 2001). Results such as these provide strong support for the family conflict perspective. Booth and Amato explain that "escape from a high-conflict marriage benefits children because it removes them from an aversive, stressful home environment. In contrast, a divorce that is not preceded by a prolonged period of overt discord may represent an unexpected, unwelcome, and uncontrollable event that children are likely to experience as stressful" (p. 210).

The family conflict perspective is particularly noteworthy for showing that the nature of the communication between the parents is what influences the well-being of their children. It is reassuring to know that when divorced parents can effectively manage their conflict and maintain some semblance of civilized communication, the ill effects of parental conflict on children's adjustment are minimized (Linker, Stolberg, & Green, 1999). On the other hand, when parents' conflict escalates out of control and occurs in the presence of their children, maintaining such a marriage appears to do little to enhance the children's well-being. Such findings have prompted family scholars to conclude that "the impact of divorce on children may not be caused by divorce per se but rather by factors associated with divorce" (Gano-Phillips & Fincham, 1995, p. 207). Often these factors involve destructive communication patterns that precede divorce by many years.

## THE EFFECTS OF PARENTAL DIVORCE ON ADULT WELL-BEING

Parental divorce does not just have an effect on young children. Research shows that the effects of parental divorce are still evident after children have grown into adults. This suggests something of a paradox. The effects of parental divorce on young children are rather weak in magnitude and tend to diminish as children become young adults. But then why would there still be noticeable negative effects for parental divorce among adults? The answer to this question may be found in a *sleeper effect*. A sleeper effect is a phenomenon that does not have a noticeable impact right away; rather, its effect becomes evident at a later point in time. It has been suggested that the delayed effects of parental divorce show up when young adults face new developmental challenges such as developing a serious intimate relationship, establishing autonomy from parents, and pursuing a career (Hetherington, Law, & O'Connor, 1993). Many of the findings on parental divorce and adulthood well-being are consistent with this explanation.

## Research Findings

In addition to their meta-analysis on young children, Amato and Keith (1991b) also conducted a meta-analysis of the research literature on parental divorce and the well-being of adults over age 18. Their analysis covered 37 studies of over 85,000 adults. Similar to the findings on children, they found that adults whose parents had been divorced had a lower level of well-being than those whose parents had not been divorced. Again, however, these effects were weak ($d = .15–.17$). Some of the domains of well-being for which there were strongest effects of parental divorce were adults' psychological adjustment, use of mental health services, conduct problems, and their own marital happiness. And once again the more recently conducted studies suggested a weakening of the effects of parental divorce. Many of the ill effects of parental divorce that are evident in studies of young children are also apparent in studies of older adults. Keep in mind that although these effects are pervasive, affecting many aspects of life, and chronic, they are not powerful. Amato recently characterized the effects of parental divorce on adult children's well-being by noting that "42% of children with divorced parents reach adulthood with a level of personal well-being higher than that of the average child from a two-parent family. In comparison, 42% of children with nondivorced parents reach adulthood with a level of subjective well-being lower than that of the average child from a divorced family" (Amato, 1999). So, the odds favor the person from the intact family, but not by a very large margin.

## Relations With Parents

One clear effect that parental divorce has on the family system is a disruption of the relationships between children and their parents. Young adults whose parents were divorced report less affection toward their mothers and fathers than young adults whose parents were happily married (Booth & Amato, 1994). This effect is especially pronounced for fathers, presumably because so few children of divorce actually grew up living with their fathers. Even when divorce occurs later in life when the children are grown it reliably decreases contact between fathers and their children (Shapiro, 2003).

How does divorce disrupt the development of the parent–child relationship? To answer this question, it is instructive to look back to earlier childhood experiences in the family. Divorce tends to put increased responsibilities and tasks in the hands of adolescents, a phenomenon referred to as *parentification* (Hetherington, 1999). Parentification is a sort of role reversal where children assume responsibilities for household tasks and the care of siblings (instrumental parentification) in addition to acting as confidant and provider of emotional support to the parent (emotional parentification). When parentification occurs, it is reasonable to assume that the child's needs do not get as much attention as those of children who live with both parents. Consequently, the affectionate bond that ordinarily develops between a child and a caring parent may be interfered with, leading to lower quality relations between the divorced parent and his or her adult child. After all, the mere presence of parentification suggests that the biological parent may be overburdened and unable to fully care for the child.

Divorce also has a tendency to create greater parent–child conflict (Kurdek & Fine, 1993) especially between single mothers and their sons (Brach, Camara, & Houser, 2000).

Ironically, these same divorced parents engaged in more permissive parenting with their child (Kurdek & Fine, 1993), a style that is notorious for producing less than optimal child outcomes. Increased conflict and a permissive parenting style indicative of low cohesion may contribute to a mild rift between the divorced parent and his or her child that would show up in the form of a more distant relationship between the two in adulthood.

Researchers are now beginning to understand that divorce affects relations within the family system beyond just the parent–child relationship. When grandparents divorce, relationships with grandchildren also suffer (King, 2003). Similar to the effects of parental divorce, it is often the relationship with the grandfather that suffers the most. King (2003) found that one of the primary reasons for deteriorating grandparent–grandchild postdivorce relationships was because of a weakened bond between the grandparent and his or her adult child (i.e., the grandchild's parent; see also chap. 8).

## The Intergenerational Transmission of Divorce

One of the most commonly cited effects of parental divorce on adult children is an increased risk for marital distress and divorce. This is known as the intergenerational transmission of divorce and ought to be a phenomenon of considerable interest and importance to students of communication. In a group of adults followed over a period of 12 years, the divorce rate was 10% among those couples with no history of parental divorce (Amato, 1996). This rate was closer to 15% if either the husband or the wife had been exposed to a parental divorce. When both the husband and wife had divorced parents, the divorce rate was close to 30%.

Why do parents "pass on" the tendency to divorce to their children? Perhaps the most compelling account of this phenomenon can be found in social leaning theory (Bandura, 1977). Recall that according to social learning theory, people learn attitudes and behaviors through *modeling*. Modeling allows people to vicariously learn behaviors by observing others perform them. Two hypotheses that could be derived from this theory are that children learn (in)effective marital communication skills by observing their own parents, and that children learn an attitude of (non)commitment to marriage by observing their parents.

Convincing evidence of the poor marital communication skills hypothesis can be found in a recent study by Sanders, Halford, and Behrens (1999). Sanders and his colleagues recruited 93 couples that were planning to marry within the next 12 months. They came to the research laboratory and participated in a 10-minute conversation about a topic that was a source of disagreement and conflict in their relationship, in addition to filling out several self-report measures about their relationship. The results indicated that couples in which the woman's parents had been divorced exhibited more disagreement, conflict, criticism, and invalidation during their interaction, and less self-disclosure and fewer proposals of positive solutions than did other couples in the study. After the conversations were over, members of the couples watched the videotape of their conversation and were asked to write down their thoughts during each 30-second interval. Again, for couples in which the woman's parents had divorced, there were fewer positive thoughts about the partner recorded during this postinteraction thought listing, relative to the other couples. There are two noteworthy aspects of these results. First, they show that parental divorce, at least for women, has an effect that is apparent in the communication behaviors of *both* members of the couple as they attempt to resolve a conflict. Second, they suggest that the effects of parental divorce on adults' communication skills are more pronounced for women. Sanders et al. (1999) argue that this may be because girls are more likely to have firsthand experience with the adversity associated with their mothers' divorces as a result of living with them after the divorce, whereas boys are far less likely to have a lot of exposure to the modeling of their fathers, postdivorce.

At least one other study indicates that parental divorce is associated with greater communication problems in young adults' own intimate relationships (Herzog & Cooney, 2002). Once again, this study showed that when broken down by sex, the effect only held for females whose parents had been divorced. Herzog and Cooney's findings implicated parental conflict as the culprit in young adults' problems with intimate communication—regardless of whether their parents had been divorced. Intense parental conflict and poorly resolved parental conflict patterns were associated with more problematic intimate communication for these young adults. A similar pattern of associations between conflict in the family of origin and relational communication problems was found by Levy, Wamboldt, and Fiese (1997) in their laboratory analysis of dating couples' conflict resolution interactions.

The idea that children learn dysfunctional communication patterns from observing their parents' interactions is consistent with findings indicating that marital discord is transmitted intergenerationally (Amato & Booth, 2001). In a 17-year longitudinal study Amato and Booth found that parents' marital discord (when the children were on average 13 years old) was predictive of their offspring's later marital discord (when the offspring were on average 30 years old). Some refined analyses showed that it was the presence of interpersonal problems in the parents' marriages such as conflict, problems, and instability that predicted children's later marital discord. The authors suggest that direct observation of parent's dysfunctional interpersonal interactions may create a predisposition for children to enact those same problem behaviors in their later marriages.

In addition to modeling poor marital communication skills, divorcing parents may also inadvertently model attitudes and beliefs toward marriage that suggest that marriages can, and perhaps should, be left when they become distressed. Amato and DeBoer (2001) tested this hypothesis by following 355 married adults and their parents over a period of 17 years. They found that parental divorce almost doubled the odds that the offspring would experience a divorce in their own marriages. Their analyses also suggested that children might learn that marriage is not permanent by observing their parents' divorce. In this study, parents' marital discord in the absence of parental divorce was not associated with a greater likelihood of offspring divorce. However, parental divorce was associated with a much higher likelihood of offspring divorce, even when parents' predivorce levels of discord were statistically controlled. This shows that it is the act of divorce, not the discord that precedes it, that appears to increase the odds of offspring divorce. One might therefore surmise that parental divorce undermines the commitment to a lifelong marriage in children who observe their parents dissolving their marriage in times of trouble. In other words, children learn from their parents that divorce is a viable option for resolving marital problems. There is clear evidence that such negative attitudes toward the permanence of marriage can explain the intergenerational transmission of divorce (Segrin, Taylor, & Altman, in press). In this study Segrin and his colleagues found that people whose parents had been divorced were about one and a half times as likely to have been divorced themselves compared to people whose parents had not divorced. However, when statistically controlling for negative attitudes toward marriage, this significant intergenerational transmission of divorce effect was rendered statistically nonsignificant. This implies that parental divorce contributes to the increased likelihood of offspring divorce through the negative attitudes toward a lifelong marriage that are presumably learned through observation.

There is some good news about how parental divorce does *not* appear to affect children. Some people have speculated that the intergenerational transmission of divorce occurs because people with divorced parents learn to distrust intimate partners. The idea is that observing parental divorce teaches young people that even romantic partners and spouses can pack up and walk away. However, a recent large-sample study indicates that parental divorce is unrelated to people's trust in intimate partners (King, 2002). However, King's study shows that parental divorce can have negative effects on people's trust in their fathers.

## THE PROCESS OF DIVORCE

People often think of and talk about divorce as a discrete event. Common statements like "I got divorced two years ago" and "I'm still waiting for my divorce to go through" give the impression that a divorce happens at a specific point in time, usually at a court hearing. However, social scientists generally agree that divorce is best understood as a process that gradually unfolds (Demo et al., 2000). This process is lucidly conveyed in many different stage models that have been developed to illustrate how marriages, and close relationships more generally, come apart (e.g., Duck, 1982; Guttman, 1993; Knapp & Vangelisti, 2000).

One of the more widely recognized stage models of divorce was developed by Bohannon (1970) and is referred to as the six stations of divorce. According to Bohannon, the first step, or station, in the divorce process is the *emotional divorce*. At this stage, spouses experience a change in feelings toward their partner. They tend to be dissatisfied, withdraw from interaction, and experience depression and loneliness. People at this stage will often invest themselves in their work or relationships with other friends or even in substance abuse in order to soothe their negative emotional states. Evidence of the emotional divorce can be found in some of the final stages of Gottman's distance and isolation cascade toward divorce (loneliness) or in the behavioral cascade model (stonewalling). Gottman (1999) notes that many couples who show up for marital therapy actually end up getting divorced because they have waited too long to seek help. Often distressed couples will seek therapy years after their problems began. The fact that many of these couples end up getting divorced suggests that they may have already passed through the emotional divorce station before seeking help.

In the next stage, the *legal divorce*, partners pursue the legal dissolution of their marriage. Ironically, this state might demand more communication between the spouses than the emotional divorce stage because they have to negotiate issues of child custody, division of property, support payments, and so forth. There is also a degree of permanence and irreversibility at the legal divorce stage that makes it different from the emotional divorce. One potential difficulty for couples at the legal divorce stage is the exposure of the marriage's problems to outsiders. Because of the need for filing court papers, consulting attorneys or mediators, or seeking other counsel, couples are more or less forced to bring outsiders into the picture at this stage. For people struggling with shame, embarrassment, or feelings of failure, this social expansion of the divorce process can be very challenging.

According to Bohannon, the third stage of divorce is the *economic divorce*. Here the partners must divide up their financial assets and negotiate what, if any, future economic arrangements will be made (e.g., alimony and child support). This stage almost always starts simultaneous to the legal divorce, but it rarely ends at the same time as does the legal divorce. This is because divorce settlements often involve issues of future earnings, a spouse's pension or social security benefits, and child support payments. For this reason, the economic divorce has the potential to last for decades.

Around the same time as the legal divorce is initiated, spouses must address the *co-parental divorce*. Of course, this stage only applies to those couples with children. Like the economic divorce, the co-parental divorce can be fraught with difficulties and obstacles. Both legal custody (who has legal responsibility for the child) and physical custody (who the child lives with) must be negotiated. Sole custody involves the child living with one parent, who has legal responsibility, often with court-ordered child support payments from the noncustodial parent. The noncustodial parent will often have visitation rights that allow him or her to spend time with the child at regular intervals of time (e.g., weekends). In the case of particularly troubled parents, these visitations may be supervised by officers of the court or state. Joint custody arrangements occur when both parents share legal and physical custody. In such cases, the child literally lives in two households, perhaps spending certain days of the week with the father and other days with the mother. Joint custody sounds attractive, but has obstacles of its own, not the least of which involves perpetually moving children back and forth between two households. This demands exquisite cooperation between the now-divorced parents. Recent findings show that such efforts may be particularly worthwhile as children living in a joint-custody arrangement are significantly better adjusted than are children with a sole-custody parent, and they are as well adjusted as children from intact families (Bauserman, 2002). Like the economic divorce, the co-parental divorce has the potential to last for years beyond the legal divorce.

The *community divorce* is another distinct stage. It occurs when the divorcing partners share the news of their divorce with their social networks. There is great variability in when and to whom people feel comfortable making this proclamation. There is still a degree of stigma attached to divorce, and people may not be comfortable sharing the news of their divorce with others. For this reason, some people may not reach this stage until after the legal divorce. On the other hand, some may experience the community divorce long before the legal divorce. Regardless of when this stage is experienced, social networks are bound to change as a result of the community divorce. Commonly, relationships with in-laws and close friends of the ex-spouse tend to dissipate at this stage.

Finally, the *psychic divorce* happens when members of the marriage reach a state of psychological closure on their marriage. They no longer think of themselves as married and now accept that they are single. For most divorcing couples, this is likely to be the final and perhaps most difficult stage in the divorce process. Like the economic or co-parental divorce, the psychic divorce has the potential to carry on for long periods of time for some people. Especially when children are involved and it is necessary to still interact with the ex-spouse, it may be extremely difficult to reach a sense of closure on the relationship. Divorces that are not mutually agreed on or desired may leave one spouse with an unrequited sense of attachment, or a sense of consuming anger, to his or her former partner. These emotions can foreclose opportunities for postdivorce relational development, thereby trapping people in what is effectively the emotional divorce stage.

## CONCLUSION

Divorce is a very common family stressor that has pervasive and long-lasting implications for the family system. Societal factors, such as individualism and women's greater occupational achievements and earnings, and individual factors, like income, education, age, premarital pregnancy, and religiosity, all contribute to the propensity to divorce. At the same time, communication patterns within the marriage appear to be as powerful, if not more so, at predicting who will divorce. Much of the evidence focuses on how couples handle disagreements and conflicts. Certain destructive communication behaviors such as contempt, defensiveness, and stonewalling appear to lay the groundwork for subsequent divorce. It is clear that the sheer amount of conflict is not a good predictor of divorce. Rather, the key issue appears to be how much negativity there is in the couple's interactions, relative to how much positivity there is. So long as the negative interactions are disproportionately balanced with positive ones, married couples can tolerate a considerable degree of conflict and disagreement in their relationship.

As the divorce rate virtually exploded between the 1960s and 1980s, social scientists responded with answers to many of the questions about how and why people get divorced. Time and again, marital communication patterns seem to play a vital role in marital disruption or longevity. Unfortunately, this knowledge has yet to stem the tide of divorce. It is still relatively easy to find couples that choose to marry despite obvious signs of trouble from the word go. It is even easier to find marriages that started out with great promise and optimism but eventually succumbed to disillusionment and disappointment. Perhaps the problem is that most of the individual and societal factors that are implicated in divorce are difficult, if not impossible, to change. Communication patterns and style of interaction can be changed, but there must be motivation to do so. One of the great challenges to family scholars and therapists alike is to figure out how to harness and preserve that motivation that couples start out with and to help them identify and correct their destructive communication behaviors while the marriage is still salvageable.

Divorce touches members of the family system beyond just husbands and wives. Children are negatively affected by parental divorce, and many of these negative effects are still present when they reach adulthood. However, these effects are weak in magnitude. Relationships between grandparents and grandchildren also suffer as a result of divorce. Above all else, it is important to realize that not all people respond to divorce in the same way. Divorce is a process, and each divorce process is somewhat unique in its effect on spouses, children, and social network members. As sociologist Paul Amato concluded (2000, p. 1282), "Divorce benefits some individuals, leads others to experience temporary decrements in well-being that improve over time, and forces others on a downward cycle from which they never fully recover." Undoubtedly, these differing outcomes are influenced to a large extent by the nature of the communication within and beyond the family system before, during, and after the divorce process.

# CHAPTER TWELVE

# Renegotiating Family Communication: Remarriage and Stepfamilies

When many people think of "family" they imagine two people getting married, having children, and growing old together. This image of the American family is perhaps more stereotypical than it is typical. Because of divorce and widowhood many people will get married more than once in their lifetime. When people with children remarry they create a stepfamily. However, not all stepfamilies are formed after divorce or widowhood. More people are having children outside marriage, and if these people eventually marry, their first marriage will generate a stepfamily. Remarriages and stepfamilies face all of the same challenges as first marriages and their associated families. However, remarriages and stepfamilies appear to have their own unique qualities and burdens that distinguish them from first marriage families. Communication and relationship development issues in stepfamilies have a different character than what might be observed in first-marriage families. Even though there has been a lot of attention to the negative aspects of remarriage and stepfamilies, there is reason to believe that they enjoy many of the benefits of first marriage families, and that their relationships are not necessarily more troubled.

We begin this chapter by briefly examining the phenomenon of remarriage and answering a common question: "Why is it that marriage does not always work out better the second time around?" Next we present an in-depth analysis of communication and relationships in stepfamilies. We address questions such as "How are stepfamilies portrayed in the media?" and "What are societal views of stepfamilies?" These views and images are mostly negative and are not accurate representations of the complex realities of stepfamilies. Next, we take on questions such as "How do stepfamily relationships and communication develop in the early years of stepfamily formation?" and "How are roles and relationships defined in different types of stepfamilies?" Finally, what are the challenges that are particular to stepfamilies with regard to communication, conflict, and adaptability and cohesion? Addressing this question leads us to consider research findings on child adjustment in stepfamilies and the importance of stepfamily communication for child well-being. Above all else, the research reviewed in this chapter shows that stepfamilies are exceptionally diverse. There are many different types of stepfamilies, and these are represented in numerous taxonomies and typologies of stepfamilies that have been developed by family scientists. Obviously, with all of the various forms and functions in stepfamilies, sweeping generalizations must be interpreted tentatively.

## REMARRIED COUPLES' RELATIONSHIPS

For the majority of people, divorce or widowhood does not mark the end of married life. Most people whose marriages end before they reach the age of 60 eventually remarry. Consequently, about half of all marriages are remarriages for at least one of the partners (Bumpass et al., 1990). About three-fourths of all divorced people eventually remarry (Furstenberg & Cherlin, 1991). Also, remarriage is becoming a more popular trend in society. For example, 10.6% of men in their 40s who were born between 1925 and 1934 were married two or more times. However, 22.3% of men in their 40s who were born between 1945 and 1954 have been married two or more times (Kreider & Fields, 2002). The corresponding figures for women are 12.1% and 22.8%. The median time span between divorce and remarriage is 3 years (Glick, 1980). This suggests that people do not move into remarriages with greater caution, as evidenced by longer courtships, than do people embarking on their first marriage. Remarriages also have a higher divorce rate than first marriages (see chap. 11). Why is it that people do not "learn from their past mistakes" and experience more success in remarriages than they did in marriage the first time around? Ganong and Coleman (1994) explain that there are multiple reasons for the higher divorce rate of remarried couples that involve a complex mix of individual, interpersonal, and societal factors.

There are several hypotheses for the relative instability of remarriages, especially those that follow a divorce. Ganong and Coleman (1994) suggest that some people have qualities that make them likely candidates for divorce. This is known as the *divorce-prone personality hypothesis*. Imagine a spouse who is very argumentative. That behavior might be perceived as obnoxious and eventually contribute to the deterioration of the marriage. Should this argumentative spouse remarry, the same behaviors and traits are now transported into the new marriage and would be expected to aggravate the new spouse and corrode that relationship as well. According to the *training school hypothesis*, first marriages are training grounds for relationships in subsequent marriages. However, as we noted earlier, people do not seem to learn from past mistakes. Rather, the most likely version of the training school hypothesis is that people learn dysfunctional patterns of interaction and problem solving in their first marriages and bring them into their subsequent marriages (Ganong & Coleman, 1994). In other words, people can develop bad habits in one marriage and continue them in another. The *willingness to leave marriage hypothesis* simply states that people who divorce have an obvious track record for seeing divorce as a solution to marital problems. If divorce was a way of escaping marital problems once, it should operate similarly in subsequent marriages. Because divorced people often marry other divorced people (Wilson & Clarke, 1992), this phenomenon may be compounded by both spouses having more favorable attitudes toward divorce. Another individual-level explanation described by Ganong and Coleman is the *dysfunctional beliefs hypothesis*. According to this explanation, people enter into remarriage with unrealistically high expectations, perhaps fueled by the certainty that they have learned from their past mistakes. When these expectations are not met, the remarried relationship is dissolved. At a more societal level, the *remarriage market hypothesis* predicts that the selection of available mates is often not as good the second or third time around. Divorced people in search of a future spouse may feel that "all of the good ones are taken." Those who are available may not have all of the desired qualities and thus contribute to lower quality marriages. Like so many social phenomena, the higher rate of divorce among remarried relationships is probably influenced by a variety of factors, at least some of which suggest that there are often troubles in these relationships.

Despite the multiple compelling explanations for the higher dissolution rate of second marriages, lower satisfaction does not seem to be a major problem for remarriages. A meta-analysis of 34 studies revealed that people in first marriages were just slightly more satisfied with their marriage than those in remarriages (Vemer, Coleman, Ganong, & Cooper, 1989). The magnitude of the difference was so weak that it could not plausibly account for the higher divorce rate among remarried people. In addition to comparable levels of happiness, Skinner et al. (2002) found that remarried couples reported a similar amount of couple communication and disagreements in their relationships as did first-married or cohabiting couples. Yet other studies show that remarried couples have more open expressions of anger, criticism, and irritation (Bray & Kelly, 1998; Hetherington, 1993). There is some reason to believe that the apparent discrepancies in these results might be explainable by the presence or absence of children in the remarried household (Coleman, Ganong, & Fine, 2000). It seems that opportunities for conflict, anger, and resentment are greater when there are stepchildren in the home.

Adjustment to remarriage is positively related to the extended interpersonal relationships that come with that marriage (Roberts & Price, 1989). These researchers found that the better remarried spouses' relationships were with the couple's families and friends, the better their marital adjustment. Not surprisingly, the quality of these same relationships was also associated with the quality of the remarried couple's own communication. However, there is one interpersonal relationship that predictably interferes with remarried couples' adjustment and that is a relationship with the former spouse. Roberts and Price (1989) found that attachment to the former spouse interfered with marital adjustment among remarried couples.

One obvious difference between remarried and first-marriage relationships is that there is a former spouse in remarried relationships. The act of getting married for a second or third time not only initiates a new marital relationship but also transforms the relationship with the former spouse (Christensen & Rettig, 1995). Christensen and Rettig found that single parents participated in substantial co-parenting (e.g., collectively making decisions about the child and discussing the child's problems), but those who had remarried were far less involved with their former spouse in terms of parenting issues. Additionally, remarried parents reported less parental support from their former spouse and held more negative attitudes toward their former spouse. Despite the seemingly negative tone of these transformations in the relationships with the former spouse, they are probably functional in some ways by creating the psychological space in which people can form a connection with a new spouse. Recall that Roberts and Price (1989) found that attachments to the former spouse could interfere with the adjustment of remarried couples. On the other hand, remarriage almost certainly marks a greater disconnection between biological parents from their children's point of view.

Overall, remarriages have been characterized as both a stressor (Crosbie-Burnett & McClintic, 2000a) and a coping response to the stress of being alone (Gentry & Shulman,

1988). Remarriages that have low levels of marital conflict and high levels of marital satisfaction can bring happiness to spouses and protect against depression (Demo & Acock, 1996). Unfortunately, the high divorce rate in remarriages suggests that the "remarriage as stressor" view is accurate in many cases.

## COMMUNICATION AND STEPFAMILY RELATIONSHIPS

Stepfamilies are quite common in American society. About 30% of all children will live with a stepparent before reaching adulthood (Bumpass, Raley, & Sweet, 1995). It is estimated that one in three Americans is presently a member of a stepfamily and that more than half of all Americans will be a part of a stepfamily at some point in their lives (Larson, 1992). Stepfamilies are also nothing new. American presidents George Washington and Abraham Lincoln each had stepfamilies. There are a lot of different terms for stepfamilies including *remarried families*, *blended families*, *binuclear families*, *second families*, and *reconstituted families,* to name but a few (e.g., Bray, 1999; Ganong & Coleman, 1997, 2000). There is something particularly interesting about phenomena that are referenced by multiple terms, such as when two middle-aged people date each other and are described with terms like "partner," "significant other," "boyfriend," "girlfriend," and "lady friend." People often look for different terms when they are somehow uneasy with the concept, or when they feel there is some stigma associated with it. Presumably it is easier to change the label than to change thinking about the concept. Stepfamilies have received a bad reputation in our culture, for reasons that we will get into shortly. However, stepfamilies are as diverse as families more generally, so broad generalizations about their harm or helpfulness are often difficult to support.

Consider some of the different ways in which stepfamilies might be formed. People often think of stepfamilies that are initiated after divorce from a first marriage. That is one of well over a dozen different ways that a stepfamily could be formed. Some people may not find themselves in a stepfamily until they reach their 30s and 40s if an older parent remarries following the death of his or her spouse. Some people may have had children outside marriage and then decide to marry someone other than the biological parent of the children. For both spouses this could be their first marriage, yet one would be a stepparent. The common denominator in all of these cases is that one adult parent has a legal or genetic tie to a child that the other adult does not (Ganong & Coleman, 2000). When these two unite, they form a stepfamily. When only one of the adults has children prior to remarriage, they form what is sometimes referred to as a *simple stepfamily*. When both have children from previous relationships, they form a *complex stepfamily*. Complex stepfamilies have a higher likelihood of redivorce (Coleman et al., 2000).

### Views of Stepfamilies

In Box 12.1, we examine how stepfamilies are portrayed in the media. Later in this section, we explore portrayals of stepfamilies in society more generally.

**Box 12.1**
**Images of Stepfamilies in the Media**

Family scientists Lawrence Ganong and Marilyn Coleman remarked that "cultural beliefs about family life exert a strong influence on the ways in which people conduct themselves, evaluate their situations, and expect to be regarded by others" (Ganong & Coleman, 1997, p. 85). Numerous family scholars have argued that stepfamilies tend to have a bad reputation, due in part to their portrayal in the media (e.g., Bernstein, 1999; Ganong & Coleman, 1997). Although there has been virtually no scientific study of the effects of stepfamily portrayals in the media, it is worthwhile to at least momentarily consider how stepfamilies are depicted in stories, movies, and television, and how that might influence both society's and individuals' beliefs, attitudes, and expectations for stepfamilies.

Without doubt, the dominant media image of stepfamily that is referenced in scholarly essays comes from the story *Cinderella* which was made into a popular film in 1950. It was *Cinderella* that popularized the "wicked stepmother" image. Other fairy tales such as *Sleeping Beauty, Snow White,* and *Hansel and Gretel* reinforced this often dim view of stepparents. Negative portrayals of stepfamily life, and stepparents in particular, have continued in earnest since *Cinderella.* Films such as *Table for Five* (1983), *See You in the Morning* (1989), *Radio Flyer* (1992), *This Boy's Life* (1993), *Bastard Out of Carolina* (1996), and *Promise to Caroline* (1996) continue to depict stepparents as mean and sometimes abusive and stepfamily life as dysfunctional. The abundance of such storylines illustrates that there is a long history of negative images of stepfamilies in American media.

With that said, it would be inaccurate to say that media images of stepfamilies are uniformly negative. A number of dramatic films such as *The Sound of Music* (1965), *Tender Mercies* (1983), *Sarah Plain and Tall* (1990), and *Stepmom* (1998) depict stepparent–stepchild relationships in a much more positive light, sometimes portraying extraordinary caring and kindness on the part of stepparents. Other films such as *Yours Mine and Ours* (1968), *With 6 You Get Eggroll* (1968), *Seems Like Old Times* (1980), *Murphy's Romance* (1985), and *My Stepmother Is an Alien* (1988) present a comedic view of stepfamilies. Furthermore, television portrayals of stepfamilies have been almost exclusively positive, as evidenced by shows such as *The Brady Bunch* (1969–1974), *Eight is Enough* (1977–1981), *Major Dad* (1989–1993), and *Hearts Afire* (1992–1995), although more recent programs such as *Once and Again* (1999–2002) have tackled some of the more difficult issues that face contemporary stepfamilies. For many Americans under the age of 50, it would be difficult to overstate the potential impact of *The Brady Bunch.* This program was first aired 35 years ago and has continued to be broadcast in syndication virtually without interruption. When family scholars discuss the role of unrealistically positive expectations in stepfamily adjustment (e.g., Jones, 1978), images of *The Brady Bunch* and similarly positive portrayals such as *The Sound of Music* immediately come to mind. However, the general belief of media cultivation theorists is that the media does not cause changes in views of the family but rather reflects and reinforces, or cultivates, already established beliefs (Signorelli & Morgan, 2001).

Despite the presence of both negative and positive images of stepfamilies in the media, on balance, their depiction on television is relatively rare. Robinson and Skill (2001) content analyzed prime time fictional TV shows with a family configuration. In the 1950s, only 1.2% of these shows featured stepfamilies. By the period 1990 to 1995 this figure had risen to 6.0%—a considerable increase, but still far below their prevalence in the actual American population.

The media has been blamed for simultaneously depicting overly negative views of step-families and stepparents in particular, as well as portraying unrealistically positive images of stepfamilies. Overall, depictions of stepfamilies on television and in the movies are still relatively rare; but in some cases, very salient and accessible. The exact role of these media images in shaping cultural as well as individual attitudes toward stepfamilies is still largely unknown to family scientists.

### Societal Views of Stepfamilies

Family scientists have argued that most societal views of stepfamilies are negative in tone and based on an idealization of nuclear families (Ganong & Coleman, 2000). For instance, one image of stepfamilies in society is that of *deviant group*. Because stepfami-lies and stepparents are sometimes stigmatized through cultural stereotypes, myths, and media images, Ganong and Coleman argue that many people see them as deviant groups. Consequently, stepfamily members sometimes attempt to conceal their status or engage in deliberate impression management strategies to overcome the stigma and prove that they are a worthwhile family. Another prominent view of stepfamilies is evident in the *incomplete institutionalization hypothesis* (Cherlin, 1978). Cherlin's thesis is essentially that stepfamilies lack guiding norms, principles, and methods of problem solving that are en-joyed by members of nuclear families. Further, there is no institutionalized social support for stepfamilies. In some cases, there are not even any appropriate terms for certain step relationships (e.g., the sibling of a stepparent). For these reasons, stepfamilies do not get adequately incorporated into our institutions and have to function under conditions of unclear or ambiguous expectations. Ganong and Coleman are quick to note that some have criticized Cherlin for overstating the case, but that there is at least a kernel of truth in the incomplete institutionalization hypothesis. Another societal view of stepfamilies is that of the *reformed nuclear family*. According to this perspective, stepfamilies are just like nuclear families by virtue of having two heterosexual adults and children. People who endorse this view assume that stepfamilies will function as any nuclear family would and that family membership and household membership are one and the same. This societal view of stepfamilies certainly sounds less negative than the incomplete institutional-ization hypothesis or the deviant groups perspective, but it is based on a fundamental misunderstanding of stepfamilies. As we reveal later in this chapter, stepfamilies face their own unique set of challenges that often distinguish them from nuclear families. And like nuclear families, stepfamilies have diverse forms and functions. For that reason the reformed nuclear family view appears to stem from a whitewashed vision of what stepfamilies are all about. At the same time, we hasten to point out that the deviant groups and incomplete institutionalization perspectives are perhaps equally off base, just in the opposite direction. In any event, the societal views of stepfamilies described by Ganong and Coleman indicate that myths and stereotypes abound when it comes to understanding stepfamilies.

## The Development of Stepfamily Communication and Relationships

Family clinicians such as Papernow (1993) recognize that stepfamilies go through distinct phases in their efforts to form a cohesive "family." At the start of the remarriage, many stepfamilies are in the *fantasy stage*. This stage is represented by hope and perhaps expectation that the new spouse will be a better partner and parent than the previous spouse. The spouse who marries a partner with children will often enter into the relationship with similarly lofty goals and an immediate effort to be a super-parent. The image of stepfamilies portrayed in *The Brady Bunch* is a good illustration of the sort of family communication dynamics that might be hoped for in the fantasy stage. However, as most people are aware, that image of stepfamily life is just that—a fantasy. Next, stepfamilies enter into the *immersion stage*. In this stage, the stepparent tends to feel like an outsider looking in and their grand expectations are often shattered. Children become more aware of the relationship between their biological parent and stepparent. This can generate feelings of jealousy, resentment, and confusion. The reality of different views toward child rearing, parental roles, and negotiation of new boundaries creates conditions that are ripe for family conflict.

The transformation from the fantasy to immersion stages described by Papernow (1993) is clearly evident in research findings on stepfathers and their stepchildren. Stepfathers often enter the stepfamily with what appear to be the best of intentions, overtly expressing positivity toward the stepchildren in the hope of developing a good relationship with them. However, research shows that they quickly become disengaged from the stepchildren when their positive overtures are rebuffed (Hetherington & Clingempeel, 1992). Despite the fact that sharing information with the children, paying attention to them, and engaging them in shared activities are all positive rapport-building communication behaviors, stepfamily relationships like all other relationships cannot be forced or rushed. Children have a knack for putting on the brakes when stepparent–stepchild relationships develop too quickly. This regulation of relationship development may be interpreted as rejection by the stepfather, resulting in his disengagement from the relationship. This pattern of early stepfamily relationship development clearly illustrates the sort of changes in behavior that would be expected as stepfamilies progress from the fantasy into the immersion stage.

The development of stepfamily relationships is often evident in how the family negotiates and develops family rituals. To explore this issue, communication researchers Dawn Braithwaite, Leslie Baxter, and Anneliese Harper (1998) interviewed 20 stepparents and 33 stepchildren and asked them to focus on family rituals during the first 4 years of the stepfamily's history. They found that families had to balance the dialectical opposition (see the dialectical approach in chap. 2) between honoring rituals of the "old" family and developing rituals in the "new" family. This management was accomplished in several ways. First, some rituals from the old family were dropped because they could no longer be performed in the new family, they were no longer appropriate, or the new spouse would not participate in the new ritual. It is sometimes the case that family rituals are built around one person (e.g., going to a certain restaurant on the father's birthday) and when that person is no longer a part of the household the ritual is dropped. In other cases, the new spouse may have different religious beliefs and practices that are at odds with the family's adherence to a former ritual. Second, some rituals were successfully imported unchanged into the new family. Braithwaite and her colleagues explain that the perseverance of such rituals functions to honor both the old and the new family. For example, a family that goes on a camping trip every summer might continue to do so after the remarriage of one of the parents. In this way they keep the "old family" tradition alive, while also incorporating the new family member(s) into that tradition ultimately making it the "new family's" ritual as well. Third, some family rituals are imported into the new family but adapted in some way. A family that always gets together for an afternoon barbeque on the 4th of July might have to modify their ritual when their new stepmother, who is a police officer, has to work on that day. Instead, this family may have a dinner and then go to their local park to watch a fireworks display in the evening. The family still celebrates the ritual of getting together for a big meal on the 4th of July, but they adapted it to meet the needs of the new family member. Finally, stepfamilies will often form new rituals of their own. These can help to create a new and unique identity for the stepfamily so long as everyone in the family is a willing participant in the ritual.

In a further analysis of these same interviews Baxter, Braithwaite, and Nicholson (1999) turned their attention to turning points in the development of these stepfamily relationships. When asked to focus on those keys events in the family's early history that brought them to where they are today, respondents most frequently cited "changes in household/family composition" (mentioned by 94% of all respondents), "conflict or disagreement" (72%), "holidays and special events" (67%), "quality time" (64%), and "family crisis" (55%). It appears that these various turning points are characteristic in the development of most stepfamilies. As part of these interviews, Baxter and her associates asked participants to draw a graph where the horizontal axis is time (0–48 months) and the vertical axis is what percent they "feel like a family" (0–100). Analyses of these revealed five distinct stepfamily development trajectories that are summarized in Table 12.1.

There are several notable qualities to Baxter et al.'s (1999) findings on stepfamily development trajectories that are evident from Table 12.1. First, it is quite obvious that not all stepfamilies develop in the same way. Some experience a smooth and rapid progression toward feeling like a family, whereas others have a more turbulent development trajectory, or never really develop the sense of being a family. Second, even though the majority of stepfamilies successfully develop a sense of cohesion and unity, it is apparent that some (i.e., "stagnating" and "declining") never successfully achieve that goal. From these data, that appears to be the case for about one in five stepfamilies.

To gain a deeper understanding of what differentiated the stepfamilies, Braithwaite and her associates conducted further analyses of the interviews from these stepfamily members to examine how family processes variables discriminated among the different types (Braithwaite, Olson, Golish, Soukup, & Turman, 2001). They found that *accelerated* stepfamilies rapidly developed traditional family roles, norms, boundaries, and expectations. They seemed to approach stepfamily life expecting traditional nuclear family roles and norms to develop. Their strong solidarity helped them to smoothly work through the conflicts that they experienced early in their development. *Prolonged* families tended to be adaptable, flexible, and generally satisfied with their stepfamily experiences. Even

**TABLE 12.1**
Baxter et al.'s (1999) Taxonomy of Stepfamily Development Trajectories

| Trajectory Type | Prevalence | Description |
|---|---|---|
| Accelerated | 31% | Started out at feeling somewhat like a family and rapidly progressed with an almost 4:1 ratio of positive to negative turning points |
| Prolonged | 27% | Started out not feeling like a family but slowly progressed toward family cohesion with a 3:1 ratio of positive to negative turning points |
| Stagnating | 14% | Started out not feeling like a family and never developed the feeling over the first four years; they experienced a 2:1 ratio of positive to negative turning points but these did not create the feeling of a family |
| Declining | 6% | Started out feeling like a family but that feeling steadily declined over the first four years; they experienced a 2:1 ratio of negative to positive turning points |
| High-Amplitude Turbulent | 22% | Drastic fluctuation in feeling like a family during the first four years; numerous positive and negative turning points that each altered their feeling of being a family |

*Note.* Adapted from Baxter, Braithwaite, & Nicholson (1999).

though they started out uncertain, they were willing to negotiate things like family roles and were open to communication about these issues. Unlike the accelerated families, those with a prolonged trajectory did not compare themselves to a nuclear family. Families with the *declining* trajectory seemed to have a lot of trouble from the word go. They started out with great expectations but almost immediately experienced loyalty conflicts, ambiguous and strained family roles, and divisive family boundaries. Their struggles were characterized by eventually developing impermeable and divisive boundaries by bloodline and generation and, ultimately, by avoidance of communication. By the end of their fourth year, these families were around zero on the "feeling like a family" scale. *Stagnating* families experienced awkwardness in their role and felt, as Braithwaite and her associates put it, "thrown together." They wanted a normal or traditional family life, but ironically, the more they tried to create that the more resistance they experienced from within. Obviously, not all members of these families were on the same page when it came to developing a "normal" family life. Loyalty conflicts, resentment, and dissatisfaction were common themes in these families that simply never took off. Finally, the *high-amplitude turbulent* families had a diverse and unstable development in their first 4 years. Like many other newly formed stepfamilies they started off with great expectations and quickly collided with realities that were at odds with these expectations. Feelings of betrayal and a lack of trust were common in these family types. Braithwaite et al. noted that a lack of solidarity between the couple was common in these families and prevented them from communicating a unified front to the children. Conflicts typically culminated in a "fork in the road" that was successfully negotiated in some turbulent families. Those who avoided these conflicts were among the least satisfied of the turbulent families. After carefully examining the development trajectories and experiences, Braithwaite et al. concluded that the three key family processes that varied across the different families were boundary management, solidarity, and adaptation. Even though these conclusions were derived from a small sample of stepfamily members, they are generally consistent with the research literature on stepfamilies that highlights the importance of these same critical issues.

## Diversity Within Stepfamilies

As we mentioned earlier in this chapter, there is no single standard or norm for stepfamilies. Like families, more generally, stepfamilies are quite diverse and can take a variety of forms. In this section we consider the variety of different roles that people might occupy in stepfamilies and some of the many different types of relationships that occur in these different stepfamilies. Finally, this section includes an analysis of different types of stepfamilies based on the members' orientation toward stepfamily life.

### Roles in Stepfamilies

Family roles simultaneously shape and are shaped by communication patterns within the family. Although the roles of child and parent are fairly clear in most family contexts, there is considerable ambiguity inherent in being a stepparent. Many stepparents are unsure about assuming the role of parent. After all, in many stepfamilies the children still have two biological parents. What is the ideal role of a stepparent in this family context? Family scientists Mark Fine, Marilyn Coleman, and Lawrence Ganong (1998) investigated this issue by asking parents, stepparents, and children in stepfamilies about what they think the ideal role of a stepparent is. They also asked respondents to describe the actual role of the stepparent in their family. For the ideal role of a stepparent, just over half of the parents and stepparents said "parent." In other words, the stepparent should assume the role of parent just as a biological parent would. In contrast, only 29% of the children offered this response. Evidently, a greater proportion of parents and stepparents, compared to children, think that "parent" is the ideal role for a stepparent. Among these same respondents, 18% of the parents and 18% of the stepparents indicated that "friend" was the ideal role of a stepparent. In contrast, 40% of the children thought that "friend" was the ideal role for a stepparent. So it seems that more children want their stepparent to assume the role of friend, whereas parents and stepparents want the stepparent to assume the role of parent. It is also interesting that 48% of the stepparents said that their actual role in the family was that of parent, whereas only 28% of the children said that their stepparent held the role of parent. Fine et al.'s study illustrates not only how there are different desires within the family for stepparent roles but also how family members do not necessarily agree on what the actual role of the family's stepparent is. For the most part, parents and children have a clearer perception of what the stepparent role is in contrast to stepparents who indicate that their role in the family is not entirely clear (Fine, Coleman, & Ganong, 1999).

The performance of some parental roles in stepfamilies may be specific to the sex of the parent. For example, mothers will often assume a variety of roles to control the development of the relationship between their children and new spouse (Coleman, Ganong, & Weaver, 2001). Mothers will sometimes perform the role of *defender* in which they try to shield their children from unfair discipline, perceived slights, and misunderstanding on the part of the stepfather. In the role of *gatekeeper*, mothers literally control the stepfather's access to their children during both courtship and marriage. For instance, it may take many years before a mother will leave her children alone with their stepfather. Mothers also act as *mediators* between children and their stepfathers. Coleman et al. note that the mediator role is particularly common early in the formation of stepfamilies when disagreements are prevalent. A related role performed by mothers in stepfamilies is that of *interpreter*. Interpreters not only step in and referee conflicts but also explain each family member's perspective to the other. When lines of communication between children and the stepfather may be hindered or nonexistent, the mother's performance of the interpreter role can be vital to salvaging some degree of civility in the family environment.

Remarriage and the formation of a stepfamily often change the interactions between a mother and her children. When mothers remarry, they decrease their use of harsh discipline tactics such as yelling, spanking, and hitting (Thomson, Mosley, Hanson, & McLanahan, 2001). However, remarried mothers supervise their children less than do stable single mothers (Thomson et al.). So remarriage brings not only some obvious improvements to mother–child interactions but also some declines in the form of less supervision.

Stepmothers have a particularly challenging role to fulfill in many remarried families. As mentioned elsewhere in this chapter, there is an abundance of negatively toned folklore concerning stepmothers. Stepmothers often feel that they have to go the extra mile to prove that they are not like the wicked stepmother in *Cinderella* (Guisinger, Cowan, & Schuldberg, 1989). In so doing, they often start by forming good relationships with their stepchildren, but their optimistic attitudes toward stepparenting erode noticeably within 3 to 5 years of marriage. Guisinger et al. also found that a quality marriage goes hand in hand with good relationships between stepmothers and their stepchildren. Many stepmothers must also contend with some of the negative emotions that stem from occupying a role that sometimes excludes them or makes them feel less than 100% legitimate. The feminist scholar Elizabeth Church (1999) interviewed 104 stepmothers and found that about half had felt jealous or envious in their role as stepmother. Feelings of jealousy were provoked by three types of circumstances: feeling second best, feeling like an outsider, and feeling like a rival. When stepmothers felt jealous due to a perceived rivalry, it was not the children's biological mother who was the rival. Rather, many felt that they had to compete with their stepchildren for their partner's attention. Church argues that often stepmothers' jealousy is an expression of feeling disconnected from the family and feeling powerless. In many families stepmothers occupy a precarious role. They are expected to form good relationships with the children and get involved in their care—but not too involved. When either biological parent pursues interaction with the children, stepmothers may be expected to step back, never having all of the full rights and privileges of a regular mother.

### Stepfamily Relationships and Stepfamily Types

It is customary to describe different types of stepfamilies by their formal structure (e.g., mother with her biological children and stepfather and both spouses with their own biological children). However, Gross (1986) described different stepfamilies from the perspective of their children. To do so, she interviewed 60 children and asked them to describe and explain who was in their family. The children's responses provide insight into the many different ways that some people might define family relationships, and how communication patterns in stepfamilies can sometimes be almost nonexistent, despite the fact that two people may share the same residence. These family structures, defined by children's subjective impressions, appear in Table 12.2. Gross (1986) found that the four different stepfamily structures were about equally common in her sample. In some

TABLE 12.2
Gross's (1986) Typology of Children's Perceptions of Family Membership

| Stepfamily Structure | Prevalence | Description |
| --- | --- | --- |
| Retention | 33% | Include both biological parents as family |
| | | Do not include stepparent as a family member |
| | | Family identified as prior to divorce |
| | | Nonresidential parent still very involved in child's life |
| | | Stepparents play a more negative role in child's life |
| Substitution | 13% | Exclude at least one biological parent from family, usually the nonresidential parent |
| | | Include at least one stepparent in family |
| | | Views family as child, one biological parent, and stepparent |
| | | Household and family are synonymous |
| | | Children are younger at separation from biological parent and remarriage to stepparent |
| | | Qualified acceptance of stepparent |
| Reduction | 25% | Fewer than the original two parents viewed as family |
| | | Stepparent not viewed as family member |
| | | At least one biological parent (usually nonresidential) not viewed as family member |
| | | Experience family as "one-parent family" |
| | | Negative feelings toward stepparent |
| Augmentation | 28% | Both biological parents identified as family, as well as at least one stepparent |
| | | Stepparent is not a "replacement" but an "addition" |
| | | Usually involved custodial father and stepmother |
| | | Many had previously lived with their mother |
| | | Maintained contact with nonresidential parent |
| | | Free movement between households, and lack of hostility between biological parents |

*Note.* Adapted from Gross (1986).

cases (*retention* and *reduction*) the stepchildren refused to characterize their stepparents as "family." In other cases (*substitution* and *reduction*) the children essentially dropped one of the biological parents from their mental representation of "family." There are also many cases (*substitution* and *augmentation*) where the stepchildren willingly characterized their stepparents as family members. This unique taxonomy developed by Gross is a reminder that children approach stepfamily relationships with vastly differing perspectives. The theory of symbolic interaction (see chap. 2) would explain these different realities of family life through the children's communication patterns with their parents and stepparents. Where there is little communication at all, as in the case of a noncustodial "deadbeat dad," some children literally revise their mental representation of "family" to exclude that member. On the other hand, where stepparent–stepchild communication patterns reflect issues such as concern, guidance, reasonable discipline, recreation, and so forth, symbolic interactionists would argue that children would more readily incorporate the stepparent into the family's membership.

Much of the research on stepfamily relationships has understandably focused on relationships between children and their stepparents and the marital relationship in stepfamilies. What is sometimes overlooked when people think about stepfamily relationships is the relationship between the two biological parents, only one of whom is currently the custodial parent. Remarriage after a divorce does not represent the end of the relationship between two biological parents. A divorced couple with children often needs to continue some form of relationship to coordinate child care and visitation, even though one or both may have remarried and formed a new family. In such cases, children become part of a *binuclear family*. The communication patterns of formerly married spouses can take on a variety of forms. Ahrons and Rodgers (1987) described these in their taxonomy of postdivorce relationships described in Table 12.3. What is most striking from the descriptions of these relationships is the diverse range of interaction patterns maintained by former spouses. Some (e.g., *dissolving duos*) permanently sever their lines of communication. This is probably a much more common communication pattern in divorced couples without any children. At the other end of the spectrum, the *perfect pals* manage to maintain open communication and continue to participate together in family activities and rituals. It is instructive to compare the types of postdivorce relations in this scheme to the children's subjective impressions of family membership described by Gross (1986). Recall that in some cases (*substitution* and *reduction*) Gross found that children would no longer consider one of their biological parents to be a member of the family. It would not be much of stretch to suppose that the biological parents in such families are *dissolving duos* or perhaps *fiery foes*. Gross also found that children would often still consider a noncustodial parent to be a member of the family, in the cases of *retention* and *augmentation*. One might suppose that the divorced biological parents in these cases would be *perfect pals* or *cooperative colleagues*. One could develop additional hypotheses linking these different stepfamily relationships, but the underlying assumption is that the nature of the postdivorce relationship of the biological parents influences to some extent the child's consideration of these parents as members of the family.

Finally, we present a recent summary of some of the distinct types of stepfamilies that have been identified in past research. Family scientists Coleman, Ganong, and Fine (2004) noted that almost every typology of stepfamilies identifies *Brady Bunch Stepfamilies*.

TABLE 12.3
Ahrons and Rogers' (1987) Typology of Postdivorce Relationships

| Relationship Type | Description |
|---|---|
| Dissolving Duos | No contact after divorce |
| Perfect Pals | Maintain mutual respect for each other after divorce |
| | Remain good friends |
| | Maintain open communication and family rituals |
| | They often remain single |
| Cooperative Colleagues | No real friendship |
| | Cooperate and coordinate efforts at parenting |
| | Compromise for the children's benefit |
| | Effectively manage conflicts |
| Angry Associates | Harbor resentment and anger toward each other |
| | Both active as parents but in parallel, not collectively |
| | Children experience loyalty conflicts |
| Fiery Foes | Intense anger |
| | No acceptance of other parent's rights |
| | Attempts to separate ex-spouse from children |
| | No cooperation between parents |
| | Children become pawns |
| | Parents still attached to each other as evidenced by their intense emotional reaction to each other |

Note. Adapted from Ahrons & Rodgers (1987).

The label that scientists use for these families is a testament to the power of the media in influencing our thinking about families. Needless to say, these are stepfamilies that try to set up a situation that is indistinguishable from a first-marriage family. Members of these families relate to each other as if they were parents and children, not stepparents and stepchildren. Their communication is open and abundant, as is their expression of affection. Coleman et al. observe that such families may be ill-prepared, unrealistic, and in denial. Like the Brady Bunch, these families may be striving not to function like a true first-marriage family but rather as a stereotype of a first-marriage family. As Coleman et al. note, often situational demands for communication and problem solving do not fit the Brady Bunch ideal, and this can be cause for dissatisfaction. For some stepfamilies, however, this mentality may work, particularly when children are very young when the stepfamily is formed.

In contrast to the Brady Bunch Stepfamilies, the *detached stepparent–engaged parent* stepfamilies function with nonequivalent parental roles. Generally the mothers in these families are involved in the upbringing of the children and the stepfathers are detached. Stepfathers in these families show little affection toward the stepchildren; they might not get involved in their supervision and engage in limited communication with them. In contrast mothers in these families are prone to engaging in frequent and intense communication with the children. Before condemning these stepfathers, it is important to realize that their detachment sometimes follows the directives of either the mother or her children (Coleman et al., 2004). Stepfathers are sometimes thrown into relationships with stepchildren merely as a function of their marriage to the mother. The stepparent–stepchild relationship is sometimes an incidental one that families manage by keeping a distance between the two and leaving most of the parenting up to the mother.

A related type of stepfamily can be found in the *couple-focused stepfamilies*. Here the marital union is of paramount importance. In these stepfamilies, the communication is largely between the spouses, and the stepparent is detached from the stepchildren. This pattern is perhaps most likely in cases where the children are older and breaking out on their own or when the children do not reside with the married couple. One might expect to see couple-focused stepfamilies, for example, in marriages that follow the death of a spouse later in life.

Finally, some stepfamilies could be characterized as *progressive stepfamilies*. Communication in these stepfamilies is modified to fit the needs to the family's particular situation and demands. Well-established stepfamilies often develop their own unique and creative style of communication to meet the complexities of their family life. One example cited by Coleman et al. (2004) is when mothers interpret the stepfathers to stepchildren and vice versa. As a way of compensating for the lack of shared history in the stepfamily, the mothers may aid their children's and spouse's understanding of each other by enacting this creative communication behavior. Progressive stepfamilies often exhibit excellent family communication and problem solving. Their relationships are sometimes closer than those of first-marriage families. At this time, family scientists and clinicians do not fully understand how such families are developed. However, it appears that a very flexible approach to family communication coupled with a respect for different family forms, devoid of any preconceived notions, are integral elements of progressive stepfamilies.

## Challenges in Stepfamilies

Stepfamilies face a number of challenges in sorting out their relationships that contribute to family stress. Some of the issues that they face, such as conflict, are comparable in kind to those of nuclear families, but perhaps differ in intensity. Other challenges such as negotiating conflicting loyalties to a stepparent and noncustodial parent are unique to stepfamilies. In this section, we examine challenges faced by stepfamilies that include relational communication issues, conflict, adaptability and cohesion, and child adjustment.

### Communication Challenges

Although all developing families face a number of communication challenges as they build relationships, trust, roles, and boundaries, stepfamilies have unique dynamics that make these challenges particularly salient. Furthermore, stepfamilies must face a number of unique challenges that differ from nuclear families with both biological parents. To identify these issues Golish (2003) interviewed 90 people (stepparents, biological parents, and children and stepchildren) from 30 different stepfamilies. They were asked how their communication, feelings, and expectations changed over time and to identify their problem areas and strengths. One of the most common challenges cited by participants was *feeling caught*. This typically involved triangulation in the relationship among a child, his or her custodial parents, and his or her noncustodial parent. This challenge caused children to avoid talking to one parent in front of the other or bringing up certain topics of discussion with one of the parents. Interestingly, it was sometimes the parents who felt caught. For example, sometimes the biological parent was used as a go-between by their child and spouse. Instead of the stepchild and stepparent communicating directly, they would air their grievances through the parent. Some families had problems with *ambiguity of parental roles*. Almost all of the stepfamilies studied by Golish (2003) experienced confusion and uncertainty about the stepparent's role in disciplining children. This sometimes causes a clash between the "friend" and "disciplinarian" role performed by the stepparent. Stepfamilies also had to contend with *regulating boundaries with the noncustodial family*. Many children in stepfamilies are still grieving the loss of their family system. This often took the form of having to renegotiate a different kind of relationship with a now noncustodial father. However, sometimes this challenge in regulating relationships was experienced between former spouses. Where there are issues of joint or shared custody, former spouses cannot simply stop communicating, but rather have to work out arrangements for care of the children.

One particularly unique challenge faced by stepfamilies is *traumatic bonding*. It was often the case that mothers and daughters formed a very close bond as the mother made the transition from divorce to single parenthood. The bond formed during these hard times would often persevere during formation of the stepfamily. At this time, the stepparent would be seen as an intruder in the family. At the same time, the stepparent may feel jealous or excluded by this intense mother–daughter bond. Stepfamilies were also challenged by *vying for resources*. Issues like money, space, and privacy are particularly salient in stepfamilies. The desire for one's own territory could be fueled by the feeling of being invaded by outsiders, which could also increase the desire for privacy. Struggling to secure these resources in an environment where they are often scarce sets the stage for abundant conflicts within the stepfamily. A related challenge faced by stepfamilies is *discrepancies in conflict management styles*. The most common scenario for this challenge was a stepparent's desire to openly confront an issue and the biological parent's and children's desire to avoid the issue. Successfully overcoming this challenge often involved all parties adjusting their communication style. The final communication challenge documented by Golish (2003) was *building solidarity as a family unit*. Particularly strong and successful families accomplished this by spending time together, developing their own family rituals, and displaying affection toward each other. In other cases stepfamilies would incorporate humor into their interactions or naturally and gradually introduce the child and stepparent without trying to force the relationship. Even though most families have to deal with at least some of these issues, they are particularly evident in stepfamilies, and their successful negotiation is vital to developing strong stepfamily relationships. Golish observed that the "meta-theme" underlying many of these communication challenges is the negotiation of boundaries within the family and across families.

In a comparable study, Cissna, Cox, and Bochner (1990) interviewed nine stepfamilies that had at least two school-aged children at home and asked them about issues such as managing relationships with the former spouse, problems in reorganizing their family, and strategies for overcoming these problems. All nine of the families mentioned issues related to balancing the marital versus the parental relationships. Cissna et al. found that there were two dominant tasks that families faced in order to manage this dialectic. First, the family needs to *establish the solidarity of the marriage relationship in the minds of the stepchildren*. Marriages are freely chosen by the spouses, but not by their children. As Golish (2003) observed, sometimes children might view the stepparents as an intruder into a close relationship that was established during tough times. For a stepfamily to develop and function effectively, stepchildren need to see the marital relationship as solid and unified. A second major task that stepfamilies face is *establishing parental authority, particularly the credibility of the stepparent*. Once the children appreciate the substantial nature of the parent–stepparent relationship, the next step is to view the stepparent as something of an authority figure. Without that, boundaries can get blurred and conflicts can arise. Cissna et al. observed that one of the difficult chores for the stepparent is building a friendship relationship with the child while at the same time exercising discipline and developing the role of authority figure. This is an unusually challenging dialectic that must be delicately balanced with acute sensitivity and social skills on the part of the stepparent.

### Conflict

Because of their unique family structure stepfamilies tend to have their own set of stressors and concerns that contribute substantially to interpersonal conflicts (Burrell, 1995). It is often the case in stepfamilies that an "outsider" comes into a long-established physical environment and relational context. Children sometimes have a close relationship with their custodial parent forged during difficult times. They are often accustomed to their custodial parent's undivided attention when they are home together. In addition children may have their own room and space in the house that does not have to be shared with others. The introduction of a stepparent, particularly one with children in tow, can dramatically upset these norms. Obviously the situation is ripe for conflict and may explain why stepfamilies experience more conflict than do intact families (Barber & Lyons, 1994). A lot of the conflicts in stepfamilies occur between the spouses and often concern the children and stepchildren (Ganong & Coleman, 2000). In stepfamilies, it is sometimes the case that the biological parent has far more history and experience raising children than does the stepparent, who may have no child-rearing experience at all. This immediately sets up a situation where the legitimacy of one person's perspective on child rearing is questioned and almost impossible to substantiate. It is no wonder that conflicts over child-rearing issues are so prevalent among spouses in stepfamilies.

Observations of family clinicians indicate that stepfamily households often have to address multiple sources of potential conflict that include outsiders and insiders, boundary disputes, power issues, conflicting loyalties, triangular relationships, and unity versus fragmentation of the new couple relationship (Visher, Visher, & Pasley, 2003). Scientific researchers have reached similar conclusions, noting that the primary sources of conflict in stepfamilies often revolve around boundary issues (Burrell, 1995; Coleman, Fine, Ganong, Downs, & Pauk, 2001). Subsidiary issues included disagreements over resources, loyalty conflicts, individuals having a "guard and protect" mentality, and conflict with extended family (Coleman et al.). Coleman and her associates documented these family conflicts through interviews of adults and children from 17 stepfamilies. Some of the major resources that they frequently argued about were possessions, space, time and attention, and finances. Loyalty conflicts were often felt by children who seemed to be torn between loyalty to their stepparent and their noncustodial parent. What Coleman et al. characterized as a "guard and protect" ideology involved the mother trying to protect an almost peer-like mother–daughter relationship, attempts to protect the children from an overly strict stepfather, or attempts to protect the children from a nonresidential parent. Instances of these interaction patterns highlighted sharp disagreements and conflicts often ensued. Finally, stepfamilies often experienced conflicts with extended family members who did not view the stepfamily as a legitimate family unit. This type of conflict is a good illustration of a dispute that involves an external boundary issue, whereas most other conflicts in the stepfamilies concerned boundaries within the family.

It is sometimes the case in stepfamilies that role ambiguity and boundary issues collectively contribute to conflicts (Burrell, 1995). For example, role ambiguity occurs when people are uncertain about what actions they are expected to take and exactly what their function is in the family. Of course, boundaries represent the often invisible psychological limits of enacted and accepted behaviors within the family and between its members and outsiders. For a new stepparent, role ambiguity and boundary issues may go hand in hand. The role of disciplinarian is often a very uncertain one for the new stepparent. Stepchildren who are unaccustomed to this new role of the stepparent may reject such forms of communication. At the same time, some stepparents may have a hard time communicating in an authoritarian or authoritative fashion toward their stepchildren. This role ambiguity is entwined in boundary issues. How permeable is the stepparent–stepchild relationship? Does the stepparent have the "right" or authority to command the stepchild to do something or to not do something? Does the stepparent have the right or authority to use corporal punishment (involving nonverbal communication)? Should there be as much physical affection in the stepparent–stepchild relationship as might be expected between biological parents and their children? These are all issues that concern both roles and boundaries. They can be very potent catalysts for conflict in most stepfamilies. These conflicts may occur between stepparent and stepchild, between two spouses who disagree on how the stepparents should interact with the stepchild, or between a child and his or her biological parent who disagree on what is acceptable behavior on the part of the stepparent.

There is an interesting power dynamic in stepfamilies that helps to explain the nature of some common conflicts that occur in these contexts. In stepfather families (perhaps the most common form of remarried families with children), family members agree that the mother has most authority and power for major decision making (Giles-Sims & Crosbie-Burnett, 1989). However, for everyday decisions, adolescents appear to have as much influence as the adults, especially early on in the history of the stepfamily. Further, Giles-Sims and Crosbie-Burnett (1989) found that when it comes to making major decisions, adolescents perceived themselves as having more power than their stepfathers—a view that was not necessarily shared by their stepfathers. This potential power struggle between adolescent and stepparent is undoubtedly manifest in conflict interactions until the family is able to establish some norms, or in systems theory terminology, homeostasis. The struggle for power and the quest to establish new family norms may explain why long-term remarried couples with stepchildren experience more conflict than long-term remarried couples with their own biological children (MacDonald & DeMaris, 1995). When children are born into an intact marriage, power, roles, norms and decision-making patterns can be gradually and consistently developed throughout childhood. On the other hand, when a remarried couple has stepchildren, where there is no relational history with one of the parents, these same roles, norms, and decision-making patterns must be negotiated and established from scratch. In long-term marriages, where the stepchildren are likely to be older children and adolescents, the potential for interpersonal conflict is extensive.

What are the communication strategies that stepfamilies use to resolve their conflicts? Coleman et al. (2001) found that stepfamilies would often compromise on rules and discipline, present a unified parental front on rules and discipline, talk directly with the person one is in conflict with, or reframe the problem as less serious, perhaps with a joke. Most communication scholars would agree that these are generally effective ways of handling conflict. This suggests, through their often extensive experience with conflict, that stepfamilies often develop and deploy effective means for managing these conflicts.

Having said that "talking directly" is one way stepfamilies resolve conflict, there are some special exceptions. Sometimes stepchildren handle conflict-laden or other sensitive topics is by avoiding the topic in family interactions. Golish and Caughlin (2002) studied this issue by interviewing 115 adolescents and young adults in stepfamilies, using Petronio's (2000) Communication Privacy Management perspective (see chap. 3) to develop hypotheses about why and when adolescents would avoid various topics with their parents and stepparents. They found that children reported the greatest topic avoidance with stepparents, followed by fathers, and finally by mothers. The most commonly avoided topic across all types of parental relationships was sex. Other commonly avoided topics included talking about the other parent or family and money (e.g., child support payments). When asked why they avoided these topics, the adolescents' and young adults' most typical replies concerned self-protection, protecting the harmony of the relationship with the parent or stepparent, and conflict. Responses that reflected concerns with conflict included the desire to keep conflicts from happening as well and the desire to keep some conflicts from escalating. Even though people often feel that discussing concerns openly is the best way to develop and manage relationships, in an often fragile context of stepfamily relationships, sometimes the avoidance of certain topics is the more sensible and comfortable strategy—at least from the perspective of a child in the stepfamily.

Before leaving the topic of conflict, it bears mentioning that conflict can be a catalyst for positive change in stepfamilies (Coleman, Fine, et al., 2001). As hard as it is for many stepfamilies to sort out their various issues, establish boundaries, and define new roles, the efforts invested in these conflicts may yield dividends so long as they do not consume the stepfamily. Stepfamilies can achieve harmony and happiness, but that may only come after intense negotiation, or conflict, over issues such as space, roles, expectations, discipline, and privacy.

### *Adaptability and Cohesion*

It is generally the case that stepfamilies have lower family cohesion and adaptability than do first-married families (Pink & Wampler, 1985; Waldren, Bell, Peek, & Sorell, 1990). People in stepfamilies report lower cooperation and greater fragmentation in family relationships than do people in nuclear families (Banker & Gaertner, 1998). Bray and Berger (1993) found not only that newly formed (within 6 months) stepfamilies had lower levels of cohesion than did nuclear families but also that levels of family cohesion dropped even lower in longer established (i.e., 2.5 and 5–7 years) stepfamilies. The fact that stepfamilies have lower cohesion than do first-married families is understandable. After all, the stepparent and any of his or her children often have very little relational history with other family members. Recall that the typical interval between divorce and remarriage is only 3 years. It is therefore plausible to assume that many stepchildren might have only known their stepparent for a year or two prior to sharing a residence with him or her. Therefore, the type of family cohesion that is associated with first marriage families of longer duration may take years to develop, and in a the majority of cases, it may never fully develop. What is perhaps more perplexing is the lower adaptability in stepfamilies. Stepfamilies experience higher levels of stress than do first married families (Waldren et al.). Although extreme adaptability can actually generate stress, some degree of adaptability is necessary to effectively cope with stressors. It is exactly this adaptability that seems to be in short supply in many stepfamilies. It is also worth noting that stepfamilies want levels of cohesion and adaptability similar to those of first-marriage families (Pink & Wampler, 1985), so it is not by design that they have lower adaptability and cohesion.

The lower adaptability and cohesion of stepfamilies is clearly evident in their communication patterns. For example, newly formed stepfamilies rate their family communication more poorly than do newly formed first-marriage families (Bray & Berger, 1993). Also, stepfathers report less positive and more negative communication with family members than do fathers in nuclear families (Pink & Wampler, 1985). Grinwald (1995) asked adolescents aged 12 to 18 to report on various positive (e.g., "my mother or father is always a good listener") and negative (e.g., "my mother or father insults me when he or she is angry with me") aspects of communication with their parent and stepparent. The reports of adolescents from first-marriage families were compared with those of stepfamilies that were formed after divorce and with stepfamilies that were formed after death of a parent. The poorest parent–child communication was reported in the stepfamilies formed after divorce, followed by those formed after death, and the best parent–child communication was reported by adolescents in first marriage families. Grinwald's study points to the fact that at least some of the cohesion and communication problems experienced by stepfamilies may be a continuation of the turmoil experienced in a prior family that ended in divorce. Remarried parents also provide less social support to their children—a level of support that is equivalent to that for divorced parents but less than that for parents in first marriages (White, 1992). White's investigation suggested that the social support deficits from remarried parents can be explained by lower levels of contact with the children and lower quality relationships and solidarity with them.

Elsewhere in this chapter we review research findings that show that levels of conflict are often higher in stepfamilies than in first-marriage families. This communication pattern is undoubtedly linked with issues of problematic adaptability and cohesion. One particularly interesting consequent of this higher family conflict and lower cohesion is that children in stepfamilies leave home sooner than do children in nuclear families (White, 1994b). In a very carefully controlled study, 65% of stepchildren were found to leave home before the age of 19, compared to 50% of the children in first-marriage families (Aquilino, 1991). Two compelling explanations for this effect concern weaker relationships or cohesion in stepfamilies, including failure to fully integrate adolescent children into the family system, and children being driven out by or seeking to escape family conflict (Crosbie-Burnett & McClinitic, 2000b; White, 1994b). Obviously, as children depart from stepfamilies, parent–child communication presumably drops as well.

### Child Adjustment in Stepfamilies

Given what is known about the special challenges faced by stepfamilies, the nature of their relationships, and their opportunities for conflict, researchers have been understandably concerned with the social and psychological adjustment of children who live in stepfamilies. Although a thorough review of this research is beyond the scope of this chapter, there are several highlights that are worth noting. First, children who live in stepfamilies tend to have slightly more externalizing behavior problems and slightly less social competence than do their counterparts in first-marriage families (Bray, 1999). Why is this the case? Obviously many children in stepfamilies undergo difficult life transitions that might include witnessing their biological parents' marriage deteriorate, experiencing the departure of one parent, perhaps living in financial hardship, moving to a new residence, and having a new adult member of the family move in to their residence (Anderson, Greene, Hetherington, & Clingempeel, 1999). These changes can sometimes all occur in a relatively short period of time.

Aside from the obvious structural and residential stressors that children in stepfamilies might have experienced, there is compelling evidence to show that their adjustment problems are also linked to family communication and relationship issues. In remarried families, parental negativity is significantly and positively correlated with child behavior problems (Anderson et al., 1999). This same research team found that adolescents in remarried families displayed more negativity toward their parent and stepparent than did adolescents in nondivorced families. Research also shows that the amount of conflict in stepfamilies is associated with child adjustment problems (Bray, 1999; Dunn, 2002).

Parents in stepfamilies tend to be less involved in the lives of their children than are parents in two-parent biological or adoptive families (Zill, 1994). This effect is especially pronounced for stepfathers (Fine, Voydanoff, & Donnelly, 1993). This is unfortunate because communication with stepfathers appears to be more vital to child adjustment outcomes than does communication with mothers in stepfather families (Collins, Newman, & McKenry, 1995). On the other hand, communication with the father was a stronger predictor of child adjustment than communication with the stepmother in stepmother families (Collins et al.). The Fine et al. investigation additionally revealed that positive parental communication behaviors such as praise, hugs, reading to the child, and private talks with the child were positively associated with child adjustment in stepfamilies, whereas negative parental communication behaviors such as spanking and yelling at the child were negatively associated with child adjustment.

Some of the difficulties that children in stepfamilies experience may be more attributable to the legacy of their original family life. A sophisticated longitudinal study that followed over 1,000 school children from age 6 to age 12 indicates that remarriage per se had no appreciable impact on children's aggressive and oppositional behavior, once the effects of parental divorce were taken into account (Pagani, Boulerice, Tremblay, & Vitaro, 1997). This study shows that many of the behavior problems that are evident in children living in stepfamilies may be a legacy of their biological parents' divorce. Contrary to what some might believe, a fairly rapid transition from the first-marriage family to the stepfamily is associated with fewer relationship problems in the new family (Montgomery, Anderson, Hetherington, & Clingempeel, 1992). Evidently, it is less disruptive to move from one two-parent household to another in rapid succession than it is to get settled into a single-parent household, only to then have to transition back into a two-parent household.

For the most part, research on child adjustment problems in stepfamilies supports the view that children in these contexts have slightly more behavior problems than do children in first-marriage families. Notwithstanding the environmental stress explanations for these effects, several theoretical explanations for these behavior problems focus on family relationship and communication problems in stepfamilies (Coleman et al., 2000). Most prominent among these are the family conflict explanation, which says that conflicts among divorced parents and within the stepfamily incite behavioral problems in children, and the deterioration of parental competencies theory, which explains child behavior problems in stepfamilies as a function of poor-quality parenting, including uninvolved parenting, minimal parental positivity, and more negatively toned communication behaviors from parents and stepparents.

## CONCLUSION

When marriages end because of death or divorce, most people tend to remarry. However, remarriages have a divorce rate even higher than do first marriages. Many of the interpersonal behaviors that might have contributed to deterioration of the first marriage might work similarly in a remarriage. A natural consequent of abundant remarriage is a large number of stepfamilies. There are many negative images and views of stepfamilies in both the media and, more generally, the society. Where there are positive images of stepfamilies in the media, as in *The Brady Bunch*, they are often unrealistic and may engender expectations for relational harmony that simply cannot be met. People in stepfamilies often start out with great expectations, but the sometimes difficult realities of living in a stepfamily quickly become evident and create distance between stepparents and stepchildren. Family scholars have found that not all stepfamilies develop their relationships in the same way. Some develop rapidly, some slowly, and some never really develop a sense of "family." As stepfamilies develop, they often face disagreements about the role of stepparents in the family. Mothers in stepfather families often assume a variety of roles to regulate and referee the relationship between their children and their spouse. Research consistently shows that there are a wide variety of different stepfamily types and forms. However, most stepfamilies face communication challenges such as feeling caught, negotiating ambiguous parental roles, regulating boundaries, and vying for resources. Research findings also indicate that many stepfamilies have to contend with greater conflict, lower adaptability, lower cohesion, and more issues of boundary regulation than do nuclear families. Finally, children in stepfamilies exhibit more behavior problems than do children in nuclear families, and these are associated to some extent with the quality of the stepfamily relationships and communication.

IV

Family Interaction, Health, and Well-Being

# CHAPTER THIRTEEN

# Family Interaction and Mental Health

Mental health problems are pervasive in America, yet poorly understood. Current estimates indicate that 48% of the U.S. population will have a diagnosable psychological disorder at some time in their lives (Regier et al., 1993). Because mental health problems are often invisible, their pervasiveness is not well appreciated, and because they are associated with a stigma, they often go untreated. Nevertheless, mental health problems can ruin relationships, careers, families, and lives. Even relatively mild psychological problems such as loneliness or social anxiety can be profoundly distressing and painfully debilitating. More severe psychological problems such as schizophrenia can permanently shatter lives sometimes rendering people virtually noncommunicative. The idea that mental health is somehow related to family interaction is nothing new. Early theorizing about mental health problems, 50–100 years ago, often postulated a connection between marital and family interactions and psychological disorders (e.g., Freud, 1917/1966; Lasegue, 1873; Sullivan, 1953). What are some of the mental health problems that are associated with problematic family interactions? How might family interactions contribute to, aggravate, or trigger relapses in mental health problems? To answer these questions, we present current research and theorizing on problems such as depression, loneliness, schizophrenia, eating disorders, and alcoholism from a family interaction perspective. These are but a mere sample of some of the many mental health problems that are linked with troubled family interaction patterns. Interested readers can consult Beach (2001), Jacob (1987), and Segrin (2001b) for further information on these topics.

## DEPRESSION

### Definition

Major depressive disorder is a pervasive illness with a lifetime risk of 10% to 25% for women and 5% to 12% for men (*DSM-IV-TR*; American Psychiatric Association [APA], 2000; Kessler et al., 1994). Depressive episodes are marked by severely depressed mood, diminished interest in any activities, significant weight loss or gain, sleep disturbance, psychomotor agitation or retardation, fatigue, feelings of worthlessness and guilt, difficulty concentrating, and recurrent thoughts of death or suicidal ideation (American Psychiatric Association). For a formal diagnosis, these symptoms must be evident for a period of at least 2 weeks, but for many people with depression these may last months or even years. Depression, like many other mental health problems, can be caused by a variety of factors. However, in virtually all cases it has substantial interpersonal implications that can and will change the nature of marital and family interactions. This point was stressed by Joiner, Coyne, and Blalock (1999), who stated that "regardless of what other factors may be involved, the interpersonal context affects greatly whether a person becomes depressed, the person's subjective experience while depressed, and the behavioral manifestations and resolution of the disorder. Consideration of the interpersonal context is simply a necessity for an adequate account of the disorder" (p. 3). As we show in this section of the chapter, in many cases the interpersonal context of depression starts in childhood through early parent–child interactions. The effects of, and in some cases antecedents to, depression are also evident in the whole family system as well as in the marital subsystem.

## Depression and Marital Interaction

Depression is strongly associated with problems in marital interactions and relationships (see Beach, 2001; Beach, Sandeen, & O'Leary, 1990; and Coyne, Kahn, & Gotlib, 1987, for reviews). Repeatedly, this research has shown that depression and marital distress go hand in hand (Beach & O'Leary, 1993; Beach et al., 1990). About 50% of all women in distressed marriages are depressed (Beach, Jouriles, & O'Leary, 1985), and 50% to 60% of all depressed women are in distressed marriages (Coyne, Thompson, & Palmer, 2002; Rounsaville, Weissman, Prusoff, & Herceg-Baron, 1979). As depressive symptoms worsen or improve, so too does relationship quality with the spouse (Judd et al., 2000).

The communication between depressed people and their spouses is often negative in tone and tends to generate negative affect in each spouse (Gotlib & Whiffen, 1989; Kahn, Coyne, & Margolin, 1985; Ruscher & Gotlib, 1988). This negative affect often takes the form of anger and hostility (Goldman & Haaga, 1995). Depressed wives also report more frequent arguments than do nondepressed wives and that their husbands do not understand or respect them (Coyne et al., 2002). As one might expect, the husbands of these depressed wives had complaints of their own. They too reported frequent arguments and complained that their depressed wives blamed them for everything that goes wrong, that they lacked ambition, and that their wives depended too much on them. McCabe and Gotlib (1993) showed that over the course of a marital interaction, the verbal behavior of depressed wives becomes increasingly negative. During conflict resolution interactions, there are more negative messages sent from and directed to the person with depression than from comparable nondepressed married people (Sher & Baucom, 1993). Other investigations of marital interaction find depression to be associated with poor communication during problem-solving interactions (Basco, Prager, Pite, Tamir, & Stephens, 1992), negative self-evaluations and statements of negative well-being (Hautzinger, Linden, & Hoffman, 1982; Linden, Hautzinger, & Hoffman, 1983), verbal aggressiveness (Segrin & Fitzpatrick, 1992), and problems in establishing intimacy (Bullock, Siegel, Weissman, & Paykel, 1972; Basco et al.). Given all of these negative communication behaviors and marital problems, it is easy to understand why depression and martial distress are so powerfully related.

Just as in martially distressed couples, for both husbands and wives, a history of depression is associated with less positive reciprocity in marital interaction (Johnson & Jacob, 2000). In other words, depressed spouses are less likely to follow their partners' positive communication with positive messages of their own. Johnson and Jacob further discovered that when depressed husbands make positive contributions to conversations, their wives respond with negativity. Consistent with the assumptions of systems theory, this pattern illustrates how all members of an interpersonal system might contribute to and maintain a member's depression.

Another relationship issue that could link depression with marital distress is the haste with which young depressed people marry (Gotlib, Lewinsohn, & Seeley, 1998). Results from Gotlib et al.'s extensive longitudinal investigation reveal that depression among adolescents predicts higher rates of marriage among younger women, diminished marital satisfaction, and increased marital disagreements. It is possible that depression motivates young people to seek out marriage, perhaps indiscriminately, as a solution to problems. Not surprisingly, such marriages are often doomed to failure.

What effect does one spouses' depression have on the other spouse? Husbands and wives who are married to a person with depression must deal with a significant burden and often experience clinical levels of depression themselves (e.g., Benazon & Coyne, 2000; Coyne, Kessler, et al., 1987). Living with a depressed person leads to profound family transformations, as spouses and other family members attempt to cope with and understand the symptoms of the disorder (Badger, 1996a, 1996b). Badger (1996a) conceptualized the stages of family transformation brought about by depression as "acknowledging the strangers within" (e.g., searching for reasons and solutions and living two lives), "fighting the battle" (e.g., reducing conflict, seeking social support, and demanding change), and "gaining a new perspective" (e.g., refocusing on others and redesigning the relationship). Before jumping to any conclusions that spouses of people with depression are just the unfortunate recipients of their partner's depressive behaviors, recall the family systems perspective (chap. 2), which suggests that the effects of depression on spouses are not unidirectional. Rather, spouses might introduce issues of their own into the marriage that agitate or maintain the depression. Coyne, Downey, and Boergers (1992) note that "family systems associated with depression can be characterized by a lack of coherence and agency and a general emotional dysregulation. . . . So that negative interactions are not repaired, disagreements are not resolved, negative affect becomes contagious, and there is little chance for negative affect to be transformed into positive affect" (pp. 228, 230). From this perspective, both the depressed individual and his or her spouse are seen as active participants in creating a dysfunctional marriage, each acting on and reacting to the other. For example, sometimes depressed persons and their spouses get caught in dysfunctional vicious cycles of interaction (Biglan et al., 1985; Hops et al., 1987). This research shows that people with depression are often "rewarded" by their spouses for emitting depressive behaviors. In other words, acting depressed tends to inhibit the hostile and irritable behaviors of the spouse (see also Nelson & Beach, 1990). When depressed people learn that their complaints and whining will be met with conciliatory responses from their souse, it is no surprise that they continue to display more depressive behaviors. Even though depression has ill effects on spouses, these same spouses might actually play a role in causing or maintaining the depressive behavior of the afflicted partner.

## Depression and Parent–Child Interactions

Another family role adversely affected by depression is parenthood. Depression has been linked in numerous research studies to dysfunctional parenting behavior (e.g., Hamilton, Jones, & Hammen, 1993; Hammen et al., 1987). Chiariello and Orvaschel (1995) explained that depression interferes with parenting skills by corrupting parents' capacity to relate to their children. In general, the social behavior of depressed parents is characterized by similar negativity, hostility, complaining, and poor interpersonal problem solving that are associated with their other relationships. The communication between depressed mothers and their children is more negative and less positive than that of nondepressed mothers (Hamilton et al.). Family interactions with a depressed father are marked by *positivity suppression,* that is, the tendency for a positive message (e.g., agree, approve, smile and laugh) by one family member to be met with either a negative (e.g., criticize, disagree, and put down) or problem-solving (e.g., question, command, and solution) message by other family members (Jacob & Johnson, 2001).

Children of depressed mothers typically exhibit a behavioral pattern indicative of rejection. During interaction with their depressed parents, young children express negative affect, are generally tense and irritable, spend less time looking at their parent, and appear less content than are children who interact with their nondepressed parents (e.g., Cohn, Campbell, Matias, & Hopkins, 1990; Field, 1984). This agitation is at least partly due to the fact that parents with depression are notoriously unresponsive to their young children during interaction. Children's irritability might be an attempt to capture their depressed parent's attention. Given what is known about the parenting behavior of people with depression, it is perhaps understandable that the children of depressed parents are at a much higher risk for behavioral, cognitive, and emotional dysfunction than those of nondepressed parents (e.g., Lee & Gotlib, 1991; Whiffen & Gotlib, 1989; see Downey & Coyne, 1990, and Gelfand & Teti, 1990, for reviews). It is common for children of depressed parents to also experience depression (Hammen et al., 1987; Warner, Weissman, Fendrich, Wickramarante, & Moreau, 1992). In fact, children are over 4 times more likely to experience depression if they have a depressed parent than if neither of their parents are depressed (Nomura, Wickramarante, Warner, Mufson, & Weissman, 2002). Normura et al. note that children with a depressed parent are also more likely to have been exposed to low family cohesion and affectionless control (i.e., low caring and warmth coupled with overprotectiveness). Naturally, these aversive family dynamics could contribute to the increased risk for depression in offspring. As Jacob and Johnson plainly stated, "family communication could be one of the channels promoting the increased risk of depression among children of depressed parents" (p. 39).

## Depression and Family of Origin Experiences

Aversive family experiences during the formative years predispose people to developing depression later in life. Many people with depression seem to have experienced difficulties in their families when growing up—more so than what would be expected by chance alone. People who are depressed typically describe their family of origin as rejecting (Lewinsohn & Rosenbaum, 1987) and uncaring (Gotlib, Mount, Cordy, & Whiffen, 1988; Rodriguez et al., 1996). Reports of low parental care coupled with overprotection are common among people with depression (Parker, 1983; Sheeber, Hops, & Davis, 2001). Parker found depressed outpatients to be 3.4 times more likely than matched control subjects to have at least one parent who exhibited low care coupled with high protection, or "affectionless control." High levels of conflict are also evident in the family backgrounds of many people with depression (Gilman, Kawachi, Fitzmaurice, & Buka, 2003; Meyerson, Long, Miranda, & Marx, 2002; Sheeber et al.). Very low or very high levels of family cohesion, to the point of enmeshment, also predispose people to develop depression (Jewell & Stark, 2003; Meyerson et al.). One particularly noxious family communication pattern occurs when the father acts to maintain high conformity in the family and the mother communicates high expectations. This family interaction pattern is predictive of suicidal ideation in young adults (Miller & Day, 2002), an obvious indicator of their depression. The lack of available social support from family members is also associated with depression (Segrin, 2003). In addition, the experience of physical and sexual abuse as a child dramatically increases the risk for developing depression later in life (Andrews, 1995; Brown, Cohen, Johnson, & Smailes, 1999; Meyerson et al.). Understandably, some people who are currently depressed might recall their childhood experiences in the family more negatively than what they really were. However, the evidence of troubled family of origin experiences is too pervasive to simply dismiss these research findings to an artifact of memory bias. For many people, distressed family of origin experiences are at least a distal cause of their depression, if not *the* proximal cause.

According to the social skills deficit hypothesis (Lewinsohn, 1974; Segrin, 2000) people who lack adequate social skills are at risk for developing depression because of their inability to create positive social experiences and avoid negative social experiences. One of the primary environments in which children learn communication skills is the family of origin (Burleson, Delia, & Applegate, 1995; Burleson & Kunkel, 2002). Consequently, parents who fail to properly teach or model effective communication skills to their children might inadvertently make those children vulnerable to subsequent depression. Fortunately, by early adulthood most children's social skills develop independently of their parents (Segrin, 1994) so this vulnerability need not be long-lasting.

## LONELINESS

Loneliness is a discrepancy between a person's desired and achieved level of social interaction (Peplau, Russell, & Heim, 1979). In other words, people who are lonely long for more and better social relationships than what they perceive to be available. Even though loneliness is not formally recognized as a psychiatric disorder, it is a psychosocial problem that can be very distressing. Because of its comparability to problems such as depression and its potential role in other problems such as alcoholism and schizophrenia, we briefly examine the role of family interaction in loneliness.

In general, loneliness is negatively associated with perceived social support from the family (Perlman & Rook, 1987; Segrin, 2003) as well as family cohesiveness (Rich & Bonner, 1987). However, within certain subpopulations, family social support does little to ameliorate feelings of loneliness. Young adults, for example, are keen to develop intimate friendships. Social support from family members can do little to replace interactions with peers. In fact, Jones and Moore (1990) found that the more social support students had from their family, the *more* lonely they were. A related finding shows that very close family relationships may be a setup for future loneliness (Andersson et al., 1990). Retrospective reports of early childhood experiences indicate that people who had an excessively close, warm, and nurturing relationship with at least one parent, were significantly *more* lonely as elderly adults than were a group of controls. Andersson et al. concluded that the effects of overinvolvement from parents can be as noxious as underinvolvement or neglect when it comes to producing lonely children. This is due in part to the fact that parental overinvolvement can create a sense of narcissism in the child that leads to interpersonal difficulties later in life. Among older adults, contact with friends and neighbors does much more to prevent loneliness than does contact with family members, especially among adult children (Mullins, Elston, & Gutkowski, 1996; Pinquart & Sorensen, 2001). Contact with family members only seems to play a role in reducing loneliness in later adulthood when elderly people are divorced, widowed, or never married (Pinquart, 2003).

There are certain family processes that seem to be conducive to loneliness. Children's loneliness tends to be positively correlated with their parents' loneliness (Henwood & Solano, 1994; Lobdell & Perlman, 1986), indicating that parents might transmit their loneliness to their children through lack of positive involvement in child-rearing practices. Family conflict is also positively associated with loneliness (Johnson, LaVoie, & Mahoney, 2001; Ponzetti & James, 1997), and healthy family communication and emotional bonding are negatively associated with loneliness in young people (Uruk & Demir, 2003). Family structure can affect loneliness in that children from single-parent and stepfamily households are more lonely than those from intact families (Antognoli-Toland, 2001). Also, Internet addicts beware: Heavy use of the Internet leads to declines in family communication and increases in loneliness (Kraut et al., 1998). It is paradoxical that a technology that allows for greater opportunity for communication should cause greater loneliness, but the displacement of face-to-face interaction appears to have undeniable consequences.

Finally, loneliness is a fairly accurate barometer of marital quality. For the most part, marriage helps protect people from the experience of loneliness, especially when there is good cohesion in the dyad (Olson & Wong, 2001; Stack, 1998). Even when married couples live under austere conditions such as long-term separation due to imprisonment, maintaining a psychological closeness to the spouse can help to prevent loneliness (Segrin & Flora, 2001). However, when marriages go bad, people often become lonely. Recall from chapter 11 that loneliness is the final stage in Gottman's (1994) distance and isolation cascade leading up to marital dissolution. What is particularly distressing about being lonely and married is that it is such a powerful violation of expectations.

# SCHIZOPHRENIA

## Definition

Schizophrenia is a formal thought disorder with various subtypes characterized by symptoms such as bizarre delusions, hallucinations, disorganized speech, grossly disorganized or catatonic behavior, inability to initiate and persist in goal-directed activity, affective flattening, and impoverished and disorganized thinking evident in speech and language behavior (*DSM-IV-TR;* APA, 2000). Such symptoms must be present for at least a month, but in some cases they may persist for years. An important diagnostic criterion for schizophrenia is social and occupational dysfunction.

Schizophrenia was the first mental health problem to attract intense theorizing and research on the role of family interactions. Some used to think that schizophrenia was the result of disturbed family interactions. Today, most scholars feel that troubled family communication patterns interact with preexisting vulnerabilities to cause the disorder and that in some cases family communication influences the course of the disorder. In this section we explore three family communication variables that have been, and continue to be, particularly influential in theory and research on schizophrenia. These are *communication deviance, expressed emotion,* and family *affective style.*

## Communication Deviance

Early research on family interaction and schizophrenia revealed that patients' families often exhibited odd and unfocused styles of interacting with each other. Family members seemed to have difficulty establishing and maintaining a shared focus of attention through their discourse. Out of this early theorizing grew a very influential line of research on communication deviance (Miklowitz, 1994; Wynne, 1981). Wynne theorized that people learn to focus their attention and derive meaning from external stimuli through their interactions, particularly with parents, during the early years of life (Wynne, 1968, 1981). Odd and deviant styles of communication among the parents were presumed to interact with biological predispositions to contribute to thought and communication disturbances in children who were unable to relate to and understand their parents.

The communication in families with a schizophrenic member is characterized by odd, idiosyncratic, illogical, and fragmented language, even when the mentally ill family member is not present. Topics of conversation will often drift or abruptly change direction with a lack of closure. Such interactions are marked by a blurred focus of attention and meaning. This characteristic style of family communication has been labeled "communication deviance" (CD; Singer, Wynne, & Toohey, 1978). Traditionally, CD has been assessed from transcripts of parents' responses to various projective tests such as the Rorschach or Thematic Apperception Test. These call for interpretations of ambiguous images presented on cards. A well-developed coding scheme classifies parents' communication behavior into such categories as *idea fragments, contradictions and retractions,* and *ambiguous references* (Jones, 1977). More recently, scientists have measured CD based on communication during family problem-solving discussions (e.g., Velligan, Funderburg, Giesecke, & Miller, 1995; Velligan et al., 1996). This measure, referred to as interactional communication deviance (ICD) has similar categories. A complete index of the categories and their definitions for both the projective test and family interaction procedures is provided in Tables 13.1 and 13.2.

Research studies indicate that CD is higher in parents of schizophrenia patients than it is in parents of either nonschizophrenic patients or healthy controls (e.g., Miklowitz, 1994; Miklowitz, Goldstein, & Neuchterlein, 1995). This work shows that aspects of parental communication deviance such as idea abandonments, extraneous remarks, and ambiguous references distinguish parents of schizophrenia patients (Miklowitz et al.,

**TABLE 13.1**
Thematic Apperception Test Communication Deviance Scoring System

| Factor | Definition | Examples |
|---|---|---|
| Contorted, Peculiar Language | Off-word usage, peculiar phrases; excessive verbiage | "They're trying to *make a goal of their life.*" <br> "This man is *in the process of thinking of the process of being a doctor.*" |
| Misinterpretations | Gross uncertainty about percepts; attributions of intention in the Thematic Apperception Test (TAT) cards, confusion about stimuli | "Is this a boy or a girl?" <br> "This must be the artist's rendering of societal progression." |
| Flighty Anxiety | Short reaction times; off-task questions and comments | "When do we finish?" |
| Overpersonalized Closure Problems | Stories left hanging; overly personalized associations | "This was me as a child." |
| Faulty Overintellectualization | Unusual task set; complicated words used incorrectly | "He wouldn't do that *facetiously.*" |
| Failure to Integrate Closure Problems | Important perceptual elements ignored; no integration of elements; "I don't know" endings | "These people have nothing to do with each other." |

*Note.* From "Communication Deviance in Families of Schizophrenic and Manic Patients, by D. J. Miklowitz, D. I. Velligan, M. J. Goldstein, K. H. Nuechterlein, M. J. Gitlin, G. Ranlett, & J. A. Doane, 1991, *Journal of Abnormal Psychology, 100,* pp. 163–173. Copyright 1991 by the American Psychological Association. Adapted with permission.

1991). It is intriguing that this distorted form of communication is very similar in style to the communication of the person who actually has schizophrenia.

An exciting development in CD research is the recognition that this form of family communication can predict the onset of schizophrenia. Research by Goldstein and his colleagues indicates that parental CD often precedes onset and is therefore an excellent predictor of schizophrenia among adolescents who have yet to develop the disorder (Goldstein, 1981, 1987; Goldstein & Strachan, 1987). In one such study parents from families with a moderately disturbed teenager each responded to Thematic Apperception Test (TAT) protocols, from which measures of CD were taken (Goldstein, 1985). High CD in the parents was strongly associated with the appearance of schizophrenia-spectrum disorders in some of the family offspring at 15-year follow-up. In a similar study, disturbed high-risk adolescents were followed over a period of 5 years (Doane, West, Goldstein, Rodnick, & Jones, 1981). By the end of the study, approximately 10% of those whose parents who were low or intermediate in CD went on to develop schizophrenia, whereas 56% of those whose parents were high in CD developed schizophrenia.

Family CD also appears to influence the course of schizophrenia. For example, Velligan et al. (1996) followed a group of schizophrenia patients and their parents for 1 year. During

**TABLE 13.2**
Interactional Communication Deviance Scoring System

| ICD Code | Definition | Examples |
|---|---|---|
| Idea Fragments | Speaker abandons ideas or abruptly ends comments without returning to them | "But the thing is as I said, *there's got* . . . you can't drive in the alley." |
| Unintelligible Remarks | Comments are incomprehensible in the context of conversation | "Well, that's just *probably a real closing spot.*" |
| Contradictions or Retractions | Speaker contradicts earlier statements or presents mutually inconsistent alternatives | "No, that's right, she does." |
| Ambiguous References | Speaker uses sentences with no clear object of discussion | "Kid stuff that's one thing but *something else* is different too." |
| Extraneous Remarks | Speaker makes off-task comments | "I wonder how many rooms they have like this?" |
| Tangential Inappropriate Responses | Non sequitur replies or speaker does not acknowledge others' statements | Patient: "Sometimes I work on the back yard." Mother: "Let's talk about your schoolwork." |
| Odd Word Usage or Odd Sentence Construction | Speaker uses words in odd ways, leaves out words, puts words out of order, uses many unnecessary words | "It's gonna be *up and downwards along the process all the while* to go through something like this." |

*Note.* From "Communication Deviance in Families of Schizophrenic and Manic Patients," by D. J. Miklowitz, D. I. Velligan, M. J. Goldstein, K. H. Neuchterlein, M. J. Gitlin, G. Ranlett, & J. A. Doane, 1991, *Journal of Abnormal Psychology, 100,* pp. 163–173. Copyright 1991 by the American Psychological Association. Adapted by permission.

the study, slightly over 50% of the patients had experienced a relapse. Parental CD at the time of the patient's discharge was significantly higher in the families of those who relapsed versus those who did not. However, looking back to the assessment of parental CD at Time 1, there were no differences among parents of those who relapsed versus those who did not. As it turns out, the parents of those patients who relapsed exhibited a dramatic increase in their CD over the course of the study. This investigation indicates that returning to a home with high CD will increase the likelihood of relapse.

Parental communication deviance functions as a type of stressor that affects the course and outcome of schizophrenia. When parents' communication is particularly amorphous and peculiar, children may become confused and uncertain about even basic and fundamental social realities. This confusion undoubtedly has functional significance in the course of the schizophrenia as it is so central in the constellation of symptoms that make up the disorder. The communication of high CD parents raises substantial questions about their own mental health. It is therefore understandable that when discharged into the care of such individuals, their offspring remain at risk for future relapse.

# EXPRESSED EMOTION

Family expressed emotion (EE; Brown, Monck, Carstairs, & Wing, 1962; Vaughn & Leff, 1976) is a pattern of criticism, overinvolvement, overprotectiveness, excessive attention, and emotional reactivity that creates a vulnerability to relapse and poor social adjustment among schizophrenia patients (see Hooley & Hiller, 1997, 1998, for reviews). EE represents an attitude of criticism and emotional overinvolvement on the part of the parent expressed during an interview. EE is measured through the frequency of critical remarks, degree of hostility, and the degree of emotional overinvolvement expressed by a family member during an interview.

Vaughn and Leff (1981) described EE as a combination of four behavioral characteristics: intrusiveness, anger and acute distress and anxiety, overt blame and criticism of the patient, and an intolerance of the patient's symptoms (Vaughn & Leff, 1981). One of Vaughn and Leff's early studies revealed that patients who returned to a home with high EE relatives exhibited a 9-month relapse rate of 51%, whereas only 13% of those who returned to a low EE family relapsed (Vaughn & Leff, 1976). Rosenfarb and his colleagues examined the functioning of a sample of young and recently discharged schizophrenia patients who returned to either high or low expressed emotion families (Rosenfarb, Goldstein, Mintz, & Nuechterlein, 1995). Recently discharged patients living in high EE families exhibited more odd and disruptive behavior during a family interaction than did patients from low EE households. Relatives in the high EE households were more critical when the patients verbalized unusual thoughts than were members of low EE families. Thus, there appears to be a vicious circle in high EE family relations: Parents respond to the patient with a lot of criticism because patients from these households appear to exhibit more bizarre and disruptive behavior than do patients from low EE homes. It is likely that the negative reactions they receive from their families contribute further to the potential for relapse among patients. Indeed, a review of 25 studies on family EE indicated a 50% relapse rate, over a period of 9 to 12 months, among schizophrenia patients discharged to a high EE family, but only 21% among those with low EE relatives (Bebbington & Kuipers, 1994). These findings indicate that the odds of relapse are increased by approximately 2.5:1 for those patients discharged to high versus low EE relatives

In addition to being a useful and reliable predictor of relapse, EE may also be fruitfully understood as a familial risk indicator for schizophrenia (Miklowitz, 1994). Even people with no history of schizophrenia are at elevated risk for developing the disorder if reared in an environment characterized by high EE. In each case one could interpret the family EE as a stressor on the patient (Hooley & Hiller, 1998).

## Affective Style

Affective style (AS) is a measure of the verbal behavior of family members during discussion of a conflict-laden issue with the patient present. AS represents the family members' actual verbal behaviors when interacting with the patient. It could be thought of as the behavioral manifestation of expressed emotion. Although AS and EE are closely related and perhaps overlapping constructs, a distinct body of literature exists on AS indicating that like EE it is often predictive of relapse among schizophrenia patients.

Affective style is typically measured from a series of brief discussions about a current unresolved problem in the family (Doane et al., 1981). As might be expected, these conversations pull for substantial emotional expression. The conversations are then transcribed and family members' speech is classified into the categories of support (e.g., "I want you to know I care about you"), criticism (e.g., "You have an ugly, arrogant attitude"), guilt induction (e.g., "You cause our family an awful lot of trouble"), and intrusiveness, which implies knowledge of the child's thoughts ("You enjoy being mean to others"; Doane et al.). Based on this coding, families are classified into one of three AS profiles: benign, intermediate, or poor. Benign AS families display a lack of negative behaviors (i.e., personal criticism, guilt induction, and critical or neutral intrusiveness) during their interactions. Intermediate AS families are those who express some negative but some positive speech behaviors (i.e., primary support) during the family discussion. Poor (also referred to as negative) AS families are those in which one or both parents exhibits negative verbal behaviors but no positive verbal behaviors.

In one of the premier AS studies (Doane et al., 1981), 65 families of high-risk, disturbed but not psychotic, adolescents participated in the family conflict discussion. Then the adolescents where assessed 5 years later. Only 8% of those with a benign family AS profile at Time 1 received a schizophrenia spectrum diagnosis at Time 2. Among those with an intermediate family AS profile at Time 1, 50% were diagnosed at Time 2. This figure increased to 59% among those with poor AS profile families. A comparable 15-year longitudinal study by Goldstein (1985) revealed no cases of schizophrenia developing over the course of the study among people from benign families. However, almost all of the schizophrenia cases emerged in the context of a family where one or both parents were high in EE and had a negative AS. Clearly, family AS is a marker of risk for schizophrenia.

In addition to predicting the development of schizophrenia AS may also predict relapse. In one study, schizophrenia patients discharged to families with benign AS profiles had a 40% rehospitalization rate over the next 12 months, whereas those who returned to negative AS families had twice the rate (83%) of rehospitalization (Doane & Becker, 1993). Even more striking are the findings for AS in concert with medication compliance: Patients with negative AS families and noncompliance with medication exhibited a 100% rehospitalization rate, compared with only 17% among those with a benign family AS profile and medication compliance.

Family AS appears to have a relationship with both the onset and the course of schizophrenia. Like CD or EE, a negative family AS must be stressful for children on the recieving end of the criticism, intrusiveness, and guilt induction. For many at-risk children with preexisting vulnerabilities, these family communication behaviors might push them over the psychological edge into full-blown mental illness, or relapse into an active episode of schizophrenia.

## EATING DISORDERS

### Definition

The American Psychiatric Association recognizes two distinct subtypes of eating disorders: anorexia nervosa and bulimia nervosa (APA, 2000). The defining features of anorexia nervosa include a refusal to maintain a normal body weight, an intense fear of gaining weight, and a disturbance in body-image perception. Bulimia nervosa is defined by recurrent episodes of uncontrolled binge eating, inappropriate compensatory behaviors to control weight gain (e.g., self-induced vomiting and misuse of laxatives or diuretics), and an undue influence of body shape and weight on self-evaluations. The primary difference between the two disorders is that individuals with bulimia nervosa are able to maintain their body weight at or above normally prescribed levels, whereas people suffering from anorexia nervosa remain significantly underweight. Like most mental health problems, there is no single cause of eating disorders. In the past 25 years, family relationships and communication patterns have been a major emphasis of researchers' efforts to understand eating disorders (Kog & Vandereycken, 1985; Vandereycken, Kog, & Vanderlinden, 1989; Waller & Calam, 1994; Wonderlich, 1992). This research shows that there are multiple destructive family processes that go hand in hand with eating disorders.

## Dysfunctional Family of Origin Interaction Patterns

The noted family systems theorist Salvador Minuchin was at that forefront of efforts to understand the origins of eating disorders through a focus on family interaction patterns (Minuchin, Rosman, & Baker, 1978). Minuchin and his associates observed dysfunctional patterns of interaction among families with an anorexia nervosa patient that often minimized conflict and adaptability. Family systems researchers and clinicians see eating disorders as built into and around family relations. In a family systems perspective, disordered eating is understood to be caused and maintained by family interpersonal behavior, which itself is assumed to be influenced by the disordered eating of one of its members. In this section we highlight some of the many different family interaction variables that appear to play a role in eating disorders.

Systems-oriented researchers have emphasized family adaptability and cohesion as two dimensions of family relationships that are crucial to healthy family functioning, provided that neither are too extreme (Olson, 1993). People with eating disorders are often reared in environments of low *family cohesion* (Blouin, Zuro, & Blouin, 1990; Latzer, Hochdorf, Bachar, & Canetti, 2002; Steiger, Puentes-Neuman, & Leung, 1991; Waller, Slade, & Calam, 1990). Although low family cohesion is often reported by young people with eating disorders as well as their parents (e.g., Attie & Brooks-Gunn, 1989; Waller et al.), eating disordered children give lower ratings to their family's cohesiveness than their parents do (Dare, Le Grange, Eisler, & Rutherford, 1994). Regardless of which family member's perception is actually "correct," the fact that the parent and child with an eating disorder differ in their view of the family's cohesiveness says something about these family relationships.

Investigations of *family adaptability* have yielded less consistent results than those of cohesion. Some evidence indicates a negative association between family adaptability and symptoms of eating disorders (e.g., Dare et al., 1994; Waller et al., 1990). However, a collection of studies revealed more chaos, less organization, more inconsistent discipline, greater role reversal, and more poorly defined boundaries in families of girls with eating disorders or symptoms of eating disorders (Humphrey, 1986; Ross & Gill, 2002; Rowa, Kerig, & Geller, 2001). All of these patterns are suggestive of excessive adaptability. As in the case of cohesion, parents of young women with eating disorders do not feel that boundary violations are a problem in the family, in sharp contrast to perceptions of their daughters who readily report boundary problems (Rowa et al.). In most studies, people with eating disorders seem to have been raised in a family that is marked by extreme levels of adaptability (either too much or too little), indicating potentially detrimental family relations.

Research on family interaction in schizophrenia identified a pattern of criticism, over-involvement, overprotectiveness, and emotional reactivity in the discourse of family members related to a person with schizophrenia. This pattern of behavior is called *family expressed emotion* and it appears to also be an important family process variable in eating disorders (e.g., Hedlund, Fichter, Quadflieg, & Brandl, 2003; LeGrange, Eisler, Dare, & Hodes, 1992; van Furth et al., 1996). The van Furth et al. investigation indicated that maternal expressed emotion during family interactions with eating disordered patients was a powerful predictor of patients' eventual outcomes and responses to therapy. Mothers' openly critical comments during a family interaction assessment were a better predictor of patients' outcomes than a host of other predictors such as body weight prior to onset of the disorder, duration of illness, body mass index, and age at onset. Family expressed emotion may be problematic in part because it is associated with high levels of conflict and poorer levels of organization in families of people with eating disorders (Hedlund et al.). The criticism element of expressed emotion is evident in studies that show that people at high risk for eating disorders tend to live with parents who are very critical, and they are often teased by their parents and siblings about their weight (MacBrayer, Smith, McCarthy, Demos, & Simmons, 2001; Polivy & Herman, 2002).

People with eating disorders sometimes experience *inappropriate parental pressure* (Horesh et al., 1996). Horesh et al. describe this phenomenon as "gender-inappropriate pressure, age-inappropriate pressure, and pressures inappropriate to the child's abilities . . . the adolescents felt that they had been forced into an exaggerated feminine style of behavior, that their parents had discussed topics (such as parental sex) before the adolescents were prepared to deal with such subjects, and that the adolescents had been made to engage in activities which reflected their parents' ambitions rather than their own" (p. 925). Horesh et al. hypothesized that the pressures for achievement at inappropriate developmental levels may lead to a counteraction from the child that is manifest in symptoms of eating disorders. Related to this, Levine's (1996) study of eating disordered families found that the family environments were characterized by a strong emphasis on achievement and perfection and overconcern with beauty, appearance, and thinness. It has been suggested that in some cases parents might project their own ambitions and ideals onto their children, which sets up the struggles for control that contribute to disordered eating (Segrin, 2001b).

It is fairly common to find *stressful mealtime or food-related communication* in the family backgrounds of people with eating disorders. For example, the family might bicker a lot during meals or have very strict rules about meals, such as when they eat and how much each person is allowed to eat (Crowther, Kichler, Sherwood, & Kuhnert, 2002; Worobey, 2002). This type of communication and these family rules have at least two pathologic consequences. First, they can teach children to obsess and ruminate about food, contributing to a preoccupation with food and eating which is common to various eating disorders. Second, this could become a bizarre form of classical conditioning in which the association of food and conflict ultimately leads to feeling stressed out about food, even when the family conflict is not present. Dysfunctional attempts to cope with this stress might entail careful management and control of eating.

Other family process variables that have been implicated in eating disorders include *poor family problem solving* (McGrane & Carr, 2002), *disturbed affective expression* (Garfinkel et al., 1983; Waller, Calam, & Slade, 1989), *inconsistent parental reward and punishment of disordered eating behaviors* (Prescott & Le Poire, 2002), lack of *parental care* (Webster & Palmer, 2000), excessive *parental overprotectivness and intrusiveness* (Calam, Waller, Slade, & Newton, 1990; Rhodes & Kroger, 1992; Rorty, Yager, Rossotto, & Buckwalter, 2000), and excessive *parental control* (Ahmad, Waller, & Verduyen, 1994; Wonderlich, Ukestad, & Perzacki, 1994). This later variable has particular significance in that the symptoms of eating disorders may be an overt manifestation of a struggle for control between a child and parent. Experts in adolescent health have developed a questionnaire measure of family communication with items such as "How often do your parents talk or share an activity with you at night?", "How much do you feel you can tell your mother or father about your problems?", and "When you do something wrong, does she or he talk with you and help you understand why it is wrong?" (Neumark-Sztainer, Story, Hannan, Beuhring, & Resnick, 2000). Results of the Newmark-Sztainer et al. investigation indicate that low levels of this sort of *family communication* are also associated with eating disorders in adolescents.

The rather paradoxical nature of some of these family processes in eating disorders is nicely illustrated in a study of parenting conducted by Humphrey (1989). Specifically, Humphrey found that parents of anorexia patients were simultaneously more nurturing and comforting but also more ignoring and neglecting of their daughters in comparison to parents of healthy controls or bulimia patients. In contrast, the bulimia patients and their parents showed signs of hostile enmeshment. Humphrey argues that these mixed messages create ambivalence about separation for the anorectic daughter. Another somewhat paradoxical tendency among parents of eating disordered girls is the combination of excessive control, overprotectiveness, and intrusiveness coupled with minimal caring and affection (e.g., Palmer, Oppenheimer, & Marshall, 1988; Latzer et al., 2002; Rhodes & Kroger, 1992; Rorty et al., 2000).

## Parent–Child Interactions

In chapter 2 we discuss social learning theory and its explanation for how children can learn behaviors by observing others perform the behaviors, along with their attendant consequences. Even a casual analysis of mother–daughter interactions in families where there is an eating disorder suggests that some daughters learn disordered eating behaviors from their mothers. For example, Hill, Weaver, and Blundell (1990) found a strong correlation between mothers' dietary restraint and that of their adolescent daughters. In another investigation, mothers' satisfaction with their body sizes was strongly correlated with that of their daughters (Evans & Le Grange, 1995). It is no surprise that this particular sample of mothers had a history of eating disorders. In a very carefully controlled study, Stein et al. (1999) discovered that 26% of the mothers of young women with bulimia nervosa had a lifetime diagnosis of some form of eating disorder. This rate is significantly higher than that of mothers of women with no history of eating disorders (see also Moorhead et al., 2003). Of course family studies confound the effects of genes and environment; thus, it is not entirely clear whether the association between maternal eating disorders is the result of genetic contributions from the mother or of the social environment that she also contributes to. Nevertheless, the data are at least consistent with a social learning effect for disordered eating.

Investigations of mothers' attitudes toward their daughters' body image arouse further suspicion about the role of some mothers in eating disorders. Mothers of eating disordered girls in one study thought that their daughters ought to lose significantly more weight than mothers of a group of noneating disordered girls did (Pike & Rodin, 1991). These same mothers rated their daughters as significantly less attractive than the daughters rated themselves. This is astonishing, given that most people with eating disorders have a negative body image and probably do not see themselves as very attractive. Related findings show that mothers of bulimics were more controlling and held higher expectations for their daughters than were control mothers (Sights & Richards, 1984). It is not difficult to imagine the effect of a mother who feels that her daughter is unattractive and needs to lose weight, and who holds perhaps unrealistically high standards for her daughter. This sort of behavior can grossly deteriorate the self-esteem and self-image of a developing adolescent. When this is coupled with parental modeling of restrictive eating, the "solution" or prescribed course of action becomes obvious. Fortunately some of the same modes of communication by which mothers convey dysfunctional views of dieting and body image, such as modeling and direct verbal discussion, are also used by some mothers to teach their daughters healthy attitudes toward body and dieting (Ogle & Damhorst, 2003).

Research on parent–child interactions and eating disorders has focused almost exclusively on mothers. In a rare investigation of father–daughter relationships, it is apparent that fathers can also play a role in the experience of these disorders. When fathers encourage open communication without making strong demands for conformity or resolve conflicts in a collaborative and compromising style, their daughters are less likely to exhibit symptoms of eating disorders (Botta & Dumlao, 2002).

## Childhood Abuse and Eating Disorders

When family members abuse their own children they communicate a powerful message of devaluation and disrespect for appropriate boundaries (see chap. 15). These messages are conveyed more clearly and dramatically through abusive conduct than any verbal behavior could ever match. Reports of childhood sexual abuse are relatively common in the research literature on family histories of people with eating disorders. The gross boundary violation that this behavior represents ought to be a clear signal that something is terribly wrong in the family system. This abuse often causes guilt, confusion, repulsion, and distrust of others. For many people, the escape from, or control of, these powerful feelings is sought in restrictive eating patterns or binging and purging.

There is some evidence to suggest that histories of sexual abuse are more common among those with eating disorders, especially bulimia, than what would be expected by chance alone (Smolak & Murnen, 2002). Some estimates indicate that rates of childhood

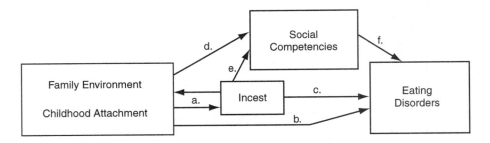

FIG. 13.1.    Mallinckrodt et al.'s Theoretical Model of Dysfunctional Family Environments, Sexual Abuse, and Eating Disorders.

*Note.* From "Co-Occurrence of Eating Disorders and Incest: The Role of Attachment, Family Environment, and Social Competencies," by B. Mallinckrodt, B. A. McCreary, & A. K. Robertson, 1995, *Journal of Counseling Psychology, 42,* pp. *178–186.* Copyright 1995 by the American Psychological Association. Adapted with permission.

sexual abuse run as high as 70% among eating disorder patients (Oppenheimer, Howells, Palmer, & Chaloner, 1985). Another study of eating disorder patients found that 65% had experienced physical abuse, 28% had been sexually abused, and 23% had been raped (Root & Fallon, 1988). However, other studies indicate that the rate of sexual abuse among people with eating disorders does not differ from that of the general population (e.g., Connors & Morse, 1993; Lacey, 1990). What conclusion can be drawn from the literature on childhood sexual abuse and eating disorders? First, some of the variability in these prevalence estimates can be explained by wildly discrepant definitions of "sexual abuse" that different researchers employ. Second, sexual abuse appears to be more common when researchers study people seeking clinical treatment for eating disorders compared to people in the general population who have symptoms of eating disorders.

How does childhood abuse contribute to the development of eating disorders? Many feel that sexual abuse creates a vulnerability to development of eating disorders (e.g., Connors & Morse, 1993; Vanderlinden & Vandereycken, 1996). For example, a theoretical model developed by Mallinckrodt, McCreary, and Robertson (1995) proposes that childhood sexual abuse, particularly incest, contributes to (and results from) dysfunctional family environments and attachments between the parent and child (see Figure 13.1). The combination of these poor family environment variables and the sexual abuse is thought to inhibit the development of social competencies in the child. These authors define social competencies as a sense of self-efficacy, an ability to communicate emotional needs, an ability to experience intimacy, and the capacity to use relationships with other people to regulate negative emotions. It is the failure to develop these basic social competencies that links sexual abuse with eating disorders. The eating disorder becomes the means by which the child develops a sense of self-efficacy and affective regulation, albeit through dysfunctional noninterpersonal means. The results of Mallinckrodt et al.'s investigation provide compelling evidence for the validity of their model. For example, they observed an eating disorder rate of 39% among incest survivors, but only 17% among those with no childhood abuse. As an aside, the rate of eating disorders was 47% in their clinical sample of incest survivors, and 24% in the student sample of incest survivors, again suggesting higher rates of abuse in the background of clinical samples. Those incest survivors in this study who reported little emotional warmth and expressiveness from their mothers were most likely to have developed an eating disorder. Furthermore, incest survivors scored lower on a number of social competence indicators compared to those with no history of childhood sexual abuse. Perhaps the cornerstone hypothesis of Mallinckrodt et al.'s model is that incestuous family environments do not provide a context adequate for the development of social competencies and skills. This "social skills" deficit hypothesis is prevalent in the mental illness literature more generally. However, this model is unique in postulating an origin of those social skills deficits, namely, a dysfunctional family environment that includes sexual abuse.

Efforts to precisely understand how childhood sexual abuse factors into the development of eating disorders are hindered by the fact that such abuse is hopelessly confounded with dysfunctional family environments (Connors & Morse, 1993; Kinzl, Traweger, Guenther, & Biebl, 1994; Schmidt, Humfress, & Treasure, 1997). The family that either perpetrates or tolerates the sexual abuse of its children surely has other drastic problems. For example, physical and emotional abuse and neglect often occur in a family environment marked by very low cohesion (Mazzeo & Espelage, 2002). These other problems may be sufficient on their own to contribute to the development of eating disorders in the family's affected children. However, two vital studies on this issue showed that even after controlling for family psychosocial factors (e.g., family communication, parental monitoring, and parental caring), youths who reported sexual abuse were still at significantly increased risk for disordered eating (Fonseca, Ireland, & Resnick, 2002; Neumark-Sztainer et al., 2000). Incidentally, Fonseca and her associates found that positive communication functioned as a protective factor to decrease the likelihood of disordered eating and dieting. At this time childhood sexual abuse appears to be a risk factor for the later development of eating disorders. This relationship may be mediated by the poor social skills that result from a history of such abuse.

## ALCOHOLISM

### Definition

Substance use disorders are divided into two groups: substance dependence and substance abuse (APA, 2000). *Substance dependence* involves a maladaptive pattern of substance use, associated with symptoms such as tolerance (the need for increased amounts to achieve the desired effect); withdrawal (physical and psychological distress associated with cessation); taking more of the substance than intended; disruption of social, occupational, or recreational activities as a result of the substance use; and continuation despite awareness of problems associated with the substance use (APA). The primary feature of *substance abuse* is a maladaptive pattern of substance use that is associated with adverse effects. These adverse effects include, for example, failure to fulfill important occupational, social, or domestic roles, using the substance in such a way as to create physical hazards or legal problems, and continued use of the substance despite interpersonal problems that are caused or exacerbated by its use (APA). Alcoholism is a specific class of the more general diagnosis of substance dependence. The term *alcoholism* is generally used to refer to *alcohol dependence* or *alcohol abuse*. Defining features of alcohol dependence are the same as those for substance dependence more generally. What distinguishes alcohol dependence from alcohol abuse is the presence of tolerance, withdrawal, and alcohol-related compulsive behavior in the person who is dependent on alcohol. Unfortunately some people use alcohol or other drugs to cope with the very problems that their heavy use creates. Like so many other psychological problems, alcoholism and substance abuse often affect and are affected by family interactions. In this section of the chapter we focus our discussion on family interaction and alcoholism. However, in chapter 14 we address the issue of adolescent substance abuse and family interaction. We reserve that discussion for chapter 14 because the sort of substance abuse that is often studied in adolescents might be more of a physical health risk than an indicator of a mental health problem.

## Alcoholism and Family Interactions

Family systems theory has been the dominant approach to understanding the role of family interactions in alcoholism (Steinglass, 1985). Recall from Chapter 2 that family systems theory locates causes and consequents of problematic behavior in the larger family system in which it is embedded. In this case, a family systems theorist would ask how the family's interactions contribute to or enable the problem drinking behavior, as well as how the problematic drinking affects the family's interactions. Applying family systems concepts to alcoholism, Steinglass (1985) noted that some families organize their lives around alcohol, just as other families might organize their lives around children or work.

The effects of alcohol and alcoholism on family interaction are not entirely straight-forward and certainly not uniformly negative. For example, in an early investigation of alcoholics and their family members (Steinglass, Weiner, & Mendelson, 1971), the expression of previously inhibited positive feelings among family members became especially pronounced during drinking periods. Apparently, when some alcoholics are drinking they become more friendly and outgoing toward their family members. Other research findings show that interactions of alcoholics and their families are actually more patterned, organized, and predictable while the alcoholic member is intoxicated (Steinglass, 1979, 1981a; Steinglass & Robertson, 1983). This prompted Steinglass et al. to suggest that there is an "alcoholic system" in some families in which drinking is an integral part of the family system that actually maintains and stabilizes the family. After viewing and rating a videotape of their own interaction, even in the absence of actual drinking, mothers and adolescent children in alcoholic families rated family members as less anxious and their interactions as more friendly than those of nonalcoholic families (Schweitzer, Wilks, & Callan, 1992). Findings such as these suggest that alcohol consumption can have paradoxically positive effects on some family interactions. However, as one might suppose, there is a little more to the story.

Even though there is clear evidence that alcohol consumption sometimes leads to positivity in alcoholics' family interactions, there are also negative effects on the family associated with drinking. For example, family scientist Theodore Jacob had families with an alcoholic father discuss items from various questionnaire inventories while drinking or not drinking (Jacob, Ritchey, Cvitkovic, & Blane, 1981). During their family discussions, the alcoholic families expressed more negative affect during the drink versus no-drink conditions. The nature of nonalcoholics' family interactions was not affected by the drinking conditions. Parental alcoholism can also have adverse effects on parent–child interactions. For example, alcoholic parents appear less sensitive to their infants during the free-play sessions (Eiden, Chavez, & Leonard, 1999). Alcoholic fathers in the Eiden et al. study made fewer verbalizations, expressed more negative emotion, and were less responsive to their infants compared to nonalcoholic fathers. Eiden et al. discovered that many of these ill effects on parent–child interactions could be explained by the alcoholic parents' depression.

As research on family interactions and alcoholism became more fine grained, scientists began to realize that there were different types of problem-drinking patters that had different effects on family interactions. Jacob classified alcoholics according to whether they were *episodic* or *steady* drinkers (Jacob, Krahn, & Leonard, 1991). Episodic drinkers tend to alternate between periods of sobriety and binge drinking. During family interactions, episodic drinkers exhibited more negativity than steady drinkers. In addition, Jacob's research team found evidence of more positive behaviors from children and greater problem solving by both children and mothers in the family interactions of steady versus episodic drinkers. It appears then that the episodic pattern of problem drinking has the most deleterious effects on family communication patters.

Just as there are different types of problem-drinking patterns, there are different phases of alcoholism that the entire family goes through. Steinglass (1981b) proposed a "family alcohol phase" model to describe this phenomenon. Accordingly, families move through various phases in conjunction with the alcoholic's drinking behavior. The *stable-wet* phase is marked by consistent drinking, whereas the *stable-dry* phase is marked by general abstinence. The family is in a *transitional* phase when the problem drinker enters a period of abstinence, or when a period of abstinence ends with episodes of drinking. Steinglass found that in the stable-wet phase, families maintain the greatest distance, interacting only for purposeful reasons, while exhibiting midrange variability in their interactions. Families in the stable-dry phase exhibited a great deal of content variability in their interactions and midrange distance regulation. Finally, those families in the transitional phase showed a decrease in distance regulation, manifesting physical closeness, with a slight decrease in the content variability of their interactions. A 2-year longitudinal study suggests that the stable-wet families are the most likely of the three to dissolve their marriages, particularly among those who exhibited little engagement with each other during home observation of family interactions (Steinglass, Tislenko, Reiss, 1985).

## Alcoholism and Marital Interaction

Alcoholism has a powerful and unavoidable impact on marital communication and relationships. Alcoholics and their spouses clearly do not see eye to eye when it comes to family relations. In one study, alcoholics described themselves as more loving, affectionate, and understanding than non-alcoholics did (Neeliyara, Nagalakshmi, & Ray, 1989). However, their spouses sharply disagreed with the alcoholics' self-perceptions, perceiving them as less loving and more aggressive. In the areas of affective involvement (e.g., "we are too self-centered") and behavior control (e.g., "anything goes in our family") alcoholics and their spouses showed very low agreement (McKay, Maisto, Beattie, Longabaugh, & Noel, 1993). These differing perceptions hold considerable potential to produce martial distress.

It is sometimes the case that alcoholism is associated with a propensity for physical aggressiveness in males and in such cases marital interactions are particularly negative in tone (Murphy & O'Farrell, 1997). When discussing a marital problem, couples with an aggressive and alcoholic husband showed a higher rate of negative communication behaviors (e.g., blaming, criticizing, and put downs) and more negative reciprocity in their communication compared to couples with a nonaggressive alcoholic husband.

Negativity in marital interaction also seems to be prevalent when the wife is alcoholic. In a rare comparison of female and male alcoholics, couples with a female alcoholic were found to be more negative in their conversations than those with a male alcoholic or no alcoholic, so long as they were not drinking (Haber & Jacob, 1997). When they drank, differences from male-alcoholic couples disappeared. For concordant couples (both husband and wife alcoholic), negativity in communication behaviors escalated when they were allowed to drink. This later finding suggests that at least one nonalcoholic spouse may be a prerequisite for adaptive outcomes associated with drinking. A related study showed greater negativity during a 10-minute conflict resolution discussion among maritally distressed couples in which the wife was alcoholic, compared to nondistressed, nonalcoholic couples (Kelly, Halford, & Young, 2002). Among these distressed couples with a female alcoholic, the men had high rates of negative encoding behaviors (e.g., criticize and offer negative solution), but not negative decoding behaviors (e.g., disagree, justify, and withdraw). In contrast, their alcoholic wives had high rates of negative decoding behaviors but not encoding behaviors. Kelly and associates concluded that in married couples with a female alcoholic, the typical sex role pattern is reversed: It is the male who demands and the female who withdraws. This is a very understandable pattern of communication when the wife is alcoholic and her husband is not. With that said, there is at least some evidence that alcoholic wives express more positive communication with their husbands and alcoholic husbands express more negative communication with their wives relative to controls (Noel, McCrady, Stout, & Fisher-Nelson, 1991). Because alcoholic wives are very likely to be divorced or deserted by their partners (Corrigan, 1980), such couples who find their way into research studies with their marriages still intact may represent particularly well functioning alcoholic marriages. For this reason, the reality of typical wife–alcoholic marital interactions remains very difficult to document.

Just as in the family interaction literature, researchers have found differential effects of alcoholism on marital interaction as a function of different patterns of problem drinking. For instance, episodic alcoholic husbands engage in less problem-solving and their wives exhibit more negativity than steady-alcoholics (Jacob & Leonard, 1988). These group differences were only evident on occasions during which the alcoholic was drinking. Also, steady-drinking alcoholics engaged in more problem-solving communication on drink nights, indicating that alcohol may actually activate their conflict resolution skills. This could inadvertently reinforce the alcohol consumption. Another useful distinction in the alcoholism literature concerns the alcoholic's drinking pattern and location, being either *in home* or *out of home*. Marital relations are most strained for the out-of-home drinkers. For out-of-home alcoholics, the husband's alcohol consumption is negatively associated with his wife's marital satisfaction (Dunn, Jacob, Hummon, & Seilamer, 1987). Dunn et al. found that the alcohol consumption pattern of out-of-home drinkers was more variable and chaotic, whereas consumption for in-home drinkers was reinforced and associated with more positive outcomes. It is certainly possible that out-of-home drinkers are seeking an escape from what they perceive to be an already bad marriage. On the other hand, spouses of in-home drinkers may find the drinking behavior to be more predictable, less stressful, and associated with less suspicion about the drinker's behavior.

Finally, there is reason to believe that the spouses or partners of people with drug or alcohol dependence can inadvertently reinforce the behavior though well-intentioned attempts at caring for them (Le Poire, Erlandson, & Hallett, 1998; Le Poire, Hallett, & Erlandson, 2000). Le Poire's Inconsistent Nurturing as Control Theory explains how many spouses are torn between the competing goals of nurturing the addicted partner and controlling his or her substance abuse. Some fear that if they are completely successful at controlling their partner's substance abuse, they will no longer be needed in the relationship for the care that they can provide. Consequently many partners oscillate between caring for their intoxicated partner and attempting to control his or her behavior. Unfortunately, this inconsistent punishment and reward pattern serves to only maintain the substance use.

## Children of Alcoholics

Family scientists, therapists, and the lay public alike have expressed considerable interest in the children of alcoholics (COAs). COAs have received a great deal of research attention as an at-risk population (e.g., Sher, 1991; Windle & Searles, 1990). This stems from the belief that parental alcoholism leads to disrupted and dysfunctional family environments that have ill effects on children. These ill effects may be driven by parental modeling of dysfunctional and destructive behaviors, corruption and deterioration of parenting behaviors, or an amalgamation of both processes (Curran & Chassin, 1996; Jacob & Johnson, 1997). Given the negative effects of alcoholism on family interaction, it is understandable why children reared in such families might be at a disadvantage. However, there is still considerable debate and disagreement about the extent to which parental alcoholism has adverse effects on children.

There is certainly some solid evidence to show that COAs have more problems with alcohol and substance abuse, as well as a range of psychological problems, than non-COAs (Sher, Walitzer, Wood, & Brent, 1991). Related findings also indicate that COAs have more problems with their marriages and intimate relationships than non-COAs do (Domenico & Windle, 1993; Martin, 1995; Watt, 2002). Children of alcoholics also appear to be particularly susceptible to the ill-effects of conflict with their parents (Barrera & Stice, 1998). Even though genetic transmission might explain why COAs are at elevated risk for drug and alcohol problems, it is plausible to assume that social learning processes also contribute to the increased risk (see chap. 2). Children who observe parents using alcohol as a means of relaxation, coping with stress, and celebration would naturally be expected to imitate this behavior that their parent(s) regularly modeled during the formative years.

It seems that for every study showing problems associated with being the child of an alcoholic there is another study showing that COAs are as functional and resilient as children of nonalcoholic parents. It may be reassuring to know that studies have found no differences between COAs and non-COAs in perceived social support (Wright & Heppner, 1991), anxiety (Clair & Genest, 1992; Velleman & Orford, 1993), social skills (Jacob & Leonard, 1986; Segrin & Menees, 1996), social maladjustment (Dinning & Berk, 1989), use of nonverbal communication behaviors (Senchak, Greene, Carroll, & Leonard, 1996), self-esteem (Menees, 1997), fear of intimacy (Giunta & Compas, 1994), or depression (Reich, Earls, Frankel, & Shayka, 1993). Such results should be harbingers of good news for the COA. While alcoholic parents may raise children with psychosocial problems of their own, this is not a deterministic relationship. Researchers are converging on the conclusion that COAs are a complex and heterogenous population who are not always distinguishable from those in the general population (Harrington & Metzler, 1997; Harter, 2000; Jacob & Johnson, 1997; West & Prinz, 1987).

Reasonable people could disagree on whether parental alcoholism has consistently negative effects on all children. However, it is more certain that children of alcoholics perceive their environments as distressed and dysfunctional. Compared to non-COAs, COAs describe their family of origin as more conflict laden (Garbarino & Strange, 1993; Giunta & Compas, 1994), less harmonious (Velleman & Orford, 1993), more troubled and stressed (Jones & Houts, 1992), and less cohesive (Dinning & Berk, 1989; Havey & Dodd, 1993). To a large extent, alcoholics and their spouses describe similar dynamics in the family environment (Moos & Moos, 1984). Even though COAs often describe a negative atmosphere in their families of origin, many are still indistinguishable from non-COAs on a variety of psychosocial outcomes. It seems that at least some COAs who grow up around dysfunctional family interaction are resilient, doing well in life despite their troubled upbringing.

West and Prinz (1987) noted that "Parental alcoholism does not occur in a vacuum. Other adverse familial and environmental factors can influence child outcomes to varying degrees" (p. 206). This highlights an interesting question: Are the problems that some COAs experience the result of parental alcoholism or some of the related family problems that go hand in hand with alcoholism? Children of alcoholics are between 2 and 4 times more likely than children of nonalcoholics to be exposed to parental divorce, separation, unemployment, or death, in addition to their parents' alcoholism (Menees & Segrin, 2000). COAs are also more likely to have experienced verbal, physical, and sexual abuse as children than non-COAs are (Bensley, Spieker, & McMahon, 1994; Johnson, 2002). Each of these stressors could independently have deleterious effects on the psychosocial adjustment of children. The Menees and Segrin study was one of the few in the COA literature to extensively control for comorbid stressors, finding that once taken into account, family environments of COAs are not described differently from those of children of nonstressed control families. Therefore, where COAs appear to be psychologically or socially disadvantaged, family stressors that go along with parental alcoholism may be as responsible, if not more so, than parental alcoholism per se (see also Heller, Sher, & Benson, 1982; Velleman, 1992).

## CONCLUSION

There is an undeniable connection between abnormal and problematic family interaction patterns and family members' mental health. It is not always clear whether troubled family interaction patterns cause or are caused by mental health problems. From a systems perspective, these two questions represent a false dichotomy. Systems theorists feel that the interaction patterns and mental health problems maintain each other. There are certain family interaction motifs that appear to cut across various mental health problems. In the family of origin these include low cohesion, inappropriate adaptability, conflict, physical and sexual abuse, low social support, criticism, overinvolvement, and affectionless control. Affectionless control is the combination of overprotectiveness and intrusiveness and low caring. This is an absolutely noxious combination of parenting behaviors that is remarkably capable of damaging children's mental health. In the family of orientation, problems such as marital distress, negativity, arguing, and failure to reach agreements go hand in hand with mental health problems. There are some unique family interaction patterns that play an important role in schizophrenia. These include communication deviance, a negative family affective style, and expressed emotion. What is not clear at this juncture is why, for example, one child reared in an environment of low cohesion might later become depressed whereas another might develop an eating disorder (and still another might not develop any mental health problem). However, one thing is clear: Dysfunctional family communication patterns can mix up, distort, and confuse people's thoughts and emotions, particularly when they are experienced during the formative years of life. It is for this reason that the blueprints for psychological well-being or distress are drawn to a large extent through interactions in the family of origin.

# CHAPTER FOURTEEN

# Family Interaction and Physical Health

What does family interaction have to do with physical health? The answer is "a lot." Family interaction contributes to the development and course of many physical health issues. This is a very fascinating time in family science, as some communication variables have even been elevated to a causal level in the path to physiological responses and health problems. In turn, physical health issues shape the nature of many family interactions. In this chapter, we explore numerous questions regarding how marital and family interactions relate to spouses' physical health, children's illnesses, adolescents' substance use and abuse, and adolescents' and young adults' sexual health. For example, are married people healthier than single people, and does a bad marriage take a toll on one's health? Does family interaction affect the development and course of childhood illnesses or adolescents' substance use and abuse? Can parents and families have an impact on adolescents' sexual behaviors? We also explore some of the major communication processes that families negotiate as they respond to physical health issues. These processes include caregiving and social support and privacy management. It is safe to say that at some point in time, the communication in every family changes in response to physical health issues or has an effect on the course of physical health problems. We are just beginning to understand the complex ways family interaction and physical health interact.

## MARITAL INTERACTION AND PHYSICAL HEALTH

Research on marriage and physical health has focused on the way three relationship variables relate to illness, disease, and mortality. These three variables are *relationship status*, *relationship quality*, and *relationship behaviors and interactions* (Burman & Margolin, 1992; Schmaling & Sher, 1997). Indeed, most early research looked only at the link between *relationship status* (i.e., married, single, and divorced) and health. This line of research proved useful at least for alerting us that marriage and health may mutually influence one another, but it only began to speculate as to how or in what way they influence one another. In 1979, Lois Verbrugge was one of the first researchers to establish a link between marriage and health. Using comprehensive data from the U.S. Census Bureau and the National Center for Health Statistics, Verbrugge found that divorced and separated people were the least healthy, with widowed, single, and married persons, respectively, more healthy. Divorced persons have the highest rates of chronic conditions, suffer the most partial work disability, visit physicians more times per year, have the highest hospitalization rates, and have the longest hospital stays. Compared to married individuals, separated and divorced persons also have poorer immune functioning, and those who have most recently experienced separation have the worst immune functioning (Kennedy, Kiecolt-Glaser, & Glaser, 1988). Numerous other studies indicate that marital status is related to mortality, such that married persons have a lower risk of mortality (Burman & Margolin, 1989, 1992). There appear to be some gender differences in the relationship between marriage and mortality. Unmarried men have a 250% greater risk for mortality than do married men, whereas unmarried women have a 50% greater risk for mortality than do their married counterparts (Ross, Mirowsky, & Goldsteen, 1990).

Before concluding that people should get married in an effort to boost their health status, it is important to understand that the relationship between marriage and health is far more complex than it may appear at first glance. Several popular explanations for why married persons are healthier argue that it is not marriage per say that enhances one's health status, but rather the type of people who tend to marry and the protections that are offered by some marriages. Kiecolt-Glaser and Newton (2001) summarize two hypotheses for the differences in the health status of married versus nonmarried persons. The *selection hypothesis* suggests that healthier people are more likely to marry and stay married, compared to unhealthy individuals. People who are seriously ill have a more difficult time dating and finding mates, which means that people who marry are in a sense "selected" for good health (Verbrugge, 1979). Later in this chapter we also discuss the strain that major health problems place on spouses and on marital interaction. In some cases, ill people find it more difficult to maintain their marriages. The *protection hypothesis* suggests that people receive protections that buffer ill health. Two primary protections include the following: (a) Married persons tend to live a less risky lifestyle compared to single persons. (b) Married persons benefit from companionship, social support, and instrumental services from their spouses. Inherent in the later protection is the assumption that not only any marriage but high-quality marriages marked by positive interactions benefit one's health. Negative or hostile interactions with spouses can damage health. Researchers very quickly surmised that *relationship status* does not predict physical health as well as overall *relationship quality* and specific *relationship behaviors and interactions*. In the following sections we explore the protection hypothesis, by examining how married people live less risky lifestyles and how the quality of relationship interactions is related to physical health. We then explore the impact that major health problems of one spouse have on marital interactions and the health of the other spouse.

## Marriage and Lifestyle

Social control theory proposes that social ties regulate behavior such that socially integrated persons engage in fewer risky or deviant behaviors compared to socially isolated persons (Tucker & Anders, 2001, p. 468). People with social ties tend to have more regular eating and sleeping habits, and they smoke and drink less (Wallston, Algania, Devellis, & Devellis, 1983). In a sense, social ties offer up other people and relationships to be accountable to. It is not uncommon for spouses to remind each other to do things to protect their health (e.g., to visit the doctor, to take their medication, to abstain from smoking or too much drinking, to drive safely; Cohen & Lichtenstein, 1990; Tucker & Anders, 2001; Verbrugge, 1979). Tucker and Anders (2001) found that when given a list of common health behaviors, most spouses could point to a few that they would like their spouses to change. The 63 husbands and 63 wives in their study most commonly reported that they wanted their spouses to exercise more frequently and eat healthier food.

Tucker and Anders (2001) also asked the spouses whether and how they persuade their partner to change their behavior. They found that the way spouses attempted social control made a big difference in the partners' responses. One dilemma spouses face is the possibility that their social control attempts could cause the partner to become irritated, feel guilty, or resent the control attempts. Tucker and Anders concluded that these negative outcomes may occur when spouses use negative social control strategies, such as nagging or placing restrictions on the partners' behaviors. When spouses use social control attempts such as joining in healthy behaviors with the partner or helping the partner think of healthy substitutes for unhealthy behavior, then the control attempts are likely more effective because the partners' perceive that the spouses are genuinely interested in their well-being.

Although married persons tend to have a healthier lifestyle than do single persons, this is not universally the case. Spouses in some marriages jointly encourage unhealthy lifestyle habits (e.g., overeating, inactivity, excessive work, or dangerous leisure habits). It is also plausible that negative marital interactions can lead spouses to a risky lifestyle. There is evidence to indicate that alcohol and drug abuse not only cause marital conflict but also are a result of marital conflict (O'Farrell, Hooley, Fals-Stewart, & Cutter, 1998). The important point is that positive and negative marital qualities each leads to very different lifestyles. Being in a *good* marriage promotes healthier lifestyle behaviors. In particular, positive interactions among spouses are related to fewer risky behaviors such as risky eating habits, substance use, and inadequate sleep (Wickrama, Conger, & Lorenz, 1995). For better or for worse, spouses directly influence each other's lifestyle, in part because they share health-related behaviors such as eating, sleeping, and leisure habits (Wickrama et al., p. 100). The quality of spouses' interaction appears to influence the positive or negative direction of these habits.

## Physiological Responses to Marital Interaction

In addition to altering health habits, marital interactions elicit physiological responses that potentially contribute to the development and course of some physical health problems. To demonstrate a causal relationship between marital interaction and physical health, Burman and Margolin (1989) explain that one must first establish that marital interaction is related to physiological functioning and then demonstrate that the physiological changes caused health problems. This requires studying couples prior to the development of health problems or even prior to the physiological responses that potentially cause the health problems. Toward this end, researchers have successfully demonstrated that specific behaviors during marital interaction alter a number of physiological responses such as stress hormones, heart rate, blood pressure, and immune functioning.

In an impressive program of research, Janice Kiecolt-Glaser and her associates have documented how marital quality and conflict interactions affect physiological responses (e.g., Kiecolt-Glaser et al., 1993). Their research methods typically involve bringing couples to the laboratory, seating the spouses face to face, and asking them to spend 30 minutes or so discussing and trying to resolve two or three marital issues that the researchers judge will be the most conflict-producing based on earlier reports from the couple. The most unique part of their research methods involves inserting a heparin well in each spouse's arm so they can periodically draw blood samples before, during, and after the problem-solving discussion. Drawing multiple samples allows the researchers to compare how physiology during and after the conflict interaction compares to baseline physiology, before the conflict interaction. The blood samples allow them to test the body's stress hormones and immune functioning. When the body produces elevated stress hormones, for example, high levels of epinephrine (i.e., adrenaline) or high levels of adrenocorticotropic hormone (ACTH; i.e., a hormone the body secretes in response to stress), researchers know the body is experiencing stress. The experience of stress then mediates immune functioning, such that the greater the stress, the poorer the immune system functions. Researchers measure immune functioning by testing blood samples in the lab for the presence of white blood cells or by testing how cells respond to the introduction of foreign substances such as viruses or bacteria. The researchers also monitor heart rate and blood pressure before, during, and after the interactions. These data indicate spouses' cardiovascular reaction to conflict. Several other researchers we refer to in this chapter use methods similar to those popularized by Kiecolt-Glaser (e.g., Kiecolt-Glaser, et al., 1996).

Overall, research indicates that couples who are more hostile, negative, and controlling during problem-solving discussions experience increased stress hormones (Malarkey, Kiecolt-Glaser, Pearl, & Glaser, 1994) and negative changes in their immune functioning (Kiecolt-Glaser et al., 1993). The stress takes a take a toll on immune functioning in part because chronic stress disrupts circadian rhythms, which are related to immune functioning (Kiecolt-Glaser & Newton, 2001). These couples also have higher increases in blood pressure and their blood pressure remains elevated for a longer time after the interaction (Brown & Smith, 1992). The heightened blood pressure is a reaction to the stress induced by negative affect. Blood pressure increases whether anger is actively expressed or passively suppressed (e.g., withdrawing gaze, hanging head, and rolling eyes; Morell & Apple, 1990, p. 399). Some couple types are especially prone to negative physiological responses to conflict. These "at-risk" couples occur when both spouses exhibit high dominance and high negative affect (Thomsen & Gilbert, 1998) or, similarly, when Type A personality husbands who are dominant, anxious, hostile competitors match with highly educated women who compete for dominance (Frankish & Linden, 1996).

Marital interaction appears to affect physiology throughout the course of a marriage. Kiecolt-Glaser et al. (1997) found that even long-term married couples have negative immune responses to negative marital interaction. In a striking study, Kiecolt-Glaser, Bane, Glaser, and Malarkey (2003) followed 90 couples over the course of their first 10 years of marriage and studied how their stress hormone levels in their first year of marriage related to and predicted marital outcomes. Compared to intact couples, couples that divorced over the course of the study had 34% higher epinephrine levels during a conflict discussion in their first year of marriage. Their stress hormones were also significantly higher throughout the day and at night in their first year of marriage. Kiecolt-Glaser et al. (2003) then compared couples who were married 10 years later, but in distressed marriages, versus those who were still married and happy. Among women whose marriages were distressed, ACTH levels during the conflict discussion in the first year were twice as high versus those whose marriages were not troubled 10 years later. As one might expect given the high stress hormones, couples who were married, but distressed 10 years later showed higher rates of negative behaviors during the Time 1 conflict interaction. Kiecolt-Glaser et al. (2003) conclude that "stress hormones may function as a kind of bellwether in early marriage, reflecting emotional responses that individuals, particularly women, have not yet acknowledged consciously" (p. 187). In other words, heightened stress hormones foreshadow negative relationship changes that the spouses themselves do not even foresee at the moment.

Do positive behaviors enhance physiology to the degree that negative behaviors damage it? Research indicates that people with a higher level of perceived family and spousal support experience cardiovascular benefits in the form of higher vascular resistance indexes (Broadwell & Light, 1999). Further, men who perceive more support have lower blood pressure compared to men who perceive low support. However, a great deal of research argues that supportive or neutral behaviors do not have much affect on physiology, or at least they do not positively alter physiology to the degree that negative or hostile behaviors negatively alter physiology (Jones, Beach, & Jackson, 2004; Kiecolt-Glaser et al., 1993; Kiecolt-Glaser & Newton, 2001; Morell & Apple, 1990). As Ewart, Taylor, Kraemer, and Agras (1991) state, "it is not how 'nice' spouses are to each other—but how 'nasty' they are not" that matters most when it comes to physical health (p. 161).

### Physiological Responses of Men Versus Women

Another fascinating and somewhat controversial topic is whether and how men and women have different physiological responses to marital conflict. Most people agree that there are gender differences in responses to conflict. A few researchers (e.g., Gottman et al., 1998; Levenson, Carstensen, & Gottman, 1994) make the case that men experience more negative physiological responses to marital conflict. They argue that the reason men are more likely to withdraw from conflict is because their physiological response to negative conflict interactions is so intense that they need to "escape" the situation, or else explode. They also suggest that husbands' or wives' ability to "soothe" husbands' negative physiological responses to conflict is key to successful marriages.

The aforementioned explanation is appealing, except for the fact that a great deal of other evidence suggests just the opposite. Women may experience more negative physiological changes as a result of negative conflict interactions than do men (Jones et al., 2004; Kiecolt-Glaser et al., 1993, 1996, 2003; Kiecolt-Glaser & Newton, 2001; Morell & Apple, 1990). During and after conflict, women's stress hormones and blood pressure are higher and their immune functioning is lower in comparison to men. Some even speculate that conflict does not trigger lingering negative health outcomes for men to the extent that it does for women, perhaps in part because some men tend to effectively withdraw from conflict before they suffer too much physiologically (Jones et al., 2004). Husband's withdrawal, however, is linked to higher stress hormones in wives (Kiecolt-Glaser et al., 1996).

### Physiological Responses to Marital Interaction and Health Problems

In many cases, it is difficult to establish a causal link between the development or worsening of health problems and physiological responses to marital interaction. Yet, researchers have made some successful efforts toward this end. Kiecolt-Glaser and Newton (2001) explain that the combination of increased stress and lower immune functioning leads to slower wound healing. Whether the stress is induced by negative marital interaction or something more external, such as academic exams or a stressful work environment, stress in general slows the healing process. Several other studies have implicated stress from marital interaction in the development and course of arthritis, cardiovascular disease, and ulcers (Burman & Margolin, 1989; see Kiecolt-Glaser & Newton, 2001). Heightened blood pressure and heart rates are particular risk factors in the course of hypertension and cardiovascular disease. After controlling for the effects of work stress, education, and income, overall marital quality is still significantly related to physical illness, with satisfied spouses less likely to become ill (Wickrama, Lorenz, Conger, & Elder, 1997).

## Marriage and Major Health Problems

Just as marital interaction may influence health problems, major health problems in one spouse may also have an effect on marital interaction and the health status of the other spouse. Roy (1985) asserts that "illnesses in families come in clusters," and illness in one member of the family often causes other members to develop related health problems (p. 204. Recall the discussion of stress pileup in chap. 9). Some of the problems that spouses of ill partners develop are associated with stress involved in the caregiver role. Spouses offering significant care to their partners often compromise their own physical health, in the form of poorer immune functioning, as well as their own mental health (Kiecolt-Glaser et al., 1987; Thompson & Pitts, 1992). We discuss this more toward the end of the chapter. Some spouses of chronic pain sufferers even report experiencing occasional pain symptoms along with their spouse, though this phenomenon is poorly understood (Roy, 1985).

Illness in one spouse also affects general marital interaction. Indeed, any change in the marital system has the potential to negatively or positively alter interaction patterns. Change that stems from meeting the demands and challenges of the illness is no exception (Cannon & Cavanaugh, 1998). Much of the change that takes a negative toll on marital interaction centers around the increasing demands placed on the nonill spouse. In some situations, the nonill spouse takes over chores and roles that were once undertaken by the other spouse. This leaves the nonill spouse with fewer opportunities for leisure and satisfying interactions outside the family. At the same time, the ill spouse, who likely is limited to fewer interactions outside the family, relies on the nonill spouse more than ever. As a result, inequities between the spouses become exacerbated (Thompson & Pitts, 1992). The type of marital interaction and the topics of marital interaction may also be dominated by the illness or chronic pain. Couples in which one spouse has experienced a stroke, heart disease, cancer, or chronic pain report decreases in frequency of and satisfaction with sexual functioning (Thompson & Pitts). Furthermore, the illness or chronic pain may itself be the major topic of conversation.

In most cases, it is crucial for spouses to respond with support and acknowledgment of their partners' pain during discussions of the illness. There may, however, be some rare exceptions in the case of chronic pain conditions. Turk, Kerns, and Rosenberg (1992) found evidence that, in some cases, the positive attention spouses offer to their partners' overt expressions of pain may actually maintain or increase the expressions of pain and even increase the potential for perceived disability. By means of operant conditioning, the pain expressions are essentially positively reinforced or rewarded by the spouse. Turk et al. found that "selectively avoiding provision of attention for expression of pain while remaining globally positive appears to be associated with a decreased experience of pain and depression" (p. 268). Note that the spouses were not getting irritated with their partners' pain expressions or making negative remarks in response to their pain expressions (i.e., they were not saying "Oh, it doesn't hurt that bad"). Rather, they were maintaining a positive demeanor without giving extra attention to the pain.

Interestingly, there is some evidence to indicate that a spouses' illness may not be so damaging to marital interaction, and in some cases, the spouses may actually enhance their interaction in response to the illness. Burman and Margolin (1992) claim, "As obvious as it seems that health problems would affect marriages, the data in this area are not nearly as powerful" as one might expect (p. 58). In other words, there is not consistent evidence that marital status or marital quality changes greatly after the onset of health problems. This could be attributed to differences in the course of various illnesses and differences in how individuals cope with illnesses. Recall that the models of family stress presented in chapter 9 explain how two families may react very differently to the same stressor depending on their coping skills and perception of the stressor. In addition, some couples experience temporary difficulties in their marriage that dissipate once they are able to adjust to the consequences of the illness or disease. Thompson and Pitts (1992) also propose that when couples face the illness of one spouse, a good marriage may get better, but a bad marriage may get worse. This reflects the idea that "preillness" marital functioning sets the stage for how a couple will react to the stressor. Badger (1992), for example, found that husbands' experience with cardiovascular disease exacerbated existing marital distress that was already present.

Clearly, some couples find extraordinary ways to deal with health problems that actually bring them closer together. Recall our discussion in chapter 9 of the double ABC-X model of family stress. This model proposes that some couples and families experience *bonadaptation*, such that they actually function better after the experience of the stressor than they did before. It is difficult to make any overarching generalizations about the impact of physical health problems on marital functioning because researchers in separate studies have found increases, decreases, as well as no change in martial functioning in response to health problems (Schmaling & Sher, 1997).

## FAMILY INTERACTION AND CHILD HEALTH

### Major Childhood Illness and the Family System

People tend to associate the experience of major health problems with older age. Nevertheless, it is sometimes the case that young children experience chronic and serious health problems. These create serious stress not only for the child but also for the greater family. When children experience major and/or chronic illness, the nature of family life is dramatically altered. Parents and siblings have to assume greater responsibility in a caregiving role, leisure activities are often restricted, and the welfare of the sick child can become a dominant theme of family interactions. Even though these family adjustments are often a necessary family response to the stress of childhood illness, they come with serious repercussions. The care of a sick child often means that the needs of other children in the family do not get as much attention as they would otherwise. The opportunities for a husband and wife to spend leisure time by themselves may be entirely eliminated. Likewise, their opportunity to attend to the maintenance of their marriage may be greatly reduced, as their interactions may be centered largely on the care and welfare of their sick child. Sometimes parents even experience anger and resentment toward the sick child (Peri, Molinari, & Taverna, 1991).

### Family Interaction and Chronic Childhood Illness: The Example of Diabetes

Childhood diabetes is a chronic health condition that demands major attention from, and reorganization of, the family. The effective management of diabetes involves careful attention to diet and exercise, monitoring of blood glucose levels, and daily injections of insulin. These are sufficiently challenging for even an adult to keep up with. When a young child has diabetes, the majority of these burdens fall on the shoulders of family members. Although some people think of diabetes as a "purely medical" condition, it can be affected by family interaction patterns. For example, high levels of family conflict are negatively associated with effective control of childhood diabetes (Anderson, Auslander, Jung, Miller, & Santiago, 1990). Part of this effect is due to family conflict interfering with treatment adherence. Wysocki (1993) studied a sample of 11- to 18-year-old adolescents who had diabetes and found that problems in family interaction structures (e.g., triangulation, coalitions) were negatively associated with the adolescents' glycohemoglobin levels, measured through blood tests. Because lower glycohemoglobin levels indicate better management of diabetes, it is obvious that dysfunctional family interaction patterns are associated with more difficulty with managing the illness. During laboratory problem-solving interactions, families without a diabetic child have been observed to talk less, ask fewer questions, and make fewer commands, compared to families without a diabetic child (Carlson, Gesten, McIver, DeClue, & Malone, 1994). Carlson and her coworkers conjecture that diabetic families may be more superficial in their family problem-solving efforts. Nevertheless, it is clear that families are taxed by the demands of managing their child's diabetes. When families were asked to role-play a diabetes problem-solving task (e.g., what type of food to eat or avoid) diabetes families rated the task as more difficult than control families did (Carlson et al.).

Perhaps the key element in the family's ability to effectively manage their child's diabetes is keeping an upbeat attitude and avoiding conflict and tension. Blechman and Delamater (1993) developed a competency model of family functioning based on their work with diabetes families. Their model begins with the assumption that a *good mood* helps to make people prepared and open to learning and optimal performance. Second, *effective family communication* promotes good moods in family members. They conceptualize effective family communication as the exchange of information, behavior management, and demonstration of good problem-solving skills. Theoretically, all of these are signs of good communication and should function to help the family maintain an upbeat outlook on their situation. Finally, positive moods promote *physiological fitness*. This is a point that has been vividly established earlier in this chapter in our discussion of marital quality and physiological outcomes. Blechman and Delamater illustrated how there are convincing research findings to establish the links between family communication and family members' moods, and positive moods and better diabetic control. The families who do the best job in managing their child's diabetes are those that have open communication, minimal conflict, good cohesion, and a generally friendly atmosphere, despite the obvious stress and burden that they must bear.

### Family Conflict and Poor Child Health Outcomes

There are few family interaction processes that appear to be as detrimental to children's health as family conflict. Family conflict is positively associated with children's physical symptoms such as headaches and stomach aches (Mechanic & Hansell, 1989). In Mechanic and Hansell's investigation, the children of divorced parents rated family conflict as significantly more unpleasant than their parents' actual divorce. In fact, the adolescents from high-conflict intact families had more physical ailments than those from low-conflict divorced families. Among already ill children, family conflict is associated with poor child adjustment to the illness (Drotar, 1997). What is even more remarkable is the long-term impact of family conflict on health problems. Lundberg (1993) analyzed longitudinal data on family living conditions and health for over 4,000 people in Sweden. He examined the effect of economic hardship, growing up in a large family (e.g., four or more siblings), parental divorce, and family conflict. Of these four stressful family processes, family conflict had the most powerful effect on subsequent physical illnesses. Children who grew up in a family marked by high levels of conflict were in a worse state of health 13 years later. Furthermore, family conflict during childhood was associated with a 46% increased risk of mortality among the elderly participants (i.e., ages of 81–84) in this study.

What does family conflict do to children's health and how does it make them susceptible to later health problems? Just like a bad marriage leads to physiological disturbances, family conflict upsets children's normal physiology. In a unique experimental study, children were exposed to angry or friendly interactions between two adult research assistants who, unbeknownst to the children, were just role-playing these emotional reactions (El-Sheikh, Cummings, & Goetsch, 1989). Children in the angry interaction condition showed more behavioral signs of distress and had a higher blood pressure than those who were exposed to the friendly exchange. In a related investigation, boys who came from families that were low in supportiveness and positive involvement with the child showed more anger and hostility and had greater cardiovascular arousal in response to simple laboratory stressors such as a isometric handgrip exercise or counting backwards by sevens (Woodall & Matthews, 1989).

The increased sympathetic arousal evidenced by children exposed to unsupportive and conflicted family interactions is functional in the short run for activating resources to deal with the stressor. The problem, however, is when this heightened responsiveness of the nervous system becomes permanently altered. This is a process known as allostasis or allostatic load, and family scientists believe that chronic exposure to stressful family environments is responsible for allostasis in children, making them vulnerable to subsequent health problems (Jones et al., 2004). The wearing down of the nervous system associated with allostasis is exceptionally taxing on children's physiology and this can culminate in illness through compromised immune response or dysfunction in the same physiological systems that are affected by the sympathetic arousal (e.g., heart and gastrointestinal system, etc.).

### Theoretical Models of Childhood Illness and Family Functioning

Historically, it has been assumed that childhood illness is a stressor that just "happens" to the family (Griffin, Parrella, Krainz, & Northey, 2002). However, researchers are beginning to understand that for at least some childhood illnesses such as asthma, diabetes, and ulcerative colitis, for example, the family can actually influence the course of the disorder. In other words there is a reciprocal relationship between the child's illness and the nature of his or her family environment (e.g., Wamboldt & Wamboldt, 2000). In the 1970s, Minuchin and his associates proposed the "Psychosomatic Family Model" to explain the relationship between the experience of certain childhood illnesses and family functioning (Minuchin et al., 1975). Their clinical observations suggested that a child's symptom expression (e.g., seizures and difficulty breathing) often functioned to distract parents from their conflicts and problems. Minuchin felt that this happened through the parents actively soliciting their sick child's involvement in their interactions, or by the child intruding into, and interrupting, their interactions. These researchers hypothesized that families of children with psychosomatic illnesses (physical ailments that are worsened by psychological distress) are characterized by four problematic family processes: lack of conflict resolution, enmeshment, overprotectiveness, and rigidity.

There is at least some scientific evidence that is consistent with elements of the Psychosomatic Family Model. For example, children with asthma have been found to intrude into their parents' conversations to a greater extent than do healthy children (Griffin et al., 2002). Griffin and his colleagues observed asthmatic children during a family dinner-time conversation and noticed that the children with asthma would start talking immediately after one of their parents disagreed with the other. Children without asthma did not do this. In this family interaction pattern, the sick child appears to deflect parents' conflicts, and shift attention to him- or herself.

Recently, Wood (2001) developed an interesting model of family relations and childhood illnesses, referred to as the "Biobehavioral Family Model." According to Wood, certain family interaction patterns *influence and are influenced by* the stressor of childhood illness. The family processes are assumed to have the power to exacerbate the child's symptoms or soothe them, depending on how extreme they are. The first family process variable is *proximity*. This refers to what extent the family shares space, information, and emotions with each other. *Generational hierarchy* describes the extent to which caregivers are in charge of the children, providing limits and nurturance. The third family feature, *parental relationship quality*, describes the nature of parent–child interactions, marked by mutual support, understanding, and adaptive disagreement as opposed to hostility, rejection, and conflict. *Triangulation* is a pattern of interaction whereby parents draw the child into their conflicts, particularly by blaming, scapegoating, or setting up battles for the loyalty of the child. *Responsivity* represents the extent to which family members are attuned and responsive to each other's behaviors and emotions. These five family processes are thought to influence the nature of the child's illness, in addition to being influenced by his or her illness. A family environment that is characterized by excessive proximity, a weak generational hierarchy, poor parental relationship quality, triangulation, and low responsivity, is assumed to worsen the child's illness experience. In so doing, the family environment contributes to stress pileup.

Families have to make serious adjustments in their communication behaviors in order to effectively cope with the stress of chronic childhood illness. Perhaps one reason why childhood illnesses such as asthma, autism, cystic fibrosis, cerebral palsy, and diabetes have such a pronounced effect on the family is because there is often no expectation for a return to normalcy. The family has to approach these as lifelong stressors. Family dynamics therefore often become more structured, rigid, overprotective, and less emotionally warm and communicative (Meijer & Oppenheimer, 1995; Wamboldt & Wamboldt, 2000). Sometimes the intrafamily strain of caring for a child with chronic illness can lead to conflict between parents and children (McCubbin et al., 1982). Are these simply family responses to the stressor? Not necessarily. Current views of childhood illness and family interaction dynamics suggest that these are both consequents of chronic childhood illnesses as well as of factors that actually exacerbate or ameliorate symptoms of the child's illness. This is an exciting development in family science as it elevates family communication variables to a causal level in the course of childhood illness.

## Family Interaction and Adolescent Substance Use and Abuse

Young people who get involved in drugs, alcohol, and smoking are assuming numerous health risks. For instance, smoking is a major risk factor for diseases of the respiratory system, including emphysema and lung cancer. The use of various hard drugs can lead to long-term addiction and dependence, and sometimes damaging neurological side effects. Although heavy alcohol consumption can have negative health implications over extended periods of use, for young people the most immediate health risk is associated with driving a car while intoxicated and involvement in high-risk behaviors (e.g., unprotected sex and fights) after drinking.

### Family Dynamics

Certain maladaptive family dynamics and atmospheres may predispose adolescents toward substance use. The families of substance-using teens tend to be less cohesive, less adaptable, and exhibit less togetherness than are families of nonusing teens (Malkus, 1994). There is evidence to suggest that lack of perceived support and encouragement from family members and weak sibling and parental relationships predispose adolescents to drug use (Rhodes & Jason, 1990). Negativity and conflict in the family are also positively correlated with adolescent drug use (Shek, 1998). Shek's study of adolescents' drug use in Hong Kong implicated many of the same family environment variables as those identified in American investigations. In chapter 13, we discussed the important role of family expressed emotion (e.g., communication that is critical, hostile, and reflective of overinvolvement) in such psychological problems as schizophrenia and eating disorders. It is apparent that this same noxious form of parental communication increases the odds of children getting involved in substance abuse (Schwartz, Dorer, Beardslee, Lavori, & Keller, 1990). Other family dynamics that predispose young people to substance abuse include low bonding in the family and few rewards for positive behaviors (Hawkins, Catalano, & Miller, 1992).

Another toxic family behavior that appeared repeatedly in the literature on mental health problems was neglect and abuse. Victimization of this sort plays a powerful role in development of substance abuse and initiation of substance use at an earlier age (Jarvis, Copeland, & Walton, 1998; Kilpatrick et al., 2000; Sheridan, 1995). In their study of over 4,000 adolescents, Kilpatrick et al. found that a history of physical or sexual abuse was associated with a 3- to 4-fold increase in alcohol abuse and an 8- to 12-fold increase of abusing hard drugs. How does child physical or sexual abuse culminate in later substance abuse? There are numerous theories. One explanation offered by Sheridan (1995) is that childhood abuse is often perpetrated in family environments where the parents themselves are substance abusers and where the family's functioning is otherwise defective. Sheridan explains that children reared in such an environment are likely to become substance abusers themselves due to problems created by these environments, such as low self-esteem. Kilpatrick et al. suggest that drug and alcohol use might represent a maladaptive coping strategy for people with a history of physical or sexual abuse. This is sometimes referred to as "self-medication." Jarvis et al. discovered an interesting pattern in their research participants who were being treated for substance abuse and child sexual abuse. They noted that people with a history of sexual abuse were clearly self-medicating and had low self-esteem, but that these individuals were three times more likely to be using stimulants than those without a history of such abuse. It seems that these women might be turning to stimulants to induce a self-protective state of hypervigilance. Jarvis and her associates noted that unfortunately self-medicating with drugs and alcohol is counterproductive in that intoxication only increases the risk of subsequent victimization. What is common to most theories and hypotheses that link child abuse with adolescent substance abuse is a hypothesized maladaptive effort at coping with psychological problems (e.g., depression, anxiety, and low self-esteem) and interpersonal problems (e.g., family conflict and boundary violations).

### Parenting

The family can also influence adolescent substance use through problematic or ineffective parenting (Hawkins et al., 1992). For example, inconsistent parental discipline and skewed parenting, in which one parent is overinvolved and the other is overly permissive, are risk factors for initial drug use in adolescents (Kandel & Andrews, 1987; Ziegler-Driscoll, 1979). A combination of low parental support and high parental control has proven to be a particularly noxious combination of parenting behaviors that is predictive of numerous mental health problems (see chap. 13) in addition to adolescent substance use (Barnes, Farrell, & Cairns, 1986). Excessive hostility from fathers and harsh punishment practices by mothers also seem to predispose adolescents to early alcohol use (Johnson & Pandina, 1991). These parenting behaviors and family environments can push the adolescent away from the family, rejecting traditional family beliefs and values, and toward socialization with deviant peers (Blackson, Tarter, Loeber, Ammerman, & Windle, 1996; Harbach & Jones, 1995). Noteworthy in the Harback and Jones study is the finding that parents of at-risk adolescents held similar beliefs and values to those of other parents, but their children did not share these values.

Some noteworthy longitudinal studies indicate that defective parenting behavior may precede offspring substance abuse by many years (Repetti, Taylor, & Seeman, 2002). A landmark study by Shedler and Block (1990) found that mothers of children who were frequent users of marijuana at age 18 were unresponsive to their child and gave them little encouragement during an observation at age 5. Mothers of would-be substance abusers in Shedler and Brock's study appeared cold, critical, and pressuring when they interacted with their young child. Similarly, parents who exhibited less directive control and assertiveness while interacting with their 4-year-old children were more likely to become the parents of heavy-marijuana-using adolescents some years later (Baumrind, 1991). Baumrind found that authoritative parenting (see chap. 7) protects adolescents from problem drug use. During the instability of adolescence, the structure and control that authoritative parents provide can be a benefit to children. The key elements of the authoritative parent that minimize adolescent substance abuse according to Baumrind are strong mutual attachments that persist throughout adolescence and coherent and consistent management policies.

One parental management strategy that appears to be quite effective at postponing or reducing the likelihood of adolescent substance abuse is parental monitoring and supervision (Hawkins et al., 1992; Ledoux, Miller, Choquet, & Plant, 2002). Parents who monitor and supervise their children know where their children are, even when away from home, and they know whom their children are with. To illustrate, Barnes, Reifman, Farrell, and Dintcheff (2000) interviewed adolescents annually from age 13 to 16. To assess parental monitoring, they asked "How often do you tell your parents where you're going to be after school?" and "How often do you tell your parents where you're really going when you go out evenings and weekends?" The results of this study showed that this sort of parental monitoring was associated with lower levels of alcohol misuse and a lower acceleration into alcohol misuse over the 13- to 16-year age range. The benefits of this parenting behavior are twofold. First, these parents maintain active awareness of what their children are up to. This gives parents an edge when it comes to steering their children away from problematic situations and peers that could pave the way to substance abuse. Second, there is a communicative function to parental monitoring and supervision. As much as adolescents may "dislike" supervision, it can send the message that (a) someone notices them, and (b) someone cares about them. These are powerful messages that can do much to build self-esteem and self-confidence—two barriers in the road to substance abuse.

Verbal interaction between the parent and child can also play a role in minimizing substance abuse, at least in some instances. Having at least one available parental figure (i.e., a parent whom the child can talk with openly) is associated with lower levels of substance use (Kafka & London, 1991) and abuse (Booth-Butterfield & Sidelinger, 1998).

Youth with the highest levels of drug involvement are those who have had either no parental or family member talk to them about drugs or those who have had a lot of parental or family members talk to them about drugs (Kelly, Comello, & Hunn, 2002). Youth who had no one talk to them about drugs may have perceived that there would not be any negative sanctions. They may also have perceived that no one cared, and the drug use could have even been an attention-seeking behavior. Youth who had many people talk to them about drugs may have been known to be using drugs already or have strong attachments to peer groups who are perceived to use drugs. Thus, it might not have been that the parental or family communication had diminishing effects because it saturated them and prompted them to use drugs (although that is plausible). More likely, the drug use preceded the parental communication in cases where parent–child communication about drugs was frequent. Ultimately Kelly and her associates (2002) argued that "parent–child communication serves as a strong protective factor with respect to youth involvement with substances, and . . . parents may be a more potent influence than they might perceive themselves to be" (p. 783). With over 82,000 research participants in their study, this assertion rests on a solid empirical foundation.

Contrary to the idea that parental communication has a positive impact, a few researchers have found that the effects of parent–child communication regarding risky behaviors such as adolescent tobacco and alcohol use are "unimportant and detrimental at worst" (Ennett, Bauman, Foshee, Pemberton, & Hicks, 2001, p. 59). Interestingly, some parents say they do not want their kids to smoke or drink, but the parents themselves engage in these behaviors. As we will see in a moment, this discrepancy between what parents say and what they do usually weakens the impact of what parents say. It is clear that parents who send mixed messages (e.g., contradictions between what they say and do) or take a heavy-handed, punitive approach to preventing or stopping their children's substance abuse are likely to find that their communication has a boomerang effect.

### Social Learning

According to social learning theory (see chap. 2), one mechanism by which people acquire behaviors is through observation of others (Bandura, 1977). This process is known as observational learning, or modeling. When we see people rewarded for performing a behavior, we are more likely to enact that behavior. Social learning theory explains that people learn if-then relationships by observing others. So, for example, an adolescent might learn "if I smoke cigarettes, then I will look cool and mature." This could be learned by observing parents, siblings, peers, and even media characters who smoke. Consistent with the predictions of social learning theory, parents who drink alcohol, smoke cigarettes, or use illicit drugs are more likely to have children who do the same. For this reason, social learning theory is currently one of the dominant theories of adolescent involvement in substance use and abuse (Botvin & Tortu, 1988; Howard, 1992; Simons, Conger, & Whitbeck, 1988).

When it comes to substance use the relationship between parents' behavior and children's behavior is striking. Ennett et al. (2001) observed "the effect of parental substance use behavior on adolescent behavior suggests that what parents communicate nonverbally by what they do is more important than what they say" (p. 60). Drug and alcohol use by peers and parents is one of the most powerful predictors of adolescent drug and alcohol involvement (Johnson & Pandina, 1991; Kandel, 1978; Kandel & Andrews, 1987). Regardless of their intentions, parents who use drugs and alcohol in the presence of their children send a powerful message that this behavior is acceptable and perhaps even desirable. This greatly increases the odds of adolescent children getting involved in substance use. For example, a study of high school students revealed a strong correlation between students' substance use and that of their parents (Malkus, 1994). In another study of prisoners enrolled in substance abuse programs, 54% indicated a family history of parental alcohol or other drug problems (Sheridan, 1995). A national household probability sample of over 4000 adolescents showed that a history of family drug use increases the odds of adolescents' abuse/dependence on alcohol, marijuana, or hard drugs by factors of 1.89, 4.14, and 7.89, respectively (Kilpatrick et al., 2000). In other words, adolescents whose family members use drugs are anywhere from 2 to 8 times more likely to be abusing or dependent on drugs themselves, compared to those in families without a history of drug use. Also, it is not just parents who teach substance use to their children through modeling. Older siblings have been demonstrated to have an even more powerful modeling effect for drug use than parents (Brook, Whiteman, Gordon, & Brook, 1988).

Earlier we noted that low family cohesion is associated with adolescent substance use and abuse. Oddly enough, family cohesion seems to offset the effect of parental modeling. Doherty and Allen (1994) followed a group of adolescents over a period of 6 years. In their sample, 53% of those who lived in a low cohesion family and had a parent who smoked were themselves smokers by the second wave of data collection. In contrast, only 18% of those living in a high-cohesion family took up smoking over the course of the study, despite having a parent who smoked.

In addition to direct effects on adolescents' substance use, family modeling appears to also have some indirect effects on their children's involvement in drugs and alcohol. Adolescents whose family members are involved in drug use not only take more drugs themselves but also are more likely to associate with drug-using peers (Bahr, Hawks, & Wang, 1993). It stands to reason that family drug use normalizes the behavior, making it seem natural to hang out with others who do the same. Of course, this only serves to intensify the modeling effect through adding additional, nonfamily, sources of modeling.

## Family Interaction and Sexual Health

The sexual behavior of young people, like consumption of drugs and alcohol, can pose a variety of health risks. Young people who are not in long-term monogamous relationships can obviously be vulnerable to sexually transmitted diseases (STDs), including HIV/AIDS. Furthermore, even though people do not often think of it as a health problem, pregnancy is a major health risk for women. For these reasons sexual behavior can be a pathway to potential health problems. Even though this is the case for all human beings, young people are particularly vulnerable to some of these health risks.

As we show in this section, family communication and the social climate in the family have an undeniable relationship with adolescents' and young adults' sexual behavior. However, we must note from the outset that in many family contexts, parental advice and influence on young people's sexual behavior is potential that is never realized. There are a multitude of factors that greatly interfere with this sort of family influence. For example, American culture in general is reluctant, or ambivalent at best, about openly discussing sex. Furthermore, some parents are personally uneasy with the topic of sex, perhaps not even discussing it with their partners. As strange as this might sound for a couple with children, it is far from out of the ordinary. People who are not secure in their own thoughts and feelings about sexuality are unlikely to provide effective input to their children on the topic. Perhaps the greatest obstacle to frank parent–child communication about sexuality is parents' reluctance to think of their children as sexual beings. Even the most cosmopolitan and progressive parents are often not ready to think of their 12- or 13-year-old as being sexual. When families cannot come to grips with this reality the consequent can be adolescents with STDs and unplanned pregnancies. Some adolescents are physically able to acquire STDs or become pregnant, but not psychologically prepared to cope with such consequences.

Can parents and families have an impact on their children's sexual behaviors? There is some evidence to suggest they can. Early parent–adolescent sexual communication is associated with later age of sexual initiation, more consistent condom use, and fewer STDs (Hutchinson, 2002). We should also note that children are exposed to many risky behaviors (e.g., unprotected sex) through the media. Several scholars indicate that children listen carefully to how their parents respond to viewing risky behaviors when watching television together. Parents who openly and critically discuss media portrayals of risky behaviors with their children appear to be able to cultivate skepticism and social resistance skills in their children (Austin, 1993, 1996; Fujioka & Austin, 2002). Also, families with generally open lines of communication are more likely to discuss sexuality as well as HIV/AIDS with their children (Powell & Segrin, in press). The beauty of this type of family communication is that it is positively associated with discussing HIV/AIDS with dating partners. In accord with social learning theory (see chap. 2), Powell and Segrin (in press) hypothesized that the modeling of communication about HIV/AIDS in the family context has a disinhibitory effect when young people converse with their dating partners. It is now apparent that both the *quality of the parent–child relationship*, as measured by their general communication, warmth, and closeness, and *sexual communication* have independent effects on age of adolescents' first intercourse (Davis & Friel, 2001). This suggests that even parents who are uneasy about talking to their adolescent about sex can still influence the adolescent's behavior through generally positive communication and parenting practices.

Family cohesion, expressiveness, and parental monitoring are all positively associated with willingness to talk with parents about STDs and the expectation that parents will respond by being helpful (Rosenthal, Cohen, Biro, & De Vellis, 1996). One way that parental warmth and involvement can serve to decrease the likelihood of adolescent pregnancy is by reducing risk-taking behaviors (i.e., delinquency and substance use) that are precursors to risky sexual behavior in adolescents (Scaramella, Conger, Simons, & Whitbeck, 1998). Comparable to the findings for substance use, parental monitoring has been linked with delayed onset of sexual activity in teens (Longmore, Manning, & Giordano, 2001). The common denominator in both cases (i.e., substance use and sexual behavior) might also be the avoidance of high-risk situations guided by parental monitoring. So, cohesion, warmth, involvement, and monitoring can have both direct and indirect effects on adolescent sexuality. Elsewhere in this chapter we discussed how excessive parental control and discipline are actually associated with increases in adolescent substance use. The same holds true for sexual behavior. Strong parental control is associated with a greater probability of adolescent sexual risk behaviors (Rodgers, 1999).

Not long ago, there was a research study conducted in the inner city of Detroit that showed that positive family environments can combat an extraordinarily high probability of risky sexual behavior. Danziger (1995) conducted in-depth life history interviews with 80 African American women, ranging in age from 15 to 20 years old, who resided in ghetto communities. Among those who had close family ties, 73% did not become sexually active until age 15 or later. In contrast, 69% of those who had weak family ties or high conflict in their families had sex prior to age 15. The same pattern holds for family routines: 69% of those whose family maintained routines delayed having sex until at least age 15 versus only 31% among those whose families were disorderly or chaotic. There seemed to be two common themes in life stories that Danziger collected from people who had experienced later or minimal sexual activity: (a) their parents put a strong emphasis on doing well in school, and (b) the family had a well-developed set of rules concerning dating and socializing. This study shows how families can help to positively structure the lives of their children through direct communication about issues such as dating, as well as emphasize other activities (e.g., school) that could at least temporarily displace early involvement in sexual activity.

It is clear that children who talk with their parents about sex are less likely to be sexually active, less likely to become pregnant, and more likely to use contraceptives (Crosby & Miller, 2002). But do parents and their children actually discuss these topics? The answer depends on the sex of the parent, the sex of the child, and the specific issue. Mothers are the primary source (within the family) of information about sex (Miller, Kotchick, Dorsey, Forehand, & Ham, 1998). Miller et al.'s findings indicate that 60% of daughters and 42% of sons have discussed with their mother when to start having sex. Issues such as birth control were discussed by 57% of daughters and 31% of sons, and condoms were discussed by 64% of daughters and 68% of sons. Thus, it appears that most family communication about sexuality is going on between mothers and daughters. However, that occurs only in about 60% of the families surveyed, and when it does, it is not clear how in-depth or extensive these conversations are. Aside from discussions with their mothers, about a third of adolescents report that they talked with their siblings about sex (Pistella & Bonati, 1998). This is a reminder that family influences on sexuality can emanate from sources other than parents.

Communication researcher Clay Warren has conducted numerous studies on family sex communication. He summarized the major findings from this research (Warren, 1992), and they are presented in Table 14.1. His findings suggest that children are willing to talk with their parents about sexuality, but that it is essential for parents to be supportive and open in order for this type of family communication to be effective. Unfortunately, an ongoing dialog about sex is uncommon in most American families. It is also clear that efforts to control via direct instructions and admonishments are likely to be ineffective.

**TABLE 14.1**
Research Findings on Family Sex Communication Summarized
by Warren (1992)

---

- A low percentage of families has any kind of ongoing discussion about sex.
- The majority of children and parents are dissatisfied with the quantity and quality of family discussions about sexual issues.
- Children are most satisfied with their family sex communication pattern when parents help them feel free to initiate discussions.
- Family sex communication must focus on supportive interaction, not on instruction; if parents intend to control their children's sexuality by a verbal-intentional process, the effort will be seen as repression and fail.
- Supportive communication about sex depends more on an attitude of openness and less on strategies.
- Healthy family sex communication facilitates children's open discussion with dating partners and favorably influences their attitudes toward birth control.
- When sex communication in the family is effective, sex is not perceived to become the primary focus of a teenage relationship.

---

*Note.* From Warren, C. (1992). Perspectives on international sex practices and American family sex communication relevant to teenage sexual behavior in the United States. *Health Communication, 4,* 121–136. Copyright 1992 by Lawrence Erlbaum Associates. Adapted with permission.

Just as the family can have positive influences on adolescents' sexual behavior so too can the family exert negative influences. Various forms of child maltreatment, including physical and sexual abuse, are associated with high rates of adolescent pregnancy and greater likelihood that these pregnancies are actually intentional (Rainey, Stevens-Simon, & Kaplan, 1995; Smith, 1996). Needless to say, family environments that perpetrate child maltreatment usually have other forms of severe dysfunction. Such families are notorious for producing children with deficits in social competence and emotional expression (Repetti et al., 2002). Unfortunately, this creates a substantial vulnerability to manipulation and exploitation later in life. In other words, it is not just that child maltreatment creates psychosocial problems for its victims, but that these young people then find their way to peers and partners with unscrupulous motivations.

## NEGOTIATING COMMUNICATION PROCESSES ASSOCIATED WITH PHYSICAL HEALTH

As we end this chapter, we emphasize two communication processes that most families face as they deal with family members' illness. We have briefly made reference to the first communication process, *caregiving and social support*, throughout this chapter. Here, we highlight just how pivotal it is for families to negotiate this process as well as the dilemmas it can present. Regarding the second process, *privacy management*, we discuss dilemmas that families face about whether and to what extent to keep family illness private from those outside the family or even from others in the family.

## Caregiving and Social Support

Family social support and care play vital roles in health and illness. People who have supportive relationships experience fewer health problems than people who lack supportive relationships and have a lot of conflict in their relationships (House, Landis, & Umberson, 1988; Walen & Lachman, 2000). By this very fact, family interactions can keep people from developing illnesses in the first place. Exactly how does this work? Cohen, Underwood, and Gottlieb (2000) offer two explanations. First, supportive relationships influence behaviors that have obvious implications for good health, such as exercise, diet, smoking, and adherence to medical regimes. So, for example, one reason why men in good marriages are on average healthier than men in bad marriages or men who are not married at all is because their wives urge them to exercise, watch their diet, and get a regular checkup at the doctor. Cohen et al. also note that supportive relationships help people to regulate their emotional responses, and these are associated with various physiological responses (e.g., immune and neuroendochrine) that have obvious health implications. As we demonstrate earlier in this chapter, unsupportive relationships can literally compromise people's physiological fitness. So, before even considering family responses to illness, it is apparent that supportive and caring family relationships can do a lot to minimize the likelihood of certain illnesses occurring in the first place.

When a family member becomes seriously ill, the entire family system can be affected. Ideally, family members respond with social support and in many cases assume the role of caregiver. There is no mistaking that this care and support are beneficial to sick family members. For example, emotional support from family members contributes greatly to cancer patients' adjustment to their illness (Gotcher, 1993), and satisfaction with social support is negatively related to depression in women with breast cancer (Badger, Braden, Longman, & Mishel, 1999). Elderly people who require institutional care in a nursing home tend to be less depressed and more motivated and happy to the extent that they are satisfied with the social support that they receive from their family members (Carpenter, 2002). For the most part, supportive communication and care from family members seems to lessen the burden of being ill.

It is important to add one caveat to the declaration that family care and support are helpful to the sick individual. As we will discuss momentarily, providing care to an ill family member is stressful. This stress can contribute greatly to conflict and poor relational quality between the caregiver and care receiver. Consequently, it is sometimes the case that receiving family care is not always beneficial to the care receiver (Edwards, 2001). Edwards noted that sometimes people being cared for by family members are no better off than those in long-term care facilities. When the care itself becomes a major source of dissention and conflict in the family, the benefits of family caregiving appear to disappear.

Unfortunately, providing care to sick family members comes at a cost. Family scientists have begun to realize that the act of providing care and support not only affects the ill family member but also the provider. For instance, effectively providing care for an elderly family member with Alzheimer's disease demands a substantial adjustment in caregiver communication patterns, requiring shorter, simpler sentences, avoiding interruptions, and asking one question or giving one instruction at a time (Small & Gutman, 2002; Small,

Gutman, Makela & Hillhouse, 2003). Some caregivers may have difficulties making these necessary adjustments to their communication, or may experience frustration when their communication no longer has the desired effects when interacting with the family member with Alzheimer's. Caregivers can become susceptible to depression when they find themselves disagreeing with other family members about how to care for the family member with Alzheimer's disease (Speice, Shields, & Blieszner, 1998). Providing care to a family member with Alzheimer's disease can be physically and emotionally draining. As it turns out, the family environment (e.g., organization, conflict avoidance, and avoiding guilt induction) is more strongly associated with the well-being of Alzheimer's caregivers than with the severity of the actual disorder (Fisher & Lieberman, 1996). These findings illustrate how family interactions can play a vital role in keeping caregivers from getting overburdened and burned out, or how they can contribute to the caregiver's rapid demise when she or he experiences further agitation through these interactions.

Just as sick family members benefit from social support, so too do family care providers. Research on family caregivers of patients who had a stroke indicates that availability of social support is positively associated with caregivers' life satisfaction and negatively with their symptoms of depression (Grant, Elliott, Giger, & Bartolucci, 2001). Acquiring information and coping with helplessness are two of the primary needs of family members of cancer patients (Northouse & Northouse, 1988). Social support from both health care providers and other friends and family could be instrumental in assisting with these needs, thus allowing family members to better withstand the burden and distress of caring for their sick relative.

Sometimes the need to provide care for a family member can be a very difficult issue for the family to discuss. After all, a serious discussion of caregiving requires an acceptance of the reality facing the sick or frail family member. Pecchioni (2001) studied this phenomenon by asking adult daughters and their mothers about their preferences for discussing the mothers' needs for care. She found that over three quarters of the mothers and daughters felt that no such conversations were even necessary. Upon closer examination, Pecchioni (2001) discovered that about a third of these mother–daughter dyads were motivated by denial. In other words, many did not want to even think about the mother's declining health and its implications for their relationship. The very fact that daughters used denial as a "coping mechanism" is indicative of the stress and burden that caregivers undertake by merely thinking about the deteriorating health of a close family member.

## Privacy Regarding Family Health

In some families, people find it less difficult to tell people outside the family about the health issue or illness, because of fear of rejection from family (e.g., in the case of teen pregnancy) or because it was someone in the family who caused the health issue (e.g., in the case of child physical or sexual abuse or spousal abuse; Caughlin & Petronio, 2004). Earlier in this chapter, we discussed the tendency for many parents, especially fathers, to avoid discussing sexuality at all with their children. Some parents' privacy boundaries regarding sexuality may be so closed that they in fact prefer that their children just "find out what they need to know" from someone outside the family.

In other families, illnesses or health problems are a family matter that members do not wish to share with persons outside the family. They keep, as we learned in chapter 3, *whole family secrets* regarding the illness. This is especially likely if the illness carries with it a stigma that the family members themselves are trying to understand, let alone share with an outsider. Caughlin and Petronio (2004) summarize research regarding adult children who accompany their aging parents in visits to the doctor. Unless the parent and adult child have carefully negotiated what is to be kept as a whole family secret and what information can be public, the adult child often discloses "too much" information to the physician or contradicts the parent against the parent's wishes. What ensues is a struggle over how to manage the parents' impression to the physician. Still another challenge for families is how to deal with information regarding physical health that is only known by some family members. When older adults require care from adult children, they often find it necessary to disclose information that they once kept private from their children (e.g., bodily needs, financial issues; Caughlin & Petronio; Petronio & Kovach, 1997).

### *Privacy Management Regarding Life-Threatening Childhood Illness*

When the illness involves the child and the parents know information about the child's health status that the child does not even know, the situation is especially complicated. It is difficult to think of a more dramatic family stressor than a child afflicted with a life-threatening illness. Among the multitude of dilemmas and challenges that families face in such situations is how to communicate with the child about his or her illness. There are two approaches that have been described in the family health communication literature (Share, 1972). Families that opt for a *protective* approach try to shield the sick child and any siblings from the reality of the illness and its ultimate consequences. The idea behind the protective view is that family members' emotional well-being is best if they are kept from the knowing just how bad off the sick child is. Parents who take this approach carefully manage the flow of information to the sick child and his or her siblings. It is predicated on the assumption that sick children do not have coping mechanisms that are sufficient for dealing with such devastating news. However, the protective approach has been criticized on grounds that it can isolate children from discussions of their condition and actually create more anxiety and uncertainty. In contrast, the *open* approach is based on allowing children and their siblings to inquire about the illness with knowledge that they will get honest and straightforward answers. The idea behind the open approach is that it is impossible to live life as if nothing is wrong and deny the sick child's natural curiosity and concern. Proponents of the open view feel that the child should be able to rely on family members as trustworthy sources of information.

In a recent study with families of pediatric oncology patients, there was clear evidence that some parents prefer the protective approach, whereas others opt for the open approach (Young, Dixon-Woods, Windridge, & Henry, 2003). Most parents in this study preferred to first learn about the diagnosis without the child being present. However, their motivation was not so much to shield the child from information about the illness as to be able to manage their own emotional reaction and convey a sense of hope to the child. Some of the families in this study developed what Young et al. characterized as a "partnership model," where the roles of the parent and child became more equal during discussions of the illness. These families had very open communication about the illness. At the same time, other parents assumed an "executive" role, managing what and when children were told about their illness. There is probably no singularly "correct" way to manage communication with a terminally ill child. Decisions about how much to tell the child, and to what extent the parent serves as a gatekeeper between the child and physician, are best made on a case by case basis taking into consideration the emotional and cognitive maturity of the child along with his or her coping skills. Nevertheless, Young et al.'s research shows that this is an exceptionally complex balancing act that parents of terminally ill children must manage. Having to continually weigh the pros and cons of these different communication styles undoubtedly adds to the stress of an already catastrophic family situation.

## CONCLUSION

In this chapter, we examine the way families communicate about health issues, for example, how much privacy they practice and how they offer caregiving and social support. We also study how family communication contributes to the development and course of family health problems. There are some take-home messages regarding the negative and positive effects of family communication on health.

In both marital and parent–child relationships, the stress induced by hostile conflict and negative family interaction leads to compromised health. Risky behaviors such as substance abuse are often an individuals' attempt to self-medicate or escape their negative family environment. Of course, the result usually leads to even poorer functioning. In parent–child relationships, controlling punitive behaviors as well as permissive parenting are associated with risky adolescent behaviors.

On the positive side, spouses who avoid excessive conflict and offer support to each other boost their health status. Even when one spouse develops a health problem, if the couple was happy before the illness, they can weather the illness better, sometimes even drawing closer. Parents who monitor their children's behavior, talk openly and supportively with their kids, and avoid mixed messages regarding their own words and behaviors can buffer their children from risky behaviors that lead to poor health. Further, spouses and parents who promote positive attitudes and communication are better able to manage existing health conditions in the family. In the end, family interaction has a lot to do with our physical health, for better or worse.

# CHAPTER FIFTEEN

# Family Violence and Abuse

In this chapter we explore one of the dark sides of family relationships by considering the causes, correlates, consequences, and explanations of family violence and abuse. The concept of family violence encompasses a wide range of noxious behaviors perpetrated within the family. As we show later in this chapter, these family problems are pervasive in American society, and they have long-lasting and long-ranging consequences.

We believe that family violence and abuse can be understood as dysfunctional communication behaviors. In Dudley Cahn's analysis of family violence, he argued that "From a communication perspective, these behaviors are redefined as acts or actions with intention (from a message sender's point of view) or with perceived intention (from a message receiver's point of view). In addition, these acts or actions may be verbal (words) or nonverbal (symbolic actions besides words) or both" (Cahn, 1996, p. 6). Cahn suggested that like any communicative act, family violence has an instrumental dimension (task accomplishment or goal attainment), a relational dimension (e.g., commitment, love, conflict, and jealousy), and an identity dimension (a reflection of how the sender feels about him- or herself). Research on family violence and abuse shows that the instrumental aspect of the behavior often involves trying to establish or maintain power in an interpersonal relationship. This might entail influencing a spouse to do something or a child to stop doing something. There is a powerful relational dimension to abusive and violent behavior. The perpetrator may feel frustrated or powerless, but the victim often harbors feelings of love or commitment to the perpetrator that prevents a departure from the relationship. Finally, problematic identity issues are almost always associated with family abuse and violence. The violence often occurs because the perpetrator is dissatisfied with his or her perceived identity in the relationship. In keeping with the theme of family violence and abuse as a communication behavior, we focus in this chapter exclusively on family, relational, and interpersonal aspects of and approaches to family violence and abuse. However, it should be pointed out that numerous biological, environmental, and psychological issues also contribute to abusive conduct in family contexts.

Communication researcher Mary Anne Fitzpatrick (2002) suggested that there are three powerful myths that inhibit a clear understanding of family violence. The first myth is that family violence is about men beating women. As we will show throughout this chapter, family violence also includes women aggressing against men, parents aggressing against their children, men aggressing against men, and women aggressing against women. Even though male → female aggression is one of the more commonly encountered forms of family violence, this aversive family behavior occurs in numerous other contexts. The second myth that Fitzpatrick dispels is that all abusers are alike. Research on martial violence reviewed later in this chapter indicates that there are distinct subtypes of abusive spouses. Family violence is a complex behavior perpetrated by different people for different reasons. The third myth described by Fitzpatrick is that violence is an isolated act. Unfortunately, abuse and violence are rarely one-time occurrences. In some cases they are perpetrated over the course of years if not decades. This is undoubtedly one reason why the consequences of family violence can be so long lasting.

In the remainder of this chapter, we examine some of the different forms and functions of family violence. What are the different types of family violence and how common are they? To answer this question we begin with definitions of different types of family violence, followed by a brief analysis of the prevalence of family violence. The majority of the chapter covers three types of family violence and abuse: physical abuse of children, sexual abuse of children, and violence in the marital subsystem. What are the family dynamics that are conducive to this type of behavior? Why do parents abuse their children? What are the effects of abuse on children? Why do spouses abuse their partners? These are some of the pressing questions that are badly in need of answers. Although scientific knowledge does not allow for definitive answers to each of these questions, currently available research provides a good starting point. This research shows that for virtually all types of family abuse and violence, interactions and relationships in the family system have problems that extend far beyond the abusive behavior itself.

## DEFINITIONS AND VARYING FORMS

*Family violence* is "the intentional intimidation, physical and/or sexual abuse, or battering of children, adults, or elders by a family member, intimate partner, or caretaker" (Alpert, Cohen, & Sege, 1997, p. S3). As this definition illustrates, terms like *domestic violence, family violence,* and *child abuse* are fairly generic concepts that refer to several different abusive family processes. The distinction between some of these subprocesses is important from a scientific perspective because different abusive family processes appear to have different antecedents and consequents. In Table 15.1, we provide definitions for most different types and subtypes of family violence and abuse. Note from these definitions how some caustic family processes are acts of commission (e.g., child physical abuse and marital violence), whereas others are acts of omission (e.g., child physical neglect and child emotional neglect). People often think of abusive family processes as negative things that family members say or do to each other. However, sometimes what family members fail to say or do can be as problematic, if not more so, than the acts they actually commit. For example, the consequences of child neglect could be every bit as severe as child abuse. Furthermore, we would argue that the relational message sent by child neglect is comparable to the message that is sent by abuse. In each case, a sense of worthlessness and devaluation is clearly imparted to the child.

Abusive family processes can be grouped into three general categories: child maltreatment, marital or intimate partner violence, and elder abuse. We focus our analysis in this chapter on child maltreatment (namely, physical abuse and sexual abuse) and

**TABLE 15.1**
Family Violence and Abuse Concepts and Definitions

---

- **Family Abuse and Violence**: act(s) carried out with the intention, or perceived as having the intention, of physically hurting another person (Gelles & Straus,1979)
  - **Child Abuse**: the physical or mental injury, sexual abuse, negligent treatment, or maltreatment of a child under the age of 18 by a person who is responsible for the child's welfare in circumstances which would indicate that the child's health or welfare is harmed or threatened thereby (Federal Child Abuse Prevention and Treatment Act of 1974, Public Law 93-237)
    - **Physical Abuse**: the infliction of physical injury as a result of punching, beating, kicking, biting, burning, shaking, or otherwise harming a child. The parent or caretaker may not have intended to harm the child; rather the injury may have resulted from overdiscipline or physical punishment (National Clearinghouse on Child Abuse and Neglect Information, 2000)
    - **Sexual Abuse**: the engagement of a child in sexual activities for which the child is developmentally unprepared and cannot give informed consent (Berkowitz, Bross, Chadwick, & Whitworth, 1992)
    - **Emotional Abuse**: acts of commission that include confinement, verbal or emotional abuse, or other types of abuse such as withholding sleep, food, or shelter (National Center on Child Abuse and Neglect, 1988)
    - **Physical Neglect**: acts of omission that involve refusal to provide health care, delay in providing health care, abandonment, expulsion of a child from a home, inadequate supervision, failure to meet food and clothing needs, and conspicuous failure to protect a child from hazards or danger (National Center on Child Abuse and Neglect, 1988)
    - **Emotional Neglect**: acts of omission that involve failing to meet the nurturing and affectional needs of a child, refusal to provide psychological care, delays in providing psychological care, and other inattention to the child's developmental needs (National Center on Child Abuse and Neglect, 1988)
  - **Marital or Intimate-Partner Violence**: intentional violent or controlling behavior by a person who is currently, or was previously, in an intimate relationship with the victim (Massachusetts Medical Society Committee on Violence, 1996)
  - **Elder Abuse**: the physical, psychological, or financial abuse or neglect of the elderly that may be intentional or unintentional (American Medical Association, 1992)

---

marital violence. We selected these focal points because they represent the major areas of research in family violence and abuse and because there is some evidence (reviewed later in this chapter) to show a connection or interrelation between these different family processes.

## INCIDENCE AND PREVALENCE

How common is family violence and abuse? The exact answer to this question may never be known. It can be said with certainty that most cases of family violence and abuse occur outside the awareness and attention of the general public. Therefore, researchers must rely on data sources such as self-reports by parents and children and police records. The use of self-report data for measuring incidence and prevalence of family violence is fraught with problems. How many people are willing to admit that they have abused their child? The stigma and fear of legal repercussions for their parents may motivate children to deny ever having been abused. Reliance on police records is equally problematic as many cases of abuse are perpetrated without ever being brought to the attention of the police.

The available data on marital violence indicate that it is a pervasive problem in American society. Up to 30% of all injuries to adult women that result in visits to hospital emergency rooms are the result of battering (McLeer & Anwar, 1989). According to the Bureau of Justice Statistics (1994) the annual rate of intimate partner violent victimization is 5 per 1,000 for women and 0.5 per 1,000 for men. Data from the National Family Violence Surveys (Gelles & Straus, 1988) indicate that in 16% of households surveyed some kind of violence transpired between spouses in the past year. This same data set shows that women initiate marital violence at least as frequently as do men (Stets & Straus, 1990). However, compared to husbands, wives are more likely to be violent in the context of self-defense and to use less severe forms of violence. This may explain the higher victimization rate for women noted previously in the Bureau of Justice Statistics. Finally, about 25% of all couples report at least one act of physical violence at some point in their marriage (Straus, Gelles, & Steinmetz, 1980).

Like intimate-partner violence, the findings on child maltreatment show that it is also a pervasive problem in our society. Approximately 3 million reports of child maltreatment are received annually by Child Protective Service and police departments throughout the United States, about 40% of which are substantiated (Miller & Knudsen, 1999). Annual incidence statistics from the National Center on Child Abuse and Neglect (1996) indicate that 9.1 per 1,000 children are physically abused, 4.5 per 1,000 are sexually abused, and 29.2 per 1,000 are neglected. Several different sources converge to suggest that over 1,000 children are killed each year by their parents or caretakers (Gelles, 1998). About 11% of all females and 4% of all males age 15 or over have been victims of severe sexual abuse (MacMillian et al., 1997).

Collectively, findings on family violence and abuse show that these corrosive behaviors are common in today's families. When one considers that many cases of abuse and violence are never observed or reported, it is likely that many of the statistics reported previously represent underestimates of the actual rates of violence and abuse in the family.

## PHYSICAL ABUSE OF CHILDREN WITHIN THE FAMILY

As highlighted in Table 15.1, physical child abuse involves the infliction of physical injury on the child. In some cases, this may be an unintended consequent of a disciplinary behavior taken too far. In other cases, physical harm to the child might be intentional. Communication researchers Steve Wilson and Ellen Whipple (1995) argued that "physical child abuse is an interactional event; that is, it arises out of communication patterns that occur during discipline episodes" (p. 301). From this perspective physical child abuse could be viewed as a dysfunctional form of parent–child communication that escalates to destructive extremes. Research on physical abuse of children reveals a number of disturbed family environment variables that help to define the family context in which this behavior occurs. Next, several theories of physical child abuse are discussed, followed by an analysis of some of the psychosocial consequences of physical child abuse.

## Associated Family Environment Factors

One issue that complicates the potential understanding of child abuse is the fact that the physical abuse of children does not occur in a vacuum. Rather, families who abuse their children reliably exhibit a host of other social and psychological problems. Whether these problems are causally related to the child abuse or the result of it is not fully known. However, understanding these family environment factors is a vital first step in comprehending how and why families sometimes abuse their children.

Low family *adaptability* and *cohesion* have repeatedly been linked to child abuse (e.g., Higgins & McCabe, 1999; Pelcovitz et al., 2000). For example, Pelcovitz et al. interviewed abused adolescents and found that they perceived their families to be less adaptable (i.e., more rigid) and less cohesive than nonabused adolescents perceived their families to be. Adults who were abused as children also report low family adaptability and cohesion (Higgins & McCabe, 2000). Higgins and McCabe found that such family environments were particularly prevalent among multiply abused (e.g., physical abuse and sexual abuse) offspring. Patchner and Milner (1992) developed a Child Abuse Potential Inventory as a screening device for physical child abuse. It contains items that measure rigidity, unhappiness, problems with the child, problems with the family, and so forth. People who score high on this inventory also score low in family cohesion and family adaptability. The pattern of low adaptability and low cohesion is often referred to as "affectionless control" (Parker, Barrett, & Hickie, 1992). In such families, there is a rigid and strict enforcement of discipline to the point of overprotection, combined with virtually no genuine affection or caring. This is a particularly noxious combination of family environmental factors that is powerfully associated with a host of mental health problems later in life (Segrin, 2001b; see also chap. 13).

A related line of research shows that there are often a number of problematic *parenting behaviors* in families of abused children. Abusive mothers tend to use authoritarian control tactics, anxiety induction, and guilt induction, in addition to practicing inconsistent discipline (Susman, Trickett, Iannotti, Hollenbeck, & Zahn-Waxler, 1985). Observations of abusive mothers interacting with their children revealed a high percentage of aversive behaviors such as hitting, grabbing, pushing, and a low percentage of positive-affect expressions such as approval, encouragement, and hugs (Lahey, Conger, Atkeson, & Treiber, 1984). In an equally clear illustration of parenting problems associated with child abuse, parents were asked about their ways of handling irritating child behaviors, such as a child who would not stop crying (Disbrow, Doerr, & Caulfield, 1977). Abusive parents said that they yelled at their child who would not stop crying whereas nonabusive parents indicate that in such cases they would pick up, hug, or distract the child. Abusive parents in Disbrow et al. (1977) study also perceived lower levels of communication between themselves and their children compared to that of nonabusive parents.

*Conflict* is another family phenomenon that is obvious in families of abused children. The potential for child abuse goes up to the extent that there is a great deal of conflict in the family (Higgins & McCabe, 2000; Patchner & Milner, 1992). Violent families have a notoriously difficult time resolving conflicts (Martin, Schumm, Bugaighis, Jurish, & Bollman, 1987). Martin et al. found evidence of this in the fact that family violence was unrelated to adolescent compliance. It therefore seems that these families have poor conflict management skills and resort to violence, even though it is an ineffective strategy for control or resolution of conflicts.

## Theories of Physical Child Abuse

In an effort to understand why family members perpetrate child abuse, social scientists have developed numerous theoretical explanations of child abuse. Even though each theory or hypothesis contains its own set of assumptions and postulates, it is important to note that child abuse is a complex phenomenon. A single explanation will never be sufficient to understand why the problem exists. Different instances of child abuse may be best explained by different theories. With that caveat in mind, the following represents some of the interpersonal or socially oriented theoretical explanations of child abuse that are currently in circulation (see Gelles, 1985, 1998; Kashani, Daniel, Dandoy, & Holcomb, 1992; Miller & Knudsen, 1999; Milner, 1998, for reviews).

### Social Learning Theory

According to social learning theory (see chap. 2) people acquire behaviors by observing them enacted by a model. The social learning model of child abuse holds that many abusive parents were themselves abused as children. In other words, they observed the actions of their parental role models and later enacted the same abusive actions when they became parents. As noxious as abusive parenting is to a child, it can create a cognitive representation of parenting that depicts the abusive behavior of children as normative. Later in this chapter we address some of the consequences of child abuse and will revisit this intergenerational transmission of abuse effect in a bit more detail.

### Family Systems Theory

The family systems theory explanation of family violence focuses on dysfunctional relationships within the family and between the family and its external environment. As we noted earlier in this chapter, family environments in abusive households are clearly suspect. Notwithstanding the child abuse, there is still something wrong with the parent–child relationships in most of these families. Families who abuse their children are often under varying forms of stress and isolation (Gelles, 1985). The issues in the relationship between the family and its external environment contribute to the risk of abusive behaviors for those internal to the family system. According to systems theory, family members play an active role in influencing one another and their environment. Accordingly, one could view many of their problems as self-generated.

### Social Situational and Stress and Coping Theory

This theory explains the situations under which abuse and other forms of family violence occur. The first factor is structural stress combined with a lack of family coping resources. So, for example, a family with a low income and a disabled member is clearly under considerable structural stress. If such a family did not have sound coping resources at their disposal, they would be at risk for abuse and violence. The second factor of this theory is a cultural norm for the use of violence and force. In societies that condone, perpetrate, or glamorize violence, this sort of behavior will be seen as more acceptable than that in societies where violence is shunned. Family abuse and violence is therefore seen as an amalgamation of structural stress and social norms. The family under stress that lacks effective coping resources will be prone to abuse and violence. If the family exists in a larger society that condones violence, they are likely to enact these behaviors as a means of coping with their stresses. Of course the hallmark sign of poor coping is the failure to recognize that misguided efforts at coping with stress only generate more stress.

### Social Cognition Theories

In models built on social cognition, abusive parents are viewed as people with unrealistic and rigid expectations for children (Slep & O'Leary, 2001). This causes them to define a broad range of child behaviors as "misbehavior" or "failure" to meet standards held by the parents. Often these parents attribute malicious intent to their children's "misbehavior" and get easily angered by it. Social cognition models also focus on poor problem-solving skills among abusive parents. Earlier we examined findings showing that abusive parents attempt to solve a child problem (e.g., nonstop crying) with strategies such as yelling at the child, whereas nonabusive parents would pick up or distract the child. The interpersonal problem-solving method of the abusive parent is grossly ineffective, serving to only worsen the problem, therefore leading to greater frustration and anger for the parent. These negative emotions are then likely to increase the risk for child abuse.

### Attachment Theory

Some have attempted to explain child maltreatment as an attachment disorder (e.g., Schmidt & Eldridge, 1986). In chapter 2 we discussed how attachment theory assumes that early experiences with a caregiver contribute to the formation of internal working models of human relationships. In ideal cases, the caregiver and infant will form a close and secure attachment during this early period. However, parent–child relationships can be marred by attachment disorder when the parent is unwilling or unable to perform the tasks necessary for promotion of the child's growth. The parent may feel ambivalent about his or her role and may be unable to fulfill the child's needs. In such cases where the parent and child never formed an attachment bond, there is an assumption of a high risk for child abuse.

## Psychosocial Consequences of Child Physical Abuse

### Child Aggression Toward Parents

There is fairly compelling evidence that parent-to-child aggression is positively associated with child-to-parent aggression (Brezina, 1999; Meredith, Abbott, & Adams, 1986). Brezina explains this connection by noting that children may learn that violence is at least partially effective at reducing noxious stimulation (i.e., physical aggression) from the abusive parent. In addition to showing that parents' aggression prompts aggression from the children, his analysis shows that aggression from the child tends to deter aggression from the parents. In such cases, children are negatively reinforced (i.e., removal of noxious stimuli) for their aggression and bound to repeat it. A meta-analysis of 88 studies involving over 30,000 people revealed an interesting connection among corporal punishment, child abuse, and child aggression (Gersoff, 2002). The use of corporal punishment (behaviors that do not result in physical injury such as slapping and spanking) is positively associated with perpetrating physical child abuse (behaviors that risk injury such as punching, kicking, or burning). Furthermore, parents' use of corporal punishment is positively associated with their children's aggression (Gershoff). Of course, many cases of physical child abuse are misguided attempts at discipline or punishment that were taken too far. Ironically, parents' use of physical aggression toward their child, while possibly effective at securing compliance in the short run, is associated with *greater* aggressive behavior from the child, including aggression directed toward the parent him- or herself in the long run. Clearly, parents who physically abuse their children send the message that aggression is an appropriate behavior in the family system, while elevating the risk of child-to-parent aggression in the service of self-defense and deterrence.

### Adult Aggression Toward Partners

Given that child abuse is associated with aggressive behavior in children, even toward their own parents, it is perhaps no surprise that child abuse is also associated with aggression toward intimate partners later in life. Several studies of dating violence show that it is more prevalent among young adults who were abused as children (e.g., Marshall & Rose, 1990; Simons, Lin, & Gordon, 1998). The Simons et al. (1998) study is noteworthy for showing that corporal punishment of children is significantly and positively associated with later violence in dating relationships. They explain that "corporal punishment teaches that it is both legitimate and effective to hit those you love" (p. 475). The ill effects of child abuse appear to persevere into marital relationships as well. A meta-analysis of 39 studies that included close to 30,000 people revealed a significant relationship between experiencing child abuse and perpetrating spousal abuse (Smith et al., 2000). In general, it appears that experiencing child abuse creates a greater likelihood of committing subsequent spousal abuse. Once again, this may be due to the fact that children learn to accept and associate violence in the context of a close relationship. What is perhaps even more alarming is the fact that child abuse also appears to increase the risk of being a *victim* of spousal abuse (Smith et al.). Some children learn a victim role from being abused by their parent(s). Even though such individuals are not to blame for subsequent victimization later in life, their behaviors and cognitions may predispose them to further abuse. One simple explanation for this could be that people with a history of accepting and tolerating abusive conduct may be attractive to would-be perpetrators.

### Psychological Problems

One of the more consistently documented consequences of child abuse is the experience of psychological problems. These include depression, alcoholism, loneliness, anxiety, and eating disorders, to name but a few (Downs & Miller, 1998; Kashani, Burbach, &

Rosenberg, 1988; Segrin, 2001b). These issues are covered in more detail in chapter 13. For the time being, it will suffice to say that parental abuse communicates a message of rejection and devaluation. In the majority of cases, psychological damage caused by such messages far outlives physical pain or injury. This is because children may internalize these aversive experiences and develop a negative self-image. In addition, abuse presents a very confusing task to the child, namely, reconciling the pain and degradation that are inflicted with a supposedly positive and nurturing idealized image of a parent. As difficult as child abuse is for adults to comprehend, it is surely far more difficult for a child to make sense of. This can therefore lead to a lack of trust in others or an excessive neediness that will bring with it a host of psychological problems associated with affect regulation. Some of these problems might contribute to difficulties with abused children's nonverbal communication such as in the processing of emotional facial expressions (Pollak & Tolley-Schell, 2003) and regulation of personal space (Vranic, 2003).

### Intergenerational Transmission of Child Abuse

According to social learning theory, children would learn how to be parents first and foremost by observing their own parents' behavior. If abusive behaviors are modeled, children may be inclined to repeat those behaviors later in life when they are parents. This is the reasoning behind the intergenerational transmission hypothesis. It is evident in findings that show, for example, that parents who were hit as teenagers by their parents are more likely to be verbally (i.e., insult, swear at, or threaten) and physically abusive toward their own children (Tajima, 2002). The idea that abused children will someday go on to abuse their own children has been met with mixed support and has been discussed from different perspectives in the research literature (e.g., Margolin & Gordis, 2000; Miller & Knudsen, 1999). It appears that about 20% to 30% of all abused children go on to be abusive parents (Oliver, 1993; Straus & Gelles, 1990). Therefore one obvious conclusion is that most abused children *do not* repeat the mistakes of their parents by growing up to abuse their own children. On the other hand, consider the fact that only 5% of parents in the general population abuse their children, implying a sixfold increase in abuse rates as a function of a childhood history of abuse (Kaufman & Zigler, 1987). From this vantage point, the intergenerational impact of child abuse looks far more compelling. This is a case where there are multiple ways of interpreting the research findings. Most abused children do not go on to abuse their own children, but a history of child abuse greatly increases the risk of later perpetrating child abuse. The fact that so many abused children do not go on to abuse their own children shows that there is no deterministic intergenerational transmission. Other factors must also be present to translate receiving abuse into perpetrating abuse (Margolin & Gordis, 2000).

## SEXUAL ABUSE OF CHILDREN WITHIN THE FAMILY

For many, the sexual abuse of children is extremely difficult to understand. Some of the clearest theoretical accounts of this noxious behavior are still wanting for more explanation. It is evident that childhood sexual abuse (CSA) virtually always occurs in family systems that have numerous other serious problems. Scientists have been working diligently to understand the unique effects of CSA, and the distressed family environments in which it occurs, on children who experience sexual abuse. From a communication perspective CSA presents a confusing array of messages, mixing affection with devaluation with gross boundary violations. The prevalence of CSA between stepparents and children is perhaps reflective of a failure to internalize the parental role and a consequent willingness to grossly exploit children for personal gain or fulfillment. Of the three types of family violence and abuse covered in this chapter, childhood sexual abuse is perhaps the least understood and therefore the most in need of further research and theory development. A synopsis of the family research on CSA is presented in two sections: one that covers family environment factors associated with CSA and one that explores psychosocial consequences of CSA.

## Associated Family Environment Factors

Despite the fact that some writers tend to discuss physical and sexual child abuse together, the two phenomena are sufficiently distinct to warrant separate analysis. However, readers will notice that some of the same family characteristics that are associated with child physical abuse are also associated with child sexual abuse. These might represent general signs of family pathology that create a nonspecific risk for several different maladaptive processes and outcomes. At the same time, there are certain family processes that have been linked only to child sexual abuse.

*Family cohesion* has proven to be a powerful discriminator between those families that perpetrate CSA and those that do not (e.g., Alexander & Lupfer, 1987; Benedict & Zautra, 1993; Harter, Alexander, & Neimeyer, 1988; Hulsey & Sexton, 1992; Ray, Jackson, & Townsley, 1991). The general pattern established by these studies is that cohesion is perceived to be lower in those families where there are cases of CSA. Low family cohesion indicates a weak emotional bond among family members. It is this weak bond, particularly between the parent and the child, that might allow the parent to sexually abuse a child absent the empathy or concern that would ordinarily prevent such acts. At the same time, recall that in Olson's circumplex model (see chap. 1) both low and high levels of cohesion are thought to be dysfunctional.

Even though most large survey studies reveal low family-of-origin cohesion among CSA victims, there is reason to believe that in perhaps a smaller number of cases, very high cohesion, or enmeshment, is a problem. Alexander (1985) presented two compelling case studies of remarkably high enmeshment in families that perpetrated CSA. In both cases, the families kept mostly to themselves and avoided people outside of the family system. In one family there was so little separation among members that one individual would answer questions asked of another. In this same family, property was shared among the members including a toothbrush and undergarments. The documentation of ultra-high cohesion in some families with CSA fits with findings discussed later on boundary ambiguity—a phenomenon that goes hand in hand with enmeshment. Faust, Runyon, and Kenny (1995) pointed out that enmeshment is often manifest as overinvolvement between the father and the child victim.

Problems with *family adaptability* have also been documented in the CSA literature. Once again, the general pattern is one of lower adaptability (i.e., rigid family dynamics) in the families of origin of CSA survivors (Alexander & Lupfer, 1987; Harter et al., 1988). This pattern might be manifest, for example, in a very strict and authoritarian style of parenting (Hulsey & Sexton, 1992; Nash, Hulsey, Sexton, Harralson, & Lambert, 1993). Participants in Hulsey and Sexton's study described their families as rigidly ruled in an authoritarian style. These family environments appeared to be particularly repressive. Once again it is important to note that very high levels of adaptability could be equally problematic according to the circumplex model. In the following section, we present findings on role confusion or role reversal in families that perpetrate childhood sexual abuse. Such role reversals are hallmark signs of chaos or extremely high levels of adaptability.

Another theme that appears repeatedly in the literature on CSA is *family isolation*. It is common for survivors of CSA to have been reared in families that were largely cut off from society (e.g., Alexander, 1985; Harter et al., 1988; Herman & Hirschman, 1981a; Hulsey & Sexton, 1992). Isolation does not necessarily imply that the family lives in a rural area, although that would be one obvious avenue to isolation. Some families achieve and maintain isolation simply by keeping to themselves and not interacting with others outside of the immediate family system. In other words, it is social isolation more than mere physical isolation that is predictive of CSA. This isolation appears to be conducive to CSA, because the family is for the most part outside of the watchful eye of those who might recognize the dysfunctional family environment and perhaps act to correct the situation. Family isolation might also be a manifestation of rejecting societal standards and norms. In the terminology of family systems theory, this isolation is evidence of a relatively closed family system.

Related to family isolation is a pattern of *parental absence* that appears to create a heightened risk for CSA in the family of origin. It is often the case that mothers are, for various reasons, unavailable in the families that perpetrate CSA (Benedict & Zautra, 1993; Herman & Hirschman, 1981b). Sometimes mothers are unavailable due to foster care, serious illness, employment outside of the home, or simply too many other children to look after. An unusually compelling case for the impact of parental absence can be found in the Benedict and Zautra study. They examined over a dozen family-of-origin variables among CSA survivors and corroborated the assessments with collateral data from siblings. Their results showed that parental absence was a more powerful risk factor for CSA than any of the other variables assessed (including cohesion, conflict, control, and stepparent family). They explain that parental absence creates a family environment that is conducive to CSA. This may be due to a lack of supervision by a parent who could potentially protect the child from the other exploitative parent. Alternatively, parental absence may make it difficult to fully meet the child's emotional needs. This could lead to a high need for affection and attention on the part of the child, making him or her susceptible to sexual exploitation from unscrupulous family members.

It is virtually true by definition that child sexual abuse represents a gross *boundary violation, role confusion, and role reversal*. Family scientists regularly find that there are significant problems with role confusion and role reversal in families that perpetrate CSA (Faust et al., 1995; Hanks & Stratton, 1988; Herman & Hirschman, 1981b; Koopmans, 1994; Parker & Parker, 1986). In Herman and Hirschman's investigation, 45% of women with a history of incestuous father–daughter contact had assumed a maternal role in the family, often by the age of 8 or 9, compared to only 5% in a control group. Koopmans found an equally strong association between CSA and role confusion (i.e., feeling like the parent–child relationship was another type of relationship, such as a sibling relationship) in the family or origin. Virtually every participant in this study who had experienced CSA had also experienced role confusion in the family of origin. Hanks and Stratton (1988) describe this family dynamic as one in which "parents come to depend on the child to provide the caregiving they need.... Sexual abuse may also involve a reversal of care or supply of needs" (p. 249). Herman and Hirschman explain that for the female CSA victims they studied "providing sexual services to their fathers seemed to develop as an extension of their maternal family role" (p. 968).

What is the course of action by which role confusion or role reversal culminates in childhood sexual abuse? Extrapolating from the findings presented thus far, it appears that in many of these families mothers are at least somewhat out of the picture, the families are away from the surveillance of others, and there may be either low cohesion, suggesting minimal parental concern for the child, or high cohesion, suggesting inappropriate emotional closeness with the child. In either case, perpetrators turn to the child for the sort of relationship one would ordinarily seek from a spouse. In perpetrating such acts, the parent commits a gross boundary violation, exploiting the naïveté of a child and the fact that she is physically present in the family environment when the mother may not be. Even though the overall family environment may create a conduciveness to this type of maltreatment, it requires no inferential leap to appreciate the fact that something must be seriously amiss in the psychological constitution of the perpetrator to allow for this conduct.

Cases of CSA often occur in families in which there is otherwise a high level of *family conflict* (Benedict & Zautra, 1993; Draucker, 1996; Edwards & Alexander, 1992; Nash et al., 1993). Survivors of CSA regularly indicate that there was more conflict in their families of origin than people reared in families with no CSA. Most of what is known about elevated family conflict and CSA comes from retrospective reports from adult survivors of CSA. For this reason, it is difficult to determine whether family conflict preceded or followed commission of CSA. CSA could understandably lead to substantial increases in family conflict. On the other hand, high levels of family conflict could create the sort of physical and psychological distance between a parent and the remainder of the family that could then create an environment that is conducive to this type of child abuse.

## Psychosocial Consequences of Child Sexual Abuse

### Psychological and Interpersonal Problems

Just as with child physical abuse, among the more dominant consequences of CSA are psychological and interpersonal problems (Bennett, Hughes, & Luke, 2000; Koopmans, 1994; Rumstein-McKean & Hunsley, 2001). The psychological problems associated with CSA include, for example, posttraumatic stress disorder, depression, low self-esteem, and social anxiety (see chap. 13 for a more in-depth analysis of these problems). It is common to observe dissociative symptoms in survivors of CSA. These symptoms are presumed to be a sort of psychological residue of the coping mechanisms that the child used when the sexual abuse was ongoing. Additionally, a number of interpersonal problems in adulthood have been linked with CSA, such as difficulty forming and maintaining relationships, relational dissatisfaction, social isolation, sexual dysfunction, insecure attachment, and divorce (Rumstein-McKean & Hunsley; Swanson & Mallinckrodt, 2001). The pervasiveness, severity, and duration of these problems are a testimony to the extremely toxic nature of CSA in the family of origin.

## Separating the Effects of Abuse From Family Environment

One issue that has plagued researchers who try to understand the psychosocial consequences of CSA is the fact that CSA is confounded with pathogenic family environments. In other words, CSA does not occur in isolation from other family problems. There is virtually always something else wrong with the family in which CSA is perpetrated (Long & Jackson, 1994). For this reason, scientists have been attempting to understand the unique effects of CSA versus other family dysfunction on children reared in these environments. A number of carefully controlled studies now suggest that dysfunctional family dynamics may be more responsible than abuse, per se, for the increased psychological adjustment problems that are seen in victims of CSA (Briere & Elliot, 1993; Draucker, 1996; Fromuth, 1986; Harter et al., 1988; Nash et al., 1993). When family environment variables such as adaptability and cohesion, parental supportiveness, conflict, and enmeshment are statistically controlled, differences in psychological adjustment problems between sexually abused and nonabused children tend to disappear (but see Kamsner & McCabe, 2000). These analyses suggest that the pathogenic family environments that tend to go hand in hand with CSA (see earlier section on Associated Family Environment Factors) are more responsible for psychological adjustments problems than the actual abuse itself. Consistent with family systems theory, it appears necessary to understand the larger family context in which childhood sexual abuse is embedded in order to appreciate the psychosocial consequences of this form of maltreatment.

## Revictimization

Among the more tragic consequences of CSA is a propensity for revictimization. People who are sexually abused in the family of origin are at increased risk for subsequent abuse by other family members (Herman & Hirschman, 1981b). A history of sexual abuse is also associated with an increased risk of rape or other nonconsensual sexual experiences in adulthood (e.g., Alexander & Lupfer, 1987; Elliot & Briere, 1993; Fromuth, 1986). Why does CSA increase vulnerability to later sexual assault? Messman-Moore and Long (2003) argue that two interpersonal mechanisms in revictimization are *exposure risk* (i.e., factors that increase the probability of contact with would-be perpetrators such as high-risk sexual behaviors) and *enhancement of perpetrator aggression* (i.e., factors that increase the probability of a would-be perpetrator acting aggressively such as poor risk recognition, intoxication, or dissociation). These later factors tend to identify the victim as an "easy target" in the eyes of potential aggressors. One other possibility suggested by Alexander and Lupfer is that CSA may instill an expectation of victimization. They also suggest that abused children may be socialized into a subservient role in a partriarchal family structure. Consequently, survivors of CSA may actually seek out other abusive relationships in their adulthood because this is what is familiar to them (Herman & Hirschman, 1977). This explanation is consistent with related findings showing that CSA victims often recreate family-of-origin characteristics such as intergenerational intimacy, personal authority, and intergenerational fusion in their families of orientation (Carson, Gertz, Donaldson, & Wonderlich, 1991). Many victims of childhood sexual abuse are socialized into a victim role by their experiences in the family of origin. The psychological template for exploitative relationships that is created by this noxious treatment tends to plague survivors long after they leave the family of origin.

## VIOLENCE IN THE MARITAL SUBSYSTEM

Violence in the marital subsystem, also known as "domestic violence" or "intimate partner" violence has been the focus of considerable research attention. This is no doubt fueled by the increased public awareness of domestic violence and its negative consequences for families. In this section of the chapter we review research findings and theories on violence that occur in the marital context. This includes an examination of communication behaviors that occur in violent marriages, followed by a discussion of different types of abusive spouses and the patriarchal social structure theory of marital violence. The final sections of this chapter cover the intergenerational transmission of spouse abuse, the association between marital violence and physical child abuse, and violence in gay and lesbian partnerships.

### Interaction Behaviors in Violent Marriages

#### Negativity in Interactions

It may come as no surprise to learn that the interactions of violent spouses are marked by a number of negative communication behaviors. In laboratory interactions, martially distressed and violent husbands expressed more negative affect (e.g., anger, distrust, contempt, belligerence, criticize, disagree, and put down) to their wives than martially distressed but nonviolent husbands did (Berns, Jacobson, & Gottman, 1999a; Cordova, Jacobson, Gottman, Rushe, & Cox, 1993). Because of the martially distressed but nonviolent control group, this heightened negativity cannot be attributed to the effect of marital distress. Understandably, negative-affect reciprocity is also a problem in violent marriages as it is in distressed marriages (Cordova et al.). However, the strength of this reciprocity is greater in distressed violent marriages than in distressed nonviolent marriages. In other words, an aversive interaction behavior by one spouse is more likely to be followed by an aversive behavior from the other spouse in violent compared to nonviolent marriages (Cordova et al.). During in-home interviews about a typical day in their family, the discourse of abusive couples expressed anger, frustration, and complaints about their spouse (Sabourin & Stamp, 1995). In contrast, nonabusive couples tended to compliment each other and express more joy and contentment with family life. It is also noteworthy that the interactions of violent couples are not entirely devoid of positivity (Lloyd, 1996). Even though Lloyd discovered high levels of negative communication behaviors (e.g., criticize and ignore) in violent marriages, she also found high levels of positive communication behaviors (e.g., compliment and apologize). This suggests that the negative interactions of violent couples may be part of a larger picture of volatility where a lot of positive and negative messages are exchanged.

### Demand–Withdraw

In chapter 10 we reviewed data showing that the demand–withdraw pattern of interaction is associated with marital distress. Recall that this is a form of interaction whereby one spouse, typically the wife, makes a demand for change and the other spouse, typically the husband, withdraws from the interaction. This dysfunctional pattern of marital communication appears to be prevalent in violent marriages. For example, martially distressed and violent husbands engage in more demand during laboratory interactions than do martially distressed but nonviolent husbands (Berns et al., 1999a). Their battered wives also make more demands than do nonbattered wives. Researchers believe that high levels of husband *and* wife demand must be understood in their different contexts. Violent husbands appear to be demanding in the context of perpetrating abuse, whereas battered wives are demanding in effort to reduce physical and emotional abuse (Berns et al.; Berns, Jacobson, & Gottman, 1999b).

When the demand–withdrawal pattern is evident, ordinarily the wife demands and the husband withdraws. However, this pattern is typically reversed in domestically violent marriages, such that the husband demands and the wife withdraws (Babcock, Waltz, Jacobson, & Gottman, 1993). Why are levels of demand so uncharacteristically high for husbands in violent marriages? The power deficit hypothesis of marital violence suggests that people become violent when they perceive themselves as lacking power in the relationship (Babcock et al.). People sometimes confuse the use of physical violence with the possession of power. However, the question is what motivates people to use physical violence in the first place? Babcock et al. argue that in the marital context violence may be seen as a means for acquiring power over a partner, especially when one's communication skills for doing so are otherwise insufficient. These researchers found that the less communicative husbands were, the more physically and psychologically abusive they were toward their spouses. Also, the less decision-making power husbands had, the more violent they were. People often try to get their way in a marriage through verbal negotiation and influence attempts. However, people with poor communication skills may make demands that go unmet because of the nonpersuasive or ineffective way in which they are pitched. In such cases, violence becomes a means that some husbands use to attempt to secure power in the relationship. The irony is that this seemingly powerful heavy-handed behavior is actually the tool of the spouse who feels powerless in the marriage.

### Relational Control

Earlier we noted that spousal violence often represents a struggle for control in a marital relationship. This relational dimension tends to be apparent in violent couples' verbal as well as in nonverbal behaviors. When aggressive and nonaggressive couples discussed topics such as how they met and decided to get married, how they handle disagreements, and what it takes to have a good marriage, there were more nonsupport and one-up messages uttered in the conversations of aggressive compared to nonaggressive couples (Rogers, Castleton, & Lloyd, 1996). One-up messages attempt to direct the partner or assert definitional rights. In essence they are verbal attempts to control the conversational partner. It is of further interest to note that the ratio of husband-to-wife one-up messages, or domineeringness, was considerably greater for aggressive couples. In nonaggressive couples, husbands and wives uttered roughly equal proportions of one-up messages. However, in aggressive couples the proportion of one-up utterances during marital interactions was much greater for husbands than for wives. In the home interview study conducted by Sabourin and Stamp (1995) the discourse of abusive couples had themes of opposition and interference. Their nonabusive counterparts on the other hand expressed cooperation, mutual facilitation, and interdependence in their talk. The works of Rogers et al. (1996) and Sabourin and Stamp (1995) illustrate how aggression is part of a larger constellation of communication behaviors that reflect the desire to assert control over a spouse. Even when they are not enacting physically violent behaviors, this struggle for control is evident in the verbal behavior of aggressive couples.

### Husband and Wife Roles in Violent Interactions

Earlier in this chapter we noted that marital violence is not entirely in the domain of husbands. Women married to violent men are often violent themselves. However, husbands and wives enact violence in different interpersonal circumstances. First, women in violent marriages tend to enact violence only in reaction to their husbands' violence, whereas husbands enact violence in response to a much wider variety of wife behaviors, including many that are not violent (Jacobson et al., 1994). Second, Jacobson et al. also found that husbands' violence appears to be less suppressable than wives' violence. Both husbands and wives in this study of violent marriages indicated that once the husband became violent, there were no wife behaviors that could be performed to stop him, including wife withdrawal. On the other hand, wives were only violent as long as their husbands were behaving violently. This research by Jacobson et al. indicates that despite the fairly high rate of mutual violence in marriages, husbands' violent behaviors clearly follow a different course and trajectory from those of wives' violent behaviors. In marital interactions husbands' violence is far less contingent on wives' behaviors, but wives' violence is clearly contingent on ongoing violent husband behavior.

### Verbal Aggression

Verbal aggression is a communication behavior that is much more common in violent than in nonviolent marriages. In a conflict interaction, there are at least two different ways that spouses might express their disagreement. An *argumentative* response takes issue with the topic or position of the partner's statement. For example, A might say "Let's go out to dinner and a movie tonight." An argumentative response from B might look something like, "I don't think we should, because I don't have a lot of money and we need to get up early tomorrow." This response comments directly on the ideas raised by A. On the other hand, a *verbally aggressive* response attacks the self-concept of the partner, causing psychological pain or harm. Following the previous example, a verbally aggressive response from B might look like, "How stupid. You must be determined to spend every penny that we have on frivolous activities." This comment does not directly address the issues raised by A, but rather attacks A's self-concept.

Verbally aggressive communication and marital violence appear to go hand in hand (Infante, Sabourin, Rudd, & Shannon, 1990; Meredith et al., 1986; Sabourin, Infante, & Rudd, 1993). In addition to sending more verbally aggressive messages to each other than nonviolent couples do, violent couples also have a strong tendency to reciprocate each other's verbal aggression (Burman, John, & Margolin, 1992; Sabourin et al.). This means that violent couples meet verbal aggression with more verbal aggression. Thus, they behave in such a way as to prompt further verbal aggression from each other (Sabourin, 1996). Unfortunately, in many circumstances this verbal aggression escalates into physical violence. This is known by communication researchers as the catalyst hypothesis (Roloff, 1996).

Why is verbally aggressive communication so prevalent in violent marriages, and why does it often escalate into violence? Sabourin (1996) argued that verbal aggression is a necessary but not sufficient condition for physical violence. It can act as a catalyst to physical aggression by increasing the arousal of the person who is verbally attacked (who often responds in kind to the partner). When arousal escalates to a certain threshold, husbands and wives may shift from verbal to physical aggression. This happens because people who use verbal aggression often lack sound argumentation skills (Infante, Chandler, & Rudd, 1989). When some people cannot get their way with words, they resort to physical violence. As noted earlier, violent couples are much more likely to exhibit verbal aggression than nonviolent couples are. However, what is less intuitive is that violent couples are *lower* in argumentativeness than nonviolent couples are (Infante et al.). This suggests that nonviolent couples approach their conflicts with argumentation, whereas violent couples attack each other physically and verbally. This pattern has been explained by an argumentation skill deficiency model: People who lack verbal argumentation skills resort to physical violence to establish control in a marriage.

## Types of Abusive Spouses

Fitzpatrick (2002) noted that one of the major myths of family violence is that all abusers are alike. People often think of the abusive spouse as a hostile, domineering, male, usually with a drinking problem. Even though this portrayal has some basis in reality, scientific research indicates that there are a number of different types of abusive spouses. In order to fully understand how and why marital violence occurs, it is necessary to examine these different profiles and patterns of spousal abuse.

One basic distinction in abusive male spouses is defined by the contextual pervasiveness of their violent behavior (Holtzworth-Munroe, Meehan, Herron, Rehman, & Stuart, 2003; Holtzworth-Munroe & Stuart, 1994). These subgroups of batterers are labeled (a) family-only, (b) dysphoric and borderline, and (c) generally violent and antisocial. The *family-only* abuser is a man who limits his violent outbursts to family contexts. Unlike the other two types of batterers whose behavior is associated with underlying personality disorders, the family-only batterer has specific interpersonal problems in the family to which he reacts with violence. As we discuss elsewhere in this chapter, one such problem may be the perception of powerlessness. Of all the types, the family-only batterer engages in the least severe forms of violence. The *dysphoric and borderline* batterer is marked by impulsiveness, unstable relationships, identity disturbance, mood swings, and boredom. As the title implies, this person suffers from a form of mental illness that causes problems with affect regulation. The third type of batterer, the *generally violent and antisocial*, is an individual who uses violence to resolve conflicts in many different situations. Thus, this is a person who is usually violent at work, with friends, and with family members and is the most persistently violent of the various subtypes (Holtzworth-Munroe et al.). Such people are often in conflict with others and the law. Their antisocial personality is such that they feel no remorse for others or guilt over their actions, and they are easily frustrated and intolerant of delayed gratification. What is particularly unique about the generally violent batterer is that he does not have interpersonal problems that are unique to the family. Rather, the marriage is merely one context in which his behavior is manifest. For individuals with such pathological tendencies, violence literally becomes a way of life.

A closely related scheme for understanding intimate partner violence has been developed by sociologist Michael Johnson and is based on the motivations of the perpetrator and his or her partner (Johnson & Ferraro, 2000). Perhaps the most benign type of partner violence is *common couple violence* in which partners lash out against each other in the context of specific arguments, unconnected to any general pattern of control. Johnson and Ferraro (2000) note that these couples are comparable to Holtzworth-Munroe et al.'s "family only" type. *Intimate terrorism* is a type of partner violence that is motivated primarily by the desire to control one's partner and is perpetrated mostly by men. The intimate terrorists would encompass both the "generally and violent antisocial" and the "dysphoric and borderline" types in Holtzworth-Munroe et al.'s taxonomy. *Violent resistance* occurs largely in the service of self-defense and is perpetrated mostly by women. Finally, *mutual violent control* involves both the husband and the wife literally battling for control over each other. Johnson observes that such couples might be composed of two intimate terrorists. Johnson's taxonomy of partner violence is valuable not only for distinguishing the motivations that drive different types of violence but also for revealing powerful sex differences in the perpetration of different patterns of violence.

An interesting and useful taxonomy of male batterers is centered on the heart rate reactivity of the batterer when engaging in marital conflict (Gottman et al., 1995). These researchers discovered two very different types of martially violent males. In laboratory interactions, Type 1 husbands were found to have a *lower heart rate* upon initiating conflict interactions with their spouses than they did at a resting baseline. On the other hand, Type 2 husbands had an *increased heart rate* when they participated in a conflict interaction. The remarkably different profiles in husbands' physiological arousal were associated with equally remarkable profiles in marital communication behaviors. For example, Type 1 (lowered heart rate) husbands showed more emotional aggression (i.e., contempt and belligerence) during marital interactions than did Type 2 (increased heart rate) husbands. However, Type 1 husbands became less aggressive over time, whereas Type 2 husbands became more aggressive with their wives over the course of an interaction (but never to the level at which Type 1 husbands started out). Wives of the Type 1 husbands were less angry and more defensive and sad in the interactions than were wives of Type 2 husbands. Outside of the laboratory interactions, there were several other notable distinctions among these different types of violent husbands. Type 1 batterers had higher rates of antisocial and aggressive–sadistic personality disorder than did Type 2 batterers. Perhaps it is therefore no surprise to learn that Type 1 batterers were more likely to threaten to use a knife or gun, and actually use a knife or gun, and to kick, hit, or slap their wives than were Type 2 batterers (Jacobson, Gottman, & Shortt, 1995). At a 2-year follow up, 27% of Type 2 marriages had broken up, versus 0% of Type 1 marriages. There were also obvious differences in the pervasiveness of their violence: 44% of Type 1 husbands had been violent toward others, whereas only 3% of Type 2 husbands were violent outside of their marriage. A brief glimpse of the potential origins of Type 1 batterers is evident in their history of observing parental violence: 46% of Type 1 men were exposed to parental violence (father → mother and mother → father) compared to only 11% of Type 2 men.

The Gottman et al. (1995) investigation paints two very different pictures of male batterers. The Type 1 husband approaches marital interactions with severe violence, yet shows reduced arousal suggestive of cool detachment. The Type 2 husband gets physiologically aroused by martial confrontations and his aggression builds over the course of the interaction. This second type of batterer is far less likely than the first to be involved in violence outside of the family or to have serious personality disorders. Afterwards, Jacobson and Gottman (1998) expanded on this typology, characterizing the two types of abusive husbands as "cobras" and "pit bulls." The cobra strikes quickly and is cool and methodical. Its aggression is lethal. The pit bull on the other hand gets worked up over the course of an interaction and strikes out in anger in the heat of the moment. Even though the consequences of being married to either type of batterer are potentially severe, the propensity for extreme violence, disordered personality, and greater involvement in substance abuse that characterizes the Type 1 batterer make him a particularly dangerous spouse.

In chapter 2, we explained how attachment theory predicts a connection between early experiences with a primary caregiver and subsequent interpersonal relationships. One of the more interesting applications of attachment theory in family relationships has been to different types of violent spouses. It appears that violent spouses have different adult attachment styles than do nonviolent spouses, and that among violent spouses there are subtypes that can be distinguished by their attachment orientation (Babcock, Jacobson, Gottman, & Yerington, 2000). Babcock et al. found that distressed but not violent husbands predominantly had a secure attachment style, whereas distressed and violent husbands had an insecure attachment style. Among these insecurely attached violent husbands were two subtypes with distinct interpersonal tendencies. Those whose attachment style was *preoccupied* engaged in mostly expressive violence (i.e., violence aimed at reducing negative affect). On the other hand, violent husbands with a *dismissing* attachment style showed more instrumental violence (i.e., violence aimed at achieving a specific goal). Babcock et al. theorize that the dismissive violent husbands use violence to thwart perceived threats to their authority. They were much more likely to exhibit stonewalling during a marital conflict interaction than were preoccupied husbands, and their wives were more likely to be defensive in these interactions. Alternatively, preoccupied husbands seem to become violent and abusive when their wives attempt to withdraw. This may trigger increased arousal due to perceived threats of abandonment. Essentially, these two types of violent husbands, defined by their attachment style, differ in the extent to which they use violence to control their wives (the dismissing) versus regulate their negative emotions (preoccupied).

## Spousal Abuse and Patriarchal Social Structure

Among some of the other theoretical explanations of intimate-partner violence already presented in this chapter is an explanation developed by feminist theorists based on the uneven distribution of power between males and females (e.g., Dobash & Dobash, 1979). The idea behind this perspective is that society is set up to support a patriarchal or male-dominated social structure. This social structure is thought to support the subordination of women and contribute to a pattern of violence perpetrated by men against women. In a patriarchal society, violence against women would be viewed as acceptable, and male perpetrators would not be punished because of their power and standing in society.

Even though the patriarchal theory is a bit more macroscopic, by virtue of its focus on societal issues, than most of the theoretical explanations that we consider in this chapter, it is important to understand for several reasons. First, all relationships within and between the sexes are embedded in a larger societal structure. It is impossible to deny that at least historically males and females have not had equal status and authority in American society. These more abstract power differences surely seeped into some close relationships and perhaps manifested themselves in physically aggressive behavior. Second, the patriarchal theory represents something of an unresolved dilemma for social scientists. On one hand, the power, status, and roles of men and women are not the same in our society. However, the validity of this argument as an explanation for intimate partner violence is challenged by data indicating comparable rates of female $\rightarrow$ male and male $\rightarrow$ female partner violence. Most cases of intimate partner violence involve mutual violence (Anderson, 2002). Of course, one obvious rebuttal would be that these statistics fail to capture the context of these two patterns of violence where men are more likely to use violence to aggress and women are more likely to use violence to defend. In addition, the negative consequences of intimate partner violence are more severe for women than for men (Anderson). Perhaps a more strenuous challenge to the patriarchal explanation comes from data showing high rates of partner violence in gay and lesbian relationships. Later in this chapter we discuss these findings in more detail, but for the time being, it should be clear that if gender-based power differentials are behind most cases of intimate partner violence, then these acts should be rare in same-sex relationships. However, this is not the case.

## The Intergenerational Transmission of Spouse Abuse

Earlier in this chapter we mentioned that one of the popular theories of child abuse, and family violence more generally, is the intergenerational transmission theory. According to this theory, children who observe violence between their parents are likely to enact similar behaviors later in life when they are married. This perspective draws heavily on social learning theory (see chap. 2) and assumes that the repeated observation of parental violence teaches the child that violence is a family norm and that the modeled behavior is an appropriate means for addressing problems. A meta-analysis of 39 research studies involving 12,981 participants showed that there is a small but significant positive association between growing up in a violent home and perpetrating spousal abuse (Smith et al., 2000). Smith et al. also found that this modeling effect was stronger for males than for females. In other words, males who grew up in a violent home were more likely to be abusive toward their spouses than were females who grew up in a violent home. However, there also appears to be an effect for being a victim of spousal abuse, and this is stronger for females. Exposure to parental violence also puts people, especially females, at higher risk for becoming victims of spousal abuse later in life.

When children grow up witnessing violence between spouses they tend to develop emotional and behavioral problems (Wolfe, Crooks, Lee, McIntyre-Smith, & Jaffe, 2003) along with positive attitudes toward marital violence (Markowitz, 2001). The favorable attitudes, in turn, are positively associated with the use of violence in adulthood against both spouses and children. Markowitz (2001) noted "By watching parents hit each other and by being hit themselves, children come to learn that violence is an appropriate means of conflict resolution, enacted in their later marital relationships" (p. 216). What is particularly interesting about this intergenerational behavioral effect is that it is largely mediated by favorable attitudes toward family violence. In other words, the favorable attitudes account for the relationship between modeled violence in the family of origin and later violence in the family of orientation. One important practical implication of this finding is that attempts to control spousal violence should be focused on changing attitudes about the appropriateness of this conduct.

The impact of parental violence on children's mental representations of family interaction is evident very early in childhood (Grych, Wachsmuth-Schlaefer, & Klockow, 2002). Grych et al. studied 3½- to 7-year-old children from homes with and without marital violence. The children were given a series of fictitious family scenarios such as disagreeing about what to have for dinner and how to punish a child for accidentally breaking a lamp. The children were then asked to complete the story in their own words and with the actions of dolls that they could manipulate. The discourse of children from homes with marital violence suggested greater conflict escalation than that of children from nonviolent homes. In other words, it appears that as children witness interparental violence, they tend to normalize the phenomenon and anticipate that small conflicts will grow into larger conflicts and go unresolved. Grych et al. interpret these children's stories as reflective of an already developing schema for the dysfunctional course and outcome of family disagreements.

Finally, the interpersonal implications of violence modeled in the family of origin are evident even before young adults marry. Engaged couples in which the male partner witnessed parental violence already show more negative and dysfunctional conflict management behaviors than those who were unexposed to parental violence (Halford, Sanders, Behrens, 2000). These researchers videotaped couples discussing an issue that was a point of contention in their relationship. Analysis of these interactions revealed more invalidation, negative nonverbal behavior, withdrawal, and conflict for the couples in which the male was exposed to family or origin violence compared to those where there was no exposure to such violence. These findings show that many of the precursors to potentially violent marital encounters are already apparent in couples with a history of exposure to violent martial interactions in their families of origin.

## The Association Between Marital Violence and Physical Child Abuse

There is good reason to believe that violence becomes a systemwide problem for some families. That is to say that violence between husbands and wives is associated with violence between parents and children. In an anonymous survey study, Meredith et al. (1986) found a significant positive association between parents' reports of physical violence toward their spouse and toward their children (see also Tajima, 2002). In a clever laboratory study, Margolin, John, Ghosh, and Gordis (1996) observed parents interacting with their children while engaging in a cooperative task. In this study parents and children had to copy a line drawing by using an Etch-A-Sketch toy, where one person controlled the vertical line drawing knob and the other controlled the horizontal line drawing knob. To draw curves or circles, the parent and child had to cooperate very carefully. Margolin et al. found that fathers' or husbands' tendencies to engage in physical aggression toward their wives were positively associated with authoritarian behaviors, negative affect, and controlling behaviors, and negatively associated with authoritative behaviors during laboratory interactions. The authors concluded that "more extreme forms of marital aggression appear to coexist with less extreme but potentially salient behavior patterns regarding how parents treat each other, how they treat the child, and how the child behaves when both the parent and child are present" (Margolin et al., p. 57).

It has recently come to light that virtually all of the risk factors associated with partner abuse (e.g., age, race, income, poverty level, family size, social isolation, and verbal aggression) are also risk factors for child abuse (Slep & O'Leary, 2001). As we discuss earlier in this chapter, in some cases marital violence is part of a larger constellation of violent behavior. In at least some cases it is clear that children are a part of that constellation, making marital violence an obvious marker of risk for child abuse.

It is not entirely surprising that people who physically abuse their spouses are also more inclined to abuse their children. However, it is now apparent that the association between martial violence and physical child abuse can span generations. Childhood exposure to either interparental violence or parent → child violence significantly increases the risk for contemporary adult partner violence and parent → child abuse (Heyman & Slep, 2002). It appears as if early childhood experience with family violence, be it direct (i.e., child abuse) or vicarious (i.e., observing interparental violence) contributes to a propensity to enact family violence later in life. This intergenerational transmission or "cycle of violence" may be the result of such children growing up with the belief that family violence is normative and appropriate.

## Violence in Gay and Lesbian Relationships

Intimate partner violence is not a phenomenon that is restricted to male–female relationships. Current scientific evidence indicates that domestic violence occurs as frequently, if not more often, in gay and lesbian partnerships as it does is heterosexual cohabiting relationships and marriages. Tabulating an exact rate of violence in gay and lesbian relationships has proven to be a difficult chore for researchers. There are often substantial differences from study to study in estimates of domestic violence in gay and lesbian relationships. This variation may be the result of different samples that are often smaller than those on which marital violence rates are assessed. Gay men in particular may be uncomfortable admitting that they have been victimized because it is inconsistent with their male identity, so they may underreport experiences with partner violence (Letellier, 1994). Reporting violence in lesbian couples is also inconsistent with the idea of women as less violent than men (Burke & Follingstad, 1999), so it too may tend to be underreported.

Estimates of partner violence rates in lesbian relationships range from 30% (Brand & Kidd, 1986; Lie & Gentlewarrior, 1991) to as high as 75% (Lie, Schilit, Bush, Montagne, & Reyes, 1991). More recently, Waldner-Haugrud, Gratch, and Magruder (1997) found 47.5% of the lesbians that they surveyed had experienced relationship violence, most commonly involving behaviors such as pushing, slapping, and punching. An explicit comparison of relationship violence in lesbian and heterosexual women indicated that a higher percentage of lesbians (40%) than heterosexual women (31%) had physical violence perpetrated against them by an intimate partner (Bernhard, 2000). However, rates of sexual violence victimization were comparable for lesbian and heterosexual women, at 24% and 23%, respectively. Regardless of the precise estimate, it is clear that intimate partner violence is at least as prevalent in lesbian relationships as it is in heterosexual relationships.

Relationship violence also appears to be common in gay male relationships. In their survey, Waldner-Haugrud et al. (1997) discovered that 29.7% of gay males had experienced partner violence. This is comparable to the 38% physical abuse rate in gay relationships reported by Gardner (1989). Some researchers have pointed out that the domestic violence movement has historically focused on the battering of women, particularly heterosexual women, resulting in virtually no attention being paid the problem of battery in gay male relationships (Letellier, 1994). For that reason, awareness and understanding of violence in gay male relationships have lagged behind those of heterosexual, and to a lesser extent lesbian, relationships.

Burke and Follingstad (1999) concluded a review of the literature on violence in gay and lesbian relationships by noting that "lesbians and gay men are just as likely to abuse their partners as heterosexual men" (p. 508). This fact presents a strenuous challenge to the doctrine of male-to-female aggression that is embraced by feminist theories of domestic violence. If the root of intimate partner violence is a patriarchal social structure that tolerates, if not condones, the victimization of women by their male partners, then interpersonal violence should be a relatively rare phenomenon in lesbian and gay relationships. As shown previously, however, this is clearly not the case. For this reason, research findings on violence in gay and lesbian relationships have particular scientific importance for evaluating theories based on power structures and gender roles. For example, psychologist Vallerie Coleman (1994) plainly argued that "gender-based sociopolitical theories of domestic violence cannot adequately explain why lesbian battering occurs at rates comparable to that of heterosexual battering" (p. 150). Theorists tend to agree that violence in these relationships is an issue of establishing and maintaining power, but that this power is not derived from sex or gender roles as some have assumed to be the case in heterosexual couples (Letellier, 1994; Waldner-Haugrud et al., 1997). Waldner-Haugud and her colleagues suggest that power in lesbian relationships may come from physical size, attractiveness, and economic or job status.

The research findings on violence in lesbian and gay male couples, along with those from heterosexual marriages, suggest that people use physical aggression to establish power and control their partner. Feeling powerless or otherwise unable to control the partner seems to be a more universal antecedent to intimate partner violence than simply being male. Research on violence in gay and lesbian relationships also indicates that power has its basis in a number of factors aside from one's biological sex.

## CONCLUSION

Family violence can take a variety of forms, but all can be conceptualized as dysfunctional and destructive communication between family members. Some of the same family environments that give rise to one type of family violence (e.g., physical child abuse) are also associated with other forms (e.g., marital violence). In most cases, family violence is not just contained to the nonverbal communication behaviors that define violence, such as hitting a family member. The verbal behaviors of family members are additionally suggestive of conflict, tension, interference, negativity, and, particularly in the case of marital violence, a struggle for control. The dynamics of families that abuse their children are marked by poor cohesion and adaptability (i.e., "affectionless control"), poor boundary regulation, and absent or ineffective parenting. Child abuse has devastating psychological and interpersonal effects on children both while they are young as well as later in life when they are at heightened risk for abusing their own children. In the marital context, violence is often perpetrated by people with poor argumentation skills. The powerlessness hypothesis explains that spouses will often enact violent behaviors in a misguided effort to establish some control in their relationship and over their partner. In fact, many of the nonverbal and verbal communication behaviors enacted by such people are in the service of attaining some degree of power over other family members, whether it is a parent disciplining a child or a spouse arguing with his or her partner.

Family violence and abuse represents one of the darkest elements of family communication. In American society, families are often revered for being the crucible of socialization, imparting values and morals, and turning out productive members of society. The research on family violence and abuse is a reminder that this same social institution can be the sight of horrific maltreatment of both children and spouses. Sadly, people who are abused, or who witness abuse, often go on to abuse others. Breaking this "cycle of violence" in the family remains as one of the great challenges in our society today.

# CHAPTER SIXTEEN

# Improving Family Communication and Family Relationships

During the life span of most marriages and families there will be times when family members are not communicating effectively with each other. Consider for example a husband and wife who slowly grow distant from each other after years of marriage and begin to simply exclude each other from their day-to-day activities. Sometimes parents have a hard time getting through to their children, especially when those children reach adolescence. For example, an adolescent child might start wearing "strange" clothes, listening to punk rock music, and associating more with friends and less with family. Parents of such children often try many different tactics to maintain contact with and control of their child, often to no avail. Earlier in this book we examine research findings that show that some of the ingredients for eventual marital distress are already evident in the communication behaviors of premarital couples. Some couples progress with wedding plans despite the incidence of domestic violence in their relationship. Is there any hope or help for such families and couples?

In this chapter, we try to answer a number of key questions about the possibility of improving family communication. Because there is no such thing as a "perfect" family, it is assumed that virtually everyone can benefit from efforts to improve family communication. But can families actually improve their communication and relationships? If so, how is this achieved? Are efforts to improve family communication only for distressed families who seek therapy? Is there anything that can be done to help couples who are planning to marry so that their communication patterns do not lead them down the road to divorce? Can communication training help parents do a better job of raising their children? These are just some of the issues that we explore as we review examples of the more organized and documented techniques and programs to improve family communication.

In this chapter we examine programs for improving family relationships and interactions. These efforts cover an interesting range of activities such as premarital counseling, parent training, and family therapy. A theme that is common to many of these efforts is improvement of family communication patterns. It seems as if family communication is viewed, at least implicitly, as either the cause of some family problems or the route to a cure. For example, interviews with 50 couples' counselors revealed that many clients seek their services for what are essentially communication problems (Vangelisti, 1994b). These therapists and counselors indicated that the most common communication problems presented by couples seeking help are not taking the partner's perspective when listening, blaming the partner for negative events, and criticizing or putting the partner down. Not surprisingly, many of the programs that are intended to improve marital relationships through either premarital counseling or marital enrichment are essentially social skills training programs that teach basic and effective interpersonal communication techniques (Segrin & Givertz, 2003).

Before looking at some of the programs and treatments for improving family communication, we want to highlight an important practical issue. Improving family communication is possible but not easy. People often learn skills such as driving a car, playing a musical instrument, or working with tools under careful supervision and with the best of intentions. Eventually, however, bad habits often develop. During courtship people tend to be on their best interpersonal behavior. Parents of newborn children typically put great care and thought into their interactions with the child. Nevertheless, like sands that are slowly washed away by time and tide, these family interaction skills sometimes get replaced by less functional interaction patterns. It is clear that efforts to improve family relationships and communication are most effective when they are pursued before real troubles start. The old saying, "a stitch in time saves nine" applies here. It is much more feasible to teach premarital couples the skills they need to maintain a happy and healthy relationship than it is to repair a marriage badly damaged by years of criticism, accusation, and disintegrated trust. Even when distressed couples undergo carefully designed and implemented therapy to enhance their communication and problem-solving skills, relapsing back to a state of distress is a common problem (Kelly, Fincham, & Beach, 2003). Well-established habits, even when they are distressing and dysfunctional, are not easily and permanently replaced. For these reasons, attempts to improve family relations and interaction are most likely to be successful when they start early.

The family scholar Luciano L'Abate (1990) characterized efforts to improve family communication and relationships as different types of prevention efforts. According to L'Abate, prevention implies "any approach, procedure, or method intended and designed to improve one's interpersonal competence as an individual, as a partner, and as a parent" (p. 20). From this perspective, prevention strategies could be understood as efforts to prevent family dysfunction by trying to improve the interpersonal competence of family members. L'Abate further delineates prevention strategies into three major categories.

*Primary prevention* involves taking steps to reduce the likelihood of experiencing distress in the family by promoting conditions that enhance the interpersonal competence and coping skills of family members. Primary prevention strategies are applied to well-functioning couples and families with the hope that they will stay that way. Often, primary prevention strategies are largely educational in nature, as we see in later sections of this chapter. A major emphasis for primary prevention has been marriage preparation.

*Secondary prevention* entails early identification of potentially "at-risk" family members and the application of training or treatment before any serious dysfunction develops. For example, we know that married couples with newly born children are at risk of experiencing declines in marital satisfaction and that low-income families that live in high-stress neighborhoods are at risk for problems such as drug and alcohol abuse. A secondary prevention strategy would attempt to identify these at-risk, but still functional, families and offer some sort of intervention before any major difficulties could develop. Sometimes the distinction between primary and secondary prevention is a little blurry. As

L'Abate (1990) notes, the distinction lies in how one defines "risk" and "need." Later in this chapter we discuss a series of secondary prevention programs designed to help couples enhance and maintain marital satisfaction and to help parents effectively raise their children. Although some might characterize these methods as primary prevention strategies, the underlying philosophies of these programs suggest that the people in these various family roles (or their children) are at some risk for potential problems.

Finally, *tertiary prevention* involves crisis-oriented therapeutic activities and interventions. These are delivered to distressed individuals and families, usually by highly trained professionals. Tertiary prevention is administered after dysfunction and breakdown occur. It is unfortunately the most common of the three prevention strategies, but comes largely after the damage is done. Common examples include couples therapy and family therapy for children with emotional or behavioral problems. Bradbury and Fincham (1990) paraphrase L'Abate's (1990) classification of primary, secondary, and tertiary prevention as "before it happens, before it gets worse, and before it is too late" (p. 376).

TABLE 16.1
Examples of Programs and Techniques to Improve Family Relationships

| Prevention Philosophy | Program | Goal | Target Population |
|---|---|---|---|
| Primary | PREP | Teach communication skills, explore cognitions, enhance relational bond | couples planning to marry |
| | PREPARE | Assess background and functioning of relationship, provide information to couples about their similarities & differences | couples planning to marry |
| Secondary | Marriage Encounter | Encourage couple dialogue and self-disclosure, explore spirituality/faith | married couples |
| | Couples Communication Program | Create self- and other-awareness, teach communication skills | married couples |
| | STEP | Understand goals of child misbehavior, teach effective techniques for managing child behavior | parents of young children–adolescents |
| | Behavioral Parent Training | Teach effective techniques for managing child behavior problems | parents |
| Tertiary | Cognitive Behavioral Family Therapy | Treat clinical family dysfunction and behavior problems | distressed couples and families |
| | Structural Family Therapy | Adjust family structure and norms of interaction to adapt to changes | distressed couples and families |

In the remainder of this chapter we discuss a number of different programs, approaches, and therapies aimed at enhancing family relationships and the communication that goes on between family members. We have organized these techniques according to L'Abate's (1990) scheme of primary, secondary, and tertiary prevention. A quick summary of these different programs and techniques is presented in Table 16.1. This review and analysis will show that many people have tried many different methods of improving family competence. However, there are some remarkable commonalities in these different programs. One of the most notable is a focus on effective communication skills. The majority of approaches to improving family relations focus, at least to some extent, on how the family members communicate with each other.

## PRIMARY PREVENTION STRATEGIES

Primary prevention programs have received substantial attention in the family science literature, and with good reason. As we discuss in chapter 11, about half of all marriages initiated in recent years are predicted to end in divorce. Divorce has obvious and profound implications for the psychological, physical, social, and economic well-being of the spouses, and further implications for their children and extended family. It is no wonder that so much effort has been put into marriage preparation programs aimed at preventing or minimizing the development of marital distress and enhancing marital stability (Fraenkel, Markman, & Stanley, 1997; Silliman & Schumm, 2000; Stahmann, 2000).

As we note earlier in this chapter, most of the primary prevention programs are educational in nature. Because these programs are for healthy, functional people, there is no "treatment" or "therapy" provided. Many of these programs fit into the larger "family life education" movement that is aimed at providing people with information and skills for dealing with the stressors and challenges that face all families (Arcus, 1995).

Primary prevention programs started from rather meager beginnings. It is apparent that practitioners have struggled to produce and offer programs that people will get involved in and to create programs that really work. Early marriage preparation programs were based largely on the conjecture of the program developers, were rarely rooted in any theory of martial success or failure, and had hardly any empirical evidence to suggest that they were effective (Bagarozzi & Rauen, 1981). More recently, Sullivan and Bradbury (1997) found the people who are most likely to participate in marital preparation programs are the ones who need it the least. Couples at high risk for eventual marital distress and dissolution do not seem to be interested in participating in such programs. No more than 50% of all marrying couples actually participate in any formalized marriage preparation or premarital counseling (Bradbury & Fincham, 1990). Among those who do participate in marriage preparation programs, future marital outcomes are not necessarily any better than those who do not participate (Sullivan & Bradbury). Despite guarded evidence for the effectiveness of prevention programs, such programs might have certain subtle benefits that are not immediately obvious. For example, a large study of people in the U.S. Army revealed that premarital counseling had no effect on couples' eventual satisfaction or distress (Schumm, Silliman, & Bell, 2000). However, those who had participated in premarital counseling were more likely (24%) to seek marital and family therapy than those who had not (8%). So, even if premarital counseling has no lasting effects on martial quality, at least it appears to motivate people to seek professional help when their marriage is in trouble.

One other positive thing about marriage preparation programs is that most people who participate in them appear to be satisfied with the experience (Williams, Riley, Risch, & Van Dyke, 1999). When asked what they liked the most or what was most helpful about marriage preparation and premarital counseling, couples cite communication skills training, conflict and problem-solving, and discussing family-of-origin issues (Lyster, Russell, & Hiebert, 1995; Valiente, Belanger, & Estrada, 2002; Williams et al., 1999). Because a focus on such communication skills is a part of most programs and is supported by good scientific evidence (Kelly & Fincham, 1999), it is understandable that participants are generally satisfied with their formal marriage preparation experiences.

In the following sections, we examine in some detail the Prevention and Relationship Enhancement Program (PREP) and briefly consider the PREPARE marriage preparation program. We selected these programs for their prominence in the family science literature, their popularity, and their historical significance. It is important to understand that these are but a mere fraction of all the marriage preparation programs in existence. There are surely hundreds of different programs, many of which are local in nature and designed and implemented by a single individual, based perhaps only on hunches about what makes a marriage work. The effectiveness of such programs may never be understood because of their lack of empirical evaluation. However, the programs presented next illustrate the thinking and planning that went into some of the better designed and more nationally available marriage preparation programs.

## Prevention and Relationship Enhancement Program

### Description

Amidst a bewildering array of marital preparation programs, the PREP (Markman, Floyd, Stanley, & Jamieson, 1984; Stanley, Blumberg, & Markman, 1999; Stanley, Markman, St. Peters, & Leber, 1995; Renick, Blumberg, & Markman, 1992) stands out for being empirically based and empirically evaluated. In other words, the people who developed PREP based the program on knowledge acquired through empirical research. Those phenomena that have been shown to predict marital satisfaction and stability (or deterioration) are the major issues addressed in PREP. Similarly, the effectiveness of PREP has been carefully tested through numerous scientific studies.

PREP is a primary prevention program. It was originally designed for couples contemplating marriage with the goal of preventing martial problems before they have a chance to negatively affect the relationship. The program incorporates many of the principles of behavioral couples therapy by assuming that couples can learn behaviors that will help to prevent the deterioration of marital satisfaction. There are four major goals to PREP: (a) teaching good communication skills, (b) clarifying and evaluating expectations for marriage, (c) creating an understanding about choices and commitment to the relationship, and (d) enhancing the couple's bond through fun, friendship, and sensuality (Stanley et al., 1999).

PREP is delivered in a group format, usually with 4 to 40 couples, over a 12-hour period. This might happen over a single weekend or six 2-hour sessions. In either case, couples attend a series of lectures on topics such as conflict management, expectations, and commitment. These lectures often include demonstrations or modeling. Shortly thereafter, couples practice, discuss, and apply the skills and concepts that were covered in the lecture. Communication is a major focus of this program. Couples are introduced to the "intent = impact" model of effective communication (Gottman, Notarius, Gonso, & Markman, 1976), which stresses the importance of clearly sending messages so that the impact on the listener matches the intention of the speaker. Couples are also taught skills for effective speaking and listening, editing destructive feelings when conversing, awareness of hidden agendas in marital interactions, and negotiating differences. One specific communication technique that is taught is the "Speaker–Listener Technique" in which the couples use an object to clearly identify who has the floor (the speaker) and who is the listener. After the speaker expresses a point, the listener is taught to paraphrase what he or she hears so that both can be sure that they are on the same page.

### Evaluation

As noted earlier, the effectiveness of PREP has been extensively evaluated through carefully designed studies. So how well does it work? Couples who participate in PREP generally show increased positive communication and decreased negative communication relative to those in a control condition, immediately following participation in the program (Stanley et al., 2001). The elements of the program that focus on communication appear to be clear favorites among the participants. When followed up over longer periods of time (1-5 years), couples that have been through PREP show higher relational satisfaction, fewer sexual difficulties, and fewer instances of physical violence than couples in a control condition (Markman et al., 1993; Renick et al., 1992). PREP couples appear to maintain many of the positive communication skills that they learn for at least 5 years beyond the program (Markman et al.). A version of PREP designed for couples in Germany (EPL; Hahlweg, Markman, Thurmaier, Engl, & Eckert, 1998; Markman & Hahlweg), has similar documented effectiveness. At a 3-year follow-up, couples in the German version of PREP exhibited more positive (e.g., self-disclosure, acceptance of partner, and agreement) and less negative (e.g., criticism and disagreement) communication behaviors during a 10-minute problem-solving interaction than did couples in a control group (Hahlweg et al.). Also, 3 years after the program, satisfaction of the PREP couples was higher and their dissolution rate was lower (9.4% vs. 21.9%) than those of couples in a control group.

It has recently come to light that the communication skills taught in PREP may have a different impact on marital outcomes for men and women (Schilling, Baucom, Burnett, Allen, & Ragland, 2003). Schilling and her associates found that people who participated in PREP indeed increased their positive communication (e.g., support–validation and expressing positive affect) and decreased their negative communication (e.g., conflict and denial) with their partner. To the extent that men increased their positive communication skills by participating in PREP, they were at decreased risk for marital distress over the following 5 years. However, for women it was the exact opposite. Their increases in positive communication were associated with an increased likelihood that the couple would experience marital distress in future years. Schilling and her associates conjecture that for women positive communication might include withholding concerns and complaints from the partner. In so doing, these issues could fail to get resolved. They found comparable results for negative communication: When men decreased their negative communication following PREP, they were at lower risk for later marital distress, but women's decreases in negative communication were unrelated to their subsequent marital distress. Although PREP appears quite effective for males, to the extent that it implicitly and inadvertently teaches females to hold off on expressing their grievances, it could have unintended negative effects on wives' subsequent marital satisfaction.

Although there is some compelling evidence for the effectiveness of PREP, there are other cases of less than ideal results. For example, 4 to 5 years after completing the program, there were no significant differences in the divorce and separation rate of couples who had participated in PREP versus couples in a control group or couples who declined to participate in PREP (Markman et al., 1993). An adaptation of PREP in the Netherlands indicated that breakups, problem intensity, and sexual dissatisfaction were higher following participation in PREP than under a control condition (Van Widenfelt, Hosman, Schaap, & van der Staak, 1996). Did participation in PREP actually hurt these Dutch couples? One unique aspect of Van Widenfelt et al.'s sample is that couples in the PREP condition had been together for 9.1 years on average, compared to 6.3 years for those in the control group. Obviously many of the PREP couples had already been married or in a marriage-like relationship. It is possible that some of these couples were already on a downward trajectory before the program started. Another issue that has plagued evaluation of PREP is a potential self-selection bias (Kelly & Fincham, 1999). In one study of PREP's effectiveness, only 39% of those couples offered PREP actually completed the program (Markman et al.). It is therefore possible that the effectiveness of PREP has been tested mostly on highly motivated couples. It not surprising that such couples benefit from its lectures and workshops. However, in fairness to the program, it should be noted that PREP has been one of the most carefully studied marital preparation programs to date. There is no reason to believe that other premarital preparation programs would fare any better if their effectiveness was tested as carefully as PREP's.

## Other Marriage Preparation Programs

As noted earlier, PREP is but one of many different marital preparation programs. Before moving on to other programs and therapies for the improvement of family communication, it is informative to briefly examine several other popular marriage preparation programs to compare and contrast approaches taken by practitioners to prevent marital distress.

A unique and straightforward program for engaged couples was developed by David Olson (who also developed the circumplex model of family functioning) and is centered on a measurement instrument called PREPARE (Fowers & Olson, 1986; Olson & Olson, 1999). PREPARE is based on the assumption that the nature of premarital relationships can predict the quality of marital relationships. The goal of the program is to assess those areas of the couple's relationship that are most predictive of marital success, to give the couple feedback on those assessments, and to have them engage in skill-building exercises. The PREPARE instrument has 125 questions designed to measure the following areas of relational functioning: realistic expectations, personality issues, communication, conflict resolution, financial management, leisure activities, sexual relationship, children and parenting, family and friends, equalitarian roles, and religious orientation. This questionnaire has been extensively studied and validated (e.g., Fowers, Montel, & Olson, 1996; Fowers & Olson, 1986, 1992) and premarital scores on the PREPARE instrument predict subsequent divorce during the first three years of marriage with 80-90% accuracy (Fowers & Olson, 1986; Larsen & Olson, 1989). A common means by which many couples encounter the PREPARE instrument is when they are preparing for marriage with a clergy member. The questionnaire is often administered as part of premarital counseling and then after its computer scoring the couple meets again with the clergy member to discuss the results. The couple is then given a workbook with exercises that involve, for example, effective conflict resolution; developing personal, couple, and family goals; and strengthening couple communication through assertiveness and active listening (Olson & Olson). PREPARE is an attractive program because, like PREP, it is based on sound scientific evidence. In addition, it is easy to administer and easy to participate in. The PREPARE instrument is extensive and is likely to bring important issues to the surface that many couples may not have discussed in much detail. For that reason, completing the questionnaire and discussing the results may prompt valuable interactions and negotiations before the couple actually gets married.

Guerney's Relationship Enhancement Program (RE; Guerney, 1977) has also been a popular program and is one of the first designed particularly for couples contemplating marriage. Ridley and Sladeczek (1992) explain that "the cardinal goal of the RE program is to teach attitudes and skills that will enable the participants to relate to significant others in ways that will maximize satisfaction of emotional and functional needs" (p. 150). RE is offered to groups of three or four couples by two group leaders in eight 3-hour weekly sessions. The program includes such techniques as leader modeling, supervised practice, and weekly "homework" sessions. A major thrust of RE involves teaching couples self-disclosure about their feelings, elimination of blaming messages, and building active listening skills. Controlled studies indicate that RE is effective in increasing expressed affection, relationship adjustment, empathy, trust, and couple communication (Ridley & Bain, 1983; Ridley, Jorgensen, Morgan, & Avery, 1982; Ridley & Sladeczek). Improvements in communication skills such as empathy and self-disclosure have been documented immediately after participating in the RE program and at a 3-month follow-up (Avery, Ridley, Leslie, & Milholland, 1980).

There are many other premarital intervention programs such as "Saving Your Marriage Before it Starts" (SYMBIS; Parrott & Parrott, 1999), the Marriage Project (Russell & Lyster, 1992), and the Premarital Education and Training Sequence (PETS; Bagarozzi, Bagarozzi, Anderson, & Pollane, 1984). In addition, enrichment programs have been developed to improve the quality of existing marriages before any major problems occur (e.g., Mace, 1975; Dyer & Dyer, 1999). Teaching effective marital communication and conflict resolution skills is an essential element of all of these primary prevention programs.

## SECONDARY PREVENTION STRATEGIES

There are some cases where families are functioning reasonably well but are clearly at risk for troubles in the future. For example, new parents and couples who have been married for a moderate amount of time may be presently happy, but are at risk for experiencing stress in the role as a parent or distress associated with changes inherent in many long-term marriages. Efforts to help such families avoid experiencing distress can be characterized as secondary prevention strategies. There is sometimes a fine line that distinguishes primary and secondary prevention strategies. The programs that we review in this section fall into the classes of marital enrichment and parent training. We characterize these programs as secondary prevention because they presume that the married couples or parents are at some risk for distress. It is often assumed that this potential distress is just a normative part of the challenges of being a parent or being married to the same person for many years. Obviously, some of these programs could also be characterized as primary prevention programs. It is interesting to note, however, that enhancing communication, interaction patterns, and relationship quality is a common theme to these secondary prevention programs as well as to the primary prevention programs discussed earlier in this chapter (Diskin, 1986).

## Marriage Encounter

### Description

There is an interesting story behind the development of the Marriage Encounter program. A Spanish priest named Father Gabriel Calvo found that many couples were seeking his help with marital and family problems. In effort to help such people, he recruited a group of 28 couples with successful marriages to work on developing a program that could help married couples develop and maintain the same kind of quality in their own relationships. So, in 1952 he founded *Encuentre Conyugal*, the Spanish precursor to the modern-day Marriage Encounter. This program was eventually brought to America in 1966, originally offered in Miami to Cuban refugee couples (see Genovese, 1975, for a historical analysis of Marriage Encounter).

A major assumption behind Marriage Encounter is that all married couples go through phases of illusion, disillusion, and joy. How they handle the disillusion phase is vital in determining whether or not they will stay together and attain the "joy" phase (Elin, 1999). This key assumption, which is actually consistent with the scientific research on martial satisfaction over the life span (see chaps. 6 and 10), situates Marriage Encounter in the realm of secondary prevention as discussed by L'Abate (1990). Because all marriages are assumed to experience a decline in satisfaction (i.e., "disillusion"), they are seen as at risk, and the program is an effort to intervene before that risk develops into serious distress.

Marriage Encounter is a faith-based weekend program that is offered through many different religious denominations. It is based on the concepts of faith and dialog (Genovese, 1975). The program is ordinarily offered over the course of a Friday evening to a Sunday afternoon at a "retreat house," hotel, or other location in which couples can get away from their regular work and family routine. The idea behind Marriage Encounter is to give husbands and wives the opportunity to focus on each other free from other distractions. Marriage Encounters are typically led by one or two lay couples and a member of the clergy. Over the weekend, couples progress through the program's four stages: "I," "We," "We–God," and "We–God–World." Participating couples hear a series of 13 presentations on various topics such as stress and marriage, disillusion, and Biblical tenets regarding marriage and family (Elin, 1999). Often couples who lead the program will model husband–wife communication. After most of the presentations, participants are given a list of questions or instructions to which they individually respond in writing. Sample questions include "What three times have I felt most united with you?" "What are my reasons to want to go on living?" and "What are the symptoms of spiritual divorce in our relationship?"(Witteman & Fitzpatrick, 1986). Spouses then share their written reflections with each other and discuss them. This is the "dialog" technique that is a staple of Marriage Encounter. There is no group sharing in the Marriage Encounter. The only time couples are together as a group is when they are listening to presentations. The rest of the time they are by themselves, either writing or discussing each other's written reflections. For this reason it is often said that couples do not receive Marriage Encounter, but rather give the encounter to each other. After several days of listening to presentations, writing personal reflections, and discussing them with each other, spouses reunite for a final ceremony. They are then encouraged to (a) continue to write daily love letters to each other and discuss them, (b) return for a reunion or refresher once a month to maintain the health of their marriage, and (c) tell other couples about their positive experience with the encounter.

If the idea of writing intimate letters to each other and discussing them over the course of a weekend sounds somewhat out of the ordinary, perhaps some historical context would be instructive. As noted earlier, the Marriage Encounter "movement" as it is sometimes called emerged in the 1960s when humanistic psychology and the human potential movements were at their peak. The idea behind this movement and the many "encounter groups" that sprang up during this time was that all people have potential that can be unlocked and realized by getting in touch with their true self and sharing this with others. This mentality is still evident today in the architecture of the Marriage Encounter program. Incidentally, like religious denominations themselves, the Marriage Encounter leadership has become divided over issues of spirituality and the use of certain techniques in the program. Hence, they have split up into the "National Marriage Encounter," "World Wide Marriage Encounter," and "United Marriage Encounter."

Literally millions of couples have participated in Marriage Encounter programs over the course of the past 40 years. Although these couples come from all walks of life, they understandably score high on measures of religiosity, physical and psychological health, and on measures of satisfaction with their spouse and family (Silverman & Urbaniak, 1983). In other words, Marriage Encounter appears to attract very motivated couples who want to keep a good thing going.

### Evaluation

The majority of couples who participate in Marriage Encounter rate their experience very favorably (Elin, 1999; Lester & Doherty, 1983). Many report that it had a positive and long-term impact on their communication. However, one test of Marriage Encounter couples against a waiting list control group found no significant differences in self-disclosure (Milholland & Avery, 1982). This is remarkable given the massive emphasis on self-disclosure through the dialog technique. However, Milholland and Avery explain that "the goal of dialogue in Marriage Encounter does not focus on better understanding and problem solving but rather on the experience of oneness and on an emotional high" (pp. 88–89). Other family scholars have been critical of the Marriage Encounter movement for its failure to teach any specific communication and problem-solving skills that are so vital to marital well-being (Witteman & Fitzpatrick, 1986). Others have criticized Marriage Encounter for its excessive mysticism and secrecy (De Young, 1979), its singular ideology of the ideal marriage (Doherty, McCabe, & Ryder, 1978), for being overly authoritarian and coercive (Doherty et al.), and for creating negative effects in about 10% of the participating couples (Doherty, Lester, & Leigh, 1986; Lester & Doherty, 1983). It appears that participating in Marriage Encounter could be a risk for already distressed couples as they are prone to "dumping" on each other through the dialogs. As communication scholars are well aware, emotional expression without problem solving can be very corrosive to an already fragile relationship. Another problem that has been cited in the literature is the development of an intense husband–wife bond to the exclusion of relations with children (Doherty & Walker, 1982). It seems then that one thing missing from Marriage Encounter is attention to communication skills that will allow couples not only to share their feelings with each other but also to actually resolve and work through these issues in cases where they are not always positive. Undoubtedly, sharing thoughts and feelings is useful to most marriages, but leveraging self-disclosure can be risky without the context of sensitive and effective communication skills.

## The Couples Communication Program

### Description

The Couples Communication Program, originally known as the Minnesota Couples Communication Program, is an educational program that focuses specifically on teaching effective communication skills (Miller, Nunnally, & Wackman, 1976; Nunnally, Miller, & Wackman, 1975). The basic premise of the Couples Communication Program is that interpersonal competence can be taught and learned. For this reason the program is focused on communication skills instead of communication content. The two main objectives of the Couples Communication Program are (a) increasing self-awareness and other-awareness and (b) enhancing communication skills to allow for mutually satisfying interactions (Nunnally et al.). The Couples Communication Program is based on elements of systems theory, symbolic interactionism, and family life-cycle theories (Nunnally et al.). The couple is viewed as a system, and a major goal is to equip them with the communication skills that will allow them to effectively face the developmental challenges that all couples experience over their life span (see chap. 10).

The Couples Communication Program is ordinarily offered to groups of five to seven couples, led by two certified instructors. The group meets weekly in 3-hour sessions for 4 weeks. The developers feel that the group session is ideal for learning communication skills because couples can receive feedback from peers and observe multiple models and identify the skills that they use, or need to use (Nunnally et al., 1975). Before beginning the program, couples are briefly screened to ensure that both members are each voluntarily participating and that each is committed to participating in the full program. Program sessions involve brief lectures, exercises, feedback, and discussions about prior sessions. Couples also do outside reading in between sessions. During the first session, couples are introduced to the "awareness wheel." This is a visual aid to help couples appreciate the various aspects of awareness such as sensing, feeling, thinking, and wanting. A series of skills are then presented for verbally expressing awareness. Nunnally et al. (pp. 64–65) present the following example of a desirable message:

*I'd like to go out more often with you.* (self-responsible speaking for self)

and the following examples of undesirable alternatives:

*You never want to go anywhere!* (overresponsible speaking for other)
*It would be nice to go out.* (underresponsible speaking for no one)

The idea here is to make people aware of what they are thinking and feeling, and then teach them to clearly express those feelings to their partner. The second session shifts to listening skills and acknowledging messages from other people. During this session the concept of "shared meaning" is introduced. This concept is comparable to the "intent = impact" model of effective communication that is taught in the PREP program. The idea here is to strive for a mutual understanding of issues through couple communication so that the two people are on the same page so to speak. The third session focuses on communication styles and the concept of metacommunication (being aware of and discussing how they communicate with each other), and the fourth session centers on the relationship between methods of dealing with conflict and those of building, maintaining, or diminishing each other's self-esteem.

### *Evaluation*

Research conducted by the developers of the Couples Communication Program is generally supportive of its intended goals (Miller et al., 1976; Nunnally et al., 1975). These authors report that people who participate in the program show greater awareness of their interaction styles and exhibit better communication skills for addressing various relational issues. Wampler (1982) reviewed the findings on 19 studies on the Couples Communication Program and found that it had an immediate positive effect on couples' communication style and relational satisfaction. However, participation in the program had no apparent effect on self-esteem or self-disclosure. Furthermore, there was no strong evidence for the durability of its positive effects. Very few studies followed couples for more than 6 months after participating in the program. A comparison of the Couples Communication Program with another enrichment program, the Communication Skills Workshop, and a waiting list control group indicated substantial improvement in nonverbal communication and positive views of partners' communication for people in the Couples Communication Program (Witkin, Edleson, Rose, & Hall, 1983). However, there were no group differences in positive verbal communication, problem-solving communication, or marital satisfaction. These findings suggest that the Couples Communication Program has some positive effects but still has considerable room for improvement. In many ways, the Couples Communication Program is the polar opposite of Marriage Encounter. In the Couples Communication Program the emphasis is on communication skills rather than on intense and prolonged self-disclosure. However, program leaders have obviously experienced some difficulty in teaching communication skills in just four sessions in such a way as to have noticeable and lasting impact on couples' problem-solving communication and marital satisfaction.

## Parent Training Programs

### Description

Raising a child is one of the most demanding tasks undertaken by the family. Effective parenting requires a complex array of skills, and of course children are not born with an instruction manual. Consequently, practitioners have developed numerous different programs to teach people how to be effective parents. Two such programs that we will cover in this section are Systematic Training for Effective Parenting (STEP) and Behavioral Parent Training. Because of their similar prevention philosophy and goals, we explore each of these briefly in this section. Each of these parent training programs represents an interesting mixture of primary and secondary prevention philosophies. On one hand, it is assumed that if parents can develop effective skills for raising children, based on good communication, effective instructional techniques, and positive regard for the child, then their children will eventually develop into healthy and functional adults. From such a vantage point, parent training programs clearly fit into the category of primary prevention (for the child). On the other hand, the people who developed parent training programs are undoubtedly aware of the many challenges and difficulties that face new, and even experienced, parents. It is reasonable to assume that the skills learned in parent training programs make the job of parenting less stressful and more enjoyable. Viewed from this perspective, parent training programs could be said to pursue secondary prevention (for the parent). For parents who are struggling to control their child's problem behaviors, many parent training programs also fit the secondary prevention philosophy for the child.

Systematic Training for Effective Parenting (STEP) is an educational program, developed by Drinkmeyer and McKay (1976, 1989), and is based on Alderian psychology and the idea that children seek a meaningful place in a group that will accept them. STEP is probably the most popular and well-known parent training technique and has spun off many related training programs (Brock, Oertwein, & Coufal, 1993). It is generally offered by a trained professional with supporting materials over weekly meetings. The primary element of STEP is to help parents understand the *goals of child misbehavior*. These include attention getting, power, revenge, and expression of inadequacy. Parents in the STEP program are encouraged to try to identify the motivation behind their child's misbehavior and to act accordingly. For example, misbehavior that is aimed at attention getting should be ignored. Even punishing the child in such cases gives him or her unnecessary attention. Rather, parents are taught to give their children attention in response to positive, desirable behaviors. Parents are also taught to identify power struggles and to withdraw from rather than escalate them. When parents "win" power struggles, the child is only further motivated to seek power. Another important element of STEP is the experience of *consequences*. Parents in STEP are taught to influence their children's behaviors by allowing them to experience the natural consequences of their own behavior. It is often said that experience is the best teacher. STEP teaches parents to avoid shielding their children from the logical consequences of their own behavior. So, for example, a child who refuses to eat all of his dinner should be allowed to go hungry later in the evening instead of being allowed to have snacks before bed. In theory, such experience will teach the child the importance of eating all of his dinner. In STEP, parents are instructed to take a matter-of-fact attitude toward these consequences and not to frame them as punishments. Just as natural consequences are preferred over parent initiated punishments, STEP teaches that *encouragement* is more desirable than praise. Praise is viewed as a power tactic that focuses on the end state rather than the effort expended to get there. Encouragement form parents causes children to focus on the effort that they put into a task and not on perfectionism. Ultimately this promotes autonomy and responsibility. Finally, STEP teaches parents to use regular *family meetings* to openly discuss issues that are of concern to the family. These meetings are to be run in a democratic fashion such that all family members are free to express their point of view.

### Behavioral Parent Training

Behavioral parent training actually refers to a collection of parenting programs that are based on learning theory principles such as conditioning, coercion, reciprocity, and modeling (Noller & Fitzpatrick, 1993). Behavioral parent training programs are applicable to everyday parenting challenges as well as treatment of more disturbed and aggressive behavior in children and can be flexibly applied to a range of family situations (Forehand & Kotchick, 2002). Readers who are familiar with behavioral learning theories will recall that *reinforcement* is vital in shaping human behavior. The use of positive reinforcement for desirable behaviors is a staple in behavioral parent training. Examples of this include complimenting a child for a job well done or giving the child $5 for bringing home a good report card. In behavioral parent training, parents are taught to eliminate or extinguish problem behaviors, not through punishment but by rewarding desirable behaviors that are incompatible with the unwanted behavior. For example, a parent who wants her child to walk instead of run at the shopping mall might complement the child for staying near her and walking slowly. The idea is that one cannot simultaneously run and walk, so if the child experiences a reward for walking, the running behavior is automatically extinguished without any use of punishment. *Token systems* are related to rewards. Parents who give their children stars, points, and so forth for performing desirable behaviors are using tokens. Tokens are a sort of bookkeeping system in which parents figuratively reward the child for positive behaviors. The token itself may have little intrinsic value, but may ultimately be cashed in for various treats, money, or even dismissal from having to do chores. Although tokens can be a very effective motivator for children, parents run the risk of prompting performance of behavior only for extrinsic reward. In other words, children may come to rely on the reward and stop performing the desired behavior unless the token is immediately forthcoming. Because people eventually have to perform most tasks (e.g., putting dirty clothes in the laundry and making the bed) in the absence of external rewards, parents must eventually abandon the technique. Another effective tool of behavioral parent training is *time out*. Time out is an alternative to punishment that removes a child from a source of positive reinforcement. Parents can create a timeout for the child by temporarily taking away a toy, separating him or her from a playmate, turning off the television, or moving the child to a different environment. The idea behind time out is to terminate ongoing positive reinforcement until the child's behavior improves, at which time previous activities can resume. *Modeling* is another important technique that involves parents demonstrating desirable behaviors to the child. For example, when a parent is upset he or she may explain why he or she is unhappy and talk things through calmly rather than resort to yelling and shouting. In theory, children who repeatedly observe this behavior will learn that talking, instead of shouting, is an appropriate way for two people to resolve their differences.

### Evaluation

Most of the parent training programs appear to be a least somewhat effective. The effectiveness of STEP has been tested in a number of research studies. Brock et al. (1993) conclude that positive changes in parent–child interaction, improved parental attitudes, and more favorable perceptions of child behaviors rank among the most consistent results of this program. Adams (2001) compared parents who participated in STEP to a group that received routine mental health services. He found that participation in STEP was associated with improved problem solving, communication, affective responsiveness, and behavior control. Further, STEP was able to generate clinical recovery in 38% of the families that were clinically distressed at the start of the program. Thus, there is clear evidence that STEP works, and that it does so in part through improving parent–child communication.

Research studies on different types of behavioral parent training programs show that it is generally effective and can be regarded as a "best practice" for most populations (Lonigan, Elbert, & Johnson, 1998). Documented effects include improved child compliance with parental directives and less aggression, as well as improvements in parent behaviors such as greater attention to rewarding positive child behaviors and more appropriate communicating with the child (e.g., Eyberg & Robinson, 1982). Unfortunately, behavioral parent training does not work for all families. Long-term follow-up assessments often show significant child behavior problems in 30% to 40% of families that participate in behavioral parent training (Assemany & McIntosh, 2002). Assemany and McIntosh found that behavioral parent training is least likely to be effective when (a) the family is economically disadvantaged, (b) there is dysfunction in the family system, and (c) the child behavior problem is severe.

There is at least some supportive evidence for the effectiveness of most parent training programs (e.g., Coren, Barlow, & Stewart-Brown, 2003). One key ingredient in these and other parent training programs (e.g., Anderson & Nuttall, 1987; Hall & Rose, 1987; van Wyk, Eloff, & Heyns, 1983) is an effort to teach parents how to more effectively communicate with their children. Even though parenting programs such as STEP and Behavioral Parent Training appear to be effective relative to no treatment, there is no conclusive evidence to support the effectiveness of one over the other (Brock et al., 1993; Noller & Fitzpatrick, 1993).

## TERTIARY PREVENTION STRATEGIES

Over the years practitioners have developed a number of different family and couple therapy techniques. Many of these techniques are associated with various "schools" of thought, such as cognitive–behavioral, psychoanalytic, and so forth. Ethical guidelines and licensing procedures for family therapists have been established by the American Association for Marriage and Family Therapy (AAMFT). A thorough review of all the different therapeutic techniques is obviously far beyond the scope of this chapter (see Jacobson & Gurman, 1995; Griffin & Greene, 1999; Kaslow, Kaslow, & Farber, 1999; Nichols & Schwartz, 1998, for reviews). Instead we briefly present two different types of family therapy that have been influential in the treatment of family dysfunction over the past 30 years and also illustrative of the strong focus on communication and relationships. After all, as Kaslow et al. (1999) noted, "most family therapists concur that a paramount goal of therapy is to change the family systems' interactional patterns, with individual change occurring as a product of systems change" (p. 770). In other words, family therapists try to resolve family problems and reduce family distress by helping the family to improve their communication and relationships with each other. The idea is that once relationships are improved or repaired distress and dysfunction naturally fade.

### Behavioral and Cognitive–Behavioral Therapy

Behavioral and cognitive–behavioral therapies utilize a variety of techniques that are based on social learning theory (see chap. 2) and social exchange theory (see chaps. 4 and 5). The fundamental assumption of behavioral approaches to treating couples or families is that people maintain each others' behavior through the use or misuse of reinforcement (Jacobson, 1992; Jacobson & Margolin, 1979; Jacobson & Martin, 1976). The goal of behavioral marital therapy is to teach the couple how to recognize and initiate rewarding interactions while decreasing aversive interactions that draw the couple apart (Kaslow et al., 1999). Behavioral couples therapy started out with an emphasis on identifying and exchanging rewarding behaviors (Gurman & Fraenkel, 2002). *Communication* and *problem-solving skills* were viewed as an essential means by which couples could achieve satisfaction in their relationships and initiate rewarding interactions. Pursuant to that, couples in this type of therapy are taught about specific communication behaviors that can be aversive such as interruptions, getting sidetracked, and inducing guilt. The goal is to try to get each spouse to become aware of these behaviors and their effects and to ultimately minimize their use. In addition to communication skills training, behavioral couples therapy often employs the technique of *behavioral contracting* (Baucom, 1984). This involves teaching the couple to perform or exchange rewarding behaviors, with the understanding, or perhaps expectation, that similarly rewarding behaviors will be forthcoming from the partner. Later developments in behavioral couples therapy added a focus on teaching partners *mutual acceptance* and *self-regulation* (Gurman & Fraenkel). Mutual acceptance occurs when partners accept each other and when there may be some aspects of the partner that cannot be changed. Self-regulation shifts the emphasis from trying to produce positive partner behaviors to managing one's own behavior for the betterment of the relationship.

Hahlweg and Markman's (1988) meta-analysis of the research studies on behavioral marital therapy indicated that the average person in this type of therapy was better off at the end of treatment than 83% of the people in control groups. This improvement appears to be stable for at least 3 to 12 months. Although there was considerable evidence that some couples who experienced behavioral marital therapy were still distressed after treatment, this type of therapy appears effective for the majority of couples (about 70%) who try it. However, about half of those couples who experience immediate benefit from behavioral couples therapy relapse back to a distressed level within 2 years (Jacobson & Addis, 1993; Kelly & Fincham, 1999).

At the same time that behavioral therapy was being widely applied to marital and family problems, the field of clinical psychology was being swept up in the "cognitive revolution." Not surprisingly, some behavioral therapists attached themselves to many of the ideas and concepts inherent in theories of cognitive psychology. What resulted is now known as cognitive behavioral therapy (CBT). CBT preserves many of the original aspects of behavioral therapy but also recognizes that people's cognitions about marital and family interactions will strongly affect subsequent behaviors and satisfaction with those relationships. Say, for example, a wife buys her husband a six-pack of his favorite beer. A husband in a distressed relationship might make an attribution such as "she's just doing this to butter me up so that I'll go over to her parent's house tonight for dinner." In this example, the wife performs what should be a rewarding behavior for the husband, but his attributional tendency is such that any positive impact of the behavior is minimized. Instead, he sees the positive gesture as a cunning ploy. People in CBT are taught to identify these maladaptive cognitive patterns and work toward their change—a technique known as *cognitive restructuring*. Although, certain elements of CBT may appear to be very intrapsychic or purely psychological, it is obvious that these cognitive patterns have profound family and relational implications.

## Structural Family Therapy

Structural family therapy was developed by Salvador Minuchin and his associates (Minuchin, 1974; Minuchin & Fishman, 1981). This type of therapy gets it name from the focus on family structure—the hierarchical organization of the family that is marked by boundaries between the family system and the outside environment, as well as by boundaries that delineate subsystems within the family. An explicit assumption of structural family therapy is that families experience changes as they progress through the family life cycle. To remain happy, healthy, and functional, the family needs to adjust its structure and norms of interactions to adapt to these naturally occurring changes. Minuchin argued that dysfunctional families have problems with *boundary regulation*, *power imbalances*, and *inappropriate alignments*. When boundaries are poorly regulated children can act like parents and parents can act like children. Minuchin felt that there should be a clear boundary between parents and children, with parents in charge. Power imbalances occur when one family member wields too much power. Although it may be tempting to conclude that this would ordinarily be a parent that is not necessarily the case. In some dysfunctional families, the parents cater to children to such an extent that the children are the ones who are running the show. When inappropriate alignments are present, two or more family members "team up" against others in the family. Even though such coalitions are common, when they become severe, involving serious issues, this can be a major problem for the family.

These types of structural dysfunctions in families are often found in *enmeshed* and *disengaged* families. Enmeshed families are so involved in each other's affairs and are so immediately reactive to each other's moods that they cannot function effectively as individuals or as a family. These families have serious problems with boundary regulation. At the opposite extreme, disengaged families do not seem to care much at all about each other.

The primary goal of structural family therapy is to reorganize the family unit, with the therapist as a sort of leader or conductor, so that the family can have more functional interactions (Fishman & Fishman, 2003; Kalsow et al., 1999). Therapy progresses through the cyclical stages of *joining*, *assessing*, and *restructuring*. Joining simply means that the family therapist will temporarily enter the family system, again, as a type of leader. Structural family therapists will often assess such family dynamics as boundary quality, flexibility, interaction patterns, presence of subsystems, coalitions, and how the family system maintains the symptoms or dysfunctional behavior of its distressed member(s). The restructuring phase is complex and involves the therapist attempting to create new awareness and change in the family and how they interact. This may be accomplished through such therapeutic techniques as *enactments* (getting the family to act out particular dysfunctional interaction patterns so the therapist can intervene), *paradox* (deliberately attempting to confuse family members to jar them out of their entrenched ways of thinking), *spatial interventions* (temporarily removing a family member from a therapy session, or having a particular family member observe the session from behind a one-way mirror), and *upsetting homeostasis* (the therapist temporarily sides with one family member or coalition to modify the typical family hierarchy). The goal of these techniques is to establish and maintain functional boundaries within the family and to replace dysfunctional ways of interacting with family interaction patterns that are satisfying to the family system and self-reinforcing.

## CONCLUSION

Most of the organized programs for improving family relations can be characterized as either primary prevention (building skills to prevent major problems from ever occurring), secondary prevention (identifying at-risk families and enhancing their communication and coping skills), or tertiary prevention (providing therapy to distressed families). Among the primary prevention strategies, marriage preparation programs have figured prominently. The PREP program is a good example of a primary prevention program that is educational in nature, teaching participants about expectations, commitment, communication skills and enhancing their relational bond. If fact, communication skills training is an important part of most programs aimed at preventing marital and family distress. The PREP program stands out for being one of the most rigorously evaluated primary prevention programs and it appears to be reasonably effective for the majority of couples who participate in it. An analysis of cognitive–behavioral premarital intervention programs such as PREP and RE showed that 79% of the couples who participated in such programs were better off than those who had not or had been in a placebo control group (Hahlweg & Markman, 1988). However, evaluating the effectiveness of most marriage preparation programs has been plagued by selection biases—In other words, the couples who participate in these programs seem to already have a very strong relationship.

Primary prevention programs for marriage appear to be on an upward trajectory of popularity. A number of states in the United States now require couples, or in some cases couples where one spouse is under 18, to enroll in marriage preparation programs or premarital counseling. Other states offer would-be brides and grooms a substantial discount on their marriage license if they complete a marriage preparation program. Many religious organizations also insist that couples participate in a premarital program prior to being married. All of this attention to primary prevention perhaps reflects the old adage that an ounce of prevention is worth a pound of cure. It is easier and more sensible to enhance and inoculate an already functional relationship than it is to work on repairing a damaged one. For this reason, marriage preparation programs are likely to proliferate even further in the future.

The secondary prevention programs reviewed include marriage enrichment programs such as Marriage Encounter and parent training programs such as STEP. Marriage Encounter places heavy emphasis on self-disclosure but has been criticized for not teaching necessary communication skills. There is some empirical support for the effectiveness of such marital enrichment programs but also some evidence to show that they are not effective, and in a few cases even harmful, for some couples. A meta-analytic review of 85 studies on marital enrichment programs (including Marriage Encounter and Couples Communication Program) indicated that 67% of the people who participated in these programs were better off than untreated control couples (Giblin, Sprenkle, & Sheehan, 1985). Because chance alone would dictate that 50% of the enrichment couples would be better off than controls, it could be said that enrichment programs represent a 17% improvement over doing nothing. Giblin et al. also found that enrichment programs have a stronger impact on communication and problem-solving variables than on relationship satisfaction.

The parent training programs all work to improve parent–child relationships through understanding children's motives and teaching parents how to interact with their children in ways that promote positive child outcomes. Empathy, positive regard, understanding, active listening, and reinforcement are issues that are addressed in the various parent training programs. The parenting programs reviewed here all assume that good parent–child communication is essential to effective parenting. These programs try to help parents understand and appreciate child psychology. Parents learn how to communicate with their children in ways that will produce desired results. Communicating understanding, appreciation, and positive regard are often presented as necessary components of good parent–child relations. The research that has been conducted on the effectiveness of parenting programs generally indicates that they produce positive outcomes for parents and children. Given the complexity and challenges of parenting coupled with the minimal preparation that most people have for the task, it is understandable why participation in parenting programs has such benefits.

Tertiary prevention strategies address problems after they have already developed. Unfortunately, many families and couples seek therapy after it is already too late. This is one reason why "success" rates for family therapy may not always be as high as they are for primary and secondary prevention strategies. Behavioral and cognitive–behavioral therapies place a strong emphasis on teaching communication skills and effective problem solving. An important part of this type of therapy is identifying and promoting behaviors that are positively reinforcing and avoiding or discouraging those that are punishing to the family. Techniques such as behavioral contracting, teaching mutual acceptance, and self-regulation are also a regular part of behaviorally oriented family therapy. This therapeutic strategy has been augmented by the cognitive–behavioral paradigm that includes many aspects of behavioral therapy but also focuses on changing the dysfunctional cognitions that harm relationships and family interactions. Structural family therapy is concerned with the arrangement of family relationships and interactions. Issues such as boundary regulation, power imbalances, and inappropriate alignments are important areas that are addressed in this type of family therapy. Structural family therapy is aimed at reorganizing the family system through the processes of joining, assessing, and restructuring. Family therapy is often a very useful means for solving even what might appear to be intrapersonal problems such as depression (e.g., Diamond, Reis, Diamond, Siqueland, & Isaacs, 2002). Many of the problems for which families seek help are really systemwide problems in that they are caused, maintained, or exacerbated by family interactions. The goal of most family therapies is to create improvements in family relationships and communication so the problems can naturally dissipate.

Concepts that cut across these organized efforts to improve family relations include self-disclosure, active listening, positively reinforcing messages, perspective taking, conflict resolution skills, and problem-solving skills. There is reason to believe that with guided instruction on these techniques people can improve their family relationships and interactions. However, such change is not easy to come by and is more difficult to produce if families or couples allow relationships to deteriorate too far before seeking intervention.

We begin this chapter by raising some fundamental questions about whether and how it is possible to improve family communication. A brief analysis of some of the available programs and therapies suggests that families can improve their communication and relationships. However, such efforts are best pursued before major problems develop.

Often people do not want to admit that they need training or therapy to help them deal with their family members. The problem then is to get the people in most need to participate in programs to improve family communication. However, people cannot be forced into such programs other than in extreme cases such as when the court system orders participation in family counseling. The challenge for the future then is to (a) make people aware of programs and practices that are effective at improving family communication and (b) increase participation in these programs, particularly to those most in need who are incidentally often the ones least likely to participate in such programs.

# Research Methods for Studying Family Communication and Relationships

The adept consumer of research on family processes must have an understanding of the different techniques that are employed in the design, collection, and analysis of family research studies and the data that they generate. Although a thorough treatment of these issues is beyond the scope of this book, in this Appendix we provide a brief summary of some of the different research methodologies, study designs, and measurement techniques that are commonly used in research on families. More in-depth analyses of these issues can be found in Acock (1999), Copeland and White (1991), Markman and Notarius (1987), Miller (1986), Noller and Feeney (2004), and Socha (1999).

## RESEARCH METHODOLOGIES

There are a variety of different methods that family researchers use to investigate family phenomena. Each of these methods has strengths and weaknesses. Understanding these different methods, what they can reveal and what they cannot reveal, is useful for interpreting the results of various research studies. In this section we briefly review some of the more common research methodologies that appear in the family communication and relationships literature.

### Surveys

The majority of what we know today about family relationships comes from survey research. The common element of all survey research is that investigators ask research participants to provide information. This produces what is known as *self-report* data. Qualities of self-report data are discussed in more detail later in this Appendix. Ordinarily survey research involves large numbers of participants. This is because surveys are fairly easy to administer to large samples even if spread out over diverse geographic regions. Survey researchers can use the mail, telephone calls, and Internet questionnaires to gather information, making it easy to reach many people. For example, the National Survey of Families and Households (e.g., Bumpass, Martin, & Sweet, 1991) involved interviews of over 13,000 households, producing one of the more intensively analyzed data sets in family science.

There are a number of different data collection methods that are used by survey researchers. Perhaps the most common is the use of *self-administered questionnaires*. These are paper-and-pencil measures that are given to respondents to complete and return to the researcher. Questionnaires often contain statements and closed-ended questions that respondents answer with various numerical scales. For example, the Family Assessment Device (Miller, Epstein, Bishop, & Keitner, 1985) contains items to measure family communication, such as "People come right out and say things instead of hinting at them," and "We are frank with each other." Respondents indicate their answer by circling a number on a scale, where 1 = strongly disagree, 2 = disagree, 3 = agree, 4 = strongly agree. This is known as a *Likert* scale. However, not all questionnaires contain closed-ended questions that are answered on Likert scales. Some might ask family members to respond to open-ended, essay-type questions such as "Describe your ideal family vacation." Such questions produce qualitative data that could be analyzed or coded for various themes that appear in the answer. In some cases *researcher-administered questionnaires* are used instead of self-administered questionnaires. Researcher-administered questionnaires are typically read out loud to the participant and the researcher records the answer. This can be a very useful technique for studying certain populations such as children who cannot read very well or elderly people with poor eyesight. Sometimes survey research is conducted over the telephone, in which case researcher-administered questionnaires are employed. Self-administered questionnaires are useful when the questions are straightforward, and not easily misunderstood by respondents, and when it is desirable to maintain the respondent's privacy and anonymity. Researcher-administered questionnaires are useful when questions are complicated and might need to be clarified by the researcher and when the data are collected over the telephone or in face-to-face interviews.

Many interview studies could be classified as a type of survey research. Like surveys more generally, interview methods are diverse and range from unstructured to highly structured. The more structured the interview is, the more the interviewer knows exactly what will be asked during the interview. An *interview schedule* is a set of questions that will be asked by the interviewer. In highly structured interviews the schedule will literally be a questionnaire that the interviewer reads to the participant, recoding answers on defined scales. In more qualitative investigations the interview schedule might involve only a general outline of issues that are to be raised in the interview. In such cases the interviewer might make decisions about what topics to pursue based on the responses of the participant. Responses to less structured interviews are often recorded through note taking or audiotape.

## Experiments

The hallmark features of a true experiment are *manipulation* of an independent variable by the researcher and *random assignment* of research participants to the different experimental conditions. In the prototypical experiment, only the independent variable is manipulated—All other variables are controlled or held constant. This way, if the different groups (e.g., experimental vs. control) differ at the end of the experiment, that difference can be attributed to the effect of the manipulated independent variable. For this reason researchers will often design and conduct experiments when they are interested in isolating the effect of some variable (independent variable) that is assumed to have a causal effect on some outcome (dependent variable). For example, Noller, Feeney, Peterson, and Atkin (2000) created a series of audiotapes that portrayed different styles of marital conflict. These included mutual negotiation, coercion, mother demand and father withdraw, and father demand and mother withdraw. In this experiment Noller and her colleagues manipulated the conflict style heard on the audiotape. The tapes were then played to father, mother, and child family triads. Results indicated that the mutual negotiation conflict was viewed more positively than were the other types, and that the mother-demand conflict was rated as more typical than the father-demand conflict. Through this experiment, the researchers were able to understand the qualities of family conflict that produce positive or negative reactions in family members.

As Noller herself points out, experiments have not been extensively used to study family communication and relationships (Noller & Feeney, 2004). However, experiments still represent an important tool for family researchers. Experiments are much more valuable than surveys for demonstrating cause–effect relationships. This is because they are high on *internal validity*. The question of internal validity concerns how confidently the researcher can conclude that the dependent, or outcome, variable was affected by the independent, or manipulated, variable. Because of their control over extraneous variables, experiments are ordinarily strong in internal validity. However, this strength comes at a price. In order to control extraneous variables (e.g., time of day, room temperature, physical environment, and noise) that could affect the dependent variable, experiments are often conducted in rather artificial laboratory environments that bear little resemblance to the "real world." Consequently, it is sometimes difficult to generalize the results of laboratory experiments to more naturalistic and realistic environments. For this reason many experiments are low in *external validity*, which represents the extent to which the results of the investigation can be generalized to environments and contexts external to the laboratory.

Is there a happy medium between the high internal validity and the low external validity inherent in most experiments? To better balance these two legitimate features of experiments, some researchers conduct *quasi-experiments*. Simply put, a quasi-experiment is not a true experiment because the researcher does not actively manipulate the independent variable or because the researcher could not randomly assign participants to conditions. There are naturalistic experiments going on all the time in society. For instance, Menees and Segrin (2000) were interested in the effects of various family stressors (e.g., death of a parent, parental alcoholism, and parental divorce) on the social climate in families. For obvious reasons researchers could never randomly assign people to these different family stressors. Instead the authors selected people from the population who had been naturally exposed to these family stressors. The problem with this technique is that internal validity is in question. If the family environment in households with an alcoholic parent has more conflict than those that experienced the death of a parent, is that because of the nature of the two different stressors, or perhaps some other variables like education or income that also differ as a function of the stressors? It is sometimes impossible to answer these questions in a quasi-experiment. On the plus side, quasi-experiments are often much higher than laboratory experiments in external validity. After all, the people in quasi-experiments usually experienced the "manipulation" as a part of their everyday life and live with it in their natural environment.

## Content Analysis

Content analysis is a technique for quantifying recorded communication or communication texts. So, for example, researchers might use content analysis to describe the prevalence of divorced characters on prime-time television, the number of interracial families in situation comedies, or the frequency of extramarital relationships portrayed on daytime soap operas. In the domain of family communication, content analysis is most often used to describe media depictions of family interactions and relationships. In chapter 12 we discuss a content analysis by Robinson and Skill (2001) that showed that depictions of stepfamilies in prime-time fictional television have been increasing over the years but still lag behind the actual prevalence of stepfamilies in the general population.

Content analysis is a useful tool for describing what appears on television, in magazines, romance novels, and motion pictures, but it does not tell us who consumes these messages or what effect they have on the viewer. For example, if a content analysis showed that more divorced people were portrayed on network television in the 1990s compared to the 1960s, it would be tempting to conclude that these media depictions are at least partly responsible for the more widespread acceptance of divorce in recent years. However, this inference goes far beyond what the data actually indicate. Similarly, if a content analysis showed that family-situated programs (e.g., *Roseanne, The Osbournes*) had more intense conflict today than they did in the past, some might conclude that this teaches young people that extensive bickering and fighting is normative in the family. As reasonable as this conclusion would appear, the content analysis alone does not tell us that young people are actually viewing these programs. That would require additional data, perhaps from a survey of television-viewing habits of young people.

One vital decision that must be made when conducting a content analysis is determining the *unit of analysis*. The unit of analysis is the basic unit or segment of the communication text that will be measured or classified. Consider, for example, a content analysis of family situated television programs (e.g., *The Brady Bunch, Roseanne*, and *The Osbournes*). At a broad level, one could treat the entire series as a unit of analysis. For example, these shows could be classified as either "fiction" or "reality" based. At a more specific level, the unit of analysis could be the episode. Researchers could, for instance, classify each episode according to its dominant plot. Getting even more specific, individual scenes or characters could be the unit of analysis. More specific yet, a researcher could classify individual utterances of the characters on these programs. Perhaps there is more profanity used in family-situated programs today than there was back in the days of *Leave it to Beaver*. In this case, a researcher could classify the individual utterances of each character in terms of whether they contain profanity. In any event, decisions about the appropriate unit of analysis are inextricably connected with the nature of the research question. If the research question concerns how often extended family members are portrayed as living in the same home, the entire series or individual episodes could be the unit of analysis. On the other hand, a research question about whether fathers are depicted as reprimanding children more often than mothers are would require a much more microscopic unit of analysis, perhaps down to the individual scene or individual utterances of each character.

A second vital element of content analysis is the *coding scheme*. A coding scheme is simply a classification system for describing the content of the communication text. For example, a content analysis of family roles in motion pictures might include the following categories: mother, father, husband, wife, son, daughter, brother, sister, grandfather, grandmother, aunt, uncle, stepmother, stepfather, cousin. Researchers could then classify each character into one of these categories to see what family roles are most and least commonly portrayed in the movies. Coding schemes used in content analysis must have categories that are *mutually exclusive*. This means that each unit to be coded can be classified into one and only one category. What if the aforementioned coding scheme was used to classify Kevin Spacey's character in the film *American Beauty*? He was both a husband and a father. As straightforward as this coding scheme appears, it could be problematic when actually getting down to the business of coding real communication texts. A coding scheme must also be *exhaustive*. This means that there is a category for every unit to be coded. What if a character in a film was the brother-in-law of another character? The scheme presented earlier has no category called "brother-in-law," so it is not truly exhaustive. Sometimes researchers will make exhaustive coding schemes by using an "other" category for all those units that cannot be fit into one of the existing categories.

Finally, there are some cases in family research where content analysis is used as a method of analyzing data that were gathered as part of an interview or survey research study. For example, Fiese and her colleagues interview families and record narratives or stories about their experiences (Fiese et al., 2001; see chap. 3). These stories would then be transcribed and essentially content analyzed for narrative coherence (how well the story is constructed and organized), narrative interaction (how well the family works together to jointly construct the narrative), and relationship beliefs (the way that the family's view of the social world is reflected in their story). In this way, content analysis is useful for summarizing and cataloging the qualitative data that are provided by research participants.

## Ethnography

Ethnography is a type of qualitative field research that is aimed more at description than at explanation. In particular, ethnographic studies examine various phenomena in their natural settings rather than in laboratories. Unlike experiments or surveys, in ethnography, investigators will often get directly involved in the subject matter that they are studying and interact frequently with the research subjects. The idea is that the closer one's contact is with the phenomenon under investigation, the better able he or she is to offer a detailed and accurate description of that phenomenon.

Ethnographic studies tend to follow the *grounded theory* approach. Researchers who develop grounded theories start with careful and detailed observations and then develop more general theoretical explanations based on those descriptions. This is more of an inductive than deductive approach to theory development.

In ethnographic research there are a number of different relationships that might exist between the researcher and his or her research subjects. When the researcher acts as a *complete observer* he or she simply observes phenomena as they occur in their natural environment. In such cases the research subjects are unaware of the ethnographer's observations and are therefore unlikely to alter their natural behavior. In a closer level of involvement with research subjects, ethnographic investigators sometimes assume the role of *observer as participant*. In such cases research participants know that they are being observed, but the researcher tries to "fit in" to the situation or context without actually participating in it. When researchers act in the role of *participant as observer* they actively participate in the phenomenon under investigation. For example, if an ethnographic investigator attended a family reunion and ate hotdogs and talked with various family members, he or she would be acting as a participant observer. This perspective gives the researcher considerable insight into the phenomenon under investigation, but this familiarity comes at a cost as the researcher may actually influence the phenomenon that is being studied. Finally, ethnographic researchers sometimes act as *complete participant*. In this case they actively participate in the phenomenon that is being studied but do not inform research participants of their dual role as both participant and researcher. This is comparable to being an undercover police officer. If the behavior being observed is public, this is not a problematic technique, but if it is private there are obvious ethical issues associated with the difficulty of securing informed consent from the potential research participants.

Ethnographic researchers use a variety of creative methods to make their observations. These might include, for example, interviews, careful note taking, and audio or video recordings. Sometimes research participants are asked to listen to or watch audio or video recordings of their own behavior, and to comment on or explain that behavior. This technique is known as *stimulated recall*.

Ethnographic methods have not been as widely employed to study family communication and relationships as surveys have been, but nevertheless they hold great promise for providing detailed descriptions of such relationships and interactions. In one notable exception, an ethnographic researcher actually lived with a family for a period of time in order to observe and better understand the family's television viewing patterns and habits (see Fiske, 1987). This sort of investigation yields a depth of knowledge that is not ordinarily available in the typical laboratory experiment or survey study. On the other hand, the ability to generalize from the results of observing a few cases in depth is extremely limited. Another potential problem inherent in some ethnographic investigations is *reactivity*. This occurs when research participants alter their behavior because they know that they are being observed. Of course, this is a problem inherent in many different research methods and is not unique to ethnographic research.

## RESEARCH DESIGNS

Regardless of the method a researcher chooses, there are several design issues that must be considered when planning the study. Three major design features that we discuss in this section are cross-sectional versus longitudinal designs, and meta-analysis. Although the longitudinal versus cross-sectional distinction is often thought of as being most applicable to survey research, experiments and content analyses could also be longitudinal in nature in some instances.

## Cross-Sectional Designs

A *cross-sectional* study examines a representative sample, or cross-section, of the population at one point in time. For this reason, cross-sectional studies are very useful for describing the status quo in a segment of the population. For example, large-scale surveys that measure rates of family violence, number of divorced people in the population, and levels of marital satisfaction in husbands and wives are often cross-sectional in nature. Such studies can tell us things like $X\%$ of husbands are dissatisfied with their marriages and $Y\%$ of wives are dissatisfied with their marriages. For many purposes, this can be useful information.

At the same time, however, there are some drawbacks to cross-sectional designs. First, if the phenomenon is one that is actively changing throughout history, the results of a cross-sectional survey might have a limited shelf life. If someone wanted to know what percentage of married women stay home to raise their children instead of working outside the home, a cross-sectional survey conducted in 1962 would be of little use. This is because women's participation in the professional workforce has changed substantially since 1962, and those results could not be assumed to accurately reflect current rates of mothers' participation in the workforce. Second, cross-sectional studies are limited in the extent to which they can provide information on cause–effect relationships. Consider two competing models of marital satisfaction and conflict. According to the first model, conflict causes marital dissatisfaction (conflict $\rightarrow$ dissatisfaction). According to the second model, martial dissatisfaction causes conflict (dissatisfaction $\rightarrow$ conflict). Suppose a researcher conducted a survey study of 1,000 married people and asked them to report on their level of marital satisfaction and the frequency of their marital conflicts. If the results indicated a significant correlation between conflict and dissatisfaction, does that support Model 1 or Model 2? In fact both Models 1 and 2 could be correct. If $A$ causes $B$, $A$ and $B$ must be correlated with each other. Also, if $B$ causes $A$, $A$ and $B$ would still be correlated. Furthermore, a significant correlation between conflict and dissatisfaction could occur even if both Model 1 and Model 2 are incorrect. If some third variable, say marital infidelity, caused both marital dissatisfaction and marital conflict, dissatisfaction and conflict would still be correlated despite having no causal relationship to each other. For this reason it is important to remember that in cross-sectional studies a significant correlation does not imply a causal relationship.

## Longitudinal Designs

A *longitudinal* study is designed to observe and study phenomena over time. As noted in our discussion of cross-sectional studies, many family phenomena change over time. Only a longitudinal study can adequately document that change. There are several different types of longitudinal study designs that are used to study different types of change. For example, the *trend* study examines changes in the general population over time. The U.S. Census Bureau measures households and living arrangements in the American population every 10 years. An examination of cohabitation rates as documented in the 1970, 1980, 1990, and 2000 census would amount to a trend study. Such an investigation would allow the researcher to examine trends in cohabitation to see if it is on the rise or decline in the U.S. population. In a *cohort* study, researchers examine changes in a certain subgroup, or cohort, in the population over time. Suppose that a researcher was interested in the "family values" of people born during the great depression of the 1930s, and how they changed over time through the varying political climates of the 1960s, 1980s, and so on. This could be accomplished by surveying a group of people born in the 1930s every 10 years. For example, the first wave of measurement might start in 1950 when members of this cohort are in their 20s. The next wave might occur in 1960 when these people are in their 30s, followed by a wave of measurement in 1970 when they are in their 40s, and so forth. This type of study would allow researchers to track changes in the family values of this cohort over extended periods of time. Perhaps their family ideologies are relatively stable despite dramatic shifts in the social climate over time. A cohort study could reveal such a finding.

Perhaps the most powerful longitudinal design is the *panel* study. In the panel study the same people are followed over time. In others words a person who is measured at Time 1 is also measured at Time 2. In the trend and cohort studies different people are measured at each point in time. The panel study allows researchers to track changes within particular individuals. Why is this such a useful and powerful research design? Scientists and philosophers generally agree that in causal models, cause must precede effect. Only a panel study can show that a supposedly "causal" agent happened and was then followed by a hypothesized "effect" in the same person. For example, in chapter 11 we discussed a study by Huston and Vangelisti (1991) that showed that wives' negativity (e.g., acting bored or uninterested, showing anger or impatience, and criticizing or complaining) during a martial interaction predicted decreases in their satisfaction 2 years later. Only a panel study could test this negativity in interaction $\rightarrow$ dissatisfaction hypothesis, because it is necessary to demonstrate that the negativity happens before the dissatisfaction does. Interested readers might want to examine Karney and Bradbury (1995) for more examples of panel studies with married couples.

The useful information that is yielded by panel studies comes at a high price—literally and figuratively. Often families have to be compensated for their time and involvement. It can take an enormous amount of money to conduct large sample studies that follow people over many waves of assessment. Panel studies also have the unique problem of *attrition*. Attrition occurs when people drop out of a panel study before it is finished. Why is this a concern? Consider Huston and Vangelisti's (1991) study mentioned earlier. What if half of the husbands and wives dropped out of the study before the 2 years were up? One might be concerned that only the happy couples stayed in the study. After all, who wants to tell the whole world about their bad marriage? In contrast, maybe more of the dissatisfied spouses stayed in the study because they have some sort of axe to grind and want to vent and unload on the researchers. Either way, there is a concern that this attrition effect is not random and may therefore bias the results. Another problem that is inherent in panel studies with two waves of measurement is *statistical regression*. This is simply the natural tendency of people with extreme scores to become less extreme over time. Imagine a couple with extraordinarily high or low levels of marital conflict. Most likely, 1 year later the couple with high conflict will be reporting slightly less conflict and the couple with virtually no conflict will be reporting higher levels of conflict. This natural occurrence happens because it is difficult to sustain extreme levels of conflict (or just about anything else) over long periods of time. For the panel study, this creates questions about "meaningful" change that is driven by some family process versus simple regression toward less extreme scores over time.

Even though longitudinal studies can document change over time, it is important to recognize their limitations. Assume, for example, that a researcher measures a variable X (marital infidelity) and its effect on variable Y (divorce) at a later point in time. An association between these two variables over time might lead some to suspect that marital infidelity is a cause of divorce. However, what if some third variable Z (psychological detachment from the marriage) causes both X and Y? This situation could make it appear that X causes Y, when in fact their association is largely coincidental by virtue of each being caused by some common third variable. The potential for misattributing causal order is especially high when effect of Z on Y takes longer to happen than X on Y. As Glenn (1998) noted, longitudinal studies, like all other studies, are limited in their ability to rule out these "third variable" explanations. Nevertheless, because temporal precedence of cause before effect is a necessary but not sufficient criterion for establishing causality, longitudinal studies are useful for at least falsifying hypothesized causal effects and still play a vital role testing causal models (Rogosa, 1979).

Despite the costs and potential pitfalls inherent in panel studies, in many ways, they represent the pinnacle of family science research. When studying phenomena that naturally develop over time such as marital distress, children's communication skills, and stepfamily cohesion, there is really no parallel to panel studies and for that reason alone they merit special attention.

## Meta-Analysis

As the name implies, a *meta-analysis* is literally an analysis of analyses that have already been conducted. In a primary research study, data points ordinarily represent variables measured from individual people. However, in a meta-analysis data points represent findings from an entire study. The purpose of a meta-analysis is to quantify how strong the association is between variables (e.g., family cohesion and child adjustment), or how strong the difference is between groups (e.g., married and divorced), and to summarize all of the findings that are available on a particular topic. These statistics that represent how strongly variables are associated or how strongly groups differ are known as *effect size estimates*. A meta-analysis provides effect size estimates that are averaged over all of the known studies on a particular topic. It is becoming increasingly common to see meta-analyses of dozens, if not hundreds, of studies in a single investigation. Often these studies collectively involve 10,000–20,000 research participants. For example, Amato and Keith's (1991a) meta-analysis of the effects of parental divorce on children's social adjustment involved 92 studies. Over 13,000 children participated in these studies. The benefit of conducting meta-analysis becomes obvious when considering the vast amounts of data that can be summarized in a single report. Further, meta-analyses report how strongly variables are associated or groups differ, not just whether they are associated or different. Because individual studies can have problems or weaknesses, their results are sometimes open to different interpretations. By accumulating results across many different studies, the weaknesses of one study are often mitigated by the strengths of others. Like panel studies, meta-analyses warrant special consideration for the wealth and conclusiveness of information that they can provide.

## MEASUREMENT IN FAMILY RESEARCH

Aside from the methodology of a study (e.g., experiment and survey) and its design (e.g., cross-sectional and longitudinal), studies also vary in the type of measurement that they employ. There are a number of different ways to measure family phenomena that are of interest to researchers who study them. Undoubtedly, the two most common types of measurement in family science are self-report and observation. We discuss the pros and cons of these measurement strategies and then briefly consider the use of other sources of data such as physiological and phenomenological data.

### Self-Report

In the section on surveys we indicate that much of what we know today about families comes from survey research and that these data are largely self-report in nature. In self-report measurement, the researcher simply asks participants to provide information in response to various questions or agreement with different statements. Family scientists have developed a multitude of different self-report instruments for assessing various family-related variables. A small sample of some of the more commonly used self-report instruments in family research appears in Table A.1. Instruments such as these are very popular in family research because they can be completed with relative ease and because they can rapidly provide useful information on variables that are sometimes difficult or impossible to actually observe.

Noller and Feeney (2004) identify many useful qualities of self-report data in family communication research. First, they are useful for collecting information about family communication across time and situations. If a researcher wanted to know if a mother was strict with her children both in the home and when they are away from home, self-report measurement would be a good way to gather this information. It would be extremely difficult to observe the mother interacting with her children in their home, at the grocery store, at their grandmother's house, at church, at the movies, and so on. It is much easier to simply ask the mother, and perhaps her children, about family discipline practices in a number of different contexts. Second, self-report data are useful for collecting information on communication that happened in the past. Does a history of childhood abuse predispose people to stormy marriages as adults? Ideally, one would follow groups of abused and nonabused children through adulthood and into marriage. However, such study could take 20 to 30 years to complete. On the other hand, a researcher could collect self-report data on childhood experiences with abuse and current marital adjustment in a sample of married adults. This method is not without its shortcomings as we will discuss momentarily. Noller and Feeney note that self-reports are also useful for gathering information on behaviors that are unlikely to be elicited in a laboratory setting. Marital violence, withdrawal, and sexually oriented nonverbal behaviors are unlikely to occur in a laboratory. Nevertheless, they could have a substantial impact on the quality of a relationship. The only sensible recourse for scientists interested in studying these behaviors is to simply ask people about their occurrence and their feelings about them. We might add to Noller and Feeney's list the fact that self-reports are also useful for measuring people's attitudes about family members and family communication, because these are otherwise not directly observable. For example, measurement of marital satisfaction is essentially an attitude toward, or evaluation of, one's marriage. Although it might have observable behavioral manifestations, the evaluation itself can really only be measured through self-report.

Just as there is obvious utility in self-report data, there are a number of limitations to self-report data that are often discussed in the research literature. For example, *social desirability* is a problem when people purposely distort the truth in order to present themselves in a positive light. For this reason a self-report study of marital violence is likely to underestimate the true incidence of the problem because some people may be unwilling to admit that they have either perpetrated or been the victim of domestic violence. There are also problems with *recall bias* any time that retrospective reports are sought. No one has a perfect memory and sometimes people remember mostly the good times from their family experiences during childhood. Others may be prone to only remember the bad times. A lot of this bias in recall could be explained by people's current emotional state. Either way, important details from the past might get lost with self-report data. A related problem with retrospective self-reports is *mentally editing* past experiences. This is different from selectively forgetting. All people think about many of their past experiences and try to make sense of them. As they do, details sometimes get edited or changed to fit a particular schema or belief system. For example, a divorced father who was distant from his children back when he still lived with them may think back to those days, overestimating how much time he actually spent with his children. It is not that the hypothetical father is being dishonest. That is the way that he really remembers the days living at home with his children. These types of distortions in memory create an interesting dilemma for researchers. Which is more important? What "really" happened, or what are people's perceptions of what happened? This is a thorny issue that boils down to one's view of "objective reality," and whether or not people feel that there even is such a thing.

Family researchers will sometimes use specialized techniques to overcome some of the limitations of the aforementioned self-report data. For example, some researchers use a *diary* method (Duck, 1991) that asks participants to record their thoughts or behaviors at some regular interval (e.g., each night). With this method scientists can analyze the accumulated diary records with reasonable confidence that participants did not forget important details because their self-report data were provided in close proximity to when the events or thoughts occurred. In some cases family researchers use *experience-sampling techniques* (Noller & Feeney, 2004) such as beepers or repeated telephone calls to collect data. Participants in such studies might receive a phone call from the researcher or respond to a pager that goes off at random times. Once again, the idea is to collect data on what is going on "right now," rather than to wait until later when the person might have forgotten certain details of the day's events. By using the specialized technique at least some of the limitations of self-report measurement can be effectively minimized.

TABLE A.1

Commonly Used Self-Report Instruments for Measuring Marital and Family Processes

| Instrument | Source | Subscales | Number of Items | Sample Items | Response Options |
|---|---|---|---|---|---|
| Dyadic Adjustment Scale | Spanier (1976) | dyadic satisfaction<br>dyadic cohesion<br>dyadic consensus<br>affectional expression | 32 | "Please indicate below the appropriate extent of agreement or disagreement between you and your partner for each item on the following list: friends, amount of time spent together, career decisions, . . . "<br><br>"Do you confide in your mate?"<br>"How often do you and your partner quarrel?" | always agree<br>almost always agree<br>occasionally disagree<br>frequently disagree<br>almost always disagree<br>always disagree<br><br>all the time<br>most of the time<br>more often than not<br>occasionally<br>rarely<br>never |
| Family Assessment Device | Epstein, Baldwin, & Bishop (1983) | problem solving<br>communication<br>roles<br>affective responsiveness<br>affective involvement<br>behavior control<br>general functioning | 60 | "We are frank with each other"<br>"We make sure members meets their family responsibilities" | strongly agree<br>agree<br>disagree<br>strongly disagree |

| Instrument | Source | Items | Dimensions | Sample items | Response options |
|---|---|---|---|---|---|
| Family Environment Scale | Moos & Moos (1994) | 90 | cohesion<br>expressiveness<br>conflict<br>independence<br>achievement orientation<br>intellectual-cultural orientation<br>active-recreational orientation<br>moral-religious emphasis<br>organization<br>control | "Family members often criticize each other"<br>"Friends come over for dinner or to visit" | true<br>false |
| Primary Communication Inventory | Narvan (1967) | 25 | none | "How often do you and your spouse talk over pleasant things that happen during the day?"<br>"Do you feel that in most matters your spouse knows what you are trying to say?" | never<br>seldom<br>occasionally<br>frequently<br>very frequently |
| Relational Dimensions Instrument | Fitzpatrick (1988a) | 77 | ideology:<br>traditionalism<br>uncertainty<br>autonomy/interdependence:<br>sharing<br>autonomy<br>undifferentiated space<br>temporal regularity<br>conflict:<br>conflict avoidance<br>assertiveness | "We try to resolve our disagreements immediately"<br>"We share many of our personal belongings with each other" | always<br>usually<br>often<br>occasionally<br>often not<br>unusually not<br>never |

## Behavioral Observation

Observational studies of marital and family interaction have become increasingly popular in the past 20 years. This is due in part to the availability of affordable audio and video-recording devices and media. In observational studies researchers observe and record family members as they interact with each other. These studies are usually done in a laboratory, but with the availability of portable audio- and videorecorders home observations are used in some cases. The purpose of an observational study is to assess family members' actual communication behavior and determine how those behaviors are related to various family processes that may be of interest to the researcher.

There are several design elements of observational studies that must be considered before the study is conducted, as well as when the data produced from the study are interpreted (Markman & Notarius, 1987). First, researchers must decide what *task* they want the family members to engage in. Observational research on marital interaction, for example, has been dominated by conflict resolution tasks. Typically husbands and wives are asked to discuss and attempt to resolve some area of conflict in their relationship. Even observational studies of larger family interactions that include children are often focused on a problem-solving task. The task that research participants engage in will determine to a large extent how far the results of the study can be generalized. A study that observes married couples attempt to resolve a conflict can reveal a lot about their conflict resolution skills but say very little about how much they enjoy leisure time together. The selection of a task obviously must serve the overall purpose of the study.

Another feature of observational studies is the *setting*. As mentioned previously, observational studies are most often carried out in a laboratory setting but could also occur in a home environment or in some other setting (e.g., a day-care center, nursing home, and pediatrician's office). Earlier we mentioned that laboratory experiments are sometimes criticized for having questionable external validity. In many ways, the same concern could be raised with observational laboratory studies. Are the behaviors that are observed in a laboratory similar to those that are enacted in the home? Will parents who hit their children also enact this behavior during a laboratory interaction? Will verbally aggressive married couples put each other down as intensely as they do when they are not sitting in front of laboratory videocameras and one-way mirrors? Answers to these questions are not always known and get to the heart of the external validity of laboratory studies. It is precisely for this reason that some researchers opt to observe families in more natural, but less controlled, settings such as their homes. For those who are particularly concerned with the artificiality of laboratory observational research, it is useful to consider that what is observed in the lab is probably an understatement of what actually goes on in the home, away from the camera and observers. Therefore, if some behavior observed in the lab (e.g., contempt for the spouse) is predictive of some outcome (e.g., divorce), it is unlikely that the laboratory research results are overstating the case for the contempt → divorce association. Again, the nature of the contempt that might be observed during a laboratory interaction is most likely an underrepresentation of the couple's actual communication behavior. So the results that are produced by such a study are probably a conservative statement about the effects of contempt.

In addition to the task and setting, observational researchers must consider the *family composition*. Some observational studies examine interactions between husbands and wives, others look at mothers and their children, and still others observe whole families interacting. Here again, the decision about family composition will have a large impact on the nature of the data that will be gathered. For example, husbands and wives will most likely alter their communication behavior when in the presence of their children. Of course, if a researcher observed that they did not, that would be diagnostic in and of itself. Children interacting with their mothers might also adjust their communication behavior when in the presence of their father. Like the interaction task, the family composition must be matched to the purpose and goals of the study.

Once the family observational data are collected, usually on audio- or videotape, they need to be organized and summarized. This is most commonly accomplished through coding or rating the interactions. *Coding* works exactly like a content analysis. Examples of various communication behaviors or acts are tabulated usually for their frequency, but sometimes for their duration or sequencing with other behaviors. *Rating* typically involves some judgment or evaluation of the observed behavior on a set of scales. For example, a researcher might rate a mother's behavior toward her child during a problem-solving task on the following scale:

unfriendly    1    2    3    4    5    friendly

Ratings such as this tend to be more global or macroscopic, whereas coded behaviors are often more microscopic in nature. Family researchers have developed dozens of excellent coding schemes for assessing family interactions (see for example Kerig & Lindahl, 2001; Markman & Notarius, 1987). Examples of some of the more commonly used coding and rating schemes appear in Table A.2. Notice how each of these schemes has a very different purpose that is obviously reflected in the types of codes that appear in the scheme. For example, Patterson's Family Interaction Coding System (FICS) scheme was developed to assess positive and negative behaviors that occur in whole family interactions that include children. Many of these are nonverbal behaviors. On the other hand, Hahlweg et al's (1984) Kategoriensystem für Partner-Schaftliche Interactions (KPI) is designed to catalog the discourse of married couples as they talk with each other.

Needless to say, observational research can be very time consuming, expensive, and difficult to conduct. So why bother? Perhaps the most compelling reason for doing observational research is the hope of assessing behaviors that actors might not always be consciously aware of, but that still have a substantial impact on family processes. Sometimes people do not realize just how often they say or do certain things. Other times they might realize it but are not willing to admit it. Observational research can be a very useful tool for getting around many of the problems inherent in self-report data collection. There is also a great purity in behavioral assessment. Reports and recollections of family behaviors can often be distorted for a variety of reasons. On the other hand, there is a greater degree of objectivity in observation of family interactions. This type of data collection does not rely on family members' recollections or perceptions. Of course there are downsides to observational studies as well. Just because a researcher documented that mothers smiled more at their children than fathers did, for example,

**TABLE A.2**
Commonly Used Classification Systems for Coding Family Interaction

| Coding Scheme | Source | Construct(s) Measured | Target Population | Unit of Analysis | Categories | Coded or Rated? |
|---|---|---|---|---|---|---|
| Couples Interaction Scoring System (CISS) | Notarius, Markman, & Gottman (1983) | verbal and nonverbal behavior during problem-solving interactions | married couples | thought unit | CONTENT CODES: problem talk; mind reading; proposing solution; communication talk; agreement; disagreement; summarizing other; summarizing self. NONVERBAL CODES: face (smile, frown, head nod, sneer); voice (caring, cold, warm, tense); body (touching, rude gestures, open arms, hand tension) | coded |
| Family Coding System | Gordis & Margolin (2001) | affective states and behaviors during triadic family interactions | families with children | 1-min of interaction | INTERPARENTAL AFFECT: hostility/contempt/criticism; self-defensive/argumentative; blame; warmth/affection; empathy/encouragement/praise. PARENT-TO-CHILD COMMUNICATION: lecture/laying down the law leading questions; parent seeks information/help from child. CHILD BEHAVIOR: withdrawal; anxiety; distraction | coded |

| Family Interaction Coding System (FICS) | Patterson, Ray, Shaw, & Cobb (1969) | deviant and cohesive behavior in families, usually with conduct-disordered children | families, sometimes used for married couples | 6-sec units of behavior | AVERSIVE: (command negative, cry, disapproval, dependency, destructiveness, high rate, humiliate, tease, whine, yell, noncompliance, negativism, ignore, physical negative) PROSOCIAL: (approval, attention, command positive, compliance, indulgence, laugh, normative, no response, play, physical positive, receive, self-stimulation, talk, touch, work) | coded |
|---|---|---|---|---|---|---|
| Kategoriensystem Für Partnerschaftliche Interaktion (KPI) | Hahlweg, Reisner, Kohli, Vollmer, Schindler, & Revenstorf (1984) | speaker and listener communication and problem-solving skills | married couples | thought unit or utterance | self-disclosure, positive solution, acceptance of other, agreement, problem description, meta-communication, rest, listening, criticize, negative solution, justification, disagreement | coded |
| System for Coding Interactions and Family Functioning (SCIFF) | Lindahl & Malik (2001) | family functioning through observation of a family problem discussion | families with children, marital dyads | the complete interaction | FAMILY CODES: negativity/conflict, positive affect, cohesiveness, focus on problem, parenting style, alliance formation DYAD CODE quality of communication PARENT CODES rejection/invalidation, coerciveness, triangulation, withdrawal, emotional support | some coded (e.g., hierarchical, democratic, lax, or inconsistent parenting) some rated (e.g., very low, low, moderate, moderately high, high) |

does not prove that this behavior means anything to the children or that they even noticed. Also, there is a serious question of generalizability from observational studies. It is often possible to only observe family members interacting for 10 or 15 minutes. Can such a small sample of behavior reveal much about the family? Remarkably, in some cases, the answer appears to be yes. Also, observational studies are difficult to conduct because they are time consuming, expensive, and create logistical challenges for getting multiple family members in a laboratory all at the same time. Once their data are recorded, coders sometimes spend hundreds of hours analyzing and cataloging the recorded behaviors. Despite all of these costs, many researchers remain convinced of the value of observational research, as family scientists Howard Markman and Clifford Notarius (1987) argued: "We remain convinced that the *proximal* source of family distress and well-being lies in the microlevel of exchange between family members" (p. 385). This microlevel exchange can only be studied effectively through observational research.

## Other Measurement Techniques

As family science progresses, researchers are finding great utility in measures other than self-reports and behavioral observations. For example, *physiological* measures indicative of arousal such as heart rate and blood pressure have proven to be useful for understanding marital interactions (Gottman & Levensen, 1988). Also, levels of stress hormones circulating in the blood during marital conflict discussions are predictive of divorce and marital satisfaction 10 years later (Kiecolt-Glaser, Bane, Glaser, & Malarkey, 2003). *Phenomenological* research often employs interviewing, for example, but might also employ techniques such a picture drawing to understand children's relationships and interactions with family members (Davilla, 1995). These symbolic creations along with other activities such as playing with dolls might contain information on children's representations of their roles in the family and relationships with other family members. Like all other measurement techniques, physiological and phenomenological measures have their strengths and weaknesses. However, in combination with other measures they often prove to be useful for revealing additional information that may not be evident from some of these more standard measurements.

# References

Abramson, L. Y., Seligman, M. E. P., & Teasdale, J. (1978). Learned helplessness in humans: Critique and reformulation. *Journal of Abnormal Psychology, 87,* 49–74.

Acock, A. C. (1999). Quantitative methodology for studying families. In M. B. Sussman, S. K. Steinmetz, & G. W. Peterson (Eds.), *Handbook of marriage and the family* (2nd ed., pp. 263–289). New York: Plenum.

Adams, B. N. (1975). *The family: A sociological interpretation* (2nd ed.). Chicago: Rand McNally.

Adams, B. N. (1999). Cross-cultural and U.S. kinships. In M. B. Sussman, S. K. Steinmetz, & G. W. Peterson (Eds.), *Handbook of marriage and the family* (2nd ed., pp. 77–92). New York: Plenum.

Adams, J. F. (2001). Impact of parent training on family functioning. *Child and Family Behavior Therapy, 23,* 29–42.

Afifi, W. A., & Guerrero, L. K. (2000). Motivations underlying topic avoidance in close relationships. In S. Petronio (Ed.), *Balancing the secrets of private disclosures* (pp. 165–180). Mahwah, NJ: Lawrence Erlbaum Associates.

Ahmad, S., Waller, G., & Verduyn, C. (1994). Eating attitudes among Asian schoolgirls: The role of perceived parental control. *International Journal of Eating Disorders, 15,* 91–97.

Ahrons, C. R., & Rodgers, R. H. (1987). *Divorced families: A multidisciplinary developmental view.* New York: Norton.

Ahuja, R. B. D., & Stinson, K. M. (1993). Female-headed single parent families: An explanatory study of children's influence in family decision making. *Advances in Consumer Research, 20,* 469–474.

AhYun, K. (2002). Similarity and attraction. In M. Allen, R. W. Preiss, B. M. Gayle, & N. Burrell (Eds.), *Interpersonal communication research: Advances through meta-analysis* (pp. 145–168). Mahwah, NJ: Lawrence Erlbaum Associates.

Ainsworth, M. D. S., Blehar, M. S., Waters, E., & Wall, S. (1978). *Patterns of attachment: A psychological study of the strange situation.* Hillsdale, NJ: Lawrence Erlbaum Associates.

Albrecht, T. L., Burleson, B. R., & Goldsmith, D. (1994). Supportive communication. In M. L. Knapp & G. R. Miller (Eds.), *Handbook of interpersonal communication* (2nd ed., pp. 419–449). Thousand Oaks, CA: Sage.

Aldous, J. (1990). Family development and the life course: Two perspectives on family change. *Journal of Marriage and the Family, 52,* 571–583.

Alexander, P. C. (1985). A systems theory conceptualization of incest. *Family Process, 24,* 79–88.

Alexander, P. C., & Lupfer, S. L. (1987). Family characteristics and long-term consequences associated with sexual abuse. *Archives of Sexual Behavior, 16,* 235–245.

Allen, E. S., Baucom, D. H., Burnett, C. K., Epstein, N., & Rankin-Esquer, L. A. (2001). Decision-making power, autonomy, and communication in remarried spouses compared with first-married spouses. *Family Relations, 50,* 326–334.

Allen, K. R., Blieszner, R., & Roberto, K. A. (2000). Families in the middle and later years: A review and critique of research in the 1990s. *Journal of Marriage and the Family, 62,* 911–926.

Allen, M., & Burrell, N. (2002). Sexual orientation of the parent: The impact on the child. In M. Allen, R. W. Preiss, B. M. Gayle, & N. A. Burrell (Eds.), *Interpersonal communication research: Advances through meta-analysis* (pp. 125–144). Mahwah, NJ: Lawrence Erlbaum Associates.

Alpert, E. J., Cohen, S., & Sege, R. D. (1997). Family violence: An overview. *Academic Medicine, 72*(Suppl. 1), S3–S6.

Altman, I., & Taylor, D. A. (1973). *Social penetration: The development of interpersonal relationships.* New York: Holt, Rinehart & Winston.

Alwin, D. F. (1996). Parental socialization in historical perspective. In C. D. Ryff & M. M. Seltzer (Eds.), *The parental experience in midlife* (pp. 105–167). Chicago: University of Chicago Press.

Amato, P. R. (1993). Children's adjustment to divorce: Theories, hypotheses, and empirical support. *Journal of Marriage and the Family, 55*, 23–38.

Amato, P. R. (1996). Explaining the intergenerational transmission of divorce. *Journal of Marriage and the Family, 58*, 628–640.

Amato, P. R. (1999). Children of divorced parents as young adults. In E. M. Hetherington (Ed.), *Coping with divorce, single parenting, and remarriage* (pp. 147–163). Mahwah, NJ: Lawrence Erlbaum Associates.

Amato, P. R. (2000). The consequences of divorce for adults and children. *Journal of Marriage and the Family, 62*, 1269–1287.

Amato, P. R. (2001). Children of divorce in the 1990s: An update of the Amato and Keith (1991) meta-analysis. *Journal of Family Psychology, 15*, 355–370.

Amato, P. R., & Booth, A. (2001). The legacy of parents' marital discord: Consequences for children's marital quality. *Journal of Personality and Social Psychology, 81*, 627–638.

Amato, P. R., & DeBoer, D. D. (2001). The transmission of marital instability across generations: Relationship skills or commitment to marriage. *Journal of Marriage and Family, 63*, 1038–1051.

Amato, P. R., & Fowler, F. (2002). Parenting practices, child adjustment, and family diversity. *Journal of Marriage and the Family, 64*, 703–716.

Amato, P. R., Johnson, D. R., Booth, A., & Rogers, S. J. (2003). Continuity and change in marital quality between 1980 and 2000. *Journal of Marriage and Family, 65*, 1–22.

Amato, P. R., & Keith, B. (1991a). Parental divorce and the well-being of children: A meta-analysis. *Psychological Bulletin, 110*, 26–46.

Amato, P. R., & Keith, B. (1991b). Parental divorce and adult well-being: A meta-analysis. *Journal of Marriage and the Family, 53*, 43–58.

Amato, P. R., & Rogers, S. J. (1997). A longitudinal study of marital problems and subsequent divorce. *Journal of Marriage and the Family, 59*, 612–624.

American Medical Association. (1992). *Diagnostic and treatment guidelines on elder abuse and neglect.* Chicago, IL: American Medical Association.

American Psychiatric Association. (2000). *Diagnostic and statistical manual of mental disorders* (4th ed., Rev. text). Washington, DC: Author.

Anderson, B. J., Auslander, W. F., Jung, K. C., Miller, P., & Santiago, J. V. (1990). Assessing family sharing of diabetes responsibilities. *Journal of Pediatric Psychology, 15*, 477–492.

Anderson, E. R., Greene, S. M., Hetherington, E. M., & Clingempeel, W. G. (1999). The dynamics of parental remarriage: Adolescent, parent, and sibling influences. In E. M. Hetherington (Ed.), *Coping with divorce, single parenting, and remarriage* (pp. 295–319). Mahwah, NJ: Lawrence Erlbaum Associates.

Anderson, K. L. (2002). Perpetrator or victim? Relationships between intimate partner violence and well-being. *Journal of Marriage and Family, 64*, 851–863.

Anderson, S. A., & Nuttall, P. E. (1987). Parent communications training across three stages of childrearing. *Family Relations, 36*, 40–44.

Andersson, L., Mullins, L. C., & Johnson, D. P. (1990). Parental intrusion versus social isolation: A dichotomous view of the sources of loneliness. In M. Hojat & R. Crandall (Eds.), *Loneliness: Theory, research, and applications* (pp. 125–134). Newbury Park, CA: Sage.

Andrews, B. (1995). Bodily shame as a mediator between abusive experiences and depression. *Journal of Abnormal Psychology, 104*, 277–285.

Andrews, J. A., Hops, H., & Duncan, S. C. (1997). Adolescent modeling of parent substance use: The moderating effect of the relationship with the parent. *Journal of Family Psychology, 11*, 259–270.

Antognoli-Toland, P. L. (2001). Parent-child relationship, family structure, and loneliness among adolescents. *Adolescent and Family Health, 2*, 20–26.

Aponte, R. (1999). Ethnic variation in the family: The elusive trend toward convergence. In M. B. Sussman, S. K. Steinmetz, & G. W. Peterson (Eds.), *Handbook of marriage and the family* (2nd ed., pp. 307–326). New York: Plenum.

Aquilino, W. S. (1991). Family structure and home-leaving: A further specification of the relationship. *Journal of Marriage and the Family, 53*, 999–1010.

Aquilino, W. S. (1997). From adolescent to young adult: A prospective study of parent-child relations during the transition to adulthood. *Journal of Marriage and the Family, 59,* 670–686.

Arcus, M. E. (1995). Advances in family life education: Past, present, and future. *Family Relations, 44,* 336–344.

Aron, A., & Aron, E. N. (1986). *Love as expansion of self: Understanding attraction and satisfaction.* New York: Hemisphere.

Aron, A., & Aron, E. N. (1997). Self-expansion motivation and including other in the self. In W. Ickes (Section Ed.) & S. Duck (Ed.), *Handbook of personal relationships* (2nd ed., Vol. 1, pp. 251–270). London: Wiley.

Aron, A., Dutton, D. G., Aron, E. N., & Iverson, A. (1989). Experiences of falling in love. *Journal of Social and Personal Relationships, 6,* 243–257.

Asante, M. K. (1988). *Afrocentricity.* Trenton, NJ: Africa World Press.

Assemany, A. E., & McIntosh, D. E. (2002). Negative treatment outcomes of behavioral parent training programs. *Psychology in the Schools, 39,* 209–219.

Attie, I., & Brooks-Gunn, J. (1989). Development of eating problems in adolescent girls: A longitudinal study. *Developmental Psychology, 25,* 70–79.

Austin, E. W. (1993). Exploring the effects of active parental mediation of television content. *Journal of Broadcasting and Electronic Media, 37,* 147–158.

Austin, E. W. (1996). Direct and indirect influences of parent-child communication norms or adolescent's tendencies to take preventive measures for AIDS and drug abuse. In G. Kreps & D. O'Hair (Eds.), *Relational communication and health outcomes* (pp. 163–183). Cresskill, NJ: Hampton Press.

Avery, A. W., Ridley, C. A., Leslie, L. A., & Milholland, T. (1980). Relationship enhancement with premarital dyads: A six-month follow-up. *American Journal of Family Therapy, 8,* 23–30.

Avins, M. (2002, April 27). Charmed silly: What made "The Bachelor' such a guilty pleasure?" For the series exhibitionist contestants and voyeuristic viewers, it was a match. *The Los Angeles Times,* pp. F1.

Axinn, W. G., & Thornton, A. (1992). The influence of parental resources on the timing of the transition to marriage. *Social Science Research, 21,* 261–285.

Babcock, J. C., Jacobson, N. S., Gottman, J. M., & Yerington, T. P. (2000). Attachment, emotional regulation, and the function of marital violence: Differences between secure, preoccupied, and dismissing violent and nonviolent husbands. *Journal of Family Violence, 15,* 391–409.

Babcock, J. C., Waltz, J., Jacobson, N. S., & Gottman, J. M. (1993). Power and violence: The relation between communication patterns, power discrepancies, and domestic violence. *Journal of Consulting and Clinical Psychology, 61,* 40–50.

Badger, T. A. (1992). Coping, life-style changes, health perceptions, and marital adjustment in middle-aged women and men with cardiovascular disease and their spouses. *Health Care for Women International, 13,* 43–55.

Badger, T. A. (1996a). Family members' experiences living with members with depression. *Western Journal of Nursing Research, 18,* 149–171.

Badger, T. A. (1996b). Living with depression: Family members' experiences and treatment needs. *Journal of Psychosocial Nursing, 34,* 21–29.

Badger, T. A., Braden, C. J., Longman, A. J., & Mishel, M. M. (1999). Depression burden, self-help interventions, and social support in women receiving treatment for breast cancer. *Journal of Psychosocial Oncology, 17,* 17–35.

Bagarozzi, D. A., Bagarozzi, J. I., Anderson, S. A., & Pollane, L. (1984). Premarital education and training sequence (PETS): A 3-year follow-up of an experimental study. *Journal of Counseling and Development, 63,* 91–100.

Bagarozzi, D. A., & Rauen, P. (1981). Premarital counseling: Appraisal and status. *The American Journal of Family Therapy, 9,* 13–30.

Bahr, S. J., Hawks, R. D., & Wang, G. (1993). Family and religious influences on adolescent substance abuse. *Youth and Society, 24,* 443–465.

Baldwin, J. H., Ellis, G. D., & Baldwin, B. M. (1999). Marital satisfaction: An examination of its relationship to souse support and congruence of commitment among runners. *Leisure Sciences, 21,* 117–131.

Baldwin, M. W., Keelan, J. P. R., Fehr, B., Enns, V., & Koh-Rangarajoo, E. (1996). Social-cognitive conceptualization of attachment working models availability and accessibility effects. *Journal of Personality and Social Psychology, 71,* 94–109.

Bandura, A. (1977). *Social learning theory.* Upper Saddle River, NJ: Prentice Hall.

Bandura, A. (1986). *Social foundations of thought and action.* Englewood Cliffs, NJ: Prentice Hall.

Bandura, A. (1994). Social cognitive theory of mass communication. In J. Bryant & D. Zillman (Eds.), *Media effects: Advances in theory and research* (pp. 61–90). Hillsdale, NJ: Lawrence Erlbaum Associates.

Bandura, A., Ross, D., & Ross, S. A. (1963). Vicarious reinforcement and imitative learning. *Journal of Abnormal and Social Psychology, 67,* 601–607.

Bank, L., Patterson, G. R., & Reid, J. B. (1996). Negative sibling interaction patterns as predictors of later adjustment problems in adolescent and young adult males. In G. H. Brody (Ed.), *Sibling relationships: Their causes and consequences* (pp. 196–230). Norwood, NJ: Ablex.

Banker, B. S., & Gaertner, S. L. (1998). Achieving stepfamily harmony: An intergroup-relations approach. *Journal of Family Psychology, 12,* 310–325.

Barber, B. K. (1992). Family, personality, and adolescent problem behaviors. *Journal of Marriage and the Family, 54,* 69–79.

Barber, B. K. (1996). Parental psychological control: Revisiting a neglected construct. *Child Development, 67,* 3296–3319.

Barber, B. K., & Harmon, E. L. (2002). Violating the self: Parental psychological control of children and adolescents. In B. K. Barber (Ed.), *Intrusive parenting: How psychological control affects children and adolescents* (pp. 15–52). Washington, DC: American Psychological Association.

Barber, B. L., & Lyons, J. M. (1994). Family processes and adolescent adjustment in intact and remarried families. *Journal of Youth and Adolescence, 23,* 421–436.

Barber, C. E. (1989). Transition to the empty nest. In S. J. Bahr & E. T. Peterson (Eds.), *Aging and the family* (pp. 15–32). Lexington, MA: Lexington Books.

Barnes, G. M., Farrell, M. P., & Cairns, A. (1986). Parental socialization factors and adolescent drinking behaviors. *Journal of Marriage and the Family, 48,* 27–36.

Barnes, G. M., Reifman, A. S., Farrell, M. P., & Dintcheff, B. A. (2000). The effects of parenting on the development of adolescent alcohol misuse: A six-wave latent growth model. *Journal of Marriage and the Family, 62,* 175–186.

Barnett, R. (1998). Toward a review and reconceptualization of the work/family literature. *Genetic, Social and General Psychology Monographs, 124,* 125–182.

Barratt, M. S. (1995). Communication in infancy. In M. A. Fitzpatrick & A. L. Vangelisti (Eds.), *Explaining family interactions* (pp. 5–33). Thousand Oaks, CA: Sage.

Barratt, M. S., & Roach, M. A. (1995). Early interaction processes: Parenting by adolescent and adult single mothers. *Infant Behavior and Development, 18,* 97–109.

Barrera, M., & Stice, E. (1998). Parent-adolescent conflict in the context of parental support: Families with alcoholic and nonalcoholic fathers. *Journal of Family Psychology, 12,* 195–208.

Bartholomew, K., & Horowitz, L. M. (1991). Attachment styles among young adults: A test of a four category model. *Journal of Personality and Social Psychology, 61,* 226–244.

Basco, M. R., Prager, K. J., Pite, J. M., Tamir, L. M., & Stephens, J. J. (1992). Communication and intimacy in the marriages of depressed patients. *Journal of Family Psychology, 6,* 184–194.

Baucom, D. H. (1984). The active ingredients of behavioral martial therapy: The effectiveness of problem-solving/communication training, contingency contracting, and their combination. In K. Hahlweg & N. S. Jacobson (Eds.), *Marital interaction: Analysis and modification* (pp. 396–428). New York: Guilford.

Baumrind, D. (1967). Child care practices anteceding three patterns of preschool behavior. *Genetic Psychology Monographs, 75,* 43–83.

Baumrind, D. (1968). Authoritarian vs. authoritative parental control. *Adolescence, 3,* 255–272.

Baumrind, D. (1971). Current patterns of parental authority. *Developmental Psychology Monographs, 4,* 1–101.

Baumrind, D. (1991). The influence of parenting style on adolescent competence and substance use. *Journal of Early Adolescence, 11,* 56–95.

Baumrind, D. (1995). *Child maltreatment and optimal caregiving social contexts.* New York: Garland.

Bauserman, R. (2002). Child adjustment in joint-custody versus sole custody arrangements: A meta-analytic review. *Journal of Family Psychology, 16,* 91–102.

Bavelas, J. B. (1990). Behaving and communicating: A reply to Motley. *Western Journal of Speech Communication, 54,* 593–602.

Baxter, L. A. (1990). Dialectical contradictions in relationship development. *Journal of Social and Personal Relationships, 7,* 69–88.

Baxter, L. A., Braithwaite, D. O., & Nicholson, J. H. (1999). Turning points in the development of blended families. *Journal of Social and Personal Relationships, 16,* 291–313.

Baxter, L. A., & Bullis, C. (1986). Turning points in developing romantic relationships. *Communication Research, 12,* 469–493.

Baxter, L. A., & Clark, L. A. (1996). Perceptions of family communication patterns and the enactment of family rituals. *Western Journal of Communication, 60,* 254–268.

Baxter, L. A., & Dindia, K. (1990). Marital partners' perceptions of marital maintenance strategies. *Journal of Social and Personal Relationships, 7,* 187–208.

Baxter, L. A., & Erbert, L. A. (1999). Perceptions of dialectical contradictions in turning points of development in heterosexual romantic relationships. *Journal of Social and Personal Relationships, 16,* 547–569.

Baxter, L. A., & Montgomery, B. M. (1996). *Relating: Dialogues and dialectics.* New York: Guilford.

Baxter, L. A., & Montgomery, B. M. (1997). Rethinking communication in personal relationships from a dialectical perspective. In S. Duck (Ed.), *Handbook of personal relationships* (pp. 325–349). Chichester, UK: Wiley.

Baxter, L. A., & Pittman, G. (2001). Communicatively remembering turning points of relational development in heterosexual romantic relationships. *Communication Reports, 14,* 1–17.

Baxter, L. A., & Wilmot, W. W. (1985). Interaction characteristics of disengaging, stable, and growing relationships. In R. Gilmour & S. Duck (Eds.), *The emerging field of personal relationships.* Hillsdale, NJ: Lawrence Erlbaum Associates.

Baydar, N., Greek, A., & Brooks-Gunn, J. (1997). A longitudinal study of the birth of a sibling during the first 6 years of life. *Journal of Marriage and the Family, 59,* 939–956.

Baydar, N., Hyle, P., & Brooks-Gunn, J. (1997). A longitudinal study of the effects of the birth of a sibling during preschool and early grade school years. *Journal of Marriage and the Family, 59,* 957–965.

Beach, S. R. H. (Ed.). (2001). *Marital and family processes in depression: A scientific foundation for clinical practice.* Washington, DC: American Psychological Association.

Beach, S. R. H., Jouriles, E. N., & O'Leary, K. D. (1985). Extramarital sex: Impact on depression and commitment in couples seeking marital therapy. *Journal of Sex and Marital Therapy, 11,* 99–108.

Beach, S. R. H., & O'Leary, K. D. (1993). Marital discord and dysphoria: For whom does the marital relationship predict depressive symptomatology? *Journal of Social and Personal Relationships, 10,* 405–420.

Beach, S. R. H., Sandeen, E. E., & O'Leary, K. D. (1990). *Depression and marriage.* New York: Guilford.

Bebbington, P., & Kuipers, L. (1994). The predictive utility of expressed emotion in schizophrenia: An aggregate analysis. *Psychological Medicine, 24,* 707–718.

Bedford, V. H. (1995). Sibling relationships in middle adulthood and old age. In R. Blieszner & V. H. Bedford (Eds.), *Handbook on aging and the family* (pp. 201–222). Westport, CT: Greenwood.

Bedford, V. H., & Avioli, P. S. (2001). Variations on sibling intimacy in old age. *Generations, 25,* 34–41.

Belsky, J. (1981). Early human experiences: A family perspective. *Developmental Psychology, 17,* 3–23.

Belsky, J. (1990). Children and marriage. In F. D. Fincham & T. N. Bradbury (Eds.), *The psychology of marriage: Basic issues and applications* (pp. 172–200). New York: Guilford.

Belsky, J., Lang, M., & Huston, T. L. (1986). Sex typing and division of labor as determinants of marital change across the transition to parenthood. *Journal of Personality and Social Psychology, 50,* 517–522.

Benazon, N. R., & Coyne, J. C. (2000). Living with a depressed spouse. *Journal of Family Psychology, 14,* 71–79.

Benedict, L. L. W., & Zautra, A. A. J. (1993). Family environmental characteristics as risk factors for childhood sexual abuse. *Journal of Clinical Child Psychology, 22,* 365–374.

Bengtson, V. L., & Robertson, J. F. (1985). *Grandparenthood.* Beverly Hills, CA: Sage.

Bennett, L. A., Wolin, S. J., Reiss, D., & Teitelbaum, M. A. (1987). Couples at risk for transmission of alcoholism: Protective influences. *Family Process, 26,* 111–129.

Bennett, S. E., Hughes, H. M., & Luke, D. A. (2000). Heterogeneity in patterns of child sexual abuse, family functioning, and long-term adjustment. *Journal of Interpersonal Violence, 15,* 134–157.

Bensley, L. S., Spieker, S. J., & McMahon, R. J. (1994). Parenting behavior of adolescent children of alcoholics. *Addiction, 89,* 1265–1276.

Berger, C. R., & Kellner, H. (1964). Marriage and the construction of reality: An exercise in the microconstruction of knowledge. *Diogenes, 46,* 1–25.

Berger, C. R., & Roloff, M. W. (1980). Social cognition, self-awareness, and interpersonal communication. In B. Dervin & M. Voigt (Eds.), Progress in communication sciences (pp. 158–172). Norwood, NJ: Ablex.

Berkowitz, C. D., Bross, D. C., Chadwick, D. L., & Whitworth, J. M. (1992). *Diagnostic and treatment guidelines on child sexual abuse.* Chicago, IL: American Medical Association.

Bernhard, L. A. (2000). Physical and sexual violence experienced by lesbian and heterosexual women. *Violence Against Women, 6,* 68–79.

Berns, S. B., Jacobson, N. S., & Gottman, J. M. (1999a). Demand-withdraw interaction in couples with a violent husband. *Journal of Consulting and Clinical Psychology, 67,* 666–674.

Berns, S. B., Jacobson, N. S., & Gottman, J. M. (1999b). Demand/withdraw interaction patterns between different types of batterers and their spouses. *Journal of Marital and Family Therapy, 25,* 337–348.

Bernstein, A. C. (1999). Reconstructing the Brothers Grimm: New tales for stepfamily life. *Family Processes, 38,* 415–429.

Bernstein, B. (1971). *Class, codes, and control.* London: Routledge and Kegan.

Berscheid, E., Snyder, M., & Omoto, A. M (1989). The relationship closeness inventory: Assessing the closeness of interpersonal relationships. *Journal of Personality and Social Psychology, 57,* 792–807.

Bertalanffy, L. von (1968). *General systems theory.* New York: George Braziller.

Bertalanffy, L. von (1975). *Perspectives on general systems theory: Scientific-philosophical studies.* New York: George Braziller.

Bethea, L. S. (2002). The impact of an older adult parent on communicative satisfaction and dyadic adjustment in the long-term marital relationship: Adult-children and spouses; retrospective accounts. *Journal of Applied Communication Research, 30,* 107–125.

Bettinghaus, E. P., & Cody, M. J. (1994). *Persuasive communication* (6th ed.). Fort Worth, TX: Harcourt Brace.

Biglan, A., Hops, H., Sherman, L., Friedman, L. S., Arthur, J., & Osteen, V. (1985). Problem-solving interactions of depressed women and their husbands. *Behavior Therapy, 16,* 431–451.

Blackson, T. C., Tarter, R. E., Loeber, R., Ammerman, R. T., & Windle, M. (1996). The influence of paternal substance abuse and difficult temperament in fathers and sons on sons' disengagement from family to deviant peers. *Journal of Youth and Adolescence, 25,* 389–411.

Blake, J. (1989). *Family size and achievement.* Berkeley, CA: University of California Press.

Blechman, E. A., & Delamater, A. M. (1993). Family communication and type 1 diabetes: A window on the social environment of chronically ill children. In R. E. Cole & D. Reiss (Eds.), *How do families cope with chronic illness?* (pp. 1–24). Hillsdale, NJ: Lawrence Erlbaum Associates.

Blouin, A. G., Zuro, C., & Blouin, J. H. (1990). Family environment in bulimia nervosa: The role of depression. *International Journal of Eating Disorders, 9,* 649–658.

Blumer, H. (1969). *Symbolic interactionism: Perspective and method.* Englewood Cliffs, NJ: Prentice-Hall.

Blumstein, P., & Schwartz, P. (1983). *American couples.* New York: William Morrow and Co.

Bochner, A. P. (1982). On the efficacy of openness in close relationships. In M. Burgoon (Ed.), *Communication Yearbook 5* (pp. 109–124). New Brunswick, NJ: Transaction Books.

Bochner, A. P., & Eisenberg, E. M. (1987). Family process: Systems perspectives. In C. R. Berger & S. H. Chaffe (Eds.), *Handbook of communication science* (pp. 540–563). Beverly Hills, CA: Sage.

Bochner, A. P., & Ellis, C. (1995). Telling and living: Narrative co-construction and the practices of interpersonal relationships. In W. Leeds-Hurwitz (Ed.), *Social approaches to communication* (pp. 201–216). New York: Guilford.

Bochner, A. P., Ellis, C., & Tillmann-Healy, L. M. (1997). Relationship as stories. In S. W. Duck (Ed.), *Handbook of personal relationships: Theory, research, and interventions* (2nd ed., pp. 107–324). Chichester: Wiley.

Bohannon, J. R., & White, P. (1999). Gender role of attitudes of American mothers and daughters over time. *Journal of Social Psychology, 139,* 173–179.

Bohannon, P. (1970). *Divorce and after.* New York: Doubleday.

Bolton, C. D. (1961). Mate selection as the development of a relationship. *Marriage and Family Living, 23,* 234–240.

Book, P. (1996). How does the family narrative influence the individual's ability to communicate about death. *Omega, 33,* 323–341.

Booth, A., & Amato, P. R. (1994). Parental marital quality, parental divorce, and relations with parents. *Journal of Marriage and the Family, 56,* 21–34.

Booth, A., & Amato, P. R. (2001). Parental predivorce relations and offspring predivorce well-being. *Journal of Marriage and the Family, 63,* 197–212.

Booth, A., & Johnson, D. (1988). Premarital cohabitation and marital success. *Journal of Family Issues, 9,* 255–272.

Booth-Butterfield, M., & Sidelinger, R. (1998). The influence of family communication on the college-aged child: Openness, attitudes, and actions about sex and alcohol. *Communication Quarterly, 46,* 295–308.

Boss, P. G. (1988). *Family stress management.* Newbury Park, CA: Sage.

Botta, R. A., & Dumlao, R. (2002). How do conflict and communication patterns between fathers and daughters contribute to or offset eating disorders? *Health Communication, 14,* 199–219.

Botvin, G. J., & Tortu, S. (1988). Peer relationships, social competence, and substance abuse prevention: Implications for the family. *Journal of Chemical Dependency Treatment, 1,* 245–273.

Bowlby, J. (1969). *Attachment and loss, Vol. 1: Attachment.* New York: Basic Books.

Bowlby, J. (1973). *Attachment and loss, Vol. 2: Separation: Anxiety and anger.* New York: Basic Books.

Bowlby, J. (1980). *Attachment and loss, Vol. 3: Loss: Sadness and depression.* New York: Basic Books.

Brach, E. L., Camara, K. A., & Houser, R. F. (2000). Patterns of interaction in divorced and non-divorced families: Conflict in dinnertime conversation. *Journal of Divorce and Remarriage, 33,* 75–89.

Bradbury, T. N., & Fincham, F. D. (1990). Preventing marital dysfunction: Review and analysis. In F. D. Fincham & T. N. Bradbury (Eds.), *The Psychology of Marriage* (pp. 375–401). New York: Guilford.

Bradbury, T. N., & Karney, B. R. (1993). Longitudinal study of marital interaction and dysfunction: Review and analysis. *Clinical Psychology Review, 13,* 15–27.

Braithwaite, D. O., Baxter, L., & Harper, A. M. (1998). The role of rituals in the management of the dialectical tension of 'old' and 'new' in blended families. *Communication Studies, 49,* 101–120.

Braithwaite, D. O., Olson, L. N., Golish, T. D., Soukup, C., & Turman, P. (2001). "Becoming a family": Developmental processes represented in blended family discourse. *Journal of Applied Communication Research, 29,* 221–247.

Bram, A., Gallant, S. J., & Segrin, C. (1999). A longitudinal investigation of object relations: Child-rearing antecedents, stability in adulthood, and construct validation. *Journal of Research in Personality, 33,* 159–188.

Bramlett, M. D., & Mosher, W. D. (2001). First marriage dissolution, divorce, and remarriage: United States. *Advance data from vital and health statistics no. 323.* Hyattsville, MD: National Center for Health Statistics.

Brand, P. A., & Kidd, A. H. (1986). Frequency of physical aggression in heterosexual and female homosexual dyads. *Psychological Reports, 59,* 1307–1313.

Bray, J. H. (1999). From marriage to remarriage and beyond: Findings from the developmental issues in stepfamilies research project. In E. M. Hetherington (Ed.), *Coping with divorce, single parenting, and remarriage* (pp. 253–271). Mahwah, NJ: Lawrence Erlbaum Associates.

Bray, J. H., & Berger, S. H. (1993). Developmental issues in stepfamilies research project: Family relationships and parent-child interactions. *Journal of Family Psychology, 7,* 76–90.

Bray, J., & Kelly, J. (1998). *Stepfamilies.* New York: Broadway.

Brezina, T. (1999). Teenage violence toward parents as an adaptation to family strain: Evidence from a national survey of male adolescents. *Youth and Society, 30,* 416–444.

Briere, J., & Elliot, D. M. (1993). Sexual abuse, family environment, and psychological symptoms: On the validity of statistical control. *Journal of Consulting and Clinical Psychology, 61,* 284–288.

Brines, J., & Joyner, K. (1999). The ties that bind: Principles of cohesion in cohabitation and marriage. *American Sociological Review, 64,* 333–355.

Brinig, M., & Allen, D. A. (1999). These boots are made for walking: Why most divorce filers are women. *American Law and Economics Review, 2,* 126–169.

Bristol, M. M. (1987). Mothers of children with autism or communication disorders: Successful adaptation and the double ABCX model. *Journal of Autism and Developmental Disorders, 17,* 469–486.

Broadwell, S. D., & Light, K. C. (1999). Family support and cardiovascular responses in married couples during conflict and other interactions. *International Journal of Behavioral Medicine, 6,* 40–63.

Brock, G. W., Oertwein, M., & Coufal, J. D. (1993). Parent education: Theory, research, and practice. In M. E. Arcus, J. D. Schvaneveldt, & J. J. Moss (Eds.), *Handbook of family life education, Vol. 1: Foundations of family life education* (pp. 87–114). Thousand Oaks, CA: Sage.

Broderick, C. B. (1993). *Understanding family processes: Basics of family systems theory.* Newbury Park, CA: Sage.

Brody, G. H., Stoneman, Z., Smith, T., & Gibson, M. (1999). Sibling relationships in rural African American families. *Journal of Marriage and the Family, 61,* 1046–1057.

Brook, J. S., Whiteman, M., Gordon, A. S., & Brook, D. W. (1988). The role of older brothers in younger brothers' drug use viewed in the context of parent and peer influences. *Journal of Genetic Psychology, 151,* 59–75.

Brown, F. H. (1988). The impact of death and serious illness on the family life cycle. In B. Carter & M. McGoldrick (Eds.), *The changing family lifecycle: A framework for family therapy* (2nd ed., pp. 457–482). New York: Gardner Press.

Brown, G. W., Monck, E. M., Carstairs, G. M., & Wing, J. K. (1962). Influence of family life on the course of schizophrenic illness. *British Journal of Preventative and Social Medicine, 16,* 55–68.

Brown, J., Cohen, P., Johnson, J. G., & Smailes, E. M. (1999). Childhood abuse and neglect: Specificity of effects on adolescent and young adult depression and suicidality. *Journal of the American Academy of Child and Adolescent Psychiatry, 38,* 1490–1496.

Brown, P. C., & Smith, T. W. (1992). Social influence, marriage, and the heart: Cardiovascular consequences of interpersonal control in husbands and wives. *Health Psychology, 11,* 88–96.

Brown-Smith, N. (1998). Family secrets. *Journal of Family Issues, 19,* 20–42.

Bruess, C. J. S., & Pearson, J. C. (1995, November). *Like sands through the hour glass: Rituals in day-to-day marriage.* Paper presented at the annual meeting of the Speech Communication Association, San Antonio, TX.

Bryant, C. M., Conger, R. D., & Meehan, J. M. (2001). The influence of in-laws on change in marital satisfaction. *Journal of Marriage and the Family, 63,* 614–626.

Buchanan, C. M., & Waizenhofer, R. (2001). The impact of interparental conflict on adolescent children: Consideration of family systems and family structure. In A. Booth, A. C. Crouter, & M. Clements (Eds.), *Couples in conflict* (pp. 149–160). Mahwah, NJ: Lawrence Erlbaum Associates.

Buehler, C., & Gerard, J. M. (2002). Marital conflict, ineffective parenting, and children's and adolescents' maladjustment. *Journal of Marriage and the Family, 64,* 78–92.

Buehlman, K. T., Gottman, J. M., & Katz, L. F. (1992). How a couple views their past predicts their future: Predicting divorce from an Oral History Interview. *Journal of Family Psychology, 5,* 295–318.

Buerkel-Rothfuss, N. L., Fink, D. S., & Buerkel, R. A. (1995). Communication in the father-child dyad: The intergenerational transmission process. In T. J. Socha & G. H. Stamp (Eds.), *Parents, children, and communication: Frontiers of theory and research* (pp. 63–86). Mahwah, NJ: Lawrence Erlbaum Associates.

Buhrmester, D. (1992). The developmental courses of sibling and peer relationships. In F. Boer & J. Dunn (Eds.), *Children's sibling relationships: Developmental and clinical issues* (pp. 19–40). Hillsdale, NJ: Lawrence Erlbaum Associates.

Buhrmester, D., & Furman, D. (1990). Perceptions of sibling relationships during middle childhood and adolescence. *Child Development, 61,* 1387–1398.

Bullock, R. C., Siegel, R., Weissman, M., & Paykel, E. S. (1972). The weeping wife: Marital relations of depressed women. *Journal of Marriage and the Family, 34,* 488–495.

Bumpass, L. L., & Lu, H. (2000). Trends in cohabitation and implications for children's family contexts in the United States. *Population Studies, 54,* 19–41.

Bumpass, L. L., Martin, T. C., & Sweet, J. A. (1991). The impact of family background and early marital factors on marital disruption. *Journal of Family Issues, 12,* 22–42.

Bumpass, L. L., Raley, R. K., & Sweet, J. (1995). The changing character of stepfamilies: Implications of cohabitation and nonmarital childbearing. *Demography, 32,* 425–436.

Bumpass, L. L., & Sweet, J. A. (1989). Children's experience in single-parent families: Implications of cohabitation and marital transitions. *Perspectives on Sexual and Reproductive Health, 21,* 256–261.

Bumpass, L. L., Sweet, J. A., & Castro Martin, T. (1990). Changing patterns of remarriage. *Journal of Marriage and the Family, 52,* 747–756.

Bumpass, L. L., Sweet, J. A., & Cherlin, A. (1991). The role of cohabitation in declining rates of marriage. *Journal of Marriage and the Family, 53,* 913–927.

Bureau of Justice Statistics. (1994). *Domestic violence: Violence between intimates.* Washington, DC: U.S. Department of Justice, Bureau of Justice Statistics.

Burgess, E. W., & Locke, H. (1953). *The family.* New York: American Book.

Burgess, E. W., & Wallin, P. (1953). *Engagement and marriage.* New York: J. B. Lippincott.

Burke, L. K., & Follingstad, D. R. (1999). Violence in lesbian and gay relationships: Theory, prevalence, and correlational factors. *Clinical Psychology Review, 19,* 487–512.

Burleson, B. R., Delia, J. G., & Applegate, J. L. (1995). The socialization of person-centered communication: Parents' contributions to their children's social-cognitive and communication skills. In M. A. Fitzpatrick & A. L. Vangelisti (Eds.), *Explaining family interactions* (pp. 34–76). Thousand Oaks, CA: Sage.

Burleson, B. R., & Denton, W. H. (1992). A new look at similarity and attraction in marriage: Similarities in social-cognitive and communication skills as predictors of attraction and satisfaction. *Communication Monographs, 59,* 268–287.

Burleson, B. R., & Goldsmith, D. J. (1998). How the comforting process works: Alleviating emotional distress through conversationally induced reappraisals. In P. A. Andersen & L. K. Guerrero (Eds.), *Handbook of communication and emotion: Research, theory, applications, and contexts* (pp. 245–280). San Diego, CA: Academic Press.

Burleson, B. R., & Kunkel, A. (2002). Parental and peer contributions to the emotional support skills of the child: From whom do children learn to express support?. *Journal of Family Communication, 2,* 81–97.

Burleson, B. R., Kunkel, A., & Birch, J. D. (1994). Thoughts about talk in romantic relationships: Similarity makes for attraction (and happiness, too). *Communication Quarterly, 42,* 259–273.

Burman, B., John, R. S., & Margolin, G. (1992). Observed patterns of conflict in violent, nonviolent, and nondistressed couples. *Behavioral Assessment, 14,* 15–37.

Burman, B., & Margolin, G. (1989). Marriage and health. *Advances, 6,* 51–58.

Burman, B., & Margolin, G. (1992). Analysis of the association between marital relationships and health problems: An interactional perspective. *Psychological Bulletin, 112,* 39–63.

Burns, A., & Dunlop, R. (2002). Parental marital quality and family conflict: Longitudinal effects of adolescents from divorcing and non-divorcing families. *Journal of Divorce and Remarriage, 37,* 57–74.

Burr, W. R., & Klein, S. R. (1994). *Reexamining family stress: New theory and research.* Thousand Oaks, CA: Sage.

Burrell, N. A. (1995). Communication patterns in stepfamilies. In M. A. Fitzpatrick & A. L. Vangelisti (Eds.), *Explaining family interactions* (pp. 290–309). Thousand Oaks, CA: Sage.

Buss, D. M., & Kenrick, D. T. (1998). Evolutionary psychology social psychology. In D. T. Gilbert, S. T. Fiske, & G. Lindzey (Eds.), *Handbook of social psychology* (Vol. 2, 4th ed., pp. 982–1026). New York: McGraw-Hill.

Buss, D. M., & Schmitt, D. P. (1993). Sexual strategies theory: An evolutionary psychology perspective on human mating. *Psychological Review, 100,* 204–232.

Buss, D. M., Shackelford, T. K., Kirkpatrick, L. A., & Larsen, J. (2001). A half-century of mate preferences: The cultural evolution of values. *Journal of Marriage and the Family, 63,* 491–503.

Byrne, D. (1969). Attitudes and attraction. In L. Berkowitz (Ed.), *Advances in experimental psychology* (pp. 178–224). New York: Academic Press.

Byrne, D. (1971). *The attraction paradigm.* New York: Academic Press.

Cahn, D. D. (1996). Family violence from a communication perspective. In D. D. Cahn & S. A. Lloyd (Eds.), *Family violence from a communication perspective* (pp. 1–19). Thousand Oaks, CA: Sage.

Calam, R., Waller, G., Slade, P., & Newton, T. (1990). Eating disorders and perceived relationships with parents. *International Journal of Eating Disorders, 9,* 479–485.

Canary, D. J., & Stafford, L. (2001). Equity in the preservation of personal relationships. In J. Harvey & A. Wenzel (Eds.), *Close romantic relationships* (pp. 133–152). Mahwah, NJ: Lawrence Erlbaum Associates.

Canary, D. J., Stafford, L., Hause, K. S., & Wallace, L. A. (1993). An inductive analysis of relational maintenance strategies: Comparisons among lovers, relatives, friends, and others. *Communication Research Reports, 10,* 5–14.

Cannon, C. A., & Cavanaugh, J. C. (1998). Chronic Illness in the context of marriage: A systems perspective of stress and coping in chronic obstructive pulmonary disease. *Family Systems and Health, 16,* 401–418.

Carlson, K. P., Gesten, E. L., McIver, L. S., DeClue, T., & Malone, J. (1994). Problem solving and adjustment in families of children with diabetes. *Children's Health Care, 23,* 193–210.

Carpenter, B. D. (2002). Family, peer, and staff social support in nursing home patients: Contributions to psychological well-being. *The Journal of Applied Gerontology, 21,* 275–293.

Carpenter, S., & Halberstadt, A. G. (2000). Mothers' reports of events causing anger differ across family relationships. *Social Development, 9,* 458–477.

Carrère, S., Buehlamn, K. T., Gottman, J. M., Coan, J. A., & Ruckstuhl, L. (2000). Predicting marital stability and divorce in newlywed couples. *Journal of Family Psychology, 14,* 42–58.

Carrère, S., & Gottman, J. M. (1999). Predicting the future of marriages. In E. M. Hetherington (Ed.), *Coping with divorce, single parenting, and remarriage* (pp. 3–22). Mahwah, NJ: Lawrence Erlbaum Associates.

Carson, D. K., Gertz, L. M., Donaldson, M. A., & Wonderlich, S. A. (1991). Intrafamilial sexual abuse: Family-of-origin and family-of-procreation characteristics of female adult victims. *The Journal of Psychology, 125,* 579–597.

Carson, J. L., & Parke, R. D. (1996). Reciprocal negative affect in parent-child interactions and children's peer competency. *Child Development, 67,* 2217–2226.

Carstensen, L. L. (1993). Motivation for social contact across the life span: A theory of socioemotional selectivity. *Nebraska Symposium on Motivation, 40,* 209–254.

Carstensen, L. L. (1995). Evidence for a life-span theory of socioemotional selectivity. *Current Directions in Psychological Science, 4,* 151–156.

Carstensen, L. L., Gottman, J. M., & Levenson, R. W. (1995). Emotional behavior in long-term marriage. *Psychology and Aging, 10,* 140–149.

Carter, B., & McGoldrick, M. (1999). Overview: The expanded family life cycle: Individual, family, and social perspectives. In B. Carter & M. McGoldrick (Eds.), *The expanded family life cycle: Individual, family, and social perspectives* (pp. 1–26). Boston, MA: Allyn & Bacon.

Cate, R. M., Levin, S. A., & Richmond, L. S. (2002). Premarital relationship stability: A review of recent research. *Journal of Social and Personal Relationships, 19,* 261–284.

Cate, R. M., & Lloyd, S. (1992). *Courtship.* Newbury Park, CA: Sage.

Caughlin, J. P. (2002). The demand-withdrawal pattern of communication as a predictor of marital satisfaction over time: Unresolved issues and future directions. *Human Communication Research, 28,* 49–85.

Caughlin, J. P. (2003). Family communication standards: What counts as excellent family communication and how are such standards associated with family satisfaction? *Human Communication Research, 29,* 5–40.

Caughlin, J. P., & Golish, T. D. (2002). An analysis of the association between topic avoidance and dissatisfaction: Comparing perceptual and interpersonal explanations. *Communication Monographs, 69,* 275–295.

Caughlin, J. P., & Huston, T. L. (2002). A contextual analysis of the association between demand/withdrawal and marital satisfaction. *Personal Relationships, 9,* 95–119.

Caughlin, J. P., Huston, T. L., & Houts, R. M. (2000). How does personality matter in marriage? An examination of trait anxiety, interpersonal negativity, and marital satisfaction. *Journal of Personality and Social Psychology, 78,* 326–336.

Caughlin, J. P., & Petronio, S. (2004). Privacy in families. In A. L. Vangelisti (Ed.), *Handbook of family communication* (pp. 379–412). Mahwah, NJ: Lawrence Erlbaum Associates.

Caughlin, J. P., & Vangelisti, A. L. (1999). Desire for change in one's partner as a predictor of the demand/withdrawal pattern of marital communication. *Communication Monographs, 66,* 66–89.

Chambers, S. M. (1999). The effect of family talk on young children's development and coping. In E. Frydenberg (Ed.), *Learning to cope: Developing as a person in complex societies* (pp. 130–149). Oxford, UK: Oxford University Press.

Cheal, D. (1988). The ritualization of family ties. *American Behavioral Scientist, 31,* 632–643.

Chen, V., & Pearce, W. B. (1995). Even if a thing of beauty, can a case study be a joy forever? A social constructionist approach to theory and research. In W. Leeds-Hurwitz (Ed.), *Social approaches to communication* (pp. 135–154). New York: Guilford.

Cheng, S. H., & Kuo, W. H. (2000). Family socialization of ethnic identity among Chinese American preadolescents. *Journal of Comparative Family Studies, 31,* 463–484.

Cherlin, A. (1978). Remarriage as an incomplete institution. *American Journal of Sociology, 84,* 634–650.

Cherlin, A. (1992). *Marriage, divorce, remarriage*. Cambridge, MA: Harvard University Press.

Cherlin, A. J., & Furstenberg, F. F. (1985). Styles and strategies of grandparenting. In V. L. Bengtson & J. F. Robertson (Eds.), *Grandparenthood* (pp. 97–116). Beverly Hills, CA: Sage.

Cherlin, A. J., & Furstenberg, F. F. (1986). *The new American grandparent*. New York: Basic Books.

Chiariello, M. A., & Orvaschel, H. (1995). Patterns of parent-child communication: Relationship to depression. *Clinical Psychology Review, 15*, 395–407.

Christensen, A. (1988). Dysfunctional interaction patterns in couples. In P. Noller & M. A. Fitzpatrick (Eds.), *Perspectives on marital interaction* (pp. 31–52). Clevedon, England: Multilingual Matters LTD.

Christensen, A., & Shenk, J. L. (1991). Communication, conflict, and psychological distance in nondistressed, clinic, and divorcing couples. *Journal of Consulting and Clinical Psychology, 59*, 458–463.

Christensen, D. H., & Rettig, K. D. (1995). The relationship of remarriage to post-divorce co-parenting. *Journal of Divorce and Remarriage, 24*, 73–88.

Church, E. (1999). The poisoned apple: Stepmothers' experience of envy and jealousy. *Journal of Feminist Therapy, 11*, 1–18.

Cicirelli, V. G. (1989). Feelings of attachment to siblings and well-being in later life. *Psychology and Aging, 5*, 458–466.

Cicirelli, V. G. (1994). Sibling relationships in cross-cultural perspective. *Journal of Marriage and the Family, 56*, 7–20.

Cicirelli, V. G. (1996). Sibling relationships in middle and old age. In G. H. Brody (Ed.), *Sibling relationships: Their causes and consequences* (pp. 47–74). Norwood, NJ: Ablex.

Cissna, K. N., Cox, D. E., & Bochner, A. P. (1990). The dialectic of marital and parental relationships within the stepfamily. *Communication Monographs, 57*, 44–61.

Clair, D. J., & Genest, M. (1992). The Children of Alcoholics Screening Test: Reliability and relationships to family environment, adjustment, and alcohol-related stressors of adolescent offspring of alcoholics. *Journal of Clinical Psychology, 48*, 414–420.

Clark-Lempers, D. S., Lempers, J. D., & Ho, C. (1991). Early, middle, and late adolescents' perceptions of their relationships with significant others. *Journal of Adolescent Research, 6*, 296–315.

Clements, M. L., Cordova, A. D., Markman, H. J., & Laurenceau, J. P. (1997). The erosion of marital satisfaction over time and how to prevent it. In R. J. Sternberg & M. Hojjat (Eds.), *Satisfaction in close relationships* (pp. 335–355). New York: Guilford.

Clements, M., & Markman, H. (1996). The transition to parenthood: Is having children hazardous to marriage? In N. Vanzetti & S. Duck (Eds.), *A lifetime of relationships* (pp. 290–310). Pacific Grove, CA: Brooks/Cole Publishing.

Cohan, C., & Kleinbaum, S. (2002). Toward a greater understanding of the cohabitation effect: Premarital cohabitation and marital communication. *Journal of Marriage and the Family, 64*, 180–192.

Cohen, S., Gottlieb, B. H., & Underwood, L. G. (2000). Social relationships and health. In S. Cohen, L. G. Underwood, & B. H. Gottlieb (Eds.), *Social support measurement and intervention: A guide for health and social scientists* (pp. 3–25). New York: Oxford Press.

Cohen, S., & Lichtenstein, E. (1990). Partner behaviors that support quitting smoking. *Journal of Consulting and Clinical Psychology, 58*, 304–309.

Cohen, S., Underwood, L. G., & Gottlieb, B. H. (2000). *Social support measurement and intervention: A guide for health and social scientists*. London: Oxford University Press.

Cohen, S., & Wills, T. A. (1985). Stress, social support, and the buffering hypothesis. *Psychological Bulletin, 98*, 310–357.

Cohn, D. A., Silver, D. H., Cowan, C. P., Cowan, P. A., & Pearson, J. (1992). Working models of childhood attachment and couple relationships. *Journal of Family Issues, 13*, 432–449.

Cohn, J. F., Campbell, S. B., Matias, R., & Hopkins, J. (1990). Face-to-face interactions of postpartum depressed and nondepressed mother-infant pairs at 2 months. *Developmental Psychology, 26*, 15–23.

Coleman, M., Fine, M. A., Ganong, L. H., Downs, K. J. M., & Pauk, N. (2001). When you're not the Brady Bunch: Identifying perceived conflicts and resolution strategies in stepfamilies. *Personal Relationships, 8*, 55–73.

Coleman, M., Ganong, L., & Fine, M. (2000). Reinvestigating remarriage: Another decade of progress. *Journal of Marriage and the Family, 62*, 1288–1307.

Coleman, M., Ganong, L., & Fine, M. (2004). Communication in stepfamilies. In A. L. Vangenisti (Ed.), *Handbook of family communication* (pp. 215–232). Mahwah, NJ: Lawrence Erlbaum Associates.

Coleman, M., Ganong, L., & Weaver, S. (2001). Relationship maintenance and enhancement in remarried families. In J. Harvey & A. Wenzel (Eds.), *Close romantic relationships: Maintenance and enhancement* (pp. 255–276). Mahwah, NJ: Lawrence Erlbaum Associates.

Coleman, V. E. (1994). Lesbian battering: The relationship between personality and the peception of violence. *Violence and Victims, 9,* 139–152.

Collins, W. E., Newman, B. M., & McKenry, P. C. (1995). Intrapsychic and interpersonal factors related to adolescent psychological well-being in stepmother and stepfather families. *Journal of Family Psychology, 9,* 433–445.

Conger, R. D., & Conger, K. J. (2002). Resilience in Midwestern families: Selected findings from the first decade of a prospective, longitudinal study. *Journal of Marriage and Family, 64,* 361–373.

Conger, R. D., & Rueter, M. A. (1996). Siblings, parents, and peers: A longitudinal study of social influences in adolescent risk for alcohol use and abuse. In G. H. Brody (Ed.), *Sibling relationships: Their causes and consequences* (pp. 1–30). Norwood, NJ: Ablex.

Connors, M. E., & Morse, W. (1993). Sexual abuse and eating disorders: A review. *International Journal of Eating Disorders, 13,* 1–11.

Cook, J., Tyson, R., White, J., Rushe, R., Gottman, J., & Murray, J. (1995). Mathematics of marital conflict: Qualitative dynamic modeling of marital interaction. *Journal of Family Psychology, 9,* 110–130.

Cooney, T., & Dunne, K. (2001). Intimate relationships in later life: Current realities, future prospects. *Journal of Family Issues, 22,* 838–858.

Cooney, T. M., & Mortimer, J. T. (1999). Family structure differences in the timing of leaving home: Exploring mediating factors. *Journal of Research on Adolescence, 9,* 367–393.

Coontz, S. (2000). Historical perspectives on family studies. *Journal of Marriage and the Family, 62,* 283–297.

Cooper, S. M. (1999). Historical analysis of the family. In M. B. Sussman, S. K. Steinmetz, & G. W. Peterson (Eds.), *Handbook of marriage and family* (pp. 13–38). New York: Plenum.

Copeland, A. P., & White, K. M. (1991). *Studying families.* Newbury Park, CA: Sage.

Cordova, J. V., Jacobson, N. S., Gottman, J. M., Rushe, R., & Cox, G. (1993). Negative reciprocity and communication in couples with a violent husband. *Journal of Abnormal Psychology, 102,* 559–564.

Coren, E., Barlow, J., & Stewart-Brown, S. (2003). The effectiveness of individual and group-based parenting programmes in improving outcomes for teenage mothers and their children: A systematic review. *Journal of Adolescence, 26,* 79–103.

Corrigan, E. (1980). *Alcoholic women in treatment.* New York: Oxford University Press.

Cowan, P. A. (1991). Individual and family life transitions: A proposal for a new definition. In P. A. Cowan & M. Hetherington (Eds.), *Family transitions* (pp. 3–30). Hillsdale, NJ: Lawrence Erlbaum Associates.

Cowan, P. (1999). What we talk about when we talk about families. *Monograph of the Society for Research in Child Development, 64,* 163–177(Serial No. 257).

Cowan, C. P., & Cowan, P. A. (1995). Interventions to ease the transition to parenthood: Why they are needed and what they can do. *Family Relations, 44,* 412–423.

Cowan, C. P., Cowan, P. A., Heming, G., & Miller, N. B. (1991). Becoming a family: Marriage, parenting, and child development. In P. A. Cowan & M. Hetherington (Eds.), *Family transitions* (pp. 79–109). Hillsdale, NJ: Lawrence Erlbaum Associates.

Cox, M. J., Paley, B., Burchinal, M., & Payne, C. C. (1999). Marital perceptions and interactions across the transition to parenthood. *Journal of Marriage and the Family, 61,* 611–625.

Coyne, J. C. (1999). Thinking interactionally about depression: A radical restatement. In T. Joiner & J. C. Coyne (Eds.), *The interactional nature of depression* (pp. 365–392). Washington, DC: American Psychological Association.

Coyne, J. C., Downey, G., & Boergers, J. (1992). Depression in families: A systems perspective. In D. Cicchetti & S. L. Toth (Eds.), *Developmental perspectives on depression* (pp. 211–249). New York: University of Rochester Press.

Coyne, J. C., Ellard, J. H., & Smith, D. A. (1990). Unsupportive relationships, interdependence, and unhelpful exchanges. In I. G. Sarason, B. R. Sarason, & G. Pierce (Eds.), *Social support: An interactional view* (pp. 129–149). New York: Wiley.

Coyne, J. C., Kahn, J., & Gotlib, I. H. (1987). Depression. In T. Jacob (Ed.), *Family interaction and psychopathology* (pp. 509–533). New York: Plenum.

Coyne, J. C., Kessler, R. C., Tal, M., Turnbull, J., Wortman, C. B., & Greden, J. F. (1987). Living with a depressed person. *Journal of Consulting and Clinical Psychology, 55,* 347–352.

Coyne, J. C., & Smith, D. A. F. (1994). Couples coping with a myocardial infarction: Contextual perspective on patient self-efficacy. *Journal of Family Psychology, 8,* 43–54.

Coyne, J. C., Thompson, R., & Palmer, S. C. (2002). Marital quality, coping with conflict, marital complaints, and affection in couples with a depressed wife. *Journal of Family Psychology, 16,* 26–37.

Craddock, A. (1988). Marital roles expectations and premarital satisfaction among Australian couples: 1979–1980 versus 1987. *Australian Journal of Sex, Marriage, and Family, 9,* 159–168.

Crawford, D. W., Houts, R. M., Huston, T. L., & George, L. J. (2002). Compatibility, leisure, and satisfaction in marital relationships. *Journal of Marriage and the Family, 64,* 433–449.

Crohan, S. E. (1996). Marital quality and conflict across the transition to parenthood in African American and White couples. *Journal of Marriage and the Family, 58,* 933–945.

Cromwell, R. E., & Olson, S. (1975). *Power in families.* New York: Wiley.

Crosbie-Burnett, M., & McClintic, K. M. (2000a). Remarriage and recoupling: A stress perspective. In P. C. McKenry & S. J. Price (Eds.), *Families and change: Coping with stressful events and transitions* (pp. 303–332). Thousand Oaks, CA: Sage.

Crosbie-Burnett, M., & McClintic, K. M. (2000b). Remarried families over the life course. In S. J. Price, P. C. McKenry, & M. J. Murphy (Eds.), *Families across time: A life course perspective* (pp. 37–50). Los Angeles: Roxbury.

Crosby, R. A., & Miller, K. S. (2002). Family influences on adolescents' sexual health. In G. M. Wingood & R. J. DiClemente (Eds.), *Handbook of women's sexual and reproductive health* (pp. 113–127). New York: Kluwer.

Crosnoe, R., & Elder, G. H. (2002). Life course transitions, the generational stake, and grandparent-grandchild relationships. *Journal of Marriage and the Family, 64,* 1089–1096.

Crowder, K. S., & Tolnay, S. E. (2000). A new marriage squeeze for black women: The role of racial inter-marriage by black men. *Journal of Marriage and the Family, 62,* 792–807.

Crowther, J. H., Kichler, J. C., Sherwood, N. E., & Kuhnert, M. E. (2002). The role of familial factors in bulimia nervosa. *Eating Disorders: The Journal of Treatment and Prevention, 10,* 141–151.

Cummings, E. J., & Goeke-Morey, M. S., & Papp, L. M. (2001). Couple conflict, children, and families: It's not just you and me, babe. In A. Booth, A. C. Crouter, & M. Clements (Eds.), *Couples in conflict* (pp. 117–148). Mahwah, NJ: Lawrence Erlbaum Associates.

Curran, P. J., & Chassin, L. (1996). A longitudinal study of parenting as a protective factor for children of alcoholics. *Journal of Studies on Alcohol, 57,* 305–313.

Cushman, D., & Whiting, G. C. (1972). An approach to communication theory: Toward consensus on rules. *The Journal of Communication, 22,* 217–238.

Cutrona, C. E. (1996). Social support as a determinant of marital quality: The interplay of negative and supportive behaviors. In G. R. Pierce, B. R. Sarason, & I. G. Sarason (Eds.), *Handbook of social support and the family* (pp. 173–194). New York: Plenum.

Cutrona, C. E., & Suhr, J. A. (1994). Social support communication in the context of marriage: An analysis of couples' supportive interactions. In B. R. Burleson, T. L. Albrecht, & I. G. Sarason (Eds.), *Communication of social support: Messages, interaction, relationships, and community* (pp. 113–135). Thousand Oaks, CA: Sage.

Dainton, M., & Aylor, B. (2001). A relational uncertainty analysis of jealousy, trust, and maintenance in long-distance versus geographically close relationships. *Communication Quarterly, 49,* 172–188.

Daly, K. J. (2001). Deconstructing family time: From ideology to livid experience. *Journal of Marriage and the Family, 63,* 283–294.

Daly, M., & Wilson, M. (1988). Evolutionary psychology social psychology and family homicide. *Science, 242,* 519–524.

Dance, F. E. X. (1967). Toward a theory of human communication. In F. E. X. Dance (Ed.), *Human communication theory* (pp. 288–309). New York: Holt.

Danziger, S. K. (1995). Family life and teenage pregnancy in the inner-city: Experiences of African-American youth. *Children and Youth Services Review, 17,* 183–202.

Dare, C., Le Grange, D., Eisler, I., & Rutherford, J. (1994). Redefining the psychosomatic family: Family process of 26 eating disorder families. *International Journal of Eating Disorders, 16,* 211–226.

Davey, A. (2000). Aging and adaptation: How families cope. In P. C. McKenry & S. J. Price (Eds.), *Families and change: Coping with stressful events and transitions* (2nd ed., pp. 94–119). Thousand Oaks, CA: Sage.

Davey, A., Fincham, F. D., Beach, S. R. H., & Brody, G. H. (2001). Attributions in marriage: Examining the entailment model in dyadic context. *Journal of Family Psychology, 15,* 721–734.

Davilla, R. A. (1995). An intersubjective methodology for studying children and families. In T. J. Socha & Glen, H. Stamp (Eds.), *Parents, children, and communication: Frontiers of theory and research* (pp. 89–99). Mahwah, NJ: Lawrence Erlbaum Associates.

Davis, E. C., & Friel, L. V. (2001). Adolescent sexuality: Disentangling the effects of family structure and family context. *Journal of Marriage and Family, 63,* 669–681.

De Bourdeaudhuij, I., & Van Oost, P. (1998). Family members' influence on decision making about food: Differences in perception and relationship with healthy eating. *American Journal of Health Promotion, 13,* 73–81.

DeFrain, J., & Olson, D. H. (1999). Contemporary family patterns and relationships. In M. B. Sussman, S. K. Steinmetz, & G. W. Peterson (Eds.), *Handbook of marriage and family* (pp. 307–326). New York: Plenum.

DeGenova, M. K., & Rice, F. P. (2002). *Intimate relationships, marriages, & families* (5th ed.). Boston: McGraw Hill.

Demo, D. H., & Acock, A. C. (1996). Singlehood, marriage, and remarriage: The effects of family structure and family relationships on mothers' well-being. *Journal of Family Issues, 17,* 388–407.

Demo, D. H., Fine, M. A., & Ganong, L. H. (2000). Divorce as a family stressor. In P. C. McKenry & S. J. Price (Eds.), *Families and change: Coping with stressful life events and transitions* (2nd ed., pp. 279–302). Thousand Oaks, CA: Sage.

Demo, D. H., & Ganong, L. H. (1994). Divorce. In T. C. McKenry & S. J. Price (Eds.), *Families and change: Coping with stressful events.* Thousand Oaks, CA: Sage.

Dennerstein, L., Dudley, E., & Guthrie, J. (2002). Empty nest or revolving door? A prospective study of women's quality of life in midlife during the phase of children leaving and reentering the home. *Psychological Medicine, 32,* 545–550.

Denton, W. H., Burleson, B. R., & Sprenkle, D. H. (1994). Motivation in marital communication: Comparison of distressed and nondistressed husbands and wives. *American Journal of Family Therapy, 22,* 17–26.

Derlega, V. J., Metts, S., Petronio, S., & Margulis, S. T. (1993). *Self-disclosure.* London: Sage.

Derlega, V. J., Winstead, B. A., & Folk-Barron, L. (2000). Reasons for and against disclosing HIV-seropositive test results to an intimate partner: A functional perspective. In S. Petronio (Ed.), *Balancing the secrets of private disclosures* (pp. 53–70). Mahwah, NJ: Lawrence Erlbaum Associates.

DeYoung, A. J. (1979). Marriage encounter: A critical examination. *Journal of Marital and Family Therapy, 5,* 27–34.

Diamond, G. S., Reis, B. F., Diamond, G. M., Siqueland, L., & Isaacs, L. (2002). Attachment-based family therapy for depressed adolescents: A treatment development study. *Journal of the American Academy of Child and Adolescent Psychiatry, 41,* 1190–1196.

Dickson, F. C., & Walker, K. L. (2001). The expression of emotion in later-life married men. *Qualitative Research Reports in Communication, Summer,* 66–71.

Dickstein, S., St. Andre, M. Sameroff, A., Seifer, R., & Schiller, M. (1999). Maternal depression, family functioning, and child outcomes: A narrative assessment. *Monograph of the Society for Research in Child Development, 64,* 84–105(Serial No. 257).

Diggs, R. C., & Socha, T. (2004) Communication, families, and exploring the boundaries of diversity. In A. Vangelisti (Ed.), *Handbook of family communication* (pp. 249–266). Mahwah, NJ: Lawrence Erlbaum Associates.

Dinning, W. D., & Berk, L. A. (1989). The Children of Alcoholics Screening Test: Relationship to sex, family environment, and social adjustment in adolescents. *Journal of Clinical Psychology, 45,* 335–339.

Disbrow, M. A., Doerr, H., & Cáulfield, C. (1977). Measuring the components of parents' potential for child abuse and neglect. *Child Abuse and Neglect, 1,* 279–296.

Diskin, S. (1986). Marriage enrichment: Rationale and resources. *Journal of Psychotherapy and the Family, 2,* 111–125.

Dixson, M. D. (1995). Models and perspectives of parent-child communication. In T. J. Socha and G. H. Stamp (Eds.), *Parents, children, and communication: Frontiers of theory and research* (pp. 43–62). Mahwah, NJ: Lawrence Erlbaum Associates.

Doane, J. A., & Becker, D. F. (1993). Changes in family expressed emotion climate and course of psychiatric illness in hospitalized young adults and adolescents. *New Trends in Experimental and Clinical Psychiatry, 9,* 63–77.

Doane, J. A., West, K. L., Goldstein, M. J., Rodnick, E. H., & Jones, J. E. (1981). Parental communication deviance and affective style: Predictors of subsequent schizophrenia spectrum disorders. *Archives of General Psychiatry, 38,* 679–685.

Dobash, R. E., & Dobash, R. (1979). *Violence against wives.* New York: Free Press.

Doherty, W. J., & Allen, W. (1994). Family functioning and parental smoking as predictors of adolescent cigarette use: A six-year prospective study. *Journal of Family Psychology, 8,* 347–353.

Doherty, W. J., & Beaton, J. M. (2004). Mothers and fathers parenting together. In A. Vangelisti (Ed.), *Handbook of family communication* (pp. 269–286 ). Mahwah, NJ: Lawrence Erlbaum Associates.

Doherty, W. J., Lester, M. E., & Leigh, G. (1986). Marriage encounter weekends: Couples who win and couples who lose. *Journal of Marital and Family Therapy, 12,* 49–61.

Doherty, W. J., McCabe, P., & Ryder, R. G. (1978). Marriage encounter: A critical appraisal. *Journal of Marriage and Family Counseling, 4,* 99–106.

Doherty, W. J., & Walker, B. J. (1982). Marriage encounter casualties: A preliminary investigation. *American Journal of Family Therapy, 10,* 15–25.

Domenico, D., & Windle, M. (1993). Intrapersonal and interpersonal functioning among middle-aged female adult children of alcoholics. *Journal of Consulting and Clinical Psychology, 61,* 659–666.

Douglas, L. K. (1999). Relational expectancy fulfillment as an explanatory variable for distinguishing couple types. *Human Communication Research, 25,* 420–442.

Douglas, W. (2003). *Television families: Is something wrong in suburbia?* Mahwah, NJ: Lawrence Erlbaum Associates.

Downey, G., & Coyne, J. C. (1990). Children of depressed parents: An integrative review. *Psychological Bulletin, 108,* 50–76.

Downs, W. R., & Miller, B. A. (1998). Relationships between experiences of parental violence during childhood and women's psychiatric symptomatology. *Journal of Interpersonal Violence, 13,* 438–455.

Draucker, C. B. (1996). Family-of-origin variables and adult female survivors of childhood sexual abuse: A review of the research. *Journal of Child Sexual Abuse, 5,* 35–63.

Drigotas, S. M., & Rusbult, C. E. (1992). Should I stay or should I go? A dependence model of breakups. *Journal of Personality and Social Psychology, 62,* 62–87.

Drinkmeyer, D., & McKay, G. (1976). *Systematic training for effective parenting: Parent's handbook.* Circle Pines, MN: American Guidance Service.

Drinkmeyer, D., & McKay, G. (1989). *Parenting young children.* Circle Pines, MN: American Guidance Service.

Drotar, D. (1997). Relating parent and family functioning to the psychological adjustment of children with chronic health conditions: What have we learned? What do we need to know? *Journal of Pediatric Psychology, 22,* 149–165.

Duck, S. W. (1982). A topography of relationship disengagement and dissolution. In S. W. Duck (Ed.), *Personal relationships 4: Dissolving personal relationships* (pp. 1–30). New York: Academic Press.

Duck, S. (1991). Diaries and logs. In B. M. Montgomery & S. Duck (Eds.), *Studying interpersonal interaction* (pp. 141–161). New York: Guilford.

Duck, S. (1998). Human relationships (3rd ed.). Thousand Oaks, CA: Sage.

Duemmler, S. L., & Kobak, R. (2001). The development of commitment and attachment in dating relationships: Attachment security as relationship construct. *Journal of Adolescence, 24,* 401–415.

du Fort, G. G., Kovess, V., & Bolvin, J. F. (1994). Spouse similarity for psychological distress and well-being: A population study. *Psychological Medicine, 24,* 431–447.

Dunn, J. (1983). Sibling relationships in early childhood. *Child Development, 54,* 787–811.

Dunn, J. (1996). Brothers and sisters in middle childhood and early adolescence: Continuity and change in individual differences. In G. H. Brody (Ed.), *Sibling relationships: Their causes and consequences* (pp. 31–46). Norwood, NJ: Ablex.

Dunn, J. (2002). The adjustment of children in stepfamilies: Lessons from community studies. *Child and Adolescent Mental Health, 7,* 154–161.

Dunn, J., & Kendrick, C. (1982). The speech of two-and three-year olds to infant siblings: "Baby talk" and the context of communication. *Journal of Child Language, 9,* 579–595.

Dunn, N. J., Jacob, T., Hummon, N., & Seilhamer, R. A. (1987). Marital stability in alcoholic-spouse relationships as a function of drinking pattern and location. *Journal of Abnormal Psychology, 96,* 99–107.

Dyer, P. M., & Dyer, G. H. (1999). Marriage enrichment: A.C.M.E.-style. In R. Berger & M. T. Hannal (Eds.), *Preventive approaches in couples therapy* (pp. 28–54). Philadelphia, PA: Taylor & Francis.

Dykstra, P. A. (1993). The differential availability of relationships and the provision and effectiveness of support to older adults. *Journal of Social and Personal Relationships, 10,* 355–370.

Eckland, B. K. (1968). Theories of mate selection. *Eugenics Quarterly, 15,* 71–84.

Edwards, H. (2001). Family caregiving, communication, and the health of care receivers. In M. L. Hummert & J. Nussbaum (Eds.), *Aging, communication, and health: Linking research and practice for successful aging* (pp. 203–224). Mahwah, NJ: Lawrence Erlbaum Associates.

Edwards, J. J., & Alexander, P. C. (1992). The contribution of family background to the long-term adjustment of women sexually abused as children. *Journal of Interpersonal Violence, 7,* 306–320.

Eggebeen, D. J., & Knoester, C. (2001). Does fatherhood matter for men? *Journal of Marriage and the Family, 63,* 381–393.

Eiden, R. D., Chavez, F., & Leonard, K. E. (1999). Parent-infant interactions among families with alcoholic fathers. *Development and Psychopathology, 11,* 745–762.

Ekman, P. (1984). Expression and the nature of emotion. In K.R. Scherer & P. Ekman (Eds.), *Approaches to emotion* (pp. 319–344). Hillsdale, NJ: Lawrence Erlbaum Associates.

Ekman, P. (2003). *Emotions revealed: Recognizing faces and feelings to improve communication and emotional life.* New York: Times Books.

Ekman, P., & Friesen, W. V. (1978). Facial action coding system. Palo Alto, CA: Consulting Psychologists Press.

Elder, G. H., & Conger, R. D. (2000). *Children of the land: Adversity and success in rural America.* Chicago: University of Chicago Press.

Elin, R. J. (1999). Marriage encounter: A positive preventive enrichment program. In R. Berger & M. T. Hannah (Eds.), *Preventive approaches in couples therapy* (pp. 55–72). Philadelphia, PA: Taylor & Francis.

Elliot, J. J., & Briere, J. (1993, August). Childhood maltreatment, later revictimization, and adult symptomatology: A causal analysis. Paper presented at the 101st Annual Meeting of the American Psychological Association, Toronto, Canada.

Ellwood, M. S., & Stolberg, A. L. (1991). A preliminary investigation of family systems' influences on individual adjustment. *Journal of Divorce and Remarriage, 15,* 157–174.

El-Sheikh, M., Cummings, E. M., & Goetsch, V. L. (1989). Coping with adults' angry behavior: Behavioral, physiological, and verbal responses in preschoolers. *Developmental Psychology, 25,* 490–498.

Elwood, T., & Schrader, D. C. (1998). Family communication patterns and communication apprehension. *Journal of Social Behavior and Personality, 13,* 493–502.

Embry, L., & Dawson, G. (2002). Disruptions in parenting behavior related to maternal depression: Influence on children's behavioral and psychobiological development. In J. G. Borkowski, S. L. Ramey, & M. Bristol-Power (Eds.), *Parenting and the child's world: Influences on academic, intellectual, and social-emotional development* (pp. 203–213). Mahwah, NJ: Lawrence Erlbaum Associates.

Ennett, S. T., Bauman, K. E., Foshee, V. A., Pemberton, M., & Hicks, K. A. (2001). Parent-child communication about adolescent tobacco and alcohol use: What do parents say and does it affect youth behavior? *Journal of Marriage and the Family, 63,* 48–62.

Epstein, N. B., Baldwin, L. M., & Bishop, D. S. (1983). The McMaster family assessment device. *Journal of Marriage and the Family, 9,* 171–180.

Epstein, N. B., Bishop, D. S., & Levin, S. (1978). The McMaster Model of Family Functioning. *Journal of Marriage and Family Counseling, 4,* 19–31.

Erel, O., & Burman, B. (1995). Interrelatedness of marital relations and parent-child relations: A meta-analytic review. *Psychological Bulletin, 118,* 108–132.

Evans, J., & le Grange, D. (1995). Body size and parenting in eating disorders: A comparative study of the attitudes of mothers towards their children. *International Journal of Eating Disorders, 18*, 39–48.

Ewart, C. K., Taylor, C. B., Kraemer, H. C., & Agras, W. S. (1991). High blood pressure and marital discord: Not being nasty matters more than being nice. *Health Psychology, 10*, 155–163.

Ex, C., Janssens, J., & Korzilius, P. (2002). Young females' images of motherhood in relation to television viewing. *Journal of Communication, 52*, 955–971.

Eyberg, S. M., & Robinson, E. A. (1982). Parent-child interaction training: Effects on family functioning. *Journal of Clinical Child Psychology, 11*, 130–137.

Farhi, P. (2002, November 20). Popping the question: Why has 'The Bachelor' become irresistible to women? Stay tuned. *The Washington Post*, pp. C1.

Farrell, M. P., & Barnes, G. M. (1993). Family systems and social support: A test of the effects of cohesion and adaptability on the functioning of parents and adolescents. *Journal of Marriage and the Family, 55*, 119–131.

Faust, J., Runyon, M. K., & Kenny, M. C. (1995). Family variables associated with the onset and impact of intrafamilial childhood sexual abuse. *Clinical Psychology Review, 15*, 443–456.

Faust, K. A., & McKibben J. N. (1999). Marital dissolution: Divorce, separation, annulment, and widowhood. In M. B. Sussman, S. K. Steinmetz, & G. W. Peterson (Eds.), *Handbook of marriage and the family* (pp. 475–499). New York: Plenum.

Feeney, J. (1999). Issues of closeness and distance in dating relationships: Effects of sex and attachment style. *Journal of Social and Personal Relationships, 16*, 571–590.

Feeney, J. A. (2002). Attachment, marital interaction, and relationship satisfaction: A diary study. *Personal Relationships, 9*, 39–55.

Feeney, J. A., & Noller, P. (1992). Attachment style and romantic love: Relationship dissolution. *Australian Journal of Psychology, 44*, 69–74.

Feeney, J. A., & Noller, P. (1996). *Adult attachment.* Thousand Oaks, CA: Sage.

Feeney, J. A., Noller, P., & Callan, V. J. (1994). Attachment style, communication, and satisfaction in the early years of marriage. In K. Bartholomew & D. Perlman (Eds.), *Advances in personal relationships, Vol. 5: Attachment processes in adulthood* (pp. 269–308). London: Jessica Kingsley.

Feeney, J. A., Noller, P., & Roberts, N. (2000). Attachment and close relationships. In C. Hendrick & S. S. Hendrick (Eds.), *Close relationships: A sourcebook.* Thousand Oaks, CA: Sage.

Feeney, J. A., Noller, P., & Ward, C. (1997). Marital satisfaction and spousal interaction. In R. J. Sternberg & M. Hojjat (Eds.), *Satisfaction in close relationships* (pp. 160–189). New York: Guilford.

Field, T. (1984). Early interactions between infants and their post-partum depressed mothers. *Infant Behavior and Development, 7*, 517–522.

Fields, J. (2003). *Children's living arrangements and characteristics: March 2002.* Current Population Reports, P20-547. U.S. Census Bureau, Washington, DC.

Fiese, B. H. (1992). Dimensions of family rituals across two generations: Relation to adolescent identity. *Family Process, 31*, 151–161.

Fiese, B. H. (2000a). Family routines, rituals, and asthma management: A proposal for family-based strategies to . . . *Family Systems and Health, 18*, 405–418.

Fiese, B. H. (2000b). Family matters: A systems view of family effects on children's cognitive health. In R. J. Sternberg & E. L. Grigorenko (Eds.), *Enviornmental effects on cognitive abilities.* Mahwah, NJ: Lawrence Erlbaum Associates.

Fiese, B. H., Hooker, K. A., Kotary, L., & Schwagler, J. (1993). Family rituals in the early stages of parenthood. *Journal of Marriage and the Family, 55*, 633–642.

Fiese, B. H., Hooker, K. A., Kotary, L., Schwagler, J., & Rimmer, M. (1995). Family stories in the early stages of parenthood. *Journal of Marriage and the Family, 57*, 763–770.

Fiese, B. H., & Marjinsky, K. A. T. (1999). Dinnertime stories: Connecting family practices with relationship beliefs and child adjustment. *Monograph of the Society for Research in Child Development, 64*, 52–68(Serial No. 257).

Fiese, B. H., Sameroff, A. J., Grotevant, H. D., Wamboldt, F. S., Dickstein, S., & Fravel, D. L. (1999). Preface. *Monograph of the Society for Research in Child Development, 64*(vii, Serial No. 257).

Fiese, B. H., Sameroff, A. J., Grotevant, H. D., Wamboldt, F. S., Dickstein, S., & Fravel, D. L. (2001). Observing families through the stories that they tell: A multidimensional approach. In P. K. Kerig & K. M. Lindahl (Eds.), *Family observational coding systems* (pp. 259–272). Mahwah, NJ: Lawrence Erlbaum Associates.

Fiese, B. H., & Tomcho, T. J. (2001). Finding meaning in religious practices: The relation between religious holiday rituals and marital satisfaction. *Journal of Family Psychology, 15,* 597–609.

Fiese, B. H., Tomcho, T. J., Douglas, M., Josephs, K., Poltrock, S., & Baker, T. (2002). A review of 50 years of research on naturally occurring family routines and rituals: Cause for celebration? *Journal of Family Psychology, 16,* 381–390.

Fincham, F. D., & Bradbury, T. N. (1991). Cognition in marriage: A program of research on attributions. In W. H. Jones & D. Perlman (Eds.), *Advances in personal relationships* (Vol. 2 , pp. 159–203). Oxford, England: Jessica Kingsley.

Fincham, F. D., Bradbury, T. N., & Scott, C. K. (1990). Cognition in marriage. In F. D. Fincham & T. N. Bradbury (Eds.), *The psychology of marriage* (pp. 118–149). New York: Guilford.

Fine, M. A., Coleman, M., & Ganong, L. H. (1998). Consistency in perceptions of the step-parent role among stepparents, parents and stepchildren. *Journal of Social and Personal Relationships, 15,* 810–828.

Fine, M. A., Coleman, M., & Ganong, L. H. (1999). A social constructionist multi-method approach to understanding the stepparent role. In E. M. Hetherington (Ed.), *Coping with divorce, single parenthood, and remarriage* (pp. 273–294). Mahwah, NJ: Lawrence Elrbaum Associates.

Fine, M., & Fine, D. (1992). Recent changes in laws affecting stepfamilies: Suggestions for legal reform. *Family Relations, 41,* 334–340.

Fine, M. A., Voydanoff, P., & Donnelly, B. W. (1993). Relations between parental control and warmth and child well-being in stepfamilies. *Journal of Family Psychology, 7,* 222–232.

Finkenauer, C., & Hazam, H. (2000). Disclosure and secrecy in marriage: Do both contribute to marital satisfaction. *Journal of Social and Personal Relationships, 17,* 245–263.

Fischer, L. (1986). *Linked lives: Adult daughters and their mothers.* New York: Harper & Row.

Fisher, L., & Lieberman, M. A. (1996). The effects of family context on adult offspring of patients with Alzheimer's disease: A longitudinal study. *Journal of Family Psychology, 10,* 180–191.

Fishman, H. C., & Fishman, T. (2003). Structural family therapy. In G. P. Sholevar (Ed.), *Textbook of family and couples therapy: Clinical application* (pp. 35–54). Washington, DC: American Psychiatric Publishing.

Fiske, J. (1987). *Television culture.* London: Routledge.

Fitzpatrick, M. A. (1984). A typological approach to marital interaction: Recent theory and research. In L. Berkowitz (Ed.), *Advances in experimental social psychology* (Vol. 18, pp. 1–47). New York: Academic Press.

Fitzpatrick, M. A. (1988a). *Between husbands and wives.* Newbury Park: Sage.

Fitzpatrick, M. A. (1988b). Approaches to marital interaction. In P. Noller & M. A. Fitzpatrick (Eds.), *Perspectives on marital interaction* (pp. 1–28). Clevedon, England: Multilingual Matters LTD.

Fitzpatrick, M. A. (2002). Communication issues in policing family violence. In H. Giles (Eds.), *Law enforcement, communication, and community* (pp. 129–153). Amsterdam: John Benjamins Publishing Company.

Fitzpatrick, M. A., & Badzinski, D. M. (1994). All in the family: Interpersonal communication in kin relationships. In M. L. Knapp & G. S. Miller (Eds.), *Handbook of interpersonal communication* (2nd ed., pp. 726–771). Thousand Oaks, CA: Sage.

Fitzpatrick, M. A., & Best, P. (1979). Dyadic adjustment in traditional, independent and separate relationships. *Communication Monographs, 46,* 167–178.

Fitzpatrick, M. A., Fey, J., Segrin, C., & Schiff, J. L. (1993). Internal working models of relationships and marital communication. *Journal of Langauge and Social Psychology, 12,* 103–131.

Fitzpatrick, M. A., Jandt, F., Myrick, F., & Edgar, T. (1994). Gay and lesbian couples relationships. In R. J. Ringer (Ed.), *Queer words, queer images* (pp. 265–276). New York: New York University Press.

Fitzpatrick, M. A., & Ritchie, L. D. (1994). Communication schemata within the family: Multiple perspectives on family interaction. *Human Communication Research, 20,* 275–301.

Fitzpatrick, M. A., Vangelisti, A. L., & Firman, S. M. (1994). Perceptions of marital interaction and change during pregnancy: A typological approach. *Personal Relationships, 1,* 101–122.

Flanagan, K. M., Clements, M. L., Whitton, S. W., Portney, M. J., Randall, D. W., & Markman, H. J. (2002). Retrospect and prospect in the psychological study of marital and couple relationships. In J. P. McHale &

W. S. Grolnick (Eds.), *Retrospect and prospect in the psychological study of families* (pp. 99–126). Mahwah, NJ: Lawrence Erlbaum Associates.

Flora, J. (1998). Relational development in dating and married couples: Implications for relational outcomes and psychosocial adjustment (Doctoral dissertation, University of Kansas, 1998). *Dissertation Abstracts International, 60(02)*, 284A. (UMI No. 9920338)

Flora J., & Segrin, C. (1998). Joint leisure time in friend and romantic relationships: The role of activity type, social skills, and positivity. *Journal of Social and Personal Relationships, 15,* 711–718.

Flora, J., & Segrin, C. (2000a). Affect and behavioral involvement in spousal complaints and compliments. *Journal of Family Psychology, 14,* 641–657.

Flora, J., & Segrin, C. (2000b). Relationship development in dating couples: Implications for relational satisfaction and loneliness. *Journal of Social and Personal Relationships, 17,* 811–825.

Flora, J., & Segrin, C. (2003). Relational well-being and perceptions of relational history in married and dating couples. *Journal of Social and Personal Relationships, 20,* 515–536.

Florsheim, P., Sumida, E., McCann, C., Winstanley, M., Fukui, R., Seefeldt, T., et al. (2003). The transition to parenthood among young African American and Latino couples: Relational predictors of risk for parental dysfunction. *Journal of Family Psychology, 17,* 65–79.

Floyd, K., & Morman, M. T. (2000). Affection received from fathers as a predictor of men's affection with their own sons: Tests of modeling and compensation hypotheses. *Communication Monographs, 67,* 347–361.

Foa, E., & Foa, U. (1976). Resource theory of social exchange. In J. Thibaut, J. Spence, & R. Carson (Eds.), *Contemporary topics in social psychology* (pp. 99–131). Morristown, NJ: General Learning.

Fonseca, H., Ireland, M., & Resnick, M. D. (2002). Familial correlates of extreme weight control behaviors among adolescents. *International Journal of Eating Disorders, 32,* 441–448.

Forehand, R., & Kotchick, B. A. (2002). Behavioral parent training: Current challenges and potential solutions. *Journal of Child and Family Studies, 11,* 377–384.

Fowers, B. J., Montel, K. H., & Olson, D. H. (1996). Predicting marital success for premarital couple types based on PREPARE. *Journal of Marital and Family Therapy, 22,* 103–119.

Fowers, B. J., & Olson, D. H. (1986). Predicting marital success with PREPARE: A predictive validity study. *Journal of Marital and Family Therapy, 12,* 403–413.

Fowers, B. J., & Olson, D. H. (1992). Four types of premarital couples: An empirical typology based on PREPARE. *Journal of Family Psychology, 6,* 10–21.

Fraenkel, P., Markman, H., & Stanley, S. (1997). The prevention approach to relationship problems. *Sexual and Marital Therapy, 12,* 249–258.

Frankish, C. J., & Linden, W. (1996). Spouse-pair risk factors and cardiovascular reactivity. *Journal of Psychosomatic Research, 40,* 37–51.

French, J. P. P., & Raven, B. (1959). The bases of social power. In D. Cartwright (Ed.), *Studies in social power* (pp. 150–167). Ann Arbor: University of Michigan Press.

Freud, S. (1966). *Introductory lectures on psychoanalysis.* New York: Norton. (Original work published in 1917)

Fromuth, M. E. (1986). The relationship of childhood sexual abuse with later psychological and sexual adjustment in a sample of college women. *Child Abuse and Neglect, 10,* 5–15.

Fujioka, Y., & Austin, E. W. (2002). The relationship of family communication patterns to parental mediation styles. *Communication Research, 29,* 642–665.

Fung, H. H., Carstensen, L. L., & Lang, F. R. (2001). Age-related patterns in social networks among European Americans and African Americans: Implications for socioemotional selectivity across the life span. *International Journal of Aging and Human Development, 52,* 185–206.

Furman, W., & Giberson, R. S. (1995). Identifying the links between parents and their children's sibling relationships. In S. Shulman (Ed.), *Close relationships and socioemotional development: Vol. 7. Human development* (pp. 95–107). Norwood, NJ: Ablex.

Furstenberg, F. F. (1998). Social capital and the role of father in family. In A. Booth & A. C. Crouter (Eds.), *Men in families. When do they get involved? What difference does it make?* (pp. 295–302). Mahwah, NJ: Lawrence Erlbaum Associates.

Furstenberg, F. F., & Cherlin, A. J. (1991). *Divided families: What happens to children when parents part.* Cambridge, MA: Harvard University Press.

Gaines, S. O., & Brennan, K. A. (2001). Establishing and maintaining satisfaction in multicultural relationships. In J. Harvey & A. Wenzel (Eds.), *Close romantic relationships: Maintenance and* enhancement (pp. 237–253). Mahwah, NJ: Lawrence Erlbaum Associates.

Galvin, K. M., & Brommel, B. J. (1999). *Family communication: Cohesion and change* (5th ed.). New York: Longman.

Galvin, K. M., Bylund, C. L., & Brommel, B. J. (2004). Family communication: Cohesion and change (6th ed.). Boston, MA: Allyn & Bacon.

Gano-Phillips, S., & Fincham, F. D. (1995). Family conflict, divorce, and children's adjustment. In M. A. Fitzpatrick & A. L. Vangelisti (Eds.), *Explaining family interactions* (pp. 206–231). Thousand Oaks, CA: Sage.

Ganong, L. H., & Coleman, M. (1994). *Remarried family relationships*. Thousand Oaks, CA: Sage.

Ganong, L. H., & Coleman, M. (1997). How society views stepfamilies. *Marriage and Family Review, 26,* 85–106.

Ganong, L. H., & Coleman, M. (1999). *Changing families, changing responsibilities: Family obligations following divorce and remarriage*. Mahwah, NJ: Lawrence Erlbaum Associates.

Ganong, L. H., & Coleman, M. (2000). Remarried families. In C. Hendrick & S. S. Hendrick (Eds.), *Close relationships: A sourcebook* (pp. 155–168). Thousand Oaks, CA: Sage.

Garbarino, C., & Strange, C. (1993). College adjustment and family environments of students reporting parental alcohol problems. *Journal of College Student Development, 34,* 261–266.

Gardner, R. (1989). Method of conflict resolution and characteristics of abuse victimization in heterosexual, lesbian, and gay male couples. (Doctoral dissertation, University of Georgia, 1989). *Dissertation Abstracts International, 50,* 746B.

Garfinkel, P. E., Garner, D. M., Rose, J., Darby, P. L., Brandes, J. S., O'Hanlon, J., et al. (1983). A comparison of characteristics in families of patients with anorexia nervosa and normal controls. *Psychological Medicine, 13,* 821–828.

Gauvain, M., Fagot, F. I., Leve, C., & Kavanagh, K. (2002). Instruction by mothers and fathers during problem solving with their young children. *Journal of Family Psychology, 16,* 81–90.

Gee, C. B., Scott, R. L., Castellani, A. M., & Cordova, J. V. (2002). Predicting 2-year marital status from partners' discussions of their marriage checkup. *Journal of Marital and Family Therapy, 28,* 399–407.

Gelfand, D. M., & Teti, D. M. (1990). The effects of maternal depression on children. *Clinical Psychology Review, 10,* 329–353.

Gelles, R. J. (1985). Family violence. *Annual Review of Sociology, 11,* 347–367.

Gelles, R. J. (1998). Family violence. In M. Tonry (Ed.), *The handbook of crime and punishment* (pp. 178–206). New York: Oxford University Press.

Gelles, R. J., & Straus, M. A. (1979). Determinants of violence in the family: Toward a theoretical integration. In W. R. Burr, R. Kill, F. I. Nye, & I. L. Reiss (Eds.), *Contemporary theories about the family* (pp. 549–581). New York: The Free Press.

Gelles, R. J., & Straus, M. A. (1988). *Intimate violence*. New York: Simon & Schuster.

Genovese, R. J. (1975). Marriage encounter. *Small Group Behavior, 6,* 45–56.

Gentry, M., & Shulman, A. D. (1988). Remarriage as a coping response for widowhood. *Psychology and Aging, 3,* 191–196.

Gershoff, E. T. (2002). Corporal punishment by parents and associated child behaviors and experiences: A meta-analytic and theoretical review. *Psychological Bulletin, 128,* 539–579.

Giblin, P., Sprenkle, D. H., & Sheehan, R. (1985). Enrichment outcome research: A meta-analysis of premarital, marital and family interventions. *Journal of Marital and Family Therapy, 11,* 257–271.

Gilbert, L. A. (1993). *Two careers/one family: The promise of gender equality*. Newbury Park, CA: Sage.

Giles-Sims, J., & Crosbie-Burnett, M. (1989). Adolescent power in stepfather families: A test of normative-resource theory. *Journal of Marriage and the Family, 51,* 1065–1078.

Gill, D. S., Christensen, A., & Fincham, F. D. (1999). Predicting marital satisfaction from behavior: Do all roads really lead to Rome? *Personal Relationships, 6,* 369–387.

Gilman, S. E., Kawachi, I., Fitzmaurice, G. M., & Buka, S. L. (2003). Family disruption in childhood and risk of adult depression. *American Journal of Psychiatry, 160,* 939–946.

Ginott, H. G. (1994). *Between parent and child*. New York: Avon Books. (Original work published in 1965)

Giunta, C. T., & Compas, B. E. (1994). Adult daughters of alcoholics: Are they unique? *Journal of Studies on Alcohol, 55*, 600–606.

Glenn, N. D. (1998). Problems and prospects in longitudinal research on marriage: A sociologist's perspective. In T. N. Bradbury (Ed.), *The developmental course of marital dysfunction* (pp. 427–440). Cambridge, UK: Cambridge University Press.

Glick, J. E., Bean, F. D., & Van Hook, J. V. W. (1997). Immigration and changing patterns of extended family household structure in the United States: 1970–1990. *Journal of Marriage and the Family, 59*, 177–191.

Glick, P. S. (1980). Remarriage: Some recent changes and variations. *Journal of Family Issues, 1*, 455–478.

Glick, P. C. (1988). Fifty years of family demography: A record of social change. *Journal of Marriage and the Family, 50*, 861–873.

Goetting, A. (1986). The developmental tasks of siblingship over the life cycle. *Journal of Marriage and the Family, 48*, 703–714.

Gold, D. T. (1989). Sibling relationships in old age: A typology. *International Journal of Aging and Human Development, 28*, 37–51.

Goldman, L., & Haaga, D. A. F. (1995). Depression and the experience and expression of anger in marital and other relationships. *Journal of Nervous and Mental Disease, 183*, 505–509.

Goldstein, J. R. (1999). The leveling of divorce in the United States. *Demography, 36*, 409–414.

Goldstein, M. J. (1981). Family factors associated with schizophrenia and anorexia nervosa. *Jounral of Youth and Adolescence, 10*, 385–405.

Goldstein, M. J. (1985). Family factors that antedate the onset of schizophrenia and related disorders: The results of a fifteen year prospective longitudinal study. *Acta Psychiatrica Scandinavica* (Suppl.), *71*, 7–18.

Goldstein, M. J. (1987). Family interaction patterns that antedate the onset of schizophrenia and related disorders: A further analysis of data from a longitudinal, prospective study. In K. Hahlweg & M. J. Goldstein (Eds.), *Understanding major mental disorder: The contribution of family interaction research* (pp. 11–32). New York: Family Process Press.

Goldstein, M. J., & Strachan, A. M. (1987). The family and schizophrenia. In T. Jacob (Ed.), *Family interaction and psychopathology: Theories, methods, and findings* (pp. 481–508). New York: Plenum.

Golish, T. D. (2000). Changes in closeness between adult children and their parents: A turning point analysis. *Communication Reports, 13*, 79–97.

Golish, T. D. (2003). Stepfamily communication strengths: Understanding the ties that bind. *Human Communication Research, 29*, 41–80.

Golish, T. D., & Caughlin, J. P. (2002). "I'd rather not talk about it": Adolescents' and young adults' use of topic avoidance in stepfamilies. *Journal of Applied Communication Research, 30*, 78–106.

Goodman, C. (1999). Intimacy and autonomy in long term marriage. *Journal of Gerontological Social Work, 32*, 83–97.

Goodman, C. C., & Silverstein, M. (2001). Grandmothers who parent their grandchildren: An exploratory study of close relations across three generations. *Journal of Family Issues, 22*, 557–578.

Goodman, S. H., Barfoot, B., Frye, A. A., & Belli, A. M. (1999). Dimensions of marital conflict and children's social problem-solving skills. *Journal of Family Psychology, 13*, 33–45.

Goodwin, R. (1999). *Personal relationships across cultures*. New York: Routledge.

Gotcher, J. M. (1993). The effects of family communication on psychosocial adjustment of cancer patients. *Journal of Applied Communication Research, 21*, 176–188.

Gotlib, I. H., Lewinsohn, P. M., & Seeley, J. R. (1998). Consequences of depression during adolescence: Marital status and marital functioning in early adulthood. *Journal of Abnormal Psychology, 107*, 686–690.

Gotlib, I. H., Mount, J. H., Cordy, N. I., & Whiffen, V. E. (1988). Depression and perceptions of early parenting: A longitudinal investigation. *British Journal of Psychiatry, 152*, 24–27.

Gotlib, I. H., & Whiffen, V. E. (1989). Depression and marital functioning: An examination of specificity and gender differences. *Journal of Abnormal Psychology, 98*, 23–30.

Gottman, J. M. (1979). *Marital interaction: Experimental investigations*. New York: Academic Press.

Gottman, J. M. (1993a). The roles of conflict engagement, escalation, and avoidance in marital interaction: A longitudinal view of five types of couples. *Journal of Consulting and Clinical Psychology, 61*, 6–15.

Gottman, J. M. (1993b). A theory of marital dissolution and stability. *Journal of Family Psychology, 7*, 57–75.

Gottman, J. M. (1994). *What predicts divorce: The relationship between marital processes and marital outcomes.* Hillsdale, NJ: Lawrence Erlbaum Associates.

Gottman, J. M. (1999). *The marriage clinic: A scientifically based marital therapy.* New York: Norton.

Gottman, J. M (2000). Why marriages fail. In K. M. Galvin & P. J. Cooper (Eds.), *Making connections: Readings in relational communication* (2nd ed., pp. 216–223). Los Angeles, CA: Roxbury Publishing Company.

Gottman, J. M., Coan, J., Carrère, S., & Swanson, C. (1998). Predicting marital happiness and stability from newlywed interactions. *Journal of Marriage and the Family, 60*, 5–22.

Gottman, J. M., & DeClaire, J. (2001). *The relationship cure.* New York: Crown.

Gottman, J. M., Driver, J., Yoshimoto, D., & Rushe, R. (2002). Approaches to the study of power in violent and nonviolent marriages, and in gay male and lesbian cohabiting relationships. In P. Noller & J. A. Feeney (Eds.), *Understanding marriage: Developments in the study of couple interaction* (pp. 323–347). New York: Cambridge University Press.

Gottman, J. M., Jacobson, N. S., Rushe, R. H., Shortt, J. W., Babcock, J., La Taillade, J. J., et al. (1995). The relationship between heart rate reactivity, emotionally aggressive behavior, and general violence in batterers. *Journal of Family Psychology, 9*, 227–248.

Gottman, J. M., Katz, L. F., & Hooven, C. (1997). *Meta-emotion: How families communicate emotionally.* Mahwah, NJ: Lawrence Erlbaum Associates.

Gottman, J. M., & Krokoff, L. J. (1989). Marital interaction and marital satisfaction: A longitudinal view. *Journal of Consulting and Clinical Psychology, 57*, 47–52.

Gottman, J. M., & Levenson, R. W. (1986). Assessing the role of emotion in marriage. *Behavioral Assessment, 8*, 31–48.

Gottman, J. M., & Levenson, R. W. (1988). The social psychophysiology of marriage. In P. Noller & M. A. Fitzpatrick (Eds.), *Perspectives on marital interaction* (pp. 183–200). San Diego: College Hill Press.

Gottman, J. M., & Levenson, R. W. (1992). Marital processes predictive of later dissolution: Behavior, physiology, and health. *Journal of Personality and Social Psychology, 63*, 221–233.

Gottman, J. M., & Levenson, R. W. (2000). The timing of divorce: Predicting when a couple will divorce over a 14-year period. *Journal of Marriage and the Family, 62*, 737–745.

Gottman, J., Levenson, R., & Woodin, E. (2001). Facial expressions during marital conflict. *Journal of Family Communication, 1*, 37–58.

Gottman, J. M., Markman, H., & Notarius, C. (1977). The topography of marital conflict: A sequential analysis of verbal and nonverbal behavior. *Journal of Marriage and the Family, 39*, 461–477.

Gottman, J. M., & Notarius, C. I. (2002). Marital research in the 20th century and a research agenda for the 21st century. *Family Process, 41*, 159–197.

Gottman, J. M., Notarius, C., Gonso, J., & Markman, H. J. (1976). *A couple's guide to communication.* Champaign, IL: Research Press.

Gottman, J. M., & Ringland, J. T. (1981). The analysis of dominance and bidirectionality in social development. *Child Development, 52*, 393–412.

Gottman, J. M., & Silver, N. (1999). *The seven principles for making marriage work.* New York: Crown.

Govaerts, K., & Dixon, D. (1988). ". . . until careers do us part:" Vocational and marital satisfaction in the dual-career commuter marriage. *International Journal for the Advancement of Counselling, 11*, 265–281.

Graham, E. E. (1997). Turning points and commitment in post-divorce relationships. *Communication Monographs, 64*, 350–368.

Gralinski, J. H., & Kopp, C. B. (1993). Everyday rules for behavior: Mothers' requests to young children. *Developmental Psychology, 29*, 573–584.

Grant, J. S., Elliott, T. R., Giger, J. N., & Bartolucci, A. A. (2001). Social problem-solving abilities, social support, and adjustment among family caregivers of individuals with a stroke. *Rehabilitation Psychology, 46*, 44–57.

Gray, J. (1992). *Men are from mars, women are from Venus: A practical guide for improving communication and getting what you want in your relationships.* New York: Harper Collins.

Gray, M. R., & Steinberg, L. (1999). Unpacking authoritative parenting: Reassessing a multidimensional construct. *Journal of Marriage and the Family, 61*, 574–587.

Greeff, A. P., & Malherbe, H. L. (2001). Intimacy and marital satisfaction in spouses. *Journal of Sex and Marital Therapy, 27,* 247–257.

Green, R. J. (2000). "Lesbians, gay men, and their parents": A critique of LaSala and the prevailing clinical 'wisdom.' *Family Process, 39,* 257–266.

Greenblat, C. (1983). The salience of sexuality in the early years of marriage. *Journal of Marriage and the Family, 45*(2), 289–299.

Griffin, W. A., & Greene, S. M. (1999). *Models of family therapy: The essential guide.* Philadelphia, PA: Brunner/Mazel, Inc.

Griffin, W. A., Parrella, J., Krainz, S., & Northey, S. (2002). Behavioral differences in families with and without a child with asthma: Testing the psychosomatic family model. *Journal of Social and Clinical Psychology, 21,* 226–255.

Grinwald, S. (1995). Communication-family characteristics: A comparison between stepfamilies (formed after death and divorce) and biological families. *Journal of Divorce and Remarriage, 24,* 183–196.

Grolnick, W. S., & Gurland, S. T. (2002). Mothering: Retrospect and prospect. In J. P. McHale & W. S. Grolnick (Eds.), *Retrospect and prospect in the psychological study of families* (pp. 5–33). Mahwah, NJ: Lawrence Erlbaum Associates.

Gross, P. (1986). Defining post-divorce remarriage families: A typology based on the subjective perceptions of children. *Journal of Divorce, 10,* 205–217.

Grote, N. K., & Clark, M. S. (2001). Perceiving unfairness in the family: Cause or consequence of marital distress. *Journal of Personality and Social Psychology, 80,* 281–293.

Grotevant, H. D., Fravel, D. L., Gorall, D., & Piper, J. (1999). Narratives of adoptive parents: Perspectives from individual and couple interviews. In B. H. Fiese, A. J. Sameroff, H. D. Grotevant, F. S. Wamboldt, S. Dickstein, & D. Fravel (Eds.), *The stories that families tell: Narrative coherence, narrative interaction, and relationship beliefs. Monographs of the Society for Research on Child Development, 64*(2, Serial No. 257). Malden, MA: Blackwell.

Groves, M. M., & Horm-Wingerd, D. M. (1991). Commuter marriages: Personal, family and career issues. *Sociology and Social Research, 75,* 212–217.

Grych, J. H., Wachsmuth-Schlaefer, T., & Klockow, L. L. (2002). Interparental aggression and young children's representations of family relationships. *Journal of Family Psychology, 16,* 259–272.

Gudykunst, W. B. (1994). *Bridging differences: Effective intergroup communication* (2nd ed.). Thousand Oaks, CA: Sage.

Gudykunst, W. B., & Lee, C. M. (2001). An agenda for studying ethnicity and family communication. *Journal of Family Communication, 1,* 75–86.

Gudykunst, W. B., Matsumoto, Y., Ting-Toomey, S., Nishida, T., Kim, K., & Heyman, S. (1996). The influence of cultural individualism-collectivism, self construals, and individual values on communication styles across cultures. *Human Communication Research, 22,* 510–543.

Gudykunst, W. B., & Nishida, T. (1986). The influence of cultural variability on perceptions of communication behavior associated with relationship terms. *Human Communication Research, 13,* 147–166.

Guerney, B. G. (Ed.). (1977). *Relationship enhancement.* San Francisco: Jossey-Bass.

Guerrero, L. K., & Afifi, W. A. (1995a). What parents don't know: Topic avoidance in parent-child relationships. In T. J. Socha and G. H. Stamp (Eds.), *Parents, children, and communication: Frontiers of theory and research* (pp. 219–245). Mahwah, NJ: Lawrence Erlbaum Associates.

Guerrero, L. K., & Afifi, W. A. (1995b). Some things are better left unsaid: Topic avoidance in family relationships. *Communication Quarterly, 43,* 276–296.

Guerrero, L. K., & Andersen, P. A. (1991). The waxing and waning of relational intimacy: Touch as a function of relational stage, gender, and touch avoidance. *Journal of Social and Personal Relationships, 8,* 147–165.

Guisinger, S., Cowan, P. A., & Schuldberg, D. (1989). Changing parent and spouse relations in the first years of remarriage of divorced fathers. *Journal of Marriage and the Family, 51,* 445–456.

Guldner, G. T., & Swensen, C. H. (1995). Time spent together and relationship quality: Long distance relationships as a test case. *Journal of Social and Personal Relationships, 12,* 313–320.

Gurman, A. S., & Fraenkel, P. (2002). The history of couple therapy: A millennial review. *Family Process, 41,* 199–259.

Guttman, J. (1993). *Divorce in psychosocial perspective: Theory and research*. Hillsdale, NJ: Lawrence Erlbaum Associates.

Haas, S. M., & Stafford, L. (1998). An initial examination of maintenance behaviors in gay and lesbian relationships. *Journal of Social and Personal Relationships, 15*, 846–855.

Haber, J. R., & Jacob, T. (1997). Marital interactions of male versus female alcoholics. *Family Process, 36*, 385–402.

Hackel, L. S., & Ruble, D. N. (1992). Changes in the marital relationship after the first baby is born: Predicting the impact of expectancy disconfirmation. *Journal of Personality and Social Psychology, 62*, 944–957.

Haefner, P. T., Notarius, C. L., & Pellegrini, D. S. (1991). Determinants of satisfaction with marital discussions: An exploration of husband-wife differences. *Behavioral Assessment, 13*, 67–82.

Hagestad, G. O. (1985). Continuity and connectedness. In V. L. Bengtson & J. F. Robertson (Eds.), *Grandparenthood* (pp. 31–48). Beverly Hills, CA: Sage.

Hahlweg, K., & Markman, H. J. (1988). Effectiveness of behavioral marital therapy: Empirical status of behavioral techniques in preventing and alleviating martial distress. *Journal of Consulting and Clinical Psychology, 56*, 440–447.

Hahlweg, K., Markman, H. J., Thurmaier, F., Engl, J., & Eckert, V. (1998). Prevention of marital distress: Results of a German prospective longitudinal study. *Journal of Family Psychology, 12*, 543–556.

Hahlweg, K., Reisner, L., Kohli, G., Vollmer, M., Schindler, L., & Revenstorf, D. (1984). Development and validity of a new system to analyze interpersonal communication: Kategoriensystem für partnerschaftliche interaktion. In K. Hahlweg & N. S. Jacobson (Eds.), *Marital interaction: Analysis and modification* (pp. 182–198). New York: Guilford.

Halberstadt, A. (1991). Toward an ecology of expressiveness: Family socialization in particular and a model in general. In R. Feldman & B. Rime (Eds.), *Fundamentals of nonverbal behavior*. Cambridge, UK: Cambridge University Press.

Hale, D. C. (1988). The impact of mother's incarceration on the family system: Research and recommendations. *Marriage and Family Review, 12*, 143–154.

Halford, W. K., Sanders, M. R., & Behrens, B. C. (2000). Repeating the errors of our parents? Family-of-origin spouse violence and observed conflict management in engaged couples. *Family Process, 39*, 219–235.

Hall, J. A., & Rose, S. D. (1987). Evaluation of parent training in groups for parent-adolescent conflict. *Social Work Research and Abstracts, 23*, 3–8.

Hamilton, E. B., Jones, M., & Hammen C. (1993). Maternal interaction style in affective disordered, physically ill, and normal women. *Family Process, 32*, 329–340.

Hammen, C. L., Gordon, D., Burge, D., Adrian, C., Janicke, C., & Hiroto, D. (1987). Communication patterns of mothers with affective disorders and their relationship to children's status and social functioning. In K. Hahlweg & M. J. Goldstein (Eds.), *Understanding major mental disorder* (pp. 103–119). New York: Family Process Press.

Hanks, H., & Stratton, P. (1988). Family perspectives on early sexual abuse. In K. Browne, C. Davis, & P. Stratton (Eds.), *Early prediction and prevention of child abuse* (pp. 245–266). New York: Wiley.

Hansson, R. O., & Remondet, J. H. (1987). Relationships and the aging family: A social psychological analysis. In S. Oskamp (Ed.), *Family processes and problems: Social psychological aspects* (pp. 262–283). Newbury Park, CA: Sage.

Harbach, R. L., & Jones, W. P. (1995). Family beliefs among adolescents at risk for substance abuse. *Journal of Drug Education, 25*, 1–9.

Hareven, T. K. (1991). The history of the family and the complexity of social change. *American Historical Review, 96*, 95–124.

Harold, R. D. (2000). Becoming a family: Parents' stories and their implications for practice, policy, and research. Mahwah, NJ: Lawrence Erlbaum Associates.

Harrington, C. M., & Metzler, A. E. (1997). Are adult children of dysfunctional families with alcoholism different from adult children of dysfunctional families without alcoholism? A look at committed, intimate relationships. *Journal of Counseling Psychology, 44*, 102–107.

Harrison-Speake, K., & Willis, F. N. (1995). Ratings of the appropriateness of touch among family members. *Journal of Nonverbal Behavior, 19*, 85–100.

Harter, S., Alexander, P. C., & Neimeyer, R. A. (1988). Long-term effects of incestuous child abuse in college women: Social adjustment, social cognition, and family characteristics. *Journal of Consulting and Clinical Psychology, 56,* 5–8.

Harter, S. L. (2000). Psychosocial adjustment of adult children of alcoholics: A review of the recent empirical literature. *Clinical Psychology Review, 20,* 311–337.

Harvey, J. H., & Omarzu, J. (1997). Minding the close relationship. *Personality and Social Psychology Review, 1,* 223–239.

Harvey, J. H., & Weber, A. L. (2002). *Odyssey of the Heart* (2nd ed.). Mahwah, NJ: Lawrence Erlbaum Associates.

Harwood, J. (2000a). Communicative predictors of solidarity in the grandparent-grandchild relationship. *Journal of Social and Personal Relationships, 17,* 743–766.

Harwood, J. (2000b). Communication media use in the grandparent-grandchild relationship. *Journal of Communication, 50,* 56–78.

Harwood, J. (2001). Comparing grandchildren's and grandparent's stake in their relationship. *International Journal of Aging and Human Development, 53,* 195–210.

Harwood, J., & Lin, M. (2000). Affiliation, pride, exchange, and distance in grandparents' accounts of relationships with their college-aged grandchildren. *Journal of Communication, 50,* 31–47.

Haslett, B. B., & Samter, W. (1997). Children communicating: The first 5 years. Mahwah, NJ. Lawrence Erlbaum Associates.

Hautzinger, M., Linden, M., & Hoffman, N. (1982). Distressed couples with and without a depressed partner: An analysis of their verbal interaction. *Journal of Behavior Therapy and Experimental Psychiatry, 13,* 307–314.

Havey, J. M., & Dodd, D. K. (1993). Variables associated with alcohol abuse among self-identified collegiate COAs and their peers. *Addictive Behaviors, 18,* 567–575.

Hawkins, J. D., Catalano, R. F., & Miller, J. Y. (1992). Risk and protective factors for alcohol and other drug problems in adolescence and early adulthood: Implications for substance abuse prevention. *Psychological Bulletin, 112,* 64–105.

Hawkins, M. W., Carrère, S., & Gottman, J. M. (2002). Marital sentiment override: Does it influence couples' perceptions? *Journal of Marriage and the Family, 64,* 193–201.

Hazan, C., & Shaver, P. R. (1987). Romantic love conceptualized as an attachment process. *Journal of Personality and Social Psychology, 52,* 511–524.

Hedlund, S., Fichter, M. M., Quadflieg, N., & Brandl, C. (2003). Expressed emotion, family environment, and parental bonding in bulimia nervosa: A 6-year investigation. *Eating and Weight Disorders, 8,* 26–35.

Heidemann, B., Suhomlinova, O., & O'Rand, A. M. (1998). Economic independence, economic status, and empty nest in midlife marital disruption. *Journal of Marriage and the Family, 60,* 219–231.

Heller, K., Sher, K. J., & Benson, C.S. (1982). Problems associated with risk overprediction in studies of offspring of alcoholics: Implications for prevention. *Clinical Psychology Review, 2,* 183–200.

Helms-Erikson, H. (2001). Marital quality ten years after the transition to parenthood: Implications of the timing of parenthood and the division of housework. *Journal of Marriage and the Family, 63,* 1099–1110.

Hendrick, S. S. (1988). The relationship assessment scale. *Journal of Marriage and the Family, 50,* 93–98.

Henshaw, S. K. (1998). Unintended pregnancy in the United States. *Family Planning Perspectives, 30,* 24–29.

Henwood, P. G., & Solano, C. H. (1994). Loneliness in young children and their parents. *Journal of Genetic Psychology, 155,* 35–45.

Hequembourg, A. L., & Farrell, M. P. (1999). Lesbian motherhood: Negotiation marginal-mainstream identities. *Gender and Society, 13,* 540–557.

Herman, J., & Hirschman, L. (1977). Fauther-daughter incest. *Signs: Journal of Women in Culture and Society, 2,* 735–756.

Herman, J. L., & Hirschman, L. (1981a). *Father-daughter incest.* Cambridge, MA: Harvard University Press.

Herman, J. L., & Hirschman, L. (1981b). Families at risk for father-daughter incest. *American Journal of Psychiatry, 138,* 967–970.

Hertenstein, M. J. (2002). Touch: Its communicative functions in infancy. *Human Development, 45,* 70–94.

Herzog, M. J., & Cooney, T. M. (2002). Parental divorce and perceptions of part interparental conflict: Influences on the communication of young adults. *Journal of Divorce and Remarriage, 36,* 89–109.

Hetherington, E. M. (1993). An overview of the Virginia longitudinal study of divorce and remarriage with a focus on early adolescence. *Journal of Family Psychology, 7,* 39–56.

Hetherington, E. M. (1999). Should we stray together for the sake of the children? In E. M. Hetherington (Ed.), *Coping with divorce, single parenting, and remarriage* (pp. 93–116). Mahwah, NJ: Lawrence Erlbaum Associates.

Hetherington, E. M., & Clingempeel, W. G. (1992). Coping with marital transitions: A family systems perspective. *Monographs of the Society for Research in Child Development, 57*(2-3, Serial No. 227).

Hetherington, E. M., Law, T. C., & O'Connor, T. G. (1993). Divorce: Challenges, changes, and new chances. In F. Walsh (Ed.), *Normal family processes* (2nd ed., pp. 208–234). New York: Guilford.

Hetsroni, A. (2000). Choosing a mate in television dating games: The influence of setting, culture, and gender. *Sex Roles, 42,* 83–106.

Heyman, R. E., & Slep, A. M. S. (2002). Do child abuse and interparental violence lead to adulthood family violence? *Journal of Marriage and Family, 64,* 864–870.

Higgins, D. J., & McCabe, M. P. (2000). Multi-type maltreatment and the long-term adjustment of adults. *Child Abuse Review, 9,* 6–18.

Hill, A., Weaver, C., & Blundell, J. E. (1990). Dieting concerns of 10-year-old girls and their mothers. *British Journal of Clinical Psychology, 29,* 346–348.

Hill, C. T., & Peplau, L. A. (1998). Premarital predictors of relationship outcomes: A 15-year follow-up of the Boston Couples Study. In T. N. Bradbury (Ed.), *The developmental course of marital dysfunction* (pp. 237–278). New York: Cambridge University Press.

Hill, R. (1949). *Families under stress.* New York: Harper & Brothers.

Hirokawa, R. Y., & Salazar, A. J. (1999). Task-group communication and decision-making performance. In L. R. Frey, D. S. Gouran, and M. S. Poole (Eds.), *The handbook of group communication theory and research* (pp. 167–191). Thousand Oaks, CA: Sage.

Hirshorn, B. A. (1998). Grandparents as caregivers. In M. E. Szinovacz (Ed.), *Handbook on grandparenthood* (pp. 200–214). Westport, CT: Greenwood Press.

Hochschild, A. R. (1997). *The time bind: When work becomes home and home becomes work.* New York: Henry Holt.

Hock, E., Eberly, M., Bartle-Haring, S., Ellwanger, P., & Widaman, K. F. (2001). Separation anxiety in parents of adolescents: Theoretical significance and scale development. *Child development, 72,* 284–298.

Hocker, J. L., & Wilmot, W. (1998). *Interpersonal conflict.* Dubuque, IA: Wm. C. Brown & Co.

Hofferth, S. J., & Sandberg, J. F. (2001). How American children spend their time? *Journal of Marriage and the Family, 63,* 295–308.

Hoffman, J. A. (1984). Psychological separation of late adolescents from their parents. *Journal of Counseling Psychology, 31,* 170–178.

Hoffman, S. D., & Duncan, G. J. (1988). What are the economic costs of divorce? *Demography, 25,* 641–645.

Hofstede, G. (1980). *Culture's consequences: International differences in work-related values.* Beverly Hills, CA: Sage.

Hofstede, G. (1994). *Cultures and organizations: Software of the mind.* London: Harper-Collins.

Holden, G. W. (1983). Avoiding conflict: Mothers as tacticians in the supermarket. *Child Development, 54,* 233–240.

Holman, T. B., & Jacquart, M. (1988). Leisure-activity patterns and marital satisfaction: A further test. *Journal of Marriage and the Family, 50,* 69–77.

Holtzworth-Munroe, A., Meehan, J. C., Herron, K., Rehman, U., & Stuart, G. L. (2003). Do subtypes of martially violent men continue to differ over time? *Journal of Consulting and Clinical Psychology, 71,* 728–740.

Holtzworth-Munroe, A., & Stuart, G. L. (1994). Typologies of male batterers: Three subtypes and the differences among them. *Psychological Bulletin, 116,* 476–497.

Honeycutt, J. M. (1993). Marital happiness, divorce status and partner differences in attributions about communication behaviors. *Journal of Divorce and Remarriage, 21,* 177–205.

Hooley, J. M., & Hahlweg, K. (1989). Marital satisfaction and marital communication in German and English couples. *Behavioral Assessment, 11,* 119–113.

Hooley, J. M., & Hiller, J. B. (1997). Family relationships and major mental disorders: Risk factors and preventive strategies. In S. Duck (Ed.), *Handbook of personal relationships* (2nd ed., pp. 621–648). Chichester, UK: Wiley.

Hooley, J. M., & Hiller, J. B. (1998). Expressed emotion and the pathogenesis of relapse in schizophrenia. In M. F. Lenzenweger & R. H. Dworkin (Eds.), *Origins and development of schizophrenia* (pp. 447–468). Washington, DC: American Psychological Association.

Hops, H., Biglan, A., Sherman, L., Arthur, J., Friedman, L., & Osteen, V. (1987). Home observations of family interactions of depressed women. *Journal of Consulting and Clinical Psychology, 55,* 341–346.

Horesh, N., Apter, A., Ishai, J., Danziger, Y., Miculincer, M., Stein, D., et al. (1996). Abnormal psychosocial situations and eating disorders in adolescence. *Journal of the American Academy of Child and Adolescent Psychiatry, 35,* 921–927.

House, J. S., Landis, K. R., & Umberson, D. (1988). Social relationships and health. *Science, 241,* 540–545.

Houts, R. M., Robins, E., & Huston, T. L. (1996). Compatibility and the development of premarital relationships. *Journal of Marriage and the Family, 58,* 7–20.

Howard, M. C. (1992). Adolescent substance abuse: A social learning theory perspective. In G. W. Lawson & A. W. Lawson (Eds.), *Adolescent substance abuse: Etiology, treatment, and prevention* (pp. 29–40). Gaithersburg, MD: Aspen Publishers.

Hsiung, R. O., & Bagozzi, R. P. (2003). Validating the relationship qualities of influence and persuasion with the family social relations model. *Human Communication Research, 29,* 81–110.

Huang, I. C. (1991). Family stress and coping. In S. J. Bahr (Ed.), *Family research: A sixty-year review* (pp. 289–334). Toronto, Canada: Lexington Books.

Hulsey, T. L., & Sexton, M. C. (1992). Perceptions of family functioning and the occurrence of childhood sexual abuse. *Bulletin of the Menninger Clinic, 56,* 438–450.

Humphrey, L. L. (1986). Family relations in bulimic-anorexic and nondistressed families. *International Journal of Eating Disorders, 5,* 223–232.

Humphrey, L. L. (1989). Observed family interactions among subtypes of eating disorders using structural analysis of social behavior. *Journal of Consulting and Clinical Psychology, 57,* 206–214.

Hunter, A. G., & Taylor, R. J. (1998). Grandparenthood in African American families. In M. E. Szinovacz (Ed.), *Handbook on grandparenthood* (pp. 70–86). Westport, CT: Greenwood Press.

Huston, T. L., & Burgess, R. L. (1979). Social exchange in developing relationships: An overview. In R. L. Burgess & T. L. Huston (Eds.), *Social exchange in developing relationships* (pp. 3–28). New York: Academic Press.

Huston, T. L., Caughlin, J. P., Houts, R. M., Smith, S. E., & George, L. J. (2001). The connubial crucible: Newlywed years as predictors of marital delight, distress, and divorce. *Journal of Personality and Social Psychology, 80,* 237–252.

Huston, T. L., & Houts, R. M. (1998). The psychological infrastructure of courtship and marriage: The role of personality and compatibility in romantic relationships. In T. N. Bradbury (Ed.), *The developmental course of marital dysfunction* (pp. 114–151). Cambridge, England: Cambridge University Press.

Huston, T. L., Niehuis, S., & Smith, S. E. (2001). The early marital roots of conjugal distress and divorce. *Current Directions in Psychological Science, 10,* 116–119.

Huston, T. L., Surra, A., Fitzgerald, N. M., & Cate, R. M. (1981). From courtship to marriage: Mate selection as an interpersonal process. In S. Duck & R. Gilmour (Eds.), *Personal relationships 2: Developing personal relationships* (pp. 53–88). London: Academic Press.

Huston, T. L., & Vangelisti, A. L. (1991). Socioemotional behavior and satisfaction in marital relationships: A longitudinal study. *Journal of Personality and Social Psychology, 61,* 721–733.

Huston, T. L., & Vangelesti, A. L. (1995). How parenthood affects marriage. In M. A. Fitzpatrick & A. L. Vangelisti (Eds.), *Explaining family interactions* (pp. 147–176). Thousand Oaks, CA: Sage.

Hutchinson, M. K. (2002). The influence of sexual risk communication between parents and daughters on sexual risk behaviors. *Family Relations, 51,* 238–247.

Infante, D. A., Chandler, T. A., & Rudd, J. E. (1989). Test of an argumentative skill deficiency model of interspousal violence. *Communication Monographs, 56,* 163–177.

Infante, D. A., Sabourin, T. C., Rudd, J. E., & Shannon, E. A. (1990). Verbal aggression in violent and nonviolent marital disputes. *Communication Quarterly, 38,* 361–371.

Jackson, A. P., Brown, R. P., & Patterson-Stewart, K. E. (2000). African-Americans in dual-career commuter marriages: An investigation of their expectations. *The Family Journal: Counseling and Therapy for Couples and Families, 8,* 22–36.

Jacob, T. (Ed.). (1987). *Family interaction and psychopathology.* New York: Plenum.

Jacob, T., & Johnson, S. (1997). Parenting influences on the development of alcohol abuse and dependence. *Alcohol Health and Research World, 21,* 204–209.

Jacob, T., & Johnson, S. L. (2001). Sequential interactions in the parent-child communications of depressed fathers and depressed mothers. *Journal of Family Psychology, 15,* 38–52.

Jacob, T., Krahn, G. L., & Leonard, K. (1991). Parent-child interactions in families with alcoholic fathers. *Journal of Consulting and Clinical Psychology, 59,* 176–181.

Jacob, T., & Leonard, K. (1986). Psychosocial functioning in children of alcoholic fathers, depressed fathers and control fathers. *Journal of Studies on Alcohol, 47,* 373–380.

Jacob, T., & Leonard, K. E. (1988). Alcoholic-spouse interaction as a function of alcoholism subtype and alcohol consumption interaction. *Journal of Abnormal Psychology, 97,* 231–237.

Jacob, T., Ritchey, D., Cvitkovic, J., & Blane, H. (1981). Communication styles of alcoholic and nonalcoholic families when drinking and not drinking. *Journal of Studies on Alcohol, 42,* 466–482.

Jacobs, J. A., & Gerson, K. (2001). Overworked individuals or overworked families?: Explaining trends in work, leisure, and family time. *Work and Occupations, 28,* 40–63.

Jacobson, N. S. (1992). Behavioral couple therapy: A new beginning. *Behavior Therapy, 23,* 493–506.

Jacobson, N. S., & Addis, A. (1993). Research on couples and couple therapy. What do we know? Where are we going? *Journal of Consulting and Clinical Psychology, 61,* 85–93.

Jacobson, N., & Gottman, J. M. (1998). *When men batter women: New insights into ending abusive relationships.* New York: Simon & Schuster.

Jacobson, N. S., Gottman, J. M., & Shortt, J. W. (1995). The distinction between type 1 and type 2 batterers— Further considerations: Reply to Ornduff et al. (1995), Margolin et al. (1995), and Walker (1995). *Journal of Family Psychology, 9,* 272–279.

Jacobson, N. S., Gottman, J. M., Waltz, J., Rushe, R., Babcock, J., & Holtzworth-Monroe, A. (1994). Affect, verbal content, and psychophysiology in the arguments of couples with a violent husband. *Journal of Consulting and Clinical Psychology, 62,* 982–988.

Jacobson, N. S., & Gurman, A. S. (Eds.). (1995). *Clinical handbook of couple therapy* (2nd ed.). New York: Guilford.

Jacobson, N. S., & Margolin, G. (1979). *Marital therapy: Strategies based on social learning and behavior exchange principles.* New York: Brunner/Mazel.

Jacobson, N. S., & Martin, B. (1976). Behavioral marriage therapy: Current status. *Psychological Bulletin, 83,* 540–566.

James, S., & Hunsley, J. (1995). The Marital Adaptability and Cohesion Evaluation Scale III: Is the relation with marital adjustment linear or curvilinear? *Journal of Family Psychology, 9,* 458–462.

Jarvis, T. J., Copeland, J., & Walton, L. (1998). Exploring the nature of the relationship between child sexual abuse and substance use among women. *Addiction, 93,* 865–875.

Jencius, M., & Rotter, J. C. (1998). Bedtime rituals and their relationship to childhood sleep disturbance. *Family Journal, 6,* 94–105.

Jewel, J. D., & Stark, K. D. (2003). Comparing the family environments of adolescents with conduct disorder or depression. *Journal of Child and Family Studies, 12,* 77–89.

Jimenez, J. (2002). The history of grandmothers in the African-American community. *The Social Service Review, 76,* 523–551.

Johnson, C. L. (1988). Relationships among family members and friends in later life. In R. M. Milardo (Ed.), *Families and social networks* (pp. 168–189). Newbury Park, CA: Sage.

Johnson, C. L. (1995). Determinants of adaptation of oldest old black Americans. *Journal of Aging Studies, 9,* 231–244.

Johnson, C. L. (2000). Perspective on American kinship in the later 1990s. *Journal of Marriage and the Family, 62,* 623–639.

Johnson, D. R., Amoloza, T. O., & Booth, A. (1992). Stability and developmental change in marital quality: A three-wave panel analysis. *Journal of Marriage and the Family, 54,* 582–594.

Johnson, H. D., LaVoie, J. C., & Mahoney, M. (2001). Interparental conflict and family cohesion: Predictors of loneliness, social anxiety, and social avoidance in late adolescence. *Journal of Adolescent Research, 16,* 304–318.

Johnson, M. P. (1991). Commitment to personal relationships. In W. H. Jones & D. W. Perlman (Eds.), *Advances in personal relationships* (Vol. 3, pp. 117–143). London: Jessica Kingsley.

Johnson, M. P., Caughlin, J. P., & Huston, T. L. (1999). The tripartite nature of marital commitment: Personal, moral, and structural reasons to stay married. *Journal of Marriage and the Family, 61,* 160–177.

Johnson, M. P., & Ferraro, K. J. (2000). Research on domestic violence in the 1990s: Making distinctions. *Journal of Marriage and the Family, 62,* 948–963.

Johnson, P. (2002). Predictors of family functioning within alcoholic families. *Contemporary Family Therapy, 24,* 371–384.

Johnson, S. L., & Jacob, T. (2000). Sequential interactions in the marital communication of depressed men and women. *Journal of Consulting and Clinical Psychology, 68,* 4–12.

Johnson, V., & Pandina, R. J. (1991). Effects of the family environment on adolescent substance use, delinquency, and coping styles. *American Journal of Drug and Alcohol Abuse, 17,* 71–88.

Joiner, T., Coyne, J. C., & Blalock, J. (1999). On the interpersonal nature of depression: Overview and synthesis. In T. Joiner & J. C. Coyne (Eds.), *The interactional nature of depression: Advances in interpersonal approaches* (pp. 3–19). Washington, DC: American Psychological Association.

Jones, D. J., Beach, S. R. H., & Jackson H. (2004). Family influences on health: A framework to organize research and guide intervention. In A. Vangelisti (Ed.), *Handbook of family communication* (pp. 647–672). Mahwah, NJ: Lawrence Erlbaum Associates.

Jones, D. C., & Houts, R. (1992). Parental drinking, parent-child communication, and social skills in young adults. *Journal of Studies on Alcohol, 53,* 48–56.

Jones, J. E. (1977). Patterns of transactional style deviance in the TAT's of parents of schizophrenics. *Family Process, 16,* 327–337.

Jones, S. M. (1978). Divorce and remarriage: A new beginning, a new set of problems. *Journal of Divorce, 2,* 217–227.

Jones, W. H., & Moore, T. L. (1990). Loneliness and social support. In M. Hojat & R. Crandall (Eds.), *Loneliness: Theory, research, and applications* (pp. 145–156). Newbury Park, CA: Sage.

Jorgenson, J., & Bochner, A. P. (2004). Imagining families through stories and rituals. In A. Vangelisti (Ed.), *Handbook of family communication* (pp. 513–538). Mahwah, NJ: Lawrence Erlbaum Associates.

Judd, L. J., Akiskal, H. S., Zeller, P. J., Paulus, M., Leon, A. C., Maser, J. D., et al. (2000). Psychosocial disability during the long-term course of unipolar major depressive disorder. *Archives of General Psychiatry, 57,* 375–380.

Jusczyk, P. W. (1997). *The discovery of spoken language.* Cambridge, MA: The MIT Press.

Kafka, R. R., & London, P. (1991). Communication in relationships and adolescent substance use: The influence of parents and friends. *Adolescence, 26,* 587–598.

Kahn, J., Coyne, J. C., & Margolin, G. (1985). Depression and marital disagreement: The social construction of despair. *Journal of Social and Personal Relationships, 2,* 447–461.

Kamo, Y. (1998). Asian grandparents. In M. E. Szinovacz (Ed.), *Handbook on grandparenthood* (pp. 97–112). Westport, CT: Greenwood Press.

Kamsner, S., & McCabe, M. P. (2000). The relationship between adult psychological adjustment and childhood sexual abuse, childhood physical abuse, and family-of-origin characteristics. *Journal of Interpersonal Violence, 15,* 1243–1261.

Kandel, D. B. (1978). Homophily, selection and socialization in adolescent friendships. *American Journal of Sociology, 84,* 427–436.

Kandel, D. B., & Andrews, K. (1987). Processes of adolescent socialization by parents and peers. *International Journal of the Addictions, 22,* 319–342.

Karney, B. R., & Bradbury, T. N. (1995). The longitudinal course of marital quality and stability: A review of theory, method, and research. *Psychological Bulletin, 118,* 3–34.

Karney, B. R., & Bradbury, T. N. (1997). Neuroticism, marital interaction, and the trajectory of marital satisfaction. *Journal of Personality and Social Psychology, 72,* 1075–1092.

Karney, B. R., Bradbury, T. N., & Johnson, M. D. (1999). Deconstructing stability: The distinction between the course of a close relationship and its endpoint. In J. M. Adams & W. H. Jones (Eds.), *Handbook of interpersonal commitment and relationship stability* (pp. 481–499). New York: Plenum.

Karney, B. R., & Coombs, R. H. (2000). Memory bias in long-term close relationships: Consistency or improvement? *Personality and Social Psychology Bulletin, 26,* 959–970.

Karney, B. R., & Fry, N. E. (2002). "But we've been getting better lately": Comparing prospective and retrospective views of relationships development. *Journal of Personality and Social Psychology, 82,* 222–238.

Karpel, M. A. (1980). Family secrets: Implications for research and therapy. *Family Process, 19,* 295–306.

Kashani, J. H., Burbach, D. J., & Rosenberg, T. K. (1988). Perception of family conflict resolution and depressive symptomatology in adolescents. *Journal of the American Academy of Child and Adolescent Psychiatry, 27,* 42–48.

Kashani, J. H., Canfield, L. A., Borduin, C. M., Soltys, S. M., & Reid, J. C. (1994). Perceived family social support: Impact on children. *Journal of the American Academy of Child and Adolescent Psychiatry, 33,* 819–823.

Kashani, J. H., Daniel, A. E., Dandoy, A. C., & Holcomb, W. R. (1992). Family violence: Impact on children. *Journal of the American Academy of Child and Adolescent Psychiatry, 31,* 181–189.

Kaslow, F. W. (1987). Couples or family therapy for prisoners and their significant others. *The American Journal of Family Therapy, 15,* 352–360.

Kaslow, N. J., Kaslow, F. W., & Farber, E. W. (1999). Theories and techniques of marital and family therapy. In M. Sussman, S. K. Steinmetz, & G. W. Peterson (Eds.), *The handbook of marriage and the family* (2nd ed., pp. 767–792). New York: Plenum Press.

Katz, L. F., Kramer, L., & Gottman, J. M. (1992). Conflict and emotions in marital, sibling, and peer relationships. In C. U. Shantz & W. W. Hartup (Eds.), *Conflict in child and adolescent development* (pp. 122–149). New York: Cambridge University Press.

Kaufman, J., & Zigler, E. (1987). Do abused children become abusive parents? *American Journal of Orthopsychiatry, 57,* 186–192.

Kawash, G., & Kozeluk, L. (1990). Self-esteem in early adolescence as a function of position within Olson's circumplex model of marital and family systems. *Social Behavior and Personality, 18,* 189–196.

Keller, H., Schoelmerich, A., & Eibl Eibesfeldt, I. (1988). Communication patterns in adult infant interaction in Western and non-Western cultures. *Journal of Cross Cultural Psychology, 19,* 427–445.

Kellermann, K. (1995). The conversation MOP: A model of patterned and pliable behavior. In D. E. Hewes (Ed.), *The cognitive bases of interpersonal communication* (pp. 181–224). Hillsdale, NJ: Lawrence Erlbaum Associates.

Kelly, A., & Fincham, F. D. (1999). Preventing marital distress: What does research offer? In R. Berger & M. T. Hannah (Eds.), *Preventive approaches in couples therapy* (pp. 361–390). Philadelphia, PA: Taylor & Francis.

Kelly, A. B., Fincham, F. D., & Beach, S. R. H. (2003). Communication skills in couples: A review and discussion of emerging perspectives. In J. O. Greene & B. R. Burleson (Eds.), *Handbook of communication and social interaction skills* (pp. 723–751). Mahwah, NJ: Lawrence Erlbaum Associates.

Kelly, A. B., Halford, W. K., & Young, R. M. (2002). Couple communication and female problem drinking: A behavioral observation study. *Psychology of Addictive Behaviors, 16,* 269–271.

Kelly, C., Huston, T. L., & Cate, R. M. (1985). Premarital relationship correlates of the erosion of satisfaction in marriage. *Journal of Social and Personal Relationships, 2,* 167–178.

Kelly, H. H., Berscheid, E., Christensen, A., Harvey, J. H., Huston, T. L., Levinger, G., McClintock, E., Peplau, L. A., & Peterson, D. R. (1983). *Close relationships.* New York: Freeman.

Kelly, K. J., Comello, M. L. G., & Hunn, S. C. P. (2002). Parent-child communication, perceived sanctions against drug use, and youth drug involvement. *Adolescence, 37,* 775–787.

Kennedy, S., Kiecolt-Glaser, J. K., & Glaser, R. (1988). Immunological consequences of acute and chronic stressors: Mediating role of interpersonal relationships. *British Journal of Medical Psychology, 61,* 77–85.

Kenrick, D. T., Groth, G. E., Trost, M. R., & Sadalla, E. K. (1993). Integrating evolutionary psychology and social exchange perspectives on relationships: Effects of gender, self-appraisal, and involvement level on mate selection criteria. *Journal of Personality and Social Psychology, 64,* 951–969.

Kenrick, D. T., Li, N. P., & Butner, J. (2003). Dynamical evolutionary psychology psychology: Individuals decision rules and emergent social norms. *Psychological Review, 110,* 3–28.

Kerig, P. K., & Lindahl, K. M. (Eds.). (2001). *Family observational coding systems: Resources for systematic research.* Mahwah, NJ: Lawrence Erlbaum Associates.

Kessler, R. C., McGonagle, K. A., Shanyang, Z., Nelson, C., Hughes, M., Eshleman, S., Wittchen, H. U., & Kendler, K. S. (1994). Lifetime and 12-month prevalence of DSM-III-R psychiatric disorders in the United States. *Archives of General Psychiatry, 51,* 8–19.

Kiecolt-Glaser, J. K., Bane, C., Glaser, R., & Malarkey, W. B. (2003). Love, marriage, and divorce: Newlyweds' stress hormones foreshadow relationship changes. *Journal of Consulting and Clinical Psychology, 71,* 176–188.

Kiecolt-Glaser, J., Fisher, L., Ogrocki, P., Stout, J. C., Speicher, C. E., & Glaser, R. (1987). Marital quality, marital disruption, and immune function. *Psychosomatic Medicine, 49,* 31–34.

Kiecolt-Glaser, J., Glaser, R., Cacioppo, J. R., MacCallum, R. C., Snydersmith, M., Kim, C., & Malarkey, W. B. (1997). Marital conflict in older adults: Endocrinological and immunological correlates. *Psychosomatic Medicine, 59,* 339–349.

Kiecolt-Glaser, J., Malarkey, W. B., Chee, M. A., Newton, T., Cacioppo, J. T., Mao, H. Y., et al. (1993). Negative behavior during marital conflict is associated with immunological down-regulation. *Psychosomatic Medicine, 55,* 395–409.

Kiecolt-Glaser, J., & Newton, T. L. (2001). Marriage and health: His and hers. *Psychological Bulletin, 127,* 472–503.

Kiecolt-Glaser, J., Newton, T. L., Cacioppo, J. T., MacCallum, R. C., Glaser, R., & Malarkey, W. B. (1996). Marital conflict and endocrine function: Are men really more physiologically affected than women? *Journal of Consulting and Clinical Psychology, 64,* 324–332.

Kilpatrick, D. G., Acierno, R., Saunders, B., Resnick, H. S., Best, C. L., & Schnurr, P. P. (2000). Risk factors for adolescent substance abuse and dependence: Data from a national sample. *Journal of Consulting and Clinical Psychology, 68,* 19–30.

Kimberly, J. A., & Serovich, J. M. (1999). The role of family and friend social support in reducing risk behaviors among HIV-positive gay men. *AIDS Education and Prevention, 11,* 465–475.

King, V. (2002). Parental divorce and interpersonal trust in adult offspring. *Journal of Marriage and Family, 64,* 642–656.

King, V. (2003). The legacy of a grandparent divorce: Consequences for ties between grandparents and grandchildren. *Journal of Marriage and Family, 65,* 170–183.

King, V., & Elder, G. H. (1995). American children view their grandparents: Linked lives across three rural generations. *Journal of Marriage and the Family, 57,* 165–178.

King, V., & Elder, G. H. (1997). The legacy of grandparenting: Childhood experiences with grandparents and current involvement with grandchildren. *Journal of Marriage and the Family, 59,* 848–859.

Kinzl, J. F., Traweger, C., Guenther, V., & Biebl, W. (1994). Family background and sexual abuse associated with eating disorders. *American Journal of Psychiatry, 151,* 1127–1131.

Kirchler, E. (1989). Everyday life experiences at home: An interaction diary approach to assess marital relationships. *Journal of Family Psychology, 2,* 311–336.

Kirchler, E., Rodler, C., Hölzl, E., & Meier, K. (2001). *Conflict and decision-making in close relationships: Love, money, and daily routines.* Philadelphia, PA: Taylor & Francis.

Kirkpatrick. L. A., & Davis, K. E. (1994). Attachment style, gender, and relationship stability: A longitudinal analysis. *Journal of Personality and Social Psychology, 66,* 502–512.

Kitzmann, K. M., Cohen, R., & Lockwood, R. L. (2002). Are only children missing out? Comparison of the peer-related social competence of only children and siblings. *Journal of Social and Personal Relationships, 19,* 299–316.

Klein, R. C. A., & Milardo, R. M. (2000). The social context of couple conflict: Support and criticism from informal third parties. *Journal of Social and Personal Relationships, 17,* 618–637.

Klein, D. M., & White, J. M. (1996). *Family theories: An introduction.* Thousand Oaks, CA: Sage.

Kliewer, W., Fearnow, M. D., & Miller, P. A. (1996). Coping socialization in middle childhood: Tests of maternal and paternal influences. *Child Development, 67,* 2339–2357.

Knapp, M. L. (1978). *Social intercourse: From greeting to goodbye.* Boston: Allyn & Bacon.

Knapp, M. L. (1984). *Interpersonal communication and human relationships.* Boston: Allyn & Bacon.

Knapp, M. L., & Vangelisti, A. L. (2000). *Interpersonal communication and human relationships* (4th ed.). Boston, MA: Allyn & Bacon.

Knok, S. L. (1988). The family and hierarchy. *Journal of Marriage and the Family, 50,* 957–966.

Koerner, A. F., & Cvancara, K. E. (2002). The influence of conformity orientation on communication patterns in family conversations. *Journal of Family Communication, 2,* 133–152.

Koerner, A. F., & Fitzpatrick, M. A. (1997). Family type and conflict: The impact of conversation orientation and conformity orientation of conflict in the family. *Communication Studies, 48,* 59–75.

Koerner, A. F., & Fitzpatrick, M. A. (2002a). You never leave your family in a fight: The impact of family of origin on conflict-behavior in romantic relationships. *Communication Studies, 53*, 234–251.

Koerner, A. F., & Fitzpatrick, M. A. (2002b). Nonverbal communication and marital adjustment and satisfaction: The role of decoding relationship relevant and relationship irrelevant affect. *Communication Monographs, 69*, 33–51.

Koerner, A. F., & Fitzpatrick, M. A. (2004). Communication in intact families. In A. L. Vangelisti (Ed.), *Handbook of family communication* (pp. 177–195). Mahwah, NJ: Lawrence Erlbaum Associates.

Kog, E., & Vandereycken, W. (1985). Family characteristics of anorexia nervosa and bulimia: A review of the research literature. *Clinical Psychology Review, 5*, 159–180.

Kohn, M. L. (1977). *Class and conformity: A study in values.* Chicago: University of Chicago Press.

Koopmans, M. (1994). Self-reports of sexual abuse, mental health status, and perceived confusion of family roles: A retrospective study of college students. *Psychological Reports, 75*, 339–347.

Kowal, A., Kramer, L., Krull, J. L., & Crick, N. R. (2002). Children's perceptions of the fairness of parental preferential treatment and their socioemotional well-being. *Journal of Family Psychology, 16*, 297–306.

Kowner, R. (2001). Psychological perspective on human developmental stability and fluctuating asymmetry: Sources, applications and implication. *British Journal of Psychology, 92*, 447–469.

Kramer, L., & Baron, L. A. (1995). Parental perceptions of children's sibling relationships. *Family Relations, 44*, 95–103.

Kramer, L., & Radey, C. (1997). Improving sibling relationships among young children: A social skills training model. *Family Relations, 46*, 237–246.

Kraut, R., Patterson, M., Lundmark, V., Kiesler, S., Mukopadhyay, T., & Scherlis, W. (1998). Internet paradox: A social technology that reduces social involvement and psychological well-being? *American Psychologist, 53*, 1017–1031.

Krcmar, M. (1996). Family communication patterns, discourse behavior, and child television viewing. *Human Communication Research, 23*, 251–277.

Kreider, R. M., & Fields, J. M. (2002). Number, timing, and duration of marriages and divorces: 1996. *Current Population Reports* P70-80. Washington, DC: US Census Bureau.

Krokoff, L. (1984). The anatomy of negative affect in working-class marriages (Doctoral dissertation, University of Illinois at Urbana-Champaign, 1984). *Dissertation Abstracts International, 45* (07), 2041A. (UMI No. 8422109)

Krokoff, L. J. (1991). Communication orientation as a moderator between strong negative affect and marital satisfaction. *Behavioral Assessment, 13*, 51–65.

Krokoff, L. J., Gottman, J. M., & Roy, A. K. (1988). Blue-collar and white-collar marital interactions and communication orientation. *Journal of Social and Personal Relationships, 5*, 201–221.

Kurdek, L. A. (1991). Predictors of increases in marital distress in newlywed couples: A 3-year prospective longitudinal study. *Developmental Psychology, 27*, 627–636.

Kurdek, L. A. (1993). Nature and prediction of changes in marital quality for first-time parent and nonparent husbands and wives. *Journal of Family Psychology, 6*, 255–265.

Kurdek, L. A. (1994). Areas of conflict for gay, lesbian, and heterosexual couples: What couples argue about influences relationship satisfaction. *Journal of Marriage and the Family, 56*, 923–934.

Kurdek, L. A. (1995). Assessing multiple determinants of relationship commitment in cohabiting gay, cohabiting lesbian, dating heterosexual, and married heterosexual couples. *Family Relations, 44*, 261–266.

Kurdek, L. A. (1998a). Relationship outcomes and their predictors: Longitudinal evidence from heterosexual married, gay cohabiting, and lesbian cohabiting couples. *Journal of Marriage and the Family, 60*, 553–568.

Kurdek, L. A. (1998b). Developmental changes in marital satisfaction: A 6-year prospective longitudinal study of newlywed couples. In T. N. Bradbury (Ed.), *The developmental course of marital dysfunction* (pp. 180–204). New York: Cambridge University Press.

Kurdek, L. A. (2000). Attractions and constraints as determinants of relationship commitment: Longitudinal evidence from gay, lesbain, and heterosexual couples. *Personal Relationships, 7*, 245–262.

Kurdek, L. A. (2003). Differences between gay and lesbian cohabiting couples. *Journal of Social and Personal Relationships, 20*, 411–436.

Kurdek, L. A., & Fine, M. A. (1993). The relation between family structure and young adolescents' appraisals of family climate and parenting behavior. *Journal of Family Issues, 14*, 279–290.

L'Abate, L. (1990). *Building family competence: Primary and secondary prevention strategies*. Newbury Park, CA: Sage.

Labrecque, J., & Line, R. (2001). Children's influence on family decision-making: A restaurant study. *Journal of Business Research, 54*, 173–176.

Lacey, J. H. (1990). Incest, incestuous fantasy and indecency: A clinical catchment area study of normal weight bulimic women. *British Journal of Psychiatry, 157*, 399–403.

Lackman, C., & Lanasa, J. M. (1993). Family decision-making theory: An overview and assessment. *Psychology and Marketing, 10*, 81–93.

Lahey, B. B., Conger, R. D., Atkeson, B. M., & Treiber, F. A. (1984). Parenting behavior and emotional status of physically abusive mothers. *Journal of Consulting and Clinical Psychology, 52*, 1062–1071.

Lang, F. R., & Carstensen, L. L. (2002). Time counts: Future time perspective, goals, and social relationships. *Psychology and Aging, 17*, 125–139.

Lang, F. R., Staudinger, U. M., & Carstensen, L. L. (1998). Perspectives on socioemotional selectivity in late life: How personality and social context do (and do not) make a difference. *Journals of Gerontology: Psychological Sciences, 53*, P21–P30.

Lansdale, D. (2002). Touching lives: Opening doors for elders in retirement communities through e-mail and the internet. In R. W. Morrell (Ed.), *Older adults, health information, and the world wide web* (pp. 133–151). Mahwah, NJ: Lawrence Erlbaum Associates.

LaRossa, R., & Reitzes, D. C. (1993). Symbolic Interactionism and family studies. In P. G. Boss, W. J. Doherty, R. LaRossa, W. R. Schumm, & S. K. Steinmetz (Eds.), *Sourcebook for family theories and methods: A contextual approach* (pp. 135–163). New York: Plenum.

Larsen, A. S., & Olson, D. H. (1989). Predicting marital satisfaction using PREPARE: A replication study. *Journal of Marital and Family Therapy, 15*, 311–322.

Larson, J. (1992). Understanding stepfamilies. *American Demographics, 14*, 36–39.

Larzelere, R. E., Klein, M., Schumm, W. R., & Alibrando, S. A. (1989). Relations of spanking and other parenting characteristics to self-esteem and perceived fairness of parental discipline. *Psychological Reports, 64*, 1140–1142.

Lasegue, E. C. (1873). On hysterical anorexia. *Medical Times Gazette, 2*, 367–369.

Latzer, Y., Hochdorf, Z., Bachar, E., & Canetti, L. (2002). Attachment style and family functioning as discriminating factors in eating disorders. *Contemporary Family Therapy, 24*, 581–599.

Lauer, R. H., & Lauer, J. C. (1991). The long-term relational consequences of problematic family backgrounds. *Family Relations, 40*, 286–290.

Laursen, B., & Collins, W. A. (2004). Parent-child communication during adolescence. In A. Vangelisti (Ed.), *Handbook of family communication* (pp. 333–348). Mahwah, NJ: Lawrence Erlbaum Associates.

Lawton, L., Silverstein, M., & Bengtson, V. (1994). Affection, social contact, and geographic distance between adult children and their parents. *Journal of Marriage and the Family, 56*, 57–68.

Lazarus, R. S. (1966). *Psychological stress and the coping process*. New York: McGraw-Hill.

Lazarus, R. S., & Launier, R. (1978). Stress-related transactions between person and environment. In L. A. Pervin & M. Lewis (Eds.), *Perspectives in interactional psychology* (pp. 360–392). New York: Plenum.

Lederer, G. S., & Lewis, J. (1991). The transition to couplehood. In F. H. Brown (Ed.), *Reweaving the family tapestry: A multigenerational approach to families* (pp. 94–113). New York: Norton.

Ledoux, S., Miller, P., Choquet, M., & Plant, M. (2002). Family structure, parent-child relationships, and alcohol and other drug use among teenagers in France and the United Kingdom. *Alcohol and Alcoholism, 37*, 52–60.

Lee, C. K. C., & Beatty, S. E. (2002). Family structure and influences in decision-making. *Journal of Consumer Marketing, 19*, 24–41.

Lee, C. M., & Gotlib, I. H. (1991). Adjustment of children of depressed mothers: A 10-month follow-up. *Journal of Abnormal Psychology, 100*, 473–477.

Leeds-Hurwitz, W. (2002). *Wedding as text: Communicating cultural identities through ritual*. Mahwah, NJ: Lawrence Erlbaum Associates.

LeGrange, D., Eisler, I., Dare, D., & Hodes, M. (1992). Family criticism and self-starvation—A study of expressed emotion. *Journal of Family Therapy, 14*, 177–192.

Le Poire, B. A., Erlandson, K. T., & Hallett, J. S. (1998). Punishing versus reinforcing strategies of drug discontinuance: Effect of persuaders' drug use. *Health Communication, 10,* 293–316.

Le Poire, B. A., Hallett, J. S., & Erlandson, K. T. (2000). An initial test of Inconsistent Nurturing as Control Theory: How partners of drug abusers assist their partners' sobriety. *Human Communication Research, 26,* 432–457.

Lerner, R. M., & Spanier, G. B. (1978). *Children's influences on marital and family interaction: A life-span perspective.* New York: Academic Press.

Lester, M. E., & Doherty, W. J. (1983). Couples' long-term evaluations of their marriage encounter experience. *Journal of Marital and Family Therapy, 9,* 183–188.

Letellier, P. (1994). Gay and bisexual male domestic violence victimization: Challenges to feminist theory and responses to violence. *Violence and Victims, 9,* 95–106.

Levenson, R. W., Carstensen, L. L., & Gottman, J. M. (1994). The influence of age and gender on affect, physiology, and their interrelations: A study of long-term marriages. *Journal of Personality and Social Psychology, 67,* 56–68.

Levenson, R. W., & Gottman, J. M. (1985). Physiological affective predictors of change in relationship satisfaction. *Journal of Personality and Social Psychology, 49,* 85–94.

Levine, P. (1996). Eating disorders and their impact on family systems. *Handbook of relational diagnosis and dysfunctional family patterns* (pp. 463–476). New York: Wiley.

Levine, T. R., & Boster, F. J. (2001). The effects of power and message variables on compliance. *Communication Monographs, 68,* 28–46.

Levy, S. Y., Wamboldt, F. S., & Fiese, B. H. (1997). Family-of-origin experiences and conflict resolution behaviors of young adult dating couples. *Family Process, 36,* 297–310.

Lewinsohn, P. M. (1974). A behavioral approach to depression. In R. J. Friedman & M. M. Katz (Eds.), *The psychology of depression: Contemporary theory and research* (pp. 157–185). Washington, DC: Winston-Wiley.

Lewinsohn, P. M., & Rosenbaum, M. (1987). Recall of parental behavior by acute depressives, remitted depressives, and nondepressives. *Journal of Personality and Social Psychology, 52,* 611–619.

Lewis, R. A., & Spanier, G. B. (1979). Theorizing about the quality and stability of marriage. In W. R. Burr, R. Hill, F. I. Nye, & I. L. Reiss (Eds.), *Contemporary theories about the family.* New York: The Free Press.

Lie, G. Y., & Gentlewarrior, S. (1991). Intimate violence in lesbian relationships: Discussion of survey findings and practice implications. *Journal of Social Service Research, 15,* 41–59.

Lie, G. Y., Schilit, R., Bush, J., Montagne, M., & Reyes, L. (1991). Lesbians in currently aggressive relationships: How frequently do they report aggressive past relationships? *Violence and Victims, 6,* 121–135.

Lin, M., & Harwood, J. (2003). Accommodation predictors of grandparent-grandchild relational solidarity in Taiwan. *Journal of Social and Personal Relationships, 20,* 537–564.

Lin, M., Harwood, J., & Bonnesen, J. L. (2002). Conversation topics and communication satisfaction in grandparent-grandchild relationships. *Journal of Language and Social Psychology, 21,* 302–323.

Lindahl, K., Clements, M., & Markman, H. (1998). The development of marriage: A 9-year perspective. In T. N. Bradbury (Ed.), *The developmental course of marital dysfunction* (pp. 205–236). New York: Cambridge University Press.

Linden, M., Hautzinger, M., & Hoffman, N. (1983). Discriminant analysis of depressive interactions. *Behavior Modification, 7,* 403–422.

Linker, J. S., Stolberg, A. L., & Green, R. G. (1999). Family communication as a mediator of child adjustment to divorce. *Journal of Divorce and Remarriage, 30,* 83–97.

Lloyd, S. A. (1996). Physical aggression, distress, and everyday marital interaction. In D. D. Cahn & S. A. Lloyd (Eds.), *Family violence from a communication perspective* (pp. 177–198). Thousand Oaks, CA: Sage.

Lobdell, J., & Perlman, D. (1986). The intergenerational transmission of loneliness: A study of college females and their parents. *Journal of Marriage and the Family, 48,* 589–595.

Lonigan, C. J., Elbert, J. C., & Johnson, S. B. (1998). Empirically supported psychosocial interventions for children: An overview. *Journal of Clinical Child Psychology, 27,* 138–145.

Long, P. J., & Jackson, J. L. (1994). Childhood sexual abuse: An examination of family functioning. *Journal of Interpersonal Violence, 9,* 270–277.

Longmore, M. A., Manning, W. D., & Giordano, P. C. (2001). Preadolescent parenting strategies and teens' dating and sexual initiation: A longitudinal analysis. *Journal of Marriage and Family, 63,* 322–335.

Lopata, H. (1973). *Widowhood in an American city.* Cambridge, MA: Schenkman.

Lopata, H. Z. (1999). In-laws and the concept of family. In B. H. Settles, S. K. Steinmetz, G. W. Peterson, & M. B. Sussman (Eds.), *Concepts and definitions of family for the 21st century* (pp. 161–172). New York: Haworth Press.

Luckey, I. (1994). African American elders: The support network of generational kin. *Families in Society: The Journal of Contemporary Human Services, 75,* 82–89.

Lundberg, O. (1993). The impact of childhood living conditions on illness and mortality in adulthood. *Social Science Medicine, 8,* 1047–1052.

Lussier, G., Deater-Deckard, K., Dunn, J., & Davies, L. (2002). Support across two generations children's closeness to grandparents following parental divorce and remarriage. *Journal of Family Psychology, 16,* 363–376.

Lye, D. N. (1996). Adult child-parent relationships. *Annual Review of Sociology, 22,* 79–102.

Lynch, E. W. (1998). Developing cross-cultural competence. In E. W. Lynch & M. J. Hanson (Eds.), *Developing cross-cultural competence: A guide for working with children and families* (pp. 47–89). Baltimore, MD: Brookes.

Lyons, R. F., Mickelson, K. D., Sullivan, M. J. L., & Coyne, J. C. (1998). Coping as a communal process. *Journal of Social and Personal Relationships, 15,* 579–605.

Lyster, R. F., Russell, M. N., & Hiebert, J. (1995). Preparation for remarriage: Consumers' views. *Journal of Divorce and Remarriage, 24,* 143–157.

Mares, M. (1995). The aging family. In M. A. Fitzpatrick & A. L. Vangelisti (Eds.), *Explaining family interactions* (pp. 344–374). Thousand Oaks, CA: Sage.

MacBrayer, E. K., Smith, G. T., McCarthy, D. M., Demos, S., & Simmons, J. (2001). The role of family of origin food-related experiences in bulimic symptomatology. *International Journal of Eating Disorders, 30,* 149–160.

Maccoby, E. E. (2002). Parenting effects: Issues and controversies. In J. G. Borkowski, S. L. Ramey, & M. Bristol-Power (Eds.), *Parenting and the child's world: Influences on academic, intellectual, and social-emotional development* (pp. 35–46). Mahwah, NJ: Lawrence Erlbaum Associates.

Maccoby, E. E., & Martin, J. A. (1983). Socialization in the context of the family: Parent-child interaction. In E. M. Hetherington (Ed.), *Handbook of child psychology: Vol. 4. Socialization, personality, and social development* (pp. 1–101). New York: Wiley.

MacDermid, S. M., Huston, T. L., & McHale, S. M. (1990). Changes in marriage associated with the transition to parenthood: Individual differences as a function of sex-role attitudes and changes in the division of household labor. *Journal of Marriage and the Family, 52,* 475–486.

MacDonald, W. L., & DeMaris, A. (1995). Remarriage, stepchildren, and marital conflict: Challenges to the incomplete institutionalization hypothesis. *Journal of Marriage and the Family, 57,* 387–398.

Mace, D. R. (1975). We call it ACME. *Small Group Behavior, 6,* 31–44.

Macmillian, H. L., Fleming, J. E., Troome, N., Boyle, M. H., & Wong, M., Racine, Y. A., et al. (1997). Prevalence of child physical or sexual abuse in the community: Results from the Ontario health supplement. *Journal of the American Medical Association, 278,* 131–135.

Magnuson, S., & Norem, K. (1999). Challenges for higher education couples in commuter marriages: Insights for couples and counselors who work with them. *The Family Journal: Counseling and Therapy for Couples and Families, 7,* 125–134.

Malarkey, W. B., Kiecolt-Glaser, J. K., Pearl, D., & Glaser, R. (1994). Hostile behavior during marital conflict alters pituitary and adrenal hormones. *Psychosomatic Medicine, 56,* 41–51.

Malkus, B. M. (1994). Family dynamic and structural correlates of adolescent substance abuse: A comparison of families of non-substance abusers and substance abusers. *Journal of Child and Adolescent Substance Abuse, 3,* 39–52.

Mallinckrodt, B., McCreary, B. A., & Robertson, A. K. (1995). Co-occurrence of eating disorders and incest: The role of attachment, family environment, and social competencies. *Journal of Counseling Psychology, 42,* 178–186.

Mancini, J. A., & Blieszner, R. (1994). Coping with aging. In P. C. McKenry & S. J. Price (Ed.), *Families and change: Coping with stressful events* (pp. 111–125). Thousand Oaks, CA: Sage.

Mares, M. (1995). The aging family. In M. A. Fitzpatrick & A. L. Vangelisti (Eds.), *Explaining family interactions* (pp. 344–374). Thousand Oaks, CA: Sage.

Margolin, G., & Gordis, E. B. (2000). The effects of family and community violence on children. *Annual Review of Psychology, 51,* 445–479.

Margolin, G., John, R. S., Ghosh, C. M., & Gordis, E. B. (1996). Family interaction process: An essential tool for exploring abusive relationships. In D. D. Cahn & S. A. Lloyd (Eds.), *Family violence from a communication perspective* (pp. 37–58). Thousand Oaks, CA: Sage.

Markman, H. J. (1981). Prediction of marital distress: A 5-year follow-up. *Journal of Consulting and Clinical Psychology, 49,* 760–762.

Markman, H. J. (1984). The longitudinal study of couples' interactions: Implications for understanding and predicting the development of marital distress. In K. Hahlweg & N. S. Jacobson (Eds.), *Marital interaction: Analysis and modification* (pp. 253–281). New York: Guilford.

Markman, H. J., Floyd, F. J., Stanley, S. M., & Jamieson, K. (1984). A cognitive-behavioral program for the prevention of marital and family distress: Issues in program development and delivery. In K. Hahlweg & N. S. Jacobson (Eds.), *Marital interaction: Analysis and modification* (pp. 396–428). New York: Guilford.

Markman, H. J., & Hahlweg, K. (1993). The prediction and prevention of marital distress: An international perspective. *Clinical Psychology Review, 13,* 29–43.

Markman, H. J., & Notarius, C. I. (1987). Coding marital and family interaction: Current status. In T. Jocob (Ed.), *Family interaction and psychopathology: Theories, methods, and findings* (pp. 329–390). New York: Plenum.

Markman, H. J., Renick, M. J., Floyd, F. J., Stanley, S. M., & Clements, M. (1993). Preventing marital distress through communication and conflict management training: A 4- and 5-year follow-up. *Journal of Consulting and Clinical Psychology, 61,* 70–77.

Markowitz, F. E. (2001). Attitudes and family violence: Linking intergenerational and cultural theories. *Journal of Family Violence, 16,* 205–218.

Markson, S., & Fiese, B. H. (2000). Family rituals as a protective factor against anxiety for children with asthma. *Journal of Pediatric Psychology, 25,* 471–479.

Markus, H., & Kitayama, S. (1991). Culture and the self: Implications for cognition, emotion, and motivation. *Psychological Review, 98,* 224–253.

Marshall, L. L., & Rose, P. (1990). Premarital violence: The impact of family of origin violence, stress, and reciprocity. *Violence and Victims, 5,* 51–64.

Martin, J. I. (1995). Intimacy, loneliness, and openness to feelings in adult children of alcoholics. *Health and Social Work, 20,* 52–59.

Martin, M. J., Schumm, W. R., Bugaighis, M. A., Jurish, A. P., & Bollman, S. R. (1987). Family violence and adolescents' perceptions of outcomes of family conflict. *Journal of Marriage and the Family, 49,* 165–171.

Massachusetts Medical Society Committee on Violence. (1996). *Partner violence: How to recognize and treat victims of abuse: A guide for physicians and other health care professionals* (2nd ed.). Waltham, MA: Massachusetts Medical Society.

Matthews, T. J., & Hamilton, B. E. (2002). *Mean age of mother, 1970–2000.* National Vital Statistics Reports, 51(1). U.S. Department of Health and Human Services, Centers for Disease Control and Prevention. National Center for Health Statistics. Available at http://www.cdc.gov/nchs/data/nvsr51/nvsr51_01.pdf.

Mazzeo, S. E., & Espelage, D. L. (2002). Association between childhood physical and emotional abuse and disordered eating behaviors in female undergraduates: An investigation of the mediating role of alexithymia and depression. *Journal of Consulting and Clinical Psychology, 49,* 86–100.

McCabe, S. B., & Gotlib, I. H. (1993). Interactions of couples with and without a depressed spouse: Self-report and observations of problems-solving interactions. *Journal of Social and Personal Relationships, 10,* 589–599.

McCoy, K., Brody, G. H., & Stoneman, Z. (2002). Temperament and the quality of best friendships: Effect of same-sex sibling relationships. *Family Relations, 51,* 248–255.

McCubbin, H., & Dahl, B. (1985). *Marriage and family: Individuals and life cycles.* New York: John Wiley.

McCubbin, H. I., Joy, C. B., Cauble, A. E., Comeau, J. K., Patterson, J. M., & Needle, R. H. (1980). Family stress and coping: A decade review. *Journal of Marriage and the Family, 42,* 855–871.

McCubbin, H. I., Nevin, R. S., Cauble, A. E., Larsen, A., Comeau, J. K., & Patterson, J. M. (1982). Family coping with chronic illness: The case of cerebral palsy. In H. I. McCubbin, A. E. Cauble, & J. M. Patterson (Eds.), *Family stress, coping, and social support* (pp. 169–185). Springfield, IL: Charles C Thomas.

McCubbin, H. I., & Patterson, J. M. (1982). Family adaptation to crisis. In H. I. McCubbin, A. E. Cauble, & J. M. Patterson (Eds.), *Family stress, coping, and social support* (pp. 26–47). Springfield, IL: Charles C Thomas.

McCubbin, H. I., & Patterson, J. M. (1985). Adolescent stress, coping, and adaptation: A normative family perspective. In G. K. Leigh & G. W. Patterson (Eds.), *Adolescents in families* (pp. 256–276). Cincinnati, OH: Southwestern.

McCullough, P. G., & Rutenberg, S. K. (1988). Launching children and moving on. In B. Carter & M. McGoldrick (Eds.), *The changing family life cycle: A framework for family therapy* (2nd ed., pp. 285–309). New York: Gardner Press.

McDonald, G. W. (1980). Family power: The assessment of a decade of theory and research, 1970–1979. *Journal of Marriage and the Family, 42,* 841–852.

McGinnis, S. L. (2003). Cohabitating, dating, and perceived costs of marriage: A model of marriage entry. *Journal of Marriage and the Family, 65,* 105–116.

McGoldrick, M. (1988). The joining of families through marriage: The new couple. In B. Carter & M. McGoldrick (Eds.), *The changing family life cycle: A framework for family therapy* (2nd ed., pp. 209–233). New York: Gardner Press.

McGoldrick, M., Heiman, M., & Carter, B. (1993). The changing family life cycle: A perspective on normalcy. In F. Walsh (Ed.), *Normal family processes* (2nd ed., pp. 405–443). New York: Guilford.

McGrane, D., & Carr, A. (2002). Young women at risk for eating disorders: Perceived family dysfunction and parental psychological problems. *Contemporary Family Therapy, 24,* 385–395.

McHale, J. P. (1997). Overt and convert coparenting processes in the family. *Family Process, 36,* 183–201.

McHale, J. P., & Grolnick, W. S. (Eds.). (2002). *Retrospect and prospect in the psychological study of families.* Mahwah, NJ: Lawrence Erlbaum Associates.

McHale, J. P., Lauretti, A., Kuersten-Hogan, R., & Rasmussen, J. L. (2000). Parental reports of coparenting and observed coparenting behavior during the toddler period. *Journal of Family Psychology, 14,* 220–236.

McHale, J. P., Lauretti, A., Talbot, J., & Pouquette, C. (2002). Retrospect and prospect. In J. P. McHale & W. S. Grolnick (Eds.), *Retrospect and prospect in the psychological study of families* (pp. 127–166). Mahwah, NJ: Lawrence Erlbaum Associates.

McHale, S. M., & Crouter, A. C. (1996). The family contexts of children's sibling relationships. In G. H. Brody (Ed.), *Sibling relationships: Their causes and consequences* (pp. 173–196). Norwood, NJ: Ablex.

McHale, S. M., Updegraff, K. A., Tucker, C. J., & Crouter, A. C. (2000). Step in or stay out? Parents' roles in adolescent siblings' relationships. *Journal of Marriage and the Family, 62,* 746–761.

McKay, J. R., Maisto, S. A., Beattie, M. C., Longabaugh, R., & Noel, N. E. (1993). Differences between alcoholics and spouses in their perceptions of family functioning. *Journal of Substance Abuse Treatment, 10,* 17–21.

McKenry, P. C., & Price, S. J. (2000). Family coping with problems and change: A conceptual overview. In P. C. McKenry & S. J. Price (Eds.), *Families and change: Coping with stressful events and transitions* (2nd ed., pp. 1–21). Thousand Oaks, CA: Sage.

McLeer, S. V., & Anwar, R. (1989). A study of battered women presenting in an emergency department. *American Journal of Public Health, 79,* 65–66.

McLeod, J. M., & Chaffee, S. H. (1972). The construction of social reality. In J. Tedeschi (Ed.), *The social influence process* (pp. 50–59). Chicago: Aldine-Atherton.

Mead, G. H. (1934). *Mind, self and society: From the standpoint of a social behaviorist.* Chicago: University of Chicago Press.

Mechanic, D., & Hansell, S. (1989). Divorce, family conflict, and adolescents' well-being. *Journal of Health and Social Behavior, 30,* 105–116.

Medway, F. J., Davis, K. E., Cafferty, T. P., Chappell, K. D., & O'Hearn, R. E. (1995). Family disruption and adult attachment correlates of spouse and child reactions to separation and reunion due to Operation Desert Storm. *Journal of Social and Clinical Psychology, 14,* 97–118.

Meeks, S., Arnkoff, D. B., Glass, C. R., & Notarius, C. I. (1986). Wives' employment status, hassles, communication, and relational efficacy: Intra- versus extra-relationship factors and marital adjustment. *Family Relations, 34,* 249–255.

Meijer, A. M., & Oppenheimer, L. (1995). The excitation-adaptation model of pediatric chronic illness. *Family Process, 34,* 441–454.

Melton, G. G., & Wilcox, B. L. (1989). Psychology in the public forum changes in family law and family life: Challenges for psychology. *American Psychologist, 44,* 1213–1216.

Menees, M. M. (1997). The role of coping, social support, and family communication in explaining the self-esteem of adult children of alcoholics. *Communication Reports, 10,* 9–19.

Menees, M. M., & Segrin, C. (2000). The specificity of disrupted processes in families of adult children of alcoholics. *Alcohol and Alcoholism, 35,* 361–367.

Meredith, W. H., Abbott, D. A., & Adams, S. L. (1986). Family violence: Its relation to marital and parental satisfaction and family strengths. *Journal of Family Violence, 1,* 299–305.

Merikangas, K. R. (1984). Divorce and assortative mating among depressed patients. *American Journal of Psychiatry, 141,* 74–76.

Merikangas, K. R., & Spiker, D. G. (1982). Assortative mating among in-patients with primary affective disorder. *Psychological Medicine, 12,* 753–764.

Merikangas, K. R., Weissman, M. M., Prusoff, B. A., & John, K. (1988). Assortative mating and affective disorders: Psychopathology in offspring. *Psychiatry, 51,* 48–57.

Messman-Moore, T. L., & Long, P. J. (2003) The role of childhood sexual abuse sequelae in the sexual revictimization of women: An empirical review and theoretical reformulation. *Clinical Psychology Review, 23,* 537–571.

Meyers, S. A., & Landsberger, S. A. (2002). Direct and indirect pathways between adult attachment style and marital satisfaction. *Personal Relationships, 9,* 159–172.

Meyerson, L. A., Long, P. J., Miranda, R., & Marx, B. P. (2002). The influence of childhood sexual abuse, physical abuse, family environment, and gender on the psychological adjustment of adolescents. *Child Abuse and Neglect, 26,* 387–405.

Mickus, M. A., & Luz, C. C. (2002). Televisits: Sustaining long distance family relationships among institutionalized elders through technology. *Aging and Mental Health, 6,* 387–396.

Mihalic, S. W., & Elliot, D. (1997). A social learning theory model of marital violence. *Journal of Family Violence, 12,* 21–47.

Miklowitz, D. J. (1994). Family risk indicators in schizophrenia. *Schizophrenia Bulletin, 20,* 137–149.

Miklowitz, D. J., Goldstein, M. J., & Neuchterlein, K. H. (1995). Verbal interactions in the families of schizophrenic and bipolar affective patients. *Journal of Abnormal Psychology, 104,* 268–276.

Miklowitz, D. J., Velligan, D. I., Goldstein, M. J., Nuechterlein, K. H., Gitlin, M. J., Ranlett, G., Doane, J. A. (1991). Communication deviance in families of schizophrenic and manic patients. *Journal of Abnormal Psychology, 100,* 163–173.

Milholland, T. A., & Avery, A. W. (1982). Effects of marriage encounter on self-disclosure, trust, and marital satisfaction. *Journal of Marital and Family Therapy, 8,* 87–89.

Millar, F. E., & Rogers, L. E. (1988). Power dynamics in marital relationships. In P. Noller & M. A. Fitzpatrick (Eds.), *Perspectives on marital interaction* (pp. 78–97). Philadelphia, PA: Multilingual Matters.

Miller, B. C. (1986). *Family research methods.* Beverly Hills, CA: Sage.

Miller, I. W., Epstein, N. B., Bishop, D. S., & Keitner, G. I. (1985). The McMaster Family Assessment Device: Reliability and validity. *Journal of Marital & Family Therapy, 11,* 345–356.

Miller, J. L., & Knudsen, D. D. (1999). Family abuse and violence. In M. B. Sussman, S. K. Steinmetz, & G. W. Peterson (Eds.), *Handbook of marriage and the family* (pp. 705–741). New York: Plenum.

Miller, K. S., Kotchick, B. A., Dorsey, S., Forehand, R., & Ham, A. Y. (1998). Family communication about sex: What are parents saying and are their adolescents listening? *Family Planning Perspectives, 30,* 218–222.

Miller, M., & Day, L. E. (2002). Family communication, maternal and paternal expectations, and college students' suicidality. *The Journal of Family Communication, 2,* 167–184.

Miller, S., Nunnally, E. W., & Wackman, D. B. (1976). A communication training program for couples. *Social Casework, 57,* 9–18.

Miller-Day, M., & Lee, J. W. (2001). Communicating disappointment: The viewpoint of sons and daughters. *Journal of Family Communication, 1,* 111–131.

Mills, J., & Clark, M. S. (1994). Communal and exchange relationships: Controversies and research. In R. Erber & R. Gilmour (Eds.), *Theoretical frameworks for personal relationships* (pp. 29–42). Hillsdale, NJ: Lawrence Erlbaum Associates.

Milner, J. S. (1998). Individual and family characteristics associated with intrafamilial child physical and sexual abuse. In P. Trickett & C. J. Schellenbach (Eds.), *Violence against children in the family and the community* (pp. 141–171). Washington, DC: American Psychological Association.

Minkler, M., & Roe, K. M. (1993). *Grandmothers as caregivers*. Newbury Park, CA: Sage.

Minnett, A. M., Vandell, D. L., & Santrock, J. W. (1983). The effects of sibling status on sibling interaction: Influence of birth order, age spacing, sex of child, and sex of sibling. *Child Development, 54,* 1064–1072.

Mintz, S. (1998). From patriarchy to androgyny and other myths: Placing men's family roles in historical perspective. In A. Booth & A. C. Crouter (Eds.), *Men in families. When do they get involved? What difference does it make?* (pp. 3–30). Mahwah, NJ: Lawrence Erlbaum Associates.

Minuchin, S. (1974). *Families and family therapy*. Cambridge, MA: Harvard University Press.

Minuchin, S. (1975). A conceptual model of psychosomatic illness in children: Family organization and family therapy. *Archives of General Psychiatry, 32,* 1031–1038.

Minuchin, S., Baker, L., Rosman, B., Liebman, R., Milmann, L., & Todd, T. C. (1975). A conceptual model of psychosomatic illness in children. *Archives of General Psychiatry, 32,* 1021–1038.

Minuchin, S., & Fishman, H. C. (1981). *Family therapy techniques*. Cambridge, MA: Harvard University Press.

Minuchin, S., Rosman, B. L., & Baker, L. (1978). *Psychosomatic families: Anorexia nervosa in context*. Cambridge, MA: Harvard University Press.

Mitchell, B. A. (1994). Family structure and leaving the nest: A social resource perspective. *Sociological Perspectives, 37,* 651–671.

Mitchell, B. A., & Gee, E. M. (1996). "Boomerang kids" and midlife parental marital satisfaction. *Family Relations, 45,* 442–448.

Mongeau, P. A., & Carey, C. (1996). Who's wooing whom II? An experimental investigation of date-initiation and expectancy violation. *Western Journal of Communication, 60,* 195–213.

Monnier, J., & Hobfoll, S. E. (1997). Crossover effects of communal coping. *Journal of Social and Personal Relationships, 14,* 263–270.

Montgomery, B. M. (1981). The form and function of quality communication in marriage. *Family Relations, 30,* 21–30.

Montgomery, B. M. (1986). Interpersonal attraction as a function of open communication and gender. *Communication Research Reports, 3,* 140–145.

Montgomery, M. J., Anderson, E. R., Hetherington, E. M., & Clingempeel, W. G. (1992). Patterns of courtship for remarriage: Implications for child adjustment and parent-child relationships. *Journal of Marriage and the Family, 54,* 686–698.

Moore, M. M. (1985). Nonverbal courtship patterns in women: context and consequences. *Ethology and Sociobiology, 1,* 237–247.

Moore, M. M. (1998). Nonverbal courtship patterns in women: Rejection signaling—An empirical investigation.*Semiotica, 3,* 205–215.

Moore, M. M. (2002). Courtship communication and perception. *Perceptual and motor skills, 94,* 97–105.

Moorhead, D. J., Stashwick, C. K., Reinherz, H. Z., Giaconia, R. M., Streigel-Moore, R. M., & Paradis, A. D. (2003). Child and adolescent predictors for eating disorders in a community population of young adult women. *International Journal of Eating Disorders, 33,* 1–9.

Moos, R. H., & Moos, B. S. (1984). The process of recovery from alcoholism: III. Comparing functioning in families of alcoholics and matched control families. *Journal of Studies on Alcohol, 45,* 111–118.

Moos, R. H., & Moos, B. S. (1994). *Family environment scale manual: Development, applications, research* (3rd ed.). Palo Alto, CA: Consulting Psychologists Press.

Morell, M. A., & Apple, R. F. (1990). Affect expression, marital satisfaction, and stress reactivity among premenopausal women during a conflictual marital discussion. *Psychology of Women Quarterly, 14,* 387–402.

Morman, M. T., & Floyd, K. (2002). A 'changing culture of fatherhood': Effects on affectionate communication, closeness, and satisfaction in men's relationships with their fathers and their sons. *Western Journal of Communication, 66,* 395–411.

Morris, D. (1977). *Manwatching*. New York: Abrams.

Mullins, L. C., Elston, C. H., & Gutkowski, S. M. (1996). Social determinants of loneliness among older adults. *Genetic, Social, and General Psychology Monographs, 122,* 453–473.

Mueller, M. M., Wilhelm, B., & Elder, G. H. (2002). Variations in grandparenting. *Research on Aging, 24,* 360–388.

Murdock, G. P. (1949). *Social structure*. New York: Macmillan.

Murphy, C. M., & O'Farrell, T. J. (1997). Couple communication patterns of maritally aggressive and nonaggressive male alcoholics. *Journal of Studies on Alcohol, 58,* 83–90.

Murray, C. I. (2000). Coping with death, dying, and grief. In P. C. McKenry & S. J. Price (Eds.), *Families and change: Coping with stressful events and transitions* (2nd ed., pp. 120–153). Thousand Oaks, CA: Sage.

Murray, S. L., & Holmes, J. G. (1999). The (mental) ties that bind: Cognitive structure that predict relationship resilience. *Journal of Personality and Social Psychology, 77,* 1228–1244.

Murray, S. L., & Holmes, J. G., & Griffin, D. W. (1996). The self-fulfilling nature of positive illusions in romantic relationship: Love is not blind, but prescient. *Journal of Personality and Social Psychology, 71,* 1155–1180.

Murstein, B. I. (1986). *Paths to marriage.* Beverly Hills, CA: Sage.

Murstein, B. I. (1987). A clarification and extension of the SVR theory of dyadic pairing. *Journal of Marriage and the Family, 49,* 929–947.

Myers, S. A., & Members of COM 200. (2001). Relational maintenance behaviors in the sibling relationship. *Communication Quarterly, 49,* 19–34.

Nadelman, L., & Bagun, A. (1982). The effect of the new born on the older sibling: Mothers' questionnaires. In M. E. Lamb & B. Sutton-Smith (Eds.), *Sibling relationships: Their nature and significance across the lifespan* (pp. 13–37). Hillsdale, NJ: Lawrence Erlbaum Associates.

Nash, M. R., Hulsey, T. L., Sexton, M. C., Harralson, T. L., & Lambert, W. (1993). Long-term sequelae of childhood sexual abuse: Perceived family environment, psychopathology, and dissociation. *Journal of Consulting and Clinical Psychology, 61,* 276–283.

National Center for Health Statistics. (1973). *100 years of marriage and divorce statistics: United States, 1867–1967.* Washington, DC: U.S. Government Printing Office.

National Center on Child Abuse and Neglect. (1988). *Study of national incidence and prevalence of child abuse and neglect: 1986.* Washington, DC: Department of Health and Human Services.

National Center on Child Abuse and Neglect. (1996). *Third national study of the incidence of child abuse and neglect: 1993.* Washington, DC: Department of Health and Human Services.

National Clearinghouse on Child Abuse and Neglect Information. (2000). *What is child maltreatment?* Retrieved August 15, 2002, from http://www.calib.com/nccanch/pubs/factsheets/childmal.cfm

Neeliyara, T., Nagalakshmi, S. V., & Ray, R. (1989). Interpersonal relationships in alcohol dependent individuals. *Journal of Personality and Clinical Studies, 5,* 199–202.

Nelson, G. M., & Beach, S. R. H. (1990). Sequential interaction in depression: Effects of depressive behavior on spousal aggression. *Behavior Therapy, 21,* 167–182.

Neugarten, B. L., & Weinstein, K. K. (1964). The changing American grandparent. *Journal of Marriage and the Family, 26,* 199–204.

Neumark-Sztainer, D., Story, M., Hannan, P. J., Beuhring, T., & Resnick, M. D. (2000). Disordered eating among adolescents: Associations with sexual/physical abuse and other familial/psychosocial factors. *International Journal of Eating Disorders, 28,* 249–258.

Newcomb, T. M. (1961). *The acquaintance process.* New York: Holt, Rinehart, & Winston.

Newman, J. L., Roberts, L. R., & Syrè, C. R. (1993). Concepts of family among children and adolescents: Effect of cognitive level, gender, and family structure. *Developmental Psychology, 29,* 951–962.

Nichols, M. P., & Schwartz, R. C. (1998). Family *therapy: Concepts and methods* (4th ed.). Needham Heights, MA: Allyn & Bacon.

Noel, N. E., McCrady, B. S., Stout, R. L., & Fisher-Nelson, H. (1991). Gender differences in marital functioning of male and female alcoholics. *Family Dynamics of Addiction Quarterly, 1,* 31–38.

Noller, P. (1984). *Nonverbal communication and marital interaction.* Oxford, England: Pergamon Press.

Noller, P. (1992). Nonverbal communication in marriage. In R. S. Feldman (Ed.), *Applications of nonverbal behavioral theories* (pp. 31–59). Hillsdale, NJ: Lawrence Erlbaum Associates.

Noller, P. (1995). Parent-adolescent relationships. In M. A. Fitzpatrick & A. L. Vangelisti (Eds.), *Explaining family interactions* (pp. 77–111). Thousand Oaks, CA: Sage.

Noller, P., & Callan, V. J. (1990). Adolescents' perceptions of the nature of their communication with parents. *Journal of Youth and Adolescence, 19,* 349–362.

Noller, P., & Callan, V. J. (1991). *The adolescent in the family.* London: Routledge.

Noller, P., & Feeney, J. A. (1998). Communication in early marriage: Responses to conflict, nonverbal accuracy, and conversational patterns. In T. N. Bradbury (Ed.), *The developmental course of marital dysfunction* (pp. 11–43). New York: Cambridge University Press.

Noller, P., & Feeney, J. A. (2002). Communication, relationship concerns, and satisfaction in early marriage. In A. L. Vangelisti, H. T. Reis, & M. A. Fitzpatrick (Eds.), *Stability and change in relationships* (pp. 129–155). New York: Cambridge University Press.

Noller, P., & Feeney, J. A. (2004). Studying family communication: Multiple methods and multiple sources. In A. L. Vangelisti (Ed.), *Handbook of family communication* (pp. 31–50). Mahwah, NJ: Lawrence Erlbaum Associates.

Noller, P., Feeney, J. A., Bonnell, D., & Callan, V. J. (1994). A longitudinal study of conflict in early marriage. *Journal of Social and Personal Relationships, 11*, 233–252.

Noller, P., Feeney, J. A., Peterson, C., & Atkin, S. (2000). Marital conflict and adolescents. *Family Matters, 55*, 68–73.

Noller, P., & Fitzpatrick, M. A. (1993). *Communication in family relationships.* Englewood Cliffs, NJ: Prentice Hall.

Nomaguci, K. M., & Milkie, M. A. (2003). Costs and rewards of children: The effects of becoming a parent on adults' lives. *Journal of Marriage and Family, 65*, 356–374.

Nomura, Y., Wickramarante, P. J., Warner, V., Mufson, L., & Weissman, M. M. (2002). Family discord, parental depression, and psychopathology in offspring: Ten-year follow-up. *Journal of the American Academy of Child and Adolescent Psychiatry, 41*, 402–409.

Northouse, P. G., & Northouse, L. L. (1988). Communication and cancer: Issues confronting patients, health professionals, and family members. *Journal of Psychosocial Oncology, 5*, 17–46.

Notarius, C. I. (1996). Marriage: Will I be happy or will I be sad? In N. Vanzetti & S. Duck (Eds.), *A lifetime of relationships* (pp. 265–289). Belmont, CA: Brooks/Cole.

Notarius, C. I., Benson, P. R., Sloane, D., Vanzetti, N. A., & Hornyak, L. M. (1989). Exploring the interface between perception and behavior: An analysis of marital interaction in distresses and nondistressed couples. *Behavioral Assessment, 11*, 39–64.

Nunnally, E. W., Miller, S., & Wackman, D. B. (1975). The Minnesota Couples Communication Program. *Small Group Behavior, 6*, 57–71.

Nussbaum, E. (2000, March). Inside the love lab: A research psychologist goes pop. *LinguaFranca*, 24–32.

O'Farrell, T., Hooley, J., Fals-Stewart, W., & Cutter, H. S. G. (1998). Expressed emotion and relapse in alcoholic patients. *Journal of Consulting and Clinical Psychology, 66*, 744–752.

Ogle, J. P., & Damhorst, M. L. (2003). Mothers and daughters: Interpersonal approaches to body and dieting. *Journal of Family Issues, 24*, 448–487.

Oliver, J. E. (1993). Intergenerational transmission of child abuse: Rates, research, and clinical implications. *American Journal of Psychiatry, 150*, 1315–1324.

Olson, D. H. (1993). Circumplex model of marital and family systems: Assessing family functioning. In F. Walsh (Ed.), *Normal family processes* (2nd ed., pp. 104–137). New York: Guilford.

Olson, D. H. (1997). Family stress and coping: A multisystem perspective. In S. Dreman (Ed.), *The family on the threshold of the 21st century: Trends and implications* (pp. 259–280). Mahwah, NJ: Lawrence Erlbaum Associates.

Olson, D. H. (2000). Circumplex model of marital and family systems. *Journal of Family Therapy, 22*, 144–167.

Olson, D. H., & Lavee, Y. (1989). Family systems and family stress: A family life cycle perspective. In K. Kreppner & R. M. Lerner (Eds.), *Family systems and lifespan development* (pp. 165–195). Hillsdale, NJ: Lawrence Erlbaum Associates.

Olson, D. H., Lavee, Y., & McCubbin, H. I. (1988). Types of families and family response to stress across the family life cycle. In D. M. Klein & J. Adams (Eds.), *Social stress and family development* (pp. 16–43). New York: Guilford.

Olson, D. H., & McCubbin, H. I. (1982). Circumplex model of marital and family systems V: Application to family stress and crisis intervention. In H. I. McCubbin, A. E. Cauble, & J. M. Patterson (Eds.), *Family stress, coping, and social support* (pp. 48–68). Springfield, IL: Charles C Thomas.

Olson, D. H., & Olson, A. K. (1999). PREPARE/ENRICH Program: Version 2000. In R. Berger & M. T. Hannah (Eds.), *Preventive approaches in couples therapy* (pp. 196–216). Philadelphia: Taylor & Francis.

Olson, D. H., Sprenkle, D. H., & Russell, C. S. (1979). Circumplex model of marital and family systems: I. Cohesion and adaptability dimensions, family types, and clinical applications. *Family Process, 18,* 3–28.

Olson, K. L., & Wong, E. H. (2001). Loneliness in marriage. *Family Therapy, 28,* 105–112.

Omarzu, J., Whalen, J., & Harvey, J. H. (2001). How well do you mind your relationship? A preliminary scale to test the minding theory of relating. In J. H. Harvey & A. Wenzel (Eds.), *Close romantic relationships: Maintenance and enhancement* (pp. 345–356). Mahwah, NJ: Lawrence Erlbaum Associates.

Oppenheimer, R., Howells, K., Palmer, R. L., & Chaloner, D. A. (1985). Adverse sexual experience in childhood and clinical eating disorders: A preliminary description. *Journal of Psychiatric Research, 19,* 357–361.

Orbuch. T. L., Verhoff, J., Hassan, H., & Horrocks, J. (2002). Who will divorce: A 14-year longitudinal study of black couples and white couples. *Journal of Social and Personal Relationships, 19,* 179–202.

Orrego, V. O., & Rodriguez, J. (2001). Family communication patterns and college adjustment: The effects of communication and conflictual independence on college students. *Journal of Family Communication, 1,* 175–190.

Orthner, D. K., & Mancini, J. A. (1990). Leisure impacts on family interaction and cohesion. *Journal of Leisure Research, 22,* 125–137.

O'Sullivan, L., & Gaines, M. E. (1998). Decision-making in college students' heterosexual dating relationships: Ambivalence about engaging in sexual activity. *Journal of Social and Personal Relationships, 15,* 347–363.

Oswald, R. F. (2000). A member of the wedding? Heterosexism and family ritual. *Journal of Social and Personal Relationships, 17,* 349–368.

Oswald, R. F. (2002). Inclusion and belonging in the family rituals of gay and lesbian people. *Journal of Family Psychology, 16,* 428–436.

Pagani, L., Boulerice, B., Tremblay, R. E., & Vitaro, F. (1997). Behavioural development in children of divorce and remarriage. *Journal of Child Psychology and Psychiatry and Allied Disciplines, 38,* 769–781.

Palmer, R. L., Oppenheimer, R., & Marshall, P. D. (1988). Eating-disordered patients remember their parents: A study using the parental bonding instrument. *International Journal of Eating Disorders, 7,* 101–106.

Papernow, P. (1993). *Becoming a stepfamily: Patterns of development in remarried families.* New York: Gardner.

Papousek, M., Bornstein, M. H., Nuzzo, C., Papousek, H., & Symmes, D. (1990). Infant responses to prototypical melodic contours in parental speech. *Infant Behavior and Development, 13,* 539–545.

Parke, R. D. (2002). Parenting in the new millennium: Prospects, promises and pitfalls. In J. P. McHale & W. S. Grolnick (Eds.), *Retrospect and prospect in the psychological study of families* (pp. 65–93). Mahwah, NJ: Lawrence Erlbaum Associates.

Parke, R. D., & Buriel, R. (1998). Socialization in the family: Ethnic and ecological perspectives. In W. Damon (Series Ed.) & N. Eisenberg (Vol. Ed.), *Handbook of child psychology: Vol 3: Social emotional and personality development* (5th ed., pp. 463–552). New York: Asher.

Parker, G. (1983). Parental "affectionless control" as an antecedent to adult depression. *Archives of General Psychiatry, 40,* 856–860.

Parker, G. B., Barrett, E. A., & Hickie, I. B. (1992). From nurture to network: Examining links between perceptions of parenting received and social bonds in adulthood. *American Journal of Psychiatry, 149,* 877–885.

Parker, H., & Parker, S. (1986). Father-daughter child sexual abuse: Am emerging perspective. *American Journal of Orthopsychiatry, 56,* 531–549.

Parks, M. R. (1982). Ideology in interpersonal communication: Off the couch and into the world. In M. Burgoon (Ed.), *Communication yearbook 6* (pp. 79–107). Beverly Hills, CA: Sage.

Parks, M. R., & Eggert, L. L. (1991). The role of social context in the dynamics of personal relationships. In W. H. Jones & D. Perlman (Eds.), *Advances in personal relationships* (Vol. 2, pp. 1–34). London, Jessica Kingsley.

Parrott, L., & Parrott, L. (1999). Preparing couples for marriage: The SYMBIS model. In R. Berger & M. T. Hannah (Eds.), *Preventive approaches in couples therapy* (pp. 237–254). Philadelphia, PA: Taylor & Francis.

Pasupathi, M., Carstensen, L. L., Levenson, R. W., & Gottman, J. M. (1999). Responsive listening in long-married couples: A psycholinguistic perspective. *Journal of Nonverbal Behavior, 23,* 173–193.

Patchner, M. A., & Milner, J. S. (1992). Family functioning and child abuse potential. *Journal of Clinical Psychology, 48,* 445–454.

Patterson, B. R. (1995). Communication network activity: Network attributes of the young and elderly. *Communication Quarterly, 43,* 155–165.

Patterson, C. J. (2000). Family relationships of lesbians and gay men. *Journal of Marriage and the Family, 62,* 1052–1069.

Patterson, C. J. (2002). Lesbian and gay parenthood. In M. H. Bornstein (Ed.), *Handbook of parenting: Vol. 3. Being and becoming a parent* (2nd ed, pp. 317–338). Mahwah, NJ: Lawrence Erlbaum Associates.

Patterson, G. R. (1982). *A social learning approach. Vol. 3: Coercive family process.* Eugene, OR: Castilia Publishing.

Patterson, G. R., Dishion, R. J., & Bank, L. (1984). Family interaction: A process model of deviancy training. *Aggressive Behavior, 10,* 253–267.

Patterson, G. R., Ray, R. S., Shaw, D. A., & Cobb, J. A. (1969). *Manual for coding of family interactions.* New York: Microfiche Publications.

Patterson, M. L. (1983). *Nonverbal behavior: A functional perspective.* New York: Springer-Verlag.

Patterson, M. L. (1988). Functions of nonverbal behavior in close relationships. In S. W. Duck (Ed.), *Handbook of personal relationships* (pp. 41–56 ). New York: Wiley.

Pavalko, E. K., & Elder, G. H. (1990). World War II and divorce: A life course perspective. *American Journal of Sociology, 95,* 1213–1234.

Pearce, W. B. (1976). The coordinated management of meaning: A rules-based theory of interpersonal communication. In G. R. Miller (Ed.), *Explorations in interpersonal communication* (pp. 17–35). Beverly Hills: Sage.

Pearlin, L. I., & Skaff, M. M. (1998). Perspectives on the family and stress in late life. In J. Lomranz (Ed.), *Handbool of aging and mental health: An integrative approach* (pp. 323–340). New York: Plenum.

Pecchioni, L. L. (2001). Implicit decision-making in family caregiving. *Journal of Social and Personal Relationships, 18,* 219–237.

Pelcovitz, D., Kaplan, S. J., Ellenberg, A., Labruna, V., Salzinger, S., Mandel, F., et al. (2000). Adolescent physical abuse: Age at time of abuse and adolescent perception of family functioning. *Journal of Family Violence, 15,* 375–389.

Pennebaker, J. W., Dyer, M. A., Caulkins, R. S., Litowitz, D. L., Ackreman, P. L., Anderrson, D. G., et al. (1979). Don't the girls get prettier at closing time: A country and western application to social psychology. *Personality and Social Psychology Bulletin, 5,* 122–125.

Peplau, L. A., Russell, D., & Heim, M. (1979). The experience of loneliness. In I. H. Frieze, D. Bar-Tal, & J. S. Caroll (Eds.), *New approaches to social problems* (pp. 53–78). San Fransisco: Josey-Bass.

Peri, G., Molinari, E., & Taverna, A. (1991). Parental perceptions of childhood illness. *Journal of Asthma, 28,* 91–101.

Perlman, D., & Rook, K. S. (1987). Social support, social deficits, and the family: Toward the enhancement of well-being. *Applied Social Psychology Annual, 7,* 17–44.

Perlman, M., & Ross, H. S. (1997). The benefits of parent intervention in children's disputes: An examination of concurrent changes in children's fighting styles. *Child Development, 68,* 690–700.

Perner, J., Ruffman, R., & Leekam, S. R. (1994). Theory of mind is contagious: You catch it from your sibs. *Child Development, 65,* 1228–1238.

Perosa, S. L., & Perosa, L. M. (1993). Relationships among Minuchin's structural family model, identity achievement, and coping style. *Journal of Counseling Psychology, 40,* 479–489.

Perosa, L. M., & Perosa, S. L. (2001). Adolescent perceptions of cohesion, adaptability, and communication: Revisiting the circumplex model. *Family Journal-Counseling and Therapy for Couples and Families, 9,* 407–419.

Peterson, G. W., & Hann, D. (1999). Socializing children and parents in families. In M. B. Sussman, S. K. Steinmetz, & G. W. Peterson (Eds.), *Handbook of marriage and the family* (2nd ed., pp. 327–370). New York: Plenum.

Peterson, G. W., & Steinmetz, S. K. (1999). Perspectives on families as we approach the twenty-first century— Challenges for future handbook authors. In M. B. Sussman, S. K. Steinmetz, & G. W. Peterson (Eds.), *Handbook of marriage and family* (pp. 1–12). New York: Plenum.

Petrie, K. J., Booth, R. J., & Pennebaker, J. W. (1998). The immunological effects of thought suppression. *Journal of Personality and Social Psychology, 72,* 1264–1272.

Petronio, S. (1991). Communication boundary management: A theoretical model of managing disclosure of private information between married couples. *Communication Theory, 1,* 311–335.

Petronio, S. (1994). Privacy binds in family interactions: The case of parental privacy invasion. In W. R. Cupach & B. H. Spitzberg (Eds.), *The dark side of interpersonal communication* (pp. 241–258). Hillsdale, NJ: Lawrence Erlbaum Associates.

Petronio, S. (2000). The boundaries of privacy: Praxis of everyday life. In S. Petronio (Ed.), *Balancing the secrets of private disclosures* (pp. 37–49). Mahwah, NJ: Lawrence Elrbaum Associates.

Petronio, S. (2002). *The boundaries of privacy: Dialectics of disclosure.* Albany, NY: State University of New York Press.

Petronio, S., Jones, S., & Morr, M. C. (2003). Family privacy dilemmas: Managing communication boundaries within family groups. In L. R. Frey (Ed.), *Group communication in context: Studies of bona fide groups* (pp. 23–56). Mahwah, NJ: Lawrence Erlbaum Associates.

Petronio, S., & Kovach, S. (1997). Managing privacy boundaries: Health providers' perceptions of resident care in Scottish nursing homes. *Journal of Applied Communication Research, 25,* 115–131.

Piaget, J. (1977). The child's conception of time. In H.E. Gruger & J. J. Voneche (Eds.), *The essential Piaget: An interpretive reference and guide* (pp. 547–575). New York: Basic Books.

Pike, K. M., & Rodin, J. (1991). Mothers, daughters, and disordered eating. *Journal of Abnormal Psychology, 100,* 198–204.

Pink, J. E.T., & Wampler, K. S. (1985). Cohesion, adaptability, and the stepfather-adolescent relationship. *Family Relations, 34,* 327–335.

Pinquart, M. (2003). Loneliness in married, widowed, divorced, and never-married older adults. *Journal of Social and Personal Relationships, 20,* 31–53.

Pinquart, M., & Sorensen, S. (2001). Influences on loneliness in older adults: A meta-analysis. *Basic & Applied Social Psychology, 23,* 245–266.

Pinsof, W. M. (2002). The death of "till death us do part": The transformation of pair-bonding in the 20th century. *Family Process, 41,* 135–157.

Pistella, C. L. Y., & Bonati, F. A. (1998). Communication about sexual behavior among adolescent women, their family, and peers. *Families in Society, 79,* 206–211.

Planalp, S., & Honeycutt, J. M. (1985). Events that increase uncertainty in personal relationships. *Human Communication Research, 11,* 593–604.

Plutchik, R., & Plutchik, A. (1990). Communication and coping in families. In E. A. Blechman (Ed.), *Emotions and the family: For better or for worse* (pp. 35–51). Hillsdale, NJ: Lawrence Erlbaum Associates.

Polivy, J., & Herman, C. P. (2002). Causes of eating disorders. *Annual Review of Psychology, 53,* 187–213.

Pollak, S. D., & Tolley-Schell, S. A. (2003). Selective attention to facial emotion in physically abuse children. *Journal of Abnormal Psychology, 112,* 323–338.

Pomerantz, E. M., & Ruble, D. N. (1998). The role of maternal control in the development of sex differences in child self-evaluative factors. *Child Development, 69,* 548–478.

Ponzetti, J. J., & James, C. M. (1997). Loneliness and sibling relationships. *Journal of Social Behavior and Personality, 12,* 103–112.

Popenoe, D. (1993). American family decline, 1960–1990: A review and appraisal. *Journal of Marriage and the Family, 55,* 527–542.

Powell, H. L., & Segrin, C. (in press). The effect of family and peer communication on college students' communication with dating partners about HIV and AIDS. *Health Communication.*

Prado, L. M., & Markman, H. J. (1999). Unearthing the seeds of marital distress: What we have learned from married and remarried couples. In M. J. Cox & J. Brooks-Gunn (Eds.), *Conflict and cohesion in families: Causes and consequences* (pp. 51–85). Mahwah, NJ: Lawrence Erlbaum Associates.

Prescott, M. E., & Le Poire, B. A. (2002). Eating disorders and mother-daughter communication: A test of inconsistent nurturing as control theory. *Journal of Family Communication, 2,* 59–78.

Presser, H. B. (2000). Nonstandard work schedules and marital instability. *Journal of Marriage and the Family, 62,* 93–110.

Pryor, J. (1999). Waiting until they leave home: The experiences of young adults whose parents separate. *Journal of Divorce and Remarriage, 32,* 47–61.

Pulakos, J. (1988). Young adult relationships: Siblings and friends. *Journal of Psychology, 123,* 237–244.

Pyke, K. (1999). The micropolitics of care in relationships between aging parents and adult children: Individualism, collectivism, and power. *Journal of Marriage and the Family, 61*, 661–672.

Rainey, D. Y., Stevens-Simon, C., & Kaplan, D. W. (1995). Are adolescents who report prior sexual abuse at higher risk for pregnancy? *Child Abuse and Neglect, 19*, 1283–1288.

Ray, K. C., Jackson, J. L., & Townsley, R. M. (1991). Family environments of victims of intrafamilial and extrafamilial child seual abuse. *Journal of Family Violence, 6*, 365–374.

Regier, D. A., Narrow, W. E., Rae, D. S., Manderscheid, R. W., Locke, B. Z., & Goodwin, F. K. (1993). The de facto US mental and addicitive disorders service system: Epidemiologic catchment area prospective 1-year prevalence rates of disorders and services. *Archives of General Psychiatry, 50*, 85–94.

Rehm, R. S., & Franck, L. S. (2000). Long-term goals and normalization strategies of children and families affected by HIV/AIDS. *Advances in Nursing Science, 23*, 69–82.

Reich, W., Earls, F., Frankel, O., & Shayka, J. J. (1993). Psychopathology in children of alcoholics. *Journal of the American Academy of Child and Adolescent Psychiatry, 32*, 995–1002.

Reifman, A., Villa, L. C., Amans, J. A., Rethinam, V., & Telesca, T. Y. (2001). Children of divorce in the 1990s: A meta-analysis. *Journal of Divorce and Remarriage, 36*, 27–36.

Reis, H. T., & Patrick, B. C. (1996). Attachment and intimacy: Component processes. In E. T. Higgins & A. W. Kruglanski (Eds.), *Social psychology: Handbook of basic principles* (pp. 523–563). New York: Guilford.

Reiss, I. L. (1980). *Family systems in America* (3rd ed.). New York: Holt, Rinehart, & Winston.

Reissman, C., Aron, A., & Bergen, M. R. (1993). Shared activities and marital satisfaction: Casual direction and self-expansion versus boredom. *Journal of Social and Personal Relationships, 10*, 243–254.

Renick, M. J., Blumberg, S. L., & Markman, H. J. (1992). The Prevention and Relationship Enhancement Program (PREP): An empirically based preventive intervention program for couples. *Family Relations, 41*, 141–147.

Reppetti, R. L., Taylor, S. E., & Seeman, T. E. (2002). Risky families: Family social environments and the mental and physical health of offspring. *Psychological Bulletin, 128*, 330–366.

Rhodes, B., & Kroger, J. (1992). Parental bonding and separation-individuation difficulties among late-adolescent eating disordered women. *Child Psychiatry and Human Development, 22*, 249–263.

Rhodes, J. E., & Jason, L. A. (1990). A social stress model of substance abuse. *Journal of Consulting and Clinical Psychology, 58*, 395–401.

Rich, A. R., & Bonner, R. L. (1987). Interpersonal moderators of depression among college students. *Journal of College Student Personnel, 28*, 337–342.

Ridley, C. A., & Bain, A. B. (1983). The effects of a premarital relationship enhancement program on self-disclosure. *Family Therapy, 10*, 13–24.

Ridley C. A., Jorgensen, S. R., Morgan, A. G., & Avery, A. W. (1982). Relationship enhancement with premarital couples: An assessment of effects on relationship quality. *The American Journal of Family Therapy, 10*, 41–48.

Ridley, C. A., & Sladeczek, I. E. (1992). Premarital relationship enhancement: Its effects on needs to relate to others. *Family Relations, 41*, 148–153.

Riedmann, A., & White, L. (1996). Adult sibling relationships: Racial and ethnic comparisons. In G. H. Brody (Ed.), *Sibling relationships: Their causes and consequences* (pp. 105–126). Norwood, NJ: Ablex.

Riggio, H. R. (2000). Measuring attitudes toward adult sibling relationships: The lifespan sibling relationship scale. *Journal of Social and Personal Relationships, 17*, 707–728.

Riggio, R. E., Widaman, K. F., Tucker, J. S., & Salinas, C. (1991). Beauty is more than skin deep: Components of attractiveness. *Basic and Applied Social Psychology, 12*, 423–439.

Rindfuss, R. R., & Stephen, E. H. (1990). Marital noncohabitation: Separation does not make the heart grow fonder. *Journal of Marriage and the Family, 52*, 259–270.

Ritchie, D. L. (1991). Family communication patterns. *Communication Research, 18*, 548–565.

Ritchie, D. L. (1997). Parents' workplace experiences and family communication patterns. *Communication Research, 24*, 175–187.

Ritchie, D. L., & Fitzpatrick, M. A. (1990). Family communication patterns: Measuring intrapersonal perceptions of interpersonal relationships. *Communication Research, 17*, 523–544.

Rivenburg, R. (2002, January 31). Family comes first, at least as an excuse: Funny how an epidemic number of ousted bigwigs is singing the same tune. Earplugs, anyone? *The Los Angeles Times*, p. E1.

Roberts, J. (1988). Setting the frame: Definition, functions, and typology of rituals. In E. Imber-Black (Ed.), *Rituals in families and family therapy* (pp. 3–46). New York: Norton.

Roberts, L. J. (2000). Fire and ice in marital communication: Hostile and distancing behaviors as predictors of marital distress. *Journal of Marriage and the Family, 62,* 693–707.

Roberts, M., & Steinberg, L. (1999). Unpacking authoritative parenting: Reassessing a multidimensional construct. *Journal of Marriage and the Family, 61,* 574–587.

Roberts, T. W., & Price, S. J. (1989). Adjustment in remarriage: Communication, cohesion, marital and parental roles. *Journal of Divorce, 13,* 17–43.

Robinson, J. D., & Skill, T. (2001). Five decades of families on television: From the 1950s through the 1990s. In J. Bryant & J. A. Bryant (Eds.), *Television and the American family,* 2nd ed. (pp. 139–162). Mahwah, NJ: Lawrence Erlbaum Associates.

Rodgers, K. B. (1999). Parenting processes related to sexual risk-taking behaviors of adolescent males and females. *Journal of Marriage and the Family, 61,* 99–109.

Rodick, J. D., Henggeler, S. W., & Hanson, C. L. (1986). An evaluation of the family adaptabilty and cohesion evaluation scales and the circumplex model. *Journal of Abnormal Child Psychology, 14,* 77–87.

Rodriguez, V. B., Cafias, F., Bayon, C., Franco, B., Salvador, M., Graell, M., et al. (1996). Interpersonal factors in female depression. *European Journal of Psychiatry, 10,* 16–24.

Rogers, L. E. (2001). Relational communication in the context of family. *Journal of Family Communication, 1,* 25–36.

Rogers, L. E., Castleton, A., & Lloyd, S. A. (1996). Relational control and physical aggression in satisfying marital relationships. In D. D. Cahn & S. A. Lloyd (Eds.), *Family violence from a communication perspective* (pp. 218–239). Thousand Oaks, CA: Sage.

Rogge, R. D., & Bradbury, T. N. (1999a). Recent advanced in the prediction of marital outcomes. In R. Berger & M. T. Hannah (Eds.), *Preventive approaches in couples therapy* (pp. 331–360). Philadelphia, PA: Taylor & Francis.

Rogge, R. D., & Bradbury, T. N. (1999b). Till violence does us part: The differing roles of communication and aggression in predicting adverse marital outcomes. *Journal of Consulting and Clinical Psychology, 67,* 340–351.

Rogge, R. D., & Bradbury, T. N. (2002). Developing a multifaceted view of change in relationships. In A. L. Vangelisti, H. T. Reis, & M. A. Fitzpatrick (Eds.), *Stability and change in relationships* (pp. 229–253). New York: Cambridge University Press.

Rogosa, D. (1979). Causal models in longitudinal research: Rationale, formulation, and interpretation. In J. R. Nesselroade & P. B. Baltes (Eds.), *Longitudinal research in the study of behavior and development* (pp. 263–302). New York: Academic Press.

Roloff, M. E. (1996). The catalyst hypothesis: Conditions under which coercive communication leads to physical aggression. In D. D. Cahn & S. A. Lloyd (Eds.), *Family violence from a communication perspective* (pp. 20–36). Thousand Oaks, CA: Sage.

Roloff, M. E., & Ifert, D. E. (2000). Conflict management through avoidance: Withholding complaints, suppressing arguments, and declaring topics taboo. In S. Petronio (Ed.), *Balancing the secrets of private disclosures* (pp. 151–164). Mahwah, NJ: Lawrence Erlbaum Associates.

Roloff, M. E., & Johnson, K. L. (2002). Serial arguing over the relational life course: Antecedents and consequences. In A. L. Vangelisti & H. T. Reis (Eds.), *Stability and change in relationships* (pp. 107–128). New York: Cambridge University Press.

Root, M. P., & Fallon, P. (1988). The incidence of victimization experiences in a bulimic sample. *Journal of Interpersonal Violence, 3,* 161–173.

Rorty, M., Yager, J., Rossotto, E., & Buckwalter, G. (2000). Parental intrusiveness in adolescence recalled by women with a history of bulimia nervosa and comparison women. *International Journal of Eating Disorders, 28,* 202–208.

Roschelle, A. R. (1997). *No more kin: Exploring race, class, and gender in family networks.* Thousand Oaks, CA: Sage.

Rosenbaum, M. E. (1986). The repulsion hypothesis: On the nondevelopment of relationships. *Journal of Personality and Social Psychology, 51,* 1156–1166.

Rosenblatt, A., & Greenberg, J. (1991). Examining the world of the depressed: Do depressed people prefer others who are depressed? *Journal of Personality and Social Psychology, 60,* 620–629.

Rosenfarb, I. S., Goldstein, M. J., Mintz, J., & Nuechterlein, K. H. (1995). Expressed emotion and subclinical psychopathology observable with the transactions between schizophrenic patients and their family members. *Journal of Abnormal Psychology, 104,* 259–267.

Rosenfeld, L. B., Bowen, G. L., & Richman, J. M. (1995). Communication in three types of dual-career marriages. In M. A. Fitzpatrick & A. L. Vangelisti (Eds.), *Explaining family interactions* (pp. 257–289). Thousand Oaks, CA: Sage.

Rosenthal, A. (2001). A review of internet-based resources for family communication research. *Journal of Family Communication, 1,* 193–206.

Rosenthal, S. L., Cohen, S. S., Biro, F. M., & DeVellis, R. F. (1996). How do family characteristics relate to interpersonal expectations regarding STD acquisition among adolescent girls? *Family, Systems and Health, 14,* 465–474.

Ross, C. E., Mirowsky, J., & Goldsteen, K. (1990). The impact of the family on health: The decade in review. *Journal of Marriage and the Family, 52,* 1059–1078.

Ross, L. T., & Gill, J. L. (2002). Eating disorders: Relations with inconsistent discipline, anxiety, and drinking among college women. *Psychological Reports, 91,* 289–298.

Roug, L., & Lowry, B. (2002, August, 18). Dating fame games: A rash of new shows stresses the comedy in courtship humiliation. Why do we watch this stuff? *The Los Angeles Times,* pp. F10.

Rounsaville, B. J., Weissman, M. M., Prusoff, B. A., & Herceg-Baron, R. L. (1979). Marital disputes and treatment outcome in depressed women. *Comprehensive Psychiatry, 20,* 483–490.

Rowa, K., Kerig, P. K., & Geller, J. (2001). The family and anorexia nervosa: Examining parent-child boundary problems. *European Eating Disorders Review, 9,* 97–114.

Roy, R. (1985). Chronic pain and marital difficulties. *Health and Social Work, 10,* 199–207.

Rubin, Z. (1970). Measurement of romantic love. *Journal of Personality and Social Psychology, 16,* 265–273.

Rubin, A., Hill, C. T., Peplau, L. A., & Dunkel-Schetter, C. (1980). Self-disclosure in dating couples: Sex roles and the ethic of openness. *Journal of Marriage and the Family, 42,* 305–317.

Ruble, D. N., Fleming, A. S., Hackel, L. S., & Stangor, C. (1988). Changes in the marital relationship during the transition to first time motherhood: Effects of violated expectations concerning division of household labor. *Journal of Personality and Social Psychology, 55,* 78–87.

Rumstein-McKean, O., & Hunsley, J. (2001). Interpersonal and family functioning of female survivors of childhood sexual abuse. *Clinical Psychology Review, 21,* 471–490.

Rusbult, C. E. (1980). Commitment and satisfaction in romantic associations: A text of the investment model. *Journal of Experimental Social Psychology, 16,* 172–186.

Rusbult, C. E., Van Lange, P. A. M., Wildschut, T., Yovetich N. A., & Verette, J. (2000). Perceived superiority in close relationships: Why it exists and persists. *Journal of Personality and Social Psychology, 79,* 521–545.

Rusbult, C. E., & Zembrodt, I. M. (1983). Responses to dissatisfaction in romantic involvements: A multidimensional scaling analysis. *Journal of Experimental Social Psychology, 19,* 274–293.

Ruscher, S. M., & Gotlib, I. H. (1988). Marital interaction patterns of couples with and without a depressed partner. *Behavior Therapy, 19,* 455–470.

Russell, C. S. (1979). Circumplex model of marital and family systems: III. Empirical evaluation with families. *Family Process, 18,* 29–45.

Russell, M. N., & Lyster, R. F. (1992). Marriage preparation: Factors associated with consumer satisfaction. *Family Relations, 41,* 446–451.

Sabatelli, R. M., & Shehan, C. L. (1993). Exchange and resource theories. In P. G. Boss, W. J. Doherty, R. LaRossa, W. R. Schumm, & S. K. Steinmetz (Eds.), *Sourcebook of family theories and methods: A contextual approach* (pp. 385–411). New York: Plenum.

Sabourin, T. C. (1996). The role of communication in verbal abuse between spouses. In D. D. Cahn & S. A. Lloyd (Eds.), *Family violence from a communication perspective* (pp. 199–217). Thousand Oaks, CA: Sage.

Sabourin, T. C., Infante, D. A., & Rudd, J. E. (1993). Verbal aggression in marriages: A comparison of violent, distressed but nonviolent, and nondistressed couples. *Human Communication Research, 20,* 245–267.

Sabourin, T. C., & Stamp, G. H. (1995). Communication and the experience of dialectical tensions in family life: An examination of abusive and nonabusive families. *Communication Monographs, 62,* 213–242.

Safilios-Rothschild, C. (1976). A macro-and micro-examination of family power and love: An exchange model. *Journal of Marriage and the Family, 76,* 355–362.

Sahlstein, E. M., & Baxter, L. A. (2001). Improvising commitment in close relationships: A relational dialectics perspective. In J. Harvey & A. Wenzel (Eds.), *Close romantic relationships* (pp. 115–132). Mahwah, NJ: Lawrence Erlbaum Associates.

Saluter, A. (1994). Marital status and living arrangements: March 1993. US Bureau of the Census, *Current Population Reports,* P20–478. Washington, DC: U.S. Government Printing Office.

Sandberg, J. F., & Hofferth, S. L. (2001). Changes in children's time with parents: United States, 1981–1997. *Demography, 38,* 423–436.

Sanders, M. R., Halford, W. K., & Behrens, B. C. (1999). Parental divorce and premarital couple communication. *Journal of Family Psychology, 13,* 60–74.

Sappenfield, M. (2002, June 10). In court, behavior trumps biology in defining 'family.' *The Christian Science Monitor, 1-3.* Retrieved September 20, 2002, from http://www.csmonitor.com/2002/0610/p01s02-usju.html

Scaramella, L. V., Conger, R. D., Simons, R. L., & Whitbeck, L. B. (1998). Predicting risk for pregnancy by late adolescence: A social contextual perspective. *Developmental Psychology, 34,* 1233–1245.

Schaefer, E. S. (1959). A circumplex model for maternal behavior. *Journal of Abnormal and Social Psychology, 59,* 226–235.

Schacter, F. F. (1982). Sibling deidentification and split-parent identification: A family tetrad. In M. E. Lamb & B. Sutton-Smith (Eds.), *Sibling relationships: Their nature and significance across the lifespan* (pp. 123–151). Hillsdale, NJ: Lawrence Erlbaum Associates.

Schilling, D. A., Baucom, D. H., Burnett, C. K., Allen, E. S., & Ragland, L. (2003). Altering the course of marriage: The effect of PREP communication skills acquisition on couples' risk of becoming martially distressed. *Journal of Family Psychology, 17,* 41–53.

Schmaling, KB., & Sher, T. G. (1997). Physical health and relationships. In W. K. Halford & H. J Markman (Eds.), *Clinical handbook of marriage and couples intervention* (pp. 323–345). New York: John Wiley.

Schmeeckle, M., & Sprecher, S. (2004). Extended family and social networks. In A. Vangelisti (Ed.), *Handbook of family communication* (pp. 349–375). Mahwah, NJ: Lawrence Erlbaum Associates.

Schmidt, A. M., & Padilla, A. (1983). Grandparent-grandchild interaction in a Mexican American group. *Hispanic Journal of Behavioral Sciences, 5,* 181–198.

Schmidt, E., & Eldridge, A. (1986). The attachment relationship and child maltreatment. *Infant Mental Health Journal, 7,* 264–273.

Schmidt, U., Humfress, H., & Treasure, J. (1997). The role of general family environment and sexual and physical abuse in the origins of eating disorders. *European Eating Disorders Review, 5,* 184–207.

Schmitt, D. P., & Buss, D. M. (2001). Human mate poaching: Tactics and temptations for infiltrating existing mateships. *Journal of Personality and Social Psychology, 6,* 894–917.

Schumm, W. R., Bell, D. B., & Gade, P. A. (2000). Effects of a military oversees peacekeeping deployment on marital quality, satisfaction, and stability. *Psychological Reports, 87,* 815–821.

Schumm, W. R., Silliman, B., & Bell, D. B. (2000). Perceived premarital counseling outcomes among recently married Army personnel. *Journal of Sex and Marital Therapy, 26,* 177–186.

Schwartz, C. E., Dorer, D. J., Beardslee, W. R., Lavori, P. W., & Keller, M. B. (1990). Maternal expressed emotion and parental affective disorder: Risk for childhood depressive disorder, substance abuse, or conduct disorder. *Journal of Psychiatric Research, 24,* 231–250.

Schweitzer, R., Wilks, J., & Callan, V. J. (1992). Alcoholism and family interaction. *Drug and Alcohol Review, 11,* 31–34.

Segrin, C. (1994). Young adults' social skills are independent of their parents' social skills. *Communication Research Reports, 11,* 5–12.

Segrin, C. (1998). Interpersonal communication problems associated with depression and loneliness. In P. A. Anderson & L. A. Guerrero (Eds.), *The handbook of communication and emotion* (pp. 215–242). New York: Academic Press.

Segrin, C. (2000). Social skills deficits associated with depression. *Clinical Psychology Review, 20,* 379–403.

Segrin, C. (2001a). Social skills and negative life events: Testing the deficit stress generation hypothesis. *Current Psychology: Developmental, Learning, Personality, Social, 20,* 19–35.

Segrin, C. (2001b). *Interpersonal processes in psychological problems.* New York: Guilford.

Segrin, C. (2003). Age moderates the relationship between social support and psychosocial problems. *Human Communication Research, 29,* 317–342.

Segrin, C. (in press). Concordance on negative emotion in close relationships: Emotional contagion or assortative mating? *Journal of Social and Clinical Psychology.*

Segrin, C., & Fitzpatrick, M. A. (1992). Depression and verbal aggressiveness in different marital couple types. *Communication Studies, 43,* 79–91.

Segrin, C., & Flora, J. (2001). Perceptions of relational histories, marital quality, and loneliness when communication is limited: An examination of married prison inmates. *Journal of Family Communication, 1,* 151–173.

Segrin, C., & Givertz, M. (2003). Social skills training. In J. O. Greene & B. R. Burleson (Eds.), *Handbook of communication and social interaction skills* (pp. 135–176) Mahwah, NJ: Lawrence Erlbaum Associates.

Segrin, C., & Menees, M. M. (1996). The impact of coping styles and family communication on the social skills of children of alcoholics. *Journal of Studies on Alcohol, 57,* 29–33.

Segrin, C. & Nabi, R. L. (2002). Does television viewing cultivate unrealistic expectations about marriage? *Journal of Communication, 52,* 247–263.

Segrin, C., Taylor, M. E., & Altman, J. (in press). Social cognitive mediators and relational outcomes associated with parental divorce. *Journal of Social and Personal Relationships.*

Seiffge-Krenke, I., Shulman, S., & Klessinger, N. (2001). Adolescent precursors of romantic relationships in young adulthood. *Journal of Social and Personal Relationships, 18,* 327–345.

Seligman, M. E. P. (1995). *The optimistic child.* Boston: Houghton Mifflin.

Seltzer, J. A. (1991). Relationships between fathers and children who live apart: The father's role after separation. *Journal of Marriage and the Family, 53,* 79–101.

Seltzer, J. A. (2000). Families formed outside of marriage. *Journal of Marriage and the Family, 62,* 1247–1268.

Senchak, M., Greene, B. W., Carroll, A., & Leonard, K. E. (1996). Global, behavioral and self ratings of interpersonal skills among adult children of alcoholic, divorced and control parents. (1996). *Journal of Studies on Alcohol, 57,* 638–645.

Settles, B. H. (1999). The future of families. In M. B. Sussman, S. K. Steinmetz, & G. W. Peterson (Eds.), *Handbook of marriage and family* (pp. 307–326). New York: Plenum.

Shackelford, T. K., & Buss, D. M. (1997). Marital satisfaction in evolutionary psychology psychological perspective. In R. J. Sternberg & M. Hojjat (Eds.), *Satisfaction in close relationships* (pp. 7–25). New York: Guilford.

Shapiro, A. (2003). Later-life divorce and parent-adult child contact and proximity. *Journal of Family Issues, 24,* 264–285.

Shapiro, A. F., Gottman, J. M., & Carrère, S. (2000). The baby and the marriage: Identifying factors that buffer against decline in marital satisfaction after the first baby arrives. *Journal of Family Psychology, 14,* 59–70.

Share, L. (1972). Family communication in the crisis of a child's fatal illness: A literature review and analysis. *Omega: Journal of Death and Dying, 3,* 187–201.

Shaw, S. M. (1992). Dereifying family leisure: An examination of women's and men's everyday experiences and perceptions of family time. *Leisure Sciences, 14,* 271–286.

Shedler, J., & Block, J. (1990). Adolescent drug use and psychological health. *American Psychologist, 45,* 612–630.

Sheeber, L., Hops, H., & Davis, B. (2001). Family processes in adolescent depression. *Clinical Child and Family Psychology Review, 4,* 19–35.

Shek, D. T. L. (1998). A longitudinal study of the relations of family factors to adolescent psychological symptoms, coping resources, school behavior, and substance abuse. *International Journal of Adolescent Medicine and Health, 10,* 155–184.

Sher, K. J. (1991). *Children of alcoholics: A critical appraisal of theory and research.* Chicago: University of Chicago Press.

Sher, K. J., Walitzer, K. S., Wood, P. K., & Brent, E. E. (1991). Characteristics of children of alcoholics: Putative risk factors, substance use and abuse, and psychopathology. *Journal of Abnormal Psychology, 100,* 427–448.

Sher, T. G., & Baucom, D. H. (1993). Marital communication: Differences among martially distressed, depressed, and nondistressed-nondepressed couples. *Journal of Family Psychology, 7,* 148–153.

Sheridan, M. J. (1995). A proposed intergenerational model of substance abuse, family functioning, and abuse/neglect. *Child Abuse and Neglect, 19,* 519–530.

Shibazaki, K., & Brennan, K. A. (1998). When birds of different feathers flock together: A preliminary comparison of intra-ethnic and interethnic dating relationships. *Journal of Social and Personal Relationships, 15,* 248–256.

Shields, G., & Clark, R. (1995). Family correlates of delinquency: Cohesion and adaptability. *Journal of Sociology and Social Welfare, 22,* 93–106.

Shorter, E. (1975). *The making of the modern family.* New York: Basic Books.

Siegert, J. R., & Stamp, G. H. (1994). "Our first big fight" as a milestone in the development of close relationships. *Communication Monographs, 61,* 345–360.

Sights, J. R., & Richards, H. C. (1984). Parents of bulemic women. *International Journal of Eating Disorders, 3,* 3–13.

Signorelli, N., & Morgan, M. (2001). Television and the family: The cultivation perspective. In J. Bryant & J. A. Bryant (Eds.), *Television and the American family* 2nd ed., pp. 333–351. Mahwah, NJ: Lawrence Erlbaum Associates.

Sillars, A. L. (1995). Communication and family culture. In M. A. Fitzpatrick & A. L. Vangelisti (Eds.), *Explaining family interactions* (pp. 375–399). Thousand Oaks, CA: Sage.

Sillars, A. L., Canary, D. J., & Tafoya, M. (2004). Communication, conflict, and the quality of family relationships. In A. Vangelisti (Ed.), *Handbook of family communication* (pp. 413–446). Mahwah, NJ: Lawrence Erlbaum Associates.

Sillars, A., Roberts, L. J., Dun, T., & Leonard, K. E. (2001). Stepping into the stream of thought: Cognition during marital conflict. In V. Manusov & J. H. Harvey (Eds.), *Attribution, communication behavior, and close relationships* (pp. 193–210). New York: Cambridge University Press.

Silliman, B., & Schumm, W. R. (2000). Marriage preparation programs: A literature review. *The Family Journal: Counseling and Therapy for Couples and Families, 8,* 133–142.

Silverman, M. S., & Urbaniak, L. (1983). Marriage encounter: Characteristics of participants. *Counseling and Values, 28,* 42–51.

Silverstein, L. B. (2002). Fathers and families. In J. P. McHale & W. S. Grolnick (Eds.), *Retrospect and prospect in the psychological study of families* (pp. 35–64). Mahwah, NJ: Lawrence Erlbaum Associates.

Simons, R. L., Conger, R. D., & Whitbeck, L. B. (1988). A multistage social learning model of the influences of family and peers upon adolescent substance abuse. *Journal of Drug Issues, 18,* 293–315.

Simons, R. L., & Johnson, C. (1996). Mother's parenting. In R. L. Simons (Ed.), *Understanding differences between divorced and intact families* (Vol. 5, pp. 81–93). Thousand Oaks, CA: Sage.

Simons, R. L., Lin, K. H., & Gordon, L. C. (1998). Socialization in the family of origin and male dating violence: A prospective study. *Journal of Marriage and the Family, 60,* 467–478.

Simpson, J. A., Ickes, W., & Orina, M. (2001). Empathic accuracy and preemptive relationship maintenance. In J. Harvey & A. Wenzel (Eds.), *Close romantic relationships: Maintenance and enhancement* (pp. 27–46). Mahwah, NJ: Lawrence Erlbaum Associates.

Singer, M., Wynne, L., & Toohey, M. (1978). Communication disorders and the families of schizophrenics. In L. C. Wynne, R. L. Cromwell, & S. Matthysse (Eds.), *The nature of schizophrenia: New approaches to research and treatment* (pp. 499–511). New York: Wiley.

Skinner, K. B., Bahr, S. J., Crane, D. R., & Call, V. R. A. (2002). Cohabitation, marriage and remarriage. *Journal of Family Issues, 23,* 74–90.

Slep, A. M. S., & O'Leary, S. G. (2001). Examining partner and child abuse: Are we ready for a more integrated approach to family violence? *Clinical Child and Family Psychology Review, 4,* 87–107.

Small, J. A., & Gutman, G. (2002). Recommended and reported use of communication strategies in Alzheimer's caregiving. *Alzheimer's Disease and Associated Disorders, 16,* 270–278.

Small, J. A., Gutman, G., Makela, S., & Hillhouse, B. (2003). Effectiveness of communication strategies used by caregivers of persons with Alzheimer's disease during activities of daily living. *Journal of Speech, Language, and Hearing Research, 46*, 353–367.

Smith, C. (1996). The link between childhood maltreatment and teenage pregnancy. *Social Work Research, 20*, 131–141.

Smith, M. J. (1982). *Persuasion and human action.* Belmont, CA: Wadsworth.

Smith, S. M., Rosen, K. H., Middleton, K. A., Busch, A. L., Lundeberg, K., & Carlton, R. P. (2000). The intergenerational transmission of spouse abuse: A meta-analysis. *Journal of Marriage and the Family, 62*, 640–654.

Smolak, L., & Murnen, S. K. (2002). A meta-analytic examination of the relationship between child sexual abuse and eating disorders. *International Journal of Eating Disorders, 31*, 136–150.

Snowden, L. R., Schott, T. L., Awalt, S. J., & Gillis-Knox, J. (1988). Marital satisfaction in pregnancy: Stability and change. *Journal of Marriage and the Family, 50*, 325–333.

Socha, T. J. (1999). Communication in family units: Studying the first "group." In L. R. Frey, D. S. Gouran, & M. S. Poole (Eds.), *The handbook of group communication theory and research* (pp. 475–492). Thousand Oaks: Sage.

Socha, T. J., & Diggs, R. C. (1999). At the crossroads of communication, race, and family: Toward understanding black, white, and biracial family communication. In T. J. Socha & R. C. Diggs (Eds.), *Communication, race, and family.* (pp. 1–24). Mahwah, NJ: Lawrence Erlbaum Associates.

Socha, T. J., Sanchez-Hucles, J., Bromley, J., & Kelly, B. (1995). Invisible parents and children: Exploring African-American parent-child communication. In T. J. Socha & G. H. Stamp (Eds.), *Parents, children, and communication: Frontiers of theory and research* (pp. 127–145). Mahwah, NJ: Lawrence Erlbaum Associates.

Solomon, J. C., & Marx, J. (2000). The physical, mental, and social health of custodial grandparents. In B. Hayslip & R. Goldberg-Glen (Eds.), *Grandparents raising grandchildren: Theoretical, empirical, and clinical perspectives* (pp. 183–206). New York: Springer.

South, S. J., & Spitze, G. (1994). Housework in marital and nonmarital households. *American Sociological Review, 59*, 327–347.

Spanier, G. B. (1976). Measuring dyadic adjustment: New scales for assessing the quality of marriage and similar dyads. *Journal of Marriage and the Family, 38*, 15–28.

Speice, J., Shields, C. G., & Blieszner, R. (1998). The effects of family communication patterns during middle-phase Alzheimer's disease. *Families, Systems and Health, 16*, 233–248.

Sprecher, S. (2001). Equity and social exchange in dating couples: Associations with satisfaction, commitment, and stability. (2001). *Journal of Marriage and the Family, 63*, 599–613.

Sprecher, S., & Felmlee, D. (1992). The influence of parents and friends on the quality and stability of romantic relationships: A three-wave longitudinal investigation. *Journal of Marriage and the Family, 54*, 888–900.

Sprecher, S., Sullivan, Q., & Hatfield, E. (1994). Mate selection preferences: Gender differences examined in a national sample. *Journal of Personality and Social Psychology, 66*, 1074–1080.

Sprey, J. (1972). Extramarital relationships. *Sexual Behavior, 2*, 34–40.

Sprey, J. (1999). Family dynamics: An essay on conflict and power. In M. B. Sussman, S. K. Steinmetz, & G. W. Peterson (Eds.), *Handbook of marriage and family* (pp. 667–686). New York: Plenum.

Stack, D. M., & Muir, D. W. (1990). Tactile stimulation as a component of social interchange: New interpretations for the still-face effect. *British Journal of Developmental Psychology, 8*, 131–145.

Stack, S. (1998). Marriage, family and loneliness: A cross-national study. *Sociological Perspectives, 41*, 415–432.

Stafford, L. (2004). Communication during childhood. In A. Vangelisti (Ed.), *Handbook of family communication* (pp. 311–332). Mahwah, NJ: Lawrence Erlbaum Associates.

Stafford, L., & Bayer, C. L. (1993). *Interaction between parents and children.* Newbury Park, CA: Sage.

Stafford, L., & Dainton, M. (1995). Parent-child communication within the family system. In T. J. Socha & G. H. Stamp (Eds.), *Parents, children, and communication: Frontiers of theory and research* (pp. 5–21). Mahwah, NJ: Lawrence Erlbaum Associates.

Stafford, L., Dainton, M., & Haas, S. (2000). Measuring routine and strategic relational maintenance: Scale revision, sex versus gender roles, and the prediction of relational characteristics. *Communication Monographs, 37*, 306–323.

Stahmann, R. F. (2000). Premarital counseling: A focus for family therapy. *Journal of Family Therapy, 22,* 104–116.

Stanley, S. M., Blumberg, S. L., & Markman, H. J. (1999). Helping couples fight for their marriages: The PREP approach. In R. Berger & M. T. Hannah (Eds.), *Preventive approaches in couples therapy* (pp. 279–303). Philadelphia, PA: Taylor & Francis.

Stanley, S. M., Bradbury, T. N., & Markman, H. J. (2000). Structural flaws in the bridge from basic research on marriage to interventions for couples. *Journal of Marriage and the Family, 62,* 256–264.

Stanley, S. M., Markman, H. J., Prado, L. M., Olmos-Gallo, P. A., Tonelli, L., St. Peters, M., et al. (2001). Community-based premarital prevention: Clergy and lay leaders on the front lines. *Family Relations, 50,* 67–76.

Stanley, S. M., Markman, H. J., St. Peters, M., & Leber, B. D. (1995). Strengthening marriages and preventing divorce: New directions in prevention research. *Family Relations, 44,* 392–401.

Stanley, S. M., Markman, H. J., & Whitton, S. W. (2002). Communication, conflict, and commitment: Insights on the foundations of relationship success from a national survey. *Family Process, 41,* 659–675.

Starrels, M. E., & Holm, K. E. (2000). Adolescents' plans for family formation: Is parental socialization important? *Journal of Marriage and the Family, 62,* 416–429.

Steiger, H., Puentes-Neuman, G., & Leung, F. Y. K. (1991). Personality and family features of adolescent girls with eating symptoms: Evidence for restricter/binger differences in a nonclinical population. *Addictive Behaviors, 16,* 303–314.

Steil, J. M. (1997). *Marital equality: Its relationship to the well-being of husbands and wives.* Thousand Oaks, CA: Sage.

Stein, C. H. (1992). Ties that bind: Three studies of obligation in adult relationships with family. *Journal of Social and Personal Relationships, 9,* 525–547.

Stein, D., Lilenfeld, L. R., Plotnicov, K., Pollice, C., Rao, R., Strober, M., et al. (1999). Familial aggregation of eating disorders: Results from a controlled family study of bulimia nervosa. *International Journal of Eating Disorders, 26,* 211–215.

Steinberg, L., Mounts, N. S., Lamborn, S. D., & Dornbusch, S. M. (1991). Authoritative parenting and adolescent adjustment across varied ecological niches. *Journal of Research on Adolescence, 1,* 19–36.

Steinglass, P. (1979). The alcoholic family in the interaction laboratory. *Journal of Nervous and Mental Disease, 167,* 428–436.

Steinglass, P. (1981a). The impact of alcoholism on the family. *Journal of Studies on Alcohol, 42,* 288–303.

Steinglass, P. (1981b). The alcoholic family at home. *Archives of General Psychiatry, 38,* 578–584.

Steinglass, P. (1985). Family systems approaches to alcoholism. *Journal of Substance Abuse Treatment, 2,* 161–167.

Steinglass, P., Bennett, L. A., Wolin, S. J., & Reiss, D. (1987). *The alcoholic family.* New York: Basic Books.

Steinglass, P., & Robertson, A. (1983). The alcoholic family. In B. Kissin & H. Begleiter (Eds.), *The biology of alcoholism: Vol. 6. The pathogenesis of alcoholism: Psychosocial factors* (pp. 243–307). New York: Plenum Press.

Steinglass, P., Tislenko, L., & Reiss, D. (1985). Stability/instability in the alcoholic marriage: The interrelationships between course of alcoholism, family process, and marital outcome. *Family Process, 24,* 365–376.

Steinglass, P., Weiner, S., & Mendelson, J. H. (1971). A systems approach to alcoholism: A model and its clinical application. *Archives of General Psychiatry, 24,* 401–408.

Steinmetz, S. K. (1999). Adolescence in contemporary families. In M. B. Sussman, S. K. Steinmetz & G. W. Peterson (Eds.), *Handbook of marriage and family* (pp. 307–326). New York: Plenum.

Stets, J. E. (1993). Control in dating relationships. *Journal of Marriage and the Family, 55,* 673–685.

Stets, J. E., & Straus, M. A. (1990). Gender differences in reporting marital violence and its medical and psychological consequences. In M. A. Straus & R. J. Gelles (Eds.), *Physical violence in American families* (pp. 151–165). New Brunswick, NJ: Transaction Publishers.

Stewart, S. D., Manning, W. D., & Smock, P. J. (2003). Union formation among men in the U.S.: Does having prior children matter? *Journal of Marriage and the Family, 65,* 90–104.

Stewart, S., Stinnet, H., & Rosenfeld, L. B. (2000). Sex differences in desired characteristics of short-term and long-term relationships partners. *Journal of Social and Personal Relationships, 17,* 843–853.

Stocker, C. M., Burwell, R. A., & Briggs, M. L. (2002). Sibling conflict in middle childhood predicts children's adjustment in early adolescence. *Journal of Family Psychology, 16,* 50–57.

Stone, (E. (1988). *Black sheep and kissing cousins.* New York: Penguin Books.

Storaasli, R. D., & Markman, H. J. (1990). Relationship problems in marriage: A longitudinal investigation. *Journal of Family Psychology, 4,* 80–98.

Straus, M. A., & Gelles, R. (1990). *Physical violence in American families: Risk factors and adaptations to violence in 8145 families.* New Brunswick, NJ: Transaction Publishers.

Straus, M. A., Gelles, R., & Steinmetz, S. K. (1980). *Behind closed doors: Violence in the American family.* Garden City, NY: Anchor Press.

Stroufe, A. L. (2002). From infant attachment to promotion of adolescent autonomy: Prospective, longitudinal data on the role of parents in development. In J. G. Borkowski, S. L. Ramey, & M. Bristol-Power (Eds.), *Parenting and the child's world: Influences on academic, intellectual, and social-emotional development* (pp. 187–202). Mahwah, NJ: Lawrence Erlbaum Associates.

Sullivan, H. S. (1953). *The interpersonal theory of psychiatry.* New York: Norton.

Sullivan, K. T., & Bradbury, T. N. (1997). Are premarital prevention programs reaching couples at risk for marital dysfunction? *Journal of Consulting and Clinical Psychology, 65,* 24–30.

Sunnafrank, M. (1985). Attitude similarity and interpersonal attraction during early communicative relationships: A research note on the generalizability of findings to opposite-sex relationships. *Western Journal of Speech Communication, 49,* 73–80.

Sunnafrank, M. (1986). Communicative influences on perceived similarity and attraction: An expansion of the interpersonal goals perspective. *Western Journal of Speech Communication, 50,* 158–170.

Sunnafrank, M. (1992). On debunking the attitude similarity myth. *Communication Monographs, 59,* 164–179.

Sunnafrank, M., & Miller, G. R. (1981). The role of initial conversations in determining attraction to similar and dissimilar strangers. *Human Communication Research, 8,* 16–25.

Surra, C. A. (1987). Reasons for changes in commitment: Variations by courtship type. *Journal of Social and Personal Relationships, 4,* 17–33.

Surra, C. A. (1988). The influence of the interactive network on developing relationships. In R. M. Milardo (Ed.), *Families and social networks* (pp. 48–82). Newbury Park, CA: Sage.

Surra, C. A. (1990). Research and theory on mate selection and premarital relationships in the 1980s. *Journal of Marriage and the Family, 52,* 844–865.

Surra, C. A. (1998). Subjectivity and practicality in mating and parenting decisions. In A. Booth & A. C. Crouter (Eds.), *Men in families* (pp. 133–148). Mahwah, NJ: Lawrence Erlbaum Associates.

Surra, C. A., Arizzi, P., & Asmussen, L. A. (1988). The association between reasons for commitment and the development and outcome of marital relationships. *Journal of Social & Personal Relationships, 5,* 47–63.

Surra, C. A., Gray, C. R., Cottle, N., & Boettcher, T. M. J. (2004). Research on mate selection and premarital relationships. In A. L. Vangelisti (Ed.), *Handbook of family communication* (pp. 53–82). Mahwah, NJ: Lawrence Erlbaum Associates.

Surra, C. A., & Hughes, D. K. (1997). Commitment processes in accounts of the development of premarital relationships. *Journal of Marriage and the Family, 59,* 5–21.

Susman, E. J., Trickett, P. K., Iannotti, R. J., Hollenbeck, B. E., & Zahn-Waxler, C. (1985). Child-rearing patterns in depressed, abusive, and normal mothers. *American Journal of Orthopsychiatry, 55,* 237–251.

Swanson, B., & Mallinckrodt, B. (2001). Family environment, love withdrawal, childhood sexual abuse, and adult attachment. *Psychotherapy Research, 11,* 455–472.

Sweet, J. A., & Bumpass, L. L. (1992). Disruption of marital and cohabitation relationship: A social demographic perspective. In T. L. Orbuck (Ed.), *Close relationship loss: Theoretical approaches* (pp. 67–89). New York: Springer-Verlag.

Swinford, S. P., DeMaris, A., Cernkovich, S. A., & Giordano, P. C. (2000). Harsh physical discipline in childhood and violence in later romantic involvements: The mediating role of problem behaviors. *Journal of Marriage and the Family, 62,* 508–519.

Szinovacz, M. E. (Ed.). (1998). *Handbook of grandparenthood.* Westport CT: Greenwood Press.

Tajima, E. A. (2002). Risk factors for violence against children: Comparing homes with and without wife abuse. *Journal of Interpersonal Violence, 17,* 122–149.

Teachman, J. (2003). Premarital sex, premarital cohabitation, and the risk of subsequent marital dissolution among women. *Journal of Marriage and Family, 65,* 444–455.

Teachman, J. D., Polonko, K. A., & Scanzoni, J. (1999). Demography and families. In M. B. Sussman, S. K. Steinmetz, & G. W. Peterson (Eds.), *Handbook of marriage and the family* (pp. 39–76). New York: Plenum.

Teti, D. M. (2002). Retrospect and prospect in the psychological study of sibling relationships. In J. P. McHale & W. S. Grolnick (Eds.), *Retrospect and prospect in the psychological study of families* (pp. 193–224). Mahwah, NJ: Lawrence Erlbaum Associates.

Teven, J. J., Martin, M. M., & Newpauer, N. C. (1998). Sibling relationships: Verbally aggressive messages and their effect on relational satisfaction. *Communication Reports, 11,* 179–186.

Thibaut, J., & Kelly, H. (1959). *The social psychology of groups.* New York: Wiley.

Thoits, P. (1983). Multiple identities and psychological well-being: A reformulation and test of the social isolation hypothesis. *American Sociological Review, 48,* 174–187.

Thomas, V., & Olson, D. H. (1993). Problem families and the Circumplex Model: Observational assessment using the clinical rating scale (CRS). *Journal of Marital and Family Therapy, 19,* 159–175.

Thompson, S. C., & Pitts, J. S. (1992). In sickness and in health: Chronic illness, marriage, and spousal caregiving. In S. Spacapan & S. Oskamp (Eds.), *Helping and being helped* (pp. 115–151). Newbury Park, CA: Sage.

Thomsen, D. G., & Gilbert, D. G. (1998). Factors characterizing marital conflict states and traits: Physiological, affective, behavioral and neurotic variable contributions to marital conflict and satisfaction. *Personality and individual differenes, 25,* 833–855.

Thomson, E., Mosley, J., Hanson, T. L., & McLanahan, S. S. (2001). Remarriage, cohabitation, and changes in mothering behavior. *Journal of Marriage and the Family, 63,* 370–380.

Thorton, A. (1989). Changing attitudes toward family issues in the United States. *Journal of Marriage and the Family, 54,* 258–267.

Tichenor, V. J. (1999). Status and income as gendered resources: The case of marital power. *Journal of Marriage and the Family, 61,* 638–650.

Ting-Toomey, S. (1991). Intimacy expressions in three cultures: France, Japan, and the United States. *International Journal of Intercultural Relations, 15,* 29–46.

Ting-Toomey, S. (1999). *Communicating across cultures.* New York: Guilford.

Ting-Toomey, S., & Oetzel, J. G. (2001). *Managing intercultural conflict effectively.* Thousand Oaks, CA: Sage.

Treas, J., & Lawton, L. (1999). Family relations in adulthood. In M. B. Sussman, S. K. Steinmetz, & G. W. Peterson (Eds.), *Handbook of Marriage and the Family* (pp. 425–438). New York: Plenum.

Trees, A. (2000). Nonverbal communication and the support process: Interactional sensitivity in interactions between mothers and young adult children. *Communication Monographs, 67,* 239–261.

Trice, A. D. (2002). First semester college student's email to parents: Frequency and content related to parenting style. *College Student Journal, 36,* 327–334.

Troll, L. E. (1988). Rituals and reunions. *American Behavioral Scientist, 31,* 621–631.

Tsushima, R., & Viktor, G. (2001). Role taking and socialization in single-parent families. *Journal of Family Issues, 22,* 267–287.

Tucker, C. J., Barber, B. L., & Eccles, J. S. (1997). Advice about life plans and personal problems in late adolescent sibling relationships. *Journal of Youth and Adolescence, 26,* 63–76.

Tucker, C. J., Updegraff, K. A., McHale, S. M., & Crouter, A. C. (1999). Older siblings as socializers of younger siblings' empathy. *The Journal of Early Adolescence, 19,* 176–198.

Tucker, J. S., & Anders, S. L. (2001). Social control of health behaviors in marriage. *Journal of Applied Social Psychology, 31,* 467–485.

Tucker, P., & Aron, A. (1993). Passionate love and marital satisfaction at key transition points in the family life cycle. *Journal of Social and Clinical Psychology, 12,* 135–147.

Turk, D. C., Kerns, R. D., & Rosenberg, R. (1992). Effects of marital interaction on chronic pain and disability: Examining the down side of social support. *Rehabilitation Psychology, 37,* 259–274.

Turner, L. H., & West. R. (2002). *Perspectives on family communication* (2nd ed.). Boston, MA: McGraw-Hill.

Turner, R. (1970). *Family interaction.* New York: Wiley.

Uhlenberg, P., & Kirby, J. B. (1998). Grandparenthood over time: Historical and demographic trends. In M. E. Szinovacz (Ed.), *Handbook on grandparenthood* (pp. 23–39). Westport, CT: Greenwood Press.

Uruk, A. C., & Demir, A. (2003). The role of peers and families in predicting the loneliness level of adolescents. *The Journal of Psychology, 137,* 179–193.

U.S. Census Bureau. (1998). Race of couples: 1990. Available at http://www.census.gov/population/socdemo/race/interractab1.txt.

U.S. Census Bureau. (1999, January). *Table MS-2: Estimated Median Age at First Marriage, by Sex: 1890 to the Present. (Current Population Reports,* Series P20–514). Retrieved September 25, 2002, from http://www.census.gov/population/socdemo/ms-la/tabms-2.txt

U.S. Census Bureau. (2001, June). *America's families and living arrangements: Population characteristics (Current Population Reports,* Series P20-537). Retrieved September 25, 2002, from http://www.census.gov/prod/2001pubs/p20-537.pdf

U.S. Census Bureau. (2002, April). *Current population survey: Definitions and explanations.* Retrieved September 25, 2002, from http://www.census.gov/population/www/cps/cpsdef.html

Vaillant, C. O., & Vaillant, G. E. (1993). Is the U-curve of marital satisfaction an illusion? A 40-year study of marriage. *Journal of Marriage and the Family, 55,* 230–239.

Valiente, C. E., Belanger, C. J., & Estrada, A. U. (2002). Helpful and harmful expectations of premarital interventions. *Journal of Sex and Marital Therapy, 28,* 71–77.

Vandereycken, W., Kog, E., & Vanderlinden, J. (Eds.). (1989). *The family approach to eating disorders.* New York: PMA Publishing.

Van der Hart, O. (1983). *Rituals in psychotherapy: Transitions and continuity.* New York: Irvington.

Vanderlinden, J., & Vandereycken, W. (1996). Is sexual abuse a risk factor for developing an eating disorder? In M. F. Schwartz & L. Cohn (Eds.), *Sexual abuse and eating disorders* (pp. 17–21). New York: Brunner/Mazel Publishers.

Van Egeren, L. A., & Barratt, M. S. (2004). The developmental origins of communication: Interational systems in infancy. In A. Vangelisti (Ed.), *Handbook of family communication* (pp. 287–310). Mahwah, NJ: Lawrence Erlbaum Associates.

Van Egeren, L. A., Barratt, M. S., & Roach, M. A. (2001). Mother-infant responsiveness: Timing, mutual regulation, and interaction context. *Developmental Psychology, 37,* 684–697.

van Furth, E. F., van Strien, D. C., Martina, L. M. L., van Son, M. J. M., Hendrickx, J. J. P., & van Engeland, H. (1996). Expressed emotion and the prediction of outcome in adolescent eating disorders. *International Journal of Eating Disorders, 20,* 19–31.

Vangelisti, A. L. (1994a). Family secrets: Forms, functions and correlates. *Journal of Social and Personal Relationships, 11,* 113–135.

Vangelisti, A. L. (1994b). Couples' communication problems: The counselor's perspective. *Journal of Applied Communication Research, 22,* 106–126.

Vangelisti, A. L., & Alexander, A. L. (2002). Coping with disappointment in marriage: When partners' standards are unmet. In P. Noller & J. A. Feeney (Eds.), *Understanding marriage: Developments in the study of couple interaction* (pp. 201–227). New York: Cambridge University Press.

Vangelisti, A. L., & Banski, M. A. (1993). Couples' debriefing conversations: The impact of gender, occupation, and demographic characteristics. *Family Relations, 42,* 149–157.

Vangelisti, A. L., & Caughlin, J. P. (1997). Revealing family secrets: The influence of topic, function, and relationships. *Journal of Social and Personal Relationships, 14,* 679–705.

Vangelisti, A. L., Caughlin, J. P., & Timmerman, L. (2001). Criteria for revealing family secrets. *Communication Monographs, 68,* 1–27.

Vangelisti, A. L., Crumley, L. P., & Baker, J. L. (1999). Family portraits: Stories as standards for family relationships. *Journal of Social and Personal Relationships, 16,* 335–368.

Vangelisti, A. L., & Huston, T. L. (1994). Maintaining marital satisfaction and love. In D. J. Canary & L. Stafford (Eds.), *Communication and relational maintenance* (pp. 165–186). New York: Academic Press.

Van Laningham, J., Johnson, D. R., & Amato, P. (2001). Marital happiness, marital duration, and the U-shaped curve: Evidence from a five-wave panel study. *Social Forces, 78,* 1313–1341.

Van Widenfelt, B., Hosman, C., Schaap, C., & van der Staak, C. (1996). The prevention of relationship distress for couples at risk: A controlled evaluation with nine-month and two-year follow-ups. *Family Relations, 45,* 156–165.

van Wyk, J. D., Eloff, M. E., & Heyns, P. M. (1983). The evaluation of an integrated parent-training program. *Journal of Social Psychology, 121,* 273–281.

Vasquez, K., Durik, A. M., & Hyde, J. S. (2002). Family and work: Implications of adult attachment styles. *Personality and Social Psychology Bulletin, 28,* 874–886.

Vaughn, C., & Leff, J. P. (1976). The measurement of expressed emotion in the families of psychiatric patients. *British Journal of Clinical and Social Psychology, 15,* 157–165.

Vaughn, C. E., & Leff, J. P. (1981). Patterns of emotional response in relatives of schizophrenic patients. *Schizophrenia Bulletin, 7,* 43–44.

Velleman, R. (1992). Intergenerational effects—A review of environmentally oriented studies concerning the relationship between parental alcohol problems and family disharmony in the genesis of alcohol and other problems. I: The intergenerational effects of alcohol problems. *The International Journal of the Addictions, 27,* 253–280.

Velleman, R., & Orford, J. (1993). The adult adjustment of offspring of parents with drinking problems. *British Journal of Psychiatry, 162,* 503–516.

Velligan, D. I., Funderburg, L. G., Giesecke, S. L., & Miller, A. L. (1995). Longitudinal analysis of communication deviance in the families of schizophrenic patients. *Psychiatry, 58,* 6–19.

Velligan, D. I., Miller, A. L., Eckert, S. L., Funderburg, L. G., True, J. E., Mahurin, R. K., et al. (1996). The relationship between parental communication deviance and relapse in schizophrenia patients in the 1-year period after hospital discharge. *Journal of Nervous and Mental Disease, 184,* 490–496.

Vemer, E., Coleman, M., Ganong, L. H., & Cooper, H. (1989). Marital satisfaction in remarriage: A meta-analysis. *Journal of Marriage and the Family, 51,* 713–725.

Ventura, S. J., Hamilton, B. E., & Sutton, P. D. (2003). *Revised birth and family rates for the United States, 2000 and 2001.* National Vital Statistics Reports, 51(4). U.S. Department of Health and Human Services, Centers for Disease Control and Prevention. National Center for Health Statistics. Available at http://www.cdc.gov/nchs/data/nvsr51/nvsr51_04.pdf.

Verbrugge, L. M. (1979). Marital status and health. *Journal of Marriage and the Family, 41,* 267–285.

Viere, G. M. (2001). Examining family rituals. *Family Journal, 9,* 284–288.

Vincent, J. P., Friedman, L., Nugent, J., & Messerly, L. (1979). Demand characteristics in observations of marital interactions. *Journal of Consulting and Clinical Psychology, 47,* 557–566.

Visher, E. B., Visher, J. S., & Pasley, K. (2003). Remarriage families and stepparenting. In F. Walsh (Ed.), *Normal family processes: Growing diversity and complexity* 3rd ed., pp. 153–175. New York: Guilford.

Vranic, A. (2003). Personal space in physically abuse children. *Environment and Behavior, 35,* 550–565.

Vuchinich, S. (1987). Starting and stopping spontaneous family conflicts. *Journal of Marriage and the Family, 49,* 591–601.

Waldner-Haugrud, L. K., Gratch, L. V., & Magruder, B. (1997). Victimization and perpetration rates of violence in gay and lesbian relationships: Gender issues explored. *Violence and Victims, 12,* 173–184.

Waldren, T., Bell, N. J., Peek, C. W., & Sorell, G. (1990). Cohesion and adaptability in post-divorce remarried and first married families: Relationships with family stress and coping styles. *Journal of Divorce and Remarriage, 14,* 13–28.

Waldrop, D. P., & Weber, J. A. (2001). From grandparent to caregiver: The stress and satisfaction of raising grandchildren. *Families in Society, 82,* 461–472.

Walen, H. R., & Lachman, M. E. (2000). Social support and strain from partner, family, and friends: Costs and benefits for men and women in adulthood. *Journal of Social and Personal Relationships, 17,* 5–30.

Waller, G., & Calam, R. (1994). Parenting and family factors in eating problems. In L. Alexander-Mott & D. B. Lumsden, (Eds.), *Understanding eating disorders: Anorexia nervosa, bulimia nervosa, and obesity* (pp. 61–76). Philadelphia, PA: Taylor & Francis.

Waller, G., Calam, R., & Slade, P. (1989). Eating disorders and family interaction. *British Journal of Clinical Psychology, 28,* 285–286.

Waller, G., Slade, P., & Calam, R. (1990). Family adaptability and cohesion: Relation to eating attitudes and disorders. *International Journal of Eating Disorders, 9,* 225–228.

Wallston, B., Algania, S. W., Devellis, B. M., & Devellis, R. F. (1983). Social support and physical health. *Health Psychology, 2,* 367–391.

Walsh, F. (1988). The family in later life. In B. Carter & M. McGoldrick (Eds.), *The changing family life cycle: A framework for family therapy* (pp. 311–332). New York: Gardner Press.

Walster, E. (1966). Importance of physical attractiveness in dating behavior. *Journal of Personality and Social Psychology, 4,* 508–516.

Wamboldt, F. S. (1999). Co-constructing a marriage: Analysis of young couples' relationship narratives. *Monograph of the Society for Research in Child Development, 64*(37–51, Serial No. 257).

Wamboldt, F., & Reiss, D. (1989). Defining a family heritage and a new relationship identity: Two central tasks in the making of a marriage. *Family Process, 2,* 317–335.

Wamboldt, M. Z., & Wamboldt, F. S. (2000). Role of family in the onset and outcome of childhood disorders: Selected research findings. *Journal of the American Academy of Child and Adolescent Psychiatry, 39,* 1212–1219.

Wampler, K. S. (1982). The effectiveness of the Minnesota Couples Communication Program: A review of research. *Journal of Marital and Family Therapy, 8,* 345–355.

Wang, H., & Amato, P. R. (2000). Predictors of divorce adjustment: Stressors, resources, and definitions. *Journal of Marriage and the Family, 62,* 655–668.

Ward, L. M. (2002). Does television exposure affect emerging adults' attitudes and assumptions about sexual relationships? Correlational and experimental confirmation. *Journal of Youth and Adolescence, 31,* 1–15.

Ward, R., & Spitze, G. (1996). Will the children ever leave? Parent-child coresidence history and plans. *Journal of Family Issues, 17,* 514–539.

Warner, V., Weissman, M. M., Fendrich, M., Wickramaratne, P., & Moreau, D. (1992). The course of major depression in the offspring of depressed parents: Incidence, recurrence, and recovery. *Archives of General Psychiatry, 49,* 795–801.

Warren, C. (1992). Perspectives on international sex practices and American family sex communication relevant to teenage sexual behavior in the United States. *Health Communicaiton, 4,* 121–136.

Watt, T. T. (2002). Marital and cohabiting relationships of adult children of alcoholics: Evidence from the National Survey of Families and Households. *Journal of Family Issues, 23,* 246–265.

Watzlawick, P., Beavin, J. H., & Jackson, D. D. (1967). *Pragmatics of human communication.* New York: Norton.

Watzlawick, P., Weakland, J. H., & Fisch, R. (1974). *Change: Principles of problem formation and problem resolution.* New York: Norton.

Webster, J. J., & Palmer, R. L. (2000). The childhood and family background of women with clinical eating disorders: A comparison with women with major depression and women without psychiatric disorder. *Psychological Medicine, 30,* 53–60.

Weigel, D. J., & Ballard-Reisch, D. S. (2001). The impact of relational maintenance behaviors on marital satisfaction: A longitudinal analysis. *Journal of Family Communication, 1,* 265–279.

Weigel, D., & Murray, C. I. (2000). The paradox of stability and change in relationships: What does chaos theory offer for the study of romantic relationship? *Journal of Social and Personal Relationships, 17,* 425–449.

Weigel, D. J., & Weigel, R. R. (1993). Intergenerational family communication: Generational differences in rural families. *Journal of Social and Personal Relationships, 10,* 467–473.

Weiss, R. L. (1980). Strategic behavioral marital therapy: Toward a model for assessment and intervention. In J. P. Vincent (Ed.), *Advances in family intervention, assessment, and theory* (Vol. 1, pp. 229–271). Greenwich, CT: JAI Press.

Welch, S. A., & Rubin, R. B. (2002). Development of relationship stage measures. *Communication Quarterly, 50,* 24–40.

West, M. O., & Prinz, R. J. (1987). Parental alcoholism and childhood psychopathology. *Psychological Bulletin, 102,* 204–218.

West, R., & Turner, L. H. (1995). Communication in lesbian and gay families: Building a descriptive base. In T. J. Socha & G. H. Stamp (Eds.), *Parents, children, and communication: Frontiers of theory and research* (pp. 147–169). Mahwah, NJ: Lawrence Erlbaum Associates.

West, R., & Turner, L. H. (2000). *Introducing communication theory: Analysis and application.* Mountain View, CA: Mayfield.

Whiffen, V. E., & Gotlib, I. H. (1989). Infants of postpartum depressed mothers: Temperament and cognitive status. *Journal of Abnormal Psychology, 98,* 274–279.

Whitchurch, G. C., & Constantine, L. L. (1993). Systems theory. In P. G. Bass, W. J. Doherty, R. LaRossa, W. R. Schumm, & S. K. Steinmetz (Eds.), *Sourcebook of family theories and methods: A contextual approach* (pp. 325–352). New York: Plenum.

Whitchurch, G. C., & Dickson, F. C. (1999). Family communication. In M. B. Sussman, S. K. Steinmetz, & G. W. Peterson (Eds.), *Handbook of marriage and the family, 2nd, ed.* (pp. 687–704). New York: Plenum.

White, L. (1992). The effect of parental divorce and remarriage on parental support for adult children. *Journal of Family Issues, 13,* 234–250.

White, L. (1994a). Coresidence and leaving home: Young adults and their parents. *Annual Review of Sociology, 20,* 81–102.

White, L. (1994b). Stepfamilies over the life course: Social support. In A. Booth & J. Dunn (Eds.), *Stepfamilies: Who benefits? Who does not?* (pp. 109–137). Hillsdale, NJ: Lawrence Erlbaum Associates.

White, L. (2001). Sibling relationships over the life course: A panel analysis. *Journal of Marriage and the Family, 63,* 555–568.

White, L., & Edwards, J. N. (1990). Emptying the nest and parental well-being: An analysis of national panel data. *American Sociological Review, 55,* 235–242.

White, L. K., & Riedmann, A. (1992a). When the Brady bunch grows up: Step/half- and full sibling relationships in adulthood. *Journal of Marriage and the Family, 54,* 197–208.

White, L. K., & Riedmann, A. (1992b). Ties among adult siblings. *Social Forces, 71,* 85–102.

Whitton, S. W., & Stanley, S. M. (1999, June). *Sacrifice in romantic relationships: The role of perceptions.* Poster session presented at the convention of the American Psychological Society, Denver, CO.

Wickrama, K. A. S., Conger, R. D., & Lorenz, F. O. (1995). Work, marriage, lifestyle, and changes in men's physical health. *Journal of Behavioral Medicine, 18,* 97–111.

Wickrama, K. A. S., Lorenz, F. O., Conger, R. D., & Elder, G. H. (1997). Marital quality and physical illness: A latent growth curve analysis. *Journal of Marriage and the Family, 59,* 143–155.

Wiener, N. (1948). *Cybernetics, or control and communication in the animal and machine.* New York: Wiley.

Williams, A., & Nussbaum, J. F. (2001). *Intergenerational communication across the lifespan.* Mahwah, NJ: Lawrence Erlbaum Associates.

Williams, L. M., Riley, L. A., Risch, G.S., & Van Dyke, D. T. (1999). An empirical approach to designing marriage preparation programs. *The American Journal of Family Therapy, 27,* 271–283.

Williams, N., & Torrez, D. J. (1998). Grandparenthood among Hispanics. In M. E. Szinovacz (Ed.), *Handbook on grandparenthood* (pp. 87–96). Westport, CT: Greenwood Press.

Wills, T. A. (1990). Social support and the family. In E. A. Blechman (Ed.), *Emotions and the family: For better or for worse* (pp. 75–98). Hillsdale, NJ: Lawrence Erlbaum Associates.

Wills, T. A., Blechman, E. A., & McNamara, G. (1996). Family support, coping, and competence. In E. M. Hetherington & E. A. Blechman (Eds.), *Stress, coping, and resiliency in children and families* (pp. 107–133). Mahwah, NJ: Lawrence Erlbaum Associates.

Wilson, B. F., & Clarke, S. C. (1992). Remarriages: A demographic profile. *Journal of Family Issues, 13,* 123–141.

Wilson, S. R., & Whipple, E. E. (1995). Communication, discipline, and physical child abuse. In T. J. Socha & G. H. Stamp (Eds.), *Parents, children, and communication: Frontiers of theory and research* (pp. 299–317). Mahwah, NJ: Lawrence Erlbaum Associates.

Wilson, S. R., & Whipple, E. E. (2001). Attributions and regulative communication by parents participating in a community-based child physical abuse prevention program. In V. Manusov & J. H. Harvey (Eds.), *Attribution, communication behavior, and close relationships* (pp. 227–247). Cambridge, UK: Cambridge University Press.

Winch, R. F. (1958). *Mate selection: A study of complementary needs.* New York: Harper.

Windle, M., & Searles, J. S. (1990). *Children of alcoholics: Critical perspectives.* New York: Guilford.

Witkin, S. L., Edleson, J. L., Rose, S. D., & Hall, J. A. (1983). Group training in marital communication: A comparative study. *Journal of Marriage and the Family, 45,* 661–669.

Witteman, H., & Fitzpatrick, M. A. (1986). A social-scientific view of the Marriage Encounter movement. *Journal of Social and Clinical Psychology, 4,* 513–522.

Wolfe, D. A., Crooks, C. V., Lee, V., McIntyre-Smith, A., & Jaffe, P. G. (2003). The effects of children's exposure to domestic violence: A meta-analysis and critique. *Clinical Child and Family Psychology Review, 6,* 171–187.

Wolin, S. J., & Bennett, L. A. (1984). Family rituals. *Family Process, 23,* 401–420.

Wonderlich, S. (1992). Relationship of family and personality factors in bulimia. In J. H. Crowther, D. L. Tennenbaum, S. E. Hobfoll, & M. A. P. Stephens (Eds.), *The etiology of Bulimia Nervosa: The individual and familial context* (pp. 103–126). Washington, DC: Hemisphere.

Wonderlich, S., Ukestad, L., & Perzacki, R. (1994). Perceptions of nonshared childhood environment in bulimia nervosa. *Journal of the American Academy of Child and Adolescent Psychiatry, 33*, 740–747.

Wood, B. L. (2001). Physically manifested illness in children and adolescents. *Child and Adolescent Psychiatric Clinics of North America, 10*, 543–562.

Wood, J. T., & Dindia, K. (1998). What's the difference? A dialogue about differences and similarities between women and men. In D. J. Canary & K. Dindia (Eds.), *Sex differences and similarities in communication* (pp. 19–40). Mahwah, NJ: Lawrence Erlbaum Associates.

Woodall, K. L., & Matthews, K. A. (1989). Familial environment associated with type A behaviors and psychophysiological responses to stress in children. *Health Psychology, 8*, 403–426.

Worobey, J. (2002). Early family mealtime experiences and eating attitudes in normal weight, underweight, and overweight families. *Eating and Weight Disorders, 7*, 39–44.

Wright, D. M., & Heppner, P. P. (1991). Coping among nonclinical college-age children of alcoholics. *Journal of Counseling Psychology, 38*, 465–472.

Wright, D. W., Nelson, B. S., & Georgen, K. E. (1994). Marital problems. In P. C. McKenry & S. J. Price (Eds.), *Families and change: Coping with stressful events* (pp. 40–65) Thousand Oaks, CA: Sage.

Wu, K. D. (2001). Evolution and evolutionary psychology: Their application to close relationships. In J. Harvey & A. Wenzel (Eds.), *Close romantic relationships: Maintenance and* enhancement (pp. 215–236). Mahwah, NJ: Lawrence Erlbaum Associates.

Wynne, L. C. (1968). Methodological and conceptual issues in the study of schizophrenics and their families. *Journal of Psychiatric Research, 6*, 185–199.

Wynne, L. C. (1981). Current concepts about schizophrenics and family relationships. *Journal of Nervous and Mental Disease, 169*, 82–89.

Wysocki, T. (1993). Associations among teen-parent relationships, metabolic control, and adjustment to diabetes in adolescents. *Journal of Pediatric Psychology, 18*, 441–452.

Yahav, R. (2002). External and internal symptoms in children and characteristics of the family system: A comparison of the linear and circumplex models. *The American Journal of Family Therapy, 30*, 39–56.

Yerby, J., Buerkel-Rothfuss, N., & Bochner, A. P. (1995). *Understanding family communication*, 2nd ed. Scottsdale, AZ: Gorsuch Scarisbrick.

Young, B., Dixon-Woods, M., Windridge, K. C., & Henry, D. (2003). Managing communication with young people who have a potentially life threatening chronic illness: Qualitative study of patients and parents. *British Medical Journal, 326*, 305–308.

Ziegler-Driscoll, G. (1979). The similarities in families of drug dependents and alcoholics. In E. Kaufman & P. Kaufman (Eds.), *Family therapy of drug and alcohol abuse* (pp. 19–39). New York: Gardner Press.

Zill, N. (1994). Understanding why children in stepfamilies have more learning and behavior problems than children in nuclear families. In A. Booth & J. Dunn (Eds.), *Stepfamilies: Who benefits? Who does not?* (pp. 97–106). Hillsdale, NJ: Lawrence Erlbaum Associates.

Zimmerman, T. S., Haddock, S. A., & McGeorge, C. R. (2001). Mars and Venus: Unequal planets. *Journal of Marriage and the Family, 27*, 55–68.

# Author Index

# Subject Index